D1520580

HANDBOOK

TO THE

UNIFORM BUILDING CODE

An illustrative commentary

International Conference of Building Officials

Second Printing

Publication Date: May 1998

ISBN 1-58001-012-1

COPYRIGHT © 1998

by

International Conference of Building Officials

5360 WORKMAN MILL ROAD
WHITTIER, CALIFORNIA 90601-2298
(800) 284-4406 • (562) 699-0541

PRINTED IN THE U.S.A.

Preface

The *Uniform Building Code*™ (UBC) is one in a family of codes and related publications published by the International Conference of Building Officials (ICBO). The *Uniform Building Code* is designed to be compatible with other codes, as together they make up the enforcement tools of a jurisdiction.

The code is divided into the following three major subdivisions:

1. The text of the UBC (sometimes referred to as "the body of the code").
2. The appendix.
3. The UBC standards.

As discussed under Section 101.3, the provisions of the appendix do not apply unless specifically included in the adoption ordinance of the jurisdiction enforcing the code. Also, as indicated in Chapter 35 of the code, the UBC standards, although published in a separate volume (Volume 3), are part of the *Uniform Building Code.*

In this handbook, wherever reference is made to "this code," "the code," "UBC" or the "*Uniform Building Code*," the reference is to the 1997 edition of the *Uniform Building Code.*

The formatting of the UBC is based on a national common code format recommended by the Council of American Building Officials (CABO).

The Council of American Building Officials was organized in 1972 by the three model code agencies: Building Officials and Code Administrators International (BOCA), ICBO, and the Southern Building Code Congress International (SBCCI). After success with a group formed by these model code agencies called the Model Code Standardization Council (MCSC), the model code agencies formed CABO to coordinate the activities of the model code agencies and to represent the building code community at the national level by a single agency.

The Board for the Coordination of Model Codes (BCMC) was formed by CABO not only to occupy the field that the old MCSC had occupied (which was to standardize many of the provisions of the model codes, including format), but also to recommend resolution of differences among the model codes. In fact, the primary intent of CABO in forming BCMC was to provide an ongoing agency that could investigate differences among the model codes where those differences had been shown to create problems for the construction industry and could recommend resolution of those differences where possible. Since its formation, BCMC has also increased its scope somewhat by evaluating new concepts and technologies that are not currently part of the model codes. The most noticeable effect of these agencies on the model building codes has been:

1. Standardization, to a degree, of the formats of the model codes.
2. Standardization, to an even greater degree, of the types of construction as delineated in the model codes.
3. Standardization, to a degree, of the occupancy classifications in the model codes.

As a result of these attempts to standardize types of construction, occupancy classifications and format, earlier editions of the UBC contain different occupancy classifications than the current code, and the earlier types of construction were classified somewhat differently than in the current edition.

The format to be followed in this handbook will be, first of all, to present commentary only for those portions of the code for which commentary would be useful in furthering the understanding of the provision and its intent. Commentary will not be provided for those sections of the code for which commentary will be redundant or where the intent is obvious. In those cases where industry already has prepared a handbook, such as the Commentary to the ACI Building Code, no attempt will be made herein to provide commentary covering the same items.

A very important part of the *Uniform Building Code* and one that is not often recognized is the EFFECTIVE USE OF THE UNIFORM BUILDING CODE procedure that is shown after the table of contents. There is no single special or unique system through which the code may be applied, but the procedure listed in this section provides a rational, straightforward method to follow in the application of the UBC.

The reader will note throughout the code that there are sideheads that precede the section numbers and are intended to be descriptive of the material encompassed in the section that follows. The sideheads are printed in the UBC for convenience only and, as they are outside of the actual section, they are not part of the code itself as far as the enforceable provisions of the code are concerned.

DEDICATION

This book is dedicated to the memory of the late Robert C. Levy, superintendent, Bureau of Building Inspection, City of San Francisco, California.

FOREWORD

How often have you heard these questions when discussing the Building Code: "What is the intent of this section?" or "What is the background behind these provisions?" This handbook is an outgrowth of having heard these and similar questions for many years.

Building codes and similar regulatory documents could never be sufficiently detailed, prescriptive and explanatory to remove all doubt as to the intent of the various provisions. If such a document were possible, it would be so large that it would be virtually useless.

The purpose of this handbook is to provide the user with the intent of the various provisions of the *Uniform Building Code* and the background of many of the provisions where this background is recorded and known. Undoubtedly, there will be those readers who will know of other sources of background information, and ICBO will be grateful to receive this information.

Because the Building Code must be reasonably brief and concise in its provisions, the user and, particularly, the enforcement official, must have knowledge of the intent and background. It will be noted in this handbook, and particularly in Chapter 3, that the UBC places great reliance on the judgment of the building official for the specific application of its provisions. Where the building official has knowledge of the rationale behind the provisions, the enforcement of the code will be based on informed judgment rather than arbitrariness or routine procedures.

It is therefore our intent that this handbook provide as much information as possible so that this information, coupled with the enforcement official's experience and education, will result in not only better utilization of the code but also more uniformity in its application. As lengthy as this document may seem, it still cannot provide all of the answers to questions of code intent. Therefore, the background, training and experience of the reader must also be called on to properly interpret and enforce the code.

It was obvious at the outset that it was necessary to consult many publications and individuals in order to prepare and maintain a viable document. The original handbook, published in 1988, was authored by Vincent R. Bush. In developing the discussions of intent, Mr. Bush drew heavily on his 40 years of experience in structural engineering, 25 years of which were involved in the field of building regulation. Mr. Bush was also in charge of ICBO's code development from 1976 to 1984. The intent of many of the code provisions was not completely documented in material available to either the original author or his collaborative sources. In some cases, the discussion is subjective and there will undoubtedly be individuals who will disagree with the conclusion presented. It is important to note, however, that the explanatory narratives are based on many decades of experience by both the author and the other contributors to the manuscript, and it is hoped that the handbook will prove beneficial to the users. In addition to the expertise of Mr. Bush, major contributions by John F. Behrens in the past include the writing of the original manuscript to the egress chapter and assistance in preparation of many other chapters should be noted. Mr. Behrens' qualifications are equally as impressive as the original author's. Mr. Behrens has vast experience as a building official, district representative for ICBO, code consultant, and seminar instructor for both ICBO and the National Fire Protection Association. The combined talents of Messrs. Bush and Behrens in drafting the original manuscript for the first edition of the handbook are reflected by the wide distribution and reference to the handbook by code officials, professional designers and builders.

The handbook, like the *Uniform Building Code* on which it is based, has become a living document subject to changes and refinement as more editions are released. The 1997 edition reflects changes made to the 1994 UBC that were ultimately published in the 1997 UBC.

Although this edition of the handbook, like the original volume, was reviewed by the staff at ICBO, it still contains viewpoints that are strictly that of the original authors and contributors. These viewpoints do not necessarily reflect the official position of ICBO. This is not intended to, and should not detract from, the benefit to building officials, design professionals and builders.

The publications examined and used in this handbook are listed in the references at the end of each chapter. Many individuals too numerous to list assisted in providing information, data and application concepts during preparation of this handbook.

The following persons provided more than the usual expert counsel and deserve special thanks for their help in producing the first edition of the handbook, which was published in 1988: James E. Amrhein, James P. Barris, James E. Bihr, Thomas A. Briggs, Gordon F. Clyde, John G. Degenkolb, Frank Drake, Beverly J. Eicholtz, Dennis Evans, James R. Johnson, Clay M. Johnston, Charles E. Layman, Harry W. Martin, Dennis J. McCreary, Ann Muirhead, Wallace A. Norum, John Nosse, Robert E. O'Bannon, Rick Okawa, Walter F. Pruter, Marvin Smith, Ronald R. Walker, Donald R. Watson, Michael Westphal and Karen L. Zisko.

TABLE OF CONTENTS

Chapter 1

ADMINISTRATION

SECTION 101 — TITLE, PURPOSE AND SCOPE

In addition to title and scope, Chapter 1 covers general subjects such as the purpose of the code, performance provisions relating to alternate materials and methods of construction, modifications and tests. This chapter also contains requirements for inspections and the issuance of permits and certificates of occupancy. The provisions in Chapter 1 are of such a general nature as to apply to the entire *Uniform Building Code™* (UBC).

101.2 Purpose. The purpose of the code is more inclusive than most people realize. A careful reading will note that in addition to providing for life safety and safeguarding property, the code also intends that its provisions protect the public welfare. This latter item, "public welfare," is not so often thought of as being part of the purpose of a building code. However, in the case of the UBC, safeguarding public welfare is a part of its purpose, which is accomplished by the code, for example, by its provisions that ameliorate the conditions found in substandard or dangerous buildings. Moreover, upon the adoption of a modern building code such as the UBC, the general level of building safety and quality is raised. This in turn contributes to the public welfare by increasing the tax base and livability. Additionally, slum conditions are reduced, and the consequent reduction of insanitary conditions contributes to safeguarding the public welfare. For example, the maintenance requirements of Section 3402 apply to all buildings, both existing and new, and as a result the continued enforcement of the UBC slows the development of slum conditions. A rigorous enforcement of Section 3402 will actually reduce the conditions that contribute to slums. Thus, public welfare is enhanced by the increased benefits that inure to the general public of the jurisdiction as a result of the code provisions.

The code intends, through the police power granted by the state, to impress reasonable standards of construction upon the building public. The imposition of construction requirements that are in excess of the minimum standards would in most cases be considered unreasonable and quite likely could not be enforced.

101.3 Scope. The intent of the code as outlined in the first paragraph of this section is that the UBC applies to virtually anything that is built or constructed, except for the work specifically exempted in the first paragraph. The definitions of "building" and "structure" in Chapter 2 are so inclusive that the code intends that any work of any kind that is accomplished on any building or structure comes within the scope of the code except for the exclusions listed in the first paragraph. Thus, the code would apply to a major high-rise office building as well as to a small wooden fence that might enclose a portion of the rear yard of a person's property. However, see the discussion of required permits in this chapter.

SECTION 102 — UNSAFE BUILDINGS OR STRUCTURES

The provisions of this section are intended to define what constitutes an unsafe building, an unsafe use of a building and unsafe building appendages. The section declares that unsafe buildings, structures or appendages are public nuisances and require repair or abatement. The abatement procedures are indicated to be as set forth in the *Uniform Code for the Abatement of Dangerous Buildings™* or in any alternate procedure that may be adopted by the jurisdiction. In case the Dangerous Buildings Code or any alternate procedures have not been adopted by the jurisdiction, this section indicates that the jurisdiction may institute any other appropriate action to abate the violation. The intent of this last provision is that even though procedures have not been adopted, the jurisdiction may abate the hazard of dangerous buildings through proper legal proceedings, being particularly careful that the owners of the buildings have had the advantage of due process.[1]*

SECTION 104 — ORGANIZATION AND ENFORCEMENT

This section establishes the authority of the building official to act as the administrative head of the code enforcement agency and mandates that the building official enforce the provisions of the *Uniform Building Code.* The section also covers such items as actions of the building official and his or her deputies with regard to right of entry, stop orders, occupancy violations and liability.

104.2 Powers and Duties of Building Official.

104.2.3 Right of entry. This section is compatible with Supreme Court decisions since the 1960s regarding acts of inspection personnel seeking entry to buildings for the purpose of making inspections. Under present case law, an inspection may not be made of property, whether it be a private residence or a business establishment, without first having secured permission from the owner or person in charge of the premises. If entry is refused by the person having control of the property, the building official must obtain an inspection warrant from a court having jurisdiction in order to secure entry. The important feature of the law regarding right of entry is that entry must be made only by permission of the person having control of the property, or lacking this permission entry may be gained only through the use of an inspection warrant.

If entry is again refused after an inspection warrant has been obtained, the jurisdiction now has recourse through the courts to remedy this situation. One avenue is to obtain a civil injunction in which the court directs the person having control of the property to allow an inspection. Alternatively, the jurisdiction can

---

*References appear at the end of each chapter.

initiate proceedings in criminal court for punishment of the person having control of the property. It cannot be repeated too strongly that criminal court proceedings should never be initiated against an owner or other person having control of the property if an inspection warrant has not been obtained. Also, because the consequences of not following proper procedures can be so devastating to a jurisdiction if suit is brought against it, the jurisdiction's legal officer should always be consulted in these matters. For further reading on this subject, see Chapter 12 of *Building Department Administration.*[1]

104.2.6 Liability. It is the intent of the UBC that the building official not become personally liable for any damage that occurs to persons or property as a result of the building official's acts so long as he or she acts in good faith and without malice or fraud. However, there seems to be an increasing trend in the courts to find civil officers personally liable for careless acts. This section requires that the jurisdiction defend the building official if a suit is brought against him or her. Furthermore, the code requires that any judgment resulting from a suit be assumed by the jurisdiction. However, regardless of this language in the code, the jurisdiction may elect to not defend the building official on the basis, for example, that he or she acted carelessly.

The second paragraph intends that the jurisdiction, by reason of its approvals authorized by the UBC, not assume the responsibility of the person owning or controlling any building or structure for any damages to persons or property caused by defects in the building. This provision is based on the doctrine that governmental actions of jurisdictions are not subject to liability. The courts have held that building department operations are governmental functions.

Case law regarding tort liability of building officials is in a state of flux at the present time and old doctrines may not now be applicable. Therefore, the legal officer of the jurisdiction should always be consulted when there is any question about liability.

104.2.7 Modifications. The provisions of this section allow the building official to make modifications to the requirements of the code under certain specified circumstances. The building official may modify requirements if it is determined that strict application of the code is impractical and, furthermore, that the modification is in conformity with the intent and purpose of the code. Without this provision in the code, the building official has very little discretionary enforcement authority and, therefore, would have to enforce the specific wording of the code, no matter how unreasonable the application may seem.

The code does not intend to allow the building official to issue a variance to the provisions of the code to permit, for example, the use of only two exits where three are required. This is clearly not in conformity with the intent and purpose of the code no matter how difficult it may be to meet the requirements of the code.

This section would permit the building official, for example, to modify the requirements of Section 107.3 relative to plan review fees when a housing project of several hundred buildings is to be constructed and only four different building plans are to be used for the construction. The amount of work expended by the building department and, consequently, the plan check fee to be charged in this particular case is not proportional to the number of buildings but rather to the number of separate building plans to be used. Therefore, a lower plan check fee could be developed by the building official to reflect the amount of work actually to be performed.

104.2.8 Alternate materials, alternate design and methods of construction. This section of the UBC may be one of the most important sections of the code. The intent is to implement the adoption of new technologies in materials and building construction that currently are not covered by the code. Furthermore, it gives the code even more of a performance character. The code thus encourages state-of-the-art concepts in construction and materials as long as they meet the performance intended by the code. This section also charges the building official to require that substantiating data and evidence be submitted to show that the alternate is in fact equivalent to the performance required by the code. Moreover, the code charges the building official with maintaining a record of such approvals in the department files.

104.2.9 Tests. The provisions of this section provide the building official with discretionary authority to require tests to substantiate proof of compliance with the code requirements. The application of these provisions should be restricted to those cases where evidence of compliance is either nonexistent or involves actions considered to be impractical.

An example would be the placement of concrete that the quality control measures (i.e., cylinder tests) did not prove compliance with minimum strength requirements. Testing of core samples or perhaps use of nondestructive test methods might be appropriate to demonstrate compliance.

The second paragraph specifies that the tests be those that are specifically enumerated within the adopted construction regulations or, as an alternate, be those of other recognized national test standards where test standards do not exist. The building official has the authority to determine the test procedures necessary to demonstrate compliance. In addition to determining appropriate test methods or procedures, the building official is mandated to maintain records of such tests in accordance with local or state statutes.

SECTION 105 — BOARD OF APPEALS

The *Uniform Building Code* intends that the board of appeals have very limited authority. This is to hear and decide appeals of orders and decisions of the building official relative to the application and interpretations of the code. Moreover, the code specifically limits the authority of the board relative to the administrative provisions of the code and does not permit waivers of code requirements. Any broader authority to be granted to the board of appeals must be granted in the adoption ordinance by a modification of this section.

SECTION 106 — PERMITS

This section covers those requirements related to the activities of the building department with respect to the issuance of permits. The issuance of permits, plan review and inspection of construction for which permits have been issued constitutes the bulk of the duties of the usual building inspection department. It is for this reason that the code goes into detail regarding the permit-issuance process. Additionally, the code provides detailed requirements for the inspection process in order to help ensure that the construction for which the inspections are made complies with the code in all respects.

106.2 Work Exempt from Permit. In earlier years the UBC required permits for any type of work that would have been covered by the scope of the code. Since the 1979 edition, however, language has been added that provides for exempted work. This section issues a caveat to the effect that even though exempted by the Building Code for a building permit, separate plumbing, electrical and mechanical permits may be required unless they are also exempted by those codes.

It is further the intent of the code that even though work may be exempted for permit, any work done on a building or structure must still comply with the code. As indicated in Section 101.3, the scope of the UBC is virtually all-inclusive. This may seem to be a superfluous requirement where a permit is not required. However, this type of provision is necessary to provide that the owner be responsible for proper and safe construction for all work being done.

106.3 Application for Permit. In this section the UBC directs that a permit be applied for and describes the information required not only on the permit application but also on the plans and specifications filed with the permit application. Essentially, the code requires that plans, engineering calculations and any other data necessary to describe the work to be done be filed along with the application for a permit. Structural observation programs are also to be submitted with the application for a permit that may be required by other sections of the code. The building official may require that the plans, specifications and other documents be prepared by a licensed competent person. In some cases, the design of portions of the building is not complete and may be dependent on the manufacturer of proposed prefabricated elements, such as for truss drawings. The code, therefore, specifically allows deferring the submittal of portions of the plans and specifications. The building official is permitted to waive the requirement for the filing of plans and other data, provided the building official is assured that the work for which the permit is applied is of such a nature that plans or any other data are not necessary in order to obtain compliance with the code.

106.4 Permits Issuance.

106.4.1 Issuance. The permit-issuance process as envisioned by the UBC is intended to provide records within the code enforcement agency of all construction activities that take place within the jurisdiction and to provide orderly controls on the construction process. Thus, the application for permit is intended to describe in detail the work to be done. The plans and other data filed with the application are intended to graphically depict the construction work to be done. In this section the building official is directed to review the application for permit and the plans and specifications filed with the permit. This review of the plans and specifications is not a discretionary procedure but rather is mandated by the code. The building official is not at liberty to check only a portion of the plans. On this basis the structural drawings as well as the engineering calculations must be checked in order for the building official to comply with the code. In fact, if the structural plans and engineering calculations are not reviewed by the building official, the building official is in effect presuming the infallibility of the design engineer in addition to violating the code.

The code also charges the building official with the issuance of a permit when it has been determined that the information filed with the application shows compliance with the *Uniform Building Code* and other laws and ordinances applicable to the building at its location in the jurisdiction. The building official may not withhold the issuance of a permit if these conditions are met. Thus, the building official would be in violation of the code to withhold the issuance of a building permit for a swimming pool because a cabana was constructed without a permit[2].

106.4.3 Validity of permit. The code intends that the issuance of a permit not be construed as permitting a violation of the code or any other law or ordinance applicable to the building. In fact, the code authorizes the building official to require corrections if there were errors in the approved plans or permit application at the time the permit was issued. The building official is further authorized to require corrections of the actual construction if it is in violation of the code although in accordance with the plans. Moreover, the building official is further authorized to suspend or revoke the permit in writing if it is found that the permit was issued in error or in violation of any regulation or provision of the code.

While it may be poor public relations to suspend or revoke a permit or to require corrections of the plans after they have been approved, it is clearly the intent of the code that the approval of plans or the issuance of a permit may not be done in violation of the code or of other pertinent laws or ordinances.

106.4.4 Expiration. The *Uniform Building Code* anticipates that once a permit has been issued, construction will soon follow and proceed expeditiously until its completion. However, this ideal procedure is not always the case, and therefore the code makes provisions for those cases where work is not started or alternately where the work after being started has been suspended for a period of time. In these cases the UBC allows a period of 180 days to transpire before the permit becomes void. The code then requires that a new permit be obtained with the fee equal to one half of the fee normally required for such work. It is assumed by the code that the code enforcement agency will have expended some effort and follow-up inspections of the work, etc., and therefore at least one half of the permit fee must be retained in order to compensate the agency for the work. However, see the discussion of fee refunds under Section 107.

SECTION 107 — FEES

107.1 General. The *Uniform Building Code* anticipates that many jurisdictions will establish their own fee schedules and, therefore, recognizes that the fees to be charged for building permits and for plan review will be either as set forth in this section or as established by the jurisdiction. It is the intent of the UBC that the fees collected by the department for building permit and plan review be adequate to cover the costs to the department in these areas. If the department has other duties in addition to building permits and plan review, then the budget of the department will need to be supplemented from the general fund.

107.2 Permit Fees. The code uses the concept of valuation to establish the building permit fee. This concept is based on the proposition that the valuation of a project is related to the amount of work to be expended in plan review, inspections and administering the permit. Also, there should be some excess in the permit fee to cover the department overhead.

The code defines the valuation or value of the building in Chapter 2 essentially as the cost of replacing the building in kind. Also, the valuation includes work such as finish work, painting, electrical and mechanical work, etc., even though separate permits are to be obtained for the mechanical and electrical trades.

In order to provide some uniformity in the determination of valuation so that there is a consistent base for the assignment of fees, the code directs the building official to determine the value of the building. To assist in obtaining uniformity, the International Conference of Building Officials publishes "Building Valuation Data" in its *Building Standards*[3] magazine periodically. Thus, building officials may utilize a common base in their determination of the value of buildings. To quote from the Building Valuation Data published in the March-April, 1998, issue of the magazine:

> The unit costs are intended to comply with the definition of "valuation" in Section 223 of the 1997 *Uniform Building Code*™ and thus include architectural, structural, electrical, plumbing and mechanical work, except as specifically listed below. The unit costs also include the contractor's profit, which should not be omitted.

107.4 Expiration of Plan Review. When a permit has not been issued within 180 days following the date of application, the application and plan review expire. However, the code authorizes the building official to extend this time for one more 180-day period when it is determined that circumstances beyond the control of the applicant prevented action to secure the permit. However, see the discussion in Section 107.6 addressing the subject of fee refunds.

107.5 Investigation Fees: Work without a Permit. When work requiring a permit is started without a permit, the code directs the building official to cause an investigation to be made of the work already done. The intent of the investigation is to determine to what extent the work completed complies with the code and to describe with as much detail as possible the work that has been completed. Because it is anticipated that the investigation may require considerable time and effort, the code specifies that a fee be paid by the person doing the work equal in amount to the permit fee that would be required. The investigation fee is to be paid in addition to the regular permit and plan check fees. Moreover, the investigation fee is to be paid whether or not a permit is later issued.

107.6 Fee Refunds. This section authorizes the building official to refund a portion of the permit fee, the plan check fee, or both, for good cause. One instance would be where the permit fee is collected in error. Another reason for authorizing the refund of the fees paid would be because circumstances beyond the control of the applicant caused delays and the eventual expiration of either the permit or the plan review. In these cases the building official may authorize the refunding of up to 80 percent of the fee paid, the intent being that at least 20 percent of the fee paid has been expended by the department in administering the plan review and permit process and in keeping track of the progress.

The building official, when authorizing a fee refund, is authorizing the disbursement of public funds. Therefore, the building official must be sure that there is good cause for the refund upon written request by the original permit holder.

SECTION 108 — INSPECTIONS

The inspection function is one of the more important aspects of building department operations along with the plan review function. The code intends that inspections, as with issuance of permits, that presume to give authority to violations of the code are invalid.

108.3 Inspection Requests. In general the UBC charges the person doing the work with notifying the code enforcement agency when it is time to make an inspection. The code also places a duty upon the person doing the work to have the work to be inspected accessible and exposed so it can be inspected.

108.4 Approval Required. The code intends that no work shall be done beyond the point where an inspection is required until the work requiring inspection has been approved. Moreover, it is intended that work requiring inspection not be covered until it has been inspected and approved.

108.5 Required Inspections. The code mandates five inspections during the progress of construction of a building, as follows:

1. Foundation inspection.
2. Concrete slab or under-floor inspection.
3. Frame inspection.
4. Lath and/or gypsum board inspection.
5. Final inspection.

108.7 and 108.8 Other Inspections and Reinspections. The code gives the building official authority to require and make other inspections where necessary to determine compliance with the code and other laws and regulations enforced by the department. In each case for the required inspections, the code is very specific as to how far the construction must have progressed in order to call for the inspection. If it is necessary to make a reinspection because work has not progressed to the point where it is ready for inspection, the code authorizes the building official to charge a reinspection fee. The reinspection fee is not mandated and normally would not be charged unless the person doing the work continually calls for inspections before the work is ready for inspection.

SECTION 109 — CERTIFICATE OF OCCUPANCY

109.1 Use and Occupancy. The tool that the building official uses to control the uses and occupancies of the various buildings and structures within the jurisdiction is the certificate of occupancy. The *Uniform Building Code* makes it unlawful to use or occupy a building or structure unless a certificate of occupancy has been issued for that use. Furthermore, the code imposes the duty of issuing a certificate of occupancy upon the building official when the building official is satisfied that the building or portion thereof complies with the code for the intended use and occupancy.

109.5 Posting. Except for Group R, Division 3 and Group U Occupancies that do not require certificates of occupancy, the code specifies that the certificate be posted in a conspicuous location in the building. This posting makes it possible for inspection personnel of the building department as well as other agencies to determine whether the building is being used in compliance with the code.

In essence, the certificate of occupancy certifies that the described building or portion thereof complies with the requirements of the code for the intended use and occupancy, except as provided in Section 3405. However, any certificate of occupancy presuming to authorize a violation of the code or other ordinances is declared by this section to be invalid. This provision is consistent with similar provisions relative to permit issuance and inspection approvals.

REFERENCES

[1]O'Bannon, Robert E. (1988). *Building Department Administration.* International Conference of Building Officials, Whittier, California.

[2]Vogelsang, John (1974). Kay Ellis vs. the City Council. *Building Standards,* 43(2):18-19.

[3]*Building Standards* magazine is published bimonthly by the International Conference of Building Officials.

Chapter 2

DEFINITIONS AND ABBREVIATIONS

SECTION 201 — DEFINITIONS

The *Uniform Building Code* provides definitions in Chapter 2 of terms that are generally used in two or more places in the code and are those that are applicable specifically to the code and may not have an appropriate definition for code purposes in Webster's unabridged dictionary. Also, there are definitions within several of the chapters of the UBC that are intended to apply only to that chapter or section. Therefore, in order to determine whether or not a definition for a specific item is contained within the UBC, Chapter 2 must be examined as well as the chapter that covers the specific subject for which a definition is desired. The definitions of some terms are contained within the text of a requirement. For example, the definition of occupancy separations is within Section 302.3. Some other frequently used and significant terms are undefined (for example, "one-hour construction"), and their meaning can be discerned only from their context. There are numerous definitions in Chapter 2, but only selected definitions are included in this commentary.

201.1 General. The important feature of this section is the requirement that Webster's unabridged dictionary shall be used to provide ordinarily accepted meanings to terms that are not specifically defined in the code. Therefore, the code defines terms that have specific intents and meanings insofar as the code is concerned and leaves it up to Webster's unabridged dictionary to provide meanings for all other terms.

SECTION 202 — A

ACCREDITATION BODY. This definition addresses the approved authority that accredits and monitors the competency and performance of grading or inspection agencies relative to carrying out a specific task and is necessary to ensure quality control.

AEROSOL. The definition of aerosol coordinates the *Uniform Building Code* and the *Uniform Fire Code*™ (UFC), which regulates aerosol products. Aerosols are distinguished from other products due to their potential to "rocket" in a fire. Flammable aerosols can "rocket" and spread fire a considerable distance. Special controls are therefore imposed on aerosols by the Fire Code, and occupancy limitations are imposed by the Building Code.

AMUSEMENT BUILDING. See Section 408.2 for definition.

APARTMENT HOUSE. The definition for apartment house is succinct and states in essence that an apartment house is any building or portion thereof that contains three or more dwelling units. The definition also includes, for the purpose of the code, residential condominiums as an apartment house. As the term "residential condominium" is not defined in the UBC except to refer back to the definition of an apartment house, the question arises then as to what a residential condominium is. In accor-

dance with Section 201, recourse must be to Webster's unabridged dictionary for the definition of residential condominium. To paraphrase Webster's, a residential condominium is individual ownership of a unit in a multiunit structure (as an apartment building). The ownership of the structure and property is held in common. Webster's further defines a residential condominium as a unit so owned and, even further, a building containing condominiums. Therefore, based on the definition in the code for an apartment house and in Webster's unabridged dictionary for a residential condominium, it appears that *any* building containing three or more dwelling units held in common (belonging to each in a group) is an apartment house. The definition in the code for an apartment house is indeed appropriate, as it includes all of the previously described residential uses where there are three or more dwelling units in the same building. Thus, the definition in the UBC for apartment house will include apartment houses in which all the units are rented by the occupants as well as those where the units are owned by the occupants and the property is held in common. It should be noted, however, that when walls and real estate property lines establish the boundaries of a living facility that is not held in common but is independently owned, it should be treated as a dwelling. Some townhouses are in this category.

SECTION 203 — B

BASEMENT. For commentary regarding the definition of basement, see commentary for the definition of story.

SECTION 204 — C

CONGREGATE RESIDENCE. This definition addresses such alternate living arrangements as convents, monasteries, dormitories, and fraternity and sorority houses. Typically, larger cities and cities with a college or university continue to see an increase in these nontraditional living arrangements. The original concept of a dwelling unit, either in a Group R, Division 1 or Group R, Division 3 Occupancy, which is occupied by only one family, did not cover many of these living arrangements.

SECTION 205 — D

DRAFT STOP. The definition was added to clarify the meaning of the term as it is used in Section 708.

SECTION 207 — F

FLOOR AREA. This definition is the area included within the surrounding exterior walls of a building, and the definition further states that the floor area of a building or portion thereof not provided with surrounding exterior walls shall be the usable area under the horizontal projection of the roof or floor above.

The intent of this latter provision is to cover the case where a building may not have exterior walls or may have one or more sides open without an enclosing exterior wall.

SECTION 208 — G

GRADE (Adjacent Ground Elevation). The code indicates that grade is the lowest point of elevation of the finished surface of the ground within an area between the building and property line or where the property line is more than 5 feet (1524 mm) from the building between the building and a line 5 feet (1524 mm) from the building.

This definition is important in determining the number of stories within a building as well as its height in feet. In some cases the finished surface of the ground may be artificially raised with imported fill to create a higher grade around a building so as to

decrease the number of stories or height in feet. The code does not prohibit this practice, and as long as a building meets the code definition and restrictions for height or number of stories, the intent of the code is met. See Figure 208-1.

SECTION 209 — H

HEIGHT OF BUILDING. The critical feature in the definition of height of building is the case where the building is on a sloping site. In the case of a sloping site, the height of the building is measured as depicted in Figure 209-1.

Where the building is stepped or terraced, the code intends that the height of such building is the maximum height of any segment of the building. It may be appropriate under certain circumstances that the number of stories in a building be determined in the same manner. Because of the varying requirements of the code that are related to the number of stories, such as exit-

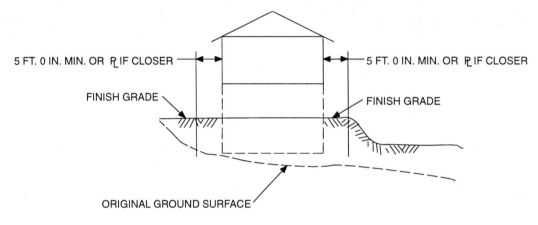

For **SI:** 1 foot = 304.8 mm.

USE OF BUILT-UP SOIL TO RAISE FINISH GRADE

FIGURE 208-1

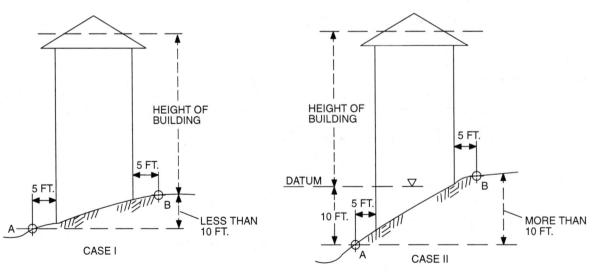

For **SI:** 1 foot = 304.8 mm.

DETERMINATION OF BUILDING HEIGHT IN FEET (mm)

FIGURE 209-1

MAXIMUM HEIGHT OF BUILDING IS 28 FT. @ SEGMENT 1.
MAXIMUM NUMBER OF STORIES IS 3 @ SEGMENTS 1 AND 2.

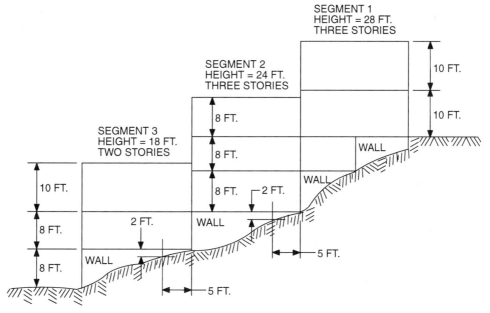

For **SI:** 1 foot = 304.8 mm.

TERRACED BUILDING

FIGURE 209-2

ing, fire resistance of construction, shaft enclosures, etc., each case should be judged individually based on the characteristics of the site and construction. In addition to those factors that are related to the number of stories, other items to consider are fire department access, location of exterior exits, routes of exit travel and type of separation between segments.

Figure 209-2 illustrates one example in which the height of the building and number of stories are determined for a stepped or terraced building. In the case of a stepped or terraced building, the language "total perimeter" used to define the case separating the first story from a basement is intended to include the entire perimeter of each segment of the building. Therefore, in the cross section of Figure 209-3, the total perimeter of the down-slope segment would be bounded by the retaining wall, the down-slope exterior wall, and the east and west exterior walls. In the case illustrated, the dwelling has two stories and a basement for the down-slope segment. The measurement for the maximum height of the building would be based upon the maximum height of the down-slope segment. In this case the highest grade of the segment is more than 10 feet (3048 mm) above the lowest grade. Thus, the reference datum would be 10 feet (3048 mm) above lowest grade, and the height would be 17 feet 6 inches (5334 mm) plus half the height of the attic.

SECTION 214 — M

MEZZANINE or **MEZZANINE FLOOR.** Although not specifically stated, the intent is also to include an intermediate floor placed within a story. A mezzanine is not counted as an additional story in a building under certain conditions. See Sections 504.4 and 507 of the UBC.

SECTION 216 — O

OCCUPANCY. In addition to the definition in this section, the code intends that the word "occupancy" carry also the connotation of a specific family of uses that are considered generally to have similar hazard characteristics. While use and occupancy are quite often used interchangeably in the code, when the word occupancy is used, it means specifically the occupancy classification of the building as defined in Chapter 3. An unoccupied building would be classified by its intended use.

SECTION 220 — S

STORY. The critical part of the definition of story involves the definition of the first story. The code defines the first story as the lowest story in a building that qualifies as a story. The first story may be either an inhabited story or may be unused under-floor space. There are two criteria that are critical to the determination if a given level is either the first story or basement:

1. If the finished floor level above the level under consideration or above under-floor space is more than 6 feet (1829 mm) above grade for more than 50 percent of the total perimeter of the building, the level under consideration is the first story.

2. If the finished floor level above the level under consideration or above under-floor space is more than 12 feet (3658 mm) above grade at any point, the level under consideration or the under-floor space shall be considered as the first story.

Conversely, if the finished floor level above the level under consideration is 6 feet (1829 mm) or less above grade for more than 50 percent of the perimeter and does not exceed 12 feet (3658 mm) at any point, the floor level under consideration is a basement. Or, as succinctly defined in the code, a basement is a floor level below the first story.

Where a building is partially excavated into a side-hill location and consists of only one level, that level is considered to be a basement by the code unless the floor level is 4 feet (1219 mm) or less below grade for more than 50 percent of the total perimeter or is 8 feet (2438 mm) or less below grade at any point. In this latter case the level is considered to be a one-story building. Figures 209-3 and 220-1 illustrate the definitions of story, first story and basement.

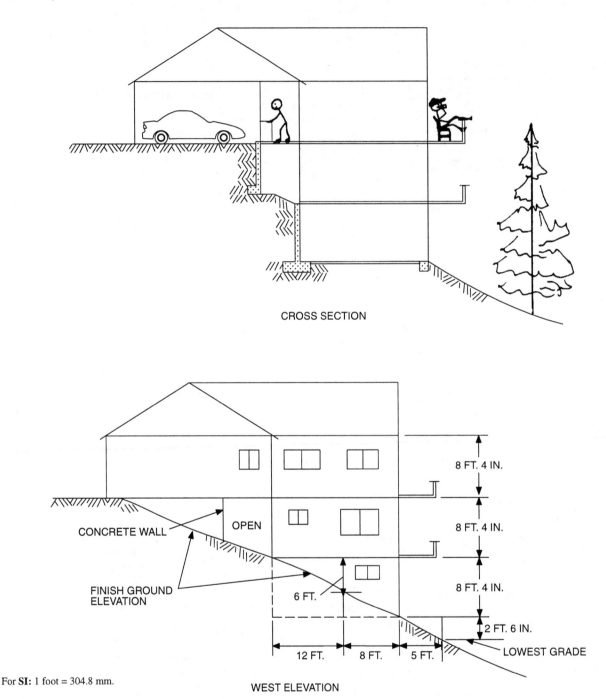

CROSS SECTION

For **SI:** 1 foot = 304.8 mm.

WEST ELEVATION

TWO-STORY AND BASEMENT BUILDING

FIGURE 209-3

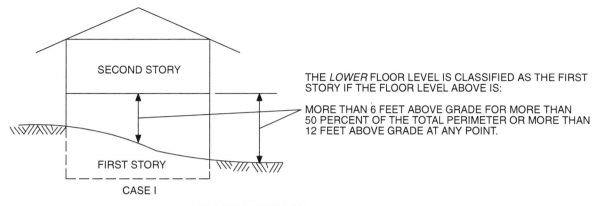

SECOND STORY

FIRST STORY

THE *LOWER* FLOOR LEVEL IS CLASSIFIED AS THE FIRST STORY IF THE FLOOR LEVEL ABOVE IS:

MORE THAN 6 FEET ABOVE GRADE FOR MORE THAN 50 PERCENT OF THE TOTAL PERIMETER OR MORE THAN 12 FEET ABOVE GRADE AT ANY POINT.

CASE I

TWO-STORY BUILDING

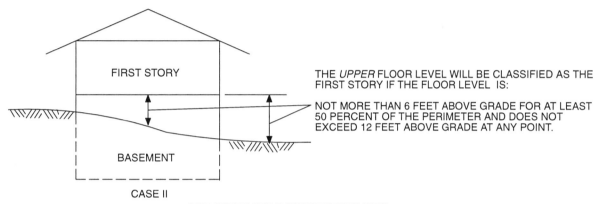

FIRST STORY

BASEMENT

THE *UPPER* FLOOR LEVEL WILL BE CLASSIFIED AS THE FIRST STORY IF THE FLOOR LEVEL IS:

NOT MORE THAN 6 FEET ABOVE GRADE FOR AT LEAST 50 PERCENT OF THE PERIMETER AND DOES NOT EXCEED 12 FEET ABOVE GRADE AT ANY POINT.

CASE II

ONE-STORY AND BASEMENT BUILDING

MULTILEVEL BUILDINGS

FIRST STORY FOR A BUILDING HAVING ONLY ONE LEVEL:

FLOOR LEVEL IS CLASSIFIED AS THE FIRST STORY WHEN THE FLOOR LEVEL IS:

NOT MORE THAN 4 FEET BELOW GRADE FOR MORE THAN 50 PERCENT OF THE TOTAL PERIMETER NOR MORE THAN 8 FEET BELOW GRADE AT ANY POINT.

FIRST STORY

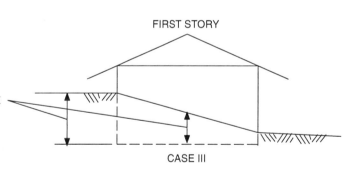

CASE III

BUILDING HAS NO FIRST STORY AND THE FLOOR LEVEL IS CLASSIFIED AS A BASEMENT WHEN THE FLOOR LEVEL IS:

MORE THAN 4 FEET BELOW GRADE FOR MORE THAN 50 PERCENT OF THE TOTAL PERIMETER OR MORE THAN 8 FEET BELOW GRADE AT ANY POINT.

BASEMENT

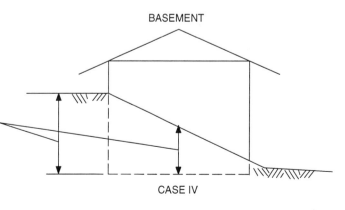

CASE IV

For **SI:** 1 foot = 304.8 mm.

SINGLE-LEVEL BUILDINGS

FIGURE 220-1

Chapter 3

USE OR OCCUPANCY

The occupancies defined, first in the 1994 edition of the code, are consistent with the recommendations of the Board for the Coordination of Model Codes (BCMC) and are essentially the same within each of the three model codes issued in the United States. The BCMC is a national committee consisting of representatives from the International Conference of Building Officials, the Building Officials and Code Administrators International, the Southern Building Code Congress International, the National Fire Protection Association, the American Institute of Architects, and the engineering discipline.

Sections 303 through 312 contain the requirements for each occupancy. The subjects covered in these sections are generally presented in the same sequence. For example, the 0.1 sections of each of these sections contain the occupancy definition. To avoid redundancy in the discussion that follows Section 303, references to a single section number are used to cover a subject that is common to all or most of the occupancies. The subjects covered by the abbreviated section reference are as follows:

.1 Sections. Occupancy Defined

.2 Sections. Construction, Height and Allowable Area

.3 Sections. Location on Property

.4 Sections. Access and Exit Facilities

.5 Sections. Light, Ventilation and Sanitation

.6 Sections. Shaft and Exit Enclosures

.7 Sections. Sprinkler and Standpipe Systems

.8 Sections. Special Hazards

Chapter 3 of the code considers the risk to occupants of the building as well as the probability of property loss. For the most part, the level of risk to occupants within a building is dependent on the number of occupants, their age, their capability of self-preservation and their control over the conditions to which they are subjected. With regard to protection against property loss, the code considers not only the internal hazards but also exposures to and from adjacent buildings and the combined hazard of buildings in a neighborhood. Regulations are based on previous experience with adjustments for current technology. In developing regulations, consideration is given to the rate of fire spread, its intensity and duration. The code recognizes the performance that may be expected from materials common in today's marketplace and recognizes materials and methods of construction that are economically feasible. Finally, the code considers the facilities that are necessary to operate and maintain a building that do not impinge on the health and public welfare of a community's citizens. The bulk of the requirements in the balance of the code are greatly dependent on the proper application of this chapter.

SECTION 301 — OCCUPANCY CLASSIFIED

This section directs the building official to:

1. Classify all buildings into one of the occupancies set forth in Table 3-A. For new buildings, the occupancy assignment is established during plan review. For unclassified existing buildings, the code does not establish a specific time within which the occupancy assignment must be made. The code intends to allow the assignment to be established whenever there is any work done that requires a permit or when there is a change in occupancy. Although the 1997 edition of the code lists in more detail the uses allowed within a specific occupancy classification, the building official will be called upon to judge whether a selected classification is appropriate under specific conditions. Assigning an occupancy classification often not only depends on the use but also on the extent and intensity of that use. A use may be so incidental to the overall occupancy that its effect on fire and life safety is negligible. For an obvious example, checkout stations in a store perform a service-type transaction, but such a use is so incidental to the general operation of the store that assigning it to a separate occupancy would be ridiculous. Therefore, the building officials' judgment will continue to be relied upon to classify occupancies even though the list of uses has been expanded.

2. Classify a use into the occupancy group that it most nearly resembles, based on life and fire hazard, when the use is not described specifically in the code or when there may be a question regarding its proper classification.

The code intends to divide the many uses possible in buildings and structures into 10 separate groupings where each group by itself represents a broadly similar hazard. The perils contemplated by the occupancy groupings are of the fire- and life-safety types and are broadly divided into two general categories: those related to people and those related to property. The people-related hazards are divided further by activity, by number of occupants, their age, their capability of self-preservation, and the individual's control over the conditions to which he or she is subjected. The property-related hazards are divided further by the quantity of combustible, flammable or explosive materials and by whether it is in use or storage.

The uses to which a building may be put are obviously manifold, and as a result the building official will, on more than one occasion, either find or be presented with a use that will not conveniently fit into one of the occupancy classifications outlined in the code. As indicated previously in this commentary, under these circumstances the code directs the building official to place the use in that classification delineated in the code that it most nearly resembles based on its life and fire risk. This requirement gives the building official broad authority to use judgment in the determination of the hazard of the affected occupancy and, as a result of this evaluation, determine the occupancy classification that the hazards of the use most nearly resemble.

The language "or about which there is any question" can involve at least two situations. The first would be where the owner of a building and the building official have a difference of opinion as to the proper occupancy classification. The second is the situation where the building official is faced with a use that appears to fit into one of the code-described occupancy classifications, but after further analysis the building official finds that the hazards representative of the code-defined occupancy classification are not present in the use proposed. On this basis the code again directs that the building official place the use in the occupancy classification that it most nearly resembles based on its life- and fire-hazard characteristics.

SECTION 302 — MIXED USE OR OCCUPANCY

302.1 General. It is more common than not for a building to contain more than one occupancy. Even the dwellings in which most of us live usually consist of the dwelling and an attached private garage. In the parlance of the UBC, these are two distinct and separate "occupancies." Office buildings of any size not only house the offices but may contain parking garages and, in many cases, cafeterias and other assembly areas. Each of these uses constitutes a distinct and separate occupancy as far as the UBC is concerned. Because this situation is so common, the code in this section specifies requirements for buildings of mixed occupancies.

Even though Section 301 directs the building official to classify a building into one of the 10 occupancy groups described in that section, Section 302 specifically modifies this requirement for buildings housing more than one occupancy. In the case of multiple-use buildings, the code directs that each portion of the building housing a separate occupancy comply with the requirements for that occupancy. Furthermore, the code intends that each occupancy be separated from any other, as required by Section 302.4. This section requires fire-resistive separations between certain occupancies, depending on the potential fire hazards representative of the separated occupancies.

The general rationale behind the use of fire-resistive occupancy separations concerns itself with the amount of combustibles encompassed in an occupancy and is termed in fire-protection circles as the "fire loading." Thus, if the amount of combustibles or fire loading is quite high, the occupancy separation between two distinct occupancies should also have a relatively high fire-resistive rating.

This general concept is not always followed by the code, and in fact many occupancy separations required by the code are specified to have fire-resistive time periods that do not appear on the surface to relate to the amount of combustibles in either occupancy. In some cases an occupancy separation is specified between two occupancies to be of four hours duration mainly because of what the code implies to be incompatibility between the two occupancies rather than a high fire loading.

For example, the code requires a four-hour fire-resistive occupancy separation between a Group I, Division 1.2 Occupancy and a Group S, Division 3 Occupancy. The amount of combustibles in either occupancy does not justify a four-hour rating for the occupancy separation. However, because of the

presumed incompatibility between the two occupancies, the four-hour fire-resistive occupancy separation is considered to be justified as no openings are permitted in the separation. Conversely, the occupancy separation between a Group H, Division 6 Occupancy and a Group A, Division 3 Occupancy is listed as three hours. The amount of hazardous materials in the Group H, Division 6 Occupancy is roughly comparable to Group H, Division 2 Occupancies and would normally require a four-hour fire-resistive occupancy separation. In this case, however, the code prescribes a three-hour fire-resistive occupancy separation that permits openings. This was done so that lunchrooms could be located in a Group H, Division 6 Occupancy building with openings permitted between the two occupancies for free movement back and forth.

Exceptions to the rule. Exceptions to the requirements for occupancy separation provisions are divided into three categories as follows:

1. Exceptions to requirements that an occupancy separation be provided. These exceptions are listed in Section 302.1.

2. Exceptions that modify the fire resistance of an assembly. These exceptions are listed in Section 302.4 and the footnotes to Table 3-B.

3. Exceptions related primarily to a condition that is peculiar to a use. These exceptions may be more or less restrictive than the general requirement for an occupancy. Exceptions in category 3, for the most part, are within the special provisions of the occupancy sections, and when they occur elsewhere they are often referenced by a section in the occupancy sections. For example, Section 302.5 is referenced by the special hazard sections of the occupancy sections.

Experience has shown that there is a practical need to have certain accessory uses without a fire-resistive separation from the primary occupancy. Because of this need and because of the reasonably good fire record exhibited by these uses, this section contains several exceptions to the requirement for a fire-resistive occupancy separation.

Exception 2 lists a number of accessory uses that need not be separated. For these uses, the code considers that there is no significant hazard created by the elimination of an occupancy separation where these uses are limited. Administrative and clerical offices not related to hazardous occupancies, small assembly rooms and kitchens serving a dining area of which the kitchen is a part are included under this exception.

Item 2.3 of Exception 2 addresses a condition that occurs in many hotels and motels. Under this exception, a Group R, Division 1 Occupancy may contain gift shops, administrative offices and similar Groups B and M type uses that are not separated from the primary residential use, provided their collective areas do not exceed 10 percent of the floor area of the primary use. For a multistory building, however, the 10 percent limitation does raise the following question: Is the 10 percent applied to the total floor area of all stories, or does it apply only to the story under consideration? Based on the intent of the exception, which is to permit a limited area of unseparated uses, the area of gift shops, offices and similar rooms should not exceed 10 percent of the floor area of the primary use on the story under consideration. See Application Example 302-1.

**Application Example 302-1
Section 302.1**

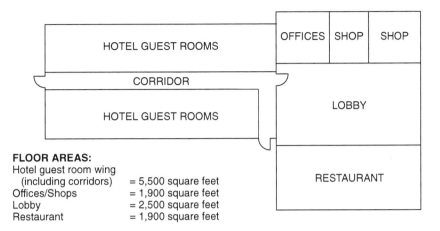

FLOOR AREAS:

Hotel guest room wing (including corridors)	= 5,500 square feet
Offices/Shops	= 1,900 square feet
Lobby	= 2,500 square feet
Restaurant	= 1,900 square feet

For **SI:** 1 square foot = 0.093 m².

REQUIRED OCCUPANCY SEPARATIONS

FIGURE 302-1

GIVEN: Information in Figure 302-1.

DETERMINE: Occupancy separation requirements.

SOLUTION: A hotel lobby presents an interesting problem in occupancy assignment. On the one hand, a lobby is a normal function of a hotel and, therefore, could be considered to be a part of the hotel use and considered to be a Group R, Division 1 Occupancy. On the other hand, at least for the particular layout presented above, it could be considered as a public area not unlike an airport terminal, which would be classified as a Group A Occupancy. Thus, it is possible to evaluate the problem in two ways, either of which can be considered appropriate and correct.

Case I—Consider the lobby area to be an extension of the hotel use and classify it as a Group R, Division 1 Occupancy. Based on this classification, we will first determine if the office and shop areas are exempt from occupancy separation requirements by having an area that does not exceed 10 percent of the major use. The area that may be used for determining the 10 percent limitation is:

5,500 (hotel guest room wing) + 2,500 (lobby) = 8,000 square feet

and the maximum area permitted for the offices and shops without an occupancy separation is:

10% x 8,000 = 800 square feet

Since the area of the offices and shops exceeds 800 square feet, an occupancy separation will be required between them and the lobby and hotel guest room wing. Table 3-B requires a one-hour occupancy separation between Groups B and M Occupancies (offices and shops) and a Group R, Division 1 Occupancy (hotel guest rooms and lobby).

The restaurant has an occupant load of approximately 126 (1,900/15 = 126), so it would be classified as a Group A, Division 3 Occupancy. Table 3-B also requires a one-hour separation between a Group A, Division 3 Occupancy and a Group R, Division 1 Occupancy. So a one-hour occupancy separation will also be required between the lobby and the restaurant.

Case II—An alternate solution to this particular problem would be to consider the lobby to be a Group A Occupancy. With an area of 2,500 square feet, the lobby would have an occupancy of approximately 167 (2,500/15 = 167) and would therefore be classified as a Group A, Division 3 Occupancy. According to Table 3-B, no occupancy separation is required between Groups B and M Occupancies and a Group A, Division 3 Occupancy, so the office and shop area would not need to be separated from the lobby. Further, since the restaurant is also a Group A, Division 3 Occupancy, it would not need to be separated from the lobby area. A one-hour occupancy separation, however, would be required between the hotel guest room wing and the entire adjoining wing (offices, shops, lobby and restaurant).

There is some conjecture as to whether or not a kitchen should have a different occupancy classification from the dining area. However, in order to make certain that a separation is not required, Item 2.4 of Exception 2 specifies the intent of the code to not require a separation between a dining area and its kitchen. The code considers that it is not practical or warranted to require an occupancy separation in this case. There are many examples, such as steak houses, where cooking is done as a display for the patrons and such uses have functioned without creating a significant hazard.

Exception 1 allows a spray booth constructed in accordance with the Fire Code to be exempt from a separation in specified occupancies. The Fire Code requirements result in comparable safety due to area limitations and construction requirements. Additional exceptions to specific uses are within the occupancy

sections; for example, see Section 311.2.3.2 for fuel dispensing at minimarkets.

Occupancy height limitations. For height limitations, the code specifies for mixed-occupancy buildings that any occupancy shall not be located higher in the building than is permitted for that occupancy by UBC Table 5-B. Figure 302-2 depicts this requirement. There is one exception to this rule, and that is for the Group H, Division 6 Occupancy. In this latter case, the code states that the portion of the building containing the Group H, Division 6 Occupancy shall not exceed three stories or 55 feet (16 764 mm).

302.2 Forms of Occupancy Separations. The code intends that fire-resistive separations between occupancies form a complete separation, and therefore, they may be horizontal, vertical or

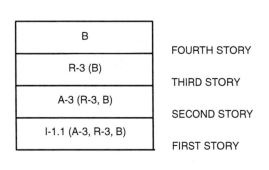

B	FOURTH STORY
R-3 (B)	THIRD STORY
A-3 (R-3, B)	SECOND STORY
I-1.1 (A-3, R-3, B)	FIRST STORY

FIGURE 302-2

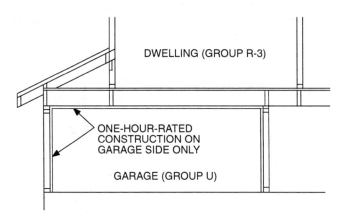

DWELLING (GROUP R-3)

ONE-HOUR-RATED CONSTRUCTION ON GARAGE SIDE ONLY

GARAGE (GROUP U)

FIGURE 302-3

such other shape as necessary in order to provide the complete separation. For example, the separation might be a stepped separation consisting of a series of short vertical and horizontal elements until the complete separation is accomplished.

In order to help ensure that occupancies will be separated as intended, this section states that occupancy separations shall be of such form "as may be required to afford a complete separation between the various occupancy divisions in the building." By this statement, the building official is granted discretion in determining whether or not the separation details for a particular project are adequate.

The code further requires that horizontal occupancy separations (usually floors) be supported by structural members or walls having the same fire rating as that required for the horizontal separation. Thus, in a Type V One-hour building of two stories where the second floor is required to be a two-hour fire-resistive occupancy separation, any walls or structural members in the first story supporting the second floor would be required to also be of two-hour fire-resistive construction. This would be the case even though the building generally is required to be only of one-hour fire-resistive construction. Obviously, if the horizontal occupancy separation is not supported by equivalent fire-resistive construction, the intent and function of the separation are negated if its supports fail prematurely.

Often overlooked is the fact that the provisions for the support of horizontal occupancy separations that apply to fully complying fire-resistive assemblies also apply to the reduced protection permitted for the separation between a dwelling (Group R, Division 3 Occupancy) and an attached private garage (Group U Occupancy). Note in Figure 302-3 that the full span of the joists and the supporting walls are protected, not just the portion common to the two occupancies.

302.3 Types of Occupancy Separations. The *Uniform Building Code* classifies occupancy separations by the fire-endurance rating of the construction and the fire-protection rating of any openings that are in the separation. It is the intent of the UBC that fire-resistive separations generally require fire-resistive protection for the openings. Where a fire-resistive wall or partition is not required to be a separation, the openings therein do not require protection. Thus, the permanent partitions in a Type I building that are required to be of one-hour fire-resistive construction do not require protected openings where they are not a specified separation.

The types of occupancy separations required by the code are classified as follows:

Fire-endurance Rating of Separation, in Hours	Fire-protection Rating for Protection of Openings, in Hours
4	No openings permitted
3	3
2	$1^1/_2$
1	1

These separations are referred to in the code as "___-hour fire-resistive occupancy separations."

It is important to note the requirement that a four-hour occupancy separation may not have openings through the separation. This prohibition includes penetrations for pipes, electrical outlet boxes, etc. According to Sections 709 and 710, such penetrations are permitted, with certain limitations, in fire-rated assemblies that require protected openings, but the code does not permit penetrations where openings are not allowed.

Special features of the required occupancy separations are that the four-hour fire-resistive occupancy separation may have no openings therein and the three-hour fire-resistive occupancy separation has limitations on the extent and type of openings. For example, a wall that is required to be a three-hour fire-resistive occupancy separation has a limit on the total width of openings that is 25 percent of the length of the wall in that story and, furthermore, no single opening may have an area greater than 120 square feet (11 m^2).

An opening in a floor assembly constituting a three-hour fire-resistive occupancy separation is required to be protected by a vertical enclosure extending above and below the floor. The walls of the vertical shaft enclosure are required to not be less than two-hour fire-resistive construction with the openings therein protected by a fire assembly having a one and one-half-hour fire-protection rating. This provision dates back to the 1927 UBC and is intended to provide protection equivalent to the floor but allow stud construction for the shaft rather than masonry or concrete. The one and one-half-hour-rated door assemblies in the shaft provide the equivalent of the three hours required, as any fire would have to breach two doors. Alternatively, under some conditions the three-hour occupancy separation can be accomplished by enclosing the shaft below the floor with three-hour fire-resistive walls with openings protected with three-hour fire-protection assemblies. Also see the discussion under Section 302.4.

302.4 Fire Ratings for Occupancy Separations. The fire-resistive ratings required by the code for the various separations are determined in accordance with UBC Standard 7-1 for walls and floors, UBC Standard 7-2 for fire assemblies for the protection of openings and approved national standards for fire and smoke dampers. These test standards will be described in more detail in this commentary under Chapter 7.

Exceptions to the rules. The code makes exceptions to the ratings for occupancy separations where the anticipated fire severity for a specific use is less than that anticipated by Table 3-B for the general occupancy classification. Thus, Exception 1 to this section permits a reduction of one hour in the occupancy separations between a Group S, Division 3 Occupancy and a Group A, Division 1 Occupancy and permits a one-hour reduction in the separation between a Group S, Division 3 Occupancy and Group A, Division 2, 2.1, 3 or 4 or Group E or I Occupancies. These reductions are based on the specific case of the Group S, Division 3 Occupancy being used only for the parking of private passenger cars. In this case, the fire loading in the Group S, Division 3 Occupancy is quite low, justifying the reduction. Also, the reduction to a rating less than four-hour fire-resistive occupancy separation would permit openings between these occupancies and a Group S, Division 3 Occupancy, thus making the building more functional.

Exception 2 to this section permits a reduction of one hour in the case of the separation between a Group S, Division 3 Occupancy and a Group R, Division 1 Occupancy. In this case, the rationale for the reduction is similar to that for Exception 1. Where the Group S, Division 3 Occupancy is limited to an area of 3,000 square feet (279 m²) (which essentially makes it a Group U Occupancy), the potential fire severity is reduced even more and the exception permits a reduction to one hour. Note, however, that the reduction permitted by Exception 2 does not apply when the provisions of Section 311.2.2 are used to divide the building horizontally into two separate buildings. In such a case, a three-hour fire-resistive occupancy separation is still required.

The third exception permits a reduced fire-resistive construction for the occupancy separation between a dwelling and private garage, which essentially results in fire-resistive protection on the garage side only and somewhat less protection for openings. This reduced protection is essentially based on the fact that a private garage in conjunction with a dwelling is usually quite a bit smaller than the maximum area permitted in a Group U Occupancy. Therefore, the potential fire severity is somewhat lower than for the general case. Because of this reduced protection, it is quite important that the limitations in the Mechanical Code and the Plumbing Code on the location of furnaces and water heaters be carefully observed in order to control potential sources of ignition.

The fourth exception eliminates the separation between Group H, Divisions 2 and 3 Occupancies and a Group H, Division 7 Occupancy when the Divisions 1 and 2 Occupancies are also constructed to the requirements of the Group H, Division 7 Occupancy. This exception was added to address materials that have multiple hazards. Thus, if a building or room is constructed to meet all hazards of a material, then the occupancy separation is not required.

302.5 Heating Equipment Room Occupancy Separation. Areas containing heating equipment are specifically named as spaces that are required to be enclosed with occupancy separations. Experience shows that the temperature of equipment and the failure or malfunction of the equipment as well as the improper use of the space increases the fire potential. Therefore, the equipment is required to be separated from the balance of the building. However, in Groups A, B, F, I, M and S Occupancies an exception allows omission of the occupancy separation when the input rating of the equipment is less than 400,000 Btus per hour (117 kW). The design of burners is such that ignition failure is not likely.

The code also requires a two-hour fire-resistive occupancy separation in Group H Occupancies between boiler and heating plants to minimize the risk of such ignition sources. Divisions 1, 2 and 3 Occupancies are prohibited from having openings directly to such rooms in an effort to prevent the migration of potentially hazardous vapors or gases into areas where ignitions or reactions could occur. The prohibition of connecting openings results in a requirement that exit and access doors to boiler and heating rooms be located in an exterior wall or open into other separated occupancies if the building contains mixed occupancies. See Figure 307-6.

SECTION 303 — REQUIREMENTS FOR GROUP A OCCUPANCIES

As its title indicates, this section contains requirements for Group A Occupancies. This section, and those following that address the subject of code requirements for the various occupancy groups, contains requirements that are judged to be unique to the occupancy even though there may be some overlapping provisions and repetitions.

The important item to be considered in this section is the definition of assembly building. Section 202 defines an assembly building as "a building or portion of a building used for the gathering together of 50 or more persons for such purposes as deliberation, education, instruction, worship, entertainment, amusement, drinking or dining, or awaiting transportation." Therefore, for a room to be considered an assembly room at least two criteria must be met:

1. The occupant load must be at least 50.
2. The individuals must be gathered together for one of the purposes described above as listed in Section 202.

Thus, the following rooms containing 50 or more occupants would be considered assembly rooms:

1. A theater for the performing arts (entertainment)
2. Motion picture theater (entertainment)
3. Church nave (worship)
4. Cocktail lounge (drinking and dining)
5. Waiting room in a bus station (awaiting transportation)
6. Gambling casino (amusement)
7. University lecture hall (education, instruction)

303.1 General. There is a very important point that should be noted here regarding the definitions of the various divisions of Group A Occupancies. For example, Division 1 through Division 3 Occupancies are defined in part as "a building or portion of a building having an assembly room." This language was developed for the 1970 edition of the code (1988 edition for Division 1 Occupancies). Prior editions of the code utilized language that did not differentiate portions of a building and thus the classification was based on the "occupant load . . . in the building." The change in language came about as a result of interpreting the code in editions prior to the 1970 edition, such that a building containing two Group A, Division 3 Occupancies each with an occupant load of, say, 250 would be classified as a Group A, Division 2.1 Occupancy. The practical effect of this former language and its interpretation was to virtually eliminate a Group A, Division 3 Occupancy classification in a building with multiple assembly rooms. The intent of the code with the present wording is that in buildings housing multiple assembly rooms, each assembly room will be classified in the occupancy that is appropriate to its occupant load. Thus, a building with several assembly rooms each with an occupant load of less than 300 will be classified as Group A, Division 3, not as Group A, Division 2.1.

The Group A, Division 1 Occupancy is considered the most hazardous of the Group A Occupancies due to the large occupant load (1,000 or more) and the presence of a legitimate stage. The significance of the stage can be inferred by its definition in Section 405. (Note that Chapter 2 refers to Chapter 4 for the definition of stage.) The hazard created by the stage is the presence of combustibles in the form of hanging curtains, drops, leg drops, scenery, etc., which have in the past been the source of ignition for disastrous fires in theaters.[1] Modern stages also have an increased hazard from the special effects utilized in so-called "spectaculars."

In the case of the "legitimate stage," the fire hazard is even greater due to the fact that the fly area that is usually above the stage is a large blind space containing combustible materials that have a fuel load considerably greater than that normally associated with an assembly occupancy. See Figure 303-1.

Previous editions of the UBC defined the stage with relation to the height of the ceiling of the stage above the top of the proscenium opening. This dimension was established as 5 feet (1524 mm), as it was considered that any space greater than 5 feet (1524 mm) in height above the top of the proscenium opening had a potential for combustible fire loading that warranted a differentiation in the classification between a stage and a platform [having a height of less than 5 feet (1524 mm) between the top of the proscenium opening and the ceiling over the stage].

However, in Section 405, the present UBC defines the difference between stages and platforms as the presence of the curtains, drops, scenery, lighting devices, etc., in a stage and not in a platform.

In the parlance of the UBC the platform would include such raised areas as the so-called "arena stage" used quite often in theaters-in-the-round, boxing rings, etc.

Recently there have developed some differences of opinion based on studies as to whether or not panic is a real problem. Further reading on the subject of panic can be found in the *Fire Protection Handbook* and *Fires and Human Behavior*.[2,3]

At least for the present, the UBC does consider the number of occupants to be a factor exacerbating panic and therefore uses occupant load in determining the division of occupancy. Thus, the Division 2 Occupancy is differentiated from Division 1 based on the occupant load only, as they both must contain a legitimate stage in order to be considered either a Division 1 or

Division 2 Occupancy. Also, occupant load is the only difference in defining Divisions 2.1 and 3 Occupancies.

However, the UBC does consider other factors besides panic in considering the hazards associated with Group A Occupancies. The presence of a legitimate stage and its distinctive hazards separates Divisions 1 and 2 Occupancies from the rest. Also, the requirement in Chapter 9 for protecting nightclubs with automatic sprinklers is another example of protecting against the specific hazards of a particular assembly use.

Another factor involving human behavior in assembly rooms is the fact that in many cases the occupants are not familiar with their surroundings and the lighting level is usually low. Thus, when an emergency arises, the occupants may perceive the danger to be greater than presented and panic may occur because of the fear of not being able to reach an exit for escape.

Division 4 Occupancies classified as stadiums, reviewing stands, amusement park structures, etc., have a unique hazard all their own and as such are classified as a separate division. As these latter structures are usually outdoor structures, the fire hazard generally is not considered to be as great as it is for Divisions 1 through 3 Occupancies, but on the other hand the type of construction normally used for Division 4 structures creates unique hazards of crowding a large number of occupants within a relatively small space and, again, the hazard of panic is assumed to be a large portion of the overall hazard for these structures.

303.1.3 Amusement buildings. Amusement buildings may be classified as a Group A Occupancy or a Group B Occupancy if the occupant load is less than 50.

303.2 Construction, Height and Allowable Area.

303.2.1 General. It is clear that the UBC considers people-related occupancies to have a hazard in relation to the number of occupants. For example, it was cited that a Division 1 Occupancy was considered to be a greater hazard than a Division 2 Occupancy, which is strictly on the basis of occupant load. Because of this gradation of hazard, with the Division 1 Occupancy being the highest and the Division 4 Occupancy being the lowest, the code also limits the types of construction and allowable areas in somewhat the same progression. A Division 1 Occupancy must be in a higher type of construction than any of the other divisions of Group A Occupancies. In fact, a Division 1 Occupancy may be located only in a Type I or II-F.R. building. Also, Divisions 2 and 2.1 Occupancies are not permitted in buildings that are unprotected (i.e., Types II-N, III-N and V-N).

303.2.2 Special provisions. The elimination of a fire-resistive ceiling for the roof-ceiling assembly in one-story portions of Types II One-hour, III One-hour and V One-hour construction is allowed, provided the roof-framing system is open to the assembly area and does not contain concealed spaces. This provision is based on the fact that assembly occupancies usually have a very low fire loading such that with a completely open roof-framing system the likelihood of a fire starting in the roof-framing system, much less being undetected, would be extremely remote.

Modifications permit running tracks of wood or unprotected noncombustible materials and permit the interior finish of exterior walls to be tongue-and-grooved wood or $3/4$-inch (19 mm) plywood installed tightly in lieu of fire-resistive construction on

(Continued on page 20)

TEMPORARY	PERMANENT
• Used within an area for **not** more than 30 days • May be constructed of any materials • Space under platform to be used only for platform equipment wiring or plumbing	• Used within an area for more than 30 days • Shall be constructed of materials as required for building type • When space under platform used for other than wiring or plumbing, floor shall not be less than one-hour construction

RAISED PRESENTATION AREA WITHIN BUILDING

FLOOR

NO OVERHANGING CURTAINS, SCENERY, DROPS, OR STAGE EFFECTS OTHER THAN LIGHTING

CASE I—PLATFORMS

STAGE HEIGHT IS 50 FEET OR GREATER

CURTAINS, SCENERY, ETC., RETRACTABLE HORIZONTALLY OR SUSPENDED OVERHEAD.

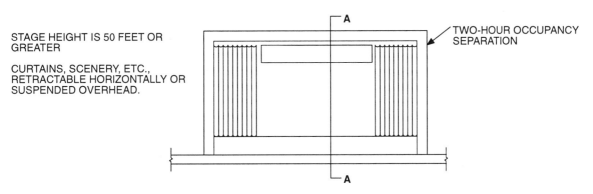

TWO-HOUR OCCUPANCY SEPARATION

CASE II— LEGITIMATE STAGE

SECTION A-A

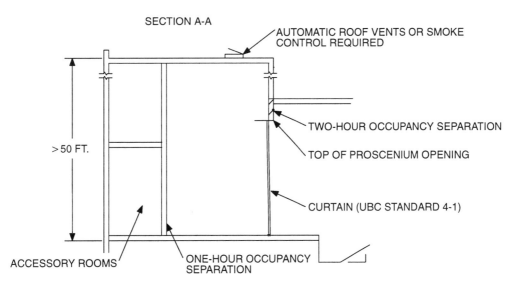

AUTOMATIC ROOF VENTS OR SMOKE CONTROL REQUIRED

TWO-HOUR OCCUPANCY SEPARATION

TOP OF PROSCENIUM OPENING

CURTAIN (UBC STANDARD 4-1)

> 50 FT.

ACCESSORY ROOMS

ONE-HOUR OCCUPANCY SEPARATION

LEGITIMATE STAGE—CROSS SECTION

For **SI:** 1 foot = 304.8 mm.

STAGES AND PLATFORMS

FIGURE 303-1

(Continued from page 18)

the interior of the wall for small buildings. These exceptions are based on the low fuel loading for gymnasiums.

303.2.2.1 Division 2.1 provisions. Reports of disastrous fires in assembly buildings such as nightclubs have shown that the problems of safety to the occupants are compounded where there are floors used for assembly purposes on other than the grade level or ground floor.[4,5] This is particularly true where the construction has minimal fire protection. Therefore, the UBC in Section 303.2.2.2 requires additional fire protection for Division 3 Occupancies located above or below the ground floor. Also, in keeping with the concept that the larger occupant loads create greater hazards, this section also requires a higher degree of fire resistance for Division 2.1 Occupancies with an occupant load of 1,000 or more.

303.2.2.2 Division 3 provisions. In the case of a Division 3 Occupancy in the basement, a minimum of one-hour fire-resistive construction is required. However, the first story or those above may be of unprotected construction if the occupancy requirements so permit for the uses on these upper floors. Conversely, if the Division 3 Occupancy is above the first story, those stories below must also be of one-hour fire-resistive construction. This is true because proper fire-protection practice for life safety would be abrogated if a lower type of construction were permitted to support a higher type of construction. This intent is expressed in the code in Section 302.2, which requires equivalent fire-resistive construction to support fire-resistive occupancy separations.

303.2.2.3 Division 4 provisions. Although Division 4 Occupancies are considered to be less hazardous than Division 1, 2, 2.1 or 3 Occupancies, grandstands, bleachers and reviewing stands of combustible construction are not permitted the liberal heights and areas that are permitted for the noncombustible types of construction. This is evidenced by the somewhat tighter limitations on combustible grandstands, bleachers and reviewing stands than there are on other Division 4 structures. Also, indoor grandstands, bleachers and reviewing stands that have combustible members in the structural framing are also limited in height.

Conversely, the code permits Division 4 structures of open skeleton frame construction without any enclosure of any kind to be of unlimited area or height except for grandstands, bleachers and reviewing stands of Type III-N and Type V-N combustible construction. Again, the philosophy of the code is that where the structures are out-of-doors and of noncombustible framing and are not high-occupant-load facilities, such as grandstands, bleachers and reviewing stands, the hazard is not as great and more liberal provisions are permitted. This provision is intended to permit amusement park structures of unlimited area and height where the construction is of Type I, II-F.R., II One-hour, II-N, III One-hour, IV or V One-hour.

303.3 Location on Property. By their nature of congregating large numbers of people in unfamiliar surroundings, assembly occupancies are considered by the code to head the relative hazard standings for people-related hazards. Thus, in order to ameliorate this high relative hazard, the code has a special requirement for the location on the property. This is designed to provide ease of access by the fire department for fire-suppression activities and rescue. Therefore, the UBC requires that buildings housing Group A Occupancies front on a public street not less than 20 feet (6096 mm) in width or have a 20-foot-wide (6096 mm) access to a public street, as shown in Figure 303-2.

Furthermore, if the building does not front on a public street, the 20-foot-wide (6096 mm) access must be maintained unobstructed and used only for the purpose of access to the public street. These provisions for location on a public street or on access to a public street provide reasonable assurance of quick response and access to the building by the fire department.

The code also requires that the main entrance to the building front on the street or strect access. The *Uniform Building Code* considers the main entrance also to be the main exit, as the occu-

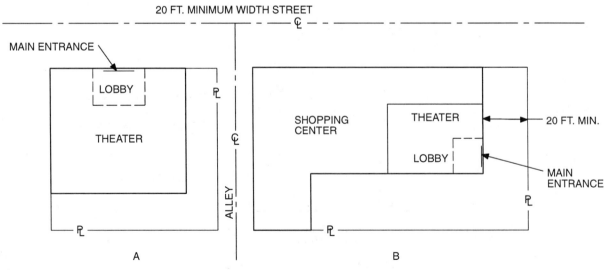

For **SI:** 1 foot = 304.8 mm.

ASSEMBLY BUILDING—LOCATION PROPERTY

FIGURE 303-2

pants of a building, particularly in an assembly building, will attempt to exit through the main entrance because they are familiar with that route. Thus, the occupants of the building will have an efficient and rapid egress to the exterior of the building and to public property, where they will be reasonably safe.

SECTION 304 — REQUIREMENTS FOR GROUP B OCCUPANCIES

304.1 Group B Occupancies Defined. In the 1994 UBC the uses allowed in Group B Occupancies (business occupancies) were considerably narrowed. Retail sales uses were moved to the Group M Occupancy, factory and industrial uses were moved to the Group F Occupancy, and storage uses were moved to the Group S Occupancy. The previous Group B Occupancy included uses with a wide variation in fire loading. In some uses the fire loading was less than 10 pounds per square foot (48.8 kg/m^2); in others the fire loading would exceed 100 pounds per square foot (488 kg/m^2). This wide range of fire loading made it difficult to deal with the hazards in general terms and made it necessary to incorporate special provisions or exceptions. Separation of the uses into hazard groupings that have a similar fire severity hazard is more logical and simplifies future revision. These groupings, in general, agree with the BCMC recommendations. The use groupings in the 1997 UBC essentially agree with those shown in the 1994 UBC.

Uses listed in the Group B Occupancy include outpatient clinics and medical offices that accommodate five or less patients in each tenant space. Some outpatient clinics and surgery centers are really Group I Occupancies as they accommodate more than five patients that are not capable of self-preservation. This is because general anesthesia is administered that causes the patients to not be in control of their faculties. Therefore, they are properly given the protection afforded by the requirements for Group I, Division 1.2 Occupancies.

Police and fire stations are also included within Group B Occupancies and should not be considered as mixed occupancies. Thus, for a fire station the entire building is classified as a Group B Occupancy and there is no separation required between the apparatus room and the rest of the building. Also, the dormitory would not be considered a separate occupancy and would not require a separation from the rest of the building. For the police station, the jail, which is most often used as a temporary holding facility, would also be included as a Group B Occupancy where it is part of the police station.

304.2.2.1 Laboratories and vocational shops. The provisions for laboratories and vocational shops are in effect exceptions that allow activities and materials that are more hazardous than those usually associated with Group B Occupancies. This provision allows laboratories in colleges or universities and allows vocational training schools such as woodworking and auto-body shops that would otherwise be classified as a Group H Occupancy to be classified as a Group B Occupancy. Laboratories in schools and vocational shops are considered less hazardous than in industrial uses due to the tighter control and safety practices associated with these uses.

304.2.2.2 Amusement buildings. This section addresses amusement buildings with occupant loads of less than 50 by referring back to the same provisions as for larger amusement

buildings. The reason for this is that the hazards associated with such structures are not due to the occupant load but are instead due to the disorienting nature of the environment inside these buildings.

304.6 Shaft and Exit Enclosures. The last paragraph of the section is in effect an exception to the requirements for shaft construction in Section 711 allowing unenclosed escalator openings. Shafts are known to be the major conduit for vertical fire spread and do deserve special attention. However, if properly treated, vertical openings in sprinklered buildings do not present an untenable condition. The purpose of the required draft curtain is to trap heat so that the sprinklers will operate and cool the gases that are rising. The curtain is not a fabric; it is constructed of materials consistent with the type of construction of the building.

SECTION 305 — REQUIREMENTS FOR GROUP E OCCUPANCIES

Early editions of the *Uniform Building Code* included educational occupancies with assembly occupancies, and it wasn't until the 1943 edition that educational occupancies were separated as a specific occupancy group. There was no age differentiation listed in the UBC up until 1970, although earlier editions of the code must have assumed children rather than adults or university students, as the terms "boys" and "girls" were used in those editions. When educational occupancies were placed into a specific occupancy group in 1943, it became necessary to differentiate the educational occupancies from assembly occupancies. Therefore, the definition of the educational occupancy excluded uses with stages and those with an occupant load of 300 or more.

In the 1970 edition of the UBC, the requirements for educational occupancies were completely rewritten, and it was at this time that the limitation of the 12th grade was placed on educational occupancies. It was also at this time that day-care uses with more than six children were placed in the educational occupancy group. Day-care facilities are most often under a similar type of supervision as educational occupancies for the younger children, and day-care uses also do provide education.

305.1 Group E Occupancies Defined. Group E Occupancies are educational uses for students through the 12th grade and uses having more than six persons for day-care purposes.

These uses are further broken down into divisions where Division 1 covers those uses of 50 or more persons that spend more than 12 hours per week or four hours in any one day in school.

Division 2 Occupancies include those educational buildings that are used by less than 50 persons but used for more than 12 hours per week or four hours in any one day.

Division 3 Occupancies include day-care uses for more than six persons.

Because of these limitations placed on the amount of time in school and on the maximum grade limit, it was necessary that those educational uses not covered under Group E Occupancies be listed in some other occupancy classification. Therefore, the committee that rewrote the educational occupancy chapter for the 1970 UBC placed educational occupancies for less than 50 students beyond the 12th grade as Group B Occupancies, and any other educational occupancy would then be placed as an assembly occupancy, depending on the occupant load. Thus, university classrooms with an occupant load of less than 50 are Group B Occupancies, and any classrooms or auditoriums with an occupant load of 50 or more are classed as an assembly occupancy and the proper division will depend on the occupant load.

There is another unique feature involved in educational occupancies, and that is the use of school buildings for assembly purposes outside the scope of the educational use. For example, many school auditoriums are used for commencement exercises and other productions to which the public at large is invited. Also, the school gymnasium in many cases is used for sporting events where the public at large is invited. These additional uses are most probably Group A Occupancies.

Because of these multipurpose uses in school buildings, it is necessary that the code requirements applicable to all the uses be enforced in order to satisfy the safety requirements for each use.

It is important to note that the occupancy divisions defined in this section would not permit uses involving the general public such as the above-described commencement ceremonies, Christmas programs, band concerts, etc. Therefore, for these assembly uses involving the general public it is necessary that the requirements of the code be obtained for those uses as well as for the educational uses.

305.2 Construction, Height and Allowable Area. The rewrite of this chapter for the 1970 edition of the UBC was based on changing concepts in educational uses that included the open-plan and flexible-plan concepts (see Figure 305-1). In order to accommodate these changing concepts, the code included provisions for the construction of atmospheric separations and included in Chapter 10 specific exit requirements to accommodate the open-plan and the flexible-plan concepts.

The use of the atmospheric separation is intended to provide safe exiting for students from schools using the open-plan and flexible-plan layouts because they do not have the inherent compartmentation provided by the so-called traditional schools. Therefore, it is necessary to provide exits from this type of school such that the exiting students will not be placed in contact with products of combustion from the fire that they are attempting to escape.

On this basis, the atmospheric separation that is accomplished by a smoke and draft barrier is required to separate the building into what are called by the code "separate atmospheres." Thus, the code most often in Chapter 10 requires that exits from large-capacity areas lead to separate atmospheres and that no more than two exits from any room enter into the same atmosphere.

An important feature of the atmospheric separation is that it is not limited to partitions and walls but actually includes the floors with the walls and the partitions and any openings therein. In the 1994 edition of the code, performance criteria for smoke barriers were added to Section 905. (See Sections 905.2.3 and 905.2.4.)

In Section 305.2.3, the code requires that rooms used for kindergarten, first- or second-grade pupils, and day-care uses not be located above or below the first story, except that basements or stories above the first story may be used for such purposes provided they are within 4 feet (1219 mm) of grade and have the required exits at grade. Smaller children are usually less mobile, and therefore the possibility of their being overtaken by the older children on the stair system has caused this requirement to be placed in the code. This requirement is fairly typical of code provisions concerning educational occupancies. It has also been theorized that the very small preschool children will have difficulty in negotiating stairs and would also have difficulty in using the handrail.

Where a building is protected by an automatic fire-sprinkler system, the second exception to Section 305.2.3 permits these children to occupy the second story, provided they have exclusive use of exits directly to the exterior. The sprinkler protection and special exits are considered to provide equivalent life safety to a first story.

Also, in Exception 3, day-care facilities are allowed above the first story in buildings of either Type I, Type II fire-resistive, Type II One-hour and Type III One-hour construction, provided the building is sprinklered throughout and an approved fire alarm and smoke-detection system is provided on the entire story of the day-care facility. In addition, the day-care facility of more than 1,000 square feet (92.9 m^2) in area must be divided into not less than two areas of approximately the same size, separated by not less than one-hour fire-resistive construction with 20-minute protected openings. Each area must have access to not less than two exits, one of which may pass through another area. In case of conflict, the specific provisions of this section will take precedence over the provisions in Section 905. This

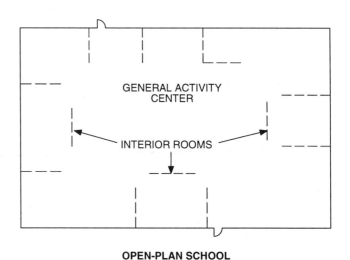

OPEN-PLAN SCHOOL

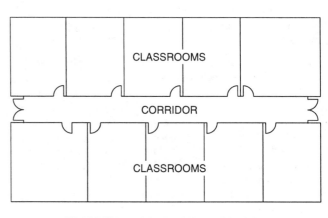

TRADITIONAL CORRIDOR CLASSROOM SCHOOL PLAN

FIGURE 305-1

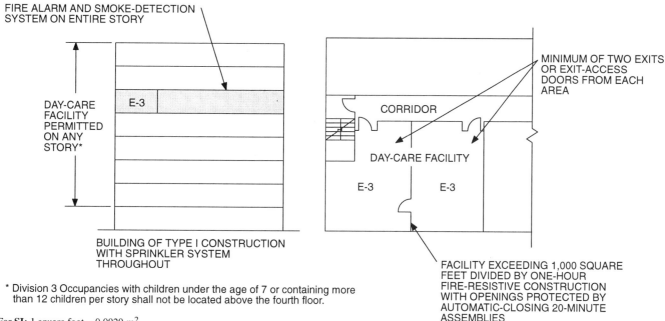

FIRE ALARM AND SMOKE-DETECTION SYSTEM ON ENTIRE STORY

DAY-CARE FACILITY PERMITTED ON ANY STORY*

E-3

BUILDING OF TYPE I CONSTRUCTION WITH SPRINKLER SYSTEM THROUGHOUT

MINIMUM OF TWO EXITS OR EXIT-ACCESS DOORS FROM EACH AREA

CORRIDOR

DAY-CARE FACILITY

E-3   E-3

FACILITY EXCEEDING 1,000 SQUARE FEET DIVIDED BY ONE-HOUR FIRE-RESISTIVE CONSTRUCTION WITH OPENINGS PROTECTED BY AUTOMATIC-CLOSING 20-MINUTE ASSEMBLIES

* Division 3 Occupancies with children under the age of 7 or containing more than 12 children per story shall not be located above the fourth floor.

For **SI:** 1 square foot = 0.0929 m².

FIGURE 305-2

exception was originally made in the 1991 UBC and revised in the 1994 edition. It is intended to allow companies to provide day-care facilities in their buildings for their employees. See Figure 305-2.

Vocational shops, laboratories and similar areas classed as Group E Occupancies are addressed by the requirements contained in Sections 305.2.4 and 1007.3, and one-hour fire-resistive occupancy separations are required between these uses and other areas as well as between each other.

305.3 Location on Property. The *Uniform Building Code* requires that buildings housing Group E Occupancies front on a street or exit discharge not less than 20 feet (6096 mm) in width for the same reasons discussed in Section 303 for assembly occupancies. It is also noted that this section requires at least one of the required exits to be located on the street or exit discharge.

305.8 Special Hazards. This section includes a requirement that exterior openings in a boiler room or room containing central heating equipment be protected by fire assemblies having a three-fourths-hour fire-protection rating under the following circumstances:

1. When the openings in the exterior wall of the boiler room are below openings in another story.

2. When the openings in the exterior wall of the boiler room are located less than 10 feet (3048 mm) from other doors or windows in the same building.

The intent of the code in this case is to prevent fire from a boiler room reaching the exterior wall opening and exposing other rooms within the same building. The primary danger is to openings in stories above the openings from the boiler room. However, due to the potentially high fire severity of the boiler room, any exterior wall opening within 10 feet (3048 mm) of the openings from the boiler room is subjected to a severe exposure hazard. Thus, the openings in the exterior wall of the boiler room require fire protection.

305.9 Fire Alarm Systems. The *Uniform Building Code* follows the philosophy of society in general that our children require special protection when they are not under parental control. Therefore, in addition to the other life-safety requirements of this chapter, fire-alarm systems are required whenever the occupant load of any Group E Occupancy is 50 or more. This requirement is reprinted from the *Uniform Fire Code* and is maintained by the International Fire Code Institute, as indicated by the F's repeating in line vertically in the margin.

SECTION 306 — REQUIREMENTS FOR GROUP F OCCUPANCIES

306.1 Group F Occupancies Defined. This occupancy designation was first included in the 1994 edition of the UBC. In general, the uses permitted are an extraction of the factory and industrial uses that were previously within the former Group B, Divisions 2 and 4 Occupancies. Although the potential hazard and fire severity of the multiple uses in the Group F Occupancies is quite varied, these uses share common elements. The occupants are adults who are awake and generally have enough familiarity with the premises to be able to exit the building with reasonable efficiency. Group F Occupancies are generally factory and industrial uses that were, for the most part, classified as Group B Occupancies prior to the 1994 edition of the code. The degree of hazard between the uses is very broad and, therefore, is divided into two divisions.

Many of the Division 1 uses would ordinarily be classified as Group H Occupancies. However, since the quantity of hazardous material permitted in the listed uses may not exceed the exempt amounts set forth in Table 3-D or 3-E, the lower classification is deserved. Due to the similarity between the names of the uses in Division 1 Occupancies and the uses in Group H Occupancies, care must be exercised when determining the appropriate classification, and operators of Division 1 uses should be appraised of the limitations on the quantities of hazardous materials that are allowed.

The hazard from uses in Division 2 Occupancies is very low; in fact, the uses are the lowest hazard group in the code. The uses allowed in Division 2 are essentially the same as uses that were previously allowed in Group B, Division 4 Occupancies, but the grouping has been narrowed by the exclusion of noncombustible storage, cold storage and creameries. The allowance for the storage of noncombustible products in Group B, Division 4 Occupancies has been controversial because the products are usually packaged or stored on combustible material. Also, cold storage and creameries have substantially changed since the provision was included in the first (1927) edition of the UBC. Creameries now contain combustible rather than glass containers, and cold storage uses are very broad, ranging from freezers to cooled warehouses that may be constructed with foam plastic insulation. Furthermore, both operations often include refrigeration equipment that contain large quantities of combustible or explosive gas. Noncombustible storage, cold storage and creamery uses are, therefore, more appropriately listed in the new Group S, Division 2 Occupancy. However, the uses may also be Group S, Division 1 Occupancies if the packaging does not qualify for inclusion in a Group S, Division 2 Occupancy.

It is noted that the Group F, Division 2 Occupancy was the Group B, Division 4 Occupancy in the 1991 edition of the code, and prior to the 1976 edition of the UBC, the uses were included in Group G Occupancies. The narrowing of these uses in the current Group F, Division 2 Occupancy in actuality returns the code to its original intent. The framers of the first (1927) edition of the UBC stated in Section 1201: "Each Group G Occupancy . . . shall include non-hazardous industrial and commercial occupancies which create a low fire and life hazard. . . ."[6]

306.2.2 Special provisions, Group F, Division 2 roof framing. Group F, Division 2 Occupancies have a low fire loading, and thus potential fire severity is low. On this basis the code permits the omission of fire protection on the underside of roof framing in all types of construction, in similar fashion as for Type II One-hour and Type III One-hour construction housing Group A Occupancies. Again, the rationale is that the fire loading is so low that the potential fire severity will not be high enough to involve the roof structure.

306.8 Special Hazards. The last paragraph of this section should not be overlooked. A product-conveying dust system complying with *Uniform Mechanical Code*™ (UMC) Section 505 is required when finely divided combustible material is generated in a Group F, Division 1 Occupancy. Also, Section 904.2.5 requires that woodworking establishments such as cabinet making and millwork that use equipment, machinery, or appliances that generate finely divided combustible waste or that use finely divided combustible materials be sprinklered when the area of the occupancy exceeds 2,500 square feet (232.3 m²). This provision stems from a revision in Group H, Division 2 Occupancies in the *1993 Accumulative Supplement to the UBC*. See additional comments under discussion of Group H, Division 2 Occupancies and Section 904.2.5.

SECTION 307 — REQUIREMENTS FOR GROUP H OCCUPANCIES

Hazardous occupancies are characterized by an unusually high degree of explosion, fire or health hazard as compared to "typical" commercial and industrial uses. Requirements for hazardous occupancies are prescribed in this section. The section is divided into 12 subsections that are supported by four tables in Chapter 3 and one table in Chapter 5. Though this section serves as the focal point for requirements pertaining to construction of hazardous occupancies in the UBC, users of the code should be aware that there are many additional requirements pertaining to construction of hazardous occupancies in the UFC that are not found in the UBC.

In general, the requirements in the UBC are limited to general construction regulations and occupancy-specific provisions. The *Uniform Fire Code* sets forth special construction requirements relating to specific materials and the specific situations of storage, use and handling. In some cases, major provisions such as fire-extinguishing system requirements and spill control, drainage control and secondary containment requirements were duplicated in both the codes for emphasis and convenience. Overall, there is an integral relationship between the UBC and UFC requirements for dealing with hazardous materials, and it is essential that persons designing, reviewing and inspecting hazardous occupancies consult both codes to ensure that all applicable regulations are considered.

What Everyone Needs to Know About the "Code Approach" to Hazardous Occupancies Before Using Section 307

There are two basic types of Group H Occupancies—those that are designated as Group H based on particular operations that are conducted and those that are designated as Group H based on excessive quantities of hazardous materials contained therein. Those occupancies that are designated as Group H based on their particular operations are Group H, Divisions 4, 5 and 6. Those occupancies that are designated as Group H based on excessive quantities of hazardous materials are Group H, Divisions 1, 2, 3 and 7.

Classification of occupancies into the Division 4, 5 and 6 categories is fairly straightforward and will be discussed later in this chapter under Section 307.1. Classification of occupancies into the Division 1, 2, 3 and 7 categories is significantly more complex. To unravel this complexity, the following discussion goes beyond the specific requirements in Section 307 and presents an overall conceptual view of dealing with the Group H, Divisions 1, 2, 3 and 7 Occupancies using the outline presented in Figure 307-1.

Determining Hazardous Materials and Processes

Figure 307-1 outlines the process for determining the code requirements that are a function of the quantities of hazardous materials stored or used. The outline is useful for both design and review. To begin, one must determine the hazardous processes and materials involved in a given occupancy and gain a thorough understanding of the operations taking place. Once the hazardous processes and materials have been identified, it is

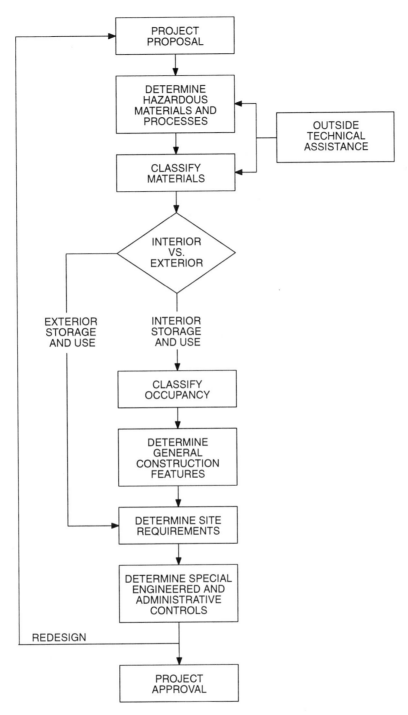

CODE APPROACH TO HAZARDOUS MATERIALS

FIGURE 307-1

necessary to classify the materials based on the categories used by the UBC and UFC.

Uniform Building Code Section 307.1.6 provides a means for the building official to acquire outside technical assistance when needed to assist in the review of a project.

Classifying Materials

The classification system used by the UBC and UFC is modeled after the United States Occupational Safety and Health Ad-

ministration regulations in the *Code of Federal Regulations, Title 29* (29 C.F.R.). It should be noted that these material classifications do not match the classifications used by other federal agencies such as the Department of Transportation and the Environmental Protection Agency.

Classifying materials is a subjective science, requiring judgment decisions by an expert familiar with the characteristics of a particular material to categorize it within the categories used by the Uniform Codes. Accordingly, material classifications must be determined by qualified individuals, such as industrial hygienists, chemists or fire-protection engineers. Though some jurisdictions employ individuals qualified to make these determinations, most jurisdictions rely on outside experts acceptable to the jurisdiction to submit a report detailing classifications compatible with the system used by the Uniform Codes. Such expert assistance must be provided by the permit applicant when required by the building official based on Section 307.1.6.

Often, a permit applicant will attempt to submit a cadre of Material Safety Data Sheets (MSDS) as a means of identifying material classifications. Though these may contain the information necessary to determine the proper classification, they do not normally contain a complete designation of classifications that is compatible with the system used by the Uniform Codes. Therefore, MSDS's are not normally acceptable as a means of providing material classifications to a jurisdiction.

The building official should understand that it is not the responsibility of the jurisdiction to provide classifications for hazardous materials. Rather, it is the responsibility of the permit applicant to provide material classification information to jurisdictions. In this way, potential liability of the jurisdiction for improper classification of materials is avoided.

In the classification system used by the Uniform Codes, hazardous materials are generally divided into two major categories, physical and health hazards, and 13 subcategories as follows:

Physical Hazards

Explosives and blasting agents
Compressed gases
Flammable and combustible liquids
Flammable solids
Organic peroxides
Oxidizers
Pyrophoric materials
Unstable (reactive) materials
Water-reactive solids and liquids
Cryogenic fluids

Health Hazards

Highly toxic and toxic materials
Corrosives
Irritants, sensitizers and other health-hazard materials

These categories are further defined in the *Uniform Fire Code* in Article 2 and Appendix Chapter VI-A. Jurisdictions should be cautioned that UFC Appendix Chapter VI-A is merely intended for general guidance and examples. This appendix should not be cited as a sole basis for classifying materials. The listings are partial and often do not address all of the hazards of a given material.

When hazardous materials possess the characteristics of more than one hazard category, which is most often the case, all applicable hazard categories must be evaluated with respect to the code requirements. For example, 10 pounds (4.54 kg) of material classified as both an oxidizer and a corrosive must be considered as both 10 pounds (4.54 kg) in the oxidizer category and 10 pounds (4.54 kg) in the corrosive category.

Interior Versus Exterior Locations

Once hazardous materials have been classified, the next step is to determine whether the materials will be at interior or exterior locations. If the hazardous materials are stored or used outside of buildings, the UBC will not be applicable. For such cases, the *Uniform Fire Code* should be consulted.

Classifying Occupancies

Exempt amounts. For interior storage and use, the first step in applying the UBC is to classify the occupancy. Occupancy classification of buildings containing hazardous materials is based on the "exempt amount" concept. Exempt amounts are the maximum quantities of hazardous materials that may be stored or used in an area before the area must be designated as a Group H Occupancy. The term "exempt" refers to quantities that are exempt from Group H Occupancy requirements, and it is not intended to imply an exemption from all code requirements. Exempt amounts vary for different states of materials (solid, liquid or gas) and for different situations (storage or use). Exempt amounts are also varied based on protection that is provided, such as fire-extinguishing systems and storage cabinets.

Control areas. Areas in a building that are designated to contain less than or equal to the exempt amounts of hazardous materials and that are properly separated from other areas containing hazardous materials are called "control areas." Any combination of hazardous materials, up to the exempt amounts, is allowed in a control area. For example, a single control area can contain storage of 5 pounds (2.27 kg) of Class 3 unstable (reactive) material, 50 pounds (22.68 kg) of Class 2 unstable (reactive) material, 120 gallons (454.2 L) of Class II combustible liquid, 5,000 pounds (2268 kg) of corrosives, etc. However, Table 3-D provides for a single quantity of combinations of flammable liquids. That is, the exempt quantities of flammable liquids do not include, for example, 60 gallons (227.1 L) of Class 1-B liquid and 90 gallons (340.7 L) of Class I-C liquid. See Table 3-D. A control area may be an entire building or only a portion of a building. It can be a part of a story, an entire story or even multiple stories.

The control area concept, as opposed to the approach used in the 1985 and prior editions of the UBC, regulates quantities of hazardous materials per control area, rather than per building. The limit for an entire building, using control areas, is then established by limiting the total number of control areas allowed per building. The control area concept was introduced in an effort to address an inconsistency in prior editions of the code that allowed the same quantities of hazardous materials in very large buildings as was allowed in very small buildings before requiring a Group H Occupancy classification.

The control area concept is based on a premise that the storage and use of limited quantities of hazardous materials (not exceeding exempt amounts) in areas that are separated from each other by one-hour fire-resistive occupancy separations do not substantially increase the risk to the occupants or change the character of a building to that of a hazardous occupancy, subject to a limitation on the number of control areas. The fire-resistive occupancy separations are relied on to minimize the risk of having multiple control areas involved simultaneously during an emergency.

The occupancy classification of a control area is the same as the occupancy classification of the portion of the building in which the control area is located. There is no special occupancy designation for a control area. For example, a control area in a Group M Occupancy is merely part of the Group M Occupancy.

Given this basic understanding of exempt amounts and control areas, the various options in the code for increasing quantities of hazardous materials in a building are as follows:

1. Buildings are generally allowed to have up to the basic exempt amounts of hazardous materials without restriction with respect to separations or protection. In this case, the entire building is designated as a control area. The boundaries of the control area are the boundaries of the building (i.e., exterior walls, roof and foundation). See Figure 307-2.

2. Using the footnotes to Tables 3-D and 3-E, exempt amounts can generally be increased by adding sprinklers throughout the building or by using cabinets or other code-approved enclosures to protect the hazardous materials.

3. Two other options are available to further increase quantities of hazardous materials in a building:
   a. Construct the building as required for a Group H Occupancy or
   b. Provide additional control areas.

4. Assuming additional control areas are used, each additional control area must be separated from all other control areas by one-hour fire-resistive occupancy separations. Up to the exempt amounts of hazardous materials are allowed in each control area. See Figure 307-3.

5. Up to four control areas are allowed in any occupancy except wholesale and retail sales occupancies, which are limited to two control areas based on a perceived increase in risk given the presence of customers. See Footnote 1 to Tables 3-D and 3-E.

Storage and use. One other fundamental concept involved in applying the exempt amounts is "situation of material." The exempt amounts in the code are based on three potential situations. These are storage, use-closed and use-open.

Though not defined by the code, "storage" is generally considered to include materials that are idle and not immediately available for entering a process. The term "not immediately available" can be thought of as requiring direct human intervention to allow a material to enter a process or, alternately, as using approved supervised valving systems that separate "stored" material from a process. In the case of liquids and gases, storage is generally considered to be limited to materials in closed vessels (not open to atmosphere). For example, clearly, materials kept in closed containers such as drums or cans are in storage since deliberate action (opening the drum or can) would be required to use the material. However, when a container or tank is connected to a process, the question of whether the material in the container or tank is in storage or use arises.

In general, the quantity of material that would be considered to be "in use" is the quantity that could normally be expected to be involved in a process or that could reasonably be expected to be released or involved in an incident as a result of a process-related emergency. Consider, for example, a process having hazardous materials that are piped from an underground storage tank outside of a building to a dispensing outlet within a building. Since the tank is connected to a process within the building, it could be argued that the contents of the tank are available for use in the building (see definition of use in Section 222) and that the quantity should be counted toward exempt amounts. However, if an approved, reliable arrangement of valving is provided between the supply and the point where the material is dispensed, it would be reasonable to conclude that the quantity on the supply of such valving that is outside of the building would be unlikely to impact incidents occurring within the building and, therefore, need not be counted toward exempt amounts. This reliable arrangement of valving can be considered as an interruption of the connection between the confined material (storage) and the point where material is placed into action or made available for service, as discussed in the definition of use in Section 222. See Figure 307-4.

The difference between use-closed and use-open is basically whether the hazardous material in question is exposed to atmosphere during a process, except that gases are defined as always being in closed systems when used since they would be immediately dispersed (unless immediately consumed) if exposed to atmosphere without some means of containment.

Determining General Construction Features

Once the occupancy is classified, general construction features for the building can be determined. For the most part, construction features are set forth in the UBC; however, some special provisions overlap with or are found exclusively in the UFC. The process of determining general construction features for Group H Occupancies is similar to that followed for any other occupancy.

Determining Site Requirements

Group H Occupancies often have special site requirements. These special requirements are set forth in Sections 307.3 and 503.4.5, Tables 3-F and 3-G, and in the UFC. The special requirements include limitations pertaining to location on property and wall and opening protection requirements.

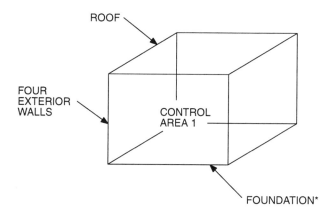

*Crawl spaces are prohibited by Sections 307.2.8 and 307.2.9 for some cases.

CONTROL AREA BOUNDARIES FOR ONE CONTROL AREA

FIGURE 307-2

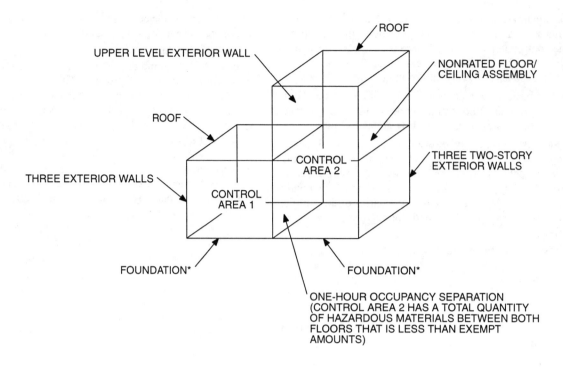

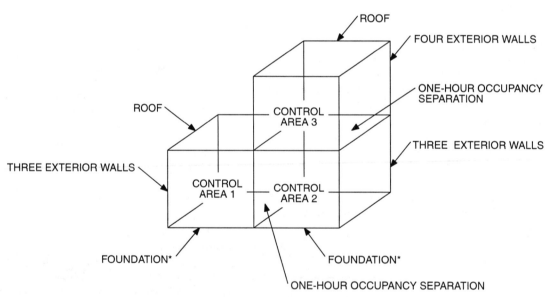

*Crawl spaces are prohibited by Sections 307.2.8 and 307.2.9 for some cases.

SAMPLE MULTIPLE CONTROL AREAS

FIGURE 307-3

Determining Special Engineered and Administrative Controls

Finally, special engineered and administrative controls set forth in UFC Article 80 and UBC Section 307 must be determined. Most of these are listed in UFC Section 8003.1. The requirements include, among others, special provisions for:

- Container and Tank Design
- Piping, Valves and Fittings

- Signage
- Security
- Control of Sources of Ignition
- Protection from Light for Light-sensitive Materials
- Shock Padding for Shock-sensitive Materials
- Shelf Construction
- Zoning

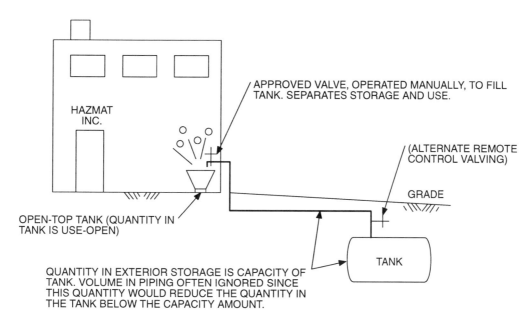

APPROVED VALVE, OPERATED MANUALLY, TO FILL TANK. SEPARATES STORAGE AND USE.

(ALTERNATE REMOTE CONTROL VALVING)

GRADE

HAZMAT INC.

OPEN-TOP TANK (QUANTITY IN TANK IS USE-OPEN)

TANK

QUANTITY IN EXTERIOR STORAGE IS CAPACITY OF TANK. VOLUME IN PIPING OFTEN IGNORED SINCE THIS QUANTITY WOULD REDUCE THE QUANTITY IN THE TANK BELOW THE CAPACITY AMOUNT.

EXAMPLE OF STORAGE VERSUS USE

FIGURE 307-4

- Storage Plans, Inventory Statements and/or Management Plans
- Spill Control, Drainage Control and Secondary Containment
- Ventilation
- Separation of Incompatible Materials
- Fire-extinguishing Systems
- Alarms
- Explosion Control
- Standby and Emergency Power
- Material-handling Requirements

307.1 Group H Occupancies Defined.

307.1.1 General. This section sets forth the definitions of the various Group H Occupancies and references Tables 3-D and 3-E for exempt amounts. Group H, Divisions 1, 2, 3 and 7 are the occupancies linked directly to the quantities and types of hazardous materials. Group H, Division 6 Occupancies are also contingent on the quantities and types of hazardous materials, but this division is limited exclusively to semiconductor fabrication facilities and comparable research facilities. The other Group H Occupancies, Divisions 4 and 5, apply to specific operations and processes that are inherently hazardous. These two occupancy classifications are not specifically contingent on quantities and types of hazardous materials stored or used, except for use of flammable and combustible liquids. Use of flammable or combustible liquids in a garage, hangar, etc., is one of the operations or processes considered to be inherently hazardous that may dictate a Group H, Division 4 or 5 Occupancy.

The reference in the first paragraph to the Fire Code for definitions, identification and control of hazardous materials generally refers to UFC Articles 2, 51 and 80 and Appendices II-E and VI-A.

The reference in the first paragraph to the Fire Code for nonflammable solid and nonflammable or noncombustible liquid hazardous materials specifically refers to a special allowance for increased exempt amounts in retail sales occupancies set forth in UFC Section 8001.14. This reference to the Fire Code allows the exempt amounts in UBC Tables 3-D and 3-E to be exceeded in accordance with UFC Section 8001.14. These special provisions were added to the UFC because the 1988 versions of UBC Chapter 9 and UFC Article 80 were considered to be overly restrictive for the storage and display of certain materials in retail sales establishments. Without these provisions, occupancies containing many types of display arrangements that had previously been allowed would have required a Group H Occupancy classification, even though there was no loss history to demonstrate the need for such restrictive treatment.

The amounts allowed by UFC Section 8001.14 vary based on the floor area used for hazardous materials storage or display. The floor area specified includes only the area actually occupied by hazardous materials that are displayed or stored. Limits are imposed on the maximum area and arrangement of materials. It should be noted that these special exceptions are not intended to apply to warehouses or wholesale operations not affiliated with a retail use.

When hazardous materials are used as refrigerants or lubricants in closed systems, Chapter 28 of the UBC and the Fire and Mechanical codes should be referred to for requirements.

Division 1 Occupancies

Division 1 Occupancies are those occupancies containing high-explosion hazard materials in quantities exceeding the exempt amounts listed in Table 3-D. Though the current Division 1 category was generally intended to include materials with detonation hazards when it was first developed, a few other types of materials with lower blast energies were added because of concerns regarding the likelihood of an explosive event, as opposed to the resultant blast energy. (For a discussion of detonations versus deflagrations, see the discussion of Section 307.10 later in this section.) For example, the material category "explosives" listed in Division 1 technically includes all materials capable of producing an explosive effect, regardless of whether such effect would be a detonation or a deflagration.

Item 1 under Division 1 has been modified in the 1997 UBC to distinguish these fireworks, Class 1.3G, (Class B, Special), that are considered Group H, Division 1 Occupancies. This category would include aerial shells or display fireworks. Item 2 under Division 1 has been added to include the manufacturing of Class 1.4G (Class C, Common) fireworks whereas the storage of Class 1.4G (Class C, Common) fireworks is considered a Group H, Division 3 Occupancy.

Exception 2 was added to Item 1 in the 1997 code to allow indoor storage and display of smokeless powder, black sporting powder, and primers or percussion caps for Group M retail sales where stored and displayed in accordance with the Fire Code. The regulations in the Fire Code should adequately protect these occupancies rather than classifying them as a Group H, Division 1 Occupancy.

This delineation clearly indicates that the UBC has taken a very conservative approach to classifying the occupancy of certain uses, assuring that buildings containing any explosives or fireworks are detached, remotely located and closely controlled as to size and type of construction. Note that the code grants some relief to the location on property provisions for materials with reduced blast energies by allowing adjustment of separation distances based on a comparison with the blast energy of TNT. See the discussion of Table 3-F later in this chapter.

Users of the code should be aware that the correlation between the requirements for explosives in UFC Article 77 and UBC Section 307 is somewhat lacking. Though both codes prescribe regulations pertaining to building construction for buildings containing explosive materials, there are some significant differences in the requirements. The most significant differences occur in four areas: construction features for magazines, location on property, retail sales of gunpowder and ammunition, and fireworks. A summary of the treatment of these subjects in the two codes is as follows:

UBC

1. Magazines are required to be constructed and protected as required for Group H, Division 1 Occupancies.

2. The required separation distance between explosive storage and inhabited buildings set forth in Table 3-F must be provided on the property where the magazine is located.

3. Occupancies used for retail sales of gunpowder are classified based on comparison to exempt amounts in Table 3-D, and once a Group H, Division 1 Occupancy is provided, quantities are not limited.

4. Class 1.3G (Class B, Special) fireworks may be stored for any purpose, so long as the storage is in a Group H, Division 1 Occupancy.

5. Storage of Class 1.4G (Class C, Common) fireworks may be considered a Group H, Division 3 Occupancy.

UFC

1. Magazines are considered special structures with special construction requirements. These are different from, and in some cases, less restrictive than provisions in the Building Code for Group H Occupancies.

2. The required separation distance to inhabited buildings may include open space on adjacent properties.

3. Retail sales of gunpowder are subject to absolute maximum quantity limits set forth in Section 7702.2 that may not be exceeded in any occupancy.

4. Storage of fireworks is prohibited unless in direct association with permitted displays.

Because these requirements are inconsistent, it is difficult to provide an absolute recommendation regarding enforcement of these provisions; however, based on discussion of these provisions at code development meetings, the following compromise is one potential solution:

1. Buildings or magazines that are regulated and inspected by the Bureau of Alcohol, Tobacco and Firearms (BATF) should be regulated in accordance with UFC Article 77, since BATF is charged with monitoring quantities of explosives with respect to newly constructed buildings on adjacent properties and requires explosive material quantities to be reduced as necessary to maintain adequate clearance.

   To allow open space on adjacent property to be used in the measurement of minimum distance required by UBC Table 3-F, the building official could apply Section 104.2.8 if appropriate assurances are given by the owner of the explosives that required separation distances will be maintained. Such assurances could include routine verification of BATF's periodic inspections that show that the amount of explosives in the structure is within the allowable quantities for the separation distance provided.

   Buildings and magazines not regulated by BATF should be constructed entirely in accordance with UBC Section 307.

2. Retail sales of gunpowder and ammunition should be subject to absolute limits set forth in UFC Section 7702.2. Gunpowder should be allowed in a Group M Occupancy up to quantities listed in Footnote 13 of Table 3-D. However, indoor storage and display of smokeless powder, black sporting powder, and primers or percussion caps exceeding the exempt amounts for Group M retail sales need not be classified as a Group H, Division 1 Occupancy where stored and displayed in accordance with the Fire Code.

3. Storage, sale and handling of fireworks should be limited to activities related to permitted displays and special effects conducted by pyrotechnic operators as defined in the UFC. Storage of such fireworks should be in magazines in accordance with UFC Article 77.

Division 2 Occupancies

Division 2 generally includes those occupancies that contain materials with hazards of accelerated burning or moderate explosion potential in quantities exceeding those listed in Table 3-D. In most cases, Division 2 Occupancies include materials with deflagration hazards. Probably what had been the most controversial subject in the Division 2 category was the inclusion of occupancies containing combustible dusts. Dusts in suspension or capable of being put into suspension in the atmosphere are a deflagration hazard.

The controversy surrounding the occupancy classification for woodworking operations began with the revision to the 1988 edition, which treated all occupancies containing dust-producing operations in a similar fashion. Since combustible dusts in suspension or capable of being put into suspension commonly present a moderate explosion risk, occupancies containing combustible dusts were placed in the Division 2 category when the 1988 edition was developed. The most significant impacts of this revision were the reduction in allowable area based on type of construction and the increase in sprinkler requirements as compared to the 1985 and prior editions, when woodworking occupancies were classified as Group H, Division 3 Occupancies. Though it was recognized that the provisions for Group H, Division 2 Occupancies are very restrictive, the change was considered to be justified based on the perceived fire and explosion risk. This viewpoint changed with the 1994 code. At this point only operations where the dust cannot be controlled such as flour and cereal mills would be considered as a Group H, Division 2 Occupancy.

To avoid classification of woodworking shops as Group H Occupancies, the code was revised to include them in Group F, Division 1 Occupancies in the 1994 edition of the UBC, and the exempt quantities of dust set forth in Table 9-A of the 1991 edition of the UBC have been deleted. See also discussion under Section 306.8.

Division 3 Occupancies

Division 3 includes those occupancies containing materials that present high fire or heat-release hazards in quantities exceeding those listed in Table 3-D.

Division 4 Occupancies

Division 4 Occupancies include repair garages that are not classified as Group S, Division 3 Occupancies. Division 4 Occupancies include those operations that involve use of Class I, II or III-A liquids in excess of the amounts in Table 3-D or open flame or welding operations. It should be noted that operations involving fuel line and a fuel filter servicing or other light maintenance where very small releases of flammable or combustible liquids may occur are generally allowed in the Group S, Division 3 Occupancy category due to the rather limited risk of such operations.

Division 5 Occupancies

Division 5 Occupancies include aircraft repair hangars having similar operations to those described in Division 4. For a discussion of heliports, see Section 311.10.

Division 6 Occupancies

Division 6 Occupancies include those occupancies containing semiconductor fabrication facilities, including the ancillary research development areas, assuming that such occupancies

use quantities of hazardous materials exceeding those listed in Tables 3-D and 3-E.

In the 1982 and prior editions, many jurisdictions classified semiconductor manufacturing as a Group H, Division 1 or 2 Occupancy based on the explosive and highly toxic materials used in such operations. Such occupancy classifications resulted in construction limitations that were considered severe, to the point where it was extremely difficult to conduct the manufacturing operation. Consequently, the Division 6 classification was created to provide specific requirements for the particular operations conducted, and it relaxed the construction requirements to a level that allows reasonable transaction of the process. Also, see UFC Article 51.

Division 7 Occupancies

Division 7 Occupancies are those containing health hazard materials in excess of the quantities listed in Table 3-E. Additional requirements for carcinogenic and radioactive materials are specifically addressed in the Fire Code.

307.1.2 Multiple hazards. Most hazardous materials possess the characteristics of more than one hazard category. This section requires that all hazards of materials must be addressed. For example, if a material possesses the hazard characteristics of a Class 2 oxidizer and an irritant, the material quantity must be considered as contributing to the exempt amounts of both categories. A quantity of 10 pounds (4.54 kg) of such material would be considered to be both 10 pounds (4.54 kg) of Class 2 oxidizer and 10 pounds (4.54 kg) of irritant. If the quantity of material exceeded the exempt amounts for both the Class 2 oxidizer and irritant categories, according to Tables 3-D and 3-E, respectively, the occupancy would be required to meet the requirements of both a Group H, Division 3 and Group H, Division 7 Occupancy. Note that in some cases, such as building height, the Division 7 provisions are more restrictive, hence the requirement that provisions for both occupancies must be satisfied.

307.1.3 Liquid use, dispensing and mixing rooms. Liquid use, dispensing and mixing rooms are classified as Group H, Division 2 Occupancies. Such rooms are required when the quantity of flammable or combustible liquids in use, dispensing or mixing operations exceeds the quantities allowed in control areas for use-open conditions specified in Table 3-D. Because of their high fire hazard, liquid use, dispensing and mixing rooms are required to be separated from other uses by one-hour fire-resistive occupancy separations for rooms up to 150 square feet (13.9 m^2) in area and two-hour fire-resistive occupancy separations for rooms exceeding 150 square feet (13.9 m^2) in area, except where the occupancy separation requirements of Table 3-B are more restrictive. Additional controls for such rooms include control of materials used for shelving, racks and wainscoting; a prohibition of locating such room in basements; and a requirement for an exterior access door for fire department access. The prohibition on basement locations is based primarily on the difficulty of fighting a fire involving large quantities of flammable and combustible liquids in basements.

For the additional requirements in the Fire Code, see UFC Section 7903.2.3.

307.1.4 Liquid storage rooms. With the exception of being classified as a Group H, Division 3 Occupancy, the requirements for liquid storage rooms are similar to those for liquid use, dispensing and mixing rooms. See discussion of Section 307.1.3 above.

For additional requirements in the Fire Code, see UFC Section 7902.5.11.

307.1.5 Flammable or combustible liquid storage warehouses. The requirements for flammable or combustible liquid storage warehouses are similar to those for liquid storage rooms discussed in Section 307.1.4 above. However, liquid storage warehouses are unique in that the storage of other materials is not allowed. Combustible storage with liquid storage is more hazardous than storage of liquids only because the combustible storage can provide a heat source that will ignite the liquids. Liquids in closed containers are difficult to ignite. A liquid storage warehouse is required when the quantities of flammable or combustible liquids stored exceed the quantity limits for liquid storage rooms established by UFC Section 7902.5.11. Quantities of flammable or combustible liquid stored in liquid storage warehouses are not limited. Liquid storage warehouses are required to be separated from all other uses by not less than a four-hour area separation wall due to the risk of a catastrophic fire therein.

For additional requirements in the Fire Code, see UFC Section 7902.5.12.

307.1.6 Requirement for report. This section is a companion provision to UFC Section 103.1.1. These sections authorize code enforcement officials to require submission of technical reports that provide the information necessary to allow a jurisdiction to perform a code compliance evaluation. The requirement for a technical report gives jurisdictions the benefit of expert opinions provided by knowledgeable persons in the particular hazard field of concern.

Technical reports are required to be prepared by an individual, firm or corporation acceptable to the jurisdiction, and must be provided without charge to the jurisdiction. Depending on the nature of the project, a combination of one or more of the following sample elements may be needed in a technical report:

1. Hazardous materials management plan (HMMP). See UFC Appendix II-E.
2. Chemical analysis and hazardous materials inventory statement (HMIS). See UFC Appendix II-E.
3. Specific methods of isolation, separation, containment or protection of hazardous materials or processes, including appropriate engineering controls.
4. Extent of changes in hazardous behavior to be anticipated under conditions of exposure to fire or from hazard control procedures.
5. Analysis of the design, operation and use of the building or premises.
6. Recommendations for mitigation of hazards.
7. Recommendations for compliance with applicable code requirements.

307.2 Construction, Height and Allowable Area.

307.2.1 General. As compared to the 1985 and prior editions, Division 1 Occupancies are now limited to noncombustible types of construction, although the allowable areas for the noncombustible types are the same as allowed under the 1985 and previous editions of the code for Division 1 Occupancies. The

number of stories allowed, however, is now limited to one. The noncombustible construction is mandated so that explosive materials in storage or use will not be exposed to fire from combustible construction members. Furthermore, noncombustible construction reduces the risk of having an exterior fire involving combustible vegetation, such as dried grass and shrubbery, spread to the building construction materials and explosives inside.

Division 2 construction requirements and area limitations are identical to those included in the 1985 and previous editions of the code for Division 1 Occupancies. The uses assigned to the present Division 2 category include many of the materials included as Division 1 materials in the 1985 and prior editions. The allowable types of construction and areas for Divisions 3, 4 and 5 are unchanged from previous editions of the code.

Construction requirements and area limitations for Divisions 6 and 7 Occupancies are the same as those for Group B Occupancies since physical hazard materials are highly protected and controlled in Division 6 Occupancies and health hazard materials in Divisions 6 and 7 Occupancies do not present an unusual fire hazard. The height of Divisions 6 and 7 Occupancies, however, is limited to three stories, primarily due to the difficulty for emergency response personnel to reach and control health hazard emergencies on floors above the third story.

307.2.2, 307.2.3 and 307.2.4 Floors, spill control, drainage and containment. The requirements of these sections, such as noncombustible and liquid-tight floors, liquid-tight sills and open-grate trench drains, are intended to prevent the accidental spread of hazardous materials releases to locations outside of containment areas. Generally, these requirements reflect those in UFC Articles 79 and 80. The provisions are placed in the UBC to provide special emphasis so that these systems will not be overlooked during design and plan review.

307.2.5 Smoke and heat vents. This section calls attention to special requirements for smoke and heat venting included in UFC Article 80. UFC Sections 8003.6.1.5, 8003.7.1.5, 8003.9.1.4 and 8003.10.1.5 all require buildings or areas containing materials regulated by these sections to be provided with smoke and heat vents, regardless of the size of the storage area.

307.2.6 and 307.2.7 Standby and emergency power. These two sections require standby and emergency power to be provided for certain occupancies and materials. Standby and emergency power systems are required to be installed in accordance with the *National Electrical Code* (NEC).

Generally, emergency power represents a higher degree of safety than standby power. Emergency power must supply loads within 10 seconds of a failure of the primary supply as opposed to 60 seconds for standby power systems. Accordingly, emergency power systems are typically required by the code to provide a backup electrical source for the most critical electrical systems. Standby power supplies are required for less critical electrical systems. For the particular circuits required to be supplied by standby and emergency power sources, see UFC Sections 8003 and 8004. Also, see NEC Articles 700 and 701.

307.2.8 Special provisions for Group H, Division 1 Occupancies. Because of the extreme hazard presented by Group H, Division 1 Occupancies, this section requires that such occupancies be used for no other purpose, and it prohibits basements, crawl spaces and under-floor spaces where flammable or explosive material might gather. Roofs are required to be of lightweight construction so that, in case of an explosion, they will rapidly vent with minimum destruction to the building. In addition, thermal insulation is sometimes required to prevent heat-sensitive materials from reaching decomposition temperatures.

A provision added in the 1991 edition requires that Group H, Division 1 Occupancies that contain materials possessing both physical and health hazards in quantities exceeding exempt amounts for health hazard materials in Table 3-E also meet the requirements for Group H, Division 7 Occupancies. This provision is somewhat parallel to Exception 4 to Section 302.4, which allows health hazard materials in excess of the exempt amounts to be stored or used in Group H, Divisions 2 and 3 Occupancies provided that these occupancies also meet the requirements for a Group H, Division 7 Occupancy.

The primary difference between these two provisions is that materials possessing only health hazard characteristics are allowed in Group H, Divisions 2 and 3 Occupancies in quantities greater than exempt amounts when the design for the building also meets the requirements for Group H, Division 7 Occupancies. For the case of Group H, Division 1 Occupancies, materials having only health hazard characteristics may not be kept in the Group H, Division 1 Occupancy in quantities exceeding exempt amounts even though the design meets the requirements for a Group H, Division 7 Occupancy.

307.2.9 Special provisions for Group H, Divisions 2 and 3 Occupancies. Group H, Divisions 2 and 3 Occupancies containing large quantities of the more dangerous types of physical hazard materials are considered to present unusual fire or explosion hazards that warrant a separate and distinct occupancy in a detached building used for no other purpose, similar to the requirements for a Group H, Division 1 Occupancy. The threshold quantities for requiring detached Group H, Divisions 2 and 3 Occupancies are set forth in Table 3-G.

This section also requires water-reactive materials to be protected from water penetration or liquid leakage. Fire-protection piping is allowed in such areas in recognition of both the integrity of fire-protection system installations and the need to protect water-reactive materials from exposure fires.

307.2.10 Special provisions for Group H, Division 4 Occupancies. Provisions for Division 4 Occupancies match those included in Footnote 4 of Table 9-C in in the 1991 UBC.

307.3 Location on Property. This section, along with Tables 3-F and 5-A and Section 503, provides regulations that limit the locations on property for Group H Occupancies and establish minimum percentages of perimeter walls of Group H Occupancies required to be located on the building exterior. In those editions of the code when fire zone regulations were in effect, Group H Occupancies were either prohibited or highly restricted in the more congested fire zones (Fire Zones 1 and 2). Since fire zones were eliminated in the 1979 edition, Group H Occupancies are allowed anywhere within jurisdictions. Land use regulations and economics made the fire zone concept unnecessary. The requirements pertaining to property line separations are further discussed under the provisions for Division 1 Occupancies earlier in this chapter.

The specific provisions in this section require that Group H Occupancies included in mixed-use buildings have 25 percent of the perimeter wall of the Group H Occupancy on the exterior of the building. Exceptions are provided for smaller, liquid use, dispensing and mixing rooms; liquid storage rooms; and spray booths. See Figure 307-5.

307.4 Access and Means of Egress Facilities. See Section 1007.4 and Chapter 11 of this handbook for a discussion of special exit and access requirements for Group H Occupancies.

307.7 Sprinkler and Standpipe Systems. This section serves as a cross reference to Chapter 9 for fire-extinguishing system requirements. Automatic fire-extinguishing systems are required for Group H, Divisions 1, 2, 3, 4, 6 and 7 Occupancies, except that Division 4 Occupancies having floor areas of 3,000 square feet (279 m^2) or less are exempted. Though not specifically required based on the occupancy classification, Group H, Division 5 Occupancies are often provided with automatic fire-extinguishing systems in order to qualify for the unlimited

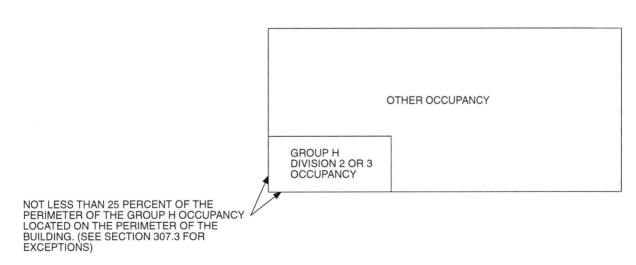

OTHER OCCUPANCY

GROUP H
DIVISION 2 OR 3
OCCUPANCY

NOT LESS THAN 25 PERCENT OF THE
PERIMETER OF THE GROUP H OCCUPANCY
LOCATED ON THE PERIMETER OF THE
BUILDING. (SEE SECTION 307.3 FOR
EXCEPTIONS)

MIXED-USE OCCUPANCY HAVING A GROUP H, DIVISION 2 OR 3 OCCUPANCY

FIGURE 307-5

area provisions in Section 504.2. An automatic fire sprinkler system should be used in all cases unless specific approval of an alternate agent is granted by the jurisdiction based on extraordinary circumstances.

307.8 Special Hazards. This section is similar in concept to Sections 302.5, 303.8, 304.8, 305.8 and 2802.

An additional requirement in this section prohibits equipment that generates a spark or glow capable of igniting gasoline vapors from being installed or used within 18 inches (457 mm) of the floor in Divisions 4 and 5 Occupancies. Since gasoline vapors are heavier than air, vapors from fuel spills or leaks would be likely to settle and achieve flammable concentrations within 18 inches (457 mm) of the floor level.

Equipment or machinery that generates or emits combustible or explosive dusts or fibers is required to be provided with a dust-collecting and exhausting system in accordance with the Mechanical Code. Particular requirements in the Mechanical Code that are applicable include UMC Section 505.1, which requires ducts conveying combustible or explosive dusts or fibers to be extended directly to the exterior of the building without en-

tering other spaces, and UMC Section 506, which specifies such features as explosion venting and fire protection for ducts. It should be noted that dust bags attached directly to equipment and dust-collection systems discharging to local collectors inside of a building are prohibited based on UMC Section 505.1.

Additional provisions relating to the subject of dust control and combustible fiber control are located in UFC Article 28, Section 3004.2 and Article 76. Requirements for combustible fibers in the Building Code have been correlated with UFC Article 28. For definitions of combustible fiber storage rooms and vaults, see UFC Article 2.

See Figure 307-6 for a sketch of a typical dust-collection system with explosion vents.

307.9 Fire Alarm Systems. Requirements for fire alarm systems and devices are correlated with UFC Section 1007.2.6.

307.10 Explosion Control. In the 1991 edition, the previous requirements for "explosion venting" were expanded to encompass "explosion control." The expansion to explosion control recognizes that there are other acceptable methods to minimize

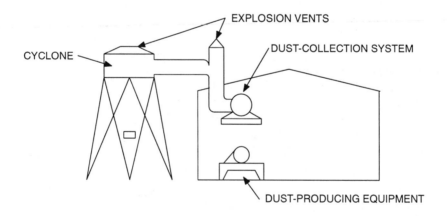

DUST-COLLECTION SYSTEM WITH EXPLOSION VENTS

FIGURE 307-6

explosion risk beyond venting. Provisions for explosion control include protective devices, suppression systems and barricades as acceptable methods of limiting damage. It should be noted that suppression systems, as referenced in this section, do not refer to typical automatic fire sprinkler systems for building fire protection. Rather, suppression systems for explosion control are intended to include only those systems specially designed for the purpose of explosion control. Such systems are capable of detecting and suppressing ignitions in microseconds.

An explosion can be summarized, based on the definition in the Fire Code, as an effect produced by a sudden violent expansion of gases that is accompanied by a shock wave. Explosions can be categorized into two basic categories: detonations (more severe) and deflagrations (less severe). Detonations are explosions that result in shock waves traveling at speeds exceeding the speed of sound, and deflagrations are explosions yielding shock waves traveling slower than the speed of sound. Beyond the alternative of explosion-suppression systems, which may be available to protect certain types of explosion hazards, the code still emphasizes explosion venting and separation distance as the main means of controlling damage from deflagrations and emphasizes barricades and separation distance as the main means for minimizing damage from detonations. Explosion-venting systems are generally considered to be incapable of minimizing damage from detonations because the speed of pressure buildup is too fast for venting systems to react to and maintain pressure levels within a building below highly destructive levels.

The code prescribes commonly accepted criteria for explosion-resistant structures and venting. The criteria specify that lightweight walls, lightly fastened hatch covers, lightly fastened and outward-opening swinging doors, or lightly fastened walls or roofs that relieve at a maximum pressure of 20 pounds per square foot (958 Pa) are to be used as a means of pressure relief. Furthermore, walls, floors and roofs that do not function as part of the explosion-relief system and that separate other uses from an explosion exposure, must be designed to resist minimum internal pressures of 100 pounds per square foot (4.79 kPa).

The code also provides requirements for clear separations around venting devices to minimize the risk of damage or injury resulting from blast debris or pressure waves. In addition, explosion venting must be designed by persons competent in such design.

For additional information, see the *Fire Protection Handbook,* published by the National Fire Protection Association (NFPA); NFPA 68, *Guide for Venting of Deflagrations*; and NFPA 69, *Standard on Explosion Prevention Systems.*[7,8,9]

307.11 Group H, Division 6 Occupancies. The Group H, Division 6 Occupancy category was created to standardize regulations for semiconductor manufacturing facilities. This section provides the specific regulations for these occupancies. The Group H, Division 6 Occupancy category requires engineering and fire-safety controls that reduce the overall hazard of the occupancy to a level thought to be equivalent to a Group B Occupancy. Accordingly, the areas permitted for Group H, Division 6 Occupancies are the same as for Group B Occupancies.

The code requires that special ventilation systems be installed in fabrication areas that will prevent explosive fuel to air mixtures from developing. The ventilation system must be con-

nected to an emergency power system. Furthermore, buildings containing Group H, Division 6 Occupancies are required to be protected throughout by an automatic fire sprinkler system and fire and emergency alarm systems. It is intended that the fire and emergency alarm systems be separate and distinct systems, with the emergency alarm system providing a signal for emergencies other than fire.

This section also provides requirements for piping and tubing that transport hazardous materials that allow piping to be located in exit corridors and above other occupancies subject to numerous, stringent protection criteria. Occasionally, it is desired to extend piping from Group H, Divisions 1, 2, 3 and 7 Occupancies through other occupancies as well. Though, technically, quantities of hazardous materials transported from Divisions 1, 2, 3 and 7 Occupancies through other occupancies in closed piping systems in excess of exempt amounts would cause such other areas to be classified as Group H Occupancies themselves, many jurisdictions allow small pipes [usually less than 2 inches (51 mm) in diameter] to extend outside of Group H, Divisions 1, 2, 3 and 7 Occupancies when the installation is performed in accordance with Section 307.11.6.2.

The provisions for Group H, Division 6 Occupancies are correlated with companion provisions in UFC Article 51. For a thorough review of the requirements for Group H, Division 6 Occupancies, see *H-6 Design Guide to the Uniform Codes for High-Tech Facilities.*[10]

SECTION 308 — REQUIREMENTS FOR GROUP I OCCUPANCIES

Group I Occupancies are institutional occupancies and in the UBC are considered to be basically of two broad types. First is the hospital, nursing home or other facility in which the very young, sick and injured are cared for. The second category of institutional occupancy considered by the UBC includes those facilities in which the personal liberties of the inmates are restricted.

In both types, the occupants or inmates are either restricted in their movements or require supervision in an emergency, such as a fire, in order to escape the hazard by proceeding along an exit route to safety. There is actually a third category in which the occupants enjoy mobility and are reasonably free of constraints but do require a measure of professional care and are asleep for a portion of the day.

As Group I Occupancies are people-related occupancies, the primary hazard is from the occupants' lack of free mobility so they can extricate themselves from a hazardous situation. On the other hand, the hazard from combustible contents is very low, and as a result the occupancy requirements for Group I Occupancies are essentially based on the limited free mobility of the occupants.[11,12] Also, the occupants of Group I Occupancies are usually institutionalized for 24 hours or longer and therefore are asleep at some time during their stay.

The code provisions for Group I Occupancies are quite restrictive due to the limited free mobility of the occupants and the fact that they are asleep for a portion of each day. Thus, the protection requirements of the code are more comprehensive than in almost any other people-related occupancy.

308.1 Group I Occupancies Defined. Except for the Division 3 Occupancies that include penal institutions and other uses where the personal liberties of the inmates are restricted, the other Group I Occupancies are defined as accommodating more than five persons (the staff is not counted). Therefore, the building official is presented with a problem of properly classifying an occupancy that is of similar nature to the Group I Occupancy except that there are fewer than five children, patients or inmates.

The primary feature that distinguishes the Division 1.1 Occupancy from the others is that it is a health-care facility in which the patients are, in general, nonambulatory. This division includes hospitals, sanitariums, nursing homes and other health-care facilities where people are treated for injuries, disease and infirmity.

Nurseries for the full-time care of small children (under the age of six) are included with hospitals, as the code assumes that the very young require the same protection as is provided for those individuals whose capability of self-preservation is severely restricted.

Outpatient health-care centers have been included as Division 1.2 Occupancies when the number of patients that are not capable of self-preservation exceeds five and are included in Group B Occupancies when the number of patients is five or less. The distinction is necessary due to the prevalence of trauma centers and surgical facilities within medical office buildings. Usually, but not always, the patients in these facilities will not stay overnight but may be recovering from surgery and, in essence, will be nonambulatory for a relatively short period of time.

Also included within Division 1.1 are nurseries for the full-time care of children under the age of six as the code assumes that these younger children are also of limited free mobility, although their parents on occasion may not agree with this assumption. Where there are five or fewer children in a full-time care nursery, the use is very similar to a residential use, and therefore the classification for this occupancy would be Group R, Division 3. The five or fewer children could be considered as a family living together in a dwelling unit, and therefore the overall hazard is virtually identical to that of a single-family dwelling. This concept is in keeping with the intent of the exception at the end of this section.

The Division 2 uses are unique in that the occupants or patients are ambulatory, and the uses include homes for children six years of age or over. In these cases where similar uses would accommodate fewer than six persons, the closest occupancy with a similar hazard would be the residential occupancy, and, again, these uses where the number of persons accommodated is five or fewer would be classified as a Group R, Division 3 Occupancy.

The Division 3 uses encompass mental hospitals, jails, prisons, reformatories and other buildings where the personal liberties of the inmates are similarly restricted. In the case of Division 3 Occupancies, there is no qualifier as to the minimum number of inmates.

The exception at the end of the section applies to all of the kinds of care and restraint associated with Group I Occupancies. It intends to avoid the impression of institutional code restrictions on private residential buildings. See also Appendix Chapter 3, Division III.

308.2 Construction, Height and Allowable Area. Because the patients and inmates of institutional occupancies will not be able to evacuate the building in case of emergency, it is important that fires not be permitted to start, or alternatively, if fires do start, rapid suppression is required, such as by automatic sprinklers. In this respect, the code secures these desirable aspects of protection in institutional occupancies by restrictions on types of construction, area and by the requirements for special fire-protection features, such as automatic sprinklers and compartmentation.

A perusal of Table 5-B will show that all institutional occupancies must be housed in protected buildings (i.e., those with a minimum of one-hour fire-resistive construction throughout) or in buildings of Type IV construction. In the case of Division 3 Occupancies, construction types are limited to Type I or Type II-F.R. construction. The reader will also note that except for Type I or Type II-F.R. construction, the heights of all institutional buildings are limited to one and two stories. Even in the case of a Type II-F.R. building, the height is restricted to three stories for Divisions 1.1, 1.2 and 2 Occupancies and restricted to two stories for Division 3 Occupancies. However, Exception 2 to Section 308.2.1 permits a Type II-F.R. sprinklered hospital or nursing home classified as a Group I, Division 1.1 Occupancy and health-care centers for ambulatory patients classified as Group I, Division 1.2 Occupancies to be five stories high and, when housed in a Type II one-hour building, to be three stories high. Furthermore, Exception 3 permits a hospital, nursing home or health-care center for ambulatory persons to be in a one-story sprinklered Type II-N building.

Because vertical evacuation of a building such as a hospital is a virtual impossibility in case of fire, multistory buildings are required to have higher types of protection such as are provided by Type I and Type II-F.R. buildings. Horizontal evacuation, on the other hand, is possible with a properly trained staff. As a result, the code makes provisions for horizontal compartmentation as illustrated in Figure 308-1, so that if necessary, patients can be moved from one compartment to another. This intent is secured by Section 308.2.2.1 wherein each story of a Division 1.1 Occupancy is required to be divided into at least two approximately equal compartments by a smoke barrier with a one-hour fire-resistive rating.

As smoke is the real killer in fires, the code requires, in addition to the one-hour fire resistance, that the partition be essentially smoketight as defined by Section 905.2.3. This would be a partition constructed with similar tightness as that described in Section 305 for educational occupancies. The code intends that there be no openings in this smoke-stop partition except for duct openings and corridor openings where the partition crosses a corridor. The doors in the portion of the partition that crosses the corridor are required to be 20-minute-rated smoke- and draft-control assemblies such as required by Section 1004.3.4.3.2 or horizontal sliding doors that comply with UBC Standard 7-8. Ducts are required to be protected with smoke-detector-activated fire dampers in the plane of the partition. The dampers shall be approved to resist passage of smoke.

308.8 Special Hazards. In keeping with the intent of the code to prevent fires because the evacuation of the patients is extremely difficult, the code also places restrictions on the storage of flammable and combustible liquids. The nature of the operation of a hospital is such that some flammable and combustible liquids

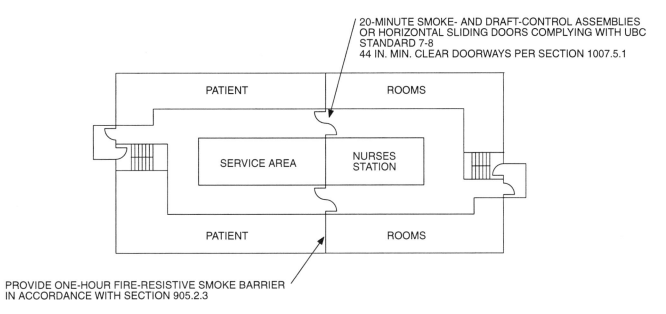

20-MINUTE SMOKE- AND DRAFT-CONTROL ASSEMBLIES
OR HORIZONTAL SLIDING DOORS COMPLYING WITH UBC
STANDARD 7-8
44 IN. MIN. CLEAR DOORWAYS PER SECTION 1007.5.1

PROVIDE ONE-HOUR FIRE-RESISTIVE SMOKE BARRIER
IN ACCORDANCE WITH SECTION 905.2.3

For **SI:** 1 inch = 25.4 mm.

HOSPITAL COMPARTMENTATION

FIGURE 308-1

are required, and such storage and handling are required to be in accordance with the Fire Code. Also, there are other types of uses that present a hazard to the patients, and Table 3-C provides separation requirements.

The provisions that require the protection of exterior openings in boiler rooms and other requirements for boiler rooms in this section have the same intent as those in Sections 302.5 and 305.8. See Sections 302.5 and 305.8 of this handbook for a discussion of the intent.

308.9 and 308.10 Fire Alarm Systems and Smoke Detectors. As patients and inmates are asleep during a large portion of the day, these two sections provide for early warning of the occupants and staff, thus enhancing life safety.

SECTION 309 — REQUIREMENTS FOR GROUP M OCCUPANCIES

309.1 Group M Occupancies Defined. The Group M Occupancy (mercantile) designation, first introduced in the 1994 UBC, should not be confused with the Group M Occupancy (miscellaneous) in the 1991 and earlier editions of the UBC. The requirements for Group M Occupancies in the 1994 edition of the UBC are an extraction of the requirements applicable to retail and wholesale stores in Chapter 7 (Group B Occupancies) of the 1991 edition of the UBC. For related discussion, see Sections 304 and 306 of this handbook. The mercantile uses listed in this section are, for the most part, self-explanatory, but further explanation as to the meaning of "paint stores without bulk handling" and "sales room" may be useful.

Paint stores typically display and store flammable liquids in the form of paint lacquer, thinners and other products associated with painting. These products would ordinarily be allowed only within Group H Occupancies; however, under the condition that there be no bulk handling of these products, they are allowed in

mercantile uses. The term "bulk handling" is defined in Section 203 of the UBC. It includes, for example, the dispensing of mineral spirits from large containers such as barrels into much smaller containers such as 1-gallon (3.8 L) containers. Accidental spills are common in such dispensing and result in the release of flammable vapors. Dispensing of flammable or combustible liquids is, therefore, not allowed within Group M Occupancies. The code intends, however, to allow the occasional opening of containers to add colonizers. Requirements on the quantities and manner of displaying and storing flammable and combustible liquids in mercantile uses are in the UFC.

The term "sales room" is used to include automobile sales rooms and similar uses that are not typically thought of as "retail stores." The term "sales room" could also apply to auction rooms; however, the usual auction room is densely populated, and when its occupant load is 50 or more it is an assembly occupancy and should be classified accordingly.

309.2.2 Special provisions. Storage areas in connection with unsprinklered wholesale or retail sales areas present a hazard to the sales area because of the potentially high fire load in the storage area. The table of occupancy separations (Table 3-B) does not require a separation in this case. The potential fire severity in the storage area is of such magnitude that the public in the sales area should be protected from the hazard; thus the code prescribes a one-hour fire resistive occupancy separation when the storage area exceeds 1,000 square feet (92.9 m^2) or 3,000 square feet (279 m^2) if sprinklered.

SECTION 310 — REQUIREMENTS FOR GROUP R OCCUPANCIES

Group R Occupancies are residential occupancies and are characterized by:

- Use by people for living and sleeping purposes.
- Relatively low potential fire severity.[13,14]

- The worst fire record of all structure fires.[15]

The basic premise of the provisions in this section is that the occupants of residential buildings will be spending one third of the day asleep and that the potential for a fire getting out of control before the occupants are awake is quite probable. Furthermore, once awakened, the occupants will be somewhat confused and disorientated, particularly in hotels.

310.1 Group R Occupancies Defined. It may be of interest to examine the BCMC descriptions of residential occupancies so as to better understand the UBC classifications. The BCMC residential occupancy classification is divided into three subdivisions:

- Group R, Division 1—Transient residential, such as hotels and motels.

- Group R, Division 2—Multiple dwellings, such as apartment houses, convents and monasteries.

- Group R, Division 3—One- and two-family dwellings.

These subdivisions are based on occupant density as well as the occupants' familiarity with their surroundings. Therefore, hotels, motels and similar uses in which the occupants are essentially transients are separated from apartment houses. The reason for this is the occupants' lack of familiarity with their surroundings in hotels. This in turn leads to confusion and disorientation when a fire occurs while the occupants are asleep. However, the UBC lumps motels, hotels, apartment houses and congregate residences into Division 1 Occupancies, and essentially this grouping is based on occupant density. As this grouping has existed since the 1927 edition of the UBC, the ICBO membership has elected to continue this combination, rather than divide apartment houses and hotels into separate divisions as in the BCMC classification. Added in the 1991 edition, congregate residences each accommodating more than 10 persons are defined in Chapter 2 and included in the Division 1 Occupancy classification. Congregate residences accommodating 10 or fewer persons are classified as Division 3 Occupancies as they most nearly resemble such uses.

Division 2 is not used by the UBC and Division 3 is assigned to dwellings, lodging houses and congregate residences (each accommodating 10 persons or less). As defined in Chapter 2, a dwelling is any building containing no more than two dwelling units. The lodging house is defined as a building containing not more than five guest rooms. The lodging house is incorporated into Division 3 as it is assumed that the number of guests will be low due to the restriction of five guest rooms. Also, the occupants of lodging houses generally remain as tenants longer than as is the case in hotels, so they are also fairly familiar with their environment.

In the case of Group R, Division 3 Occupancies, the code makes provision for the adoption of the CABO *One and Two Family Dwelling Code,*[16] which, if adopted through Appendix Section 332, takes precedence over the requirements of the UBC. This type of language is necessary, as there are many provisions of the *One and Two Family Dwelling Code* that conflict with those of the UBC. Also, this adoption procedure is placed into the UBC to encourage uniformity of construction requirements for one- and two-family dwellings nationwide.

310.2 Construction, Height and Allowable Area. It will be noted from the perusal of Table 5-B that the code places more restrictive requirements on Division 1 Occupancies than it does on Division 3 Occupancies. This is consistent with the intent of the code that the hazard be roughly in accordance with the occupant density. Furthermore, the special provisions of Section 310.2.2 also require more fire protection in Division 1 Occupancies with large area above the first story and those three stories or more in height, regardless of area. Again, these provisions are based on the fact that the Division 1 Occupancy has a greater density of occupants, and therefore the code considers the hazard to be greater.

The fire record, however, belies the relative hazards of residential occupancies as established by the UBC. The fire record would seem to indicate that hotels are the safest of residential buildings and one- and two-family dwellings are the most hazardous. Based on the number of fatalities and injuries, the number of buildings involved, and the dollar fire loss, the one- and two-family dwelling would seem to be the most hazardous occupancy of all.

However, the best answer to this seeming anomaly is that the Building Code provisions do, in fact, ameliorate the relatively greater hazard of the apartment house and hotel, and therefore the fire losses are lower in those occupancies. Also, the fact that the dwelling, as compared to other occupancies, is relatively unregulated by the code, must also have an effect on the seeming contradiction. Furthermore, the far greater number of dwellings as related to other structures most certainly has an effect on the fire loss statistics and creates the impression of an excessive fire hazard in dwellings.

310.2.2 Special provisions. This section has special provisions for the construction of Group R, Division 1 Occupancies. First is a requirement for walls and floors separating units or guest rooms to be of one-hour fire-resistive construction. This provides a modified tenant separation (openings do not require protection) which is necessary as it protects the occupants of one unit or guest room from the actions of their neighbors. See also the discussion which follows regarding Section 601.5.2.2. Secondly, Division 1 Occupancies more than two stories in height or having more than 3,000 square feet (279 m^2) of floor area above the first story must be of at least Type II One-hour, Type III One-hour or Type V One-hour construction. The code intends that Group R, Division 1 Occupancies housed in protected types of construction such as those just enumerated contain desirable features, such as fire-resistive compartmentation, which help prevent the spread of fire.

Section 601.5.2.2 has exceptions to the provision that requires one-hour fire-resistive construction throughout and will be discussed later in Chapter 6. Suffice it to say that the exceptions still provide for a degree of compartmentation by requiring one-hour fire-resistive construction around each dwelling unit or guest room in a Group R, Division 1 Occupancy.

310.4 Access and Means of Egress Facilities and Emergency Escapes. Because so many fire deaths occur as the result of the occupants of residential buildings being asleep at the time of a fire, the UBC requires that basements in dwelling units and all sleeping rooms below the fourth story have windows or doors which may be used for emergency escape or rescue. The reason for the requirement in basements is that they are so often used as sleeping rooms.

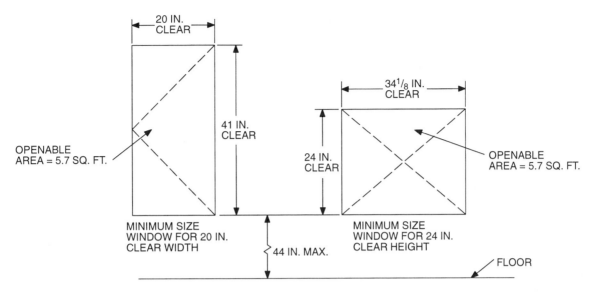

For **SI:** 1 foot = 304.8 mm, 1 square foot = 0.093 m².

EMERGENCY ESCAPE AND RESCUE WINDOW

FIGURE 310-1

The requirement for emergency escape and egress openings in sleeping rooms is because a fire will usually have spread before the occupants are aware of the problem, and the normal exit channels will most likely be blocked. The dimensions prescribed in the code, and as illustrated in Figure 310-1 for exterior wall openings used for emergency egress and rescue, are based on extensive testing by the San Diego Building and Fire Departments to determine the proper relationships of height and width of window opening to adequately serve for both rescue and escape. The minimum of 20 inches (508 mm) for the width was based on two criteria: the width necessary to place a ladder within the window opening and, secondly, the width necessary to admit a firefighter with full rescue equipment. The minimum 24-inch (610 mm) height dimension was based on the minimum necessary to admit a firefighter with full rescue equipment.

It is the intent of the code that the windows required for emergency escape or rescue be located on the exterior of the building so that rescue can be effected from the exterior or, alternatively, so that the occupants may escape from that window to the exterior of the building without having to travel through the building itself. If these windows open into an interior exit court, the exit court must have an exit passageway, that provides access to the public way.

As stated in the code, these windows used for emergency escape or rescue must be operable windows. The intent is that they be of the usual double-hung, horizontal sliding or casement windows operated by the turn of a crank. The building official should evaluate special types of windows other than those just described based on the difficulty of operating or removing the windows. If no more effort is required than that required for the three types of windows just enumerated, they could be approved as meeting the intent of the code as long as no tools, special knowledge or effort are required.

Window wells in front of emergency escape windows also have minimum size and escape requirements. These requirements were added to address those emergency escape windows that occur below grade. Obviously, just providing the standard emergency escape window criteria to these windows will get occupants through the window but the window well may actually trap them against the building without providing for their escape from the window well or providing for firefighter ingress.

The minimum size requirements in cross section are similar in intent to the emergency escape window criteria: that is, to provide a nominal size to allow for the escape of occupants or ingress of firefighters. The ladder or stair requirement is the main difference.

Emergency escape windows below the fourth story are not required to have an escape route down to grade; however, those windows below adjacent grade are so required. When the depth of a window well exceeds 44 inches (1118 mm), a ladder or stair from that window well is required. The type of ladder or stair is not identified in these provisions. However, a permanently fixed ladder as required by the *Uniform Mechanical Code* for access to rooftop equipment would be acceptable or any type of usable stair would suffice.

Remember, these ladders or stairs are provided for emergency use and need not fully comply with the code.

The ever-increasing concern for security, particularly in residential buildings, has created a fairly large demand for security devices such as grilles, bars and steel shutters. Unless properly designed and constructed, these security devices over bedroom windows can completely defeat the purpose of the emergency escape and rescue window. Therefore, the UBC makes provisions for security devices, provided the release mechanism has been approved and is operable from the inside without the use of a key or special knowledge. Furthermore, the code requires that in this case the building be equipped with smoke detectors in accordance with Section 310.9.1. Fire deaths have been attributed to the inability of the individual to escape from the building because the security bars prevented emergency escape.

The very essence of the requirement for emergency escape windows is that a person must be able to effect escape or be rescued in a short period of time because in all probability the fire will have spread to the point where all other exit routes are blocked. Thus, time cannot be wasted to figure out means of opening rescue windows or obtaining egress through them. Thus, any impediment to escape or rescue caused by security devices, inadequate window size, difficult operating mechanisms, etc., is not permitted by the code.

310.6 Room Dimensions. Room size, tightness of construction, minimum ceiling height, number of occupants and ventilation all interact with each other to establish the interior living environment insofar as odors, moisture and transmission of disease are concerned. Therefore, the UBC regulates room sizes to assist in maintaining a comfortable and safe interior environment, and the minimum room sizes become increasingly important as buildings become ever tighter in their construction due to energy conservation requirements.

Section 310.6.1 regulates ceiling heights not only to assist in maintaining a comfortable indoor living environment, but also to provide safety for the occupants of the dwelling. As our population becomes increasingly taller, it is important that tall individuals be able to move about without striking projections from the ceiling with their heads.

The basic requirement for a smooth ceiling of relatively constant height is that the ceiling height not be less than 7 feet 6 inches (2286 mm) for habitable space (see definition of habitable space in Section 209). Kitchens, baths, halls, etc., may have a ceiling height less than 7 feet 6 inches (2286 mm), but under no circumstances may it be less than 7 feet (2134 mm) measured to the lowest projection from the ceiling.

For those ceilings having exposed beams that project down from the ceiling surface, there are two criteria:

1. Where the ceiling beam members are spaced closer than 48 inches (1219 mm) on center, the ceiling height of 7 feet 6 inches (2286 mm) is measured to the bottom of these members.

2. Where the exposed beam ceiling members are spaced at 48 inches (1219 mm) or more on center, the minimum ceiling height of 7 feet 6 inches (2286 mm) is measured to the bottom of the ceiling deck that is supported by the beams.

However, in no case shall the bottom of the members be less than 7 feet (2134 mm) above the floor.

For rooms with sloping ceilings, the code requires only that the prescribed ceiling height be maintained in one-half the area of the room. However, no portion of the room that has a ceiling height of less than 5 feet (1524 mm) shall be used in the computations for minimum floor area. In the case of a room with a furred ceiling, the code requires the prescribed ceiling height in two thirds of the area and, as in all cases for projections below the ceiling, the furred area may not be less than 7 feet (2134 mm) above the floor.

The provisions of Sections 310.6.2 and 310.6.3, limiting the minimum sizes of rooms, apply to habitable rooms except for kitchens. Thus, kitchens, water closet compartments, bathrooms, utility rooms, janitor closets, hallways, etc., have no minimum size or area.

310.7 Efficiency Dwelling Units. This section of the code provides for a specific type of dwelling unit which, as defined in Section 205, is a dwelling unit consisting of only one habitable room. Many of the requirements in this section are redundant, as Section 310 already requires many of these provisions. However, there are some requirements that are unique to the efficiency dwelling unit:

1. A minimum living room size (which also serves as a bedroom and kitchen) of not less than 220 square feet (20.4 m^2) of superficial floor area. Although not defined in the UBC, superficial floor area is intended to mean the gross floor area less the area occupied by built-in cabinets and other built-in appliances that are not readily removed and that preclude any other use of the floor space occupied by the built-in cabinets and fixtures.

2. The minimum room size shall be increased by 100 square feet (9.3 m^2) of superficial floor area for each occupant in the unit in excess of two.

3. A closet is required.

4. A refrigerator is required.

5. Thirty inches (762 mm) of clear working space is required in front of the kitchen sink, kitchen stove and refrigerator.

310.8 Shaft and Exit Enclosures. Exceptions to Sections 711.3 and 1005.3.3 permit unenclosed openings in floors for shafts, stairs, etc., where the opening is only in one floor in Division 1 Occupancies. These unenclosed openings have been an avenue of fire spread from the first floor to the second floor, particularly in motels.[17] Thus, the second paragraph of this section intends to obtain a cutoff between floors when the occupant load is 10 or more. This cutoff acts more as a draft stop than as an enclosure. However, when properly constructed, the cutoff separation will prevent the spread of fire and smoke to an adjacent upper floor.

310.9 Smoke Detectors and Sprinkler Systems. As indicated in the introduction to this chapter, residential fire deaths far exceed those of any other building classification. Furthermore, more than one half of the fire deaths that occur in residential buildings have occurred because of a delay in detection due to the occupants being asleep at the time of the fire. Thus, the UBC requires smoke detectors in all residential buildings.

For Group R Occupancies, the code has a unique provision of retroactivity. Except for repairs to the exterior surfaces such as reroofing, where any addition or repair work exceeds $1,000 or where one or more sleeping rooms are added or created, the code requires that the entire building be provided with smoke detectors located as required for new buildings. This provision is intended to speed up the installation of smoke detectors in residential buildings, as they have proven to be very effective in the reduction of fire deaths. By having these retroactive-type provisions, it is felt that the number of fire deaths per year will be even more drastically curtailed and thousands of lives will be saved annually as a result.

In general, the code requires that smoke detectors receive their power from the building wiring with a battery backup, except for installation of smoke detectors in existing buildings or in buildings regulated by the retroactive provisions just described. In these latter cases, detectors may be battery operated. An important feature of the requirement for detectors being connected into the building's electrical wiring is that there shall be no disconnecting means other than the primary overcurrent protection. See Figure 310-2.

Moreover, the code requires that smoke detectors be centrally located in each sleeping room and on the ceiling or wall of the corridor or area giving access to sleeping rooms. Where sleeping rooms are on an upper floor, the code requires the detector to be placed on the ceiling in close proximity to the stairway. See Figure 310-3. This requirement is based on the fact that any fire initiating on the lower floors will send products of combustion up the stairway, and this position above the stairway will give the earliest warning to the occupants of sleeping rooms on the upper floor. Where high, vaulted ceilings of living rooms and entries adjoin halls, they act as a reservoir for smoke, and this will delay the response of hallway detectors. Therefore, detectors are required in these adjacent rooms to ensure quick response and early warning.

In addition, for buildings with basements, a detector must be installed in the basement where the basement has a stairway communicating with the dwelling. In this case, the detector alarm must be audible in the sleeping area. The *Uniform Fire Code* should also be consulted for other requirements for the location and design of smoke-detection systems.

310.10 Fire Alarm Systems. When asleep, the occupants of residential buildings will usually be unaware of a fire, and it will have an opportunity to spread before being detected. As a result,

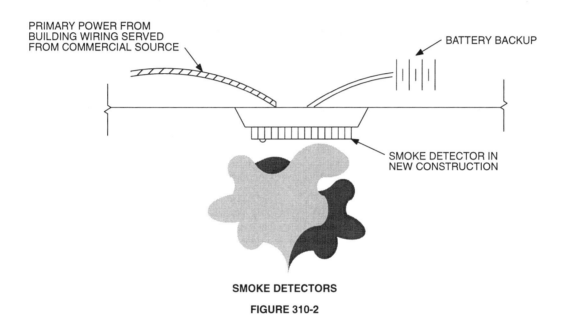

PRIMARY POWER FROM BUILDING WIRING SERVED FROM COMMERCIAL SOURCE

BATTERY BACKUP

SMOKE DETECTOR IN NEW CONSTRUCTION

SMOKE DETECTORS

FIGURE 310-2

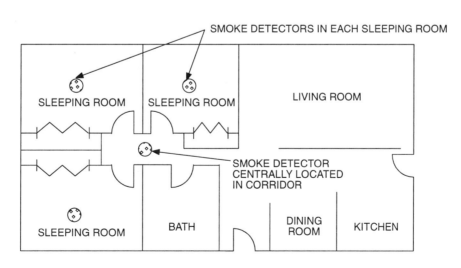

SMOKE DETECTORS IN EACH SLEEPING ROOM

SLEEPING ROOM

SLEEPING ROOM

LIVING ROOM

SMOKE DETECTOR CENTRALLY LOCATED IN CORRIDOR

SLEEPING ROOM

BATH

DINING ROOM

KITCHEN

LOCATION OF SMOKE DETECTORS WITHIN A RESIDENCE

FIGURE 310-3

more than one out of two fire deaths occurring in residential buildings have occurred because of this delay in detection. It is for this reason that this section requires fire alarm systems in certain residential buildings in addition to smoke detectors. Thus, apartment houses three or more stories in height or those containing 16 or more dwelling units, hotels three or more stories in height or those containing 20 or more guest rooms, and congregate residences three or more stories in height or having an occupant load of 20 or more are required to have an approved fire alarm system.

Note that a building less than three stories in height will require a fire alarm system if as an apartment house it contains more than 15 dwelling units or as a hotel it contains 20 or more guest rooms. Consequently, there is an exception for apartment houses less than three stories in height from the requirement for fire alarm systems where all dwelling units are completely separated by a one-hour fire-resistive occupancy separation and each dwelling unit has an exit directly to a yard or public way. This exception is based on the compartmentation provided by the separations between units and by the relatively rapid means of exit available to the occupants.

In view of the provisions of Section 904.2.8, and the second exception to Section 310.10, very few buildings will require fire alarm systems. These will be buildings of a size requiring fire alarm systems, but divided by area separation walls so that sprinklers will not be required. The fire alarm provisions are maintained by IFCI.

310.11 Heating. The provisions of this section require that the heating equipment be "capable" of maintaining a room temperature of 70°F (21°C) at a point 3 feet (914 mm) above the floor in all habitable rooms. The code does not require that this temperature be maintained.

310.12 Special Hazards. As stated earlier in this handbook, it is the intent of the code to separate various uses and hazards with fire-resistive occupancy separations. The intent, of course, is to prevent the spread of fire. In this section, the UBC is concerned with special hazards, such as flammable liquids and boiler rooms. Also, see the commentary on Section 302.5.

Combustible or flammable liquids are required by the UBC to be stored and handled in accordance with the *Uniform Fire Code*. There is also a special requirement for doors leading from Division 1 Occupancies into rooms where Class I (the more volatile) flammable liquids are used or stored. In addition to the requirement for a one-hour fire-protection rating for the protective assembly, the code also requires that it be self-closing and be posted with a sign on each side of the door stating FIRE DOOR—KEEP CLOSED.

SECTION 311 — REQUIREMENTS FOR GROUP S OCCUPANCIES

311.1 Group S Occupancies Defined. This occupancy designation first appeared in the 1994 UBC. In general, it includes storage occupancies that are not highly hazardous and uses related to the storage or repair of vehicles. The occupancy designation is in keeping with the recommendations of the Board for the Coordination of the Model Codes (BCMC).

Before discussing the five divisions of Group S Occupancies, we should consider the classification of borderline uses. In a number of instances, the code does not give a list of the uses allowed within an occupancy; an exclusionary rule is used instead. For example, a Group S, Division 1 Occupancy is used for storage of materials not classified as a Group S, Division 2 or as a Group H Occupancy. Similarly, a Group H, Division 4 Occupancy is a repair garage not classified a Group S, Division 3 Occupancy. The building official will often be called upon to decide which classification is most appropriate when a use can fall within two occupancy classifications. As guidance in making this decision, it is usually more appropriate to choose the least restrictive occupancy. This is particularly true when the area and height of the building in question is far below the allowable. Classifying the use into the more restrictive use would allow the operator to employ the most hazardous operations allowed within the occupancy and thereby increase the hazards in the building.

Division 1. Group S, Division 1 Occupancies are used for the storage of combustible commodities. A complete list of all products allowed in this use would be very lengthy. The list would include electrical appliances, lumber, wood furniture, upholstered furniture, mattresses and carpeting. The list would also include paint storage without bulk handling. In general, buildings classed in this division would be used for the storage of commodities that are manufactured within buildings classified as Group F, Division 1 Occupancies. Commodities that constitute a high hazard would be stored in the appropriate Group H Occupancy.

Division 2. Group S, Division 2 Occupancies, include not only the storage of noncombustible commodities that can be packaged in wood, paper or cardboard cartons and often stored on wood pallets but also ice plants, power plants and pumping plants. Since the manufacturing of ice is also included in Group F, Division 2 Occupancies it is more appropriate to classify ice plants as Group F, Division 2 Occupancies. Power plants and pumping plants would also seem more appropriate as Group F, Division 2 Occupancies and classifying them as such is allowed by the code.

Division 3. Group S, Division 3 Occupancies include uses that under the 1994 edition of the code were classified as Group B, Division 1 Occupancies. A provision that prohibited the use of Class I, II or III liquids in this occupancy has been removed. Limited quantities of these liquids are allowed when the quantity is below the exempt amount per control area and the storage and use complies with the *Uniform Fire Code*.

Divisions 4 and 5. Group S, Division 4 Occupancies (open parking garages) were classified as Group B, Division 4 Occupancies in the previous editions of the UBC, and Group S, Division 5 Occupancies were previously classified as Group B, Division 3 Occupancies.

311.2.2 Special provisions. This section contains provisions that might be considered the only exception to the principle that an area separation is strictly a wall without horizontal offsets. In Section 311.2.2.1, Item 1, the code makes provisions for the use of a horizontal occupancy separation as a sort of equivalent construction feature to the area separation wall.

Section 311.2.2.1 in effect is an exception that allows a parking garage in a basement or first story of a building to be considered a separate building. The floors above such parking must be a Group A, Division 3, Group B, Group M or Group R, Division 1 Occupancy. As these occupancies are quite common in Type V construction, the intent is to grant the maximum number of stories for the Type V construction without the penalty of sacrificing one story for the garage.

It is fairly common in terrain that has a rolling or hillside character to erect apartment houses and small office/retail buildings with a garage in the basement or first story. Due to the slope of the ground surface, the lowest level is usually partially within the ground, and therefore the walls are normally designed as reinforced concrete or reinforced masonry retaining walls. Thus, the construction of the lowest level is close to conforming to the code construction requirements for a Type I building.

If this lowest level is classified as the first story, the code would normally permit only two additional stories of apartments for a building classified as Type V One-hour construction. However, as depicted in Figure 311-1, the provisions of Section 311.2.2 permit three additional stories of apartments to be erected above the garage level, provided the garage level is of Type I construction and a three-hour fire-resistive occupancy separation is constructed between the garage and the occupancy above.

Under these circumstances, the first-level garage would be considered a Group S, Division 3 Occupancy housed within a Type I building, and an apartment house above would be classified as a separate Type V One-hour building housing a Group R, Division 1 Occupancy. The code lists four conditions that must be met in order to take advantage of these provisions, including an often-forgotten provision that the overall height in feet (mm) of both buildings shall not exceed the height limit set forth in Table 5-B for the least type of construction. The third condition has two exceptions that allow other occupancies in the Type I portion of the building. The first exception allows rooms and uses that are incidental to the operation of the building to be located below the three-hour occupancy separation. The second exception allows office, restaurant and retail occupancies below the three-hour separation, provided that portion of the building is sprinklered throughout.

Section 311.2.2.2 is an exception to the requirement that a building classified as a Group S, Division 4 Occupancy (open parking garage) be used for no other purpose. The section allows the basement or first story to be a Group S, Division 3 Occupancy when all of the listed conditions are met.

311.2.3.2 Marine or motor vehicle fuel-dispensing stations. Due to the potential exposure of gasoline and vehicle fires during fuel-dispensing operations, the canopies and supports over pumps are required by this section to be noncombustible fire-retardant-treated wood or of one-hour fire-resistive construction.

To avoid damage to vehicles and canopies, the height of canopies should not be less than 13 feet 6 inches (4114 mm). The 13-foot 6-inch (4114 mm) dimension will provide adequate clearance for recreational vehicles.

The provisions in the third paragraph of this section are essentially an exception to the requirements for an occupancy separation required between covered fuel-dispensing pumps and an associated retail store. Since minimarkets started replacing service bays at many modern gasoline stations, building officials have wrestled with the problem of what type of occupancy separation, if any, should be required between such minimarkets and fuel-dispensing operations. To provide a one-hour occupancy separation presented a problem since it prevented the use of the large expanse of glass that is necessary for operators to provide visual control of fueling activities that is required by the Fire Code. A second exit would help the situation by providing a secondary escape route in case of emergency, yet most minimarkets are too small to need a second exit. Under the provisions of this exception, both problems should be solved since no occupancy separation is required if the retail sales area (minimarket) is provided with two complying exits that are not located on the same exterior wall. Further, in order to spatially separate the hazard of fuel spillage from the retail sales area, pump islands are required to be located at least 20 feet (6096 mm) from the retail sales area. A further restriction is imposed because the retail store is limited to a maximum area of 2,500 square feet (225 m^2).

311.2.3.5 Vehicle barriers. In this section, all parking areas more than 5 feet (1524 mm) above adjacent grade are required

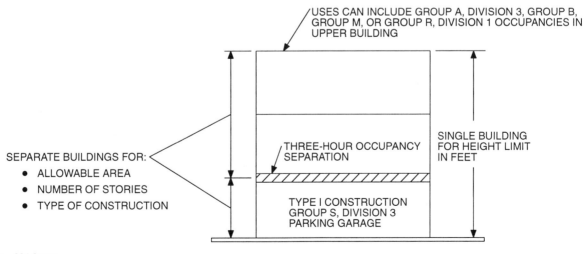

For **SI:** 1 foot = 304.8 mm.

FIGURE 311-1

to be provided with vehicle barriers, with the exception of Group U, Division 1 Occupancy parking garages. This provision establishes specific design requirements for these barriers and refers to Table 16-B for the required design loads. See Figure 311-2.

311.9 Group S, Division 4 Open Parking Garages. Studies and tests of fires in open parking garages have shown that, in addition to a low fire loading, the potential for a large fire is exceedingly remote.[18] Based on these data, the UBC establishes special provisions for open parking garages in this section, which in general are less restrictive than those for the usual parking structure (Group S, Division 3 Occupancy). The key is that the open parking garage is well ventilated naturally, and as a result the products of combustion dissipate rapidly and do not contribute to the spread of fire.

To secure the proper amount of openness, the code, as illustrated in Figure 311-3, specifies that (a) the building must have openings on at least two sides, (b) the openings must be uniformly distributed along each side, (c) the area of openings in the exterior walls on any given tier must be at least equal to 20 percent of the wall area of the total perimeter of each tier, and (d) the aggregate length of openings considered to provide natural ventilation shall constitute a minimum of 40 percent of the perimeter of that tier.

Because the potential fire severity is extremely low, the code permits area and height limitations in excess of those for Group S, Division 3 Occupancies in Type II buildings. For example, an open parking garage in a Type II-F.R. building would be permitted an area of 125,000 square feet (11 613 m²) per tier with a height limit of 12 tiers for a ramp-access garage. For open parking garages the total area of a multistory building is not limited to twice that for a one-story building but can actually be computed as the permitted area per tier times the number of tiers. Therefore, in the example just given, the total area permitted would be one and one-half million square feet (46 450 m²). This is compared to a permissible area of 159,600 square feet (14 827 m²) for a Group S, Division 3 parking garage in a Type II-F.R. building facing three streets at least 60 feet (18 288 mm) in width.

In the same fashion, the heights permitted for the less-protected Type II buildings are two and one-half to four times the heights permitted for a Group S, Division 3 Occupancy. The maximum height in tiers has been limited somewhat arbitrarily by the code, based on the length of time it would take for fire department personnel to reach the top of the structure for fire-suppression purposes. However, if an automatic fire-extinguishing system is installed throughout the building, the total number of tiers may be increased by 50 percent.

The only area and height increases above those listed in Table 3-H permitted for parking structures are outlined in Section 311.9.5 and are basically keyed to the provision of more natural ventilation area than the minimum required by the code. For unlimited-area buildings permitted by this section, see Figure 311-4.

In addition to limiting the use to the parking of private or pleasure-type motor vehicles, the code also provides the following other limitations that are prohibitions:

1. There shall be no automobile repair work performed in the building.

2. There shall be no parking of buses or trucks or similar vehicles.

(Continued on page 46)

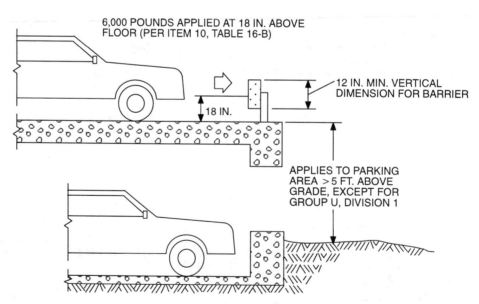

For **SI:** 1 foot = 304.8 mm, 1 pound = 0.45 kg.

ALL PARKING GARAGES EXCEPT GROUP U, DIVISION 1

VEHICLE BARRIERS

FIGURE 311-2

EXTERIOR WALLS
MUST HAVE UNIFORMLY DISTRIBUTED OPENINGS ON TWO OR MORE SIDES

INTERIOR WALL AND COLUMN LINES
SHALL BE AT LEAST 20% OPEN (AREA) WITH UNIFORMLY DISTRIBUTED OPENINGS

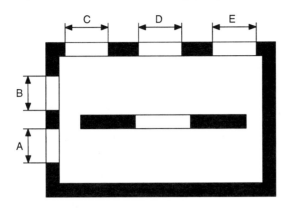

1. AREA:
   A + B + C + D + E ≥ 20% TOTAL
   (PERIMETER AREA OF EACH TIER)

2. LENGTH:
   A + B + C + D + E ≥ 40% TOTAL
   (PERIMETER AREA OF EACH TIER)

GENERAL CASE

OPEN PARKING GARAGES

FIGURE 311-3

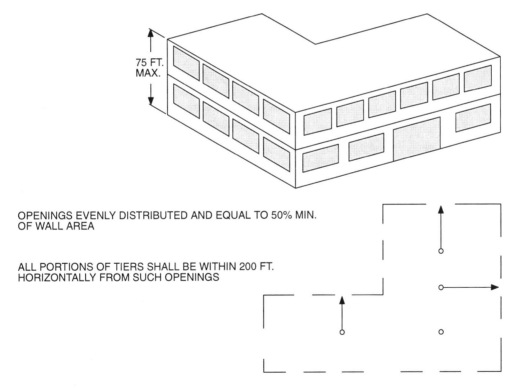

OPENINGS EVENLY DISTRIBUTED AND EQUAL TO 50% MIN.
OF WALL AREA

ALL PORTIONS OF TIERS SHALL BE WITHIN 200 FT.
HORIZONTALLY FROM SUCH OPENINGS

TYPE II-F.R., II ONE-HOUR OR II-N CONSTRUCTION REQUIRED. UNLIMITED AREA PERMITTED.

For **SI:** 1 foot = 304.8 mm.

SPECIAL CASE

TYPE II OPEN PARKING GARAGES

FIGURE 311-4

(Continued from page 44)

3. There shall be no partial or complete closing of the required exterior wall openings by tarpaulins or by any other means.

4. There shall be no dispensing of fuel.

The intent of these limitations is to further ensure low fire loading, low possibility of fire spread and good natural cross ventilation.

311.10 Helistops. Helistops are differentiated from heliports by the presence of refueling facilities, maintenance operations, and repair and storage of helicopters; thus, heliports pose the same hazards as aircraft repair hangars. However, when installed on rooftops, they present special exposure hazards. Accordingly, in cases where heliports are constructed on buildings, they must be in accordance with Section 1609.3.

SECTION 312 — REQUIREMENTS FOR GROUP U OCCUPANCIES

This section covers those utility occupancies that are not normally occupied by people, such as sheds and other accessory buildings, carports, small garages, fences, tanks and towers, and agricultural buildings when not regulated by Appendix Chapter 3, Division II. The fire load in these structures and uses varies considerably but is usually not excessive. Because they are normally not occupied by people, the concern for fire load is not very great, and as a group these uses constitute a low hazard.

312.1 Group U Occupancies Defined. Group U Occupancies are divided into two divisions. Division 1 includes those that are buildings and are used for shelter of chattels. These include private garages, carports, sheds and agricultural buildings when not regulated by Appendix Chapter 3, Division II.

If the jurisdiction has adopted Appendix Chapter 3, Division II, then it will govern the design and construction of agricultural buildings that come under its purview; however, many urban jurisdictions do not adopt Appendix Chapter 3, Division II. In this case, should an occasional agricultural building be constructed, it would be regulated by Section 312 of the UBC.

Division 2 covers those structures that are not occupied and that are not used for shelter, such as fences, tanks and towers.

312.2 Construction, Height and Allowable Area. In order to secure the low fire hazard intended by the Group U Occupancy classification, the code limits buildings in Division 1 to 1,000 square feet (92.9 m^2) in area and one story in height. The code goes on to develop what are in effect exceptions to the 1,000-square-foot (92.9 m^2) limitation. For a mixed-occupancy building such as a Group R, Division 1 apartment house and a Group U private parking garage, the code permits the Group U, Division 1 Occupancy to have an area of 3,000 square feet (279 m^2).

This increase in area is permitted on the basis of restricting the use to private or pleasure-type motor vehicles with no repair or fueling. Furthermore, the exterior wall and opening protection of the Group U Occupancy are required to be the same as required for the major occupancy of the building (Group R, Division 1 in the example). Thus, the increase in area is justified on the basis of restricting the use of the building and increasing the exterior wall and opening protection. Where this provision of the code is utilized, it also permits the allowable floor area of the total building to be as permitted for the major occupancy.

The code also allows an increase in area to 3,000 square feet (279 m^2) if the building is limited to a Group U Occupancy and is used for the parking of private- or pleasure-type vehicles, provided the exterior wall and opening protection are as provided for a Group R, Division 1 Occupancy. This increase in area for a single-occupancy building is predicated on the same restrictions provided for a mixed-occupancy building.

Table 3-A—Description of Occupancies by Group and Division. This table summarizes the more detailed descriptions in the occupancy sections. When there is a conflict between the table and the more detailed description in the occupancy sections, the detailed description applies. See Section 101.3.

Table 3-B—Required Separation in Buildings of Mixed Occupancy (in Hours). This table is generally self-explanatory. The "Notes" to Table 3-B are important as they refer to exceptions and modifications to the ratings in the table.

This table was revised in the 1997 code to reduce the occupancy separation requirements between Group S, Division 2, storage occupancies and other specified occupancies on the basis that a reduced occupancy separation requirement exists in the table for the more hazardous Group S, Division 1 storage occupancies. As an example, the code does not require any separation between a Group B and a Group S, Division 1 Occupancy, and should not require a separation between a Group B Occupancy and the less hazardous Group S, Division 2 Occupancy, which is predominately used for storing noncombustible materials.

Table 3-C—Required Separation of Specific-use Areas in Group I, Division 1.1 Hospital and Nursing Homes. This table was in Chapter 10 of the 1988 and 1991 editions of the code. The table is referenced by Section 308.8. It requires occupancy separations for uses in hospitals or nursing homes that may not otherwise be recognized as a use that poses a hazard to patients and deserves to be isolated.

Table 3-D—Exempt Amounts of Hazardous Materials Presenting a Physical Hazard: Maximum Quantities per Control Area. This table sets forth exempt amounts for physical hazard materials. All three situations (storage, use-closed and use-open) are considered. For the specific case of gases, exempt amounts are all listed under storage and use-closed because the definition of use-closed in Chapter 2 specifically includes all gases in use.

With two exceptions, any combination of materials or situations listed in this table is allowed in each control area. These two exceptions are (1) as provided by Footnote 15, combination flammable liquids, and (2) as provided by Footnote 2, which requires that aggregate quantities of materials in both use and storage must not exceed the allowable quantity for storage.

It is extremely important to note that, for certain occupancies, the Fire Code contains more stringent requirements than those in this table. For example, consider Class 4 oxidizers not protected by storage cabinets. The exempt amount in Table 3-D is listed as 1 pound (0.45 kg); however, UFC Section 8001.15.2.6.2.1 prohibits Class 4 oxidizers in Group R Occupancies and UFC Sections 8001.15.2.2.2, 8001.15.2.3.2, 8001.15.2.4.2, 8001.15.2.5.2.1 and 8001.15.2.7.2.1 prohibit Class 4 oxidizers in Groups A, B, E, F, I, M, S and U Occupancies with certain exceptions. The exceptions allow Class 4 oxidizers in these occupancies to be stored within hazardous materials storage cabinets not containing other storage. These types of restrictions are included in the Fire Code for toxic and highly toxic gases, liquid and solid oxidizers, organic peroxides, and unstable (reactive) materials.

Specific footnotes to the table provide the following information:

Footnote 1. This footnote briefly defines the construction requirements for control areas and limits the number of control areas within buildings to four, unless such buildings are used for retail and wholesale sales in which case the number of control areas is limited to two. For additional information, see the discussion of control areas at the beginning of Section 307.

Footnote 2. This footnote requires quantities of materials that are in use to be counted as both storage and use when comparing quantities to exempt amounts.

Footnote 3. This footnote defers to Section 8001.12 of the UFC for requirements.

Footnote 4. This footnote exempts small size containers of certain consumer products that are considered to present minimal hazards based on the types of materials and the container sizes.

Footnote 5. This footnote defers to Article 88 of the UFC for requirements.

Footnote 6. This footnote allows certain materials to have exempt amounts doubled when stored or used in sprinklered buildings. Compounding with the increases provided by Footnote 10 is allowed when both footnotes are applicable. Materials and situations referencing both Footnotes 6 and 10 can receive four times the listed exempt amount when both footnotes are applied.

Footnote 7. This footnote provides a cross-reference to the special hazards sections in the occupancy chapters of the UBC. These sections typically reference the *Uniform Fire Code.* Flammable and combustible liquids are regulated by UFC Article 79, and requirements dealing with general storage and use situations are located in Sections 7902 and 7903. The Fire Code contains specific limits and controls for flammable and combustible liquids that often go beyond the limitations in the *Uniform Building Code.* For example, the Fire Code specifies that exempt amounts are subject to limited storage arrangements. See UFC Section 7902.5.10. Also, UFC Table 7903.3-A, Footnote 2, authorizes the chief to impose special restrictions on flammable and combustible liquids used in quantities less than exempt amounts.

Footnote 8. This footnote recognizes special quantity increases allowed for wholesale and retail sales of flammable and combustible liquids in UFC Table 7902.5-B. When applying these criteria, the building official should consult with the fire department.

Footnote 9. This footnote is provided as a cross-reference to UFC Section 4502. Spray finishing with flammable and combustible liquids is considered to constitute a special hazard for which specific provisions have been included in the Fire Code; therefore, exempt amounts in Table 3-D do not apply in these cases. Rather, UFC Section 4502 requires spray finishing to be conducted in spray booths or spraying rooms, except as provided for limited spraying areas in UFC Section 4502.6. These requirements are applicable, regardless of the quantity of liquid being sprayed.

Footnote 10. This footnote allows exempt amounts for certain materials in storage and use to be doubled when approved storage cabinets, gas cabinets, etc., as applicable are employed. For cabinet requirements, see UFC Sections 7902.5.9, 8003.1.10 and 8003.3.1. Also, see Footnote 6.

Footnote 11. This footnote allows certain materials to be stored or used in unlimited quantities in sprinklered buildings.

Footnote 12. This footnote limits storage and use of certain materials to sprinklered buildings.

Footnote 13. This footnote limits quantities of black sporting powder and smokeless powder per building rather than per control area. For additional requirements, see UFC Section 7702.2. Also, see discussion of Group H, Division 1 Occupancies covered previously in this chapter.

Footnote 14 is self-explanatory.

Footnote 15. This footnote limits the quantities of Class I-A, -B and -C liquids making up the total quantity of Class I liquids.

Footnote 16. This footnote allows increased quantities of Class 3 oxidizers in all occupancies for maintenance purposes and operation of equipment. The revision to this footnote removes the limitation on the use of this exception to Groups I, R and U Occupancies since this exception is limited to the storage of such materials used for the maintenance or operation of equipment only. Also, see UFC Sections 8001.15.2.3.4, 8001.15.2.5.2.2 and 8001.15.2.7.4.

Table 3-E—Exempt Amounts of Hazardous Materials Presenting a Health Hazard: Maximum Quantities per Control Area. This table is similar in nature to Table 3-D, except that the exempt amounts listed in Table 3-E are for health hazard materials. For discussions of specific footnotes, see the above discussion of Table 3-D. Table 3–E was revised in the 1997 UBC to be consistent with the UFC.

Table 3-F—Minimum Distances for Buildings Containing Explosive Materials. This table sets forth the minimum distances to property lines from buildings that are required by Table 3-G to be detached. Separations from inhabited buildings and other buildings containing explosives that are subject to a sympathetic explosive reaction are also specified. The distances in the table may be reduced when adequate barricades are installed in accordance with Footnote 4. Furthermore, the distances may be adjusted based on the TNT equivalency of explosive materials involved. TNT equivalency for some materials is published; however, for many materials, TNT equivalency must be evaluated based on actual testing, calculations performed by a chemist or both. Alternately, the full values in the table can be used if TNT equivalency can not be reliably estimated. To use TNT equivalency, the weight of the material in question is multiplied by the ratio of relative blast energy with respect to TNT. The resultant weight is used when applying the table to determine the required separation distances.

For those occupancies required by Table 3-G to have detached storage based on quantities of materials that do not possess explosive characteristics, the minimum distances in Table 5-A should be used.

The distances in this table are derived from the American Table of Distances for Storage of Explosives Materials, which is included in C.F.R. Titles 27 and 30. Similar requirements are included in UFC Appendix VI-E, which is provided as reference material for UFC Article 77.

One significant difference between application of the American Table of Distances as published in the C.F.R. and the *Uniform Fire Code* versus UBC Table 3-F is that measurements to inhabited buildings under the American Table of Distances allow the use of vacant space on adjacent properties. Table 3-F, on the other hand, requires separation distances to be measured only on the property containing the building housing explosive materials. This will usually have the effect of the UBC requiring greater distances between buildings on adjacent properties. Also, see discussion in Section 307.1 for Group H, Division 1 Occupancies in this chapter.

Table 3-G—Required Detached Storage. This table establishes the threshold quantities of hazardous materials requiring detached buildings. Once the quantities listed in the table are exceeded, a detached building is required. Though the table only specifically addresses storage amounts, conditions involving use should be treated in a similar manner to that prescribed by Footnote 2 of Table 3-D, which requires "use" quantities to be aggregated with "storage" quantities when comparing to exempt amounts.

Example for Using Control Areas and Exempt Amounts

A company desires to store 1,000 pounds (453.6 kg) of Chemical "A" in a Group S, Division 1 warehouse. The material will not be protected by sprinklers or hazardous materials storage cabinets. The company has stated that no other hazardous materials will be stored in the warehouse.

According to a technical report submitted by the permit applicant, Chemical "A" presents only a physical hazard. It is categorized as a Class 2 Oxidizer.

Question: Can the company store the desired quantity in the Group S, Division 1 warehouse?

Answer: The exempt amount for Class 2 Oxidizers, unprotected by sprinklers or hazardous materials storage cabinets, is listed as 250 pounds (113.4 kg) in Table 3-D. The appropriate occupancy classification for Class 2 Oxidizers stored in excess of the exempt amounts allowed in control areas would be Group H, Division 3; however, the code allows the use of four control areas in a warehouse. Therefore, if the warehouse is divided into four control areas having not more than 250 pounds (113.4 kg) of Chemical "A" per control area, the occupancy can be designated as a Group S, Division 1 Occupancy. See Figure 312-1.

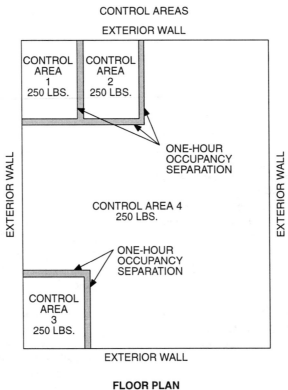

For **SI:** 1 pound = 0.454 kg.

FLOOR PLAN

FIGURE 312-1

REFERENCES

[1]Colling, R. C., and Hal Colling, Eds. (1951). *Modern Building Inspection,* Second Edition. Building Standards Publishing Company, Los Angeles, California (Chapter 12, "Building Failures," No. 18, the Iroquois Fire).

[2]Bryan, John L. (1986). *Fire Protection Handbook.* National Fire Protection Association, Quincy, Massachusetts ("Human Behavior and Fire," Section 1/Chapter 2).

[3]Canter, David, Ed. (1980). *Fires and Human Behavior.* John Wiley and Sons, New York, New York (Chapter 5, "The Concept of Panic," by Jonathon Sime).

[4]Kentucky State Police (1977). *Investigative Report to the Governor, The Beverly Hills Supper Club Fire.* Commonwealth of Kentucky, Frankfort, Kentucky.

[5]National Fire Protection Association (1978). Reconstruction of a tragedy: Beverly Hills Supper Club. National Fire Protection Association, Quincy, Massachusetts.

[6]*Uniform Building Code* (1927 Edition). Pacific Coast Building Officials Conference, Long Beach, California.

[7]*Fire Protection Handbook*, 17th Edition (1991). National Fire Protection Association, Quincy, Massachusetts.

[8]*Guide for Venting of Deflagrations,* NFPA 68 (1988). National Fire Protection Association, Quincy, Massachusetts.

[9]*Standard on Explosion Prevention Systems,* NFPA 69 (1986). National Fire Protection Association, Quincy, Massachusetts.

[10]Goldberg, A. G., and L. Fluer (1986). *H-6 Design Guide to the Uniform Codes for High-Tech Facilities.* Codes and Standards Information Company and GRDA Publications, Mill Valley, California.

[11]National Bureau of Standards (1957). *Fire Resistance Classifications of Building Construction* (BMS 92). Washington, D.C., page 67.

[12]Boring, Delbert F., James C. Spence and Walter G. Wells (1981). *Fire Protection through Modern Building Codes,* Fifth Edition. American Iron and Steel Institute, Washington, D.C., pages 64-66.

[13]Ibid., pages 67-70.

[14]National Bureau of Standards (1942). *Fire-resistance Classifications of Building Construction (BMS 92).* Washington, D.C.

[15]Karter, Michael J., Jr. (1985). Fire Loss in the United States during 1984. *Fire Journal,* September.

[16]Council of American Building Officials (1989). *One and Two Family Dwelling Code.* Washington, D.C.

[17]Cote, Ron, and Thomas Klem. Investigation Report—Ramada Inn Central Fire, Fort Worth, Texas, June 14, 1983. National Fire Protection Association, Quincy, Massachusetts.

Chapter 4

SPECIAL USE AND OCCUPANCY

SECTION 402 — ATRIA

This section has been designed to fill a need for code provisions applicable to the current trends in architectural design of office buildings and hotels wherein the designer makes use of an atrium. Prior to the 1982 edition, the UBC did not provide for atria, and, moreover, atria were prohibited due to the requirements for protection of vertical openings in Section 711. However, they have in the past been permitted on an individual basis, usually under the provisions of Section 104.2.8 where alternate protection was provided. The general concept of alternate protection is to provide for both the equivalence of an open court and at the same time provide protection somewhat equivalent to shaft protection to prevent products of combustion from being spread throughout the building via the atrium.[1]

The basic requirement in this section is that the building be provided with an automatic sprinkler system throughout. See Figure 402-1. During the development of the provisions, it was felt that the protection requirements of a building with atria were so unique that trade-offs should not be permitted. Therefore, amendments were made to Chapter 5 so that area and height increases and the substitution of automatic sprinklers for one-hour protection throughout would not be permitted for buildings with atria.[2,3]

On the basis of equivalency to an open court, the minimum size of the clear opening for the atrium is limited in accordance with Table 4-A and as depicted in Figure 402-2. Elevators located totally within the atrium are permitted without an enclosure; however, stairs and ramps required for egress and located in the atrium space will require a shaft enclosure except where connecting only the two lowest floor levels. It should be empha-

sized that this new requirement in the 1997 code applies to only "required" stairs within the atrium space if serving the third floor or above. The travel distance of any open exit-access balcony within the atrium is limited to 100 feet (30 480 mm) by Section 402.5.1 from the point where a required exit from any tenant space, hotel room or hotel corridor enters the open exit-access balcony. When the separation between the tenant space has been omitted, this travel distance is measured from the point where the exit leaves the tenant space and enters the common atmosphere with the atrium. See Figure 402-3.

Because the atrium is roofed, it was believed desirable during the development of the provisions not only to limit exit travel distance within the atrium but also to control combustibles and interior finish. Therefore, the *Uniform Fire Code* contains special provisions limiting combustibles in atria. Section 402.8 of the UBC requires all interior finish within the atrium to be Class I with no reduction because of the sprinkler system.

Another component of the equivalency to an open court is the smoke-control system required by Section 402.2. The design of the smoke-control system is to be in accordance with Section 905.

With some exceptions, an enclosure separation is required between the atrium and the remainder of the building. See Figure 402-4. The basic requirement is for a one-hour fire-resistive separation with door openings equipped with 20-minute smoke- and draft-control assemblies, which are to be self-closing or automatic closing by smoke detector actuation. This type of enclosure and the special sprinkler-wetted glass enclosure as depicted in Figure 402-5 and outlined in Exception 2 to Section 402.3 are

(Continued on page 54)

SPRINKLER SYSTEM THROUGHOUT—PREVENT SPREAD OF FIRE.

(NOT PERMITTED FOR OTHER INCREASES—SECTIONS 505.3 AND 506)

SMOKE-CONTROL SYSTEM—KEEP BUILDING AND ATRIUM CLEAR OF SMOKE SO THAT SAFE EXITING MAY BE ACCOMPLISHED THROUGH ATRIUM.

ATRIUM CONCEPT

FIGURE 402-1

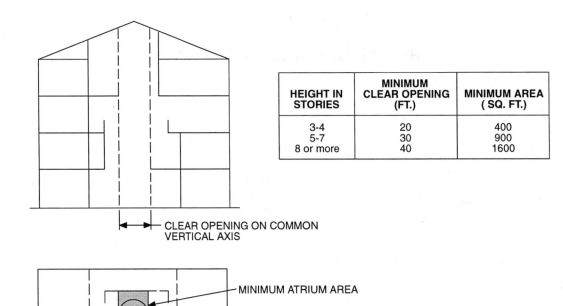

HEIGHT IN STORIES	MINIMUM CLEAR OPENING (FT.)	MINIMUM AREA (SQ. FT.)
3-4	20	400
5-7	30	900
8 or more	40	1600

CLEAR OPENING ON COMMON VERTICAL AXIS

MINIMUM ATRIUM AREA

For **SI:** 1 foot = 304.8 mm, 1 square foot = 0.093 m².

ATRIUM SIZE

FIGURE 402-2

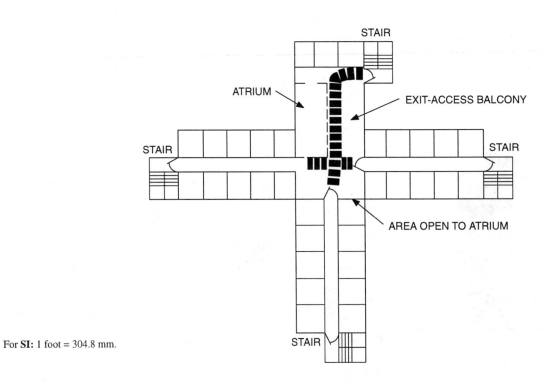

For **SI:** 1 foot = 304.8 mm.

TRAVEL DISTANCE MAXIMUM 100 FEET ON AN OPEN EXIT-ACCESS BALCONY IN ATRIUM

FIGURE 402-3

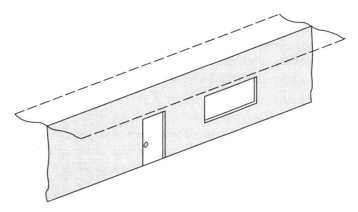

WALL CONSTRUCTION: One-hour fire-resistive construction.
DOOR REQUIREMENTS: Smoke- and-draft-control assemblies conforming to Section 1004.3.4.3.2—or—tightfitting with automatic-closing by smoke detector or self-closing (no fire rating needed if protected by sprinkler system).
GLAZING REQUIREMENTS: Listed three-fourths-hour fire windows and maximum 25 percent of common wall. Glazing maximum length or height is 12 feet and 84 square feet (Section 713.8).

EXCEPTIONS: 1. R-1, unprotected openings when floor area per unit is less than 1,000 square feet and unit has an approved means of egress not entering the atrium.
2. For guest rooms. dwelling units, congregate residences or tenant spaces, glazing may be wired glass in steel frames. In lieu thereof, tempered or laminated glass may be used, provided:
  (a) Glass is protected with sprinkler system (quick-response sprinklers) on each walking surface side.
  (b) Tempered or laminated glass is supported by gasketed frame.
  (c) Three-fourths-hour-rated glass block wall may be used.
  (d) Obstructions are prohibited between sprinklers and glass openings.

For **SI:** 1 foot = 304.8 mm, 1 square foot = 0.0929 m^2.

ATRIUM ENCLOSURE

FIGURE 402-4

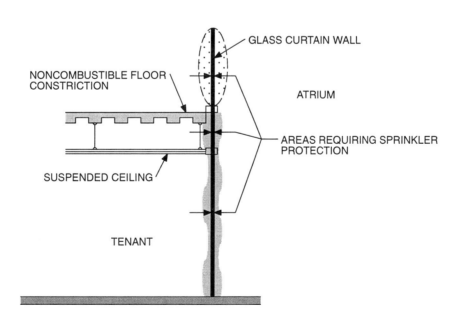

GLASS PROTECTION

FIGURE 402-5

(Continued from page 51)

intended to provide protection somewhat equivalent to the shaft protection.

In keeping with the court concept, it is intended by the UBC that open exit balconies and open exit stairs be permitted within the atrium. However, the minimum dimension and area of the atrium are measured between projections such as balconies. This is because the minimums outlined in Table 4-A are based on unobstructed vertical movement of air within the atrium. The protection illustrated in Figure 402-5 and outlined in Exception 2 to Section 402.3 for sprinkler-wetted glass enclosure walls of atria is intended to cool the glass to prevent breakage when a fire breaks out in a tenant space. However, if there is a walking surface on the atrium side of the enclosure, such as an exit balcony, the special sprinkler protection is required on both sides. However, it should be noted that the code does *not* require sprinkler protection for the wired glass separation, as wired glass is considered to provide resistance to breakage equivalent to the wetted tempered or laminated glass.

There are two exceptions to the requirements for the protection of openings in the enclosure of the atrium:

1. The first permits unrated doors, provided they are tightfitting and are maintained as self-closing or automatic closing in accordance with Section 713.2 by actuation of a smoke detector. The doors must be protected by sprinklers as are required for sprinkler-wetted glass enclosures in Exception 2.

2. The second case is for Group R, Division 1 Occupancies where protection of fixed glazed openings in the enclosure of the atrium is waived where the floor area of each hotel room or dwelling unit does not exceed 1,000 square feet (93 m²) and there is an approved means of egress from the room or unit which does not enter the atrium. This exception is based on the supposition that if smoke from an atrium fire were to fracture ordinary annealed window glass between the atrium and the hotel room or dwelling unit, the occupants could exit to a protected exit system. Also, this event is considered to be fairly remote because of the sprinkler system and smoke-control systems required for the building.

The separation between tenant spaces (spaces used for other than Group R, Division 1 Occupancies) and the atrium may be omitted on a maximum of any three floor levels, provided the remaining floor levels are separated as provided in this section. Even though the Group R, Division 1 Occupancy is permitted to be separated from the atrium by a glass enclosure, the provision permitting the omission of the separation applies only to tenant spaces. Omission of the separation between tenant spaces and the atrium is consistent with parallel provisions for covered mall buildings in Section 404 that permit a maximum of three stories or floor levels with a common atmosphere.

Where a Group B Occupancy office, Group M Occupancy sales area, or Group A, Division 3 Occupancy is located below a Group R, Division 1 Occupancy, Section 402.6 provides for the omission of the vertical portion of the occupancy separation that would be required by Section 302 and which is adjacent to the atrium. This provision is consistent with the special provisions for the glass-walled atrium enclosure. However, structural supports that are part of the structural frame would require protection as required in Table 6-A. See Figure 402-6.

Many of the concepts embodied within this section have been used with success under the provisions of Section 104.2.8 of the code prior to their inclusion in the UBC. It is expected that as these provisions are tested by experience, refinements will continue to be made through the code change process. However, until more experience is obtained, a certain amount of redundancy in the life-safety protection is included in the provisions.

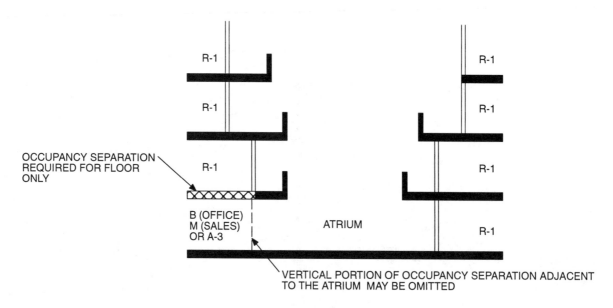

NOTE: Atrium enclosure protection (Section 402.3) must still be maintained.

OCCUPANCY SEPARATION EXCEPTION

FIGURE 402-6

SECTION 403 — SPECIAL PROVISIONS FOR GROUP B OFFICE BUILDINGS AND GROUP R, DIVISION 1 OCCUPANCIES

This section encompasses special life-safety requirements for high-rise office buildings, apartment houses and hotels. The comparatively good fire record notwithstanding, particularly in office buildings, fires in high-rise buildings have prompted government at all levels to develop special regulations concerning life safety in high-rise buildings. Despite the fact that "it would take 400 years for the number of fire deaths in high-rise buildings to equal the total deaths due to fire in one year in one- and two-family dwellings,"[4] the potential for disaster due to the large number of occupants in high-rise buildings has resulted in the provisions now included in this section.

The high-rise building is characterized by several features:

- It is impractical, if not impossible, to completely evacuate the building within a reasonable period of time.[4,5]

- Prompt rescue will be difficult, and the probability of fighting a fire in upper stories from the exterior will be low.[4,5]

- High-rise buildings are occupied by large numbers of people, and in hotels and apartment houses, the occupants may be asleep during an emergency.

- A potential exists for stack effect. The stack effect can result in the distribution of smoke and other products of combustion throughout the height of a high-rise building during a fire.[5,6]

The provisions in this section are designed to account for the features described above.

403.1 Scope. While a high-rise building can be defined in accordance with the special features just described, the UBC elects to define a high-rise building as one having floors used for human occupancy located more than 75 feet (22 860 mm) above the lowest level of fire department vehicle access. Most moderately large and larger cities have apparatus which can fight fires up to about 75 feet (22 860 mm); thus, the fire can be fought from the exterior. Any fires above this height will require that they be fought internally. Also, in some circles, 75 feet (22 860 mm) is considered to be about the maximum height for a building that could be completely evacuated within a reasonable period of time. Thus, the fire department capability plus the time for evacuation of the occupants constitute the criteria used by the *Uniform Building Code* for defining a high-rise building.

This section thus defines the high-rise building and, furthermore, specifies that it be fully protected throughout with an automatic fire sprinkler system designed in accordance with the parameters of Section 403.2 and UBC Standard 9-1.

403.2 Automatic Sprinkler System.

403.2.1 System design. The automatic fire sprinkler system required by Section 403.1 must be completely reliable, as the other life-safety systems must be, because it is also a mechanical system. In order to develop this reliability, the code requires that the system be designed and installed in accordance with the following criteria:

- The system must be completely supervised as described in Chapter 4 of UBC Standard 9-1.

- Shutoff valves and flow-detection devices are required on each floor.

- In Seismic Zones 2, 3 and 4, an on-site secondary water supply shall be provided, with a supply of water equal to the hydraulically calculated sprinkler design demand plus 100 gallons per minute (378.5 L/min) in addition to the total standpipe system for a duration of 30 minutes.

As fires can and do break out as a result of earthquake damage to the various mechanical systems within a building, it is imperative that the reliability of the sprinkler system be such that any fires resulting can be automatically extinguished. Therefore, the code requires that the secondary on-site water supply be automatic so there is no time delay in the operation of the fire sprinkler system should a fire break out.

403.2.2 Modifications. Because the high-rise building is sprinklered, the UBC permits certain modifications of the code requirements, which are sometimes referred to as "trade-offs." The trade-offs in this case are considered to be justified on the basis that the sprinkler system, although a mechanical system, is highly reliable due to the provisions of Section 403.2, which require supervision* and a secondary on-site supply of water.

The provisions of this section were originally developed when the basic requirement for high-rise buildings was compartmentation and the installation of an automatic fire sprinkler system was considered to be an alternate to the basic requirement. Nevertheless, there are certain modifications of the code requirements permitted because of the installation of the automatic fire sprinkler system as follows:

- A reduction in the fire-resistive time periods of one hour from those outlined in Table 6-A for various components of the building as described in Item 1 are permitted. It will be noted that no reduction in fire-resistive protection for the structural frame is permitted. The code assumes that even with the reliability required by the code for the sprinkler system, a failure cannot be tolerated, and the structural integrity of the building must be maintained.

- Interior nonbearing partitions that are required by Table 6-A to be of one-hour fire-resistive construction are permitted to be of noncombustible construction without a fire-resistive time period. This reduction does not apply to corridors, which are required to be fire resistive in accordance with the requirements of Section 1004.3.4.3, or to partitions separating dwelling units or guest rooms. The code considers the integrity of the exit system to be too important a life-safety feature of the building to permit reductions in the fire resistance of the corridor system. The code considers that the fire-resistive separations between dwelling units and guest rooms is also too important a life-safety feature to permit a reduction in the fire-resistive requirement. Again, it should be pointed out that where the fire-resistive rating of the nonbearing partitions is permitted to be omitted, the code still requires that the partitions be made of noncombustible materials. Thus, the fire-retardant-treated-wood option permitted by the code

---

*Supervision requires that appropriate sensors installed within the components be electrically connected, and sound an alarm to one of the locations specified in Section 904.3 of the UBC in the event of a failure.

would not apply, as fire-retardant wood is a combustible material.

- Except in certain cases, fire dampers are not required. However, ceiling dampers that protect floor-ceiling assemblies must be maintained.

- The requirement in Section 310.4 for emergency escape-and-rescue windows is waived. This is in reality a small trade-off, as the protection afforded by the sprinkler system is considered by the code to be preferable to jumping from a second- or third-story window.

403.3 Smoke Detection. The requirements for smoke-detection systems in this section are primarily intended for early warning by actuating the voice alarm system; secondarily, they are intended to place into operation all equipment provided in the building that is necessary to prevent the recirculation of smoke. For this reason, the detector locations are specified:

- In the building service equipment rooms.

- In the return-air and exhaust-air ducts or plenums of the air-conditioning systems.

- At each connection to a vertical duct or riser in the return-air portion of an air-conditioning system.

- In corridors of Group R, Division 1 Occupancies that serve as a means of egress for 10 or more occupants.

In addition to providing early warning, these latter detectors (within the air-conditioning system) are also required to prevent recirculation of smoke by either shutting down the entire system, of which the ductwork is a part, or by placing the system in an exhaust-only mode so as to exhaust the smoke from the building.

403.4 Smoke Control. A smoke-control system complying with Section 905 is required.

403.5 Fire Alarm and Communication Systems. Among the more important life-safety features required by the code are the alarm and communication systems required by this section. Where it is expected that people will be unable to evacuate the building, it is imperative that they be informed as to the nature of any emergency that may break out, as well as the proper action to take to exit to a safe place of refuge. Furthermore, a system is necessary in most cases to provide for communication between the fire officer in charge at the scene and the firefighters throughout the building. The code requires the communication systems to comply with the Fire Code.

403.5.2 Emergency voice alarm signaling system. This section requires that operation of the automatic fire detector or sprinkler result in an alert tone followed by appropriate voice instruction. The alert tone and voice instruction may be directed generally on a selective basis to the following areas:

- Elevators and elevator lobbies.

- Corridors and exit stairways.

- Rooms and tenant spaces exceeding 1,000 square feet (92.9 m²) in area.

- Dwelling units, guest rooms and suites in apartment houses and hotels.

- Areas of refuge as defined in Section 1102.

403.5.3 Fire department communication system. The code prescribes the fire department communication system to provide for efficient operation of the fire-suppression forces by the fire officer in charge. Thus, a two-way system is required for operation between the central control station and specified locations in the building.

403.6 Central Control Station. The central control station is the heart of the life-safety systems in a high-rise building, and as such, the code specifies that it be provided for fire department use and contain the listed controls, panels, indicators and items of equipment.

403.7 Elevators. Elevators are an important life-safety system in high-rise buildings, and the provisions of this section combined with Chapter 30 (Elevators, Dumbwaiters, Escalators and Moving Walks) outline the requirements of the code to provide the necessary life safety. Essentially, elevators as a life-safety system for a high-rise building are intended to function as follows:

- To operate as a means of access to the upper stories of the buildings for fire-suppression forces.

- To provide a means for evacuating the injured and handicapped individuals unable to use the standard exit systems.

To accomplish the above, this section establishes three criteria:

- Elevators and elevator lobbies shall comply with the provisions of Chapter 30. Chapter 30 contains general requirements for the design, construction, installation and operation of elevators whether or not they are located in high-rise buildings. This chapter will be covered in more detail later in this handbook, but for the purposes of Section 403, it includes such features as requirements for the maximum number of cars in the hoistway, size of cab and control locations and hoistway venting. The size-of-cab provisions are written specifically to provide for the evacuation of handicapped individuals from the building by way of the elevator system. The code requires that at least one car serving all floors of the building be of such a size that a 24-inch by 76-inch (610 mm by 1930 mm) ambulance stretcher can be accommodated in the horizontal position. This is an essential life-safety requirement.

- Elevators on all floors are required to open into elevator lobbies, which are separated from the remainder of the building by a one-hour fire-resistive partition with openings therein protected by 20-minute smoke- and draft-control assemblies as required by Section 1004.3.4.3.2 for corridors. The intent of the code is that the elevator lobby completely separate the elevator hoistway from the rest of the building and the exit corridors. In the past, elevator hoistways have been prime conduits for the transmission of smoke and other products of combustion into the upper floors of a building.[7] The requirement for the enclosed elevator lobby also permits the fire-suppression forces to have a protected means of gaining access into the upper floors of the building to fight the fire and provides a protected means of evacuating the handicapped and injured. There are three exceptions to the requirement for an enclosed elevator lobby:

1. The enclosure is not required on the ground floor of office buildings because the combustible loading in the area where the elevators discharge on the ground floor is usually so low that the generation of smoke at this location is unlikely.

2. Elevators in atria are not required to have enclosed elevator lobbies for similar reasons as for the ground floor in office buildings. The requirements for atria, particularly insofar as combustible contents and smoke control are concerned, are such that the atrium should be considered to be essentially a smoke-free environment. Also, there is little probability of smoke within an elevator hoistway contaminating the corridors in the rest of the building where the elevator is located within an atrium.

3. Corridors in office buildings may pass through elevator lobbies provided there is access to another exit that does not pass through the elevator lobby. Life loss in sprinklered office buildings has been very low, and under the limitations expressed, a safe exiting path is maintained.

- The elevators are required to have an automatic recall system that goes into operation when any of the required smoke detectors located on the ceiling of each elevator lobby is activated by smoke. Also, it is the intent of the code that the smoke detector located on the ceiling of the elevator lobby is used to close the elevator lobby doors and the additional door at the hoistway opening as allowed by Section 3007.

In general, the automatic recall system recalls all cars to the ground floor, except that if the ground floor is the fire floor, the cars shall stop at another designated floor as approved jointly by the fire department and the building official. Whenever the cars operate on automatic recall, they are then placed under manual control. Chapter 30 requires that at least one car in each bank of elevators be provided with standby power, and, furthermore, the standby power

be switchable between elevator cars. Thus, the fire department is provided with at least one elevator car to gain access to the upper floors for firefighting and rescue purposes.

There is another provision in this section relating to hoistway venting. If hoistways are not vented, smoke entering the hoistway has no escape and the hoistway soon becomes untenable. Venting of the hoistway through elevation machine rooms is not permitted to ensure smoke and heat, which affect elevator control equipment, do not permeate the machine room, thereby causing the elevator to be inoperative. See discussion in Chapter 30.

403.8 Standby Power, Light and Emergency Systems. Furthering the intent of the UBC that the life-safety systems in high-rise buildings be highly reliable, the code requires that the power supply to the life-safety systems be automatically transferable to a standby power system in the event of the failure of the normal power supply in accordance with the Electrical Code. The requirement is that the capacity rating of the standby system be such that it will be capable of supplying power to all of the equipment required to be operational at the same time. However, the capacity need not be capable of operating all the connected electrical equipment simultaneously. Thus, the code intends that an analysis be made of all the systems connected to the standby power system so that a determination can be made as to what equipment will be required to be operational at the same time. A review of the code requirements for those systems required to be connected to the standby power system indicates that virtually all of the systems will be required to operate at the same time, with the possible exception of the smoke-detection system. The code requirements and details for the standby power system are depicted in Figure 403-1.

In addition to the standby power system, the code further requires that lighting for exit signs, exit illumination and elevator car lighting be automatically transferable to an emergency power system capable of operation within 10 seconds of the fail-

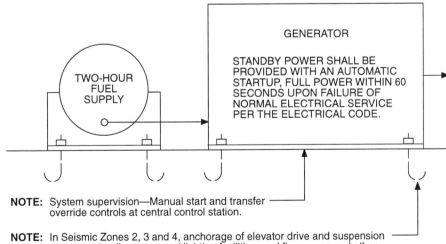

POWER TO:
1. MECHANICAL SMOKE-DETECTION SYSTEM
2. ALARM AND COMMUNICATION SYSTEMS
3. CENTRAL CONTROL STATION
4. SMOKE CONTROL AND VENTILATION
5. ELEVATORS
6. EXIT SIGN LIGHTING AND EXIT ILLUMINATION
7. PRESSURE MAINTENANCE FIRE PUMPS
8. MECHANICAL EQUIPMENT ROOM LIGHTING
9. ELEVATOR CAR AND LOBBY LIGHTING

NOTE: System supervision—Manual start and transfer override controls at central control station.

NOTE: In Seismic Zones 2, 3 and 4, anchorage of elevator drive and suspension systems, standby power and lighting facilities, and fire pumps and other fire-protection equipment are to be designed for lateral forces in accordance with Chapter 16, Division IV.

STANDBY POWER

FIGURE 403-1

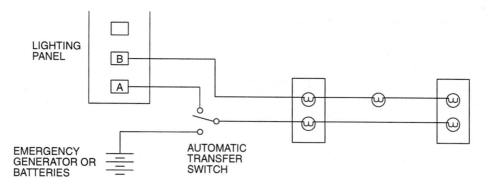

EMERGENCY LIGHTING SYSTEM

FIGURE 403-2

ure of the normal power supply. Figure 403-2 illustrates one means of transfer to emergency power.

403.9 Means of Egress. In those cases where it is impractical to totally evacuate the occupants from the building through the stairway system, it must be possible then to move the occupants to different floors of the building that are safe by way of the stairway system. For this to happen, the doors to the stair enclosures either must be maintained unlocked or be designed for automatic unlocking from the central control station.

The *Uniform Building Code* further requires a telephone or other two-way communication system (such as a two-way system with speaker and microphone) at every fifth floor in each required stair enclosure in those cases where the stair enclosure doors are to be locked. Moreover, the code requires that this communication system be connected to an approved emergency service that operates continuously. Thus, anyone trapped in the stairway during a nonfire emergency may call for help without traversing more than four levels. In the case of office buildings and apartment houses, the emergency service may be provided by the office of the building as long as the office has continuous attendance by responsible individuals who are familiar with the life-safety systems. For hotel buildings, the most likely choice for the emergency service will probably be the hotel telephone operators, and, again, they must be trained to assist the persons trapped within the stair enclosure.

403.10 Seismic Considerations. Quite often fires are the result of earthquake action, and the code requires that mechanical and electrical equipment required for life-safety systems be designed to resist earthquake forces in accordance with Chapter 16, Division IV. This is again a requirement of the code to ensure the highest reliability for the life-safety systems. Surely, a design that did not properly account for earthquake lateral forces for the life-safety equipment would not be in keeping with the overall concept of life safety in high-rise buildings. Thus, the equipment must be so anchored to the structure that it will remain in place and be functional not only during the earthquake but after the earthquake as well. It is this postearthquake period that is so critical insofar as fire is concerned. Special attention must be made to Footnote 3 of Table 16-O and the design and detailing requirements of Chapter 16, Division IV. The requirement for anchorage of life-safety equipment to resist earthquake forces is illustrated in Figure 403-1.

SECTION 404 — COVERED MALL BUILDINGS

This section first appeared in the 1982 edition of the UBC in Appendix Chapter 7. The material was moved to the body of the code for the 1988 edition.

The provisions were included in the UBC to set forth *specific* code requirements for covered mall buildings. Provisions for covered malls in this chapter apply to covered mall buildings having not more than three levels. Furthermore, the provisions for covered malls are only those that are considered to be unique to covered mall buildings. For those features that are not unique, the general provisions of the code apply. Covered mall buildings complying in all respects with the other provisions of the code are not required to comply with these provisions.

For example, a designer could choose to construct a mall-type building that has unprotected corridors. The corridors in such case must be more than 30 feet (9144 mm) in width and occupants must have at least one exit independent of the corridor. See Section 1004.3.4.3, Exception 2. Other provisions of the code would also apply, such as shaft protection, occupancy separation and allowable areas.

404.1 General. In addition to giving the purpose and scope, this section provides definitions. Among the more important of these definitions is that for "covered mall building." This section also identifies what is not a covered mall building, specifically listing terminals for transportation facilities and lobbies of hotel, apartment and office buildings.

The covered mall building must contain a mall that is defined by the code as a common pedestrian passageway within a covered mall building that serves as access for two or more tenants. The covered mall building includes many different occupancies and uses and may contain offices or even consist completely of offices as long as there is a common pedestrian way providing access to at least two of the tenants. A covered mall building comprised completely of offices is shown in Figure 404-1.

Anchor buildings may be considered to be part of the covered mall building as they are permitted by Section 404.3.9 to have openings into the mall that are unprotected; however, the definition of "anchor building" and Section 404.2.1 require that they stand on their own as far as types of construction, exiting, area, height, etc., are concerned. The definition of "anchor building" is such that it could include uses other than stores. Group R, Division 1 uses such as hotels are allowed to be classified as an anchor building. Parking structures are not included in the definition of anchor building so the allowances applicable to anchor stores do not apply to parking structures.

404.2 Types of Construction and Required Yards for Unlimited Area. The code permits mall buildings to be of any type of construction permitted by the code, except that three-level mall buildings shall be of at least Type II One-hour construction. Furthermore, anchor buildings are limited in height and area in accordance with Sections 504, 505 and 506. This same provision also applies to parking garages. The code requires a minimum of Type II One-hour construction for three-level mall buildings primarily because it was felt that where three levels open into a common atmosphere, conservatism should be applied to the provisions. Therefore, in addition to the requirement for an automatic fire sprinkler system and smoke-control system, the provisions also require a minimum of a noncombustible building of one-hour fire resistance.

Covered mall buildings are permitted by this section to have unlimited area, and the conditions for such are somewhat similar to those in Section 505.2, which require 60-foot (18 288 mm) yards surrounding a building of unlimited area. In this case the code requires the 60-foot (18 288 mm) yards to surround the entire building, including any attached anchor buildings and parking garages. Figure 404-2 shows a typical regional shopping center consisting of a covered mall building with attached anchor buildings and parking garages, with 60-foot (18 288 mm) yards completely surrounding the structure.

404.3 Special Provisions.

404.3.1 Automatic sprinkler systems. The automatic fire sprinkler system is the primary means of fire protection for the covered mall building. Additionally, the code requires a smoke-control system and standpipes. Because of the reliance placed on the sprinkler system, this chapter requires the following additional safeguards:

1. The control valves are required to be supervised electrically in an approved manner that will give an audible sig-

nal to the fire department or signal company, for example. Also, any constantly attended location may be approved by the building official.

2. The code requires that the sprinkler system be complete and operative throughout all of the mall before occupancy of any of the tenant spaces. In those areas that are unoccupied, the building official and the fire chief are jointly required by the code to determine if the separation between the mall and tenant space is appropriate.

3. The mall and the tenant spaces shall be protected by separate sprinkler systems, except that the code will permit tenant spaces to be supplied by the same system as the mall, provided they can be independently controlled.

Even though the requirement for the sprinkler system is a basic requirement for fire protection for covered mall buildings, the code in this case permits area and height increases for covered mall buildings, including the anchor buildings. This provision may seem redundant because, for most cases, covered mall buildings, including the anchor buildings and attached garage buildings, will be surrounded by 60-foot (18 288 mm) yards and thus qualify for unlimited area. There may be occasions, however, when the full complement of yards surrounding the facility will not be available. When this occurs, the area increases permitted for the sprinkler systems will be important. Nevertheless, the covered mall building is limited in height by type of construction and these heights may not be exceeded. The increase in height for sprinkler systems may be applied to the anchor buildings and parking garages.

404.3.2 Standpipes. A combined Class I standpipe system with $2^1/_2$-inch (64 mm) outlets is required in the mall at the entrance to any exit passageway or corridor. Further outlets are required at each floor level or landing within enclosed stairways which open directly into the mall. Outlets are also required adjacent to the exterior public entrances to the mall. Figure 404-3 shows typical locations for these outlets, which are for fire department use. The code requires that they be connected to a system sized to deliver 250 gallons per minute (946.4 L/min) at each stand-

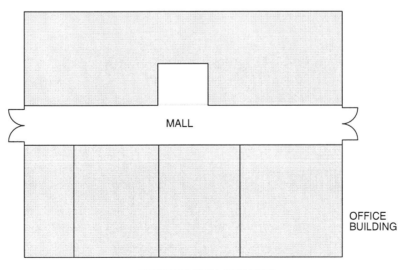

COVERED MALL BUILDING

FIGURE 404-1

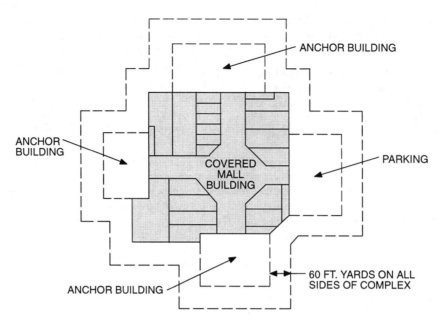

For **SI:** 1 foot = 304.8 mm.

UNLIMITED AREA WHERE THERE ARE 60 FT. YARDS ALL AROUND

COVERED MALL BUILDING

FIGURE 404-2

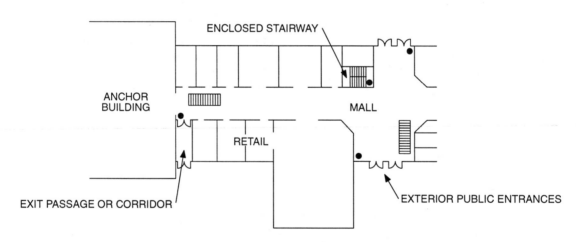

LOCATION OF CLASS I STANDPIPE OUTLETS
COVERED MALL BUILDING

FIGURE 404-3

pipe location. The standpipe system must be connected to the sprinkler system as required for a combined system.

404.3.3 Smoke-control system. The fire-protection goal of these provisions for covered mall buildings is twofold:

1. To isolate any fire at its point of origin.

2. To maintain tenable means of egress for the occupants in case of fire.

The sprinkler system will certainly aid in the first objective, and the mechanical smoke-control system will help accomplish the second objective.

The smoke-control system must comply with Section 905.

404.3.4 Fire department access to equipment. Understandably, the control rooms or areas that control the systems just described (sprinkler, fire detection and smoke control) should be identified for use by the fire department. Although not required by the code, the preferable arrangement would be to provide a single control room identified for the use of the fire department and located near a main entrance to the mall.

404.3.5 Tenant separation. The provisions of this section provide for separation of tenants in malls. In addition to protecting one tenant from the activities of a neighbor, the tenant separation requirements for malls are also intended to assist in the goal of

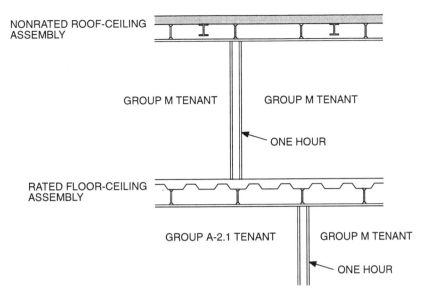

NONRATED ROOF-CEILING ASSEMBLY

GROUP M TENANT

GROUP M TENANT

ONE HOUR

RATED FLOOR-CEILING ASSEMBLY

GROUP A-2.1 TENANT

GROUP M TENANT

ONE HOUR

TENANT SEPARATIONS—COVERED MALL BUILDING

FIGURE 404-4

restricting the fire to the area of origin and to assist in the compartmentation that is required for the smoke-control system.

The basic requirement is for a one-hour fire-resistive wall that is used to separate one tenant space from another and that is required by the code to extend from the floor to the ceiling above. Unless the ceiling is an element of a fire-resistive floor-ceiling or roof-ceiling assembly that would be required for purposes of an occupancy separation or because of the type of construction, the ceiling otherwise need not be part of a fire-rated assembly. An example of these requirements is shown in Figure 404-4 for a Type II-N building. The roof-ceiling assembly shown in Figure 404-4 is nonrated because the building is Type II-N construction (no more than two stories in height). The floor-ceiling assembly is required by Table 3-B to provide a one-hour fire-resistive occupancy separation between the Group M Occupancy and the Group A, Division 2.1 tenant space on the lower floor.

The wall between the tenant space and the mall is permitted by the code to be nonrated. The code does not require that the wall between the tenant space and the mall be one-hour fire resistive as part of the smoke-control zone perimeter, but the actual design of the smoke-control system might require either a one-hour fire-resistive wall or a smoke-stop partition.

404.3.6 Public address system. It is common for several thousand people to be present in a covered mall building at any one time. Certainly, a large regional shopping center will have a sufficiently large number of tenant spaces and anchor buildings to draw large numbers of people into the facility. Where such large numbers of people are gathered together in one facility, it is necessary to have a method for conveying instructions to the occupants in case of fire or other emergency. Thus, the code requires that covered mall buildings with an area of more than 50,000 square feet (4645.2 m²) be provided with a public address system to accomplish this. Furthermore, this system is required to be accessible to fire department personnel for their use. When the owner of a smaller covered mall building [less than 50,000 square feet (4645.2 m²)] provides a public address system vol-

untarily, it must also be available to fire department personnel for their use. The public address system is another system that preferably should have controls and a microphone within the room or area discussed in Section 404.3.4.

404.3.7 Plastic panels and plastic signs. In this section the UBC limits plastic panels and plastic signs because they are within an exitway (the mall) and they are combustible even though of approved plastic. It is important to note that the percentage of wall covered is based on the area common to each single tenant space. Thus, for a tenant space whose common wall with the mall is 60 feet (18 288 mm) wide and 11 feet (3353 mm) high, the total area is 660 square feet (61.3 m²). As the code permits 20 percent of that area to be plastic panels or signs, the sum of all of the plastic signs and panels on the common wall is limited to 132 square feet (12.3 m²). Figure 404-5 illustrates the code limitations for plastic signs and panels.

A new code change clarifies the use of plastic panels and plastic signs in malls and requires that the plastic meet the requirements of an approved plastic material as defined in Section 217. The use of foam plastic in malls is based on testing in accordance with UL 1975, Standard for Fire Tests of Foam Plastics Used for Decorative Purposes.

404.3.8 Lease plan. The lease plan is required so that firefighting, rescue and other emergency personnel can locate with dispatch the various spaces within the covered mall building.

404.3.9 Openings between anchor building and mall. Section 601 essentially requires that area separation walls be provided to separate two different types of construction within the same structure. However, in the case of the covered mall building, Section 404.3.9 permits the openings in these area separation walls between other than Group R, Division 1 sleeping rooms and the mall to be unprotected where the anchor building is one of the following types of construction:

- Type I
- Type II-F.R.

- Type II One-hour
- Type II-N

Figure 404-6 depicts this situation.

404.3.10 Standby power. This chapter considers covered mall buildings in excess of 50,000 square feet (4645.2 m^2) to have a potential for life-safety hazards similar to those in a high-rise building. Therefore, the code requires that standby power be provided for a covered mall building in excess of 50,000 square feet (4645.2 m^2) and be capable of operating the public address system, the smoke-control activation systems and the smoke-control equipment as required by Section 905.

404.4 Means of Egress.

404.4.1 General. This section is somewhat unique primarily because of the unique nature of malls and the exiting requirements for malls. Therefore, the UBC requires that the provisions of Chapter 10 be followed as far as the determination of means of egress from each tenant space into the covered mall building is concerned. Furthermore, the provisions of Section 404.4 shall also be followed. Where there is a conflict, the provisions of Section 404.4 apply.

404.4.2 and 404.4.3 Determination of occupant load and number of exits. The determination of occupant load and number of exits can be divided into two areas:

1. Tenant spaces.
2. The covered mall building.

Tenant spaces. The *Plan Review Manual* presents the method for computation of the number of occupants and the number of exits required for tenant spaces.[8] Figures 404-7 and 404-8 are taken from this source.

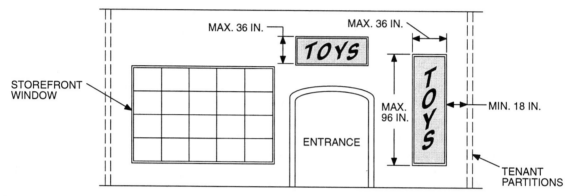

For **SI:** 1 foot = 304.8 mm.

LIMITATIONS FOR PLASTIC SIGNS AND PANELS IN MALLS

FIGURE 404-5

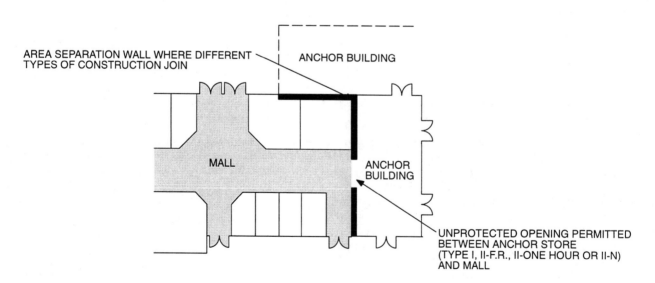

MIXED TYPES OF CONSTRUCTION—COVERED MALL BUILDING

FIGURE 404-6

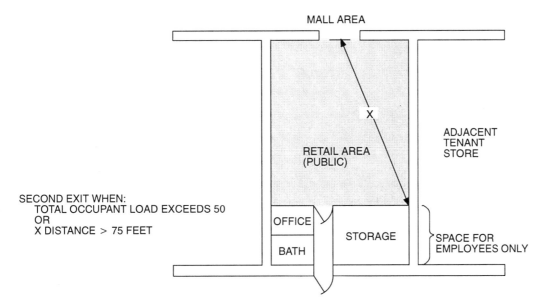

For **SI:** 1 foot = 304.8 mm.

REQUIREMENT FOR SECOND MEANS OF EGRESS FROM TENANT SPACE

FIGURE 404-7

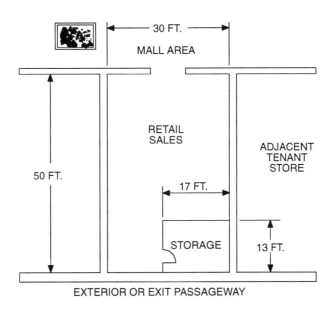

For **SI:** 1 foot = 304.8 mm.

NUMBER OF MEANS OF EGRESS FROM TENANT SPACE

FIGURE 404-8

Figure 404-7 depicts the requirements of Section 404.4.3 for the determination of the number of exits from the tenant space. Figure 404-8 shows a typical tenant space of 1,500 square feet (139.4 m²) with an occupant load of 44. The provisions of Chapter 10 would require only one means of egress from this tenant space, and the provisions of Section 404.4.3 would also require only one means of egress. Therefore, the number of means of egress complies with the code. However, if the distance x exceeds 75 feet (22 860 mm), two means of egress would be required even though the occupant load might be less than 50.

The covered mall building. Not only must the occupant load and exits be determined for each individual tenant space, the occupant load and the number of exits from the covered mall building must be determined also. It is highly unlikely that all tenant spaces will be fully occupied at the same time in a covered mall building. Even though Section 404.4.2 indicates that it must be assumed that all portions of the covered mall building will be occupied at the same time, the occupant load factor to be used is something less than that normally required by Chapter 10. As a result, the net effect is that the total occupant load computed for the covered mall building will be something less than the summation of the occupant loads previously determined for each individual tenant space.

The occupant loads determined in accordance with Section 404.4.2 for the covered mall building are also based on the gross leasable area. As the gross leasable area increases, the occupant load factor or square feet (m²) per occupant increases because the likelihood of full occupancy of all tenant spaces at the same time decreases with the increasing size of the covered mall building. The code recognizes this fact, and Table 404-A in this handbook shows the determination of the square feet (m²) per occupant based on the gross leasable area as defined in Section 404.1.3.

TABLE 404-A—OCCUPANT LOAD FACTORS FOR COVERED MALL BUILDINGS

GROSS LEASABLE AREA (as defined)	SQUARE FEET PER OCCUPANT
< 150,000	30
150,000 to 350,000	40
> 350,000	50

For **SI:** 1 square foot = 0.093 m².

With the revision to Section 404.4.2 to include the occupant load of a food court, as determined from Section 1003.2.2, in addition to the occupant load from the covered mall building as calculated above, the egress capacity from the mall would be further increased by the calculated occupant load of the food court.

The determination of occupant loads and exits for the anchor buildings is in accordance with Chapter 10 and is not affected by the provisions of Section 404.

As there are no provisions in Section 404 for the determination of the number of exits from the covered mall building, reference must be made to Section 1003. Virtually all covered mall buildings will require four exits because even small covered mall buildings of 30,001 square feet (2787 m²) will require four exits based on the provisions of Section 1003.1. However, covered mall buildings with very large gross leasable areas, such as 200,000 or 300,000 square feet (18 580 or 27 870 m²), will more than likely have more than four exits because the exit width requirements of Section 1004.2.3 are such that where only four exits are provided, the width required for each exit would become unmanageable [42 feet (12 802 mm) for a mall with a gross leasable area of 500,000 square feet (46 450 m²)]. Also, travel distance may require more than the minimum number of four exits, and this will be discussed in Section 404.4.5.

404.4.4 Arrangement of means of egress. The provisions of this section are unique to the covered mall building and are depicted in Figure 404-9. The uses described in this section generally encompass a large number of occupants, and this section prevents these occupants from having to traverse long portions of the mall to reach a means of egress. The provisions also prevent the overcrowding of the mall, such as if a large number of patrons from these uses were to be discharged into the mall at the same time and at some distance from a means of egress.

In securing the intent of Section 404, this section also repeats the requirement that means of egress for anchor buildings shall be provided independently from the mall exit system. Furthermore, the mall shall not egress through the anchor buildings. Moreover, the termination of a mall at an anchor building where no other means of egress has been provided except through the anchor building shall be considered to be a dead end, which is limited in accordance with Section 404.4.6.

404.4.5 Travel distance. Figure 404-10 depicts the multifaceted provisions of this section as follows:

- The first case is illustrated for travel within the tenant space and includes the provisions applicable to tenant space A and tenant space B. For tenant space A, the diagram depicts the application of the code for a tenant space with a closed front with only a swinging exit door to the mall. The "entrance to the mall" would be the point at which occupants from the tenant space pass through the exit door from the tenant space to the mall.

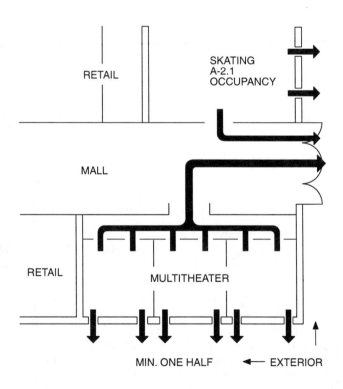

ARRANGEMENT OF EXITS

FIGURE 404-9

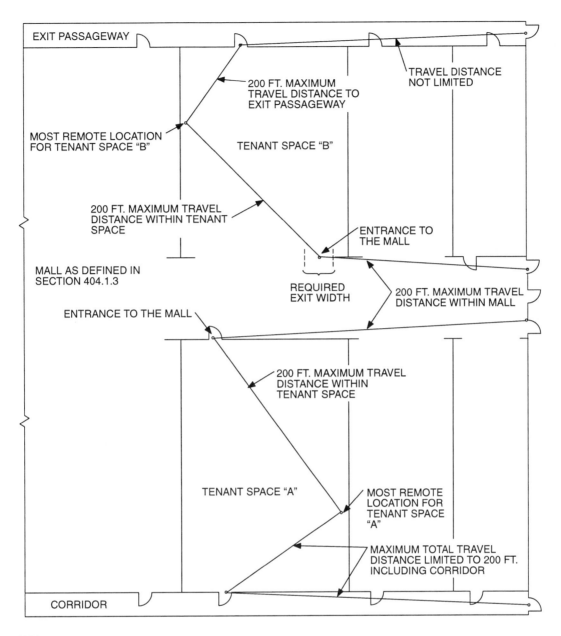

For **SI:** 1 foot = 304.8 mm.

TRAVEL DISTANCE

FIGURE 404-10

Tenant space B represents the condition for an open store front using a security grille instead of a standard exit door. The "entrance to the mall" in this case is the point at which occupants of the tenant space pass by an imaginary plane that is common to both the tenant space and the pedestrian mall. The location of the assumed required clear exit width along the open front of tenant space B may be placed at any point along the front, and its location would depend only on that which would render the least-restrictive application of the provisions.

For either tenant space A or B, the code permits the travel distance within the tenant space to the "entrance to the mall" to be a maximum of 200 feet (60 960 mm).

• After the occupants exit from a tenant space into the mall, the code permits another 200 feet (60 960 mm) of exit travel distance to one of the exit segments described in Section 404.4.5.

It can be seen from this discussion plus a perusal of Figure 404-10 that the travel distances permitted for a covered mall building are generally more liberal than those permitted by Section 1005.2.2. This more liberalized and increased travel distance is based on the rationale that travel within a mall will be within an area where smoke-control measures are provided; therefore, the atmosphere in the mall will be relatively smoke free.

- Another limitation of these provisions regarding travel distance within covered mall buildings is also illustrated by Figure 404-10. In this instance, if the path of travel is through a secondary exit from tenant space B to an exit passageway, travel distance within the exit passageway is not limited in accordance with the general provisions of Section 1005.2.2.

- In the case of exiting via the corridor as depicted for tenant space A, Section 404.4.5 limits the total travel distance to 200 feet (60 960 mm). This limitation is based on the consideration that a corridor does not offer as much protection as either an exit passageway or the mall.

It is somewhat unfortunate that the code uses the expression "entrance to the mall" to have two separate meanings. As far as travel distance within a tenant space is concerned, "entrance to the mall" means the exit from the tenant space into the mall. The term is also used to represent one of the main entrances to the covered mall building.

404.4.6 Exit access. This section uses the same approach as does Chapter 10 of requiring that the means of egress be so arranged that the occupants may go in either direction to a separate exit. However, in this section the dead end is measured in a different manner than in Chapter 10. Figure 404-11 shows the manner in which dead-end conditions are measured and limited.

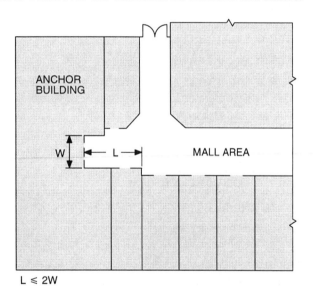

$L \leq 2W$

DEAD-END MALL CRITERIA

FIGURE 404-11

Another exiting provision that is unique to the covered mall building is that all means of egress from the mall shall be a minimum of 66 inches (1676 mm) in width. The exit passageway shown in Figure 404-3 must be at least 66 inches (1676 mm) wide. The main entrances shown in the same figure are also required to not be less than 66 inches (1676 mm) in width. (This may be a needless restriction as the exit width limitations of Section 1003.2.3 will most often require a greater exit width.)

404.4.7 Malls. With its added life-safety systems, the mall may be considered a corridor without meeting the requirements of Sections 1004.3.4.3.1 and 1004.3.4.3.2 when the mall complies with the conditions of this section as depicted in Figure 404-12.

In this case, the code requires that the minimum mall width be 20 feet (6096 mm) and this typical cross-section shows that the minimum required width may be divided so that a clear width of 10 feet (3048 mm) is provided separately on each side of any kiosks, vending machines, benches, displays, etc., contained in the mall. A minimum separation of 20 feet (6096 mm) between kiosks, vending machines and similar uses as well as a 300-square-foot (28 m^2) area limitation for each is required to limit the mall uses and provide free-flowing access consistent with the basis on which the mall provisions were developed. Understandably, the mall width shall also accommodate the occupant load immediately tributary thereto in accordance with Section 1003.2. In addition, food court seating in the mall would have to be located so as not to encroach upon any required mall width.

In the case of malls, the designer has two options:

1. Comply with the provisions of Section 404.4.7.
2. Comply with the requirements of Sections 1004.3.4.3.1 and 1004.3.4.3.2.

404.4.8 Security grilles and doors. Quite often mall tenants wish to have the dividing plane between the mall and the tenant space completely open during business hours. Horizontal sliding or vertical security grilles or doors are usually placed across this opening. This section permits their use, provided they do not detract from safe exiting from the tenant space into the mall. To secure that intent, the code requires the four limitations outlined in this section.

404.5 Occupancy. Covered mall buildings are generally classified by this section as Group B or M Occupancies. However, it should be noted that the "tenant" spaces in such buildings should take on the occupancy classification they most nearly resemble. The covered mall building may also contain accessory uses consisting of Group A, B, E or R, Division 1 Occupancies. This section provides a limitation in area for these accessory uses that is three times the basic area permitted by Table 5-B. Moreover, the aggregate area of all accessory uses is limited to 25 percent of the gross leasable area.

The code places these limitations on accessory uses for the same reason as it does in Chapter 5 so that a single occupancy classification can be given for the purpose of area and height limitations.

The code addresses mixed occupancies in a similar manner as in Chapter 5 in that each distinct occupancy shall be separated by an occupancy separation. However, the main entrance from a tenant space that opens into a mall is not required to be protected. Furthermore, an attached automobile parking structure may be considered a separate building without the requirement for an area separation wall if it is separated from the covered mall building by a two-hour occupancy separation. Figure 404-13 shows a portion of a covered mall building which depicts the requirements of the code for occupancy separation and separation between a parking structure and the covered mall building.

SECTION 405 — STAGES AND PLATFORMS

This section was rewritten for the 1985 edition of the UBC in an attempt to bring the code requirements in line with the present state of the art regarding the use of stages and platforms. The

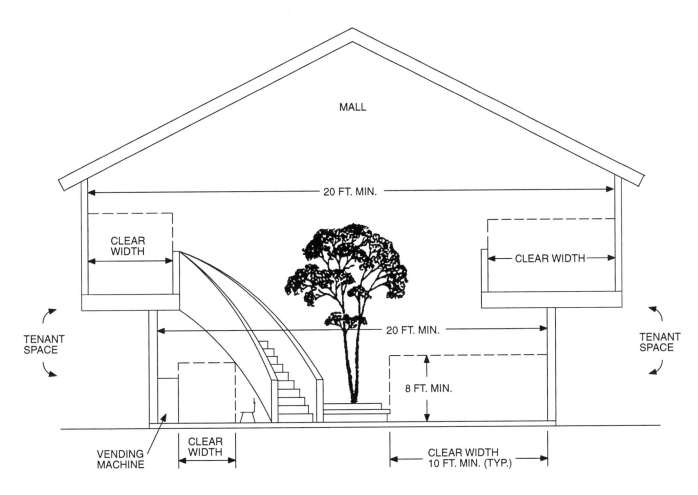

For **SI:** 1 foot = 304.8 mm.

MALL WIDTH REQUIREMENTS

FIGIRE 404-12

section was further revised in 1994 to agree with the recommendation of the BCMC. The basic provisions for life safety, however, are unchanged, except for modifications necessary to accommodate the present state of the art.

405.1 Scope. The primary purpose of this section is the definitions. While these definitions are complete and reasonably understandable, there are terms that are unique to the performing arts and are not generally understood, such as drops and leg drops. For a thorough discussion and definition of these terms, the reader is referred to John Degenkolb's article in *Building Standards*.[9]

405.2 Platforms. As it is impractical to construct temporary platforms of fire-resistive materials, the code permits temporary platforms to be constructed of any materials but restricts the use below the platform to that of electrical wiring or plumbing to operate platform equipment. Therefore, no storage of any kind is permitted beneath temporary platforms because of the potential for a fire to start and spread undetected.

When the area below a permanent platform is used for storage, it becomes a blind space in which a fire might burn for a relatively long period of time before discovery. The code requires that the floor of such platforms be constructed of not less than one-hour fire-resistive construction.

405.3 Stages.

405.3.1 Construction. The construction requirements for stages are depicted in Figure 405-1. In addition to the features shown, any stage may have a finished floor of wood. As the area above and at the sides of legitimate stages are filled with combustible materials which can be moved both vertically and horizontally, such as curtains, drops, leg drops, scenery and other stage effects, the code requires that such stages be constructed as required by the type of construction of the building and separated from the balance of the building.

405.3.2 Accessory rooms. For all stages the code requires accessory rooms to be separated from each other and from the stage by a minimum of one-hour fire-resistive construction. The exception for stages not exceeding 500 square feet (46.5 m^2) is based on the rationale that the smaller stages will have fewer accessory rooms and, consequently, no significant amount of combustible materials.

405.3.3 Ventilation. The Iroquois Theater fire in 1903 was directly responsible for the requirement for automatic smoke

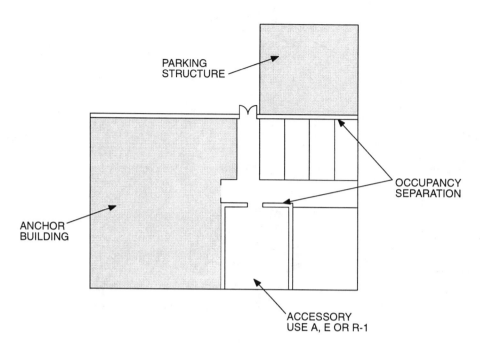

OCCUPANCY SEPARATION REQUIREMENTS

FIGURE 404-13

vents in the roofs of theater stages. Due to the presence of large amounts of combustible materials, excessive quantities of smoke will accumulate in and above the stage area unless it is automatically vented or removed by a smoke-control system. The removal of the smoke is necessary for firefighting as well as the prevention of panic by drawing off the smoke so that it will not infiltrate the theater auditorium.

The maximum floor area of stages that would be permissible without the installation of venting increased from 500 square feet to 1,000 square feet (41.5 m² to 92.9 m²) for the 1991 edition. In the 1994 edition of the code, an additional requirement was added specifying that stores be equipped with smoke-removal equipment or roof vents when they are greater than 50 feet (15 240 mm) in height. Experience over the years has shown the 500-square-foot (46.5 m²) area as being overly restrictive, particularly for stages installed within schools. The automatic sprinkler requirements of the code are believed to address the fire concern, and the need for venting is only necessary in stages of larger sizes or greater heights.

The detailed requirements for the smoke vents in the UBC are intended to provide reliability and reasonable assurance that after many years of inoperation the vents will operate when needed.

405.3.4 Proscenium walls. The proscenium wall is intended by the UBC to provide a complete fire separation between the legitimate stage and the auditorium. As such, the code requires that it be constructed essentially as a two-hour fire-resistive occupancy separation wall (except for the protection of the proscenium opening). The requirement for the proscenium wall to extend 4 feet (1219 mm) above the roof of the auditorium was eliminated in the 1991 UBC since experience had shown it to be overly restrictive for "other than legitimate" stages.

Because the proscenium opening is too large to protect with any usual type of fire assembly, the code requires that it be protected with a fire-resistive fire curtain or water curtain constructed and installed as outlined in UBC Standard 4-1. The performance requirements for the fire curtain are:

- That it successfully pass the fire test for nonbearing partitions specified in UBC Standard 7-1 for a period of five minutes.

- That it be smoke tight so as not to permit the passage of hot gases, flames and smoke.

- That it prevent the glow from a severe fire on the stage side from showing on the auditorium side for a period of 30 minutes.

The standard also requires that the curtain close automatically by gravity obtained by overbalancing the curtain after fusible link activation.

Several changes to the proscenium wall requirements were made in the 1991 edition to allow the use of alternative methods of protection in lieu of the traditional proscenium curtain. The alternate of the woven, high-temperature coated fiberglass fabric is now covered by UBC Standard 4-1 rather than by being specifically included in the code.

SECTION 406 — MOTION PICTURE PROJECTION ROOMS

Up until the 1970 edition, the UBC addressed the subject of motion picture projection rooms based on the hazard of the cellulose nitrate film being used prior to that time. Actually, pro-

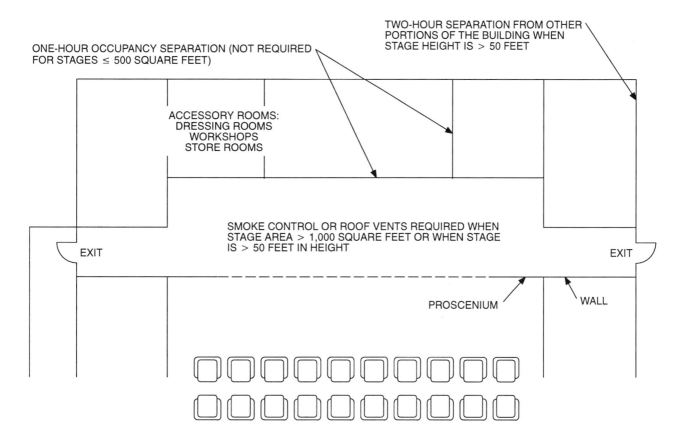

ONE-HOUR OCCUPANCY SEPARATION (NOT REQUIRED FOR STAGES ≤ 500 SQUARE FEET)

TWO-HOUR SEPARATION FROM OTHER PORTIONS OF THE BUILDING WHEN STAGE HEIGHT IS > 50 FEET

ACCESSORY ROOMS:
DRESSING ROOMS
WORKSHOPS
STORE ROOMS

SMOKE CONTROL OR ROOF VENTS REQUIRED WHEN STAGE AREA > 1,000 SQUARE FEET OR WHEN STAGE IS > 50 FEET IN HEIGHT

EXIT

EXIT

PROSCENIUM

WALL

FINISH FLOOR OF ALL STAGES MAY BE WOOD

STAGE REQUIRED TO BE CONSTRUCTED AS REQUIRED FOR THE BUILDING

For **SI:** 1 foot = 304.8 mm, 1 square foot = 0.093 m^2.

STAGES

FIGURE 405-1

duction of cellulose nitrate films ceased around 1950, although its use continued thereafter. In fact, even today, some cellulose nitrate film is used at film festivals and at special occasions requiring the projection of historically significant films which are still imprinted on cellulose nitrate film. Although the provisions in the code since the 1970 edition are based on the use of safety film, some of the protection requirements for cellulose nitrate film have been retained in the new requirements, such as ventilation requirements for the projection room.

406.1 General.

406.1.1 Scope. As indicated by the scope in the UBC, the intent is to provide safety to the occupants of a theater from the hazards consequent on the light source where electric arc or Xenon projection lamps are used. Although not used to any extent today, electric arc projection lamps emit hazardous radiation. Xenon lamps, which are now the most prevalent projection lamps, emit ozone. As a result, the provisions of Section 406 are based on the lamps used for projection of the film rather than the type of film to be used, as long as the film is not nitrate based.

406.1.2 Projection room required. The intent of this section is to isolate the projection room so that it does not present a danger to the theater audience. As the room is designed for the projection of safety film, there is no intent to provide a special fire-resistive enclosure, and fire protection of openings between the projection room and the auditorium is not required. However, due to the projection lamps, it is the intent of the code to provide an emission-tight separation so that any opening should be sealed with glass or other approved material such that the emissions from the projection lamps will not contaminate the auditorium. In order to secure the intent that the projection room is constructed and intended for use only with safety film, the code requires that a conspicuous sign be posted stating that only safety film is permitted in the room.

406.3 Means of egress. This section was revised for the 1985 edition to be explicit in the requirement that only one means of egress is required from the projection room where safety film is used. This provision is based on the fact that the usual occupant load of a projection room is one or two persons. Furthermore, as soon as the occupants of the projection room have exited the room, they are able to have their choice of at least two means of egress, where the projection room is located above the second story.

406.5 Ventilation. These provisions for supply and exhaust ventilation have been brought up-to-date to recognize modern projection room equipment.

The intent of the expression "the projection lamp or projection room exhaust system . . . shall not be interconnected with any other exhaust or return system" is to make the system independent of any other exhaust or return system in the theater building outside of the projection room. It is not intended to prevent the combining of the projection room exhaust with the projection lamp exhaust systems. The intent of the UBC is to provide ventilation so that the hazardous emissions from the projection lamps will be conveyed to the exterior. Thus, it makes sense that the exhaust system for the projection machines also be utilized to provide exhaust for the projection room, as the intake for the projection lamp ventilation is from the projection room.

406.6 Miscellaneous Equipment. Safety film is a combustible material and burns somewhat like paper, giving off a black, sooty smoke. As it burns it melts, and the melted drippings continue to burn. Therefore, the code requires that film rewinding and storage facilities be included within the projection room. A separate room in connection with the projection room would be permitted as long as the protection is equivalent to that provided in the projection room. The intent is to protect the theater audience from being exposed to the hazards of burning film.

406.7 Sanitary Facilities. Both a water closet and lavatory will be required in all projection rooms that require a projectionist in attendance.

SECTION 407 — CELLULOSE NITRATE FILM

The requirements in this section have been deleted because cellulose nitrate film is very seldom used, and when it is used, the Fire Code contains adequate requirements for the handling and storage of the material. Because of the extreme hazard, the subject was felt important enough to use the cross-reference to the Fire Code in Section 407.

SECTION 408 — AMUSEMENT BUILDINGS

Amusement buildings are usually classified as Group A Occupancies but may be classified as Group B Occupancies when the occupant load is less than 50. The major factors contributing to the loss of life in fires within amusement buildings has been the failure to detect and extinguish the fire in its incipient stage, the ignition of synthetic foam materials, and subsequent fire and smoke spread and the difficulty of escape. Provisions for the detection of fires, the illumination of the exit path and the sprinklering of these structures are required to protect the occupants in such structures. However, amusement buildings or portions thereof without walls or a roof are not required to comply with this section provided they are designed to prevent smoke from accumulating in the assembly areas. Approved smoke-detection and alarm systems are also required in amusement buildings. A provision of Section 408.5 is that on the activation of the sysem as described, all confusing sounds and visual effects shall stop, an approved directional exit marking system

shall activate, and the exit path itself shall be illuminated. This should identify a clear exit path for the occupants to use. A public address system, which may also serve as the alarm system, is required so that the occupants can be notified and given instructions in case of an emergency.

SECTION 409 — PEDESTRIAN WALKWAYS

This section, which was entitled "Arcades" prior to the 1985 edition of the code, contained a very short set of provisions for arcades connecting buildings. These provisions were not always understood and appeared to many to not cover areas which needed addressing. The designation as a "pedestrian walkway" is considered to more accurately define the use of the structure.

This section (1) establishes specific requirements for the protection of openings between the building and the pedestrian walkway when opening protection would be required in the exterior wall of the building due to its location on the property, (2) requires protection of openings in accordance with Section 1004.3.4.3.2 when the walkway is enclosed, (3) specifies minimum and maximum widths, (4) specifies a minimum horizontal separation between any two walkways, and (5) provides specifically that walkways may be used as exits when they are at grade or conform to requirements in Section 1005.3.5 for a horizontal exit.

Section 409.2 requires that pedestrian walkways be constructed of either noncombustible materials, one-hour fire-resistive construction or heavy-timber construction. There is an exception that permits pedestrian walkways located at grade with both sides open at least 50 percent connecting buildings of Type III, IV or V construction to be constructed of any materials permitted by the code. Where pedestrian walkways are designed and constructed in accordance with the provisions of Section 409, the code intends that, except for roof covering, they not be considered as part of the connected buildings. Furthermore, they need not be considered in the determination of the allowable area of either of the connected buildings.

In effect, this section is an exception to the general construction requirements and its use is optional. That is, the designer may choose to treat the pedestrian walkway as part of the building.

SECTION 410 — MEDICAL GAS SYSTEMS IN GROUPS B AND I OCCUPANCIES

This section was extracted from the *Uniform Fire Code* as it contains construction provisions that are properly regulated by the building code. It regulates gases commonly associated with dental and medical offices. The provisions require that nonflammable gases be isolated so that an accidental release of the gas will be contained or vented to the exterior. Also, as heated cylinders may explode, they are required to be separated from the balance of the building by fire-resistive construction.

SECTIONS 411–418

Sections 411 through 418 contain cross-references that give direction to the code users to the applicable appendix sections. These sections are also included to give the jurisdiction a convenient section to amend the code and make one or more appendix sections applicable.

Provisions in the appendix of the code do not apply unless specifically adopted. See the last paragraph of Section 101.3. These sections, therefore, may be revised in the statute, ordinance or resolution adopting the code to specify that certain appendix provisions apply.

REFERENCES

[1]Degenkolb, John G. (1975). Firesafety for the atrium type building. *Building Standards,* 44(3):16-18.

[2]Degenkolb, John G. (1983). Atriums, *Building Standards,* 52(1):7-10, 14.

[3]International Conference of Building Officials (1991). *Plan Review Manual,* Whittier, California, Chapter 11.

[4]Boring, Delbert F., James C. Spence and Walter G. Wells (1981). *Fire Protection through Modern Building Codes,* Fifth Edition. American Iron and Steel Institute, Washington, D.C., pages 88 and 161.

[5]Degenkolb, John G. (1974). The reasoning behind requirements for high rise buildings. *Building Standards,* 43(5):4-9.

[6]*Fire Protection Handbook,* 16th Edition (1986). National Fire Protection Association, Quincy, Massachusetts, pages 7-129.

[7]Bush, Vincent R. (1981). Preliminary report—MGM Grand Hotel fire, Las Vegas, Nevada. *Building Standards,* 50(1):6-9.

[8]International Conference of Building Officials (1991). *Plan Review Manual,* Whittier, California, Chapter 11.

[9]Degenkolb, John G. (1986). Stages and platforms. *Building Standards,* 55(3):13-15, 47.

Chapter 5

GENERAL BUILDING LIMITATIONS

Chapter 5 provides general provisions that are applicable to all buildings. These include requirements for exterior wall and opening protection; allowable floor areas and increases, including area separation walls; increases for open spaces and for the use of automatic sprinkler systems; and allowable height of buildings and increases. Other miscellaneous topics addressed in Chapter 5 are premises identification, mezzanines and guardrails.

In addition to general provisions set forth in Chapter 5, there are several special uses and occupancies which need to be addressed. These special provisions are found in both Chapters 3 and 4 with a cross-reference to the special uses and occupancies being presented in Section 501.

SECTION 502 — PREMISES IDENTIFICATION

In this section, which first appeared in the 1982 edition, the UBC intends that buildings be provided with plainly visible and legible address numbers posted on the building or in such a place on the property that the building may be identified by emergency services such as fire, medical and police. The primary concern is that responding fire-suppression forces may locate the building without going through a lengthy search procedure. In furthering the concept, the code intends that the approved street numbers be placed on a sign readily visible from the street fronting on the property if a sign on the building would not be visible from the street.

SECTION 503 — LOCATION ON PROPERTY

503.1 General. The *Uniform Building Code,* as far as exterior wall protection is concerned, operates on the philosophy that an owner can have no control over what occurs on adjacent property, and therefore the locations of buildings on the owner's property must be regulated relative to the property line. In fact, the location of all buildings and structures on a given piece of property are located with relation to the real property lines as well as assumed or imaginary property lines between buildings. The use of assumed property lines will be discussed later.

The property line concept provides a convenient means of protecting one building from another insofar as exposure is concerned. Exposure is the potential for heat to be transmitted from one building to another under fire conditions in the exposing building.[1] Radiation is the primary means of heat transfer.

Section 503 begins with a requirement that every building shall adjoin or have access to a public way or yard on at least one side. The objective is to provide space through which the fire department may gain access to the property to fight a fire.

The access requirement precludes the concept of surrounding one building by another where the surrounded building is separated from the surrounding building with area separation walls. The building in the center would not have access and thus would be in violation of the code. This access requirement would also prohibit a building which extends from property line to property line from being divided by an area separation wall in such a manner as to completely isolate the back portion. See Figure 503-1 for examples of these two situations.

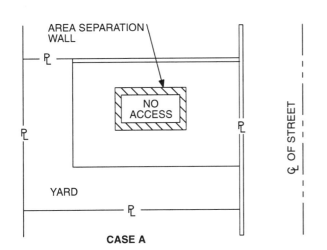

CASE A

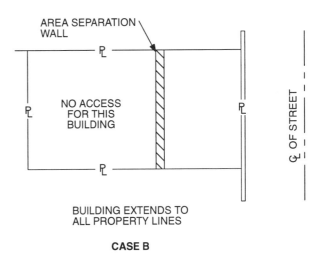

CASE B

ACCESS REQUIREMENTS FOR BUILDINGS

FIGURE 503-1

Because the open space between a street front lot line and center line of the street is available to property on both sides of the street, the code provides that the center line of the street shall be assumed to be the property line. As the code refers to "public way," this would also be applicable to an alley or other appropriate open spaces that the building official may determine is reasonably likely to remain unobstructed through the years.

503.2 Fire Resistance of Walls. The rules for exterior wall and opening protection based on proximity to the property line are contained in UBC Table 5-A. As it turns out, the exterior wall requirements based on location on property as set forth in Table 5-A also become the governing condition for exterior walls based on type of construction, as set forth in Table 6-A. More discussion about this topic appears in Chapter 6.

The *Uniform Building Code* is somewhat unique in that not only are the distances measured at right angles to the property line but the fire-protection requirements for exterior walls and openings do not apply to walls which are at right angles to the property line. Thus, openings may be placed in walls which are at right angles to the property line right up to the property line.

Figure 503-2 illustrates where openings are permitted in walls that are at least 90 degrees to the property line.

Figure 503-3 illustrates the application of exterior wall and opening protection where the exterior walls of the building are not parallel to the property line but rather are at some angle other than 90 degrees to the property line. In this case, the illustrations assume that the building is one-story Type V-N construction used for offices (Group B Occupancy). Referring to UBC Table 5-A, it is noted that exterior walls less than 20 feet (6096 mm) from the property line must be of one-hour fire-resistive construction. Moreover, no openings are permitted in exterior walls less than 5 feet (1524 mm) from the property line, and protected openings are required where the distance is less than 10 feet (3048 mm).

To give substance to the requirement that exterior walls within a specified distance of the property line be of fire-resistive construction, Section 503.2.2 limits the total area of openings in the exterior walls where openings are required to be protected to 50 percent of the area of that wall in that story. Further, the area of individual glazed openings is limited by Section 713.8.

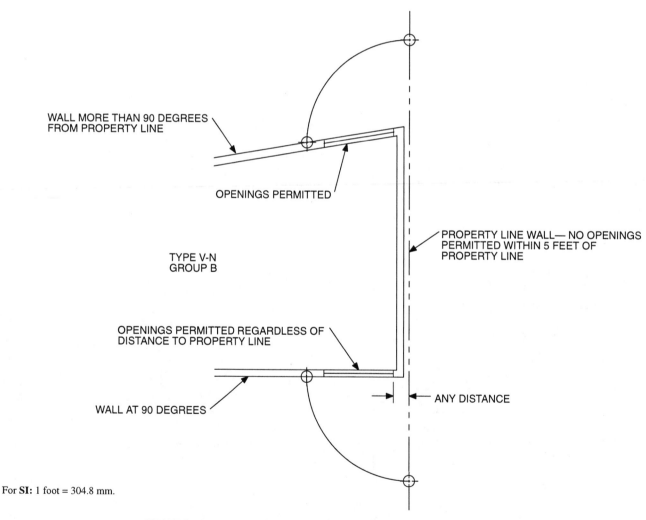

WALL MORE THAN 90 DEGREES FROM PROPERTY LINE

OPENINGS PERMITTED

TYPE V-N GROUP B

PROPERTY LINE WALL— NO OPENINGS PERMITTED WITHIN 5 FEET OF PROPERTY LINE

OPENINGS PERMITTED REGARDLESS OF DISTANCE TO PROPERTY LINE

ANY DISTANCE

WALL AT 90 DEGREES

For **SI:** 1 foot = 304.8 mm.

PROTECTION OF OPENINGS IN WALLS AT RIGHT ANGLES TO PROPERTY LINES

FIGURE 503-2

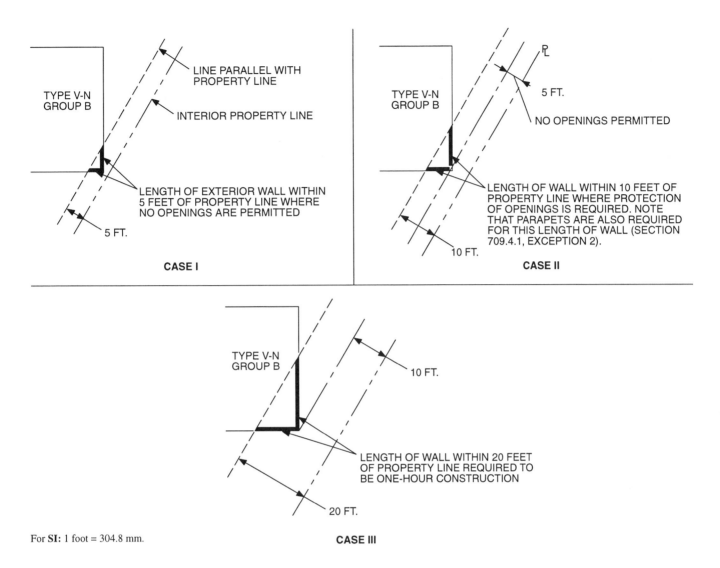

CASE I

CASE II

CASE III

For **SI:** 1 foot = 304.8 mm.

**MEASURING DISTANCE TO PROPERTY LINE AT ANGLE TO BUILDING FOR DETERMINING
FIRE-PROTECTION REQUIREMENTS FOR EXTERIOR WALLS**

FIGURE 503-3

While the perspective of the UBC does not generally concern itself with the exposure created by a building under consideration to another on adjacent property, the limitation of openings in an exterior wall does have the beneficial effect of limiting the amount of thermal radiation from the building under consideration to one on adjacent property. Thus, additional safety for adjoining property is fostered, even though this is not the primary intent of Section 503.

Exterior projections. Architectural considerations quite often call for projections from the exterior walls such as cornices, eave overhangs and balconies. Where these projections are from walls that are in close proximity to a property line, they create problems due to trapping the convected heat from a fire in an adjacent building. As this trapped heat increases the hazard for the building under consideration, the code limits the amount these projections may extend from the face of the building when the exterior wall is within the area where exterior wall openings require fire-resistive protection. The rule established by the code is that exterior wall projections may not project beyond a point

one-third the distance from an assumed vertical plane located where fire-resistive protection of exterior wall openings is first required or more than 12 inches (305 mm) into areas where openings are prohibited.

The rule governing projections was revised with the 1991 UBC in the interest of simplification. Unfortunately, the revised language does not indicate whether the least restrictive or the most restrictive condition shall govern. It was probably intended that the least restrictive condition govern, as was the case with prior code editions, but, unlike previous editions, no specific statement as to the governing condition now appears in the code. Lacking specific direction, the provisions of Section 101.3 would require that the most restrictive provision govern.

Figure 503-4 illustrates the rule. Case I is for a Group B Occupancy of Type V-N construction. For such a building, openings must be protected less than 10 feet (3048 mm) from the property line and are prohibited less than 5 feet (1524 mm) from the property line. Drawing A represents the first criteria while Drawing B illustrates the second. Assuming that the most restrictive condition governs, the condition shown in Drawing A governs since a property line separation of 6 feet 8 inches (2033 mm) is greater than the 4 feet (1219 mm) indicated in Drawing B.

Case II is for a Group R, Division 1 Occupancy, also of Type V-N construction. In this case, openings are not permitted less than 5 feet (1524 mm) from the property line. With no specific reference in Table 5-A to a location where opening protection is required, the point where fire-resistive protection of exterior wall openings is first required should also be taken as 5 feet (1524 mm). For Case II, Drawing D represents the more restrictive of the two conditions and thus governs.

503.3 Buildings on Same Property and Buildings Containing Courts. The UBC regulates the exterior wall construction and protection based on the proximity of the walls to property lines, either real or assumed. This section provides the code requirements for the establishment of assumed property lines between buildings on the same property and for buildings containing courts. Where two or more buildings are to be erected upon the same property, the determination of the code requirements for protection of the exterior walls is based on placing an assumed property line between buildings. Figure 503-5 illustrates an example for two buildings, and it is noted that the assumed property line can be located anywhere between the two buildings so

that the best advantage can be taken of wall and opening protection, depending on the use and architectural considerations for the exterior walls of the buildings. For example, if it were desired to have unprotected openings in the walls of each building, the property line would be so located that the distance between the property line and each building would permit unprotected openings. Thus, for the case where the two buildings each house Group B Occupancies and are of Type V construction, the code would require that each building be placed a minimum of 10 feet (3048 mm) from the property line in order to have unprotected openings. If one of the buildings were planned to have no openings in the exterior wall, the property line could be placed at the exterior wall of the building without openings. The other building would be located at a distance of 10 feet (3048 mm) from the property line and the other building. However, in all of the cases described, the exterior walls would be required to be of one-hour fire-resistive construction, as they are located less than 20 feet (6096 mm) from the assumed property line. Also, in the last example, Section 709.4 could possibly require that the exterior wall on the assumed property line be provided with a parapet. See discussion of Section 709.4.

Similar reasoning and procedures are used for the determination of wall and opening protection for court walls, except that

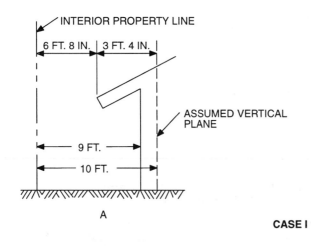

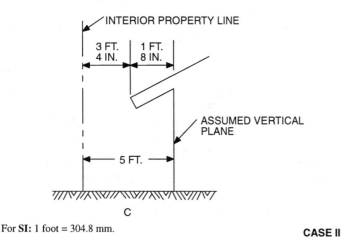

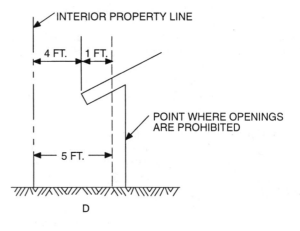

For **SI:** 1 foot = 304.8 mm.

CASE II

PROJECTIONS BEYOND THE EXTERIOR WALL

FIGURE 503-4

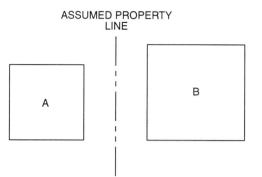

ASSUMED PROPERTY
LINE

A

B

CASE I: An assumed property line between buildings
A. Fire resistance and opening protection for walls adjacent to the property line must comply with the code.
B. Property line may be placed to take best advantage of wall and opening protection.

CASE II: As a single building
A. Allowable area and type of construction are based on the most restrictive requirements for the occupancies housed.
B. Total floor area may not exceed that allowed for a single building.

BUILDINGS ON THE SAME PROPERTY

FIGURE 503-5

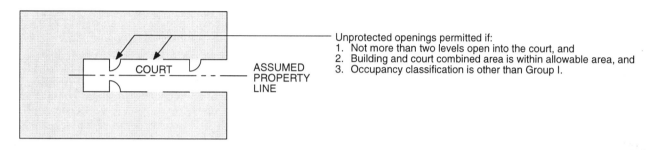

COURT

ASSUMED PROPERTY LINE

Unprotected openings permitted if:
1. Not more than two levels open into the court, and
2. Building and court combined area is within allowable area, and
3. Occupancy classification is other than Group I.

BUILDINGS CONTAINING COURTS

FIGURE 503-6

the code does permit omission of opening protection as depicted in Figure 503-6. The rationale for the omission for the opening protection as shown in Figure 503-6 is based on the fact that if the court were roofed over, Section 711.3 of the code would not require protection of the openings where only two stories or levels are involved and the building is other than a Group I Occupancy. Carrying the comparison one step further, you will notice that even though the court is not roofed over, its area must be included with that of the building in determining allowable area if openings are to be unprotected. This limitation was included in order to help address future problems when at some later date an owner wishes to cover the court.

In the case where a new building is to be erected on the same property as an existing building, the same rationale applies as depicted in Figure 503-5 except that the wall protection of the existing building determines the location of the property line. In any case where two or more buildings are located on the same property, they may be considered to be a single building subject to the limitations depicted in Figure 503-5.

503.4 Special Provisions and Exceptions to Table 5-A. Prior to the 1994 edition, the UBC contained a number of exceptions for various construction-type exterior wall requirements that were spread over four different chapters. Most of these exceptions were incorporated into Table 5-A. However, a few remaining limited application exceptions, together with some very specific requirements for the separation of hazardous occupancies

from adjacent property lines, have been accumulated in this section.

503.4.2 and 503.4.8 One-story Groups B, F, M and S Occupancies and Group U, Division 1 Occupancies. These two sections provide for a relaxation in exterior wall requirements under certain, well-defined conditions. Section 503.4.2 is an exception that applies only to one-story buildings of Type II-N construction housing Groups B, F, M and S Occupancies. This exception provides that there is no requirement for the fire resistance of exterior walls, provided the floor area of the building does not exceed 1,000 square feet (92.9 m²) and the wall is located at least 5 feet (1524 mm) from the property line.

This exception, or a similar one, has been in the UBC for several decades, and in fact, earlier editions of the code required only a 3-foot (914 mm) setback from the property line. These small Group B, F, M, and S Occupancy noncombustible buildings have a good fire history, based primarily on a relatively low fire loading and the lack of fuel contribution from the noncombustible construction. The noncombustible exterior wall construction prevents the spread of fire even though the wall is of nonfire-resistive construction because of the two attributes described above.

Section 503.4.8 is similar to the exception previously discussed in that it applies to a specific occupancy group, in this case Group U, Division 1, and is also limited to one-story buildings having floor areas that do not exceed 1,000 (92.9 m²) square feet. The 1,000-square-foot (92.9 m²) area limitation comes from Section 312.2.1, which limits both the height and floor area of Group U, Division 1 Occupancies. Section 503.4.8 permits materials approved on one-hour fire-resistive construction to be installed only on the exterior face of exterior walls required to be one-hour fire-resistive construction due to location on property line. Specifically, this would be an exterior wall located from zero to 3 feet (914 mm) from an interior property line. [It is true that Section 312.2.2 permits Group U, Division 1 Occupancies under certain conditions to have floor areas up to 3,000 square feet (279 m^2). But when this occurs, exterior wall and opening protection shall be as required for the major building occupancy for mixed occupancy buildings or as required for a Group R, Division 1 Occupancy for stand-alone Group U, Division 1 buildings. In either case, Section 503.4.8 is not applicable.]

A revision to this section excludes work that is exempt from a permit as listed in Section 106.2, Item 1, from meeting the wall and opening protection requirements. There is no known fire loss history available for the small sheds that could be built under this exclusion.

503.4.3 and 503.4.4 Fire-retardant-treated wood framing and wood columns and arches. These two sections establish exceptions for exterior wall construction for Types III and IV construction. Section 503.4.3 provides that fire-retardant-treated wood framing may be used within the assembly of exterior walls when Table 5-A allows a fire-resistive rating of two hours or less. When using this exception, the required fire resistance must be maintained and the exposed outer and inner faces of the wall must be of noncombustible material.

The rationale for this exception is that fire-retardant-treated wood, although a combustible material, will not support its own combustion, and the exposure hazards are low enough that the fire-retardant-treated wood will provide adequate performance. Also, the requirement that the exposed inner and outer faces be noncombustible provides that the likelihood of direct flame impingement of the fire-retardant-treated wood is unlikely. This is particularly true for the common case where the noncombustible exposed faces will be gypsum wallboard for the interior and either masonry veneer or metal siding for the exterior. Section 503.4.4 involves the external use of unprotected wood columns and arches. The code requires that these members conform to the requirements for heavy-timber sizes and that their use is permitted only where the exterior walls are permitted to be of either one-hour fire-resistive noncombustible construction or unprotected noncombustible construction. For most occupancies, Table 5-A permits one-hour noncombustible construction at 20 feet (6096 mm) from the property line and unprotected noncombustible construction at 40 feet (12 192 mm). Here again, the location of the exterior walls represents a low exposure hazard, and although heavy-timber sizes cannot be equated to one-hour fire-resistive construction, they are allowed to be used interchangeably in some cases in Type IV buildings.

503.4.5 Group H Occupancies—Minimum distance to property lines. This section contains four items that address various minimum set-back requirements for Group H, Divisions 1, 2 and 3 Occupancies. In discussing the special requirements of this section, it must be understood that the minimum separation distance from property lines for Group H, Divisions 1, 2 and 3 Occupancies is measured from the walls enclosing the occu-

pancy to all property lines, including those on a public way. This requirement for Group H Occupancies is more stringent than for other occupancies since the measurement on sides adjacent to public streets does not allow measuring to the center line of the street. This provision also affords a greater degree of protection for pedestrians and vehicles in the event of an explosion or conflagration. Note that the fire-protection requirements for bearing and nonbearing walls and for openings may be measured to property lines, including an allowance to measure to the center of adjoining public ways, since these provisions primarily relate to protection of the Group H Occupancy from exposure to fires. See Figure 503-7.

Group H, Division 1 Occupancies are required to be separated from property lines by the distance specified in Table 3-F, but by not less than 75 feet (22 860 mm). Group H, Division 2 Occupancies not exceeding 1,000 (92.9 m^2) square feet and not required by Table 3-G to be in detached buildings are not restricted with respect to location on property. Group H, Division 2 Occupancies exceeding 1,000 square feet (92.9 m^2) in area and not required by Table 3-G to be in detached buildings must be separated from property lines by not less that 30 feet (9144 mm). In the case of mixed occupancies, the separation distance must be measured from the walls enclosing the Group H, Division 2 or 3 Occupancy, which may or may not be an exterior wall. Group H, Divisions 2 and 3 Occupancies that are required by Table 3-G to be in detached buildings must be separated from property line by the greater of 50 feet (15 240 mm) or the distance required by Table 3-F when these occupancies contain materials with explosive characteristics.

See Figures 503-8 and 503-9. There is no requirement for minimum distances to property lines for Group H, Divisions 4, 5, 6 and 7 Occupancies.

503.4.6 Group H, Division 1, 2 or 3 Occupancies—Detached buildings. This section is an exception that states that when a detached building is required for a Group H, Division 1, 2 or 3 Occupancy there shall be no requirements for wall and opening protection based on location on property. As discussed above, the minimum property line separation would be 50 feet (15 240 mm) (for a Group H, Division 2 or Group H, Division 3 Occupancy); reference to waiving opening protection seems redundant as a quick look at Table 5-A reveals that there is no requirement beyond 20 feet (6096 mm).

503.4.9 Exterior wall assemblies. This section cross-references Section 2602.5.2, which addresses the use of foam plastic insulation in exterior wall panels. Such panels, when they comply with the limitations set forth in Section 2602.5.2, may be used in all types of construction.

SECTION 504 — ALLOWABLE FLOOR AREAS

The *Uniform Building Code* limits the size of buildings in order to limit to a reasonable level the size of a fire that potentially may develop in a building. The size of a building is controlled by its floor area and height and both are limited by the UBC.

While floor-area limitations are concerned primarily with property damage, life safety is also enhanced by floor-area limitations because of the fact that for the larger building there are typically more people at risk during a fire.

(Continued on page 80)

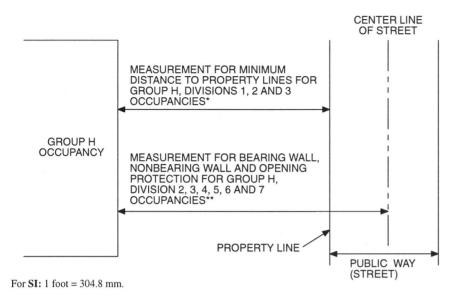

For **SI:** 1 foot = 304.8 mm.

MEASUREMENT FOR WALL PROTECTION, OPENING PROTECTION AND LOCATION ON PROPERTY FOR GROUP H OCCUPANCIES

FIGURE 503-7

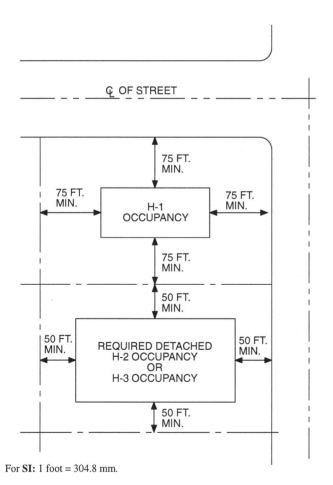

For **SI:** 1 foot = 304.8 mm.

LOCATION ON PROPERTY FOR DETACHED BUILDINGS

FIGURE 503-8

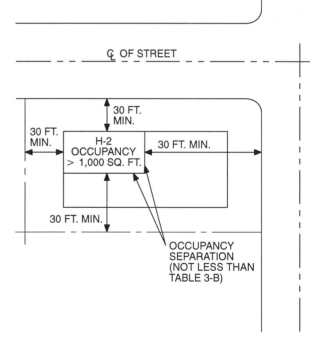

NOTE: Section 307.10 requires a 50-foot separation between all property lines and explosion side wall vents. Also, per Section 307.3, 25 percent of perimeter of Group H Occupancy must be on an exterior wall.

For **SI:** 1 foot = 304.8 mm, 1 square foot = 0.093 m².

LOCATION ON PROPERTY FOR MIXED OCCUPANCIES THAT INCLUDE A GROUP H, DIVISION 2 OCCUPANCY

FIGURE 503-9

(Continued from page 78)

The essential ingredients in the determination of allowable areas are:

- The amount of combustibles attributable to the use which determines the potential fire severity.

- The amount of combustibles in the construction of the building which also contributes to the potential fire severity.

In addition to the two factors just itemized, there may be other features of the building that have an effect on area limitation, such as the presence of built-in fire protection (an automatic fire sprinkler system) and compartmentation (fire-resistive interior walls and floors), which tend to prevent the spread of fire.

A desirable goal of floor-area limitations in a building code is that they should provide a relatively uniform level of hazard for all occupancies and types of construction. A glance through Table 5-B of the UBC will reveal that, in general, the higher hazard occupancies have lower permissible areas for equivalent types of construction and, in addition, the less fire-resistive and more combustible types of construction also have more restrictive area limitations.

504.1 One-story Areas. The *Uniform Building Code* establishes in Table 5-B what the code refers to as "basic" permissible areas for one-story buildings. By use of the term "basic," the code means that the building in question has no features that might be considered as improving the overall fire hazard (such as a fire sprinkler system) from the case of an unsprinklered building which faces only one yard or public way. On this basis, this section states the rule that the area of any one-story building shall not be greater than the basic area specified in Table 5-B unless the building is entitled to area increases, which are described in Section 505.

504.2 Areas of Buildings over One Story. For multistory buildings, the UBC permits the total combined floor area to be twice that specified in Table 5-B for a one-story building. However, the code also limits any single story to that permitted for a one-story building. This latter provision prevents the first story of a two-story building from having essentially double the area permitted for the ground floor where only a small room comprises the second story.

504.3 Allowable Floor Area of Mixed Occupancies. For area considerations in a mixed-occupancy building, the code uses a formula that is very similar to the interaction formula used in structural engineering where two different types of stress are imposed on a member at the same time. In the case of a mixed-occupancy building, the code uses this type of formula for the determination of the allowable area for the total building.

For example, if there are three different occupancies in a building, the formula is as follows:

$$\frac{a1}{A1} + \frac{a2}{A2} + \frac{a3}{A3} \le 1$$

WHERE:

$a1$, $a2$ and $a3$ represent the actual areas for the three separate occupancies, and $A1$, $A2$ and $A3$ represent the allowable areas for the three separate occupancies.

See Application Examples 504-1 and 504-2 for examples of this computation.

This formula essentially prorates the areas of the various occupancies so that the sum of the percentages must not exceed 100 percent. It is also interesting to note that if one of the occupancies is a single-family dwelling (Group R, Division 3 Occupancy), the ratio of areas for the dwelling in the equation approaches zero as a limit because the allowable area is unlimited.

Application Example 504-1

I. GIVEN A ONE-STORY BUILDING HOUSING AN OCCUPANCY GROUP CLASSIFIED AS GROUP E, DIVISION 1, OFFICES AND AN ASSEMBLY HALL. THE BUILDING IS OF TYPE V ONE-HOUR CONSTRUCTION. NO YARDS ARE AVAILABLE FOR AREA INCREASE PURPOSES. FLOOR AREAS ARE AS FOLLOWS:

OFFICE (B)	4,500 SQUARE FEET
ASSEMBLY (A-2.1)	3,000 SQUARE FEET
E-1	6,000 SQUARE FEET

II. IS THE BUILDING AREA WITHIN THE ALLOWABLE AREA?

III. SOLUTION IN ACCORDANCE WITH SECTION 504.3.

$$\frac{\text{ACTUAL AREA OF OFFICE}}{\text{ALLOWABLE AREA OF OFFICE}} + \frac{\text{ACTUAL AREA OF ASSEMBLY}}{\text{ALLOWABLE AREA OF ASSEMBLY}} + \frac{\text{ACTUAL AREA OF E-1}}{\text{ALLOWABLE AREA OF E-1}} \le 1$$

$$\frac{4,500}{14,000} + \frac{3,000}{10,500} + \frac{6,000}{15,700} \overset{?}{\le} 1$$

$$.321 + .286 + .382 \overset{?}{\le} 1$$

$$.989 < 1$$

BUILDING IS WITHIN THE ALLOWABLE AREA

For **SI:** 1 square foot = 0.093 m^2.

DETERMINING ALLOWABLE AREAS FOR A MIXED-OCCUPANCY BUILDING

Application Example 504-2
Section 504.3

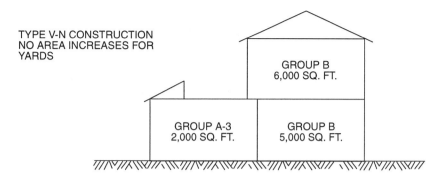

TYPE V-N CONSTRUCTION
NO AREA INCREASES FOR
YARDS

GROUP B
6,000 SQ. FT.

GROUP A-3
2,000 SQ. FT.

GROUP B
5,000 SQ. FT.

For **SI:** 1 square foot = 0.093 m².

ALLOWABLE AREA FOR MIXED OCCUPANCIES

FIGURE 504-2

GIVEN: Information in Figure 504-2.

DETERMINE: Whether the building area is within the allowable area.

SOLUTION: Because the building is more than one story in height, each story must be reviewed to be sure that the individual story is within allowable areas for a one-story building and then the building as a whole must be reviewed to be sure that the total area is also within allowable areas. The first step in determining if the building area is within the allowable area is to review the first story. Since it contains a mixed occupancy, it must be checked to be sure that the sum of the ratios for the occupancies does not exceed one.

$$\frac{\text{Actual Area (A–3)}}{\text{Allowable Area (A–3)}} + \frac{\text{Actual Area (B)}}{\text{Allowable Area (B)}} \leq 1$$

$$\frac{2,000}{6,000} + \frac{5,000}{8,000} = 0.333 + 0.625 = 0.958 \qquad \text{(First Story O.K.)}$$

The second step is to review the area of the second story. Since the 6,000 square feet of the Group B Occupancy located on the second story is less than the 8,000 square feet allowable area, by inspection the second story is obviously O.K. If the second story had also contained mixed occupancies, the same calculation performed for the first story would have been required.

The last step is to check the entire building to see if the total area is within the allowable area. However, in applying the multistory increases permitted by Section 504.2, a question arises since the Group A, Division 3 Occupancy occurs only on the first story. Can a multiple story allowable area be applied to the Group A, Division 3 Occupancy in order to reduce the sum of the ratios to less than one even though the Group A, Division 3 Occupancy does not exist on the second story? This question can be answered if we restate the provisions of Section 504.2 to reflect its intent by saying that the allowable area for multistory buildings may be twice that permitted for a one-story building. This has the effect for mixed occupancies of doubling the allowable area in the denominators of the fractions making up the equation for the sum of the ratios. All denominators may be doubled whether or not the occupancy under consideration occurs on only one story or on several. Another method that is mathematically equivalent to multiplying the denominators by two is for the sum of the ratios not to exceed two. Applying this method to the particular problem, we get:

$$\frac{2,000}{6,000} + \frac{5,000}{8,000} + \frac{6,000}{8,000} = 0.333 + 0.625 + 0.750 = 1.708 < 2 \qquad \text{(Multistory O.K.)}$$

Thus, the presence of a Group R, Division 3 Occupancy in a mixed-occupancy building has no effect insofar as the area permitted for the other occupancies is concerned.

Exceptions. In some cases, the mixed-occupancy building may actually consist of a primary occupancy with one or more minor accessory uses. If the aggregate of these accessory uses does not occupy more than 10 percent of the floor area of any floor of the building or more than the basic area permitted for the occupancy in UBC Table 5-B, the building is classified in accordance with the major occupancy for the determination of the allowable area. The code further requires that these minor accessory uses be separated as required by Section 302.4.

This provision for minor accessory uses appears as Exception 1 under Section 504.3. Exception 2 of the same section also addresses minor accessory uses, only in this case it addresses such minor uses in a building permitted to be of unlimited area under the provisions of Section 505.2 [i.e., a fully sprinklered building surrounded on all sides with 60-foot (18 288 mm)

Application Example 504-3
Section 504.3

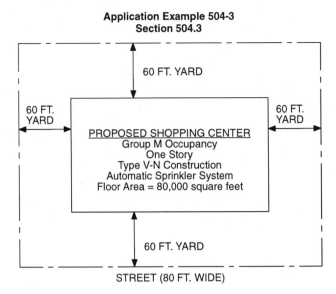

60 FT. YARD

60 FT. YARD | 60 FT. YARD

PROPOSED SHOPPING CENTER
Group M Occupancy
One Story
Type V-N Construction
Automatic Sprinkler System
Floor Area = 80,000 square feet

60 FT. YARD

STREET (80 FT. WIDE)

For **SI:**   1 foot = 304.8 mm, 1 square foot = 0.093 m².

MINOR ACCESSORY USES

FIGURE 504-3

GIVEN: Information in Figure 504-3.

DETERMINE: The shopping center developer is proposing to include two 3,000-square-foot Group A, Division 3 restaurant occupancies in a shopping center built using the unlimited area provisions of Section 505.2. Does this design comply with Exception 2 of Section 504.3?

SOLUTION:

Check 10 percent limitation per Exception 2, Section 504.3:
10 percent of 80,000 square feet = 8,000 square feet
8,000 square feet ≥ 6,000 square feet (O.K.)

Check basic area limitation from Table 5-B:
For Type V-N, Group A, Division 3 Occupancy
Basic allowable area = 6,100 square feet
= 6,000 square feet proposed Group A, Division 3 floor area (O.K.)

Interestingly, if this particular Group M Occupancy qualified as a covered mall building, the restaurant in question, if it were the only accessory use, could have an area as great as 18,300 square feet rather than the 6,100 square feet allowed under Section 504.3, Exception 2. (Per Section 404.5.1, allowable area is 3 × 6,100 = 18,300 square feet, or 25 percent of gross leasable area. Although we don't know the gross leasable area in this example, if we assume 60,000 square feet, then the restaurant could have an area of 0.25 × 60,000 = 15,000 square feet.)

yards]. This exception is somewhat similar to Section 404.5.1 for covered mall buildings, which are often of unlimited area, but is not nearly as generous. Under Section 404.5.1, the aggregate area of all accessory uses may be as much as 25 percent of the gross leasable area, with an individual accessory use not exceeding three times the basic area permitted by Table 5-B. Although the 25 percent limitation is not based on the entire covered mall building's floor area or on a per-floor basis as is the 10 percent permitted by Exception 2, a covered mall building may have accessory uses with a total area two and one-half times greater than allowed under Exception 2. See Application Examples 504-3 and 504-4.

504.4 Mezzanines. A mezzanine that complies with the limitations imposed by Section 507 may be considered to be a part of the story within which it is located. In such a case, its area is required to be included when calculating the allowable area permitted for the story in which the mezzanine is located. A mezzanine is not, however, required to be considered a part of the story

in which it is located. It may be considered to be a separate story provided it meets all requirements and limitations attributable to an additional story. This is important to remember because, for example, if one had a one-story building that was already at maximum allowable area, a mezzanine could still be added if it were made to comply as a second story.

504.5 Basements. The code intends that basements that do not exceed the allowable floor area permitted for a one-story building need not be included in determining the area of a building. This provision is a holdover from many years back when basements were most commonly used for service of the building. Today it is not at all uncommon to find basements occupied for the same uses as the upper floors; consequently, for example, a two-story with a basement department store is literally permitted by the UBC to have an area of three times that permitted for a one-story building. There apparently has been no adverse experience for cases of this type (most likely because of the fire sprinkler protection required), and, therefore, the code provision

Application Example 504-4
Sections 504.1 and 504.3

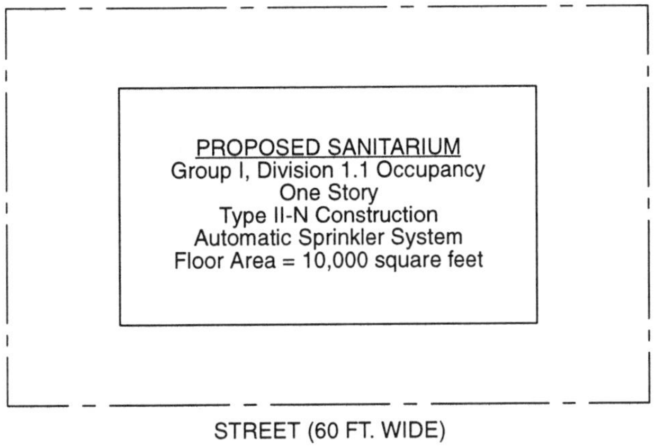

PROPOSED SANITARIUM
Group I, Division 1.1 Occupancy
One Story
Type II-N Construction
Automatic Sprinkler System
Floor Area = 10,000 square feet

STREET (60 FT. WIDE)

For **SI:** 1 foot = 304.8 mm, 1 square foot = 0.093 m^2.

MINOR ACCESSORY USES

FIGURE 504-4

GIVEN: Information in Figure 504-4.

DETERMINE: Could the minor accessory use provisions of Section 504.3 be used as justification for allowing no more than 10 percent of the floor area of the Group I, Division 1.1 Occupancy to be used as a lock-down sanitarium, a Group I, Division 3 Occupancy?

SOLUTION: The first exception to Section 504.3 states that "the major occupancy classification of a building may be used to determine the allowable area of such building when the major use occupies not less than 90 percent of the area of any floor of the building and provided that other minor accessory uses shall not exceed the basic area permitted by Table 5-B for such minor uses and that various uses are separated as specified in Section 302.4." Looking at Table 5-B, you will notice that the table does not permit a Group I, Division 3 Occupancy in a building that is of Type II-N construction. Therefore, since there is no basic area permitted for the proposed minor accessory use, the minor accessory provisions of Section 504.3 cannot be used to justify the proposed addition of a Group I, Division 3 Occupancy.

appears to be satisfactory. The code does not address how to handle a basement that exceeds the area permitted for a one-story building. As the code does not permit any story to exceed that permitted for a one-story building, a basement should also be limited to the same area. If anything, a fire in a basement is more difficult to fight than one in an above-ground story. Thus, it does not seem reasonable or appropriate to permit a basement with an area exceeding that for a one-story building.

504.6 Area Separation Walls. In Section 302 the code introduced the concept of the fire-resistive *separation,* designated the "occupancy separation," where the openings in the separation wall are protected by fire-protection assemblies. The *Uniform Building Code* has a second type of fire-resistive separation, which is called the "area separation wall." The intent of the code is that the function of the wall is exactly as its name implies—a vertical wall that *separates* areas. This is to distinguish it from an occupancy separation that may be horizontal. Structural members that penetrate area separation walls could limit the effectiveness and would not comply with the provision that states such walls "shall provide a complete separation." Any member that passes through an area separation wall could affect the integrity of the required fire-resistive construction. However, the code does not prohibit western platform framing to divide a two-hour area separation wall if solid blocking is provided within the floor or roof cavity. See Footnote 2 for a

reference to an article by Paul Sheedy which illustrates this concept.

The *Uniform Building Code* permits such walls to be installed in a large-area building, thereby creating one or more smaller-area buildings. The code further intends that each portion of the building so separated may be considered a separate building. However, remember the earlier discussion under Section 503. Each separate building created by an area separation wall must adjoin or have access to a public way or yard on at least one side.

It follows that the area separation wall performs the very important function of acting as a barrier to fire spread so that a fire on one side of the wall will not be transmitted to the other. On this basis, the area separation wall must have a fire-resistive rating commensurate with the type of construction in which it is installed. The *Uniform Building Code* provides that area separation walls in Types I, II-F.R., III and IV buildings shall not be of less than four-hour fire-resistive construction. Openings in this wall are required to be protected with assemblies having a three-hour fire-protection rating. Chapter 7 of the code requires that fire doors in three-hour fire-rated assemblies be of the "automatic" type. An automatic fire assembly requires that an actuating mechanism (a fusible link which is heat actuated, or a smoke detector) be installed (on each side of the wall for the fusible link), which will cause the door to close automatically in case of fire.

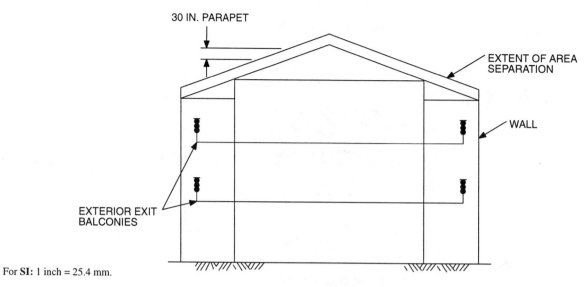

For **SI:** 1 inch = 25.4 mm.

**EXTENT OF AREA SEPARATION WALL
GENERAL RULE**

FIGURE 504-5

In other types of construction, the code requires that the area separation wall be of two-hour fire-resistive construction with openings protected with one and one-half-hour fire-protection assemblies. The *Uniform Building Code* intends by the use of the term "assemblies" that the opening protection consist of not only a fire door but the requisite hardware, anchorage, frames and sills for the opening. The *Uniform Building Code* further limits the total width of all openings in an area separation wall to 25 percent of the length of the wall in each story. When a wall serves both as an area separation wall and as part of an occupancy separation, the most restrictive requirements of each separation shall apply.

Having established the intent of the *Uniform Building Code* that area separation walls prevent the spread of fire around or through the wall to the other side, the UBC further ensures the "separate building" concept by specifying that the wall extend continuously from the foundation to and through the roof to a point 30 inches (762 mm) above the roof. The 30-inch (762 mm) parapet prevents the spread of fire along the roof surface from the fire side to the other side of the wall. Furthermore, the lateral extent of the wall as well is intended to completely separate all portions of the building. Therefore, the wall must extend to the outer edges of horizontal projecting elements, such as balconies and roof overhangs. See Figure 504-5 for an example of the general rule for this case. It is emphasized that the term "area separation wall" also limits its use to vertical walls. Therefore, there can be no horizontal offsets nor can the plan view of the wall change from level to level.

The original objective of area separation walls was that a complete burnout could occur on one side of the wall without any effects of the fire being felt on the opposite side. Furthermore, the only damage to the wall would be the effects of fire and the shock of hose stream application on the fire side. The separate building concept has been modified as described above for western platform framing. Nevertheless, structural members, especially members that conduct heat, that penetrate area separation walls could limit the effectiveness and would not comply with the provision that states such walls "shall provide a complete separation." Any member that passes through an area separation wall could affect the integrity of the required fire-resistive construction.

There are exceptions to the provisions defining the required extent of the wall that are based on:

- Equivalent fire protection being provided by an alternate construction system such as western platform framing;

- Aesthetic considerations such as parapets that look ugly; and

- A combination of the two previous reasons.

For the same reasons that Section 503.1 requires that the building have access on at least one side, the code applies this same rule to a large-area building that has been divided by area separation walls. As the walls divide the large building into smaller but separate buildings, each of the separate buildings then must have access on at least one side, as discussed in Section 503.1.

Because the area separation wall is such a critical element in the prevention of the spread of fire from one separated building to another, it is of great importance that the wall be situated and constructed properly. Refer to Footnote 2 for a highly definitive treatment of the subject.

504.6.7 Combustible framing in area separation walls. This section was added to define the limitations on penetration of combustible framing into masonry area separation walls. Adjacent combustible members framing into a masonry area separation wall from opposite sides require a minimum distance of 4 inches (102 mm) between embedded ends. All hollow spaces at this location shall be solidly filled for the full thickness of the wall and for a distance not less than 4 inches (102 mm) above, below and between the structural members with noncombustible materials approved for fireblocking.

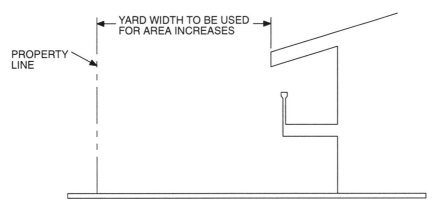

MEASUREMENT OF YARDS

FIGURE 505-1

SECTION 505 — ALLOWABLE AREA INCREASES

505.1 General. The minimum requirement of the code insofar as siting a building is concerned is that it have access on at least one side to a street or yard. Thus, it could extend completely between side property lines and to the rear property line and have access from only one side. It, therefore, follows that if a building is provided with yards or open space on two or more sides, some benefit should accrue based on better access for the fire department. Also, if the yards or streets are wide enough, there will be a benefit due to the decreased exposure from adjoining properties.

Because of the beneficial aspects of open space adjacent to a building, the UBC permits increases in the basic areas established from Section 504 based on the number and width of the yards and streets around the building. For yards to be effective for use by the fire department, it is a good idea that they be connected to a public way so that the fire department will have access to that portion of the perimeter of the building that is adjacent to open space. However, the code does not require this condition.

Yards and public ways—What can and can't be used. By definition, a yard is an open, unoccupied space from the ground to the sky that is located on the lot on which the building is situated. This definition precludes the storage of pallets, lumber, manufactured goods or any other objects that similarly obstruct the yard. Most jurisdictions, however, do permit automobile parking, low-profile landscaping, fire hydrants, light standards and similar features to occupy the yard. Since a yard must be unobstructed from the ground to the sky, yard widths should be measured from the edge of roof overhangs or other projections as shown in Figure 505-1.

Something that seems to cause confusion is what width of public way should be used for determining area increases. Do you use the full width of the public way or only the distance to the center line? The confusion evolves from Section 503.1, which states "For the purpose of this section, the center line of an adjoining public way shall be considered an adjacent property line." The key words here are "for the purpose of this section." Thus, the requirement to use the center line is limited to Section 503 and is not applicable to Section 505. For determining area increases for open space, the full width of the public way may be used by buildings located on each side of the public way.

The following type of question is sometimes asked: "Why can't I use the big open field next door for area increases?" Remember that by definition a yard must be on the same lot as the building, so an adjoining area that is not a part of the lot upon which the proposed building is situated may not be used. There is a good reason for this—the owner of one parcel lacks control over a parcel owned by another and, thus, a yard can disappear when the owner of "the big open field" decides to build on it. One way some jurisdictions have allowed such "big open spaces" to be used is by accepting joint use of shared yards when a recorded restrictive covenant is executed to ensure that the shared space will remain open and unoccupied as long as it is required by the Building Code. This does not seem unreasonable since the aim is to maintain open spaces between buildings. Any covenant should be reviewed by counsel to be sure it will accomplish what is intended and should clearly describe the reason and code section applicable so that any future revisions or deletions may be considered if the owners wish to terminate such an agreement.

In such an event, each building should be brought into current code compliance or the agreement would be required to remain in effect.

Prior to the 1985 edition, the code referred to "public space, streets or yards." Reference to "public space" was deleted because the building official usually has no control over the long-range use of publicly owned property and there is little assurance that such property will be available as open space for the life of the building. Remember that what is today's publicly owned open parking lot could become tomorrow's new city hall and the open space used to justify area increases would no longer exist. The term "public way" was used in place of "streets" because its definition in Chapter 10 allows the use of a broad range of publicly owned open space while still allowing the building official some discretion as to the acceptability of a particular parcel. "Public way" usually conjures up visions of streets and alleys, but how about other open spaces such as power line right of ways, or flood-control channels or railroad right of ways? Many such open spaces are generally acceptable provided there is good probability that they will remain as open space during the life of the building for which they will serve. Power lines and flood-control channels are usually good bets for longevity, but railroads are often abandoned and, therefore, may not be as good a bet.

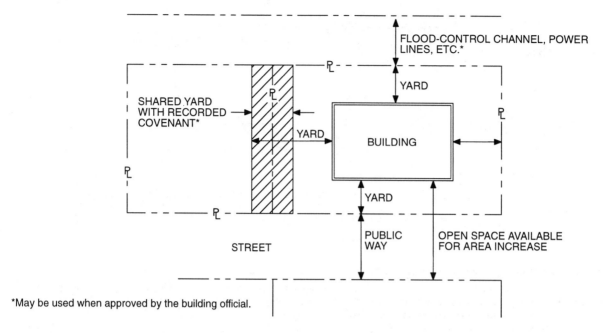

YARDS AND PUBLIC WAYS AVAILABLE FOR AREA INCREASES

FIGURE 505-2

Figure 505-2 provides a visual summary of yards and public ways that could be used for open space area increases.

How much increase? In the case where streets or yards adjoin two sides of the building, the code permits an increase in area of up to 50 percent. It should be noted that such yards need not be on adjacent sides of the building. Where streets or yards exist on three or four sides, the code for most occupancies and types of construction permits an area increase of up to 100 percent.

Where yards exist on four sides, the code does allow extra area increases for three cases where the amount of combustibles and, consequently, potential fire severity is relatively low. Also, the height of the building is limited to either one or two stories. In these three cases, the area may be increased beyond 100 percent, provided, of course, the minimum width yard or street exceeds a width of 40 feet (12 192 mm). This is based on the code criterion of permitting a rate of increase equal to 5 percent for each foot (304 mm) that the minimum width yard or street exceeds 20 feet (6096 mm). See Application Examples 505-3, 505-4 and 505-5.

505.2 Unlimited Area. There are many cases where very large undivided floor areas are required for efficient operation in such facilities as warehouses and industrial plants. The *Uniform Building Code* recognizes this necessity and allows unlimited areas for these uses under two different sets of circumstances.

The first case is for buildings up to a maximum of two stories in height when the building is completely surrounded by streets or yards not less than 60 feet (18 288 mm) in width and protected throughout by an automatic fire sprinkler system. The first case applies to any business (Group B), factory and industrial (Group F), mercantile (Group M) or storage (Group S) occupancy and to an aircraft repair hangar (Group H, Division 5). The code as-

sumes in this case that the amount of combustibles and, consequently, the potential fire severity is relatively low. In addition, the protection provided by the automatic fire sprinkler system plus the fire department access furnished by the 60-foot (18 288 mm) yards or streets surrounding the building reduce the potential fire severity to such a level that unlimited area is reasonable.

The second case involves a Group F, Division 2 or a Group S, Division 2 Occupancy in a one-story building of Type II, Type III One-hour or Type IV construction. Both Group F, Division 2 and Group S, Division 2 Occupancies by definition are low-hazard uses, which the code considers to be low fire risks. Fire risk is further reduced by limiting the provision to buildings of noncombustible construction that are otherwise protected (one-hour or heavy timber) to reduce structure contribution to any fire. This second case also requires that the building be surrounded by yards or streets with a minimum width of 60 feet (18 288 mm), but does not require the installation of an automatic fire sprinkler system.

There is also a third case where unlimited areas are permitted but are not discussed in this section of the code. This is the Type I building except when it houses Group H, Divisions 1 and 2 Occupancies. The restriction of areas for the Group H, Divisions 1 and 2 Occupancies is based on the explosive, highly flammable and combustible contents exemplified by these uses.

In all other cases the Type I building enjoys an unlimited floor area regardless of the number of streets or yards around the building and regardless of whether or not an automatic fire sprinkler system is installed. The rationale for permitting an unlimited area for a Type I building is based on the highly fire-resistive nature of the Type I building and the compartmentation provided by the fire-resistive floors. Thus, it is assumed that a complete burnout of the contents on any given floor may occur without causing the collapse of the building and without the fire spreading to any other floors or to adjacent buildings.

505.3 Automatic Sprinkler Systems. Because over the years automatic fire sprinkler systems have exhibited an excellent record of in-place fire suppression, the UBC allows area increases where an automatic fire sprinkler system is installed throughout the building. In this case the area of a one-story building may be tripled, and for a building of two or more stories in height, the area may be doubled. This restriction of permitting only a 100 percent increase in area for multistory buildings protected by an automatic fire sprinkler system is based on the assumption by the code that the fire department suppression activities are still going to be required even when an automatic fire sprinkler system is installed. Therefore, a multistory building presents more problems to the fire department than a one-story building, and a smaller increase in area is permitted.

The *Uniform Building Code* permits area increases for sprinklers, provided that the systems are not otherwise required by the code in the following cases:

1. To increase the allowable number of stories.

2. Group H, Divisions 1 and 2 Occupancies.

3. Substitution for one-hour fire-resistive construction.

4. Buildings with atria.

In these cases the code considers that the conditions and hazards requiring the installation of fire sprinklers are such that the sprinkler system should not also be used to increase the allowable area.

In recognition of the excellent fire record in buildings protected throughout with fire sprinkler systems, the UBC further intends that the area increases permitted for sprinkler systems be compounded with the increases outlined in Section 505.1 for spatial separations consisting of public ways or yards on two or more sides of a building.

Consider a two-story office building of Type III-N construction protected with an automatic fire sprinkler system and situated on a lot that has a 60-foot (18 288 mm) street across the front. There is one 60-foot (18 288 mm) yard on one side of the building. The allowable area would be computed as follows:

1. Determine the basic allowable area for a one-story Group B Occupancy of Type III-N construction from Table 5-B. Basic area = 12,000 square feet (1114.8 m^2).

2. Determine the allowable increase in area due to 60-foot (18 288 mm) yards on two sides from Section 505.1.

Application Example 505-3

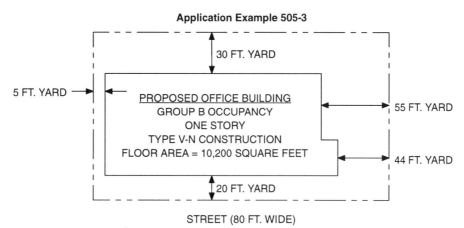

For **SI:** 1 foot = 304.8 mm, 1 square foot = 0.093 m^2.

AREA INCREASES FOR OPEN SPACES

FIGURE 505-3

GIVEN: Information in Figure 505-3.

DETERMINE: If building may be of Type V-N construction as proposed.

SOLUTION: Basic allowable area for a Group B Occupancy of Type V-N construction (Table 5-B) is 8,000 square feet.

The provisions of Section 505.1 are permissive; therefore, any combination of yards that results in the largest increase may be used. In evaluating yard increases for conditions with varying yard widths, the minimum width within each configuration to be checked should be used, but all available yards need not be used. For this example, there are two possible yard configurations that should be checked.

Option 1—Two 44-foot yards (44-foot right side and 100-foot front yard/public way)

(44 feet – 20 feet) × 1^1/$_4$ percent = 30 percent increase

Option 2—Three 30-foot yards (30-foot rear yard, 44-foot right side and 100-foot yard/public way)

(30 feet – 20 feet) × 2^1/$_2$ percent = 25 percent increase

Option 1, the two-yard condition, will permit the greater area increase. Therefore, the maximum allowable floor area per story will be:

8,000 square feet × 1.30 = 10,400 square feet > 10,200 (Type V-N O.K.)

Application Example 505-4

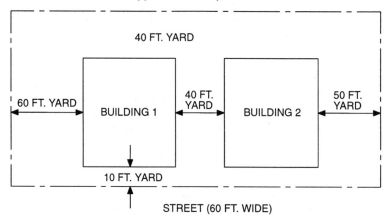

For **SI:** 1 foot = 304.8 mm, 1 square foot = 0.093 m^2.

AREA INCREASES FOR OPEN SPACES

FIGURE 505-4

GIVEN: BUILDING 1   Group B Occupancy
Type III-N Construction
One Story

          BUILDING 2   Group B Occupancy
Type V-N Construction
One Story

DETERMINE: Maximum allowable floor area for each building.

SOLUTION: Since both buildings are located on the same lot, both buildings may use the 40-foot yard that separates them for area increases. As a result, each building may use four 40-foot yards for area increase.

Building 1—Basic allowable area for a Group B Occupancy of Type III-N construction (Table 5-B) is 12,000 square feet [(40 feet – 20 feet) × 5 percent = 100 percent increase].

        Allowable Area = 12,000 square feet × 2.0 = 24,000 square feet

Building 2—Basic allowable area for a Group B Occupancy of Type V-N construction (Table 5-B) is 8,000 square feet [(40 feet – 20 feet) × 5 percent = 100 percent increase].

        Allowable Area = 8,000 square feet × 2.0 = 16,000 square feet

Increase = (60 – 20) × 1^1/$_4$ percent = 50 percent = 6,000 square feet (557.4 m^2).

3. Add the increase in area from Step 2 to the basic area determined from Step 1. Area = 12,000 + 6,000 = 18,000 square feet (1114.8 + 557.4 = 1672 m^2).

4. Multiply the area for Step 3 by 3 for the single-story condition. Area = 18,000 × 3 = 54,000 square feet (1672.2 × 3 = 5016.6 m^2). This is the maximum allowable area for any single story in the three-story building.

5. Multiply the area from Step 3 by 2 for the multistory condition. Area = 18,000 × 2 = 36,000 square feet (1672.2 × 2 = 3344.4 m^2).

6. Multiply the area determined in Step 5 by 2 in accordance with Section 504.2 for a multistory sprinklered building. Area = 36,000 × 2 = 72,000 square feet (3344.4 × 2 = 6688.8 m^2).

7. The area determined in Step 6 is the total allowable area permitted for the building. Any single story, however, may have an area of 54,000 square feet (5016.6 m^2), provided the area of both stories does not exceed 72,000 square feet (6688.8 m^2).

Once again there are a myriad of situations that can arise involving the determination of the allowable area for a building.[3] Also, as illustrated in Application Example 505-5, the introduction of an area separation wall in a large-area building will result in the loss of a yard on one side for one section of the building. Figures 505-6 and 505-7 present two further examples of the determination of allowable areas.

SECTION 506 — MAXIMUM HEIGHT OF BUILDINGS AND INCREASES

The *Uniform Building Code* limits the maximum height and number of stories for similar reasons as discussed under "Area Limitations." In addition, the higher the building becomes, the more difficult access for firefighting becomes. Furthermore, the time required for the evacuation of the occupants increases, and therefore, the fire resistance of the building should also be increased.

The code presumes that when the height of the highest floor used for human occupancy in Group R, Division 1 Occupancies and Group B office buildings exceeds 75 feet (22 860 mm), the life-safety hazard becomes even greater because most fire de-

Application Example 505-5

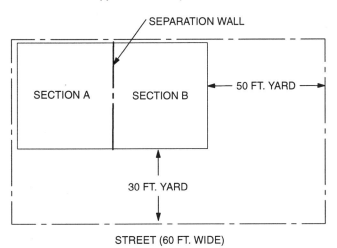

For **SI:** 1 foot = 304.8 mm, 1 square foot = 0.093 m^2.

AREA INCREASES FOR OPEN SPACES

FIGURE 505-5

GIVEN: SECTION A   Group S, Division 3 Occupancy
Type II-N Construction
One Story

SECTION B   Group B Occupancy
Type II-N Construction
One Story

CASE 1   Separation wall is an *occupancy* separation wall.
CASE 2   Separation wall is an *area* separation wall.

DETERMINE: Maximum allowable floor area for Cases 1 and 2.

SOLUTION: *Case 1*—When the two sections are divided by only an occupancy separation wall, the building may be evaluated as one building. This building is bounded on two sides by yards, with the right side having the minimum width of 50 feet. (The front yard/public way combination is 90 feet.) Because Group S, Division 3 and Group B Occupancies have the same allowable area, there is no need to evaluate the building for mixed-occupancy allowable areas as required by Section 504.3.

(50 feet − 20 feet) × 1^1/$_4$ percent = 37^1/$_2$ percent increase

Allowable Area = 12,000 square feet × 1.375 = 16,500 square feet

Case 2—When the separation wall is an area separation wall, each section may be evaluated individually, and Section A would not be eligible for an area increase for open space. This is so because Section 504.6 considers that each portion of a building separated by an area separation wall is a separate building. As a separate building, Sections A and B (read as Buildings A and B) do not reflect similar conditions. Section B is bounded on the right side by a 50-foot-wide yard and at the front by a 90-foot-wide open space consisting of a 30-foot yard and 60-foot street (public way). However, Section A is bounded by open space only at the front. The right side is occupied by another building (Section B).

Section (Building) A—No increases for open space.
Allowable Area = 12,000 square feet

Section (Building) B
(50 feet − 20 feet) × 1^1/$_4$ percent = 37^1/$_2$ percent increase

Allowable Area = 12,000 square feet × 1.375 = 16,500 square feet

partments are unable to adequately fight a fire above this elevation from the outside. Furthermore, the evacuation of occupants from the building is generally not feasible. Thus, the code in Section 403 prescribes special provisions for these high-rise buildings.

Coming back to this section, the code specifies in Table 5-B the maximum height in feet (mm) for each different type of construction and further specifies the maximum number of stories for each occupancy. In general, the greater the potential fire- and life-safety hazard, the lower the permitted overall height in feet (mm) as well as the fewer number of stories permitted. Excep-

tions to Table 5-B are provided for towers, spires and steeples, and one-story aircraft hangars and building used for manufacture of aircraft. This latter exception provides for unlimited height in a similar fashion as provided for unlimited area in Section 505.2.

In Section 302.1, the code provides for multistory buildings containing more than one occupancy. This section states that "an occupancy shall not be located above the story or height set forth in Table 5-B, except as provided in Section 506." This reference to Section 506 has been inserted to let the code user know that a one-story increase is permitted under certain conditions.

I. Given a building as follows:
   A. Medical offices—group B occupancy
   B. Type V-N construction
   C. One yard, 60 feet wide, and a 60-foot-wide street
   D. Automatic fire sprinklers
   E. Two stories

II. Find allowable area

III. Solution:

Basic Allowable: 8,000 sq. ft. . . . . Table 5-B

Increase for yards:
50 percent (8,000)   <u>4,000 sq. ft.</u> . . . . Sec. 505.1.1
             Subtotal: 12,000 sq. ft.

Multistory: 2 × 12,000 = 24,000 sq. ft. . . . . Sec. 504.2
Sprinklers: 2 × 24,000 = 48,000 sq. ft. . . . . Sec. 504.2

Simplified solution:

8,000 × 1.50 × 2 = 24,000 sq. ft.
(Table 5-B) (yards and multistory)

2 × 24,000 = 48,000 sq. ft. (total) (sprinklers)

For **SI:** 1 foot = 304.8 mm, 1 square foot = 0.093 m^2.

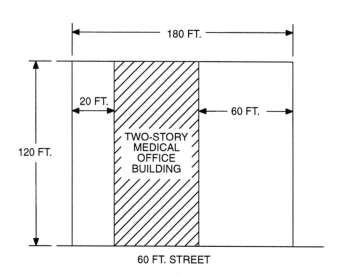

**DETERMINING ALLOWABLE AREA INCREASES
FOR YARDS AND SPRINKLER PROTECTION**

FIGURE 505-6

I. GIVEN:
   A TWO-STORY APARTMENT HOUSE OF TYPE V-N CONSTRUCTION. THE BUILDING IS PROVIDED WITH ONE 30-FOOT YARD AND ONE 40-FOOT STREET.
II. DETERMINE THE TOTAL ALLOWABLE FLOOR AREA.
III. SOLUTION:
   BASIC ALLOWABLE: 6,000 SQ. FT. . . . . Table 5-B
   MULTISTORY INCREASE: 6,000 × 2 = 12,000 SQ. FT. . . . . SEC. 504.2
   YARD INCREASE: (30 − 20) × 0.0125 = 12.5%
                      12,000 × 1.125 = 13,500 SQ. FT. . . . . SEC. 505.1.1
   ALLOWABLE AREA FOR THE FIRST STORY:
                      6,000 × 1.125 = 6,750 SQ. FT. . . . . SEC. 504.2
   HOWEVER, TABLE 5-B, FOOTNOTE 9, AND SECTION 310.2.2 STATE THAT IF THE SECOND FLOOR OF A GROUP R, DIVISION 1 OCCUPANCY HAS AN AREA OF GREATER THAN 3,000 SQUARE FEET, THE ENTIRE BUILDING SHALL BE OF TYPE V ONE-HOUR CONSTRUCTION.
   ∴ THE TOTAL ALLOWABLE AREA FOR TYPE V-N CONSTRUCTION
   = 6,750 + 3,000 = 9,750 SQ. FT.

For **SI:**   1 foot = 304.8 mm, 1 square foot = 0.093 m^2.

**DETERMINING ALLOWABLE AREAS
GROUP R, DIVISION 1 OCCUPANCY**

FIGURE 505-7

The code permits an increase of one story in the number of stories where the building is provided with an automatic fire sprinkler system throughout. This increase, based on an automatic fire sprinkler's system being installed throughout, applies *only* to an increase by one in the number of stories and does not permit an increase of the height limit in feet (mm).

The increase by one permitted in the number of stories where the building is provided with an automatic fire sprinkler system throughout does not apply when the systems are installed under one of the following provisions:

1. To increase the allowable area.

2. To substitute for one-hour fire-resistive construction.

3. Buildings with atria.

4. Group H, Divisions 1, 2, 3, 6 and 7 Occupancies.

5. Group I, Divisions 1.1 and 1.2 Occupancies used for hospitals, nursing homes or health-care centers that are of other than Type II One-hour, III One-hour, IV or V One-hour construction.

This is based on a rationale similar to the provisions for allowable area increases described in the prior discussion for floor area increases for automatic fire sprinklers. The increase by one in the number of stories also applies to the conditions outlined in Section 302.1 for a mixed occupancy. In other words, the maximum level that a particular occupancy may occupy in a mixed-occupancy building as specified in the second paragraph of Section 302.1 may also be increased by one story due to automatic sprinklers.

SECTION 507 — MEZZANINES

A mezzanine as defined in Chapter 2 is an intermediate floor placed within a room.[4] As long as the area of the mezzanine floor is limited to some extent (the code limits the area of a mezzanine to one-third that of the room in which it is located), an intermediate floor without enclosure causes no significant safety hazard. The occupants of the mezzanine by means of sight, smell or hearing will be able to determine if there is some emergency or fire that takes place either on the mezzanine or in the room in which the mezzanine is located. However, once portions or all of the mezzanine are enclosed, or the mezzanine exceeds one-third the area of the room in which it is located, life-safety problems such as not being aware of an emergency or finding a safe exit route from the mezzanine become important. Therefore, the code places the restrictions encompassed in this section on mezzanines to ameliorate the life-safety hazards that can be created by large and enclosed mezzanines. Also, by virtue of the conditions placed on mezzanines in this section, a mezzanine is not considered to be an additional story.

In keeping with the concept of openness and limited area, the code establishes the following conditions:

1. This first condition is in reality a set of three conditions:

   - The construction of the mezzanine shall be consistent with the requirements for the type of construction in which the mezzanine is located. For example, a mezzanine in a Type I building would be constructed with a floor of noncombustible construction, while a mezzanine in a Type V building could be constructed of wood.

   - The fire-resistive rating need be no greater than one hour for unenclosed mezzanines.

   - There must be a minimum clear height above and below the mezzanine floor construction of 7 feet (2134 mm).

2. Mezzanines are limited to two levels within any given room. However, there is no limitation on the number of separate mezzanines within a room as long as the total area complies with Item 3. See Figure 507-1.

3. The total area of all mezzanines within a room must not exceed one-third the area of the room in which they are located. See Figure 507-2.

4. The mezzanine must be open to the room in which it is located, and any side that opens to the room will be considered open if it is unobstructed except for columns, posts and protective walls or railings not more than 44 inches (1118 mm) in height. Figure 507-3 illustrates this requirement. There are, however, three exceptions to the requirement for openness that may result in some small mezzanines being completely enclosed:

   - The first exception is divided into two provisions. As illustrated in Figure 507-3, 10 percent of the mezzanine area may be enclosed. This is usually done for toilet rooms, closets, utility rooms and other similar uses that must, of necessity, be enclosed. As long as the aggregate area does not exceed 10 percent of the area of the mezzanine, the enclosure is permitted by the code.

     The second provision is also illustrated in Figure 507-3. In this case, the criterion is that the enclosed area contain an occupant load that does not exceed 10. As this criterion governs over the 10-percent-of-floor-area rule if it results in a greater area, it may result in an entire mezzanine's being enclosed, as shown in Figure 507-3.

   - As shown in the top figure in Figure 507-4, a mezzanine may be enclosed if it has two means of egress, one of which gives direct access to the exit components indicated on the drawing. Although the drawing shows the second means of egress to an adjacent room, the second means of egress could just as well be a stairway down into the room in which the mezzanine is located.

   - Mezzanines used for control equipment in industrial buildings may be glazed on all sides. This exception is necessary due to the delicate nature of much of today's control equipment and the fact that it may require a dust-free environment.

5. Two means of egress from the mezzanine must be provided when required by Table 10-A.

6. Understandably, the code requires that the occupant load of the mezzanine be added to the occupant load of the story or room into which any required means of egress enters.

Historically, the UBC has permitted mezzanine floors (the original concept of a mezzanine was a floor only) to be of wood or unprotected steel in all buildings since the 1927 edition and up to the 1982 edition. In Type I buildings (the only fire-resistive noncombustible type in early years), only two mezzanines were permitted with an aggregate area of one-third the area of the room in which the mezzanines were located. These provisions were in a section with the sidehead "Combustible Materials Regulated," and, further, the early codes provided that the limitations on number and area of mezzanines were mandatory if they were to be of wood or unprotected steel. Thus, the one-third area limitation is in part a holdover from early editions of the UBC, which permitted wood and unprotected steel mezzanines; thus, the intent was to limit combustible materials and unprotected steel in Type I buildings.

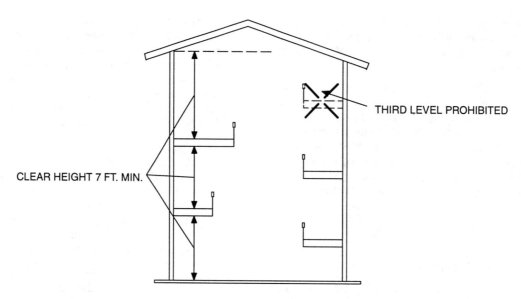

THIRD LEVEL PROHIBITED

CLEAR HEIGHT 7 FT. MIN.

NO MORE THAN TWO MEZZANINE LEVELS PERMITTED; HOWEVER, NO LIMIT
ON THE NUMBER OF MEZZANINES AS LONG AS FLOOR AREA LIMITS ARE MET.

For **SI:** 1 foot = 304.8 mm.

MEZZANINE LEVELS

FIGURE 507-1

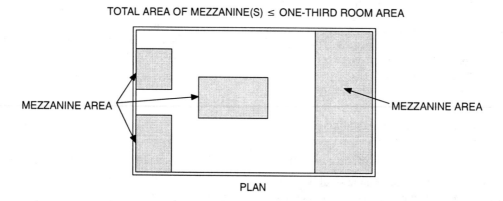

TOTAL AREA OF MEZZANINE(S) ≤ ONE-THIRD ROOM AREA

MEZZANINE AREA

MEZZANINE AREA

PLAN

MEZZANINE AREA

FIGURE 507-2

SECTION 508 — FIRE-RESISTIVE SUBSTITUTION

In this section the UBC permits, for Types II One-hour, III One-hour and V One-hour buildings, the substitution of an automatic fire sprinkler system throughout for the one-hour fire-resistive construction, provided the sprinkler system is not otherwise required throughout the building. Although an automatic fire sprinkler system may be substituted for one-hour construction, the code lists 10 specific instances where the substitution may not waive or reduce the required fire-resistive construction.

These 10 listed items represent specific fire-resistive requirements to counter specific hazards, while on the other hand the one-hour fire-resistive construction required for Types II One-hour, III One-hour and V One-hour buildings applies gen-

erally to the entire building. Thus, in accordance with the third paragraph of Section 101.3 of the code, the specific requirements outlined by the enumerated items in this section take precedence and require that the fire resistance not be reduced in these cases. This rationale is consistent with other provisions of the code that would not permit, for example, a reduction in the fire-resistive construction for these enumerated items in a Type I or Type II-F.R. building that has an automatic fire sprinkler system installed throughout.

There is a key word in this section that should be noted. That word is "throughout." The section allows fire sprinkler substitution when the system is not required *throughout* a building by other sections of the code. As an example, Section 904.2.3.1 requires that an automatic fire sprinkler system be installed in

(Continued on page 94)

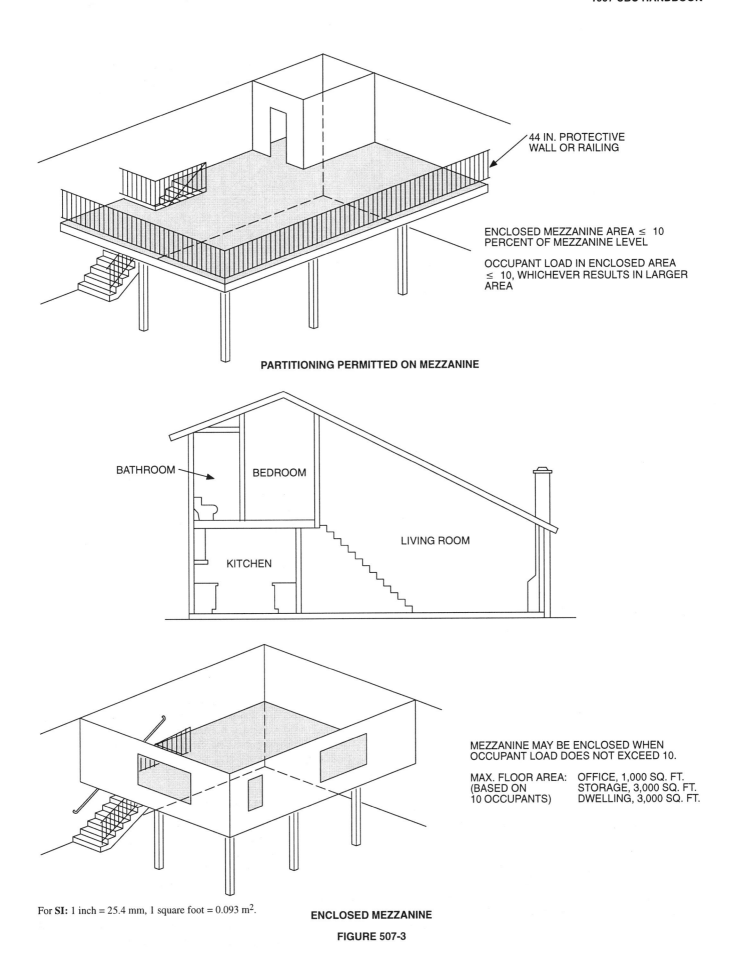

44 IN. PROTECTIVE
WALL OR RAILING

ENCLOSED MEZZANINE AREA ≤ 10
PERCENT OF MEZZANINE LEVEL

OCCUPANT LOAD IN ENCLOSED AREA
≤ 10, WHICHEVER RESULTS IN LARGER
AREA

PARTITIONING PERMITTED ON MEZZANINE

BATHROOM

BEDROOM

LIVING ROOM

KITCHEN

MEZZANINE MAY BE ENCLOSED WHEN
OCCUPANT LOAD DOES NOT EXCEED 10.

MAX. FLOOR AREA: OFFICE, 1,000 SQ. FT.
(BASED ON   STORAGE, 3,000 SQ. FT.
10 OCCUPANTS)   DWELLING, 3,000 SQ. FT.

For **SI:** 1 inch = 25.4 mm, 1 square foot = 0.093 m^2.

ENCLOSED MEZZANINE

FIGURE 507-3

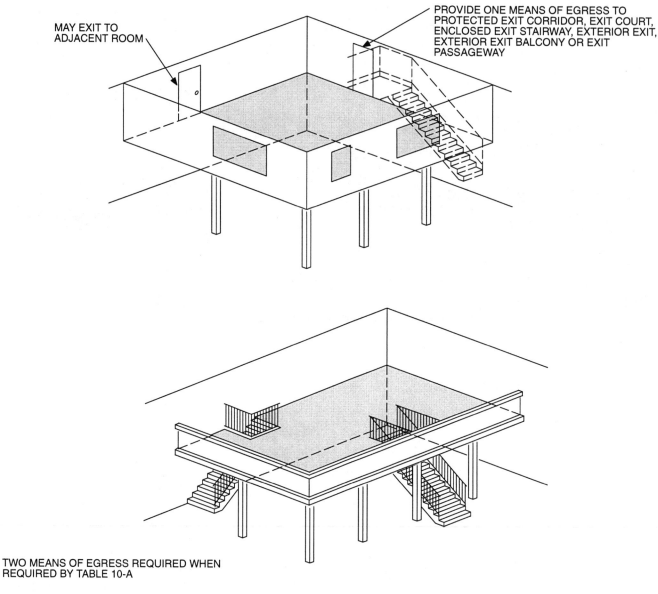

MAY EXIT TO
ADJACENT ROOM

PROVIDE ONE MEANS OF EGRESS TO
PROTECTED EXIT CORRIDOR, EXIT COURT,
ENCLOSED EXIT STAIRWAY, EXTERIOR EXIT,
EXTERIOR EXIT BALCONY OR EXIT
PASSAGEWAY

TWO MEANS OF EGRESS REQUIRED WHEN
REQUIRED BY TABLE 10-A

MEZZANINE EXITS

FIGURE 507-4

(Continued from page 92)

drinking establishments having an area exceeding 5,000 square feet (465 m²). If such a drinking establishment were situated in one corner of a retail sales building that was otherwise not required to be sprinklered, then an automatic sprinkler system installed throughout the complex could substitute for one-hour construction. This is because the provisions of Section 904.2.3.1 do not require sprinklers to be installed throughout the building in which the drinking establishment is located.

In the final analysis, the UBC intends through this section that a building utilizing the automatic fire sprinkler system as a substitution for one-hour fire-resistive construction may still be classified as a Type II One-hour, Type III One-hour or Type V One-hour building. When fire sprinklers are used for one-hour substitution, an increase in area due to the presence of the automatic sprinkler system is not permitted. An automatic sprinkler system may not be used to both increase the area and eliminate the one-hour fire-resistive construction, but one or the other use

may be selected, at the designer's option. When there is no requirement that fire sprinklers be installed, it is generally more advantageous to classify the building as nonrated and use the area increases permitted by Section 505.3. See Application Example 508-1.

SECTION 509 — GUARDRAILS

In this section, the code provides for guardrail protection for unenclosed floor and roof openings, open and glazed sides of stairways, landings and ramps, and porches, which are more than 30 inches (762 mm) above grade or a floor or other surface below. Also, the protection is required for roofs that are used other than for service of the building and thus are subject to use by individuals walking on the roof. The need for guardrails in these circumstances is evident, although the arbitrary limit of 30 inches (762 mm) above grade or floor below is subject to con-

Application Example 508-1

GIVEN: One-story building of Type V-N construction with an automatic fire-sprinkler system installed throughout. The building has no yards.

DETERMINE: Maximum allowable floor area for the building housing either a Group B Occupancy or a Group A, Division 2.1 Occupancy.

SOLUTION: *Case I*—Group B Occupancy:

The building can be evaluated with the automatic fire sprinklers used either to increase area according to Section 505.3 or to substitute for one-hour construction according to Section 508, thus upgrading the construction from Type V-N to Type V One-hour.

A. Section 505.3. Basic allowable area according to Table 5-B is 8,000 square feet for Type V-N construction.
   Allowable Area = 8,000 x 3 = 24,000 square feet.

B. Section 508. Basic allowable area according to Table 5-B is 14,000 square feet for Type V One-hour. Obviously, it is more advantageous to use the provisions of Section 505.3.

Case II—Group A, Division 2.1 Occupancy:

Referring to Table 5-B, it is seen that a Group A, Division 2.1 Occupancy is not permitted to be of Type V-N construction. Thus, the automatic fire-sprinkler system must be used as a substitute for one-hour construction in order for the building to qualify as Type V One-hour construction. The allowable area for this type of construction is 10,500 square feet housing a Group A, Division 2.1 Occupancy.

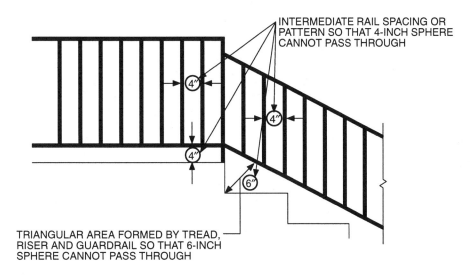

For **SI:** 1 inch = 25.4 mm.

GUARDRAILS

FIGURE 509-1

jecture. Nevertheless, in the case of the UBC, it is assumed that the height of 30 inches (762 mm) does not create a significant safety hazard.[5]

The guardrail must be of adequate height to prevent someone from falling over the edge of the protected areas and be designed to prevent someone, including small children, from falling through under the top rail. Therefore, the code establishes 42 inches (1067 mm) as the minimum height that is recognized nationally as the proper height for guardrail protection. The code also requires that for open-type rails, intermediate members be provided so that a sphere 4 inches (102 mm) in diameter cannot pass through between the intermediate members, a requirement that prevents small children from falling through the guardrail assembly. See Figure 509-1. The code also lessens the height for open sides of stairs; they may be protected with a guardrail having a height the same as for stair railings as provided for in Section 1003.3.3.7. There are several more exceptions to the requirements for guardrails, as follows:

- Guardrails are not required on the loading side of docks or along vehicle service pits not accessible to the public for obvious reasons.

- Guardrails are required to be only 36 inches (914 mm) high in dwellings, Group U Occupancies, and within individual apartments or guest rooms in Group R, Division 1 Occupancies. This lower height is based on the good experience that has been exhibited in these uses; for several decades, the guardrail height in them has been no higher than 36 inches (914 mm).

- In commercial and industrial uses where the public is not invited (therefore, the guardrail is not subject to small children falling through), guardrails may have intermediate members spaced so that a 12-inch (305 mm) diameter sphere cannot pass through.

- In order to provide for proper viewing in theaters, a guardrail in front of the first row of fixed seats, and which is not at the end of an aisle, may be 26 inches (660 mm) in height.

- A new provision in the 1997 code requires 26-inch-high (660 mm) guardrails between aisles parallel to seats (cross aisles) and the adjacent floor or grade below where an elevation change of 30 inches (762 mm) or less occurs. An exception exists where the backs of seats on the front

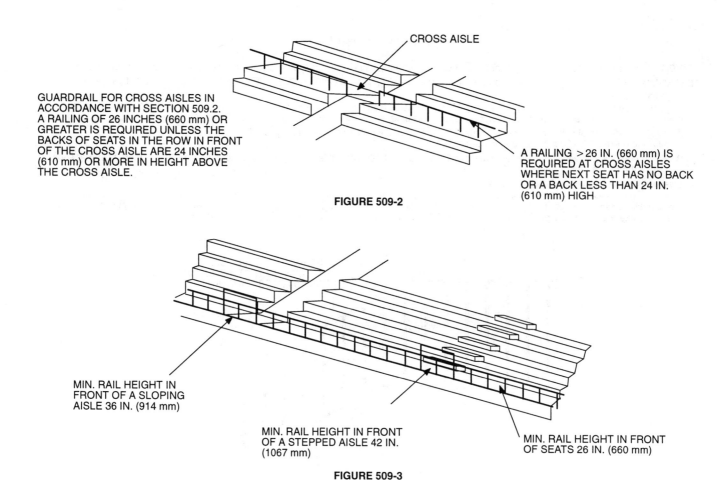

GUARDRAIL FOR CROSS AISLES IN ACCORDANCE WITH SECTION 509.2. A RAILING OF 26 INCHES (660 mm) OR GREATER IS REQUIRED UNLESS THE BACKS OF SEATS IN THE ROW IN FRONT OF THE CROSS AISLE ARE 24 INCHES (610 mm) OR MORE IN HEIGHT ABOVE THE CROSS AISLE.

CROSS AISLE

A RAILING > 26 IN. (660 mm) IS REQUIRED AT CROSS AISLES WHERE NEXT SEAT HAS NO BACK OR A BACK LESS THAN 24 IN. (610 mm) HIGH

FIGURE 509-2

MIN. RAIL HEIGHT IN FRONT OF A SLOPING AISLE 36 IN. (914 mm)

MIN. RAIL HEIGHT IN FRONT OF A STEPPED AISLE 42 IN. (1067 mm)

MIN. RAIL HEIGHT IN FRONT OF SEATS 26 IN. (660 mm)

FIGURE 509-3

of the cross aisle project 24 inches (610 mm) or more above the adjacent floor of the aisle. See Figure 509-2.

- To protect occupants using the aisle, guardrails with a minimum height of 42 inches (1067 mm) are required at the end of stepped aisles terminating at the fascia of boxes, balconies and galleries, and shall extend for the full width of the aisle. For sloping aisles, the minimum required rail height is 36 inches (914 mm). See Figure 509-3.

- Again for obvious reasons, guardrails are not required on the auditorium side of a stage or enclosed platform.

TABLE 5-A — EXTERIOR WALL AND OPENING PROTECTION BASED ON LOCATION ON PROPERTY FOR ALL CONSTRUCTION TYPES

In all tables in the UBC, the footnotes contain important modifications and exceptions to the tabulations and are worthy of study each time the tables are used. Footnote 5 to this table is worth noting in particular, as it specifies that openings in exterior walls required to be protected shall be protected with a fire assembly having a three-fourths-hour fire-protection rating.

Footnote 6, which was previously in the 1991 UBC, is re-introduced in the 1997 code.

TABLE 5-B — BASIC ALLOWABLE BUILDING HEIGHTS AND BASIC ALLOWABLE FLOOR AREA FOR BUILDINGS ONE STORY IN HEIGHT

Footnote 9 to Table 5-B is referenced for the Group R, Division 1 Occupancy in the column identifying nonrated construction such as Types II-N, III-N and V-N. By this footnote the code calls the attention of the code user to the special provisions in Section 310.2 that the total area of the building above the first story is limited to 3,000 square feet (279 m²) unless the building is of one-hour fire-resistive construction throughout. Section 601.5.2.2 provides exceptions to this rule and will be discussed later. The purpose of this footnote is to call attention to the fact that there is another provision in the code that limits area in addition to this table. Footnote 10 was added to limit the maximum building height of Group I, Division 1.1 Occupancies to 75 feet (22 860 mm) in Type II F.R. buildings and 45 feet (13 716 mm) in Type II, One-hour buildings. This revision, based on BCMC reports issued in 1990, provides a maximum height for the allowed number of stories to assist in facilitating emergency operations and to reduce the risk associated with building heights.

REFERENCES

[1]Boring, Delbert F., James C. Spence and Walter G. Wells (1981). *Fire Protection through Modern Building Codes*, Fifth Edition. American Iron and Steel Institute, Washington, D.C.

[2]Sheedy, Paul (1982). Area separation walls revisited. *Building Standards,* 51(5):12-20.

[3]International Conference of Building Officials (1991). *Uniform Building Code Interpretation Manual*. Whittier, California.

[4]International Conference of Building Officials (1991). *Plan Review Manual.* Whittier, California, Section 9.6.

[5]Sheedy, Paul (1985). Stair railings. *Building Standards,* 54(2):4-9.

Chapter 6

TYPES OF CONSTRUCTION

SECTION 601 — CLASSIFICATION OF ALL BUILDINGS BY TYPES OF CONSTRUCTION AND GENERAL REQUIREMENTS

As its title implies, this section not only develops provisions for classification of buildings by types of construction but also contains general requirements for construction that are applicable to all types.

The *Uniform Building Code* is unique in that from its first edition in 1927 to the present, it has regulated buildings by types of construction as well as by occupancy classifications. To quote Section 1701 of the 1927 edition: "The various Types of Construction herein specified represent varying degrees of public safety and resistance to fire."[1] The 1927 code also stated in Section 1702 that "all buildings for the purpose of this Code shall be divided into the following Types of Construction based upon their resistance to fire, and for the purpose of this Code Type I shall be deemed to be the most fire-resistive and Type V the least fire-resistive Type of Construction." Therein followed the description of five types of construction that are somewhat different than those described in the present edition. The current UBC, however, follows the same concept of the highest type of construction being Type I and the lowest type of construction being Type V.*

Even in the 1927 edition, the fire protection required for the various types of construction is based on hourly fire-endurance ratings as established by the American Society for Testing and Materials (ASTM). The 1927 *Uniform Building Code* was the first major building code to adopt this system of hourly fire-endurance ratings. Other building codes established fire-resistance requirements by specifying the type and thickness of materials used.

Many of the concepts embodied in the 1927 edition of the *Uniform Building Code* that have carried over to today were developed from the reports issued by the committee known as the Department of Commerce Building Code Committee, which was appointed by Herbert Hoover, then Secretary of Commerce.[2,3] The committee was also dubbed the "Little Hoover Commission" and was appointed to investigate building codes. This was an outgrowth of the findings of the Senate Committee on Reconstruction and Production, which was appointed in 1920 to study the various factors entering into the recovery of our economy from the depression of the early 1920s. While the committee studied a wide-ranging set of those institutions and groups affected by the economy, it was also especially interested in construction. During its tenure, the committee held numerous hearings and expressed the following sentiment at their conclusion: "The building codes of this country have not been developed on scientific data but rather on compromise; they are not uniform in practice and in many instances involve an additional cost of construction without assuring more useful or more durable buildings."[4] Thus, the stage was set for improvement in building regulations, and the timing was especially favorable for the 1927 edition of the UBC to take advantage of the reports of the Department of Commerce Building Code Committee.

The *Uniform Building Code* classifies construction into five types, and as indicated earlier in this handbook, they are listed in descending order from the most fire resistive to the least fire resistive. These five types are further divided into two main groupings. These are noncombustible construction (Types I and II) and combustible construction (Types III, IV and V). It will be noted that the various types of construction within these two main groupings are further subdivided as fire resistive, protected and unprotected. These subdivisions, based on combustibility of construction and fire protection, may be represented as follows:

- Noncombustible, fire resistive.
  Types I and II-F.R. construction.
- Noncombustible, protected.
  Type II One-hour construction.
- Noncombustible, unprotected.
  Type II-N** construction.
- Combustible, protected.
  Types III One-hour, IV and V One-hour construction.
- Combustible, unprotected.
  Types III-N and V-N construction.

A perusal of UBC Table 5-B will show the reader that the UBC considers Types II, III and IV buildings (except for Type II-F.R.) to be of comparable protection. For example, Types II One-hour, III One-hour and IV are permitted the same areas and heights. The same is also true for Types II-N and III-N.

601.1 General. In similar manner as in Section 301, Section 601.1 also charges the building official:

1. To classify all buildings within the jurisdiction into one of the types of construction set forth in Table 6-A.
2. To classify a building that does not entirely conform to a type of construction outlined in Table 6-A into a type having an equal or lesser degree of fire resistance.

This second duty imposed on the building official grants the building official liberal authority to use judgment in the determination of the characteristics of the construction so as to classify it into the proper type of construction. The building official may find, for example, that a proposed building may have fire-resistive features that resemble a Type I building except that the floor assemblies and roof-ceiling assembly are all of one-hour

---

*Prior to the 1994 edition, the general type of construction requirements appeared in Chapter 17 with requirements for each specific type of construction being addressed in Chapters 18 through 22. The 1994 edition of the UBC placed both the general and specific types of construction requirements in Chapter 6.

**"N" denotes that there are no general requirements for fire resistance (may be unprotected).

fire-resistive construction. After evaluating the various construction features and fire-endurance ratings for the components of the building, the building official would classify the building as a Type II One-hour building and might be tempted to classify the building as a Type II-F.R. building because of the three-hour fire-resistive protection for the structural frame. However, the deficiency in fire-resistive ratings for the floor assemblies is such that it should be classified as a Type II One-hour building— even though some features are in excess of the requirements for Type II One-hour construction.

The *Uniform Building Code* intends, as expressed in the scope, that the provisions of the code are minimum standards. Thus, the second paragraph of this section directs that buildings not be required to conform to the requirements for a type of construction higher than the type that meets the minimum requirements of this code based on occupancy. A fairly common case in this regard is where a developer may construct industrial buildings that comply in most respects to the requirements of the code for a Type III-N building, but the occupancy requirements are such that a Type V-N building would meet the requirements of the code. In this latter case, it would be clearly inappropriate and, in fact, a violation of the code for the building official to require compliance with requirements for a Type III-N building. However, where the building does comply in all respects to Type III-N, the building official may so classify it.

This section also permits alternate materials, types of construction or fire-resistive protection that provide equal or greater public safety than those specifically outlined in the code.

601.2 Mixed Types of Construction. This section addresses the separate building concept with which portions of a building may be separated by area separation walls. In this case, the code intends that buildings so divided be considered separate buildings insofar as type of construction is concerned. On the other hand, where there is no such separation, the area of the entire building will be limited in accordance with the least type of construction.

601.4 Structural Frame. This section defines what is considered to be a part of the structural frame. This consists of the columns and all of the horizontal floor and roof girders and roof trusses which frame into the columns and bracing members designed to carry gravity loads. Any horizontal floor and roof members that do not frame into the columns but frame into other girders or trusses are not considered part of the structural frame and are secondary members.

Lateral force bracing in the exterior wall or in the interior of the building is not considered to be part of the structural frame where the bracing serves no other purpose but to resist the lateral loads. In this case, lateral load bracing in the exterior walls would be protected in accordance with Tables 5-A and 6-A by the exterior nonbearing walls.

In the case of the secondary members in the floor and roof assemblies, the protection required would be protected the same as required in Table 6-A by the floor or roof assemblies.

Table 6-A. This table provides the basic fire-resistive requirements for the various types of construction. It also delineates those fire-resistive ratings required to qualify for a particular type of construction. As discussed above, even though a building may have some features that conform to a higher type of construction, the building shall not be required to conform to that higher type of construction as long as a lower type will meet the minimum requirements of the code based on occupancy. Nevertheless, any building must comply with all the basic fire-resistive requirements in this table if it is indeed the intent to classify it for that particular type of construction.

As stated, this table provides the basic fire-resistive requirements for the various types of construction. Section 601.5 should be consulted for any exceptions. In this respect, Section 503.4 also contains important exceptions.

Footnote 1 to the table provides that structural frame elements in the exterior wall must be protected from external fire exposure as required for the structural frame or for exterior bearing walls, whichever requires the greater fire resistance. The intent is that the structural frame should never have a lower fire rating than that required in either Table 5-A or 6-A to protect the frame from internal fires. Nevertheless, if the exposure hazard from an external source is so great as to require a rating for exterior bearing walls higher than that required by Table 6-A for the structural frame, the higher rating must be provided for the frame. For example, if a Type I building housing a Group B Occupancy is so situated on the property that a two-hour fire-resistive bearing wall would be permitted, the structural frame would then be required to have three-hour fire-resistive protection. In this case, the internal fire exposure to the frame is greater than that from the exterior. On the other hand, if the building were situated closer to a property line so that protection of openings is required—for example, within 5 feet (1524 mm)—the external fire exposure becomes the more severe criterion, and a four-hour noncombustible bearing wall would be required; thus, four-hour fire-resistive protection for the structural frame elements in the exterior wall would also be required.

601.5 Exceptions to Table 6-A. This section, in addition to providing exceptions to Table 6-A, also provides exceptions to the construction requirements specified in Chapter 3 and Sections 602 through 606. As these provisions are exceptions, they are not basic requirements of the code.

Section 601.5.2.1 addresses the subject of exceptions to the fire-resistive requirement for fixed partitions in stores and offices or other similar places occupied by one tenant only. The key words in this item are "occupied by one tenant only." It is the intent of the UBC that this expression applies to an area or a building which is under the complete control of one person, organization or other occupant. This would be contrasted to multiple-tenant occupancies where an area would be under the control of two or more individuals, companies or occupants.

A multistory building owned by a large company would also qualify as being occupied by one tenant only if the large company that owned the building also completely occupied the building. A government office building owned by a city or county occupied by several departments of the government would also be considered as occupied by one tenant only. If the government office building contained an assembly room, the assembly room itself would not qualify for the exceptions listed in Section 601.5.2.1. These exceptions apply only to stores, offices and similar uses.

The intent of these provisions is to provide exceptions to the construction requirements not only in Table 6-A but also found in Chapter 3 and Sections 602 through 606. Thus, one of the four types of partitions listed in Section 601.5.2.1 could be constructed regardless of other code sections regulating the construction of partitions. For example, a one-hour fire-resistive combustible partition constructed of ordinary wood studs would be permitted to be installed in a Type I building in accordance with the provisions of this section.

These provisions are based on the common practice in offices and stores to create large open areas. When subdivided, low-height partitions are utilized. Sometimes a few areas are completely partitioned off with full ceiling-height partitions in order to provide privacy or security for storage, etc. As these partitions are subject to being moved almost continually, the code permits these exceptions to the general construction requirements of the code.

Except for the three-fourths-room-height light-wood partitions, the other partitions do provide some type of barrier to the spread of fire. In the case of the three-fourths-room-height light-wood partition, the concept is that being only three-fourths of the room height, persons in one portion of the area are aware of what is going on in the other portions, and if a fire develops, the occupants would be aware of that fact and take appropriate action.

The exceptions for hotels and apartments in Section 601.5.2.2 are intended to provide a complete separation between each dwelling unit or guest room or suite and the remainder of the building so that an effective compartment is created. On this basis, the exceptions for the interior nonload-bearing partitions within the dwelling units, guest rooms or suites do not significantly reduce life safety, as they are still of such construction as to provide a reasonable barrier to fire within each unit.

These exceptions are based on the concept of protecting an individual or family from possible hazardous practices (such as smoking in bed) of other occupants in the building.

Section 601.5.3 provides for the installation of folding, portable or movable partitions without a fire-resistive rating in buildings where such a rating would otherwise be required. The conditions of this exception ensure that the partitions will not be used to establish an exit corridor, will not block required exits or exit-access doors, will be restricted in location by tracks or other permanent guides, and will have flame spread limited as set forth in Table 8-B.

These exceptions permit flexibility of use, particularly in assembly uses. As the combustible loading in assembly uses is extremely low, the exceptions permitting the use of these folding partitions do not reduce life safety to any degree.

Section 601.5.4 provides exceptions for certain elements of exterior walls fronting on streets or yards having a minimum width of 40 feet (12 192 mm). These reductions apply to all construction types and fire-resistive ratings and are granted because the required open spaces reduce exposure hazard and because only a limited amount of combustible materials at a restricted height are allowed in the wall construction.

In addition to Section 601.5.4, other code sections also permit the use of combustible construction for otherwise noncombustible buildings. For example, Section 2602.5.2 permits the use of wall assemblies employing foam plastic insulation in or on the exterior walls.

The exceptions in Section 601.5.5 for trim are based on the concept of permitting very limited amounts of combustible materials and, in the case of foam plastics, limiting the flame spread to no greater than 75.

Section 601.5.6 permits exterior loading platforms of either noncombustible materials or heavy timber construction, and the code further specifies that the wood construction shall not be carried through the exterior walls to the interior of the building. This exception is based on the fact that when a loading dock is exterior and separated from the interior of the building by exterior walls, and the material is required to be either noncombustible or heavy timber, the hazard is quite low.

Section 601.5.7 allows the use of combustible insulation boards under the finished flooring. The key words here are "finished flooring." Since the code allows the finished flooring itself to be combustible, even in Type I or Type II-F.R. construction, and since Item 6 of Section 708.2.1 regulates how this flooring must be installed, allowing the use of combustible insulation is reasonable.

Section 601.5.8 establishes construction requirements for interior nonload-bearing partitions within health-care suites that comply with the new requirements of Section 1007.5.

Exterior walls. Before discussing specific requirements for each of the five basic construction types, it is very important that the fire-resistive requirements for exterior walls is discussed.

Chapter 5, via Table 5-A, establishes fire-resistive ratings for exterior walls based on location on property. Chapter 6, via Table 6-A, establishes fire-resistive ratings for exterior walls based on types of construction. Because of major revisions that occurred with the 1994 edition, the exterior wall requirements set forth in Table 6-A do not seem to allow any exceptions like those found in the 1991 UBC. However, exterior walls, both bearing and nonbearing, were intended to be addressed in Table 5-A and Section 503.4. Table 5-A was amended in the 1994 edition so that it lists all exterior wall fire-resistive requirements for all occupancies and construction types and includes the various exceptions that appeared in the -03 sections of Chapters 18, 19, 20 and 21 of the 1991 UBC and earlier editions. It is recommended that, to avoid confusion and possible mistakes, Table 5-A, in conjunction with Section 503.4, be used to determine required exterior bearing and nonbearing fire-resistive ratings or opening protection requirements.

SECTION 602 — TYPE I FIRE-RESISTIVE BUILDINGS

Type I buildings are of fire-resistive noncombustible construction. The fire-resistive ratings required for Type I buildings historically have provided about the same protection over the years and, thus, have proved to be satisfactory for occupancies with low to moderate fire loadings, such as office buildings, hotels and retail stores.[5]

Although Type I buildings are defined as noncombustible, even a cursory reading of the UBC will show that combustible materials are permitted in limited quantities. Wood door frames, trim and wall finish are permitted, as well as combustible partitions, insulation and roofing materials. Where these combustibles are properly controlled, they have proved, over the years, to not add significantly to the fire hazard.

602.1 Definition. The code restricts structural elements of Type I buildings to steel, iron, concrete or masonry. Except for those exceptions outlined in Section 601.5, interior permanent partitions and all walls of Type I buildings are required to be of noncombustible fire-resistive construction. However, permanent nonbearing partitions of one-hour or two-hour fire-resistive construction that are not part of a shaft enclosure may be constructed with fire-retardant-treated wood. Nevertheless, the partition still must maintain its required fire-resistive rating.

602.2 Structural Framework. This section, as well as Section 602.1, specifies that the structural elements and the structural framework of Type I buildings are required to be concrete, masonry, or iron or structural steel as defined in Chapters 19, 21 and 22, respectively. Therefore, in addition to requiring that the materials be noncombustible, the UBC further restricts the materials to those listed. Thus, the use of nonferrous metals that are noncombustible is not permitted by the UBC for structural elements.

602.4 Stairway Construction. Here is another case where the code is very specific as to the type of noncombustible materials required for stairs, stair platforms, etc. They must be constructed of reinforced concrete, iron or steel. If an additional finish is provided on stairs, it is limited to brick, marble, tile or hard noncombustible materials. Effective in the 1997 code, an exception to the noncombustible finish requirements for treads and risers exists for stairs not required to be enclosed by Section 1005.3.3. This exception allows the finish material to be of any material, such as carpet, that is permitted by the code.

602.5 Roofs. The provisions of this section are in reality exceptions to the general rule that roofs or roof-ceiling assemblies must be of two-hour fire-resistive construction. This section provides what amounts to three exceptions to the general rule, the second of which is multifaceted:

- The first case covers those situations where the roof and its components are more than 25 feet (7620 mm) above any floor, balcony or gallery. Under these circumstances, the roof and its components may be of unprotected noncombustible construction. However, the structural frame requires protection as required by Table 6-A.

  Except in retail sales and storage areas classified as Groups M and S, Division 1 Occupancies and Group H Occupancies where fire loading is typically higher, this paragraph applies to all other occupancies housed within Type I buildings and is based on the fact that where the roof is more than 25 feet (7620 mm) above the nearest floor, the temperatures at this elevation during most fires are quite low. As a result, fire protection of the roof and its members, except for the structural frame, is omitted. For those occupancies where the fire loading and the consequent potential fire severity is relatively high, such as mercantile or storage uses, the code generally requires an additional means of fire protection, such as an automatic fire sprinkler system. In addition to noncombustible materials, the code also permits heavy-timber members complying with Section 605.6 in the roof construction of one-story buildings without fire protection.

- The second case involves Groups A and E Occupancies and any occupancies within an atrium where every part of the structural framework of the roof is 25 feet (7620 mm) or more above any floor, balcony or gallery. In this case,

fire protection of all members of the roof construction, including those of the structural frame, may be omitted.

The rationale here is very similar to that just discussed in the preceding item, except that the provision is limited to Groups A and E Occupancies and atria, which (except for exhibit halls which require sprinkler protection) have demonstrated very low potential fire severity. The types of structures most commonly using this exception are gymnasiums and sports arenas. Again, the code permits heavy-timber members to be used in lieu of the noncombustible members for one-story buildings. The reason for accepting this reduction for all occupancies within an atrium is also based on the low fire severity expected. This is due to the protection features associated with atria, namely, the sprinkler system and the smoke-control system.

The next paragraph of the code is what amounts to a three-pronged exception within an exception. This case involves one-story Group A, Division 2.1 Occupancies having an occupant load of 10,000 or more. Subject to the conditions itemized, roofs constructed of unprotected noncombustible or heavy-timber members may be less than 25 feet (7620 mm) above any floor balcony or gallery. The limitation to a one-story Group A, Division 2.1 Occupancy provides that the potential fire severity will be low. Although these provisions have general application, they were developed to apply to heavy-timber dome roofs where it would be impractical to provide one-hour fire-resistive construction for that area less than 25 feet (7620 mm) above the floor around the perimeter of the dome. The limitation that only 35 percent of the roof area be less than 25 feet (7620 mm) above any floor, balcony or gallery, plus the requirement for a supervised automatic fire sprinkler system, is considered to offer equivalent protection to that required by the code for roofs less than 25 feet (7620 mm) above the floor.

- This third case also pertains to Groups A and E Occupancies and involves those situations where every part of the structural steel framework of the roof is between 18 and 25 feet (5486 and 7620 mm) above the floor balcony or gallery. Under these circumstances, the protection required for the roof assembly is a ceiling whose fire resistance is equivalent to that required for a one-hour fire-resistive roof-ceiling assembly. Thus, again, the provision relates to occupancies with low fire loading, and the code assumes that the fire-resistive ceiling membrane located no closer than 18 feet (5486 mm) above the floor will provide adequate protection for the roof construction.

SECTION 603 — TYPE II BUILDINGS

Type II buildings are of noncombustible construction and run the gamut from fire-resistive construction (Type II-F.R.) through protected buildings (Type II One-hour) to unprotected construction (Type II-N).

Type II-F.R. construction is very similar to Type I construction except for a reduction of one hour in the required ratings for interior bearing walls, the structural frame and roof-ceiling construction. Thus, and particularly because of the reduction in the fire-resistive rating required for the structural frame, the Type II-

F.R. building does not enjoy the unlimited height and areas that accrue to the Type I building. It will be noted from Table 5-B that Type II-F.R. construction has height and area limits placed on it.

With regard to the Type II-F.R. building, the previous discussion in this handbook for Type I buildings is equally applicable to Type II-F.R. buildings. There are some exceptions to this general rule, and they will be discussed in the specific section in which they occur.

603.1 Definition. Type II One-hour and Type II-N buildings are required by the code to be of noncombustible construction, and in the case of Type II One-hour buildings, they are also required to be of one-hour fire-resistive construction throughout. In the case of Type II One-hour construction, there is an exception for permanent nonbearing partitions that permits the use of fire-retardant-treated wood within the assembly as long as the one-hour fire-resistive rating is maintained.

Although the code is silent regarding the use of fire-retardant-treated wood in permanent partitions in Type II-N buildings, surely they should be permitted if they are of one-hour fire-resistive construction, as for Type II One-hour buildings.

The exceptions in Section 601.5 are equally applicable to Type II buildings.

603.2 Structural Framework. Although there is a difference in language in Section 603.2 from that in Section 602.2, the intent and requirements are the same. That is, the structural framework must and is specifically called out to be as specified in Chapter 19 for concrete, Chapter 21 for masonry and Chapter 22 for iron and steel. Thus, while other structural elements within Type II One-hour and Type II-N buildings may be of any noncombustible materials permitted by the code, the members of the structural frame are limited to those materials specified in Section 603.2. In the case of Type II-F.R. buildings, the requirements are the same as for Type I buildings (i.e., structural elements must also be limited to steel, iron, concrete or masonry).

603.4 Stairway Construction. These provisions depart from those in Section 602.4 only insofar as this section provides that stairs for Type II One-hour and Type II-N buildings shall be of noncombustible construction. In essence, then, any noncombustible materials approved for use by the UBC could be used for stairs rather than the specific itemized materials listed for Type II-F.R. and Type I buildings. The exception for finish materials as allowed on treads and risers is discussed in Section 602.4.

603.5 Roofs. The requirements for Type II-F.R. and Type II One-hour buildings are identical to those for Type I buildings in this section. In the case of Type II-N buildings, the code requires that roofs be of noncombustible construction. Again, this means any noncombustible materials approved for use by the UBC are permitted. However, Section 603.2 requires that the materials of the roof which are part of the structural framework be those specifically itemized in Section 603.2.

SECTION 604 — TYPE III BUILDINGS

The Type III building grew out of the necessity to prevent conflagrations in heavily built-up areas where buildings were erected side by side in congested downtown business districts.

After the severe conflagrations in Chicago and Baltimore, it became apparent that some control must be made to prevent the spread of fire from one building to another. As a result, the Type III building was defined. The Type III building is, in essence, a wood-frame building (Type V) with fire-resistive exterior walls.

Around the turn of the century, and prior to the promulgation of modern building codes, Type III buildings were known as "ordinary construction." They later became known in some circles, such as those who were familiar with the 1927 edition of the *Uniform Building Code,* as "ordinary masonry"construction. However, as stated previously, the intent behind the creation of this type of construction was to prevent the spread of fire from one combustible building to another. Thus, the early requirements for these buildings were for a certain thickness of masonry walls, such as 13 inches (330 mm) of brick for one-story and 17 inches (432 mm) for two-story buildings of bearing-wall construction. Later, in the 1927 edition of the UBC, the required fire endurance was specified as four hours. Thus, any approved noncombustible construction which would successfully pass the standard fire test for four hours was permitted.

604.1 Definition. Type III buildings are considered combustible buildings and are either protected (Type III One-hour) or unprotected (Type III-N). The structural elements may be of any materials permitted by the code. This expression "permitted by the code" is very important; even though the buildings are considered to be of combustible construction, not all combustible materials are permitted. Only those regulated in the code are permitted. Therefore, such materials as structural plastics are not permitted except under the provisions of Section 104.2.8 of the code.

604.2 Structural Framework. In Types I and II buildings, the code is very specific insofar as the materials required for the structural framework. In Type III construction, steel, iron, masonry, concrete and wood are permitted for use in the structural frame.

604.4 Stairway Construction. Interior stair construction for Type III buildings is predicated on two situations:

1. Interior stairs in buildings three stories or less in height may be constructed of any material permitted by the code. Thus, they may be constructed of wood, either framing lumber or heavy-timber framing, or of noncombustible material such as steel.

2. Interior stairs in buildings more than three stories in height shall be constructed as required for Type I buildings. Thus, the specific materials specified in Section 602.4 must be used. See Section 602.4 in this handbook for discussion.

Exterior stairs must be of noncombustible materials, except that wood not less than 2 inches (51 mm) nominal thickness is permitted for stairs on buildings no more than two stories high.

604.5 Roofs. Roof construction may comply with requirements similar to that found for Type I roof construction for all occupancies except retail sales and storage areas classified as Group M or S, Division 1 Occupancies provided the roof framing is 25 feet (7620 mm) or more above the floor or any other encroachment such as a balcony. The same roof construction provisions also apply to Type V construction.

SECTION 605 — TYPE IV BUILDINGS

Type IV buildings are also referred to as "heavy-timber" buildings. In the eastern United States during the 1800s, a type of construction evolved which was known as "mill" construction. Mill construction was developed by insurance companies to reduce the heavy losses they were facing in the heavy industrialized areas of the northeast.[6]

This type of construction has also been referred to as "slow burning." Wood under the action of fire loses its surface moisture, and when the surface temperature reaches about 400°F (204°C), flaming and charring begin. Under continued application of the heat, charring continues, but at an increasingly slower rate, as the charred wood insulates the inner portion of the wood member. There is quite often enough sound wood remaining during and after a fire so that sudden structural collapse very seldom occurs. In recognition of these characteristics, the insurance interests reasoned that replacement of light wood framing on the interior of factory buildings with heavy-timber construction would substantially cut down their fire losses.

605.1 Definition. The Type IV building is essentially a Type III building with a heavy-timber interior. In fact, the UBC classified the heavy-timber building as a Type III building from the 1952 edition through the 1973 edition. As late as the 1976 edition of the UBC, Types III and IV buildings were lumped together in one chapter.

It is of interest to see how the 1943 edition of the *National Building Code,* developed by the National Board of Fire Underwriters, defined heavy-timber construction:

"Heavy-timber construction," as applied to buildings, means that in which walls are of approved masonry or reinforced concrete; and in which the interior structural elements, including columns, floors and roof construction, consist of heavy timbers with smooth flat surfaces assembled to avoid thin sections, sharp projections and concealed or inaccessible spaces; and in which all structural members which support masonry walls shall have a fire-resistance rating of not less than three hours; and other structural members of steel or reinforced concrete, if used in lieu of timber construction, shall have a fire-resistance rating of not less than one hour.[7]

From this definition, it can be seen that in the early developments of heavy-timber construction, not only did the heavy-timber members have large cross sections to achieve the "slow-burning" characteristic, but, furthermore, surfaces were required to be smooth and flat. Sharp projections were to be avoided, as well as concealed and inaccessible spaces. Thus, the intent of the concept is to provide open structural framing without concealed spaces and without sharp projections or rough surfaces which are more easily ignitable. In this case, flame spread along the surface of heavy-timber members is reduced, and without concealed blind spaces, there is no opportunity for fire to smolder and spread undetected.

In accordance with the second paragraph of Section 605.1, modern-day heavy-timber construction can be a mixture of heavy-timber floor and roof construction and one-hour fire-resistive structural frame and interior partitions. Although heavy-timber construction is not equal to one-hour fire-resistive construction, the code considers heavy timber to provide equivalent protection in Type IV buildings.

Sections 605.2, 605.3 and 605.4 are virtually identical to the comparable sections for Type III buildings, except for the use of heavy-timber construction for the structural frame and for stair construction in buildings three stories or less in height.

605.6 Heavy-timber Construction. In keeping with the concept of slow-burning construction by means of wood members with large cross sections, the UBC in this section specifies minimum nominal dimensions for wood members used in heavy-timber construction. As the code specifies the size of members as "nominal" sizes, the actual net surfaced sizes may be used. For example, an 8-inch by 8-inch (203 mm by 203 mm) member nominally will actually be a net size of 7 1/2 inches by 7 1/2 inches (191 mm by 191 mm). Therefore, even though the code calls for a nominal 8-inch by 8-inch (203 mm by 203 mm) member, the net 7 1/2-inch by 7 1/2-inch-size (191 mm by 191 mm) member meets the intent of the code. Wherever framing lumber or sawn timber is specified, structural glued-laminated timber may also be used.

As indicated earlier, the minimum sizes for heavy-timber construction as listed in this section are based on experience and the good behavior in fire for heavy-timber construction.

In addition to the minimum size requirements in Section 605.6, Section 605.6.7 requires construction details which thoroughly tie the building together both horizontally and vertically. A building detailed in accordance with the code requirements to resist lateral forces of wind or earthquake will of necessity be tied together to meet the intent of Section 605.6.7.

Furthermore, the code requires that girders and beams be tightly fitted to columns, and, in fact, the joinery of all wood members should be tightly fit in order to eliminate points of ignition.

Section 605.6.9 specifies that partitions shall be either of solid-wood construction or one-hour fire-resistive construction. However, Section 302 of the code requires that if there are mixed occupancies within the building, an occupancy separation shall be required. In this case, fire-resistive occupancy separations in heavy-timber buildings should be constructed as required by the code for the required rating. Where this is a requirement for corridors in heavy-timber buildings, one-hour fire-resistive construction must be used rather than solid-wood construction for the partitions.

SECTION 606 — TYPE V BUILDINGS

Type V buildings are essentially construction systems that will not fit into any of the other higher types of construction specified in the code and may be constructed of any materials permitted by the code. The usual case for Type V construction is the light wood-frame building consisting of walls and partitions of 2-inch by 4-inch (51 mm by 102 mm) or 2-inch by 6-inch (51 mm by 152 mm) wood studs. The floor and roof framing are usually of light wood joists of 2-inch by 6-inch (51 mm by 152 mm) size or deeper. Roofs may also be framed with light wood rafters of 2-inch by 4-inch (51 mm by 102 mm) cross section or, as is now quite prevalent, framed with pre-engineered wood trusses of light-frame construction. Wood-frame Type V buildings may be constructed with larger framing members than just described, and these members may actually conform to heavy-timber sizes. However, unless the building complies in all respects to Section 605, it is still a Type V building.

Type V construction is divided into two subtypes:

1. **Type V One-hour.** This is protected construction and is required to be of one-hour fire-resistive construction throughout.

2. **Type V-N.** This type of construction has no general requirements for fire resistance and may be of unprotected construction except where Section 503 and Table 5-A require wall protection due to proximity to a property line.

REFERENCES

[1]*Uniform Building Code,* 1927 Edition. Pacific Coast Building Officials Conference, Long Beach, California.

[2]*Uniform Building Code,* op. cit., Preface.

[3]Colling, R. C. and Hal Colling, Eds. (1951). *Modern Building Inspection,* Second Edition. Building Standards Publishing Company, Los Angeles, California.

[4]Colling and Colling, op. cit., page 103.

[5]Boring, Delbert F., James C. Spence and Walter G. Wells (1981). *Fire Protection through Modern Building Codes,* Fifth Edition. American Iron and Steel Institute, Washington, D.C., page 102.

[6]National Fire Protection Association (1986). *Fire Protection Handbook,* 16th Edition. Quincy, Massachusetts, pages 7-54.

[7]National Board of Fire Underwriters (1943). *National Building Code,* 1943 Edition. New York, page 32.

Chapter 7

FIRE-RESISTANT MATERIALS AND CONSTRUCTION

The types of construction and the fire-resistive requirements of the UBC are based on the concept of "fire endurance." Fire endurance is the length of time during which a fire-resistive construction assembly will confine a fire to a given area or continue to perform structurally when exposed to fire, or both.[1] In the UBC, fire endurance of an assembly is usually expressed as "a ___ -hour fire-resistive assembly." The *Uniform Building Code* in Chapter 7 provides test criteria for the determination of the fire-resistive rating of construction assemblies and materials, details of construction of many assemblies and materials which have already been tested, and other details necessary to secure the intent of the code as far as the fire resistance and the fire endurance of construction assemblies and materials are concerned. Additionally, Chapter 7 addresses other construction items that must be incorporated into a building's design in order to safeguard against the spread of fire and smoke.

This chapter has been revised and reformatted based on a report by BCMC on "Protection of Penetrations and Joints in Building Wall, Floor and Roof Assemblies" dated March 7, 1995. This report was developed in response to the need for consistent, reasonable and easy-to-understand provisions for the protection of penetrations and other items. Industry representatives, code enforcement officials and the design community were involved in the development of these provisions. The result is, hopefully, a fairly easy-to-understand set of criteria that should result in more uniform enforcement.

SECTION 702 — DEFINITIONS

Several definitions that pertain to Chapter 7 are presented in this section. Of these, four are definitions for concrete made from different aggregates. Aggregate types are important not only for structural considerations, but also from a fire endurance standpoint. Because the aggregate type bears on concrete performance, minimum concrete thickness listings in Tables 7-A, 7-B and 7-C provide listings for different aggregates. Generally, the use of siliceous aggregate results in lower fire-resistive ratings while structural lightweight concretes have better fire resistance than normal weight concrete.[2] This is well illustrated by the minimum thicknesses for concrete walls as shown in Item 7-1.1 in Table 7-B, Rated Fire-Resistive Periods for Various Walls and Partitions. For a four-hour wall, the following minimum thicknesses are required:

Concrete type	Thickness (inches) (× 25.4 for mm)
Siliceous aggregate	7.0
Carbonate aggregate	6.6
Sand-lightweight	5.4
Lightweight	5.1

Two other definitions that appear in Section 702 are "F Rating" and "T Rating." "F Rating" and "T Rating" address different properties of fire stops. An F rating is defined as the time required for flames to penetrate a through-penetration fire stop system, while T ratings are defined as the time required for a specific temperature rise on the unexposed side of the system. Each of these ratings should not be less than the ratings of the assembly in which the fire stop is installed. The establishing of the rating of a through-penetration fire stop is determined by tests in accordance with UBC Standard 7-5. A more detailed discussion of this subject is found later in this chapter.

New definitions are added that are similar to many existing definitions and terms used in the previous code but are typically much simpler to use.

SECTION 703 — FIRE-RESISTIVE MATERIALS AND SYSTEMS

703.1 General. It is the intent of the UBC that, unless accepted under the procedures given in Section 104.2.8, 703.2 or 703.3, materials used for fire-resistive purposes are limited to those specified in this chapter. For the most part, the materials and assemblies listed in UBC Tables 7-A, 7-B and 7-C have been tested in accordance with UBC Standard 7-1 for the fire-resistive ratings indicated. In addition, Footnote (a) to the tables allows the acceptance of generic assemblies that are listed in the *Fire-Resistance Design Manual* published by the Gypsum Association. Unless materials or assemblies are listed in Table 7-A, 7-B or 7-C or in the Gypsum Association's design manual, they may not be used unless proven by tests in accordance with Section 703.2 or established by calculations in accordance with Section 703.3. It is also important to note that certain specific assemblies which have been reviewed by ICBO ES and found to comply with the code are also acceptable for use when approved by the building official.

703.2 Qualification by Testing. Figures 703-1 through 703-5 depict the testing requirements of UBC Standard 7-1. The first paragraph of this section gives the intent of the UBC that any material or assembly that successfully passes the end-point criteria depicted for the specified time period shall have its fire-endurance rating accepted and the assembly classified in accordance with the time during which the assembly successfully withstood the test.

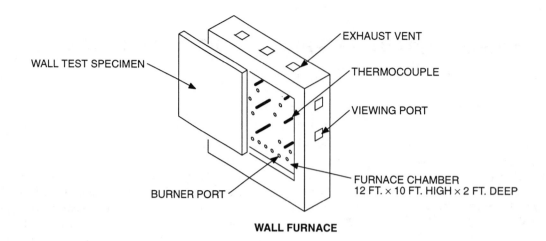

WALL TEST SPECIMEN

EXHAUST VENT

THERMOCOUPLE

VIEWING PORT

FURNACE CHAMBER
12 FT. × 10 FT. HIGH × 2 FT. DEEP

BURNER PORT

WALL FURNACE

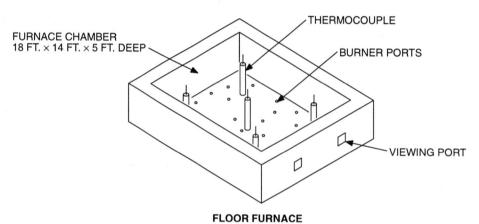

FURNACE CHAMBER
18 FT. × 14 FT. × 5 FT. DEEP

THERMOCOUPLE

BURNER PORTS

VIEWING PORT

FLOOR FURNACE

For **SI:** 1 foot = 304.8 mm.

TEST FURNACES

FIGURE 703-1

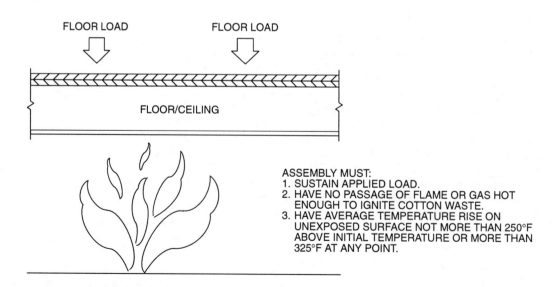

FLOOR LOAD

FLOOR LOAD

FLOOR/CEILING

ASSEMBLY MUST:
1. SUSTAIN APPLIED LOAD.
2. HAVE NO PASSAGE OF FLAME OR GAS HOT
   ENOUGH TO IGNITE COTTON WASTE.
3. HAVE AVERAGE TEMPERATURE RISE ON
   UNEXPOSED SURFACE NOT MORE THAN 250°F
   ABOVE INITIAL TEMPERATURE OR MORE THAN
   325°F AT ANY POINT.

For **SI:** °F = 1.8°C + 32.

FLOOR ASSEMBLY FIRE TEST

FIGURE 703-2

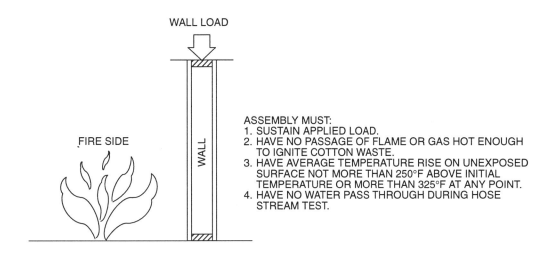

WALL LOAD

FIRE SIDE

WALL

ASSEMBLY MUST:
1. SUSTAIN APPLIED LOAD.
2. HAVE NO PASSAGE OF FLAME OR GAS HOT ENOUGH TO IGNITE COTTON WASTE.
3. HAVE AVERAGE TEMPERATURE RISE ON UNEXPOSED SURFACE NOT MORE THAN 250°F ABOVE INITIAL TEMPERATURE OR MORE THAN 325°F AT ANY POINT.
4. HAVE NO WATER PASS THROUGH DURING HOSE STREAM TEST.

For **SI:** °F = 1.8°C + 32.

CONDITIONS OF ACCEPTANCE—WALL FIRE TEST

FIGURE 703-3

Uniform Building Code Standard 7-1 is essentially ASTM Standard E 119. The one important difference on how the standards address restrained assemblies will be discussed in this handbook. Although earlier fire testing in the United States began as long ago as the 1890s, the standard fire-endurance test procedure using a standard time-temperature curve and specifying fire-endurance ratings in hours was developed in 1918. The significance of the 1918 and later standards is the fact that they were and are intended to be reproducible so that the test conducted at Underwriters Laboratories (UL) can be compared with the test of the same assembly conducted at the University of California, Ohio State University or other testing facility.[1] An often-expressed criticism of a standard such as UBC Standard 7-1 is that "it does not represent the real world." This is true in many cases, and for that reason it should not be thought of as representing the absolute behavior of a fire-resistive assembly under most actual fires in buildings. There are too many variables which affect the fire endurance of an assembly during an actual fire, such as fuel load, room size, rate of oxygen supply and restraint, to consider that the test establishes absolute values of the real-world fire endurance of an assembly. However, it is a severe test of the fire-resistive qualities of a material or an assembly, and because of its reproducibility, it provides a means of comparing assemblies.

In addition to the fire-endurance fire ratings obtained from the standard fire test of UBC Standard 7-1, it is also possible to obtain, as expressed in the standard, the protective membrane performance for walls, partitions, and floor or roof assemblies. In the case of combustible walls or floor and roof assemblies, it is also referred to as the "finish rating." Although the test standard does not limit the determination of the protective membrane performance to combustible assemblies, its greatest significance is with combustible assemblies.

The end-point criteria for determining the finish rating are that the average temperature at the surface of the protected materials shall not be greater than 250°F (121°C) above the begin-

ning temperature. Furthermore, the maximum temperature at any measured point shall not be greater than 325°F (163°C) above the beginning temperature. These temperatures roughly relate to the lower limit of ignition temperatures for wood. Figure 703-4 illustrates the determination of the finish rating for a wall assembly, which is usually determined during a fire-endurance test of the assembly.

The conditions of acceptance, also referred to as failure criteria and end-point criteria, of fire-resistive assemblies are as follows:

- For load-bearing assemblies, the applied load must be successfully sustained during the time period for which classification is desired. There shall be no passage of flame or hot gases hot enough to ignite cotton waste on the unexposed surfaces.

- The average temperature rise on the unexposed surface shall not be more than 250°F (121°C) above the initial temperature during the time period of the test.

- The maximum temperature on the unexposed surface shall not be more than 325°F (163°C) above the initial temperature during the time period of the test.

- Walls or partitions shall withstand the hose stream test without passage of flame or hot gases hot enough to ignite cotton waste on the unexposed side or the projection of water from the hose stream beyond the unexposed surface.

In addition to the conditions of acceptance just described, load-carrying structural members in roof and floor assemblies are subject to special end-point temperatures for:

- **Structural steel beams and girders**—1100°F (593°C) average at any cross section and 1300°F (704°C) for any individual thermocouple, for unrestrained assemblies.

- **Reinforcing steel in cast-in-place reinforced concrete beams and girders**—1100°F (593°C) average at any section.

- **Prestressing steel in prestressed concrete beams and girders**—800°F (427°C) average at any section.
- **Steel deck floor and roof units**—1100°F (593°C) average on any one span.

As columns are exposed to fire on all surfaces, the standard has special temperature and testing criteria for these members:

- The column is loaded so as to develop as nearly as practicable the working stresses contemplated by the structural design. The condition of acceptance is simply that the column sustain the load for the duration of the test period for which a classification is desired.

- Alternatively, a steel column may be tested without load, and the column will be tested in the furnace to determine the adequacy of the protection on the steel column. The test and end points are depicted in Figure 703-5.

The exception to the first paragraph of this section is intended to modify the acceptance criteria for exterior bearing walls so that the walls will receive a rating based on which of the two following sets of criteria occurs first during the test:

1. Heat transmission or flame and hot gases transmission for nonbearing walls.

2. Structural failure or hose stream application failure.

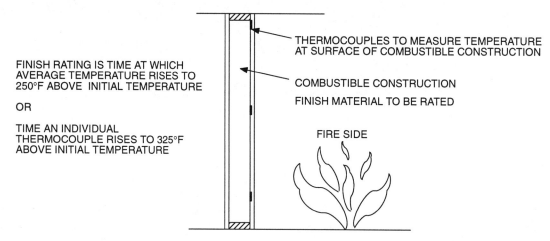

FINISH RATING IS TIME AT WHICH AVERAGE TEMPERATURE RISES TO 250°F ABOVE INITIAL TEMPERATURE

OR

TIME AN INDIVIDUAL THERMOCOUPLE RISES TO 325°F ABOVE INITIAL TEMPERATURE

THERMOCOUPLES TO MEASURE TEMPERATURE AT SURFACE OF COMBUSTIBLE CONSTRUCTION

COMBUSTIBLE CONSTRUCTION

FINISH MATERIAL TO BE RATED

FIRE SIDE

For **SI:** °F = 1.8°C + 32.

COMBUSTIBLE ASSEMBLY FOR DETERMINING FINISH RATING

FIGURE 703-4

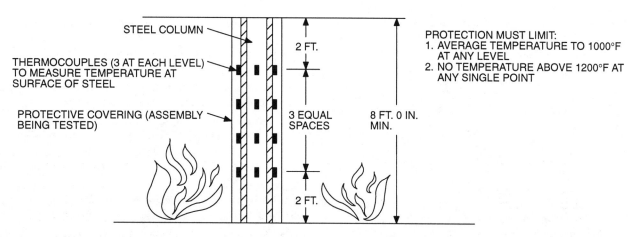

STEEL COLUMN

THERMOCOUPLES (3 AT EACH LEVEL) TO MEASURE TEMPERATURE AT SURFACE OF STEEL

PROTECTIVE COVERING (ASSEMBLY BEING TESTED)

2 FT.

3 EQUAL SPACES

8 FT. 0 IN. MIN.

2 FT.

PROTECTION MUST LIMIT:
1. AVERAGE TEMPERATURE TO 1000°F AT ANY LEVEL
2. NO TEMPERATURE ABOVE 1200°F AT ANY SINGLE POINT

For **SI:** 1 foot = 304.8 mm, °F = 1.8°C + 32.

ALTERNATE FIRE TEST OF STEEL COLUMN PROTECTION

FIGURE 703-5

The first set of end points measures the wall's ability to prevent the spread of fire from one side to the opposite side. It is considered overly restrictive to require that exterior bearing walls comply with this first set of end points for a longer time than would be required for a nonbearing wall located at the same distance from the property line, if it is still structurally capable of carrying the superimposed loads.

On the basis of this exception, an exterior bearing wall located at such a distance from the property line that the code would permit an unprotected nonbearing wall would only be required to have a structural fire-resistance rating as required for the structural frame.

In 1973, UBC Standard 7-1 was brought up to date with ASTM Standard E 119-71 and included for the first time a dual classification system for roof and floor assemblies, including their structural members. This dual classification system involves the use of the terms "restrained" and "unrestrained." The use of the word "restrained" entails the concept of thermal restraint (restraint against thermal expansion as well as against rotation at the ends of an assembly or structural member).

For example, if a structural beam of uniform cross section is subjected to heat on its bottom surface, such as would be the case in the standard test furnace, it will attempt to expand in all directions, with the longitudinal expansion being the primary component. If the beam is restrained at the ends so that it cannot expand, compressive stresses will build up within the beam and, in effect, it will behave in similar fashion to a prestressed beam. As a result the thermal restraint will be beneficial in terms of improving the beam's ability to sustain the applied load during the fire test. If the same beam is restrained only for the lower one half of its cross section, it will tend to deflect upward due to the conditions of restraint. This upward deflection tendency is also considered to enhance the beam's ability to sustain the applied load during a fire-endurance test.

Conversely, if the end restraint is applied only to the upper half of the beam cross section, the beam will tend to deflect downward, and, in this case, the restraint will be detrimental to the beam's ability to sustain the applied load during the fire-endurance test. As the heat is applied to the bottom surface during a fire, it creates a downward deflection, and the two downward deflections are additive. In an actual building this could lead to premature failure. It can be seen, then, that thermal restraint may be either beneficial or detrimental to the fire-resistive assembly, depending on its means of application in the building.

Uniform Building Code Standard 7-1 in Section 7.141 provides general guidance for the building official as to what conditions in the constructed building provide restraint. It is generally agreed that an interior panel of a monolithically cast-in-place reinforced concrete floor slab would be considered to have thermal restraint. Also, Footnote 12 to UBC Table 7-A provides that "interior spans of continuous slabs, beams and girders may be considered restrained." Conversely, because the restraint present in many construction systems cannot be determined so neatly, the UBC requires that these assemblies be considered unrestrained, unless the structural design engineer shows by the requisite analysis and details that the system qualifies for a restrained classification. Furthermore, the code requires that any

construction assembly that is to be considered restrained be identified as such on the drawings.

American Society for Testing and Materials Standard E 119 contains an appendix that outlines various types of construction for horizontal assemblies and indicates whether they are considered to be restrained or unrestrained. This table was deleted from the 1979 edition of UBC Standard 7-1 by the membership of ICBO because some of the restrained construction systems that were outlined were not considered to qualify as being restrained.

703.3 Calculating Fire Resistance. Fire research and the theory of heat transmission have combined to make it possible with the present state-of-the-art technology to calculate the fire endurance for certain materials and assemblies. As a result of this testing and research, this section permits the calculation of the fire-resistive rating for structural steel, reinforced concrete, wood, concrete masonry and clay masonry in accordance with UBC Standard 7-7.

At the present time, it is doubtful that the fire resistance of many buildings will be based on calculations. Even so, the code user should be aware of the useful information presented in UBC Standard 7-7, including:

Reference	Subject
Table 7-7-S-2	Details for installation of sheet metal column protective covers around gypsum wallboard.
Table 7-7-S-3	Attachment of gypsum wallboard around structural steel columns.
Figure 7-7-C-2	Thickness of ceramic blanket joint material for precast concrete wall panels.
Figure 7-7-M-2	Control joints for fire-resistance-rated concrete masonry walls.
Sections 7.729 and 7.730	Design of exposed wood members for one-hour fire-resistive rating.

The procedure set forth in Section 7.729 and 7.730 of UBC Standard 7-7 should be used when someone wishes to consider exposed "heavy timber" as one-hour construction in something other than a Type IV building. One of the factors affecting a wood member's fire-resistive rating is the load on the member as a percentage of its allowable structural capacity. See Application Example 703-6.

703.4 Standards of Quality. This section provides a list of tests or standards of quality. The standards listed as a UBC standard are also listed in Chapter 35, Part II, and are a part of the code; all other standards are recommendations and are not a part of this code. A more detailed discussion of standards of quality is found in the discussion of Chapter 35 in this handbook.

SECTION 704 — PROTECTION OF STRUCTURAL MEMBERS

704.1 General. The code intends that the fire-resistive protection for structural members shown in Table 7-A be applied to the individual structural member. This is based on the differences in both the testing procedure and the conditions of acceptance which were discussed in Section 703.2. In other words, the code does not intend that the structural member be protected by a wall assembly or other fire-resistive assembly, except as described in Section 704.2.6 for ceiling membrane protection and Section

Application Example 703-6
UBC Standard 7-7

DETERMINE: Column's fire-resistive rating at 50 percent, 75 percent and 100 percent of its structural capacity.

SOLUTION: According to Section 7.729, column fire-resistive rating is calculated from the formula, $2.54 \, Z_d \, [3 - (d/b)]$

WHERE:

b = larger side of column [inches (mm)]

d = smaller side of column [inches (mm)]

Z = $0.9 + 30/r$

r = ratio of applied load to allowable load expressed as a percent of allowable

When r = 50% or less, Z = 1.5

Calculated Z:

50% Capacity	$Z = 1.5$
75%	$Z = 0.9 + 30/75 = 1.3$
100%	$Z = 0.9 + 30/100 = 1.2$

Calculate rating:

$2.54Z \, (7.5) \, [3 - (7.5/7.5)] = 38.1Z$

50% Capacity   38.1 (1.5) = 57.15 minutes
75%   38.1 (1.3) = 49.53 minutes
100%   38.1 (1.2) = 45.72 minutes

The same column loaded to 50 percent of capacity, but exposed on only three sides, would have a fire-resistive rating of 100 minutes.

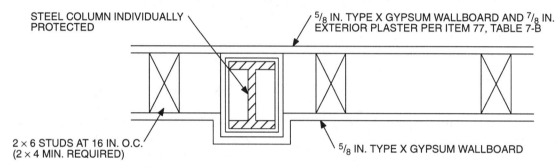

STEEL COLUMN INDIVIDUALLY PROTECTED

$5/8$ IN. TYPE X GYPSUM WALLBOARD AND $7/8$ IN. EXTERIOR PLASTER PER ITEM 77, TABLE 7-B

2 × 6 STUDS AT 16 IN. O.C. (2 × 4 MIN. REQUIRED)

$5/8$ IN. TYPE X GYPSUM WALLBOARD

STRUCTURAL MEMBERS WITHIN A FIRE-RESISTIVE WALL MUST BE PROVIDED WITH INDIVIDUAL PROTECTION

For **SI:** 1 inch = 25.4 mm, 1 foot = 304.8 mm.

PROTECTION OF STRUCTURAL MEMBERS

FIGURE 704-1

704.2.8 for truss protection. Also, trusses may be used in a roof-ceiling or floor-ceiling assembly without individual protection of the structural members of the truss. Therefore, the column shown in the fire-resistive wall in Figure 704-1 requires individual protection as shown. Figures 704-2 through 704-6 provide details and illustrations of the requirements of the code for protection of structural members. Figure 704-5 provides details of fire protection of structural members that indicate the principle of "mass effect." Mass effect is beneficial to the protection requirements for structural members of a heavy cross section. In the case of steel members, the amount of protection depends on the weight of the structural steel member. A heavy, massive structural steel cross section behaves such that the heat applied to the surface during a fire is absorbed away from the surface, resulting in lower steel surface temperatures. Thus, the insulating thicknesses indicated by test or in Table 7-A should not be used for members with a smaller weight than that specified in the test or table.

704.2.6 Ceiling membrane protection. Under certain restrictions the code permits the use of a fire-resistive ceiling membrane that is part of a fire-resistive floor-ceiling or roof-ceiling assembly to provide protection for horizontal structural members, rather than requiring that they be individually protected. The criteria for the use of ceiling protection are depicted in Figure 704-7 and are as follows:

- The use of ceiling protection applies only to horizontal structural members.

- Such structural members shall not support directly applied loads from a floor and roof or more than one floor.

- The required fire resistance of the assembly shall be at least equal to that required by the code for the individual protection of the structural members.

704.2.8 Truss protection. It is the intent of the UBC that this item be applied to trusses that are part of the structural frame as defined in Section 601.4. In this case, the code permits the encapsulation with fire-resistive materials of the entire truss assembly for its entire length. It is the intent of the code that the thickness and details of construction of the fire-resistive protection be based on the results of full-scale tests or of tests on truss

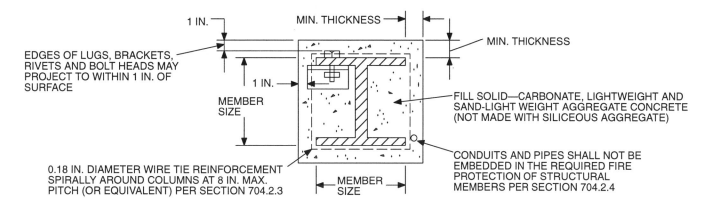

MEMBER SIZE	MINIMUM THICKNESS (In inches)			
	4 Hr.	3 Hr.	2 Hr.	1 Hr.
6 in. × 6 in. or greater	$2^1/_2$	2	$1^1/_2$	1
8 in. × 8 in. or greater	2	$1^1/_2$	1	1
12 in. × 12 in. or greater	$1^1/_2$	1	1	1

For **SI:** 1 inch = 25.4 mm.

PROTECTION OF STRUCTURAL STEEL COLUMNS

FIGURE 704-2

components. Approved calculations based on such tests that show that the truss components provide the fire endurance required by the code are also acceptable. One application of this concept is in the use of the encapsulated trusses as dividing partitions between hotel rooms in multistory steel-frame buildings. Since the truss becomes part of the structural frame where it is used to span between exterior wall columns, it provides a column-free interior. The fire-resistive design of the encapsulating protection can be based either on tests or on analogies derived from fire tests.

704.3 Protected Members. Figures 704-2 and 704-3 depict the details discussed in Sections 704.3.1 and 704.3.2.

704.3.3 Bonded prestressed concrete tendons. Figure 704-8 depicts the requirements specified in Items 1 and 2 for variable concrete cover for the tendons. It must be noted that for all cases of variable concrete cover, the average concrete cover for the tendons must not be less than the cover specified in UBC Table 7-A.

As prestressed concrete members are designed in accordance with their ultimate moment capacity, as well as with their performance at service loads, Item 3 provides two sets of criteria for variable concrete cover for the multiple tendons:

- Those tendons having less concrete cover than specified in Table 7-A shall be considered as furnishing only a reduced portion of the ultimate moment capacity of the member, depending on the cross-sectional area of the member.

- No reduction is necessary for those tendons having reduced cover for the design of the member at service loads.

As the ultimate moment capacity of the member is critical to the behavior of the member under fire conditions, the code requires the reduction for those tendons having cover less than that specified by the code. However, behavior at service loads is less affected by the heat of a fire; therefore, the code permits those tendons with reduced cover to be assumed to be fully effective.

704.4 and 704.5 Members Carrying Masonry or Concrete and Fire Protection Omitted. Regardless of the type of construction and the code-required fire-resistive rating for the walls, Section 704.4 requires that any member-carrying masonry or concrete walls in buildings over one story in height be fire protected with not less than one-hour fire-resistive material or the fire-resistive requirement of the wall, whichever is greater. Exempted from this requirement are the bottom flanges of short span lintels, and shelf angles or plates that are not part of the structural frame.

Usually this requirement will be taken care of by the requirements in Table 6-A. However, in the case of a Type V-N building which may not require fire-resistive construction of the exterior walls, Section 704.4 requires at least one-hour fire-resistive protection for any structural member carrying a masonry or concrete wall. The potential for disaster is too great if the structural member were to fail prematurely due to fire and allow the wall to collapse.

In those cases which are exempted from this provision—for example, the short span lintels—it is assumed by the code that arching action of the masonry or concrete above the lintel will prevent anything more than just a localized failure of the concrete or masonry wall. Furthermore, only the bottom flange is permitted to be unprotected, and as a result the concrete or masonry wall supported by the lintel will act as a heat sink to draw heat away from the lintel and thereby increase the length of time until failure due to heat.

This latter rationale also applies to shelf angles and plates that are not part of the structural frame.

SECTION 705 — PROJECTIONS

Projections from buildings are regulated in order to prevent a fire hazard from inappropriate use of combustible materials attached to the exterior walls. Thus, the UBC requires that projections from walls of Type I or II buildings be of noncombustible materials. However, it should be noted that certain combustible materials are permitted on walls fronting on streets or yards, in accordance with Section 601.5.4.

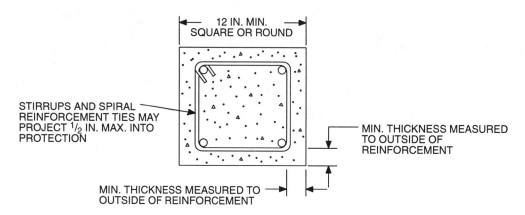

CONCRETE	MINIMUM THICKNESS (In inches)			
	4 Hr.	3 Hr.	2 Hr.	1 Hr.
Carbonate, lightweight and sand-lightweight aggregate concrete	$1^1/_2$	$1^1/_2$	$1^1/_2$	$1^1/_2$
Siliceous aggregate concrete	2	$1^1/_2$	$1^1/_2$	$1^1/_2$

REINFORCING STEEL IN CONCRETE JOISTS

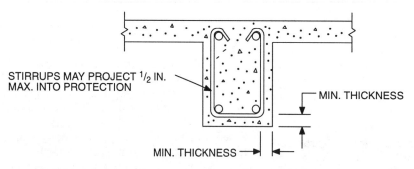

CONCRETE	MINIMUM THICKNESS (In inches)			
	4 Hr.	3 Hr.	2 Hr.	1 Hr.
Carbonate, lightweight and sand-lightweight aggregate concrete	$1^1/_4$	$1^1/_4$	1	$3/_4$
Siliceous aggregate concrete	$1^3/_4$	$1^1/_2$	1	$3/_4$

REINFORCING STEEL IN CONCRETE COLUMNS, BEAMS, GIRDERS AND TRUSSES

For **SI:** 1 inch = 25.4 mm.

PROTECTION OF STRUCTURAL MEMBERS

FIGURE 704-3

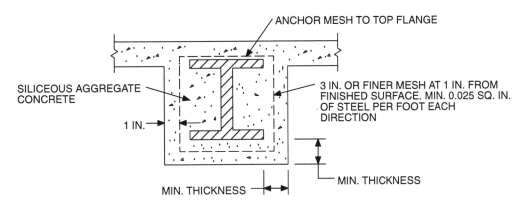

EDGES OF LUGS, BRACKETS, RIVETS AND BOLT HEADS ATTACHED TO STRUCTURAL
MEMBERS MAY EXTEND TO WITHIN 1 IN. OF THE SURFACE OF THE FIRE PROTECTION

MINIMUM THICKNESS (In inches)			
4 Hr.	3 Hr.	2 Hr.	1 Hr.
$2^1/_2$	2	$1^1/_2$	1

STEEL BEAMS AND GIRDERS

For **SI:** 1 inch = 25.4 mm, 1 square inch per foot = 2.12 mm^2 per mm.

PROTECTION OF STRUCTURAL MEMBERS

FIGURE 704-4

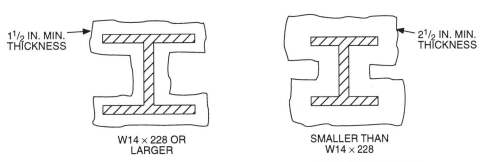

STEEL COLUMNS—FOUR-HOUR PROTECTION, SPRAY-ON PROTECTION

For **SI:** 1 inch = 25.4 mm.

MASS EFFECT

FIGURE 704-5

For buildings which the code considers to be of combustible construction (Type III, IV or V construction), either combustible or noncombustible materials are permitted. Where combustible projections are utilized and they extend into an area where openings are either not permitted or where they must be protected, the code requires that they be of one-hour fire-resistive construction or of heavy-timber construction. This latter requirement is based on the potential for a severe exposure hazard and, consequently, the code intends that combustible materials be protected or, alternatively, be of heavy-timber construction which has comparable performance when exposed to fire.

SECTION 706 — FIRE-RESISTIVE JOINT SYSTEMS

This section has been revised and retitled in the 1997 edition as Fire-Resistive Joint Systems. A fire-resistive joint system is defined in Section 702 as an "assemblage of specific materials or products that are designed, tested and fire resistive in accordance with UBC Standard 7-1 to resist, for a prescribed period of time, the passage of fire through joints." The term joint is also defined in Section 702 as the linear opening between adjacent fire-resistive assemblies and is a division of a building that allows independent movement of the building as caused by ther-

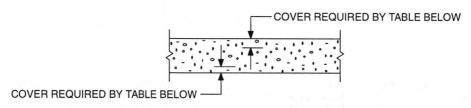

COVER REQUIRED BY TABLE BELOW

COVER REQUIRED BY TABLE BELOW

STRUCTURAL PARTS TO BE PROTECTED	INSULATING MATERIAL USED	MINIMUM THICKNESS OF INSULATING MATERIAL FOR FOLLOWING FIRE-RESISTIVE PERIODS (In inches)			
		4 Hr.	3 Hr.	2 Hr.	1 Hr.
Reinforcing and tie rods in floor and roof slabs	Carbonate, lightweight and sand-lightweight aggregate concrete	1	1	$3/4$	$3/4$
	Siliceous aggregate concrete	$1^1/4$	1	1	$3/4$

REINFORCING STEEL AND TIE RODS IN FLOOR AND ROOF SLABS

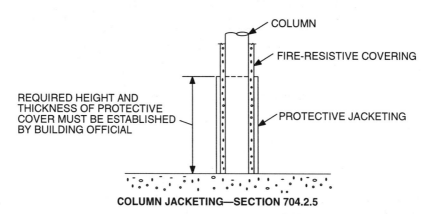

COLUMN

FIRE-RESISTIVE COVERING

REQUIRED HEIGHT AND THICKNESS OF PROTECTIVE COVER MUST BE ESTABLISHED BY BUILDING OFFICIAL

PROTECTIVE JACKETING

For **SI:** 1 inch = 25.4 mm.

COLUMN JACKETING—SECTION 704.2.5

PROTECTION OF STRUCTURAL MEMBERS

FIGURE 704-6

mal, seismic, wind or any other loading. The approved joint system should be designed to resist the passage of fire for a time period not less than the required fire resistance rating of the floor, roof or wall in or between which it is installed.

Fire-resistive joint systems shall be tested in accordance with UBC Standard 7-1 under the conditions described in Section 706.2. The exceptions to providing a fire-resistive joint system are listed in Section 706.1.

The revision of Section 706 again clarifies the scope of these provisions by adding a number of exceptions and defining the test procedures for joint protective devices. One of the more interesting changes is the requirement of preconditioning the joint protection system by cycling. This is already in an ICBO Evaluation Service Acceptance Criteria for such joint protection devices and is now proposed to be included in the code. Recognized standard ASTM E 1399 has been developed specifically for these systems and will make these provisions consistent with the move toward the cyclic testing of lateral force-resisting structural elements. The number of cycles in Table 7-D is different than in ASTM E 1399 as the numbers chosen were believed to more realistically represent the number of cycles under full

design load. They are also in concert with those recently accepted by BOCA.

This revision is intended to be a move toward more uniform code provisions not only among the three model codes but within the *Uniform Building Code* itself.

TABLE 7-D—PRECONDITIONING CYCLES FOR FIRE-RESISTIVE JOINT SYSTEMS

TYPE OF JOINT SYSTEM	NUMBER OF CYCLES
Expansion/construction	500
Seismic	100
Wind sway	500

SECTION 707 — INSULATION

The intent of this section is to establish code requirements for thermal and acoustical insulation located on or within building spaces. This section regulates all insulation except for foam plastic insulation that is regulated by Section 2602, and duct insulation and insulation in plenums, which must comply with the requirements of the UMC.

(Continued on page 118)

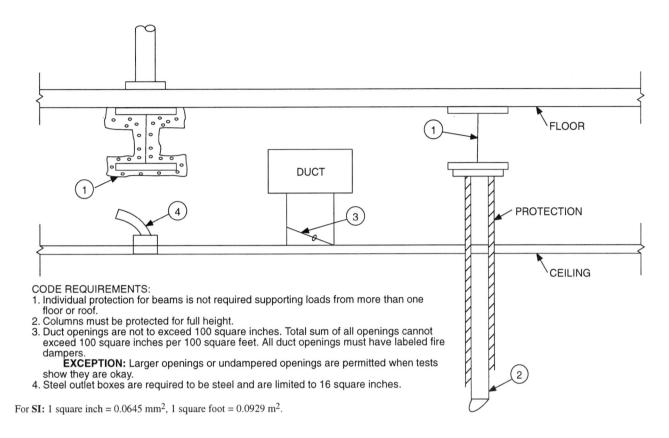

CODE REQUIREMENTS:
1. Individual protection for beams is not required supporting loads from more than one floor or roof.
2. Columns must be protected for full height.
3. Duct openings are not to exceed 100 square inches. Total sum of all openings cannot exceed 100 square inches per 100 square feet. All duct openings must have labeled fire dampers.
   EXCEPTION: Larger openings or undampered openings are permitted when tests show they are okay.
4. Steel outlet boxes are required to be steel and are limited to 16 square inches.

For **SI:** 1 square inch = 0.0645 mm², 1 square foot = 0.0929 m².

PROTECTION OF STRUCTURAL MEMBERS

FIGURE 704-7

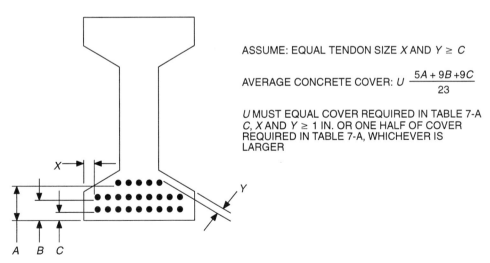

ASSUME: EQUAL TENDON SIZE X AND $Y \geq C$

AVERAGE CONCRETE COVER: $U \dfrac{5A + 9B + 9C}{23}$

U MUST EQUAL COVER REQUIRED IN TABLE 7-A C, X AND $Y \geq 1$ IN. OR ONE HALF OF COVER REQUIRED IN TABLE 7-A, WHICHEVER IS LARGER

For **SI:** 1 inch = 25.4 mm.

VARIABLE PROTECTION OF BONDED PRESTRESSED TENDONS, MULTIPLE TENDONS

FIGURE 704-8

(Continued from page 116)

As a general requirement, insulation including facings used as vapor retarders or as breather papers must have a flame-spread rating not in excess of 25 and a smoke-developed rating not to exceed 450. Exception 2 in Section 707.3 waives the flame-spread and smoke-developed limitations for facings on insulation installed in Types III, IV and V construction, provided that the facing is installed in substantial contact with the unexposed surface of the ceiling, floor or wall finish.

SECTION 708 — FIRE BLOCKS AND DRAFT STOPS

Fire blocks and draft stops are required in combustible construction to cut off concealed draft openings (both vertical and horizontal). The code requires that fire blocks and draft stops form an effective barrier between floors and between the top story or attic space. The code also requires that attic spaces be subdivided, as will be discussed later along with concealed spaces within roof-ceiling and floor-ceiling assemblies. Figures 708-1 through 708-4 depict UBC requirements for fire blocks.

Experience has shown that the greatest damage occurs to conventional wood-framed buildings during a fire when the fire travels unimpeded through concealed draft openings. This often occurs before the fire department has an opportunity to control the fire, and greater damage is created as a result of the lack of fire blocking.

For these reasons, the code requires fire blocks and draft stops to prevent the spread of fire through concealed combustible draft passageways. Virtually any concealed air space within a building will provide an open channel through which high-temperature air and gases will spread. Fire and hot gases will spread through concealed spaces between joists, between studs, within furred spaces and through any other hidden channel that is not fire blocked.

708.2 Fire Blocks. The platform framing that is used most often today in wood-frame construction provides adequate fire blocking between stories in the stud walls, but care must be exercised to ensure that furred spaces are effectively fire blocked to prevent transmission of fire and hot gases between stories or along a wall. For this reason, the code requires that fire blocks be provided at 10-foot (3048 mm) intervals horizontally and vertically along walls that are either furred out, of double-wall construction or are greater than 10 feet (3048 mm) in height.

Care must also be exercised to fire block openings around vents and pipes that penetrate wood members that would otherwise act as a fire block. In this latter case, and for fire blocking around chimneys, fireplaces and similar openings, the code requires that the fire blocking be of noncombustible materials.

Item 6 contains the fire blocking provisions for wood flooring used typically in gymnasiums, bowling alleys, dance floors, etc. As long as the wood flooring described in this item is in direct contact with a concrete or masonry fire-resistive floor, there is no significant hazard. However, if there is a space between the wood flooring and the fire-resistive floor, a blind space is created that is enclosed with combustible materials and provides a route for the undetected spread of fire. Therefore, the code requires that where the wood flooring is not in contact with the fire-resistive floor, the space be filled with noncombustible material or be fire-blocked. Two exceptions to the fire blocking requirement are:

1. The first exception exempts floors of gymnasiums where they are at or below grade. In this case, the code presumes a low hazard, as gymnasiums are usually only one story in height. If the floor is at or below grade, it is unlikely that any ignition sources would be present to start a fire that would spread through the blind space under the wood flooring.

2. Bowling lanes are exempted from fire blocking except as described in the code, which provides for areas larger than 100 square feet (9.3 m^2) between fire blocks. Fire blocking intermittently down a bowling lane would create problems for accurate bowling. Also, the exception is rationalized on the basis that the space between fire blocks is approximately equivalent to that which would be permitted in wood-frame construction in Section 708.3.1.1.3.

Except as described above for fire blocking around chimneys, fire blocking materials are required to consist of lumber or wood structural panels of the thicknesses specified; gypsum board; cement asbestos board; mineral fiber; glass fiber; or any other approved materials securely fastened in place. The use of the word "approved" is defined in Chapter 2.

Section 708.2.2 has been revised to clarify the use of mineral and glass fiber insulation and loose-fill insulation. Only batts or blankets of mineral fiber and glass fiber materials should be allowed to be used as fire blocks, especially where parallel or staggered stud walls are used. Loose-fill insulation should not be used as a fire block under any circumstance. Even in the case where it fills an entire cavity, a hole knocked into the membrane enclosure for the cavity could allow the loose-fill insulation material to fall out, negating its function. Therefore, loose-fill insulation material shall not be used as a fire block unless it has been properly tested to show that it can perform the intended function. The main concern is that the loose-fill material, even though it may perform adequately in a fire test to show sufficient fire-retardant characteristics to meet the intent of this section, would not be adequately evaluated for various applications due to the physical instability of the material in certain orientations.

708.3 Draft Stops. Draft stops are utilized to subdivide large concealed spaces such as attics, concealed spaces within roof and floor-ceiling assemblies, false fronts set out from walls, and similar concealed spaces. Figures 708-5 through 708-8 show UBC requirements for draft stopping.

Draft stops are to be installed in floor-ceiling assemblies as follows:

1. **Single-family dwellings.** Where there is usable space above and below the concealed space within the floor-ceiling assembly, the code requires that draft stops be installed so that the area of any concealed space does not exceed 1,000 square feet (93 m^2) and so that the draft stops divide the concealed space into approximately equal areas.

2. **Two or more dwelling units and hotels.** In this case, the code requires that draft stops be installed in line with the wall separating tenants from each other and separating tenants from other areas. In this case, a fire originating in a dwelling unit or hotel room will find draft stops in the concealed space blocking the transmission of fire and hot gases into another hotel room or apartment.

(Continued on page 120)

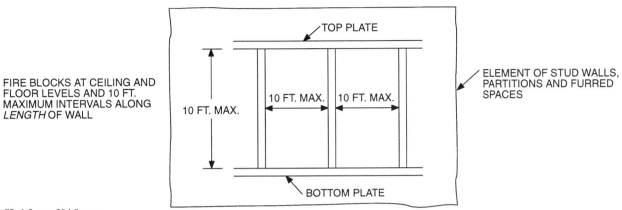

FIRE BLOCKS AT CEILING AND FLOOR LEVELS AND 10 FT. MAXIMUM INTERVALS ALONG *LENGTH* OF WALL

TOP PLATE

ELEMENT OF STUD WALLS, PARTITIONS AND FURRED SPACES

10 FT. MAX.

10 FT. MAX.   10 FT. MAX.

BOTTOM PLATE

For **SI:** 1 foot = 304.8 mm.

FIRE BLOCKS—WALLS

FIGURE 708-1

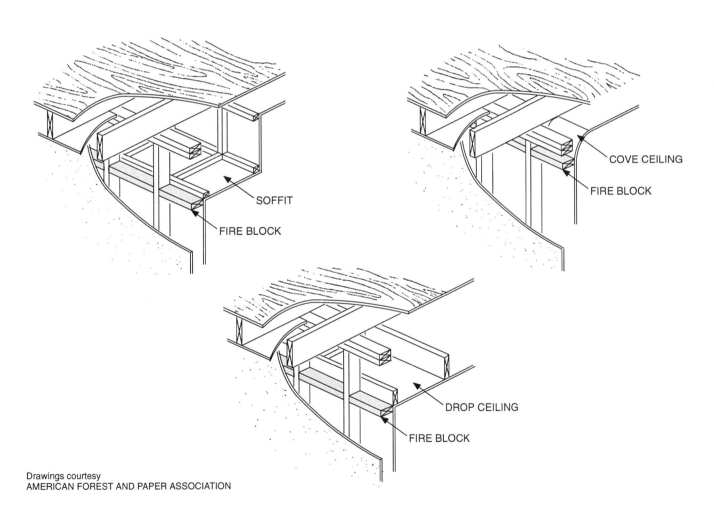

SOFFIT

FIRE BLOCK

COVE CEILING

FIRE BLOCK

DROP CEILING

FIRE BLOCK

Drawings courtesy
AMERICAN FOREST AND PAPER ASSOCIATION

FIRE BLOCKS—VERTICAL AND HORIZONTAL SPACE CONNECTIONS

FIGURE 708-2

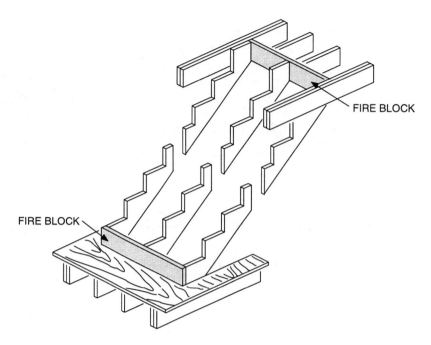

FIRE BLOCKS—STAIRS

FIGURE 708-3

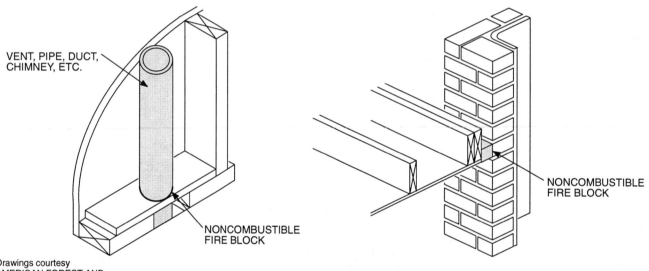

Drawings courtesy
AMERICAN FOREST AND
PAPER ASSOCIATION

FIRE BLOCKS—PIPES, CHIMNEYS, ETC.

FIGURE 708-4

(Continued from page 118)

3. **Other uses.** For uses other than residential occupancies, the code intends that the concealed space within the floor-ceiling assembly be separated by draft stops so that the area of any concealed space does not exceed 1,000 square feet (93 m^2) and the horizontal dimension between draft stops does not exceed 60 feet (18 288 mm). An exception permits tripling the area between draft stops where automatic fire sprinklers are installed and increasing the horizontal dimension to 100 feet (30 480 mm).

In attics, the code requires draft stops under the following circumstances:

1. **Single-family dwellings.** None required.

2. **Multiple dwelling units and hotels.** Draft stops to be installed above and in line with the walls separating dwelling units or between walls separating hotel rooms or suites. Figure 708-7 explains the intent of Exception 1. Exception 2 applies where automatic fire sprinklers are installed in the attic. In this case, attic areas may be increased by installing draft stops to subdivide the attic into a maximum of 9,000-square-foot (836 m^2) spaces with a maximum horizontal dimension between draft stops of 100 feet (30 480 mm).

(Continued on page 122)

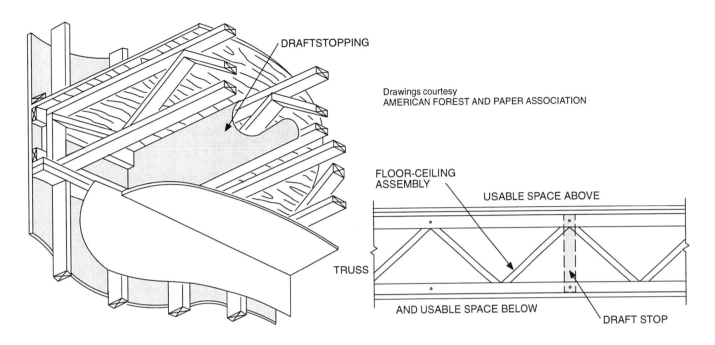

DRAFTSTOPPING

Drawings courtesy
AMERICAN FOREST AND PAPER ASSOCIATION

FLOOR-CEILING
ASSEMBLY

USABLE SPACE ABOVE

TRUSS

AND USABLE SPACE BELOW

DRAFT STOP

SINGLE-FAMILY DWELLING—MAX. 1,000 SQUARE FEET AND DIVIDED INTO
APPROXIMATELY EQUAL AREAS

For **SI:** 1 square foot = 0.0929 m^2.

DRAFT STOPS—SINGLE-FAMILY DWELLINGS

FIGURE 708-5

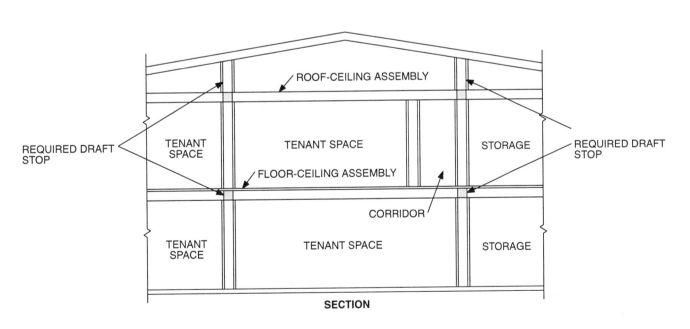

ROOF-CEILING ASSEMBLY

REQUIRED DRAFT
STOP

TENANT
SPACE

TENANT SPACE

STORAGE

REQUIRED DRAFT
STOP

FLOOR-CEILING ASSEMBLY

CORRIDOR

TENANT
SPACE

TENANT SPACE

STORAGE

SECTION

TWO OR MORE DWELLING UNITS AND HOTELS—Draft stops in line with tenant separation walls

DRAFT STOPS—MULTIPLE UNITS

FIGURE 708-6

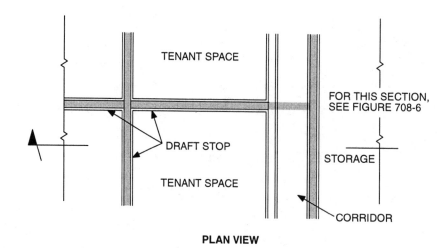

PLAN VIEW

ATTIC DRAFT STOPS—MULTIPLE UNITS

FIGURE 708-7

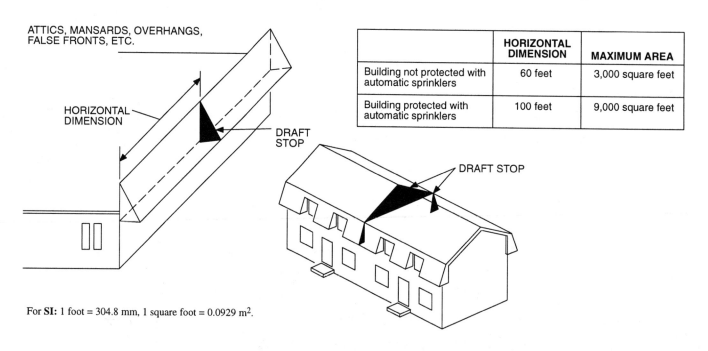

	HORIZONTAL DIMENSION	MAXIMUM AREA
Building not protected with automatic sprinklers	60 feet	3,000 square feet
Building protected with automatic sprinklers	100 feet	9,000 square feet

For **SI:** 1 foot = 304.8 mm, 1 square foot = 0.0929 m².

DRAFT STOPS—OTHER USES

FIGURE 708-8

(Continued from page 120)

3. **Other uses.** Draft stops are required by the code to be installed in attics of nonresidential buildings, mansards, false fronts set out from the walls and similar concealed spaces so that the area between draft stops does not exceed 3,000 square feet (279 m²) with the maximum horizontal dimension limited to 60 feet (18 288 mm). The exception triples the permitted area and allows an increase in the distance between draft stops to 100 feet (30 480 mm).

708.4 Draft Stops or Fire Blocks in Other Locations. This section provides cross-references to other provisions of the code that require fire blocking or draftstopping.

SECTION 709 — WALLS AND PARTITIONS

709.1 General. The fire-resistive ratings for the fire-resistive walls and partitions outlined in Table 7-B of the UBC are based on actual tests. Figure 709-1 shows two samples from the table. For reinforced concrete walls, it is important to note the type of aggregate as discussed earlier in this chapter. The difference in aggregates is quite significant for a four-hour fire-resistive wall, as it amounts to a difference in thickness of almost 2 inches (51 mm).

For hollow-unit masonry walls, the thickness required for a particular fire-endurance rating is the equivalent thickness. Fig-

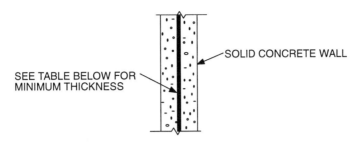

SOLID CONCRETE WALL

MATERIAL	ITEM NUMBER	CONSTRUCTION	MINIMUM FINISHED THICKNESS FACE-TO-FACE[2] (inches)			
			× 25.4 for mm			
			4 Hr.	3 Hr.	2 Hr.	1 Hr.
7. Solid Concrete[11,18]	7-1.1	Siliceous aggregate concrete	7.0	6.2	5.0	3.5
		Carbonate aggregate concrete	6.6	5.7	4.6	3.2
		Sand-lightweight concrete	5.4	4.6	3.8	2.7
		Lightweight concrete	5.1	4.4	3.6	2.5

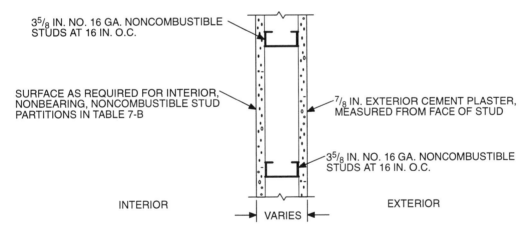

METAL STUDS AND EXTERIOR CEMENT PLASTER FROM ITEM 18-1.4 OF TABLE 7-B

For **SI:** 1 inch = 25.4 mm.

WALLS AND PARTITIONS

FIGURE 709-1

ure 709-2 outlines the manner in which the equivalent thickness is determined. The information shown in Figure 709-2 can be found in Footnote 2 of Table 7-B and applies to concrete masonry, hollow clay or shale brick.

The new paragraph in this section is actually a reiteration of Section 104.2.8 on the use of alternate materials, design, and methods of construction when approved by the building official.

709.2 Combustible Members. It is important that combustible members framing into fire-resistive walls do not significantly reduce the fire resistance of the wall. For example, if combustible members frame into a wall from each side and from oppo-

site of each other, the fire-resistive integrity of the wall is easily breached at the points of penetration, and a ready path for a fire through the wall is created. This is particularly important for occupancy separations and other fire-resistive walls which require protection of openings. It is also important in other fire-resistive walls to help prevent the spread of fire through a building. The upper drawing in Figure 709-3 depicts this requirement of the code for protection at the ends of combustible members.

709.3 Exterior Walls. Building designers may often omit the fire-resistive membrane on the interior surface of wood-stud exterior wall construction where the exterior wall passes through

Equivalent Thickness—For fire-resistance rating, the equivalent thickness is defined as the average thickness of solid material in the wall and is represented by the formula

$$T_E = \frac{V}{L \times H}$$

WHERE:

L = length of block or brick, using specified dimensions as defined in Chapter 21 in inches (mm).
H = height of block or brick, using specified dimensions as defined in Chapter 21 in inches (mm).
T_E = equivalent thickness, in inches (mm).
V = net volume (gross volume less volume of voids), in cubic inches (mm³).

When all cells are solid-grouted or filled with silicone-treated perlite loose-fill insulation; vermiculite loose-fill insulation; or expanded clay, shale or slate lightweight aggregate, the equivalent thickness shall be the thickness of the block or brick using specified dimensions as defined in Chapter 21. Equivalent thickness may also include the thickness of applied plaster and lath or gypsum wallboard, where specified. Section 2101.3 defines **specified dimensions** as "the dimensions specified for the manufacture or construction of masonry, masonry units, joints or any other component of a structure."

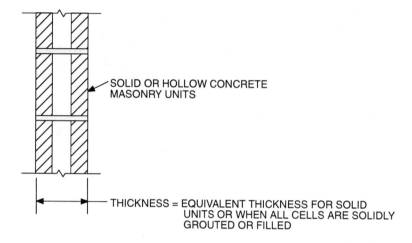

SOLID OR HOLLOW CONCRETE MASONRY UNITS

THICKNESS = EQUIVALENT THICKNESS FOR SOLID UNITS OR WHEN ALL CELLS ARE SOLIDLY GROUTED OR FILLED

EQUIVALENT THICKNESS OF MASONRY WALLS

FIGURE 709-2

an attic or other areas containing concealed spaces. However, the full fire-resistive rating of the wall is considered important by the UBC in the attic area or other area containing concealed spaces, particularly if the wall is load bearing. For this reason the code requires that the fire-resistive rating be maintained where the wall passes through an attic or concealed area, as depicted in the lower drawing of Figure 709-3.

709.3.2 Vertical fire spread at exterior walls. The intent of this section, added in the 1991 UBC, is to limit the vertical passage of fire, smoke and hot gases between floors. Vertical passages without barriers allow fire and hot gases to circumvent the protection provided for occupants in the floors above. When floor-ceiling assemblies do not extend to the exterior face of a building, Section 709.3.2.2 requires an approved barrier at the intersection at least equal to the fire resistance of the floor-ceiling assembly. For a comprehensive discussion about vertical fire spread, see Donald Belles' articles in *Building Standards* magazine.[3] See Figure 709-4.

Section 709.3.2.3 requires exterior flame barriers either projecting out from the wall or in line with the wall. These flame barriers are intended to prevent the "leap frogging" effect of a fire at the outside of a building. See Figure 709-5. However, there are three exceptions to Section 709.3.2.3. The first is for fully sprinklered buildings, and the second is for buildings three stories or less in height. The third exception is for open parking garages.

709.4 Parapets. This section intends that exterior walls of buildings extend a minimum of 30 inches (762 mm) above the roof to form a parapet. There are two reasons for the parapet:

1. To prevent the spread of fire from the roof of the subject building to a nearby adjacent building.

2. To protect the roof of a building from exposure due to a fire in an adjacent nearby building.

Three of the five exceptions listed in the code involve cases where the parapet would serve no useful purpose. In Exception 3, a concession is made to the small-floor-area building and in Exception 5, an alternate method for providing equivalent protection is delineated. It is not necessary that all of the exceptions listed apply. Only one of the exceptions is necessary for the elimination of a parapet.

Certainly, walls not required to be of fire-resistive construction would not benefit from a parapet. In the case of walls that terminate at two-hour fire-resistive roofs or roofs constructed entirely of noncombustible materials, the parapet would be of little benefit, as the construction of the roof would prevent the spread of fire into the building. The expression "roofs constructed entirely of noncombustible materials" is not intended to preclude the use of a fire-retardant roof covering.

In the case of walls located where unprotected openings are permitted, the code assumes that the exterior wall will be far enough away from either an exposing building or an exposed

(Continued on page 126)

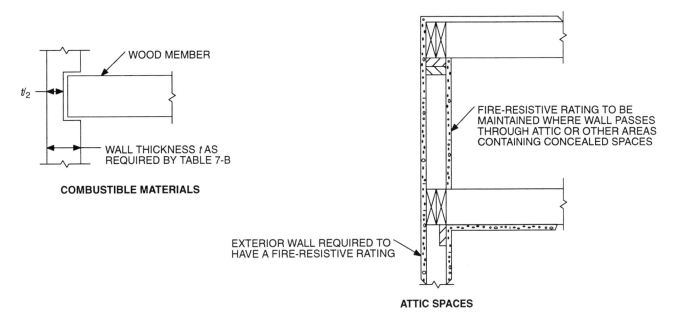

$t/2$

WOOD MEMBER

WALL THICKNESS t AS
REQUIRED BY TABLE 7-B

COMBUSTIBLE MATERIALS

FIRE-RESISTIVE RATING TO BE
MAINTAINED WHERE WALL PASSES
THROUGH ATTIC OR OTHER AREAS
CONTAINING CONCEALED SPACES

EXTERIOR WALL REQUIRED TO
HAVE A FIRE-RESISTIVE RATING

ATTIC SPACES

WALLS AND PARTITIONS

FIGURE 709-3

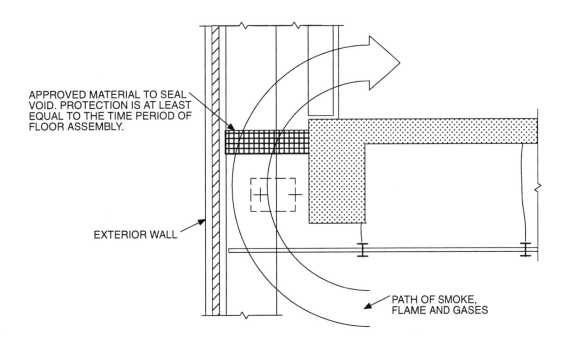

APPROVED MATERIAL TO SEAL
VOID. PROTECTION IS AT LEAST
EQUAL TO THE TIME PERIOD OF
FLOOR ASSEMBLY.

EXTERIOR WALL

PATH OF SMOKE,
FLAME AND GASES

THIS DRAWING SHOWS COMPLIANCE WITH SECTION 709.3.2.2. THE BUILDING MUST ALSO COMPLY WITH
THE REQUIREMENTS OR EXCEPTIONS IN SECTION 709.3.2.3. ASSUME DETAIL IS WITHIN A SPRINKLERED
BUILDING OR BUILDING HEIGHT IS THREE STORIES OR LESS.

FIGURE 709-4

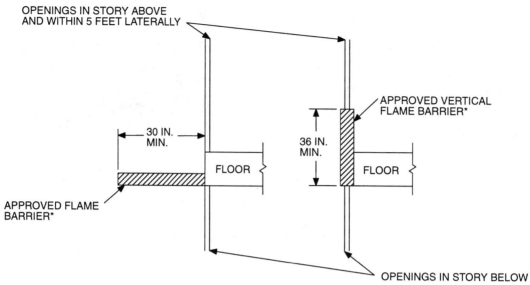

OPENINGS IN STORY ABOVE
AND WITHIN 5 FEET LATERALLY

30 IN.
MIN.

FLOOR

APPROVED FLAME
BARRIER*

APPROVED VERTICAL
FLAME BARRIER*

36 IN.
MIN.

FLOOR

OPENINGS IN STORY BELOW

* BARRIERS NOT LESS THAN THREE-FOURTHS
  HOUR RATED. FLAME BARRIERS NOT
  REQUIRED IN SPRINKLERED BUILDINGS OR IN
  BUILDINGS THREE STORIES OR LESS IN HEIGHT.

For **SI:** 1 inch = 25.4 mm, 1 foot = 304.8 mm.

FLAME BARRIERS

FIGURE 709-5

(Continued from page 124)

building so that the protection provided by the parapet will not be necessary.

The final exception makes a provision for one-hour fire-resistive exterior walls that are constructed similar to area separation walls to terminate at the underside of the roof sheathing, deck or slab. This provides designers with an alternate to the use of parapets while recognizing that these walls provide adequate protection of the structure and its occupants as well as providing consistency with Section 504.6 for area separation walls. See Figure 709-6.

In addition to having the same degree of fire resistance as required for the wall, the code also requires that the face of the parapet that faces the roof be of noncombustible materials for the upper 18 inches (457 mm). Thus, a fire that might be traveling along the roof and reaching the parapet will not be able to continue upward along the face of the parapet and over the top and expose a nearby adjacent building. The reason the requirement only applies to the upper 18 inches (457 mm) of the parapet and allows for extending the roof covering up the base of the parapet so that it can be effectively flashed. The 18-inch (457 mm) figure is based on a parapet height of 30 inches (762 mm). As stated in the code, the 30-inch (762 mm) requirement is measured from the point where the roof surface and wall intersect. This would also agree with the parapet wall definition found in Section 224. Therefore, when a cricket is installed adjacent to the parapet, the 30-inch (762 mm) dimension would be taken from the top of the cricket.

In those cases where the roof slopes upward away from the parapet and slopes greater than 2 units vertical in 12 units horizontal (16.7% slope), the parapet is required to extend to the same height as any portion of the roof that is within the distance

where protection of openings in the exterior wall would be required. However, in no case shall the height of the parapet be less than 30 inches (762 mm). See Figure 709-7 for an illustration of this latter requirement.

709.5 Nonsymmetrical Wall Construction. During the last decade or so, various manufacturers of exterior wall panels, manufacturers of pre-engineered buildings and others have proposed exterior wall construction that is nonsymmetrical as far as its fire resistance is concerned. The concept is to provide lesser protection on the exterior surface than on the interior surface of the exterior wall construction. A study by Richard Bletzacker indicates that there may be merit to these proposals.[4] However, the UBC does not recognize this concept and establishes generally in Table 7-B that exterior walls have the same fire-endurance rating from either side. Therefore, this section makes specific the intent of the UBC, which is that nonsymmetrical walls shall be tested from both sides, and the lower fire-endurance rating obtained from the tests shall be the fire-resistive rating assigned to the assembly.

709.6 Through Penetration. The subject of penetrations of fire-resistive walls and partitions has troubled building officials for years. The *Uniform Building Code* has had provisions for such penetrations since the 1979 edition. In a further attempt to clarify the problem of penetrations, the 1991 edition split the subject into two sections, "Through Penetration" and "Membrane Penetrations."

Through penetrations (penetrations through both membranes of a wall) are required to be fire-stopped with an approved through-penetration firestopping material complying with UBC Standard 7-5 when the penetration is through fire-resistive walls. This material is required to have an F rating at least equivalent to that of the fire-resistive rating of the wall penetrated. The previous edition of the code required through penetration fire stops for load-bearing fire-rated walls and walls requiring protected openings, which created considerable confusion in its application. These through-penetration fire stops required an F or T rating for certain specified wall penetrations, which was also confusing. The code change in the 1997 edition eliminating the T rating for through-penetration firestops in walls was justified on the basis that there was no need for such a restrictive rating for penetration of wall assemblies.

The 1997 edition also revised exceptions to the firestopped wall penetrations to allow small noncombustible penetrations, as stated in Section 709.6.1, not larger than 6-inch (152 mm) nominal diameter or 16 square inches (10 323 mm^2) in area to penetrate concrete or masonry walls provided the full thickness of the wall or the thickness required to maintain the fire resist-

ance is filled with concrete, grout or mortar. A second exception will allow the annular space around the same penetration to be fire stopped with a material that presents the passage of flame or hot gases sufficient to ignite cotton waste when tested under the time-temperature fire conditions of UBC Standard 7-1 and under a positive pressure differential of 0.01-inch (0.25 mm) water column. In this exception, the maximum size limitation of 4-inch (102 mm) diameter and 144-square-inch (92 903 mm^2) area of opening specified in the 1994 code have been removed. When properly installed around these penetrations, these materials provide adequate firestopping between the penetrating item and the fire-resistive membrane of the wall.

Like the membrane-penetration requirements discussed in the following section, through-penetration requirements can be confusing and at first reading can be a bit difficult to understand. For this reason, the reader is referred to Footnote 5 for an extended discussion of penetration protection.

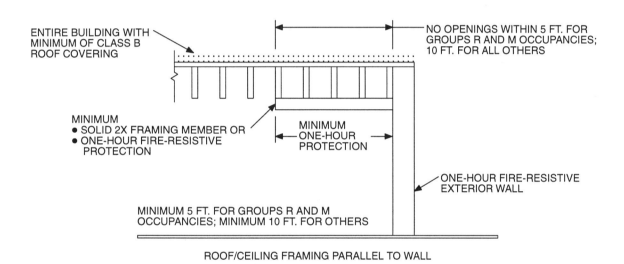

ENTIRE BUILDING WITH MINIMUM OF CLASS B ROOF COVERING

NO OPENINGS WITHIN 5 FT. FOR GROUPS R AND M OCCUPANCIES; 10 FT. FOR ALL OTHERS

MINIMUM
• SOLID 2X FRAMING MEMBER OR
• ONE-HOUR FIRE-RESISTIVE PROTECTION

MINIMUM ONE-HOUR PROTECTION

ONE-HOUR FIRE-RESISTIVE EXTERIOR WALL

MINIMUM 5 FT. FOR GROUPS R AND M OCCUPANCIES; MINIMUM 10 FT. FOR OTHERS

ROOF/CEILING FRAMING PARALLEL TO WALL

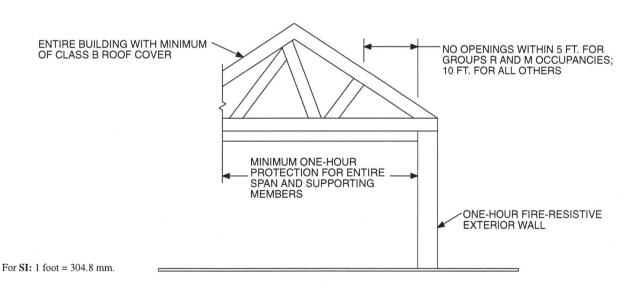

ENTIRE BUILDING WITH MINIMUM OF CLASS B ROOF COVER

NO OPENINGS WITHIN 5 FT. FOR GROUPS R AND M OCCUPANCIES; 10 FT. FOR ALL OTHERS

MINIMUM ONE-HOUR PROTECTION FOR ENTIRE SPAN AND SUPPORTING MEMBERS

ONE-HOUR FIRE-RESISTIVE EXTERIOR WALL

For **SI:** 1 foot = 304.8 mm.

ROOF/CEILING FRAMING PERPENDICULAR TO WALL

FIGURE 709-6

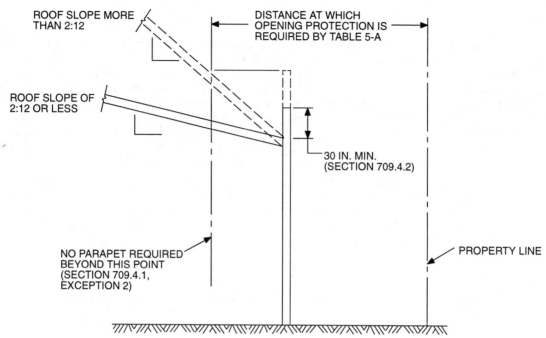

For **SI:** 1 inch = 25.4 mm.

PARAPET REQUIREMENTS

FIGURE 709-7

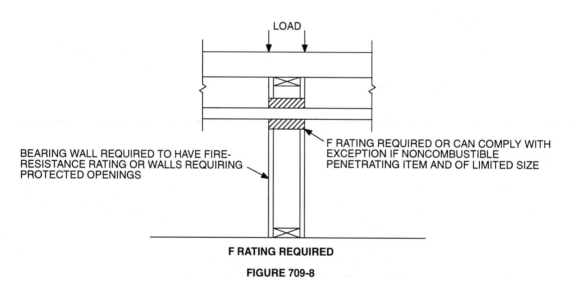

F RATING REQUIRED

FIGURE 709-8

Section 709.6.2, Fire-rated assembly, was added to define requirements for installation of penetrations in a UBC Standard 7-1 rated assembly. Section 709.6.3, Penetration firestop systems, defines the installation requirements for a tested firestop penetration system and further requires the system to have an F rating of not less than that of the required rating of the wall penetrated. See Figure 709-8.

709.7 Membrane Penetrations. This section addresses penetrations through a single membrane of fire-resistive walls. Some of these penetrations are allowed without a rated firestopping material in the annular space around such penetrations. Openings for steel electrical outlet boxes are such, provided that they

are no more than 16 square inches (10 320 mm²) in area and the aggregate area of the boxes does not exceed 100 square inches (64 500 mm²) for any 100 square feet (9.3 m²) of wall area. Also, to prevent an indirect through penetration, outlet boxes on opposing sides of a fire-resistive wall shall be separated by not less than 24 inches (610 mm). See Figure 709-9 for an example.

A new provision in the exception for membrane penetrations of electrical outlet boxes will allow outlet boxes of any material provided they are tested for use in fire-resistive assemblies and installed in accordance with the tested assembly. Also, a new exception was added to allow the annular space created by the penetration of a fire sprinkler to be unprotected provided such space is covered by a metal escutcheon plate. Since the escutch-

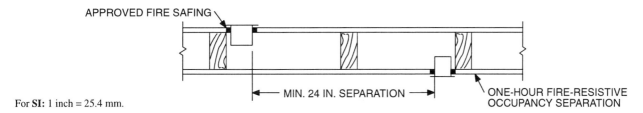

For **SI:** 1 inch = 25.4 mm.

MIN. 24 IN. SEPARATION

APPROVED FIRE SAFING

ONE-HOUR FIRE-RESISTIVE
OCCUPANCY SEPARATION

**PLAN SECTION OF WALL
STEEL ELECTRICAL OUTLET BOX PENETRATION**

PENETRATION OF FIRE-RESISTIVE WALLS

FIGURE 709-9

eon is a part of the listed sprinkler, it is inappropriate to require fire blocking at this location. It should be noted that this new exception applies to penetration of sprinklers, not sprinkler piping or cross mains that might be penetrating fire-resistive construction.

Also allowed, as with through penetrations, are noncombustible penetrations, provided they meet the same requirements as mentioned earlier for through penetrations.

An additional provision has been added to address the improper installation of noncombustible penetrating items to combustible materials on both sides of the membrane unless it can be confirmed that the fire-resistive integrity of the wall is maintained in accordance with UBC Standard 7-1.

SECTION 710 — FLOOR-CEILINGS OR ROOF-CEILINGS

710.1 General. Table 7-C of the UBC provides fire-resistive ratings for floor-ceiling and roof-ceiling assemblies, and Figure 710-1 depicts the construction of a one-hour fire-resistive wood floor or roof assembly.

Often, materials such as insulation are added to fire-resistive assemblies. It is the intent of the UBC to require substantiating fire test data to show that when the materials are added to a floor-ceiling or roof-ceiling assembly, they do not reduce the required fire-endurance time period. This is because adding insulation (for example) to a floor-ceiling or roof-ceiling assembly may change its capacity to dissipate heat, and, particularly for noncombustible assemblies, the fire-resistive rating may be changed. Although the primary intent of the provision is to cover those cases where thermal insulation is added, the language is intentionally broad so that it applies to any material which might be added to the assembly. Also, Footnote 14 of Table 7-C exempts unusable space from the flooring and ceiling requirements. See Figure 710-2.

The protection of a ceiling membrane also includes the adequacy of the panelized ceiling system to withstand forces generated by a fire and other forces that may try to displace the panels. These forces can generate positive pressures in a fire compartment that need to be counteracted. As a result, lay-in ceiling panels that provide a portion of the fire resistance of the floor-ceiling or roof-ceiling assembly should be capable of resisting this upward or positive pressure so that the panels stay in position and continue to maintain the integrity of the system. The

code defines the pressure to be resisted as 1 pound per square foot (47.9 Pa).

710.3 Membrane Protection. When the code permits the use of a fire-resistive ceiling as a part of the protection of a fire-resistive floor-ceiling or roof-ceiling assembly, penetrations of the ceiling membrane shall comply with the requirements stated in Section 710.2 for through penetrations, except as follows:

1. Membrane penetrations of steel, ferrous or copper conduits, electrical outlet boxes, pipes, tubes, vents, concrete or masonry penetrating items where the annular space is protected in accordance with Section 709.6 or 710.2 or is protected to prevent the free passage of flame and the products of combustion. Such penetrations shall not exceed an aggregate area of 100 square inches in any 100 square feet (694 mm^2/m^2) of ceiling area in assemblies tested without penetrations.

2. Membrane penetrations for electrical outlet boxes of any material are permitted, provided that such boxes are tested for use in fire-resistive assemblies and installed in accordance with the tested assembly.

3. The annular space created by the penetration of a fire sprinkler shall be permitted to be unprotected, provided such space is covered by a metal escutcheon plate.

710.2 Through Penetrations. These requirements have been reformatted from Section 710.3, Floors, in the 1994 edition to allow for easier use and more uniform enforcement. The provisions do, however, have some technical changes from the 1994 code.

The proper protection of openings in floors is one of the most important requirements in the code as far as spread of fire is concerned. One of the largest factors contributing to deaths in fires is the vertical spread of fire. Therefore, it is of paramount importance that the fire-resistive integrity of the floor assembly be maintained and not destroyed by "poke-through" openings and improperly fire-stopped penetrations. The code requires that fire-resistive floors be continuous. Thus, they must extend to the exterior walls and have no offsets with openings, such as are commonly found in parking garages. If the floor is not joined tightly to the exterior wall, the joint must be fire-stopped with an approved noncombustible safing material. See Section 709.3.2.

The usual procedure for protection of openings in floor assemblies is to provide a fire-resistive shaft as required in Section 711 or to comply with the fire-rated assembly requirements of Section 710.2.2 or the penetration firestop system requirements

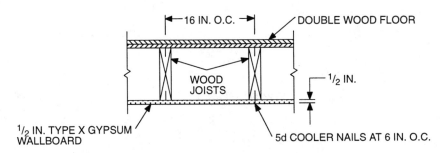

END JOINTS OF WALLBOARD CENTERED ON JOISTS

WOOD FLOOR AND JOISTS—$^1/_2$ IN. TYPE X GYPSUM WALLBOARD FROM ITEM 13-1.4 OF TABLE 7-C

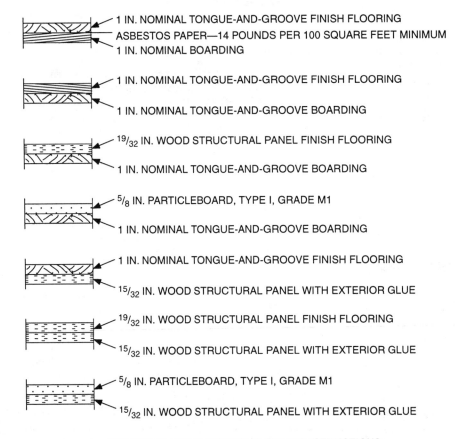

ALTERNATE DOUBLE WOOD FLOOR CONSTRUCTIONS

For **SI:** 1 inch = 25.4 mm, 1 pound per square foot = 4.88 kg/m^2.

ONE-HOUR FIRE-RESISTIVE FLOOR AND ROOF ASSEMBLIES

FIGURE 710-1

of Section 710.2.3. However, the code does except certain penetrations when installed according to the requirements of this section. The shaft enclosure provisions of Section 711 are obviously allowed as well as exit enclosures as stated in Chapter 10. Furthermore, Section 711 contains exceptions that allow penetrations within walls under certain conditions. Atria constructed according to the requirements of Section 402 are also allowed as penetrations through fire-resistive floors or floor-ceiling assemblies. These are all specific cases that are discussed in this handbook. Penetrations of pipes, conduit, sleeves and electrical

boxes that are not discussed in the sections mentioned above are specified in this section. It should be noted that Exceptions 1 and 2 in this section have been revised from similar exceptions in the previous code to allow the penetrating items, so specified, in a single fire-rated floor assembly or concrete floor up to a maximum of 6 inches (152 mm) in diameter.

Penetrations through fire-resistive floors or floor-ceiling assemblies are to be protected since they provide a means of communicating a fire between stories. Such penetrations are allowed

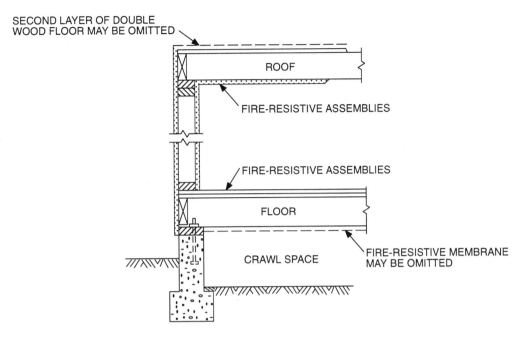

OMISSION OF CEILING AND FLOORING—COMBUSTIBLE ASSEMBLIES

FLOOR-CEILING OR ROOF-CEILING

FIGURE 710-2

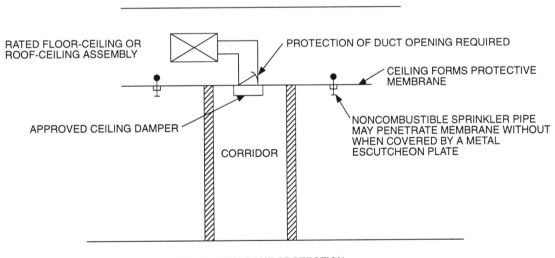

CEILING MEMBRANE PROTECTION

FIGURE 710-3

if they maintain the same fire resistance as the floor in which they are installed. Firestopping of the annular space around these penetrations must provide an F or a T rating as described in Section 702. An F rating is based on flame occurrence on the unexposed surface while the T rating is based on the temperature rise on the unexposed side of the through-penetration firestop. A T-rated fire stop must first pass the F rating criteria specified in Section 7.512-1 of UBC Standard 7-5, "Fire Tests of Through Penetration Fire Stops." and is further subject to the temperature

rise performance test of Section 7.512.2. T-rated fire stops are required for floor penetrations unless meeting the exceptions of Section 710.2.1; however, the 1997 code will allow F-rated fire stops to be used for floor penetrations contained and located within the cavity of the wall.

710.6 Construction Joints. Openings in fire-resistive floors for construction joints are to be protected as required by Section 706, which is discussed earlier in this handbook.

SECTION 711 — SHAFT ENCLOSURES

It is well known that one of the primary means for the spread of fire in multistory buildings, particularly the older buildings, has been the transmission of hot gases and fire upward through unprotected or improperly protected vertical openings.[6] The primary cause of death in the hotel portion of the MGM Grand Hotel in Las Vegas, Nevada, as a result of the fire in November 1980 was the upward transmission of smoke through inadequately protected elevator shafts, stair shafts and heating and ventilating shafts.[7] It is because of this potential for fire spread vertically through buildings that this section requires that vertical openings be protected with fire-resistive shafts. The protection of interior stairways will be discussed in the appropriate portions of Chapter 10.

The fire-resistive ratings required for shafts that protect vertical openings vary in accordance with the types of construction, but generally Types I and II-F.R. buildings require two-hour fire-resistive construction for the shafts and all other buildings require one-hour fire-resistive construction for shafts.

Section 711.1 is the charging section requiring shaft protection for vertical openings, and Section 711.2 contains the requirements for the extent of the enclosure. Shaft enclosures are required to extend from the lowest floor opening through each successive floor opening and be enclosed at the top and bottom. Although this seems intuitively obvious, it was clarified in the 1991 and 1997 editions. Two exceptions are included in this section. The first addresses those shafts that extend through or to the roof, by waiving the enclosure requirements at the top of the shaft. Shaft protection is not needed at the roof, but is needed only within the interior portions of the building. The second exception allows the use of a horizontal fire damper at the lowest floor level in lieu of the enclosure at the bottom of the shaft enclosure.

For the most part, Section 711.3 includes the former exceptions found in the shaft provisions of the 1988 edition of the UBC. These are now called special provisions and are easier to understand. The first provision permits two adjacent stories to intercommunicate with each other without protection of the openings between the two stories except in the case of Group I Occupancies. A note of caution here. For nonsprinklered Group R, Division 1 Occupancies, Section 310.8 requires that corridors serving an occupant load of 10 or more be separated from corridors and other areas on adjacent floors. Thus, in this special condition, a shaft enclosure complying with Section 711 may not be required, but a separation is required.

The language "not concealed within building construction" is intended to prevent unprotected shafts such as chutes or dumbwaiter shafts that are completely enclosed by partitions or closets. Where the openings are concealed in this manner, they permit a fire within the shaft to burn undetected and distribute products of combustion to the upper floor.

As long as these intercommunicating openings serve only the one adjacent floor, shaft protection is not required. This exception is commonly used where office buildings have a lobby that extends up through the second story so that individuals on the second floor may look down into the lobby. Any building containing an opening similar to that just described, which extends through two or more floor levels, must be constructed as required for a building containing an atrium, as discussed in Section 402.

The second provision is really not a provision but a cross-reference to Section 1005.3.3 for exit enclosures.

The third paragraph is similar to the first provision except it allows one more floor to be penetrated but is limited to shafts for gas vents, ducts, factory-built chimneys or piping that extend through not more than two floors, provided the openings around the penetration are fire-stopped at each floor. This exception applies only to one- and two-story buildings.

The next two provisions provide for gas vents, noncombustible piping and conduit to be installed in the walls of buildings without complying with the requirements for shaft construction. They also require draft stops at each floor or ceiling. In this case, a noncombustible sealant is required where the walls are penetrated by the pipes and conduits. These provisions are based on the extreme difficulty in constructing very small shafts to comply with the fire-resistive requirements for shafts. The code requires that where these vents and pipes are installed within the walls of the building:

- The pipes be noncombustible (gas vents must comply with the Mechanical Code).

- The penetrations of the walls and floors be sealed with a noncombustible material that also must be impervious to smoke.

When these conditions are met, the code assumes that reasonably equivalent fire protection is secured.

The last provision provides for cables, cable trays, conduit, pipes or tubing to penetrate a floor without complying with the requirements for shaft construction, provided the openings around such penetrations are protected with approved through-penetration fire stops that have the same degree of fire resistance as the floor construction which they penetrate.

Section 711.4 requires protection of openings into shafts for the very same reason that occupancy separations require protection of openings. Because fire-resistive shafts act as barriers to the vertical spread of fire in a building, the entire assembly, including openings, requires protection. There is an exception covering openings in the exterior wall that constitute no hazard unless proximity to a property line requires their protection. Exception 2 provides for the use of through-penetration fire stops providing the same degree of fire resistance as the shaft in lieu of fire-resistive fire door assemblies. See Figure 711-1.

In the 1997 edition, a new Exception 3 has been added to Section 711.4, which essentially relocates Exception 2 in Section 711.2 of the 1991 edition. This relocation of the exception to the section titled "Protection of Openings" should make the intended applications clearer. This exception addresses the penetration of non-combustible ducts, vents and chimneys in the bottom of the shaft enclosures that are used to convey vapors, ducts or combustion products. This exception, when first placed in the 1991 edition, resolved several conflicts with the *Uniform Mechanical Code*, which often resulted in the construction of dedicated shafts for individual floors or pieces of equipment. The exception was intended to allow non-combustible ducts, vents and chimneys to enter a shaft at the bottom without requiring a fire damper at the point of penetration. The exception was not intended to allow the bottom of the shaft to be unenclosed.

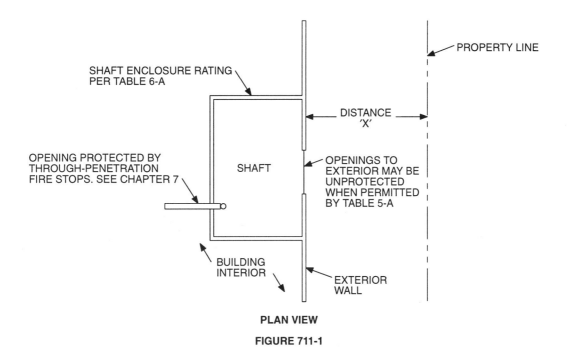

SHAFT ENCLOSURE RATING
PER TABLE 6-A

PROPERTY LINE

DISTANCE
'X'

OPENING PROTECTED BY
THROUGH-PENETRATION
FIRE STOPS. SEE CHAPTER 7

SHAFT

OPENINGS TO
EXTERIOR MAY BE
UNPROTECTED
WHEN PERMITTED
BY TABLE 5-A

BUILDING
INTERIOR

EXTERIOR
WALL

PLAN VIEW

FIGURE 711-1

AUTOMATIC SPRINKLER SYSTEM REQUIRED.
SECTION 904.2.2, ITEM 2, REQUIRES THE
INSTALLATION OF AUTOMATIC SPRINKLER
HEADS IN THE TERMINAL ROOM, AT THE TOP
OF THE CHUTE AND AT ALTERNATE FLOORS
WHEN A CHUTE EXTENDS THROUGH THREE
OR MORE FLOORS.

RUBBISH OR LINEN CHUTE

OCCUPANCY SEPARATION AROUND
TERMINATION ROOM. ONE- OR TWO-HOUR
RATED DEPENDING ON SHAFT PROVISIONS
BUT NOT LESS THAN A ONE-HOUR RATING.

TERMINATION ROOM

OPENINGS PROTECTED PER OCCUPANCY
SEPARATION REQUIREMENTS

RUBBISH AND LINEN CHUTES

FIGURE 711-2

The requirements in Section 711.5 for the termination rooms for linen and rubbish chutes are intended to provide protection of exit routes in buildings. The redundancy of requiring the termination rooms to be enclosed with a minimum one-hour fire-resistive occupancy separation and not opening into exit corridors or stairways helps secure the intent of not exposing exit routes to fire (in this case from rubbish and linen chutes). Also, the termination rooms are frequently littered with trash and do represent the termination of the shaft and its protection. As a result, the minimum one-hour fire-resistive occupancy separation enclosure prevents any fire beginning in the termination room from spreading to the rest of the building. To further secure the intent, Section 904.2.2 requires sprinkler protection for the chutes and terminal rooms. See Figure 711-2.

Section 711.6 allows for an alternate type of protection by providing for the use of small chutes and shafts in Type V buildings. The shaft is required to be of one-hour fire-resistive construction; however, this section allows 26-gage sheet steel to be substituted for the fire-resistive membrane on the interior of the shaft. For small chutes and dumbwaiter shafts, this provides a smoke-tight shaft liner that is durable and easy to maintain.

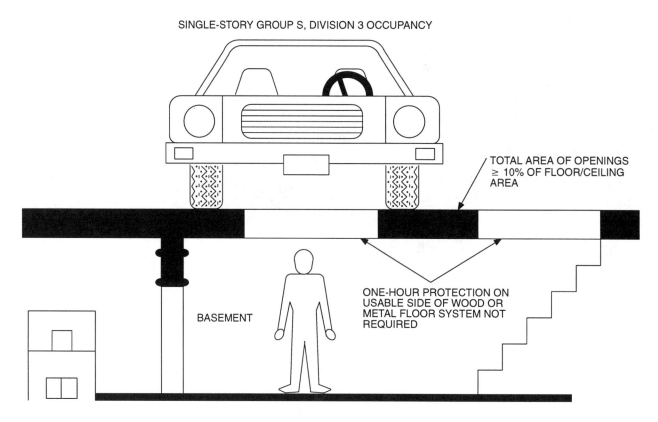

SINGLE-STORY GROUP S, DIVISION 3 OCCUPANCY

TOTAL AREA OF OPENINGS ≥ 10% OF FLOOR/CEILING AREA

ONE-HOUR PROTECTION ON USABLE SIDE OF WOOD OR METAL FLOOR SYSTEM NOT REQUIRED

BASEMENT

USABLE SPACE UNDER A VEHICLE SERVICE PIT

FIGURE 712-1

Thus, fire and other products of combustion will not readily be spread to other floors within the building.

SECTION 712 — USABLE SPACE UNDER FLOORS

This section requires that, except for Group R, Division 3 and Group U Occupancies, under-floor spaces protected with an automatic sprinkler system, and vehicle service pits (see Figure 712-1), usable space under the first story be enclosed. When the enclosure is constructed of metal or wood, it must be protected on the side of the usable space, as would be required for one-hour fire-resistive construction. Doors must be tightfitting, self-closing and either a solid wood door not less than $1^3/_8$ inches (35 mm) thick or a 20-minute-rated door.

The rationale for this requirement has become blurred and uncertain with time, but seems to relate to a 1943 version of the same section that required that all building floor areas be enclosed with exterior walls whenever openings in exterior walls required protection or were prohibited. This section was revised for the 1994 edition.

SECTION 713 — FIRE-RESISTIVE ASSEMBLIES FOR PROTECTION OF OPENINGS

713.1 General. In the context of the UBC, the expression "fire assembly" refers to a fire door, fire window or fire damper, including the required frames, sills, anchorage and hardware for its proper operation. Generally, whenever a fire door, fire win-

dow or fire damper is referred to, it is the intent of the code that the entire fire assembly be included. Figure 713-1 illustrates the code requirements for fire door assemblies. Figure 713-2 depicts a typical installation of an automatic hinged fire damper. As far as identification is concerned, the code intentionally separates fire doors, fire windows and fire dampers from the hardware, frames, sills and anchorage. This separation is considered necessary, as fire door frames and hardware are usually interchangeable with many different fire doors. Where they are not interchangeable, the entire assembly of door frame and hardware is labeled and shipped as a unit from the factory.

Fire doors, windows and dampers are required to have an approved label or listing mark permanently affixed at the factory. Listing agencies will only label assemblies that have been tested. However, some assemblies, generally doors, are too large to be tested in available furnaces. As a result, a provision was added to the UBC in 1985 that permits the installation of oversized fire doors when approved by the building official. As oversized fire doors are not subjected to the standard fire test, UL, for example, will provide a certificate of inspection for them certifying that, except for the fact that the doors are oversized, they comply with the requirements for materials design and construction for a fire door of the specified fire-endurance rating. Where the certificate of an approved agency such as UL has been provided, there is assurance that the fire door will protect the opening as required by the code.

A new provision in the 1997 edition requires labels for exit enclosure fire doors to indicate that the temperature rise on the

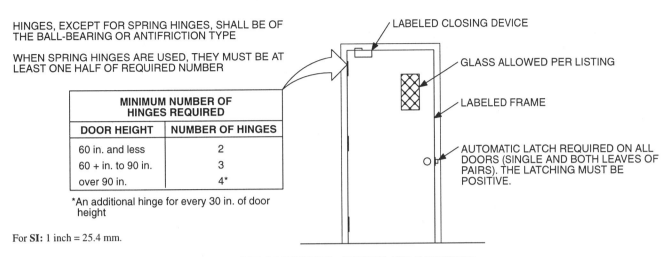

HINGES, EXCEPT FOR SPRING HINGES, SHALL BE OF THE BALL-BEARING OR ANTIFRICTION TYPE

WHEN SPRING HINGES ARE USED, THEY MUST BE AT LEAST ONE HALF OF REQUIRED NUMBER

MINIMUM NUMBER OF HINGES REQUIRED	
DOOR HEIGHT	NUMBER OF HINGES
60 in. and less	2
60 + in. to 90 in.	3
over 90 in.	4*

*An additional hinge for every 30 in. of door height

For **SI:** 1 inch = 25.4 mm.

LABELED CLOSING DEVICE

GLASS ALLOWED PER LISTING

LABELED FRAME

AUTOMATIC LATCH REQUIRED ON ALL DOORS (SINGLE AND BOTH LEAVES OF PAIRS). THE LATCHING MUST BE POSITIVE.

FIRE DOOR ASSEMBLIES—FRAMES AND HARDWARE

FIGURE 713-1

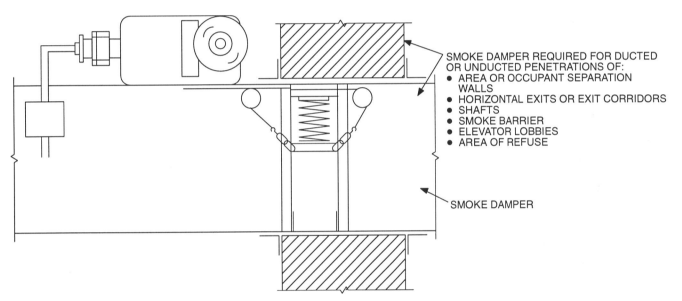

SMOKE DAMPER REQUIRED FOR DUCTED OR UNDUCTED PENETRATIONS OF:
- AREA OR OCCUPANT SEPARATION WALLS
- HORIZONTAL EXITS OR EXIT CORRIDORS
- SHAFTS
- SMOKE BARRIER
- ELEVATOR LOBBIES
- AREA OF REFUSE

SMOKE DAMPER

Figure Courtesy
SHEET METAL AND AIR CONDITIONING CONTRACTORS NATIONAL ASSOCIATION

NOTE: These illustrations are not intended to exclusively endorse or indicate preference for a combination fire and smoke damper. Two separate dampers that satisfy requirements for the respective functions may also be used for fire and smoke control.

COMBINATION FIRE AND SMOKE DAMPERS

FIGURE 713-2

unexposed surface will not exceed 450° F (232°C) above ambient at the end of 30 minutes of the fire exposure specified in UBC Standard 7-2 in order to show compliance with Section 1005.3.3. The change was made to be consistent with current practices and will improve the ability of an inspector to quickly identify that the proper door is installed in an exit enclosure. This will also help the designer and contractor identify the proper door as well.

As the UBC contains no standards for installation, construction and anchorage of fire doors and windows, the code requires that they be installed in accordance with their listing by an approved agency.

713.6 Hardware.

713.6.1 Closing devices. Figure 713-1 depicts in general the code requirements for closing devices and specifically details the code requirements for hinging and latching.

As far as closing devices are concerned, the code requires one of two types of closing devices:

A. An automatic device that closes automatically when subjected to either:

- An increase in temperature. This is most often a fusible link rated with a maximum temperature of 165°F (74°C).

- Actuation of a smoke detector. In this case the closing device is activated by a smoke detector and is set to operate at a specified density of smoke. The code prohibits the use of smoke detectors, which delay the release of the door for more than 10 seconds, to prevent excessive smoke from passing through the opening prior to door closing.

B. A self-closing device. A self-closing device is usually either an approved set of spring hinges or a pneumatic device that operates to close the door and cause it to latch after each opening.

The code requires mandatory use of automatic-closing devices for the following doors:

- **Those doors required by the code to have a three-hour fire-protection rating.** Most often these doors are horizontal or vertical sliding doors on which it is virtually impossible to utilize self-closing devices. Therefore, the code makes the installation of automatic closers mandatory.

    Although three-hour fire doors are also manufactured as side-hinged swinging fire doors, the code still requires automatic-closing devices. This is to increase the reliability of the opening protection. Swinging fire doors with self-closers are all too often propped open with wood blocks or wedges. As a result the door will not protect the opening in case of fire. In this case the increased reliability is considered by the code to be necessary for a door with such a fire-protection rating. It is either protecting an opening in an area separation wall or an occupancy separation separating an occupancy with a relatively high potential fire severity.

    Additionally, automatic-closing three-hour fire assemblies that are activated by an increase in temperature shall have one heat-actuating device installed on each side of the wall at the top of the opening and one on each side of the wall at the ceiling where the ceiling is more than 3 feet (914 mm) above the top of the opening.

    When the closing device will operate by the actuation of a smoke detector, Section 713.2 requires that the device be installed and maintained as set forth in approved nationally recognized standards. There are a number of parameters that will affect the number of and location for smoke detectors. These include the height from the top of the door opening to the ceiling above; when multiple doors are involved, the separation between doors, the

number of doors and the total width of these doors all must be considered.

- **One and one-half hour, one-hour or three-fourths-hour assemblies** may be either automatic or self-closing. Regardless of rating, doors that are a part of an automobile ramp enclosure shall be automatic closing. When temperature-activated automatic-closing devices are used, they shall have heat-actuated devices as required for three-hour doors, or they may be activated by a single fusible link in the opening incorporated in the closing device.

- **Fire assemblies** required by Chapter 10, Means of Egress, shall have closing devices as in Chapter 10. Primarily this would be doors for corridors, Section 1004.3.4, and enclosures, Section 1005.3.3.

- **Cross-corridor fire doors.** In this case the code makes the automatic-closing device mandatory to increase reliability. This requirement is intended to eliminate the problem of wedged-open fire doors installed across corridors. To further increase reliability, the code requires that the automatic devices be activated by smoke detectors and, furthermore, that they be of an approved type which will release the door in the event of a power failure.

713.6.2 Hinges. This item was added to the 1985 edition. As the UBC contains no standard for the installation of fire doors, this item makes specific the intent of the code. The requirement that at least one half of the hinges be spring hinges where spring hinges are used as self-closers is intended to avoid excessive strain and premature failure of the springs. Figure 713-1 depicts the requirements set forth in Section 713.6.2.

713.6.3 Latch. This item was also added to the 1985 edition of the UBC and is also intended to clarify the intent of the code that fire doors be provided with an automatic latch that will positively secure the door when closed in order to maintain the required protection of the opening.

713.7 Glazed Openings in Fire Doors. Except for doors required to have a three-hour fire-protection rating, the UBC permits glazed openings in fire doors as described in this section. These limitations are based on years of testing; as a result, the code intends that openings not exceeding the sizes indicated are permitted without further testing. The reason for the 4-inch (102 mm) minimum dimension for the 100-square-inch (64 500 mm²) opening is to preserve the structural integrity of the door. For example, a 2-inch by 50-inch (51 mm by 1270 mm) opening in the door would be structurally detrimental and, most likely, would lead to a premature failure of the door under fire conditions.

713.8 Fire Window Size. Prior to the 1994 edition, all fire windows that were required to have a three-fourths-hour fire-protective rating were limited in size to 84 square feet (7.8 m²) with neither width nor height exceeding 12 feet (3658 mm). The code now places these area and dimensional limitations only on exterior wall openings required to be protected by Table 5-A. Interior openings required to have a three-fourths-hour rating are now limited only to the actual size tested.

713.9 Glazing. The labeling of glazing materials with the required fire-protection rating is mandated by this section. The labeling requirement is new with the 1994 UBC. The section also provides a direct reference to the requirements for safety glazing, Sections 2406.3 and 2406.4, to clearly define the code's intent that glazing used in fire doors and fire windows subject to human impact must comply with safety glazing requirements.

713.10 and 713.11 Smoke Dampers and Fire Dampers. Provisions for smoke dampers and for fire dampers have been greatly expanded in the 1994 UBC. Many of the changes, particularly those related to smoke dampers, were related to the new smoke-control provisions of Section 905. The net result of the new provisions will be the required installation of smoke dampers in many locations where only fire dampers were previously required. Table 7-13 lists the locations where smoke dampers and fire dampers are required. Note that in many locations both types of damper are required. This will mean either two dampers must be installed or a damper listed for both heat and smoke control must be installed. Figure 713-2 illustrates the installation of an automatic-closing combination fire and smoke damper.

Specific UBC standards for fire, ceiling or smoke dampers no longer exist. Part III of Chapter 35, however, does list recognized standards for these items, including three UL standards: UL 555 for fire dampers, UL 555C for ceiling dampers, and UL 555S for leakage-rated dampers for use in smoke control. Underwriters Laboratories' *Building Materials Directory* lists dampers under the categories of "Fire Dampers" and "Leakage-Rated Dampers." Dampers intended for installation in air-handling openings penetrating fire-resistive membrane ceilings are listed by UL in their *Fire-Resistive Directory* under "Ceiling Dampers."

Both Sections 713.10 and 713.11 require that dampers be installed so they are accessible for inspection and servicing, while Section 713.12 requires fire assemblies to be installed in accordance with their listing.

713.10 Smoke Dampers. Just what is a smoke damper, and what is the significance of the Class II, 250°F (121°C) designation? First, what is a smoke damper? Test standard UL 555S states that leakage-rated dampers (smoke dampers in the terminology of the UBC) are intended (a) to restrict the spread of smoke in heating, ventilating and air-conditioning (HVAC) systems that are designed to automatically shut down in the event of a fire or (b) to control the movement of smoke within a building when the HVAC system is operational in engineered smoke-control systems. The Class II and 250°F (121°C) designation relate to the test criteria used to evaluate dampers in fulfilling these two functions.

The class designation indicates the maximum leakage permitted in cubic feet per minute per square foot (cubic mm per minute per mm²) for the particular class. The four classes progress from Class I (least leakage or best performance) through Class IV (greatest leakage or poorest performance). The UBC requires compliance with Class II, so a damper rated as Class I would be acceptable. These leakage ratings are determined at ambient temperature after exposing the damper to temperature degradation at an elevated temperature, with 250°F (121°C) being the lowest elevated temperature allowed by the standard. Dampers can be tested using higher degradation temperatures, one as high as 850°F (454°C), but most listed dampers seem to have been tested at either 250°F (121°C) or 350°F (177°C).

A new provision has been added to specifically instruct the designer or installer on how to control smoke dampers. Smoke dampers are required to be closed by activation of smoke detectors installed in accordance with the Fire Code and any of the five specified methods defined in this new provision. These methods of control, each having benefits and drawbacks, were proposed by those involved with damper installation and should provide consistent and logical control methods for the dampers.

713.11 Fire Dampers. Test standard UL 555 covers fire dampers ranging from one-half hour to three hours, but UL seems to only list (and it is assumed test) dampers at one-and-one-half hours up to three hours. Because fire dampers carry an hourly rating, plans should reflect the rating required at a particular location if more than one rating is required within a building. Underwriters Laboratories 555 indicates that dampers tested under that standard are intended for use in HVAC duct systems passing through fire-resistive walls, partitions or floor assemblies. This intent of the test standard is interesting because this section indicates that fire dampers are to be installed for various "penetrations" but does not indicate that these are to be "duct penetrations." Editions prior to the 1994 edition specifically said "duct penetrations." The point of all this is that if an unducted penetration is to occur through, say, a shaft wall, the listing for any fire damper to be installed to protect that penetration should be reviewed to be sure it is intended for the particular installation.

There are two exceptions listed under Item 3 for penetrations of shaft enclosures. These two exceptions are illustrated in Figures 713-3 and 713-4. A note of caution when applying the first exception: the exception listed for shaft penetrations under the smoke damper requirements of Section 713.10 is different. It exempts "exhaust-only openings serving continuously operating fans and protected using the provisions of Chapter 9." Since this was a new provision in the 1994 edition, it did not undergo the test of field usage, but it is assumed that the reference to Chapter 9 is intended to mean that the exception applies only when a smoke-control system as detailed in Chapter 9 is installed. Therefore, fire dampers may be omitted from the shaft enclosure penetration under the first exception of Section 713.11, but smoke dampers may still be required.

Item 4 mentions penetrations of the ceiling of fire-resistive floor-ceiling or roof-ceiling assemblies and refers back to Section 710.3. This cross-reference is provided because such dampers are really not fire dampers as tested under the fire damper test standard (UL 555), but rather they are "ceiling dampers" tested under their own unique standard (UL 555C). Section 710.2 specifically mentions "ceiling fire dampers."

Just as fire dampers are tested for different hourly ratings, they are also tested for different installation positions. A damper listed for vertical installation cannot arbitrarily be installed in the horizontal position.

713.12 Installation. This section states that fire assemblies shall be installed in accordance with their listing. The test standards for each of the three types of damper carry specific requirements that manufacturers provide installation and operating instructions, and that a reference to these instructions be a part of the required marking information on the damper. For fire dampers, required information on the damper includes the hourly rating; the words "Fire Damper"; whether or not the damper is to be in a dynamic or static system (or both); maximum rated airflow and pressure differential across the closed damper for dampers

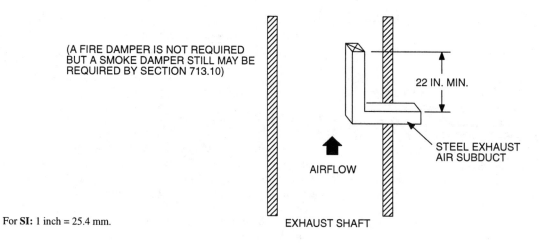

(A FIRE DAMPER IS NOT REQUIRED BUT A SMOKE DAMPER STILL MAY BE REQUIRED BY SECTION 713.10)

22 IN. MIN.

STEEL EXHAUST AIR SUBDUCT

AIRFLOW

For **SI:** 1 inch = 25.4 mm.

EXHAUST SHAFT

EXHAUST SUBDUCTS PENETRATING SHAFTS

FIGURE 713-3

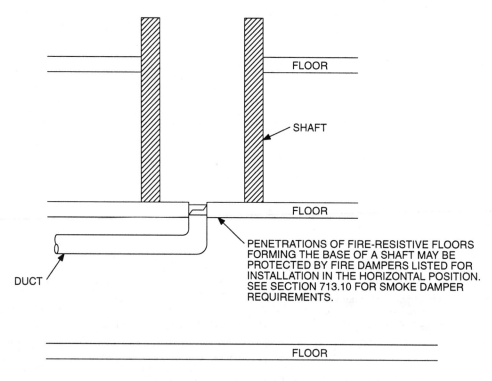

FLOOR

SHAFT

FLOOR

PENETRATIONS OF FIRE-RESISTIVE FLOORS FORMING THE BASE OF A SHAFT MAY BE PROTECTED BY FIRE DAMPERS LISTED FOR INSTALLATION IN THE HORIZONTAL POSITION. SEE SECTION 713.10 FOR SMOKE DAMPER REQUIREMENTS.

DUCT

FLOOR

VERTICAL PENETRATIONS INTO SHAFT ENCLOSURES

FIGURE 713-4

intended for use in dynamic systems; an arrow showing direction of airflow for dampers intended for use in dynamic systems, the intended mounting position (vertical, horizontal, or both), top of damper; and of course, the manufacturer's name and model number. Standard 555 requires that all of this information be available on the damper label, which is installed at the factory, and that all labels be located on an internal surface of the damper and be readily visible after the damper is installed.

This section also states that only fire dampers labeled for use in dynamic systems shall be installed in systems intended to operate with fans on during a fire. The test standard for fire dampers states that fire dampers are intended for use in either (a) static systems that are automatically shut down in the event of a fire or (b) in dynamic systems that are operational in the event of a fire. If the HVAC system has not been designed and constructed to shut down in case of fire, then dynamically listed fire dampers are necessary. Special attention should be paid to damper listings when smoke-control systems are installed under the provisions of Section 905.

SECTION 714 — THROUGH-PENETRATION FIRE STOPS

As discussed earlier, all through-penetration fire stops must have an F or a T rating, unless otherwise exempted. These ratings are determined by UBC Standard 7-5. Since through pene-

trations must conform to these requirements and membrane penetrations have no specific provisions for the testing of such, except for small noncombustible penetrations, through-penetration fire stops are permitted for use as membrane-penetration fire stops. A new provision has been added to the 1997 edition to clarify how to handle those penetration firestop systems that use sleeves in their assembly and insulation and coverings of penetrations. An exception was added to make it clear that the sleeves covered by this section do not include damper sleeves because the filling of the space around the damper could adversly affect its ability to close.

TABLE 7-13—REQUIRED LOCATIONS FOR SMOKE AND FIRE DAMPERS

ITEM	LOCATION	SECTION 713.10 SMOKE DAMPERS[1,2]	SECTION 713.11 FIRE DAMPERS[3]
1.	Penetrations of area or occupancy separation walls	Required	Required
2.	Penetrations of the fire-resistive construction of horizontal exit walls or corridors serving as a means of egress	Required[4]	Required[4]
3.	Penetrations of shaft enclosures	Required[5]	Required[6,7]
4.	Penetrations of areas of refuge	Required[8]	Required[8]
5.	Penetrations of smoke barriers	Required	—
6.	Penetrations of elevator lobbies required by Section 3002	Required	—
7.	Penetrations of the ceiling of fire-resistive floor-ceiling or roof-ceiling assemblies	—	Required[9]
8.	Penetrations of an atrium enclosure element	—	Required
9.	Penetrations of the building exterior required to have protected openings per Table 5-A	—	Required

[1]A smoke damper need not be provided when it can be demonstrated that the smoke damper is not essential to limit the passage of smoke under passive conditions and the proper function of a smoke-control system complying with Chapter 9 does not depend on the operation of the damper.

[2]Smoke dampers may be omitted at openings that must be maintained open for proper operation of a mechanical control system provided that adequate protection against smoke migration, in event of system failure, has been provided.

[3]A fire damper is not required where fire tests have demonstrated that fire dampers are not required to maintain the fire resistance of the construction.

[4]Openings for steel ducts penetrating the required fire-resistive construction of corridors are not required to have smoke or fire dampers when such ducts are of not less than 0.019-inch (0.48 mm) thickness (No. 26 galvanized sheet steel gage) and have no openings serving the corridor.

[5]Exhaust-only openings serving continuously operating fans and protected using the provisions of Chapter 9 is an exception.

[6]Duct penetrations by steel exhaust air subducts extending vertically upward at least 22 inches (559 mm) above the top of the opening in a vented shaft where airflow is upward is an exception.

[7]Penetrations of a fire-resistive floor forming the base of a shaft enclosure may be protected by fire dampers listed for installation in the horizontal position.

[8]Ventilation systems specifically designed and protected to supply outside air to the areas during an emergency is an exception.

[9]Penetrations shall be protected in accordance with Section 710.3.

REFERENCES

[1]Boring, Delbert F., James C. Spence and Walter G. Wells (1981). *Fire Protection through Modern Building Codes,* Fifth Edition. American Iron and Steel Institute, Washington, D.C., page 25.

[2]Ibid, page 138.

[3]Belles, Donald W. (1986). External walls of buildings—Prevention of fire spread from story to story. *Building Standards,* 55(3):7-12.

[4]Bletzacker, Richard W. (1986). Fire exposure of exterior walls. *Building Standards,* 55(5):7-11.

[5]Armstrong, Paul, and Jay A. Woodward (1992). Penetration protection: An overview of the 1991 UBC requirements. *Building Standards,* July-August, and Penetration protection: An update, *Building Standards,* November-December.

[6]Boring, Spence and Wells, op. cit., page 151.

[7]Bush, Vincent R. (1981). Preliminary report—MGM Grand Hotel Fire, Las Vegas, Nevada. *Building Standards,* 50(1):6-9.

Chapter 8

INTERIOR FINISHES

Unfortunately, many building code provisions are enacted only after a disaster (usually with a large loss of life) indicates the need to regulate in a specific area. This is true of the interior wall and ceiling finish requirements of Chapter 8. In this case the 1942 Coconut Grove nightclub fire in Boston, with a loss of almost 500 lives, provided the impetus to develop code requirements for the regulation of interior finish. Based on fire statistics, lack of proper control over interior finish (and the consequent rapid spread of fire) is second only to vertical spread of fire through openings in floors as a cause of loss of life during fire in buildings.[1]

The dangers of unregulated interior finish are as follows:

- **The rapid spread of fire.** Rapid spread of fire presents a threat to the occupants of a building by either limiting or denying their use of exitways within and out of the building. This limitation on the use of exits can be created by:

  1. The rapid spread of the flame itself so that it blocks the use of exitways.

  2. The production of large quantities of dense, black smoke (such as smoke created by certain plastic materials), which obscures the exit path and exit signs.

- **The contribution of additional fuel to the fire.** Unregulated finish materials have the potential for adding fuel to the fire, thereby increasing its intensity and shortening the time available to the occupants to exit safely. However, because UBC Standard 8-1, "Test Method for Surface-burning Characteristics of Building Materials," no longer requires the determination of the amount of fuel contributed, the UBC does not regulate interior finish materials on this basis.

SECTION 801 — GENERAL

This section has been revised in the 1997 edition to achieve uniformity with the other two model building codes regarding how interior finish is defined. Both the 1994 Southern Building Code Congress International (SBCCI) *Standard Building Code* and the 1993 BOCA *National Building Code* with the 1994 Supplement contain essentially identical wording for defining interior finish. The only significant technical change to the current definition is the inclusion of a reference to structural fire-resistive materials that may be used in buildings and are exposed to the interior of the building. In those cases, such materials should meet the requirements for interior finish in Chapter 8. This is currently recognized by the ICBO ES Acceptance Criteria for Spray-applied Fire-protection Materials (AC23), which specifies a maximum flame-spread index of 200 and a smoke-density rating not greater than 450.

It is the intent of the UBC to regulate only the interior finish materials on walls and ceilings and not to regulate floor coverings applied to the floor. Experience tells us that the traditional type of interior floor finish materials such as wood, vinyl asbestos tile, linoleum and other resilient floor-covering materials do not contribute to the early spread of fire.[2]

Fire tests have demonstrated that carpet on the floor which passes the Federal Flammability Standard is not likely to become involved in a room fire until the fire has reached or approached "flashover."[3] This federal standard was developed in 1970, and all carpet manufactured in the United States since 1971 must meet the requirements of the test. Therefore, carpet on the floor in rooms requires no further evaluation as to its flame-spread characteristics.

Although there is evidence that corridor floor coverings can propagate flame when exposed to a fully developed fire in a room that opens into the corridor,[4] the UBC and most codes do not regulate finish materials applied to floors. One argument holds that when the radiant heat energy from an exposing room opening into the corridor is so high as to involve the corridor floor finish, the corridor has also become untenable for the occupants of the building.

It is the intent of the UBC to regulate interior finish materials, which cover wide expanses or areas, and not to regulate such items as trim including picture molds, chair rails, baseboards and handrails, which cover only a small proportion of the walls and ceilings. Nor does the UBC intend to regulate thin materials such as wallpaper, which is less than $1/28$ inch (0.9 mm) thick. These thin materials behave essentially as the backing to which they are applied and, as a result, are not regulated. The 1997 edition clarifies this intent by eliminating the surface-burning characteristics comparison to paper, required in previous editions, since there are no specific standards or even approved tests available that compare the surface-burning characteristics of paper with a thickness of less than $1/28$ inch (0.9 mm). However, repeated applications of wallpaper where the original materials are not removed can accumulate to a thickness of such magnitude that they do require regulation. Also, some wall-covering materials (such as vinyl plastics and other plastic materials) are regulated, as they do not meet the thickness criterion. Also excluded from compliance with Chapter 8 are doors, windows and their frames.

SECTION 802 — TESTING AND CLASSIFICATION OF MATERIALS

802.1 Testing. The standard test for the determination of the flame-spread characteristics of interior finish materials is as indicated in the introduction to this chapter, UBC Standard 8-1, which is based on ASTM Standard E 84. This test is commonly known as the Steiner Tunnel Test. Section 8.101 of the standard should be referred to for a thorough discussion of the scope, purpose, intent and limitations of the test standard. The *Uniform Building Code* also permits the use of any other recognized test method or procedure for determining the surface-burning characteristics of finish materials that will give comparable results to those from the Steiner Tunnel Test. Textile materials used for interior finish are not ordinarily suitable for testing in accordance with the procedures of UBC Standard 8-1. In this case the UBC specifies testing in accordance with UBC Standard 8-2. See Section 805.

The *Uniform Building Code* also requires that the method of fastening the finished materials to the interior surfaces be capable of holding the material in place for 25 minutes under a room temperature of 300°F (149°C). If there is any question as to the adequacy of the fastening, appropriate tests should be required to determine compliance with this provision of the code. ICBO ES has evaluated some adhesive materials, and reference to these reports by the manufacturer will establish compliance with the code if approved by the building official.

802.2 Classification. In addition to the flame-spread classifications depicted in Table 8-A, the UBC also requires that for all cases the smoke density be no greater than 450 when tested in accordance with UBC Standard 8-1. The intent of the limitation on smoke density is strictly based on visual obscuration of the exit path. Where the smoke density is greater than 450, obscuration of the exit path and exit signs by the smoke will be such that the occupants of the building will have extreme difficulty in locating exits and exiting the building.

TABLE 8-A
FLAME-SPREAD CLASSIFICATION

MATERIAL QUALIFIED BY:	
Class	Flame-spread Index
I	0-25
II	26-75
III	76-200

SECTION 803 — APPLICATION OF CONTROLLED INTERIOR FINISH

When interior finish is not applied directly to a backing surface (such as a fire-resistive or noncombustible wall or ceiling), concealed spaces are created that provide the opportunity for fire to originate and spread without detection until the interior finish material has burned through. Item 1 of this section is intended to protect against this condition.

Where interior finish materials are set out or suspended distances greater than specified in Item 1, the potential exists for the fire to gain access to the space through joints or imperfections and to spread along the back surface as well. In this case the flame spreads at a much faster rate than on one surface, as the flame front will be able to feed on the material from two sides. Therefore, the provisions of Item 2 of this section are intended to protect against this type of hazard. In the case where a wall is set out, the wall, including the portion that is set out, is required by the code to be of fire-resistive construction as would be required by the code for the occupancy and type of construction.

It should be noted for Items 1 and 2 that the provisions are applicable only where the walls and ceiling assemblies are required to be either of fire-resistive or of noncombustible construction. Where the walls and ceiling assemblies are of unprotected combustible construction, the fire blocking provisions of Section 708.2 are applicable.

Item 4 requires that thin materials—less than $1/4$ inch (6.4 mm) thick—other than Class I materials be applied directly against a noncombustible backing unless they were qualified by tests where the material was suspended from the noncombustible backing. The reason for this requirement is similar to that in Item 2. There are millions of square feet of thin paneling, such as luan plywood, installed on walls and ceilings. When not installed against a noncombustible backing, these materials readily burn through and permit an almost uncontrolled rapid flame spread because the flame proceeds on both surfaces of the material.

After flame-spread requirements were applied to the interior finish of mobile homes, the fire death rate in mobile homes dropped from 3.2 per 100 fires to 1.0 per 100.[5] Although other factors such as firestopping, smoke detectors and emergency escape windows contributed to the reduction, one contributor to the higher death rate was the rapid spread of fire along thin paneling materials applied without a backing.

SECTION 804 — MAXIMUM ALLOWABLE FLAME SPREAD

804.1 General. The required flame-spread classes of finish materials, based on location within the building, are shown in Figure 804-1 and Table 8-B.

Exception 1 is based on the assumption that limited amounts of Class III materials will not substantially increase the hazard in the areas specified.

Exception 2 is based on the cooling that the automatic sprinkler system provides. Because of this cooling, the code permits the reduction of one classification.

Exception 3 relative to Type IV buildings recognizes that the flame-spread classification of most woods is under 200, or a Class III classification, and that the heavy-timber construction is not subject to rapid flame spread. This exception applies only to other exitways, rooms or areas since the code requires vertical stair enclosures of Type IV buildings to have a minimum of one-hour fire-resistive construction for the enclosure.

Figure 804-2 provides flame-spread classifications of the woods commonly used in construction and finish work. A glance at the table will show that most woods qualify for a Class III rating. There are a few woods that qualify for a Class II rating, and no woods available in the United States qualify for a Class I rating. There are on the market, however, many paints and varnishes that the manufacturers refer to as fire-retardant coatings. In the parlance of the UBC, these are flame-spread reducers, and ICBO ES and the Council of American Building Officials (CABO) National Evaluation Committee have evaluated several of these intumescent paints or coatings. Due to intumescence, these paints or coatings bubble up or swell up under the action of flame and heat to provide an insulating coating on the surface of the material treated. Certain intumescent paints can reduce the flame spread of combustible finishes to as low as Class I and the smoke density to considerably below 450. These flame-spread-reducing intumescent coatings are particularly useful when correcting an existing nonconforming combustible interior finish.

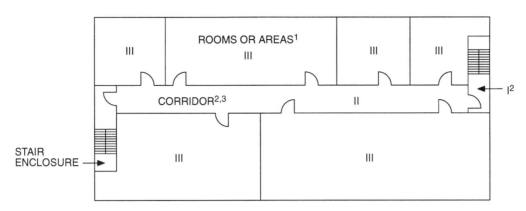

NOTES:
1. Class II required for Group A, Divisions 1, 2 and 2.1 and Group I, Divisions 1.1, 1.2 and 2 Occupancies.
2. Class III permitted in Group F and Group R, Division 3 Occupancies.
3. Class I required in Group I Occupancies, except in Group I, Divisions 2 and 3 Occupancies, where Class II may be used.

FLAME-SPREAD REQUIREMENTS BY LOCATION WITHIN THE BUILDING

FIGURE 804-1

TABLE 8-B—MAXIMUM FLAME-SPREAD CLASS[1]

OCCUPANCY GROUP	ENCLOSED VERTICAL EXITWAYS	OTHER EXITWAYS[2]	ROOMS OR AREAS
A	I	II	II[3]
B	I	II	III
E	I	II	III
F	II	III	III
H	I	II	III[4]
I-1.1, I-1.2, I-2	I	I[5]	II[6]
I-3	I	I[5]	I[6]
M	I	II	III
R-1	I	II	III
R-3	III	III	III[7]
S-1, S-2	II	II	III
S-3, S-4, S-5	I	II	III
U	NO RESTRICTIONS		

[1]Foam plastics shall comply with the requirements specified in Section 2602. Carpeting on ceilings and textile wall coverings shall comply with the requirements specified in Sections 804.2 and 805, respectively.

[2]Finish classification is not applicable to interior walls and ceilings of exterior exit-access balconies.

[3]In Group A, Divisions 3 and 4 Occupancies, Class III may be used.

[4]Over two stories shall be of Class II.

[5]In Group I, Divisions 2 and 3 Occupancies, Class II may be used.

[6]Class III may be used in administrative spaces.

[7]Flame-spread provisions are not applicable to kitchens and bathrooms of Group R, Division 3 Occupancies.

804.2 Carpeting on Ceilings. The code requires that the materials listed have a Class I flame-spread rating. This is based on the fact that untreated surfaces having a napped, tufted, looped or similar fuzzy surface will contribute to a flash fire over the complete surface. Thus, when a portion of the material has been ignited, it will almost instantaneously cause a flash which completely engulfs the entire ceiling.

SECTION 805 — TEXTILE WALL COVERINGS

Textile wall coverings present a unique hazard due to the potential for extremely rapid fire spread, and the flame-spread indices obtained from UBC Standard 8-1 may not be reliable when applied to textile wall coverings. *Uniform Building Code Standard 8-2*, which was developed at the University of California, Berkeley, is considered to provide a more realistic appraisal of these materials, and the code now provides for its use in establishing acceptance criteria for textile wall coverings.

SECTION 807 — SANITATION

The primary thrust of this section is to provide easily cleanable, sanitary and water-resistant surfaces in toilet rooms and showers.

FLAME-SPREAD CLASSIFICATION OF WOODS

Species of Wood	Flame Spread	Soruce*
Birch, yellow	105-110	UL
Cedar, eastern red	110	HUD/FHA
Cedar, Pacific Coast yellow	78	CWC
Cedar, western red	70	HPMA
Cottonwood	115	UL
Cypress	145-150	UL
Fir, Douglas	70-100	UL
Gum, red	140-155	UL
Hemlock, West Coast	60-75	UL
Lodgepole pine	93	CWC
Maple flooring	104	CWC
Oak, red or white	100	UL
Pine, eastern white	85	CWC
Pine, Idaho white	72	HPMA
Pine, northern white	120-215	UL
Pine, ponderosa	105-200	HUD/FHA
Pine, red	142	CWC
Pine, southern yellow	130-190	HUD/FHA
Pine, western white	75	UL
Poplar	170-185	UL
Redwood	70	UL
Spruce, northern	65	UL
Spruce, western	100	UL
Spruce, white	65	CWC
Walnut	130-140	UL
Plywoods		
Douglas fir, $^1/_4$-inch	120	HUD/FHA
Lauan, three-ply urea glue, $^1/_4$-inch	110	HUD/FHA
Particleboard, $^1/_2$-inch	135	HPMA
Redwood, $^3/_8$-inch	95	CRA
Redwood, $^5/_8$-inch	75	CRA
Walnut, $^3/_4$-inch	130	HUD/FHA

*Source:

CRA:	California Redwood Association	HPMA:	Hardwood Plywood Manufacturers Association
	Data Sheet-2D2-7L (Lumber)		Test No. 337, Test No. 592, Test No. 596
	Data Sheet-2D2-7P (Plywood)	HUD/FHA:	Flame-spread Ratings for Various Materials
CWC:	Canadian Wood Council	UL:	Underwriters Laboratories
	Data File FP-6		UL 527, May, 1971

For **SI:**   1 inch = 25.4 mm.

FIGURE 804-2

807.1.1 Floors. Except for dwelling units, the code requires toilet room floors to have a smooth, hard, nonabsorbent surface. Finishes such as concrete and ceramic tile are specifically mentioned, but other approved materials may also be used. When the code refers to "other approved material," the intent is that the building official determine that any other material be the equivalent of the materials specified in this section insofar as cleanability and water resistance are concerned.

Whatever floor finish is used, the code requires that it extend upward onto the walls at least 5 inches (127 mm). The intent here is that the flooring form an integral cove so that there will be no sharp joint at the floor/wall intersection. If sheet materials are approved for use in toilet rooms, the top set base that is so often used would not satisfy the intent of the code.

Toilet room floor finish requirements apply to all uses and occupancies except for dwelling units. Since motel and hotel rooms are not dwelling units, toilet room flooring in these uses should comply.

807.1.2 Walls. Walls within 2 feet (610 mm) of the front and sides of urinals and water closets are required to have a smooth, hard, nonabsorbent finish of portland cement plaster, concrete or ceramic tile. As is permitted for floor coverings, other approved materials may be used. Required finishes shall extend to a height of at least 4 feet (1219 mm) above the floor and shall be of a type not adversely affected by moisture. Water-resistant gypsum backing board may be used as a base for tile or wall panels provided it satisfies the limitations set forth in Section 2512. Although the code does not specifically state that concrete walls must be sealed, concrete is not, strictly speaking, a nonabsorbent material and needs some type of surface treatment. Sealing is particularly important for concrete block walls.

Special wall finishes at water closets and urinals are not required for dwelling units and guest rooms or toilet rooms not accessible to the public that contain only one water closet. Note that the exceptions for floor finishes and wall finishes are not the same. A private toilet room containing one water closet would be required to have flooring that complies with Section 807.1.1, but there would be no special requirements for wall finish.

In all occupancies, including dwelling units, penetrations of the water-resistant surfacing of the walls for the installation of accessories such as grab bars, towel bars, etc., are required to be sealed to protect the structural elements from moisture. The intent of the code is that because the structural elements are not required to be moisture resistant, the penetrations should be sealed to protect the structural elements. Although sealing is required for all walls in a toilet room, sealing is obviously most critical in areas of water splash such as in showers or behind or adjacent to lavatories.

807.1.3 Showers. All showers must have floor and wall finishes that are smooth, nonabsorbent and not affected by moisture. Wall finishes must extend not less than 70 inches (1778 mm) above the drain inlet. Water-resistant gypsum backing board installed in compliance with Section 2512 may be used on shower walls.

REFERENCES

[1]Boring, Delbert F., James C. Spence and Walter G. Wells (1981). *Fire Protection through Modern Building Codes,* Fifth Edition. American Iron and Steel Institute, Washington, D.C., page 156.

[2]Lathrop, James K., Ed. (1986). *Life Safety Code Handbook,* Third Edition. National Fire Protection Association, Quincy, Massachusetts, page 206.

[3]Ibid., page 211.

[4]Ibid., pages 211-212.

[5]Cote, Arthur E., and Jim L. Linville, Eds. (1986). *Fire Protection Handbook.* National Fire Protection Association, Quincy, Massachusetts, pages 9-51.

Chapter 9

FIRE-PROTECTION SYSTEMS

Chapter 9 provides requirements for two distinct systems considered vital for the creation of a safe building environment. The first of these systems is intended to control and limit fire spread and to provide building occupants and firefighters with the means for fighting fire. Included are fire-extinguishing and standpipe systems. The second system is intended to control smoke migration. Included are design and installation standards for smoke-control systems required by other chapters of the UBC as well as smoke- and heat-venting systems.

SECTION 904 — FIRE-EXTINGUISHING SYSTEMS

904.1.1 General. It is the intent of this chapter to require fire-extinguishing systems in those buildings and with those uses which through experience have been shown to present hazards requiring the additional protection provided by fire-extinguishing systems. Furthermore, it is the intent of the code to prescribe installation standards for those systems which are required by the code. Conversely, as long as the installation does not create a hazard, the UBC does not intend to regulate the design, installation or operation of a fire-extinguishing system that is not required by the code. A note of caution is necessary, however, regarding the installation of a nonstandard system. It is not unusual for buildings to be enlarged or the use to be changed. As a result, a code-complying fire-extinguishing system may be required at some future time. At that time the existing nonstandard system will either need to be abandoned or will need to be brought into compliance. Thus, the installation of a nonstandard system may not be a wise choice in the long run. Additionally, the installation of a nonstandard system may negate any cost saving in fire insurance premiums that would otherwise be due an owner for voluntarily installing a code-complying fire-extinguishing system.

In general, automatic fire suppression is required when:

- There are inadequate numbers and sizes of openings in the exterior walls from which a fire may be fought from the exterior of a building. The provisions requiring sprinklers in these "windowless" buildings apply to all buildings, regardless of occupancy, except for Group R, Division 3 and Group U Occupancies.

- Certain special features and hazards of the various occupancy groups are such that the additional protection provided by automatic suppression is warranted.

As fire-extinguishing systems are mechanical systems and are subject to breakdown when not properly installed and maintained, the code requires that they be approved and subject to such periodic tests as may be required. The fire department hose connection is required to be approved by fire department personnel, as they know better than anyone else the best location for such a connection.

The approval process is usually a joint approval process conducted by both the building and fire departments, as both agencies have a stake in ensuring that the systems are properly designed and installed.

High-piled combustible storage. The last paragraph of Section 904.1.1 directs the code user to the Fire Code for the fire protection of buildings used for high-piled combustible storage. Such storage is defined in the *Uniform Fire Code* as "storage of combustible materials in closely packed piles or combustible materials on pallets, in racks or on shelves where the top of storage is greater than 12 feet (3658 mm) in height. When required by the chief, high-piled combustible storage also includes certain high-hazard commodities, such as rubber tires, Group A plastics, flammable liquids, idle pallets and similar commodities, where the top of storage is greater than 6 feet (1829 mm) in height."

904.1.2 Standards. As indicated earlier, the UBC provides standards for the design, installation and maintenance of fire-extinguishing systems which are required by the code. Three exceptions to this requirement are as follows:

1. Where an automatic fire-extinguishing system is not covered by either UBC Standard 9-1 or 9-2, the code requires that it be installed in accordance with approved standards. These systems would be special systems required by the Fire Code and other types of systems, such as dry chemical, carbon dioxide or aqueous-foam systems.

2. The code permits a sprinkler system to be connected to the domestic water system as long as the connection is made as shown in Figure 904-1 and is approved by the building official. Although the code permits a domestic water connection as shown in Diagram A, the presence of the meter ahead of the sprinkler connection introduces an unnecessary friction loss to the system, as well as an additional cost due to the size of the meter necessary to be installed in a service line which supplies both domestic and fire sprinkler systems.

   The connection shown in Diagram B is preferable, as the meter is provided only in the domestic water service connection and permits relatively unimpeded flow to the sprinkler system. The two connections shown in Figure 904-1 provide for the reliability of the sprinkler system, as a shutdown of the domestic water supply system would not affect the water supply to the sprinklers.

   Furthermore, the check valves protect the domestic water system from the potential high pressures in the sprinkler system. They also protect the public water system from any backflow due to pumping into the fire department connection.

   Although this exception also permits the omission of the fire department connection when approved by the fire

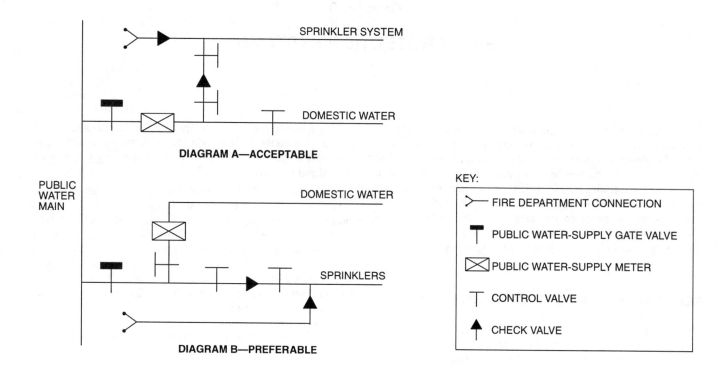

AUTOMATIC SPRINKLER SYSTEM CONNECTION TO DOMESTIC WATER SUPPLY

FIGURE 904-1

department, this approval is almost never granted. The reliability of the fire department connection is a very important factor. It allows the fire department to pump water into the system and supplement the system where the normal water supply might have too low a pressure due to excessive demands. Furthermore, where the piping is laid out so that the fire department connection is downstream from the control valves, it permits the fire department to bypass a control valve that might have been inadvertently closed. Omission should be permitted only in those few cases where the protected building is relatively small and has exterior walls mostly open on all sides. Thus, the fire department will have relatively easy access for supplementing the sprinkler system with handlines.[1]

3. Exception 3 allows the use of sprinkler systems that comply with UBC Standard 9-3 in residential occupancies that are four stories or less in height. Since UBC Standard 9-3 does not require sprinklers within all spaces of the building, the exception does not allow an area increase or a reduction in fire-resistive rating when such a sprinkler system is installed. The system, however, can be used to satisfy the requirements of Section 904.2.8 provided the residential building is not more than four stories in height.

904.1.3 Modifications. This section calls attention to the fact that area increases or substitutions for one-hour fire-resistive construction are not permitted when a residential-type sprinkler system complying with UBC Standard 9-3 is used. Because complete coverage is not provided, trade-offs should not be

allowed when the system is a residential system as described in UBC Standard 9-3.

904.2 Automatic Fire-extinguishing Systems. It is the intent of this section to specify those occupancies and locations where automatic fire-extinguishing systems are required. The Fire Code is referenced in Section 904.2.1 for special provisions for hazardous chemicals and materials.

A fire-extinguishing system is a system that discharges an approved fire-extinguishing agent (such as water, dry chemicals, aqueous foams or carbon dioxide) onto or in the area of a fire. A fire sprinkler system discharges only water. The code specifies a fire sprinkler system in certain circumstances, as it is the intent of the code that water be applied and not one of the other extinguishing agents. In fact, the code-referenced standard, UBC Standard 9-1, provides for the design and installation of a system supplied by water, and almost all references in Section 904.2 (with the exception of 904.2.1, and 904.2.5, Group H Occupancies) require the installation of "an automatic sprinkler system." Generally, water is the most effective extinguishing agent for fires. Only where water creates problems, such as in magnesium or calcium carbide storage areas, would some other type of extinguishing agent be required.

904.2.2 All occupancies except Group R, Division 3 and Group U Occupancies. The provisions of Item 1 make specific the intent of the code to require an automatic sprinkler system in windowless buildings. Items 2, 3 and 4 of this section are directed to providing automatic fire suppression to protect specific hazardous uses or hazardous installations. A new Item 5 was added to the 1994 UBC, which recognizes the difficulty of fire-fighting and rescue in taller buildings.

The code intends through Item 1 to regulate buildings with limited access from the exterior:

- **On the basis of each individual story above ground.** Each individual story is analyzed for the size and the number of exterior wall openings. Thus, in a multistory building, it is possible to have a requirement that a sprinkler system be installed in one story and not in another.

  The code requires that the openings be:

  1. **Installed above the finished exterior grade or ground level.** This provision is necessary so that effective fire suppression and rescue can be accomplished from the exterior of the building.

  2. **Of adequate size and spacing.** While it may be argued that the openings required by the code are not the equivalent of automatic fire sprinkler protection, the access for firefighting provided by the openings has proven satisfactory.

     The intent of the code is that there shall be at least one opening in each 50 lineal feet (15 240 mm) of exterior wall. Note that the word *in* rather than *for* has been used in the code. Thus, an exterior wall 100 feet (30 480 mm) long with a 20-square-foot (1.82 m^2) opening at each end will comply with the intent of the code. Since each 50-foot (15 240 mm) length of the wall would have an opening while the same wall with only one 40-square-foot (3.72 m^2) opening at one end would not comply.

  3. **Accessible to the fire department from the exterior.** Certainly the openings would be of no value for firefighting if the firefighting forces cannot gain access to them. The mere fact that the openings may be 30 or 40 feet (9144 mm or 12 192 mm) above grade does not mean the openings are inaccessible. However, if, with

the resources available to the fire department, access cannot be obtained to the openings, they would be considered inaccessible. The determination of accessibility rests with the building official. However, personnel in the fire department should be consulted for their professional opinions and also for their knowledge of the capabilities of their equipment.

4. **Adequate to allow access for firefighting to all portions of the interior of the building.** For this reason the code requires that where openings are provided on only one side and the opposite exterior wall is more than 75 feet (22 860 mm) away, sprinklers shall be provided or openings shall be provided on at least two sides. For those floors of the building that qualify as stories by definition, the code requires openings only on two sides, which can either be adjacent sides or opposite sides on the assumption that, with two exterior sides having openings, adequate access may be gained to effectively fight the fire.

   The provisions requiring openings in the exterior walls do not extend beyond the exterior wall line into the building. Thus, the code does not dictate specific openings for interior partition arrangements because the normal openings provided through interior partitions provide adequate accessibility to all interior portions of the building.

5. **Applicability.** The provisions of Item 1 apply to every story or basement of all buildings when the floor area exceeds 1,500 square feet (139.4 m^2). See Figures 904-2, 904-3 and 904-4 for graphic representations of Item 1 requirements.

- **On the basis of each basement.** Basements are considered to be somewhat more difficult than stories above grade when it comes to fighting fires from the exterior of the building. Therefore, the code provides that when any portion of a basement is located more than 75 feet (22 860

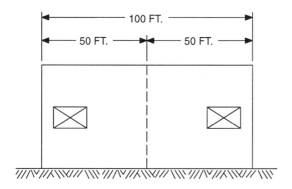
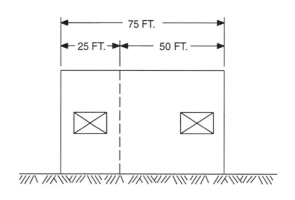

☒ Required exterior opening:
1. Twenty square feet of opening in each 50 lineal feet or fraction thereof.
2. Minimum dimension of 30 inches.
3. Accessible to the fire department from the exterior.
4. Cannot be obstructed in a manner that prevents firefighting or rescue from the exterior.

For **SI:** 1 inch = 25.4 mm, 1 foot = 304.8 mm.

FIGURE 904-2

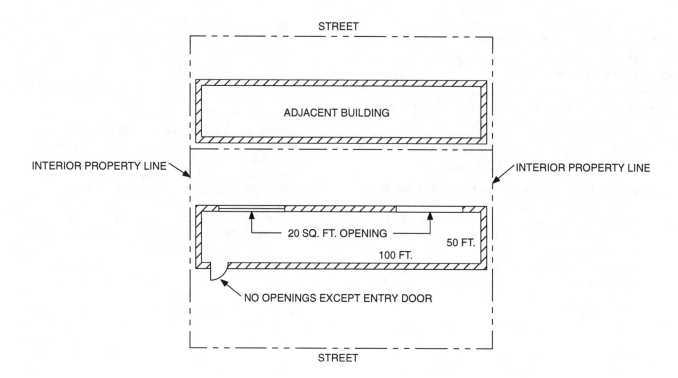

STREET

ADJACENT BUILDING

INTERIOR PROPERTY LINE

INTERIOR PROPERTY LINE

20 SQ. FT. OPENING

50 FT.

100 FT.

NO OPENINGS EXCEPT ENTRY DOOR

STREET

REQUIRED OPENINGS MAY NOT OPEN ONTO A NONACCESSIBLE YARD AS SHOWN IN THE PLAN. FOR THE CONDITION SHOWN, EITHER COMPLYING OPENINGS WOULD NEED TO BE PROVIDED ON THE STREET FRONT WALL OR THE BUILDING WOULD HAVE TO HAVE AN AUTOMATIC SPRINKLER SYSTEM.

For **SI:** 1 square foot = 0.0929 m².

FIGURE 904-3

mm) from exterior wall openings, the basement is required to be provided with a fire sprinkler system.

With regard to the requirement that the exterior wall openings be entirely above grade, areaways and light wells may be considered as meeting this requirement. However, the light well and areaway should be provided with a stairway or other equivalent means for gaining ready access to the openings. Furthermore, the plan dimensions of the areaway or light well should be adequate to permit the necessary maneuvering to accomplish firefighting or rescue from the opening. On this basis, it is advisable to consult with fire department personnel to obtain their expertise in these situations.

Firefighting in buildings that are over 55 feet (16 764 mm) in height is difficult, and many jurisdictions do not have the personnel or equipment to control fires on upper floors and rescue occupants. Item 5 was added to Section 904.2.2 in the 1994 code in recognition of this problem. This provision applies to all occupancies, not just high-rise office and residential buildings covered by Section 403. (There are three exceptions, however, where Item 5 is not applicable. The three exceptions are airport control towers, open parking structures, and low-hazard factories and industrial occupancies—Group F, Division 2.)

Item 5 lowers the threshold at which automatic sprinklers are required for high-rise office and residential buildings from 75 feet (22 860 mm) to 55 feet (16 764 mm), but it does not alter the applicability of any of the other special requirements set forth in Section 403. These still do not apply until the office or residential building has an occupied floor more than 75 feet (22 860 mm) above the lowest level of fire department vehicular access.

Requirements for specific occupancies. The requirements set forth in Section 904.2.2 are not occupancy dependent, while those which follow do apply to specific occupancy groups or parts of those groups. The provisions in Sections 904.2.3 through 904.2.9 are applicable for the specific conditions stated in each section and apply whether or not complying exterior openings have been provided.

904.2.3 Group A Occupancies.

904.2.3.1 Drinking establishments. These provisions are relatively new to the UBC, having first appeared in the 1982 edition. The intent is to provide sprinklers in any room where alcoholic beverages are served, even if the service of alcoholic beverages is incidental to dining. Thus, dining rooms and nightclubs serving alcoholic beverages, cocktail lounges, and saloons are intended by the code to be sprinklered. The sole criterion is whether or not alcoholic beverages are served. The record of casualties during fires in buildings housing these types of uses demonstrates the need for the additional protection provided by fire sprinklers or, alternatively, the separation into small areas. The code intends that all areas not separated by a one-hour fire-resistive occupancy separation be included in the computation

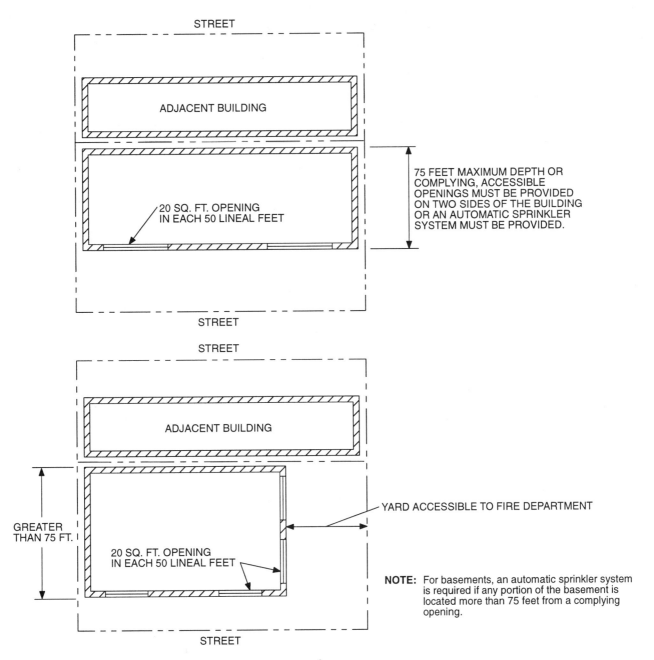

STREET

ADJACENT BUILDING

20 SQ. FT. OPENING
IN EACH 50 LINEAL FEET

75 FEET MAXIMUM DEPTH OR
COMPLYING, ACCESSIBLE
OPENINGS MUST BE PROVIDED
ON TWO SIDES OF THE BUILDING
OR AN AUTOMATIC SPRINKLER
SYSTEM MUST BE PROVIDED.

STREET

STREET

ADJACENT BUILDING

GREATER
THAN 75 FT.

20 SQ. FT. OPENING
IN EACH 50 LINEAL FEET

YARD ACCESSIBLE TO FIRE DEPARTMENT

NOTE: For basements, an automatic sprinkler system
is required if any portion of the basement is
located more than 75 feet from a complying
opening.

STREET

For **SI:** 1 foot = 304.8 mm, 1 lineal foot = 304.8 mm, 1 square foot = 0.929 m².

FIGURE 904-4

of the area included with the rooms used for consumption of alcoholic beverages.

904.2.3.2 Basements. It is the intent of the UBC that the basement actually be used and classified as a Group A Occupancy in order to require sprinklers where the basement is larger than 1,500 square feet (139 m²) in floor area. A basement under a Group A Occupancy which itself is not classified as a Group A Occupancy would not be subject to this provision.

In the case of a multi-occupancy basement, which includes a Group A Occupancy, the entire area of the basement would require sprinklers.

904.2.3.3 Exhibition and display rooms. This code requirement came about as a direct result of the McCormick Place fire in Chicago on January 16, 1967. McCormick Place was not sprinklered and consisted of three levels, including a main exhibit area of 320,000 square feet (29 728 m²) on the upper level. Both the upper and lower levels were in the final stages of readiness for a housewares exhibition and were heavily laden with combustibles when the fire broke out. The fire was reported to have originated in the storage area behind an exhibit booth on the upper level. The upper level was almost totally destroyed, and considerable damage occurred to the lower level.[2]

Ordinarily, assembly occupancies are considered to have a very low fire loading; therefore, automatic fire sprinkler protection has not been required for the building. The need for built-in fire suppression in an assembly occupancy that can be used for exhibition or display purposes was clearly demonstrated by the McCormick Place fire. Display booths are most often constructed with combustible materials, and the storage area behind the booths is a receptacle for combustible materials and packing boxes. Thus, without built-in fire suppression, the large quantities of combustible materials and the large areas combine to create an excessive hazard.

904.2.3.4 Stairs. As assembly occupancies contain large numbers of occupants, it is imperative that the exits be available for use and that stairways not be subjected to any fire hazards which could render them unusable. Thus, the code requires sprinklers to be installed in enclosed usable space under or over a stairway in the listed assembly occupancies to protect against the common practice of storing combustible materials in these enclosed spaces. The reference to Section 1005.3.3.6 is to call attention to the code prohibition against enclosed usable space under a stairway in an exit enclosure.

904.2.3.5 Multitheater complexes. This section requires the installation of sprinkler systems in multitheater complexes due to the potential life loss hazard in these uses.

904.2.3.6 Amusement buildings. As a result of the life loss in the 1984 fire at the "Haunted Castle" at Six Flags Great Adventure Park in New Jersey, this provision was added to require the installation of sprinkler systems in amusement buildings. A study of this fire shows that a major factor in the loss of life was the failure to detect and extinguish the fire in its incipient stage.

904.2.3.7 Stages. Since its inception, the *Uniform Building Code* has required the installation of automatic sprinkler systems for stage areas. These requirements resulted from the disastrous Iroquois Theater fire in Chicago, Illinois, in 1903, in which over 60 persons lost their lives. Because of the appallingly large loss of life, the Iroquois Theater fire had an enormous impact on fire- and life-safety provisions in codes, particularly with regard to sprinkler protection, smoke removal from the stage area and exiting from the theater. As stages and accessory areas have a potential for high combustible content due to scenery, stage props and furniture, they require special protection.

The wording of the requirement for providing automatic sprinklers for stages was revised in the 1994 edition to streamline the provisions. These changes resulted from a comprehensive code change to Section 405 (Stages and Platforms) submitted by the BCMC. Unfortunately, due to the nature of the code development process, Section 904.2.3.7 only references "stages" when, in fact, it should reference both "stages" and "legitimate stages." In the BCMC proposal, a "stage" was defined as "a space within a building used for entertainment or presentations." The definition for "legitimate stage" was to be omitted. Revisions made at the 1993 Annual Business Meeting held in Sacramento, California, retained the definition for legitimate stage in Section 405 and amended the definition for stage so that it would apply only to those stages having a height of 50 feet (15 240 mm) or less. Stages with a height greater than 50 feet (15 240 mm) were defined as legitimate stages. Unfortunately, when changes were made to the language used in Section

405, they were not coordinated with Section 904.2.3.7. Section 904.2.3.7 should reference both "stages" and "legitimate stages." Historically, the UBC has always required sprinkler protection for both, and there was no intent by BCMC to change the requirement that both stage types be provided with an automatic sprinkler system.

For a discussion of modern-day stages and platforms, see John Degenkolb's article in *Building Standards* magazine.[3]

Two exceptions have been provided. Exception 1 exempts smaller stages (but not legitimate stages) from the requirement to install sprinklers. Note that the stage area is limited to a maximum of 1,000 square feet (92.9 m^2) and that the exception applies only to stages since the stage height cannot exceed 50 feet (15 240 mm).

Exception 2 covers low-height storage areas under stages or platforms, where, if sprinklers were installed, they would be subject to excessive damage due to the movement of chairs and tables in and out of the storage area. Therefore, the code provides that where the understage or platform storage areas are lined with $5/8$-inch (15.9 mm) Type X gypsum wallboard or other materials approved for one-hour fire-resistive construction, sprinklers are not required. As there generally would be no source of ignition and no human occupancy, the area presents no significant hazard, particularly when lined with fire-resistive materials.

904.2.3.8 Smoke-protected assembly seating. This new provision was added to the 1997 edition to require an approved automatic sprinkler system for smoke-protected assembly seating. Smoke-protected assembly seating is defined in Section 1002 as seating served by a means of egress system and is not subject to blockage by smoke accumulation within or under a structure. Exceptions to this requirement include press boxes and storage facilities less than 1,000 square feet (92.9 m^2) in area in conjunction with outdoor seating facilities where all means of egress in the seating area are essentially open to the outside.

904.2.4 Group E Occupancies. The provisions applicable to automatic sprinkler systems in educational occupancies underwent a major change with the 1994 edition. Prior editions required sprinklers only in selected areas of any Group E Occupancy, namely basements and enclosed usable space under or above a stairway. Under the 1994 edition, sprinklers are only required in Group E, Division 1 Occupancies, but they are required throughout the building, with a couple of exceptions. The requirement to provide an automatic sprinkler system throughout Group E, Division 1 Occupancies was added to the code in order to address the problem created by the increasing number of school fires.

The first exception permits the omission of sprinklers when the building has direct exterior exits at the ground level.

The second exception will allow the omission of sprinklers when the building is divided into areas no greater than 20,000 square feet (1858 m^2) by either area separation walls or by occupancy separation walls having a fire-resistive rating of not less than two hours. This second exception seems to introduce a new concept into the UBC: that in this case a two-hour occupancy separation wall is equivalent to an area separation wall.

Basements and stairs. Prior to the 1994 edition, Section 904.2.4.2 applied to all Group E Occupancy basements larger than 1,500 square feet (139 m^2). The section now applies only to basements in Group E, Division 1 Occupancies regardless of basement size. Like the basement provision, the provision requiring that sprinklers be installed in enclosed usable space below or over stairways, which appears in Section 904.2.4.3, formerly applied to all Group E Occupancies. This provision now applies only to Group E, Division 1 Occupancies. Both Sections 904.2.4.2 and 904.2.4.3 are applicable regardless of the floor area of the Group E, Division 1 Occupancy. The 20,000-square-foot (1858 m^2) compartmentalization of Section 904.2.4.1 is not applicable.

904.2.5 Group F Occupancies.

904.2.5.1 Woodworking occupancies. This new section was added to the 1997 edition and requires that an automatic fire sprinkler system be installed in Group F woodworking occupancies over 2,500 square feet (232.3 m^2) in area that use equipment, machinery or appliances that generate finely divided combustible waste or that use finely divided combustible materials. This code requirement essentially relocates the sprinkler requirements from Section 306.8 in the 1994 edition to Chapter 9 of the 1997 edition.

904.2.6 Group H Occupancies. Group H Occupancies are hazardous occupancies, and one special feature of the hazardous occupancy is that in addition to presenting a local hazard within the building, it has a potential for presenting a high level of hazard to the surrounding properties. Therefore, the code requires sprinkler protection for all Group H Occupancies except for Division 5 Occupancies (aircraft repair hangars). Because of the exterior wall requirements of Table 5-A or, alternatively, the spatial separations required, the usual extreme height of the roof—150 feet (45 720 mm) is not unusual—and insurance company requirements for protection of the aircraft by other means, sprinklers are considered unnecessary by the code for Division 5 Occupancies. Buildings containing Division 6 Occupancies require sprinklers in other portions of the building in addition to the Division 6 area proper. This requirement is based on the original premise that the primary protection feature of this highly protected use is the automatic fire-extinguishing system.

904.2.7 Group I Occupancies. Because the mobility of the occupants of Group I Occupancies is greatly diminished (in the case of hospitals and detention facilities, the mobility is essentially zero), the code requires automatic fire suppression.

For many years prior to the 1988 edition, the UBC permitted certain rooms in hospitals to be unsprinklered. However, experience has not shown the omission of sprinklers to be necessary.[4] Also, the partial sprinkler system which results offers only marginal protection and is often overtaxed by fires that start in unsprinklered areas.[5]

The exception is intended to prevent the loss of water from the system due to the inmates tampering with the sprinkler devices. This may be an arguable supposition, as informal studies by the NFPA Committee on Safety to Life indicate that there have been no significant problems.[6]

904.2.8 Group M Occupancies. The typical American supermarket evolved during the construction boom which followed World War II. The typical supermarket consisted of a one-story building of moderately large area, e.g., 15,000 to 25,000 square feet (1394 to 2323 m^2). During the 1950s, fire statistics indicated that large-area supermarkets without sprinkler protection were subject to a larger proportion of fires than were usually attributable to this use in the past. As a result, this provision requiring sprinklers in retail sales rooms classified as Group M Occupancies where the floor area exceeds 12,000 square feet (1115 m^2) was placed in the 1970 edition of the UBC. For multiple sales rooms, each area of 12,000 square feet (1115 m^2) or less has, for ease of enforcement, been generally required to be separated by at least a one-hour fire-resistive occupancy separation to eliminate the requirement for sprinklers.

Although the provision now applies to all rooms of Group M Occupancies, it was the very poor fire record of the supermarket that generated the impetus to initiate the changes to the UBC. Fortunately, most retail department stores were already protected with fire sprinklers, usually as the result of insurance company requests.

The revision in the 1997 edition clears up enforcement problems with retail versus wholesale uses. This was felt to be appropriate since there is a proliferation of wholesale uses that are open to the general public. Also, these sprinkler requirements are still based on the size of the room rather than the size of the occupancy as a whole.

The more than three-story criterion pertains to the complete occupancy, and where a Group M Occupancy exceeds three stories in height, the entire occupancy is required to be protected throughout with fire sprinklers, regardless of area. Thus, storage rooms, office areas and other areas auxiliary to the Group M Occupancy would require sprinkler protection as well.

904.2.9 Group R, Division 1 Occupancies. As the large majority of fires and life loss occur in residential buildings, the UBC requires sprinklers in apartment houses and hotels of the sizes specified. The occupants may be asleep at the time of a fire and, in the case of hotels, may not be familiar with their surroundings. The last sentence of this section requires that within the dwelling unit and guest room portions of the building, residential or quick-response sprinklers must be used.

904.4 Permissible Sprinkler Omissions. It is the intent of the sprinkler standard that "the basic principles for providing proper protection are namely: (1) sprinklers installed throughout the premises, including basements, lofts and all other locations herein specified."[2] It is also the intent of the UBC that when an automatic extinguishing system is required "throughout," the same meaning is implied. One of the reasons for requiring protection throughout is the possibility of a fire in an unprotected area gaining such a foothold that the automatic fire sprinkler system would be overpowered. However, over the years, certain areas, locations or conditions have shown that they require special consideration and omission of sprinklers.

In this section the code itself provides the rationale for the omission of sprinklers.

Item 1 of this section was revised in the 1991 edition by adding the phrase "or contains electrical equipment" at the end to specifically indicate that sprinklers should generally not be omitted from a room simply because it contains electrical equipment.

In the case of Item 4, the communication industry has consistently recommended against fire sprinkler protection of areas housing communications equipment. As a result the code permits the omission of sprinklers in these areas under the conditions specified.

It is important to note that all of the sprinkler omissions specified in this section require approval of the building official with the concurrence of the fire chief. Therefore, these omissions are not automatic and each request should be carefully considered. For example, the omissions itemized in Item 4.2 of Item 4 might be approved as long as the rooms or areas are separated from the remainder of the structure by a minimum of a one-hour fire-resistive occupancy separation and a fire alarm system is installed.

904.5 Standpipes.

904.5.1 General. A standpipe system is a system of piping valves and outlets which is installed exclusively for fighting a fire within a building. Standpipes are not considered a viable substitute for an automatic fire sprinkler system. They are needed in large-area buildings with combustible contents, and when used by trained personnel, they provide an effective means of fighting a fire.

904.5.2 Where required. Table 9-A of the code provides the basic requirements for when a standpipe system is required in a building. It will be noted from the table that a fire hose is required in all cases for nonsprinklered buildings except for stages more than 1,000 square feet (93 m^2) in area. It is the intent of the code for all Class II and Class III standpipes in nonsprinklered buildings that the $1^1/_2$-inch (38 mm) outlets be connected to a hose for use by the occupants of the building. The use of fire hose cabinets in which the hose is attached to the $1^1/_2$-inch (38 mm) outlets on Class II standpipes is considered to be first aid (along with any portable fire extinguishers that may be present), as it is the intent that these hose lines be used by the occupants of the building before fire department personnel arrive.

However, it will be noted that only in one case—that of a Group A, Division 2.1 Occupancy over 5,000 square feet (465 m^2) in area used for exhibition—is there a hose requirement in a sprinklered building. This requirement is based on the fact that there are large amounts of combustibles present when the area is used for exhibition. Furthermore, the sprinklers may be at such a high elevation above the exhibition floor that there will be a delay in sprinkler activation. Thus, the hose lines that are present will provide the means of first aid fire control by the occupants of the building prior to either sprinkler activation or the arrival of fire department personnel.

904.5.3 Location of Class I standpipes. It is the intent of the code that Class I standpipes are for the use of the fire department to fight fires within a building. Thus, the code requires that standpipe outlets be within exit enclosures or, in the case of a smokeproof enclosure, be within the vestibule or exterior balcony which provides access to the stairway. With these locations for standpipe outlets, the fire department personnel can bring hose into the stair enclosure and make a hookup to outlets in a relatively protected area. Figure 904-5 depicts the location of Class I standpipes.

The stairway enclosure also provides protection for the standpipe and piping system. In those cases where the risers and laterals are not within stair enclosures, the code requires that they be protected by equivalent fire-resistive construction. The exception to this requirement assumes that the automatic fire sprinkler system will keep the riser and laterals cool enough so that they will not be damaged by fire.

On those roofs which have a flat enough slope for firefighters to move about, the code requires at least one roof outlet so that exposure fires can be fought from the roof.

The interconnection of the standpipe risers at the bottom for multiple standpipe systems is intended to increase the reliability.

904.5.4 Location of Class II standpipes. It is the intent of the code to require the location of hose cabinets for Class II standpipes at intervals ensuring that all portions of a building will be within 30 feet (9144 mm) of a nozzle attached to 100 feet (30 480 mm) of hose. In plan review this would necessitate allowing for pulling the hose down corridors and through rooms such that several right-angle turns may be necessary before the hose stream can be placed on the fire. Therefore, judgment is necessary in the determination of standpipe locations. One

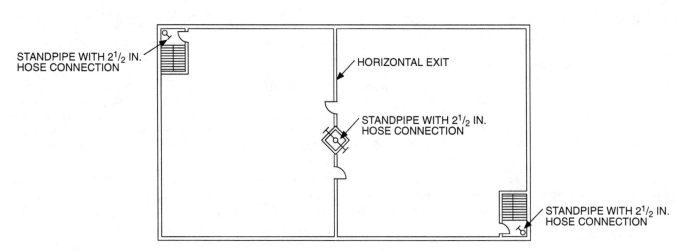

STANDPIPE WITH $2^1/_2$ IN. HOSE CONNECTION

HORIZONTAL EXIT

STANDPIPE WITH $2^1/_2$ IN. HOSE CONNECTION

STANDPIPE WITH $2^1/_2$ IN. HOSE CONNECTION

For **SI:** 1 inch = 25.4 mm.

CLASS I (DRY) STANDPIPE LOCATION

FIGURE 904-5

method to account for this type of partitioning in a building where the future location of partitions is unknown is to subtract 30 feet (9144 mm) from the straight line distance between the hose cabinet and the remote location and then multiply the remainder by 1.4. If the result is more than 100 feet (30 480 mm), an additional standpipe will be required. Diagram A of Figure 904-6 illustrates the location of a Class II standpipe in a building where an office floor has a central corridor with offices on each side. In this particular arrangement, it is obvious from the layout that the one standpipe will suffice. In Group A Occupancies equipped with a stage, Diagram B depicts the code requirement for the location of Class II standpipes.

Since Class II standpipe systems are charged with water, the code does not require fire-resistive protection because the water within the system is considered adequate to keep the pipe cool enough to prevent damage.

904.5.5 Location of Class III standpipes. As Class III standpipes are combination standpipes containing both $1^1/_2$-inch (38 mm) outlets for occupant use and $2^1/_2$-inch (64 mm) outlets for fire department use, it is only logical that they be located so as to serve the building as required for both Class I and Class II standpipes. Figure 904-7 shows the typical arrangement for a Class III standpipe in a building. Usually the hose rack for $1^1/_2$-inch (38 mm) outlets and $2^1/_2$-inch (64 mm) hose outlets are both located within the stair enclosure. Where the coverage requirements for Class II standpipes are such that stair enclosure locations will not cover the entire building, laterals are usually run to other locations from hose cabinets in order to provide for

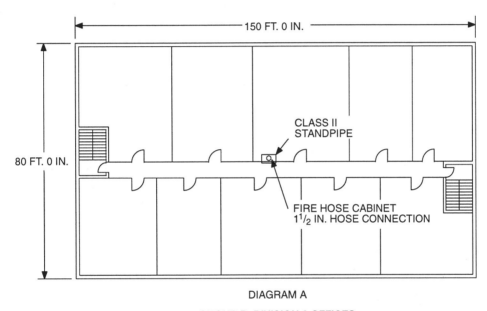

DIAGRAM A

GROUP B, DIVISION 2 OFFICES

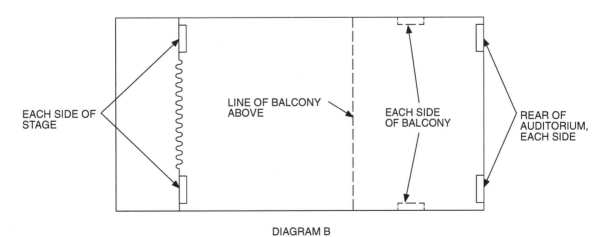

DIAGRAM B

GROUP A, DIVISIONS 1, 2 AND 2.1 OCCUPANCIES

For **SI:** 1 inch = 25.4 mm, 1 foot = 304.8 mm.

CLASS II STANDPIPE LOCATION

FIGURE 904-6

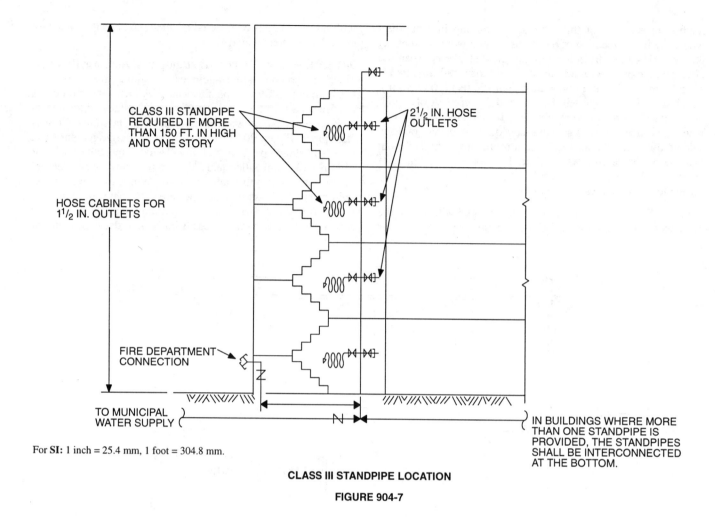

For **SI:** 1 inch = 25.4 mm, 1 foot = 304.8 mm.

CLASS III STANDPIPE LOCATION

FIGURE 904-7

the required coverage. In this case the laterals are not required to be protected, as they are charged with water.

As was the case with Class I standpipes, Class III standpipe systems and their risers and laterals in sprinklered buildings are not required to have fire-resistive protection for the same reasons as discussed for the Class I standpipes.

904.6 Buildings under Construction. Considerable amounts of combustible materials are present during the construction of a building. Where building height will be such that firefighting operations would be hampered from the outside, standpipe systems are required to provide water for firefighting.

Thus, the code requires that, where a building is to be four stories or more in height, a standpipe system be installed before the construction height exceeds 35 feet (10 668 mm) above the lowest level of fire department access. During construction operations, the amount of combustible materials from concrete forms, scaffolding, plastic and canvas tarpaulins, and other combustible materials are prevalent not only throughout the building but throughout the construction site itself. Thus, the standpipe system in many cases provides the only source of water for firefighting purposes.

The code requirement is for the equivalent of a Class I standpipe, although the standpipe may be charged with water. The preferable case is to plan the construction of the building such that the standpipe system required for construction will be a per-

manent system available for use after the building is constructed. However, during construction the code does not require that a permanent water supply be connected to the standpipe, except for buildings to be over 150 feet (45 720 mm) in height, but the standpipes must still be provided with fire department hose connections as specified in the code.

Where the height of the completed building will be over 150 feet (45 720 mm) and a Class III standpipe is required, the code requires that during construction the standpipe be connected to fire pumps and the public water main.

The code makes provisions for the use of temporary standpipes during construction as long as the system is designed to furnish the required water and pressure as outlined in the code.

904.7 Basement Pipe Inlets. Where it is desired to require basement pipe inlets, Appendix Section 907 should be adopted.

SECTION 905 — SMOKE CONTROL

This section was new with the 1994 edition and has revisions in the 1997 edition. The provisions which eventually led to the section on smoke control were first developed in 1989.

The section applies to mechanical or passive smoke-control systems when they are required by other provisions of the UBC. Other sections of the UBC that formerly contained detailed requirements for smoke control are now referenced to Section

905. An exception is the stage ventilation requirements of Section 405.3.3, which are in reality smoke-control provisions, which do not reference Section 905. Section 905 specifically exempts smoke and heat venting requirements which appear in Section 906 and are discussed in the next section of this handbook. Also, Section 905 states that smoke-control systems are not required to comply with Section 609 of the Mechanical Code (product-conveying duct requirements) unless their normal use would otherwise require compliance.

This section establishes minimum requirements for the design, installation and acceptance testing of smoke-control systems, but nothing within the section itself is intended to imply that a smoke-control system be installed. Some sections that specifically reference Section 905 are the requirements for atria (Section 402.2), high-rise buildings (Section 403.4) and malls (Section 404.3.3). Smoke barrier requirements, such as those in Section 308.2.2.1 for institutional occupancies, are also referenced to Section 905. Smoke-control systems are intended to provide a tenable environment for the evacuation or relocation of occupants. The provisions are not intended for the preservation of contents or for assistance in fire suppression, and Section 905.1 specifically states that "smoke-control systems are not a substitute for sprinkler protection."

The provisions of this section were based on the American Society of Heating, Refrigerating and Air-Conditioning Engineers (ASHRAE) publication, *Design of Smoke Control for Buildings;* NFPA publication 92-A, *Recommended Practice for Smoke Control Systems*; and the companion draft publication 92-B, *Technical Guide for Smoke Control Systems in Malls, Atriums and Large Areas.*[7]

Although this section covers both passive and active smoke-control systems, the majority of the material presented in the section addresses the three mechanical methods—pressurization (Section 905.3), airflow (Section 905.4) and the exhaust (Section 905.5)—with other sections addressing related subjects such as the design fire; equipment, including fans, ducts and dampers; power supply; detection and control systems; and the firefighter's control panel.

Section 905.2.4 on opening protection in smoke barriers was revised in the 1997 edition to eliminate the requirement for gaskets at the sill since such gaskets served little practical use and were not intended to be part of the original proposal. The protection at door openings is, instead, referenced to Section 1004.3.4.3.2 and provides the same protection as required for corridor doors.

Section 905.7.3 on ducts was revised in the 1997 edition to allow ducts in a smoke-control system to be supported by substantial, noncombustible supports rather than from fire-resistive structural elements as required in the previous edition. The previous requirement seemed overly restrictive, particularly since smoke-control systems may be utilized in buildings that do not require fire-resistive construction.

Section 905.9 on detection and control systems was revised in the 1997 edition to clarify the intent of the previous code text. Since UL has now established the subcategory UUKL for fire alarm control panels under UL Standard 864, it is appropriate to refer the user to listed systems for smoke-control system activation and control. Minor changes were made to clarify the intent.

The final segment of Section 905 addresses acceptance testing of the smoke-control system. Smoke-control system installation requires special inspection per Section 1701.5. Item 14.1 of Section 1701.5 requires special inspection during erection of ductwork and prior to concealment for the purpose of testing for leaks and recording device location. This latter provision creates, in effect, as-built drawings for the system. Item 14.2 of Section 1701.5 requires additional testing and verification prior to occupancy. Section 905.15.9 requires the work of the special inspector to be documented in a final report. The report shall be reviewed by the responsible designer, who is required to certify the work. The final, designer-approved report, together with other information addressed in Section 905.15.10, shall be maintained on file at the building. Although Section 905.15.10 doesn't specifically require it, it would seem prudent for this information to be maintained by the responsible code enforcement agency.

Those who would like additional information about the smoke-control provisions of Section 905 should refer to code change 57-95-1 (Item 213) in the 1991 code development cycle.[8]

SECTION 906 — SMOKE AND HEAT VENTING

Smoke and hot gases created by fires rise to the underside of the roof structure above and then build up so as to interfere with firefighting and reduce visibility to the point where firefighting is relatively ineffective. Also, as the hot gases accumulate near the roof structure, the unburned products of combustion become superheated, and if a supply of air is introduced, these hot, unburned products of combustion will ignite violently. Thus, it has been found that it is imperative that industrial and warehouse-type occupancies be provided with smoke and heat vents in the roofs. Although the UBC only requires smoke and heat vents for one-story buildings, their use in multistory buildings is also recommended, particularly in the top story.

Smoke and heat vents must also be installed in conjunction with draft curtains, which are often referred to as "curtain boards." Curtain boards installed at code-specified intervals confine the smoke and hot gases so they are not diluted and, thus, increase the effectiveness of automatic vents. Without the confining of the smoke and hot gases by curtain boards, the vents would be relatively ineffective due to delay in operating, or even due to nonoperation.

In the case of buildings with automatic fire sprinkler systems, the curtain boards confine the smoke and hot gases so that when sprinklers are actuated they are in a relatively confined area. Without curtain boards, the hot gases would spread laterally and possibly actuate so many sprinklers that the sprinkler system may be overcome due to excessive water-flow demand.

906.1 When Required. The *Uniform Building Code* requires smoke and heat venting in industrial buildings and warehouses and in hazardous occupancies. An exception is granted to Group S, Division 2 Occupancies used for bulk frozen food storage when the building is protected by an automatic fire sprinkler system. The intent is that those occupancies that have a potential to include large areas, such as industrial uses and hazardous occupancies, be provided with the means to rid the building of hot gases and smoke. The exception for office buildings is due to the favorable loss experience attributable to office buildings and to the compartmentation provided. Large retail sales areas are protected by the fire sprinklers required by Section 904.2.8 for retail sales occupancies. In the case of Group S, Division 2 bulk frozen food storage uses, when the building is protected by an automatic fire sprinkler system, the potential for fire is greatly reduced. Should a fire break out, the probability of rapid fire spread is very low.

For those buildings containing high-piled combustible stock, requirements for smoke and heat venting are contained in the Fire Code.

906.3 Types of Vents. The code requires that smoke and heat vents either be fixed in the open position or operate automatically in order to release the smoke and hot gases. Vents may be skylight-type vents, may be exterior wall openings or may be any other type of opening that leads directly to the exterior of the building. When used, exterior wall openings are placed at the top of the exterior walls, as the code requires that any smoke and heat vent be placed at or above the elevation of the upper one third of the curtain board.

As smoke and heat vents are intended to release smoke and hot gases from a fire within the building, the code requires that they be placed a minimum of 20 feet (6096 mm) from any property line in order to reduce exposure to adjacent property.

906.4 Releasing Devices. *Uniform Building Code* Standard 15-7 requires that the releasing devices for automatic smoke and heat vents be activated by temperature. Field reports and technical analysis of vent operations indicate that actuation by other means, such as by smoke, sprinkler flow or flame detection, is unsatisfactory. For obvious reasons the standard requires noncorrodible materials to be used for the hinges and other parts related to the opening of the vents.

906.5 Size and Spacing of Vents. Aerodynamic studies of flow through rectangular openings have shown that the minimum

cross-sectional area for smoke and heat vents should be 16 square feet (1.5 m^2), with a minimum dimension of 4 feet (1219 mm). Thus, the code has the same requirement. The code also permits projections such as ribs and rain gutters to project into the required 4 feet (1219 mm) as long as the total width for all projections does not exceed 6 inches (152 mm).

The venting ratios and spacing of vents required by the code are based on the heat release expected from the various occupancies.

The *Uniform Building Code* considers two types of heat release:

1. Moderate heat release—Groups B, F, M and S Occupancies.

2. High heat release—Group H Occupancies.

Table 9-8 in this handbook provides criteria for the spacing and venting ratios of smoke and heat vents.

TABLE 9-8
SMOKE AND HEAT VENTS SPACING AND VENTING RATIOS

OCCUPANCY	SPACING (feet) × 304.8 for mm	VENTING RATIO
B,F,M,S	120	1:100
H	100	1:50

906.6 Curtain Boards. In order to be effective, curtain boards are required to be of a type of construction that will prevent the passage of smoke through the curtain board. Therefore, the code requires that they be constructed of sheet metal, asbestos board, lath and plaster, gypsum wallboard or of another approved material that will prevent the passage of smoke. Also, the joints and connections are required to be smoketight.

Table 9-9 and Figure 906-1 in this handbook provide details for size and spacing of curtain boards.

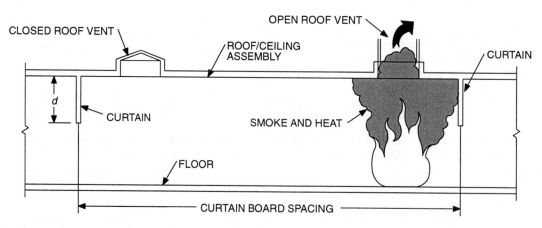

NOTE: In general, several small vents are more effective than a larger vent of equal area.

ROOF VENTS AND CURTAIN BOARDS

FIGURE 906-1

TABLE 9-9
SIZE AND SPACING OF CURTAIN BOARDS

OCCUPANCY CLASSIFICATION	MAXIMUM CURTAIN BOARD SPACING (feet)	MINIMUM CURTAIN BOARD DEPTH, *d* (feet)	MAXIMUM AREA WITHIN CURTAIN BOARDS (sq. ft.)
	× 304.8 for mm		× 0.0929 for m²
B,F,M,S	250	6[1]	50,000
H	100	12[2]	15,000

[1]Need not extend closer than 8 feet to floor.

[2]Need not extend closer than 8 feet to floor, provided minimum 6-foot depth is obtained.

REFERENCES

[1]Hodnett, Robert M., Ed. (1980). *Automatic Sprinkler Systems Handbook.* National Fire Protection Association, Quincy, Massachusetts.

[2]American Iron and Steel Institute (1968). *An Engineering Report on the January 16, 1967, McCormick Place Fire.* Washington, D.C.

[3]Degenkolb, John G. (1986). Stages and platforms. *Building Standards,* 55(3): 13-15, 47.

[4]Lathrop, James K., Ed. (1983). *Life Safety Code Handbook,* Third Edition. National Fire Protection Association, Quincy, Massachusetts, page 44.

[5]International Conference of Building Officials (1987). *1987 Accumulative Supplement to the Uniform Codes.* Whittier, California, page 251.

[6]Lathrop, op. cit., page 233.

[7]International Conference of Building Officials (1992). *1992 Accumulative Supplement to the Uniform Codes.* Whittier, California, page 299.

[8]International Conference of Building Officials (1991). *Code Change Agenda, 1991 Annual Education and Code Development Conference.* Whittier, California, pages 77 and 78.

Chapter 10

MEANS OF EGRESS

This chapter establishes the basic approach to determining a safe exiting system for all occupancies. It addresses all portions of the egress system and includes design requirements as well as provisions regulating individual components that may be used within the egress system. The chapter specifies the methods of calculating the occupant load that is used as the basis of designing the system and, thereafter, discusses the appropriate criteria for the number of exits, location of exits, width or capacity of the egress system and arrangement of the system. This arrangement is treated in terms of remoteness and accessibility of the egress system. The accessibility is handled both in terms of the system's being usable by building occupants and in terms of it being available within a certain maximum distance of travel. After having dealt with general issues that affect the overall system or multiple zones of the system, the chapter then establishes the design requirements and components that may be used to meet those requirements for each of the three separate zones.

In interpreting and applying the various provisions of this chapter, it would help to understand the four basic concepts on which safe exiting from buildings is based:

1. A safe egress system for all building occupants must be provided.

2. Throughout the system, every component and element that a building occupant will encounter in seeking egress from the building must be under the control of the person wishing to exit.

3. Once a building occupant reaches a certain degree or level of safety as that occupant proceeds through the exiting system, that level of safety is not thereafter reduced until the occupant has arrived at the exit discharge, public way or the eventual safe place.

4. Once the exit system is subject to a certain maximum demand in terms of numbers of persons, that system must thereafter, throughout the remainder of the system, be capable of accommodating that maximum number of persons.

Because many of the elements comprising the egress system (doors, landings ramps and the like) may also form part of an accessible route as required by Chapter 11 for use by persons with disabilities, Chapter 11 and appropriate sections of CABO/ANSI A117.1 need to be consulted whenever Chapter 11 is applicable. This requirement is specifically stated in Section 1003.2.10.

This chapter was substantially revised in the 1997 edition to include the three-part definition of "means of egress." The *Uniform Building Code* was the last model building code not using the three-part means of egress system and the change was believed to be long overdue. The three-part system, or zonal approach as is now used, was first used by NFPA in 1956 and has been incorporated over the years into all of the model codes and has established terms that are used throughout the design and en-

forcement communities to deal with the means of egress system. The three parts of the means of egress system are the "exit access," the "exit" and the "exit discharge." For conceptual ease, the exit access is generally considered as any location within the building from where you would start your egress path and continues until you reach the door of an exit. The exit access would include all the rooms or spaces that you would pass through on your way to an exit. This may be the room you are in, an intervening room, a corridor, and any doors, ramps, stairs or aisles that you use along that path. An exit is the point where the code believes that you have obtained an adequate level of safety so that travel distance measurements are no longer a concern. They will generally consist of rated construction and opening protection requirements that will separate the occupants from any problem within the building. The four items which are considered as exits are exit enclosures, exit passageways, horizontal exits and exterior exit doors. The exterior exit doors will not provide the fire-protection levels that the other three elements provide, but since the occupant will be outside the building after passing through the door, it will provide a level of safety by removing the occupant from the problem area. The last of the three parts is the exit discharge. For conceptual ease, the UBC will generally view exterior areas as a part of the exit discharge. Therefore, the exit access will be the area within the building that gets the occupants to an exit, while the exit discharge will be exterior areas where the occupant goes upon leaving the building in order to reach the public way.

SECTION 1001 — ADMINISTRATIVE

1001.1 Scope. This section requires that every building or portion thereof comply with the provisions of Chapter 10. In dealing with portions of buildings, it is important to understand that the code intends this chapter to apply to all portions that are actually occupiable by people. This section also provides the definition of a means of egress and establishes the three parts, which will be discussed and regulated later. The requirement for the undiminished path reinforces one of the basic concepts addressed previously.

1001.2 Standards of Quality. The standards listed are all UBC Standards and are therefore adopted and enforceable as a part of the code. The standards for power-operated doors are important since doors that comply with these standards can often be substituted for regular swinging-type egress doors. The stairway numbering standard provides information code users should be aware of regarding code required signage within exit stairs. Without knowledge of these standards, the design of the egress system may not comply with the code. The panic hardware standard is a product standard that ensures that these vital-releasing devices will continue to serve their purpose for a great length of time under various conditions. Without a standard such as this, the durability and continued performance of the panic hardware would not be regulated.

SECTION 1002 — DEFINITIONS

Section 1002 contains a number of definitions that are especially important to this chapter. The majority of these definitions will be discussed later in connection with those sections that deal with the particular provisions relative to the terms defined. The rewrite of Chapter 10 for the 1997 edition resulted in reformatting the definitions with the chapter. Instead of having the definitions listed in this section as was done in earlier editions, the proponent's idea was to place the definitions within the text of the section where it was used. Although some may argue that these are not true "definitions," the intent is that the code user will see the definition within the text, read it and know exactly how that term is used within the code requirements of that section. Exam-

ples of this style of definitions can be found in Section 1006.3.3.1 for exterior exit stairs and Section 1006.3.5.1 for exit courts. The previous system relied on the user remembering a definition that was located elsewhere and was often overlooked.

Two of the definitions, however, are important throughout the chapter, and are discussed here. The first of these is "means of egress." The *Uniform Building Code* defines a means of egress in Section 1001.1 as a continuous, unobstructed and undiminished path of exit travel to a public way. It includes all components of the exiting system that might intervene between the most remote occupiable portion of the building and the public way or the eventual place of safety. Therefore, the means of egress includes all such intervening components as doors, corridors, stairways, exit courts and yards, as well as any other component that might be in the path of travel as depicted in Figure 1001-1. It is particularly important to note that the means of

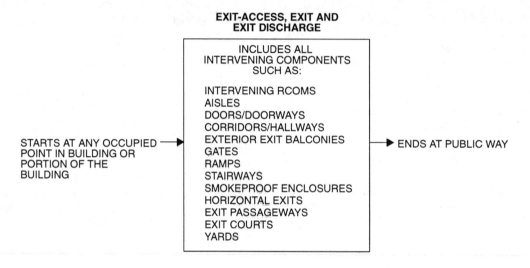

DEFINITION OF A MEANS OF EGRESS

FIGURE 1001-1

egress begins at the most remote occupiable portion of the building and continues until the building occupant eventually arrives at a public way. It is also important to note that the definition of "means of egress" defines an entire system and that that system includes all three parts for design and regulation purposes.

The code does not address the term "entrance" as it relates to exiting. Generally, the main entrance into a building would be one of the most likely paths of egress to which occupants would turn in an emergency. Accordingly, such entrances should generally comply with the exit requirements of the code.

The other important term is "public way." The code defines a public way essentially as a street, alley or any parcel of land that is permanently appropriated to the public for public use. Therefore, the public's right to use such a parcel of land is guaranteed. The building occupants, having reached a public way, are literally free to go wherever they might choose. They are certainly free to go so far as to escape any fire threat in any building that they may have been occupying.

In practical application, it is not always necessary to literally enforce this particular definition. There are many installations, large building complexes, large residential developments, and university campuses where the street and general circulation system within the project may not meet the strictest interpretation of the definition of public way. However, within such developments there are many open spaces, such as private streets or greenbelts, that will afford safety to building occupants. Under the equivalency concepts contained in Chapter 1 of the UBC, the intent of the exit chapter is certainly satisfied when building occupants arrive at such a safe place. This issue was also given support when the exception found in Section 1006.1 was added to the 1997 UBC. (Additional information will be provided at that section.)

The definition also imposes two additional limitations on a parcel of land in order for that parcel to comply with the definition of public way. The first is that the property be essentially open and unobstructed to the sky. The second imposes a minimum width requirement of at least 10 feet (3048 mm). In requiring that the public way be essentially open and unobstructed, the code is saying that it is permissible to have occasional building features, such as bridges crossing alleys and streets, and still allow the parcel of land to qualify as the required public way. The minimal dimensional limitations are simply to ensure that there is both adequate width and height so that the parcel of land is actually usable.

SECTION 1003 — GENERAL

The requirements and topics addressed in this section are used as basic provisions and may be applied to the entire egress path or to more than one of the three parts of the system. Examples of the types of general issues that are found here include occupant load, egress width, stairways and egress path identification. Since the occupant load will often drive the design requirements and will be applicable to all three parts of the egress system, the provisions for determining the occupant load will be found in this one location. In addition, certain components, such as stairways, can be found in the exit access, the exit and exit discharge. Instead of repeating the provisions at each location or providing additional cross-references, these general provisions are all consolidated into this one section. Section 1003.2 explains this by pointing out that the provisions of Section 1003 apply to all three parts of the egress system and that these provisions are in addition to the requirements for the separate provisions for the three zones and the components within those zones.

1003.2.1 Use. As the person responsible for interpreting and enforcing the code, the building official will be called on to make decisions regarding the categories in UBC Table 10-A. While Table 10-A contains occupant load factors that will serve the code user for most uses, there will be occasions when either the table does not have an occupant load factor appropriate for the intended use or where the occupant load factor contained in the table will not have a realistic application. In such instances, the code charges the building official with the responsibility of establishing an appropriate occupant load factor or an appropriate occupant load for those special circumstances and those special buildings. The table provides some guidance to the building official in the establishment of these special factors by stating that the occupant load factor should be approximately that listed for the use contained in the table that most nearly resembles the intended use under consideration.

Distinction between use and occupancy. It is meaningful to point out that the first column of Table 10-A is headed "USE." Thus, the categories listed in that first column are not occupancy classifications but are basic generic uses of building spaces. It has been pointed out in discussion of the various occupancy groups that it is possible to have a classroom in a Group A Occupancy, a Group E Occupancy or a Group B Occupancy. In terms of occupant density, however, a classroom is a classroom, and it is reasonable to expect the same density of occupancy in a classroom, regardless of the occupancy group in which that classroom might be classified. Therefore, the table specifies that when considering classroom use, one must assume there is at least one person present for each 20 square feet (1.86 m^2) of floor area.

1003.2.1.2 Change in use. This section serves as a reminder that changing the use of a building or area can greatly affect the re-

quirements for an egress system and that a change in use should not be made unless the egress system will be capable of handling the new use. This section is slightly different then the typical change of use requirements found in Section 3405. While those provisions apply when the change would result in the occupancy classification being changed, this section applies anytime that the building or area is used for a purpose other than what it was intended for. Perhaps the best example of this may be an assembly-type space that is originally approved based on the use of tables and chair seating [therefore, an occupant load factor of 15 square feet (1.39 m^2) per person] that ends up being used simply with loose seating in rows [occupant load factor of 7 square feet (0.65 m^2) per person]. This type of change may not result in the occupancy classification being changed, but it will definitely add to demand that is placed on the egress system.

1003.2.2 Occupant load.

1003.2.2.2 Determination of occupant load. This section perscribes a series of methods for determining the occupant load that will be used as the basis for the design of the egress system. The basic concept, again, is that the building must be provided with a safe exiting system for all persons in the building. If the maximum number is known, the system must be designed to accommodate it. However, in most instances, that maximum probable number of occupants may not be known. Therefore, the code provides a formula for determining an occupant load that constitutes the minimum number of persons for which the exiting system must be designed. In instances where the intended occupant load is less than the number obtained by the formula, it is the number produced by the formula that is the required minimum occupant load. As a consequence, many building officials refer to the number obtained by the formula as the "design" occupant load. Egress systems from all buildings or building spaces must be designed to accommodate at least this minimum number. Section 1003.2.2.4 clearly establishes this design occupant load as the "minimum" that can be used when applying the provisions of this chapter.

1003.2.2.2.1 Areas to be included. In specifying how the occupant load is to be determined, this section states first that it is to be assumed that all portions of a building are fully occupied at the same time and combines with Section 1003.2.2.2.2 to specify that the occupant load to be served by the exit system is the cumulative total of the separate occupant loads of the individual portions of the building. The exception to this section, however, recognizes that in many instances not all portions of the building are, in fact, fully occupied simultaneously. Therefore, when the building official can determine that there are accessory spaces that ordinarily are used only by persons who at other times occupy the main areas of the building, it is not necessary to accumulate the occupant load of the separate spaces when calculating the total occupant load of the building. It is always necessary, however, to provide each individual space of the building with exits as if that individual space were fully and completely occupied.

Occupant loads of accessory uses. Perhaps one of the better examples of the approach to determining the occupant load as provided by this exception is the calculation of occupant load in a school building. Typically, most building officials will calculate occupant load in such buildings utilizing only the classroom area. It is generally assumed that when corridors, rest rooms and other miscellaneous spaces are occupied, they are occupied by the same people who are at other times occupying the classrooms. As a consequence, it is general practice that the individual occupant loads of the separate spaces *not* be added together in calculating the total occupant load of the building. It should be noted that the code contains no occupant load factor for calculating the number of persons that must be considered to be present in such a space as a corridor or in other spaces that actually constitute part of the exit system.

Similarly, some building officials take the same approach in calculating the total occupant load of an office building and do not ascribe additional occupants to corridors, restrooms, storage rooms and other miscellaneous spaces. In certain instances, it is appropriate that conference rooms or minor assembly areas, such as lunch rooms in office buildings, also be considered as accessory spaces if they are, in fact, occupied by persons who at other times occupy the general office area. The code establishes this approach as a legitimate method of determining occupant load. The key, however, lies in the ability of the building official to conclude that in the actual use of the building or the respective building spaces, they are not in fact fully occupied simultaneously. Having concluded that, it is entirely appropriate that the occupant load of such spaces not be included in the total building occupant load.

1003.2.2.2.2 Areas without fixed seats. The occupant load that can be expected in different buildings or use spaces depends on two primary factors: the nature of the use of the building space and the amount of space devoted to that particular use. Different types of building uses have a variety of characteristics. Of primary importance is the density characteristic. Therefore, in calculating the occupant load of use areas by means of the formula, the minimum number of persons that must be assumed to occupy a building or portion thereof is determined by dividing the area devoted to the use by that density characteristic, or occupant load factor. The third column of UBC Table 10-A prescribes the occupant load factor to be used with the respective corresponding uses listed in the first column. As explained in Footnote 3, the occupant load factor does not represent the amount of area which is required to be afforded each occupant. The *Uniform Building Code* does not limit, and has never attempted to limit, the maximum occupant load on an area basis. Rather, the occupant load factor is that unit of area for which there must be assumed to be at least one person present. For example, when the code prescribes an occupant load factor of 100 for office use, it is not saying that each person in the office must be provided with at least 100 square feet (9.29 m^2) of area. Rather, it is saying that at least one person must be assumed to be present for each 100 square feet (9.29 m^2) of floor area in the office use. The floor area to be used in occupant load calculations is that floor area defined in Section 207 with counters and showcases in retail stores, furniture in dwellings, equipment in hospitals, and similar furnishings already taken into account in the occupant load factors in Table 10-A. Therefore, the gross area of the space should be used in the determination of the occupant load.

The numbers contained in the third column of Table 10-A represent those density factors that represent the probable densities that can usually be expected in areas devoted to the respective uses listed. For this purpose, these occupant load factors are really a means of estimating the probable maximum density in the respective use areas. They have been developed over a period of years and, for the most part, have been found to consistently represent the densities which one might expect in building spaces devoted to the respective uses.

Warehouse occupant load. The reason for a larger occupant load factor for warehouses than for storage areas and stockrooms is that in very large facilities used primarily for storage purposes, particularly those which are automated, the density of occupancy is less than that generally experienced in smaller storage areas or in spaces frequently referred to as stockrooms. The latter are frequently incidental to other uses and are often more densely occupied. Footnote 5 was added to reflect that even the higher occupant load factor that is assigned to warehouses will often result in an occupant load that is not resonable for the mechanical-access high-rack storage systems.

Occupant loads in mixed/multiple use buildings. The determination of occupant load is relatively easy when the building contains a single, continuous use. However, in the real world, this is often not the case. Many buildings contain more than one use or a combination of uses. Also, many buildings are used for different purposes or different uses at different times. All of this must be considered when calculating the maximum number of people that might be expected in a building or building space. It is the maximum occupant load obtained as a result of these several variables that will be the occupant load that dictates the requirements for the design of the egress system. Obviously, the exiting system must be adequate to accommodate the maximum number of persons that results from the use that will produce the greatest density. Where two or more occupancies or uses occur in the same building, the occupant load of the separate uses must then be combined to determine the total occupant load of the building.

Occupant loads when there are variations of use. An additional factor frequently involved, probably most often in Group A Occupancies, is that the assembly areas, in addition to being subject to different kinds of assembly uses, are also frequently arranged so that the floor areas can be used in different spatial arrangements. Typically, in a hotel, for example, the grand ballroom will be divisible by folding partitions or other methods into various combinations of smaller spaces by manipulating the folding partitions. This sometimes presents a difficult problem in determining the ultimate maximum occupant load for which the exiting systems must be designed. In order to do this, it is necessary to consider all the various arrangements or combinations of spaces that can be created by using the dividing partitions. This is complicated by the fact that within those various arrangements of spaces there can be a variety of different types of uses that will have different occupant densities.

The building official must ascertain that arrangement of space coupled with the types of uses that would be anticipated to determine what the maximum occupant load would be and to ensure that the required safe egress system is designed accordingly. It is important that each possible arrangement of space, when used for that purpose which will produce the greatest number of persons, be provided with its own individual exiting system.

From the information above, it is apparent that in certain occupancies the ultimate determination of occupant loads, occupancy densities and exiting systems can be fairly tedious. It is essential that this be completely analyzed and that a safe exiting system be provided for every combination of spatial arrangement and use. In establishing appropriate occupant load factors, as contained in Table 10-A, the code recognizes that even within a specific type of use, such as assembly, there are variations of use that will produce different occupant densities. Therefore, the code divides assembly occupancies into two basic categories— concentrated use or less-concentrated use. Concentrated use involves those spaces where the entire room or area is available for the gathering together of people. These spaces are generally without furnishings, furniture or built-in features so that it is possible for persons to occupy the entire area in rather dense concentration. In such a use, the code says that one must assume at least one person present for each 7 square feet (0.65 m²) of floor area. Table 10-A lists examples of the uses that would fall within this concentrated category. Among these are dance floors, lodge rooms, lobbies accessory to other assembly spaces, some churches and auditoriums.

In the less-concentrated use category, it is anticipated that these assembly spaces will also involve furnishings, such as tables and chairs, equipment, and similar things. In these less-concentrated uses, it is necessary to assume at least one person present for each 15 square feet (1.39 m²) of floor area, recognizing that portions of the area are occupied by things rather than by people. The examples presented in the table will readily explain the nature of uses to be classified in this category. Conference rooms, dining rooms, drinking establishments, lounges and exhibit rooms are all types of spaces that, in addition to having people present, will have things that will occupy a portion of the floor area. This floor area occupied by furniture and furnishings is, however, to be included in the area used to determine the occupant load. The application would be the same for gaming areas which will have a variety of table games and machines that occupy a portion of the floor area. The factor of 11 square feet (1.02 m²) per occupant in these gaming areas provides the casinos with the flexibility to move and relocate the various games without affecting the occupant load that would be located in the area.

1003.2.2.2.3 Areas with fixed seats. The method of calculating occupant load discussed to this point—that is, the formula that divides an appropriate occupant load factor into the amount of space devoted to a use—is used when dealing with building spaces without fixed seating. Where fixed seats are installed, the code specifies that the occupant load is determined simply by counting the number of seats. While the code does not define the term "fixed seats," it is intended by this term that the seats provided are, in fact, fastened in position, not easily movable and maintained in those fixed positions on a more or less permanent basis. A primary example of a fixed-seat facility would be a theater. In determining the occupant load of this type of facility, the number of fixed seats is utilized because the code also requires that the space occupied by aisles may not be used for any purpose other than aisles and, therefore, may not be used for accommodating additional persons. The aisle system through a fixed seating facility is, in fact, the exiting system for those fixed seats and, as such, must remain unobstructed. Therefore, the code does not assume any occupancy in the areas that make up the aisles.

In addition to those fixed-seating arrangements where the seating is provided by a chair-type seat, there will be those that utilize continuous seating surfaces, such as benches and pews.

When this type of seating is provided, it is necessary to assume at least one person present for each 18 inches (457 mm) of length of seating surface.

Where seating is provided by use of booths, as is frequently done in restaurants, it must be assumed that there is a person present for each 24 inches (610 mm) of booth seating surface. Prior to the 1997 edition of the code, this section specified that when determining the occupant load on a booth seat, that a person was assumed to be present for each 24 inches (610 mm) "or major portion thereof." The wording dealing with this excess length was removed simply to be consistent with the wording related to benches or pews. Since the previous paragraph did not specify how the extra length was determined, it is left to the building official to interpret the application. If the booth, pew or bench seat is curved, the code does specify that the larger radius is used to determine the length of the seat. See Application Example 1003-1 for determining the occupancy load in a small restaurant.

1003.2.2.2.4 Outdoor areas. Yards, patios and courts that are accessible to or used by occupants of a building shall be provided with exits as required by Chapter 10. This provision was added to address the use of outdoor areas for dining by restaurants where, for example, the occupant load of the structure itself may require only one exit, while the occupant load of the outdoor area is well over 50, thereby requiring two exits. The building official shall assign an occupant load in accordance with the anticipated use of outdoor areas; if an area's occupants need to pass through the building to exit, the cumulative total of the outdoor area and the building shall be used to determine the exiting requirements.

The judgment of the building official is very important to the application of these provisions, because the building official must determine exactly what occupant load should be considered, and whether the area is accessible and usable by the building occupants to establish the exiting requirements. Some cases that will require judgment include large spaces that might have a very limited anticipated occupant load, such as areas that are primarily for the service of the building, or even the everyday back yard serving a single family dwelling when the yard is fenced. While the language in the code might seem to imply that the occupant load of an exterior space is added to the buildings occupant load when there is only the one path available back through the building, this is really more of a reminder to include the added occupant load than it is a limiting code requirement. Outdoor areas that have access to a means of egress system without entering the building should be handled similar to the way passing through an intervening room is reviewed. The distribution of the occupant load from the outdoor area will depend on how many exits are required and how many paths are available.

1003.2.2.3 Maximum occupant load. The provisions of Section 1003.2.2.2 specify the methods to be used in determining what the anticipated occupant load would be. As specified in Section 1003.2.2.4, the occupant load as determined by these various methods is the minimum number of persons for which the exiting system must be designed. It does *not*, as previously pointed out, intend that the maximum permitted occupant load be regulated or controlled on an area basis. Section 1003.2.2.3 does, on the other hand, specify how the maximum permitted occupant load in a building or a portion of the building is to be determined. Two rules for determining the maximum permitted

Application Example 1003-1
Section 1003.2.2

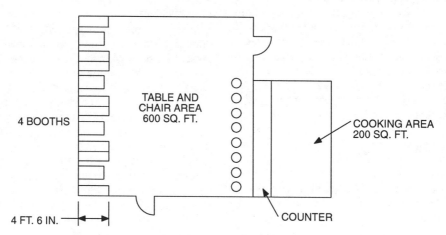

For **SI:**   1 inch = 25.4 mm, 1 foot = 304.8 mm, 1 square foot = 0.0929 m².

DETERMINATION OF OCCUPANT LOAD

FIGURE 1003-1

GIVEN: Information in Figure 1003-1.

DETERMINE: The occupant load for the small restaurant shown in Figure 1003-1.

SOLUTION: Section 1003.2.2.2.3 states that where booths are used in dining areas, the occupant load shall be based on one person for each 24 inches (610 mm) of booth length. Based on this requirement, each booth would have an occupant load of four, or a total occupant load for the booth area of 16.

The fixed seats at the counter number eight, which, based on the first paragraph of Section 1003.2.2.2.3, would establish an occupant load of eight.

The open dining area (tables and chairs), having a floor area of 600 square feet (55.7 m²) and using an occupant load factor of 15 square feet (1.39 m²) per occupant, as set forth in Item 4 of Table 10-A, would have an occupant load of 40.

The cooking area, having a floor area of 200 square feet (18.6 m²) and using an occupant load factor of 200 square feet (18.6 m²) per occupant, as set forth in Item 16 of Table 10-A, would have an occupant load of one.

The total occupant load in accordance with the second paragraph of Section 1003.2.2.2.2 is as follows:

Booths	16
Counter	8
Dining area (tables and chairs)	40
Cooking area	1
	Total Occupants 65

occupant load are presented in this section. One is for assembly uses and the other is for all other uses.

Maximum occupant load in assembly occupancies. Assembly uses probably present the most difficult problem in determining and controlling appropriate occupant loads and in preventing overcrowding of building spaces. The original determination of maximum permitted occupant load is made by the building official. After the facility has been constructed and is in use, it is frequently subject to inspection by representatives of the fire department. Many fire departments use the *Uniform Fire Code*. In UFC Section 2501.16.2, there is a provision that allows the fire chief to permit an occupant load 10 percent greater than that determined by the building official.

The basic purpose of this 10 percent tolerance is not for the fire chief to add 10 percent onto the stated maximum permitted occupant load as determined under the UBC. Rather, it is a tolerance that is permitted the on-site inspector in recognition of the extreme difficulty in accurately counting the number of persons present. The code intends that this be an on-site, enforcement-type tolerance, permitting a variation of plus or minus 10 percent of the occupant load as determined under the UBC. Users of both the UBC and the UFC should be cognizant of this relationship between these two documents.

Exception for occupant load increase. In general, the code limits the *maximum* occupant load within an assembly occupancy to the number that is established as the *minimum* or design occupant load by Section 1003.2.2.2. The method for increasing the occupant load in assembly uses is contained within the exception to Section 1003.2.2.3.1. Here, the same basic approach is taken in that the occupant load determined as previously provided may be increased if and when approved by the building official. If any increase is permitted, the code pointedly states that the entire egress system must be adequate, in all of its parts, to accommodate the increased number.

To this point, the rule for assembly uses is the same as the rule for all other uses. However, with assembly uses the code places the option of increasing the occupant load at the discretion of the building official by stating it can only occur "when *approved*."

Implicit in the term "approved," as defined in Section 202, is that it must be acceptable to the building official. Therefore, in order to authorize an increase of occupant load in an assembly use, the building official will generally want to review and accept a diagram showing the aisle, seating and fixed equipment arrangement of the space. It is important that any such diagram also identify the location of the exits, their arrangement with respect to other egress paths that are provided, their individual widths and capacities, and the travel distances involved.

In analyzing a request for an increase of occupant load in an assembly use, the building official should make two decisions. The first is to decide if any increase in the occupant load is justified. The second, more difficult decision is to determine to what extent the occupant load can be increased. In arriving at this second decision, the building official must carefully analyze all aspects of the arrangement of space as well as the details of the total egress system, not only from the immediate space but continuously through all other building spaces that might intervene between the assembly use and the eventual safe place.

By virtue of the inclusion of these provisions relative to an increase of occupant load, a building designer or building operator has a right to request consideration for such an increase. Should such building designer or building operator be able to justify the increase under all the parameters imposed by the code on the exiting system, it would seem reasonable to assume that the building official would be willing to approve the proposed increased occupant load.

Maximum occupant load in other than assembly occupancies. For other than assembly uses, the maximum permitted occupant load is determined solely by the capacity of the exiting system. As long as the egress system has sufficient capacity for the larger number of persons, an occupant load greater than that determined by the formula methods specified in Section 1003.2.2.2 must be permitted. When this increased number of persons is permitted, however, it is absolutely essential that the means of egress, in every component and in every aspect, be adequate to accommodate the increased number of persons.

1003.2.2.5 Revised occupant load. Having determined the occupant load as prescribed in Section 1003.2.2, it is now possible to design the overall egress system. Primary features of the exiting system are regulated by Sections 1003, 1004, 1005 and 1006. Knowing the maximum number of persons to be accommodated by the system, it is now possible to consider this section and design the individual components of the system according to the parameters outlined. In doing so, it must be remembered that no requirement relative to the egress system can be considered out of context with all of the others. It is essential that each be individually designed to comply with the requirements of the code so that collectively the various components can work together to provide a system that will give reasonable assurance that building occupants can safely evacuate and reach a safe place outside the building. Therefore, because the design of the system relies so heavily on the occupant load, it is essential that the occupant load and the use of the building not be changed without reviewing what the possible effects might be. To that extent, Sections 1003.2.2.5 and 1003.2.1.2 serve as reminders of the basic egress concepts.

1003.2.3 Width. This section establishes the method for determining the capacity of the exit system as well as the capacity of each individual component in that exit system. The formula is very succinct. It says simply that the required width, in inches (mm), of the exit shall not be less than that obtained by multiplying the total occupant load served by a component by the appropriate factor from UBC Table 10-B nor less than the minimum widths specified elsewhere in this code. Such exit widths shall be divided approximately equally among the separate exits. In designing the exit system, it is first necessary to determine the occupant load that must be accommodated through each individual portion of the system. Multiplying that occupant load by the above factors will result in the minimum required width, in inches (mm), necessary to accommodate the occupant load. See Application Example 1003-2.

The requirements of Section 1003.2.2.3 limit that the maximum permitted occupant load in any building or portion thereof is not to exceed the maximum exit width serving that building or portion of a building. The formula stated in Section 1003.2.3.2 is the one used to determine if the exit system—and each individual component in that egress system—is adequate to accommodate the maximum permitted occupant load. To determine if the entire exiting system is adequate or does provide adequate capacity, it will be necessary to verify each individual element by the use of this formula.

In a given exiting system, different components will afford different capacities. It is, of course, the capacity that is provided by the most restrictive component in the system that establishes the capacity of the overall system. It accomplishes nothing in increased exit capacity to arrange for a wide corridor that leads to a relatively narrow door. The capacity of this means of egress arrangement is established by the capacity of the doorway and not by the apparent capacity of the wider corridor.

When the required capacity of the system has been determined by the use of the formula, and the required number of paths has been determined in accordance with the provisions of Section 1004.2.3, the required egress capacity must be divided approximately equally among the number of required exits. It is the express intent of these sections, working together, that there be reasonable distribution of the egress capacity necessary to serve a given occupant load.

The reason for requiring multiple exit-access paths is the fact that in a fire or other emergency, it could be possible that at least one of the routes will be unavailable or blocked by the fire. If the egress capacity were not equally distributed among the number of exits, it could very easily be that path that affords the greatest portion of the egress capacity that would be lost. The resulting limitation on the occupants' ability to exit a building or portion thereof is simply unacceptable.

When applying the egress width provisions based on the factors shown in Table 10-B, it is important to note that the factors vary depending upon the occupancy that is under consideration. The egress width for certain hazardous and institutional occupancies were increased when this table was added to the 1997 UBC. The increased factors for the hazardous occupancies will provide a greater width for the system and therefore reduce the time spent in leaving the area. On the other hand, the factor for the stairs in the Group I, Division 2 Occupancy reflects the capability of the occupants of this use, and provides a larger width so that the stair does not become a bottleneck or limiting factor. It is important to realize that the Group I, Division 1 Occupancies

Application Example 1003-2
Section 1003.2.3

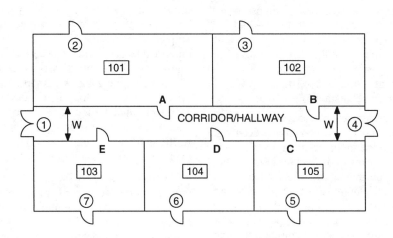

REQUIRED WIDTH OF EXIT

FIGURE 1003-2

GIVEN: In Figure 1003-2, the occupant load of Room 101 is 160; of Room 102 is 120; and of Rooms 103, 104 and 105 are 100 each. Each room has two required exits.

DETERMINE: The required minimum exit width for each doorway.

SOLUTION: The occupant load of Room 101 is 160. Thus, the total required exit width from Room 101 is 160 multiplied by 0.2 which equals 32 inches (813 mm). This required width may be divided equally between Doorways 2 and A. Therefore, each of the doorways at 2 and A may be 16 inches (406 mm) (32 divided by 2). However, Section 1003.3.1.3 requires a minimum doorway for the installation of a door 3 feet (914 mm) wide by 6 feet 8 inches (2032 mm) high so that the clear width shall not be less than 32 inches (813 mm). Therefore, the doors must be 3 feet wide (914 mm) by 6 feet 8 inches (2032 mm) high.

Since the solutions for the required exit widths of Rooms 102 through 105 are similar to that just explained for Room 101, the required doorway widths at Doors 3, 5, 6, 7, B, C, D and E each must be of sufficient size for the installation of a door 3 feet (914 mm) wide by 6 feet 8 inches (2032 mm) high so that the clear width is not less than 32 inches (813 mm).

The solution for the required widths of the doorways at 1 and 4 is determined as follows:

One half of the occupants of each of Rooms 101 through 105 exit through the hallway or corridor and eventually through doorways at 1 and 4. The total occupant load which is required to be considered to be exiting through the hallway or corridor for the purpose of determining exit width is:

$$1/2 \ (160 + 120 + 100 + 100 + 100) = 290 \text{ occupants}$$

Since, however, the occupants who exit by way of the hallway or corridor through Doorways A, B, C, D and E may continue in either direction to either Doorway 1 or 4, each of these doorways need serve only one-half of the total hallway or corridor occupant load, or 145 occupants (290 divided by 2). The required individual width of Doorways 1 and 4 then becomes 29 inches (737 mm) (145 × 0.2). The minimum exit door width is governed by Section 1003.3.1.3 as before.

See Application Example 1004-9 for determining required corridor width.

are regulated the same as the "all other uses." This is due to the defend-in-place nature of these occupancies, and it is important to list separately due to these factors being different than what is found in some of the other model codes.

It cannot be emphasized too strongly that when the code discusses width in terms of an egress system or component, it is referring to the clear unobstructed usable width afforded along the exit path by the individual components. Therefore, if it is determined, for example, that a means of egress must have a width of at least 3 feet (914 mm), it shall be arranged so that it is possible to pass a 36-inch-wide (914 mm) object through that egress path and each of its components. As stated in Section 1003.2.5, unless the code specifically states that a projection is permitted into that required width, nothing may reduce the width of the component required to provide the necessary exit capacity.

Maintaining width. As stated earlier, it is the width of the most restrictive component that establishes the capacity of the

overall exit system. To ensure that a design does not reduce the capacity at some point throughout the remainder of the exit system, Section 1003.2.3.3 stipulates that the width may not be reduced and that the design must accommodate any accumulation of occupants along the path. Therefore, once the required width is determined from any story or, in fact, from any room or other space, that required width must be maintained until the occupants have reached the public way or an ultimate safe place. This requirement is affected by both the exception in this section, and the provisions related to adjacent levels in Section 1003.2.3.4. The exception simply serves as a reminder that it is really the capacity of the egress system that is not permitted to be reduced. This is important to remember since different factors are used to determine the width requirements for stairways and for all other components. A door, hallway, corridor or passageway located at the bottom of any stairway may generally be reduced in width from what is required for the stairway. This is simply due to the width factor of the stairway being greater than the factor for the other elements. In the Group H, Division 1, 2, 3 and 7 Occupancies these elements may use the factor of 0.4 inch (10.2 mm) per person, whereas on all other uses the appropriate factor would be 0.2 inch (5.1 mm)

Width of exit stairways from a multistory building. This section also presents the method for establishing the required widths of exit stairways in multilevel buildings. The basic provision is that as long as the occupants are headed the same way, there is no need to combine the loads from adjacent levels. The UBC assumes that in exiting multilevel buildings there will be occupants feeding into the exit stairs at various levels. This is accommodated by requiring stairways to be 50 percent wider than the paths of level travel leading to them. As a result, flow rates should be equivalent. Also, the speed of exiting on a stair is substantially less than the speed of exiting on level or nearly level surfaces because of the forced reduction in normal stride as the length of stride on a stair must coincide with the stair's run. A study of this difference shows that the stair width requires an increase of 50 percent from level or ramped floors. Therefore, in determining the required minimum width of a stair, the tributary occupant load served by the stair is multiplied by the appropriate factor from Table 10-B to yield the required minimum width measured in inches (mm). The end result should be checked to see if it complies with the minimum width requirements as governed by Section 1003.3.3.2.

Codes prior to the 1991 edition addressed a cascading effect when analyzing and determining the required width of stairs, but this concept is no longer applicable. The required width of a stair is calculated on a floor-level-by-floor-level application of the formula.

In the design of multistory buildings, it is quite common that different floor levels have different occupant loads. Thus, the occupant load calculated for each floor level must be considered. As a matter of fact, it is not uncommon that buildings will have assembly uses on the top floor. As a consequence of that configuration, it is entirely possible that the top floor of the building will have an occupant load greater than any other. Under such a condition, it will be necessary to calculate the required stair width based only on the occupant load of the uppermost floor. This required width must be maintained through the successive levels, or until it serves a greater occupant load from a lower floor, until the occupants have reached the public way or an ultimate safe place. Application Example 1003-3 illustrates this requirement.

It should be noted that the same concept of determining stair width discussed above applies where building occupants exit upward through the stairway. This is the situation in buildings with basements and subbasements. Occupants of those below-grade floors must exit up the stairway, onto the landing on the ground floor, and then out through the exterior exit door from that landing. The widest width calculated from any floor level will be the controlling factor of the exit at ground level as well as the exit doorway from the stairway. Of course, it is possible that occupants on the ground level will exit through an exit enclosure. If so, the required width determined based on that condition may govern. However, the ground floor usually has adequate width of exits independent of the stairway. Thus, the

occupant load of the ground floor is not usually included in the determination of the exterior exit door width from the stairway.

In those situations where occupants from above and below converge, versus heading in the same direction as discussed above, the occupant load must be added together. In these cases it is assumed that the occupants do arrive at the same point at the same time and therefore the capacity of the system must accommodate the sum of these converging floors. Since the code does not specify exactly which floors are to be used when there are multiple floors both above and below, the building official will need to evaluate each case and reach a decision based on the occupant loads that are served and their locations relative to the point of convergence. In a case where a large occupant load is located at the tenth floor, it is unlikely that group would reach the point of convergence at the same time that occupants coming up just one level from a basement would. Therefore, the building official would need to determine which floors would place the greatest capacity demand on the exit system and design to accommodate that occupant load.

1003.2.4 Height. This section was added into the 1997 edition and provided a general requirement to provide a minimum headroom height. Prior editions of the code contained provisions that regulated the height in certain circumstances, such as at doorways, above stairs and ramps, above and below mezzanines, in parking garages, and in residential occupancies but, in general, headroom height was unregulated. This general requirement will apply in all three parts of the means of egress system, but it can be modified by the exception and by specific provisions such as those for doorways and stairways.

1003.2.5 Exit continuity. This section emphasizes that wherever the code imposes minimal widths on components in an exiting system, such widths are to be clear, usable and unobstructed widths. Nothing may project into these required widths so as to reduce the usability of the full dimension, unless the code specifically and expressly states that a projection is permitted. Two notable examples of permitted projections are doors, either during the course of their swing or in the fully open position, and handrails. The limitations on the amount of such projections are specified within the appropriate sections of the chapter. Additionally, this section places into code language one of the four basic concepts that were previously discussed and points out that the egress system is a complete package that applies to all elements until the safety of the public way is reached.

1003.2.6 Changes in elevation. The first sentence of this section directs the code user to Sections 1003.3.3.3 (stairways) and 1003.3.4 (ramps) for elevation changes along an exit. The intent is that all changes of elevation must comply with one of these two sections, regardless of occupancy load or the use of the building. However, the code is concerned that within a building there be no change in elevation along the path of exit travel, which is not readily apparent to persons seeking to exit under emergency conditions. Therefore, within any building, in an exiting system that is serving an occupant load of 10 persons or more, any change in elevation of less than 12 inches (305 mm) must be accomplished by means of a ramp. A single riser or a pair of risers is not permitted. See Figure 1003-4. Steps used to achieve minor differences in elevation frequently go unnoticed and, as a consequence, can cause missteps or accidents. This limitation on the method for a change of elevation, however,

(Continued on page 171)

Application Example 1003-3

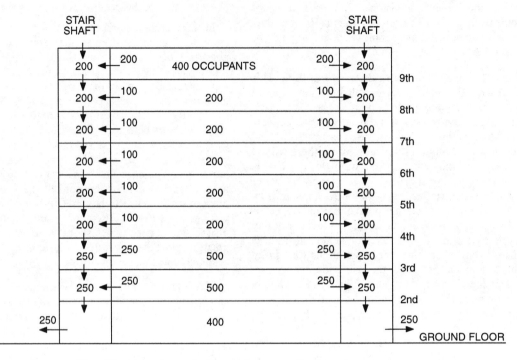

NOTE: First-story occupants may exit through stair enclosures or through independent exits.
Width required at ground level is the same for each case.

OCCUPANT LOAD × 0.3 = REQUIRED EXIT WIDTH, INCHES

STAIRWAY WIDTH REQUIRED
  4TH THROUGH 9TH STORIES: 200 × 0.3 = 60 INCHES
  1ST THROUGH 3RD STORIES: 250 × 0.3 = 75 INCHES

STAIR EXIT DOOR WIDTH
  250 × 0.2 = 50 INCHES

For **SI:** 1 inch = 25.4 mm.

WIDTH OF EXITS—MULTISTORY OFFICE BUILDING

FIGURE 1003-3

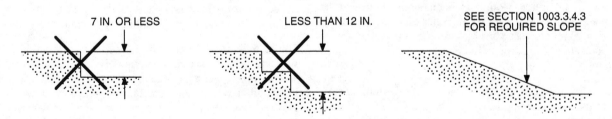

For **SI:** 1 inch = 25.4 mm.

**LONGITUDINAL SECTION THROUGH CORRIDOR OR OTHER EXIT PATH
SERVING AN OCCUPANT LOAD OF 10 OR MORE**

FIGURE 1003-4

(Continued from page 169)

does not apply in exterior locations, within one- and two-family dwellings, within an individual unit of a Group R, Division 1 Occupancy, or along aisles that serve seating areas. Steps may be used to accomplish a change in elevation of less than 12 inches (305 mm) when the occupant load is nine or less, provided the steps comply with the rise and run limitations of Section 1003.3.3.3. Where a single step occurs, no handrails would be required since Section 1003.3.3 applies only to stairways with two or more risers.

1003.2.8 Means of Egress Identification.

1003.2.8.2 Where required. To properly identify the egress path from a building and its portions thereof, it is necessary to provide exit signs. While somewhat vague, these provisions are probably more performance-oriented than most requirements. The basic provision is that signs are required so that the exiting path is clearly indicated. By combining this requirement with Exception 2, it will mean that, in general, when access to two or more exits are required from any portion of a building, such as from a room, area, floor or other space, exit signs must be installed at all required exit doorways and at any other location throughout the exiting system where deemed necessary by the building official to clearly identify the path of travel to the exit.

Care must be taken in the placement of the exit signs to see that they are properly located and properly oriented to the direction of travel in the egress system so that they can be easily read by the persons seeking the exit. Particular care should also be taken to see that nothing occurs in the means of egress that might tend to obscure or screen the exit sign or that might cause confusion in identifying the exit sign. It is not uncommon in many building plans to find that exit signs are shown at what appear to be the appropriate locations. However, they are actually installed behind ducts or other building equipment in such a manner that they are not really visible to building occupants or they occur near or over doors which are not the exit.

In certain instances, the exit signs may be present, but they are not oriented to the path of travel and to the approaching building occupant. Therefore, they are not visible and are certainly not legible to the person seeking the exit. It is strongly advised that, as one of the last points of inspection before approving occupancy of any building, the building official or designated agent carefully walk the egress path to ensure the proper installation and effective location and orientation of exit signs. It is also important that ceiling-suspended exit signs do not project below the 7-foot (2134 mm) level.

Omission of exit signs. While the installation of exit signs is of paramount importance in most instances, there will be cases where the exit is abundantly obvious to any building occupant. Where the exit is clearly identifiable as the exit, the exit is essentially its own identifying sign. When approved by the building official, it may not be necessary to install an exit sign at such an obvious exit. Exit signs may be omitted in Group R, Division 3 Occupancies and within individual units of Group R, Division 1 Occupancies. In addition, in rooms or areas of Group I, Divisions 1.1, 1.2 or 2 Occupancies and Group E, Division 3 day-care occupancies, exit signs may be omitted when the occupant load is less than 50. These latter occupancies, based on Table 10-A, require access to two exits when the occupant loads are eight or ten in the health care occupancies and seven in a daycare use. Requiring exit signs for such small occupant loads may

be overly restrictive when the basic provision is applied. Exception 2, which eliminates the need for exit signs in areas that need access to only one exit, has application to a great number of areas including "within" exits such as a stair enclosure. It will be important to remember this second exception especially when determining if all points are within 100 feet (30 480 mm) of a visible sign.

1003.2.8.3 Graphics. While no particular color is specified for exit signs, it is required that the color and design of the signs, the lettering, the arrows and other symbols on the sign provide good contrast so as to increase legibility. The letters of the word "exit" are required to be 6 inches (152 mm) in height and have a width of stroke of not less than $3/4$ inch (19.1 mm). The width of the individual letters and their spacing was added in the 1997 UBC. These dimensions will not greatly affect the appearance of the signs on the market since most national standards had used these dimensions. By specifying the letter spacing it will ensure they are not placed too close together so that the signs will be more legible and probably more effective. Additionally, when a larger sign is provided, it is important that the lettering be increased proportionally.

1003.2.8.4 Illumination. When required, exit signs must be illuminated. The source of the illumination is not material, provided the level of illumination at the sign meets the minimum requirements of the code. When the illumination of the sign is from an external source, that source must be capable of producing a light intensity of at least 5 footcandles (54 lx) at all points over the face of the sign. When illumination of the sign is from an internal source, that internal source must produce luminance of the face of the sign equivalent to the 5 footcandles (54 lx) produced by an external source. The exception addresses the fact that the illumination of approved self-luminous are measured differently. The measurement of light falling *on* an object is measured differently from the level that is measured *from* a light source.

The measurement of the the 5 footcandles (54 lx) from an external source can be made by a light meter. The measurement of the equivalent luminance, however, from an internal source is more difficult. In many instances, it may be necessary for the building official to rely on the testing laboratory that has examined, certified and labeled the exit sign. In labeling such a sign, the testing agency is certifying, among other things, that the light level is at least that required by the code.

Exit sign light sources. The UBC requires that the light source for exit signs be provided by either of two electric lamps. It also recognizes approved self-luminous exit signs. Under the provisions of Section 104.2.8, the building official may also approve alternate type signs or lighting systems. Such alternates must, in fact, provide the equivalent of the specified light levels.

The lighting of a self-luminous sign is provided by a radioactive source, usually tritium. It has a half-life of approximately 10 years, and the signs are manufactured so that the letters of the word "exit" are illuminated uniformly. This uniformity of illumination of the letters' surface contributes greatly to the legibility of the sign.

There are also other types of signs available today, such as the electroluminescent sign. This is one where the letters on the sign are coated with phosphorous. The sign is maintained plugged into a power source. The current excites the phosphorous so that in event of a power failure the sign will produce a sufficient light level on the letters of the sign for a time period as specified by the code, generally one and one-half hours. Also, LED exit signs have become available.

1003.2.8.5 Power source. Regulations concerning the need to provide power for illumination of exit signs are applicable to all exit signs. All the signs are required to be illuminated and must provide continued operation for a minimum of one and one-half hours after the loss of the normal power supply. This backup power supply shall be from approved storage battery system, or another approved on-site, independent source. The exception addresses the use of self-luminous signs which, by definition, are independent of external power supplies and therefore do not require compliance with the general power or emergency power provisions.

1003.2.9 Means of egress illumination.

1003.2.9.1 General. In order for the exit system to afford a safe path of travel and for the building occupant to be able to negotiate the system, it is necessary that the entire egress system be provided with a certain minimum amount of lighting. Without such lighting it would not be possible for building occupants to identify and follow the appropriate path of travel. Therefore, the code requires that, except in Group R, Division 3 Occupancies and within individual units of Group R, Division 1 Occupancies, the egress paths be illuminated throughout their entire length any time the building is occupied. Such illumination must be capable of producing a light intensity of not less than 1 footcandle (10.76 lx) at floor level throughout the entire path of travel through the system. The second exception recognizes that such levels of illumination might interfere with presentations in such places as motion picture theaters; therefore, the exception allows a reduction in such building places to a level of not less than 0.2 footcandle (2.15 lx). Such a reduced lighting level, however, is permitted only during a performance and would be brought up to the 1 footcandle (10.76 1x) level if a fire alarm system was activated.

One footcandle (10.76 lx) of light on a surface is not a great deal of light. It is probably not sufficient light to enable a person to read. However, it is sufficient light to allow a person passing through the exit system to distinguish objects and to identify obstructions in the actual path of travel. The light cast by a full moon on a clear night might approximate the 1-footcandle (10.76 lx) light level. When the amount of light intensity is in doubt, it is possible to measure it with a light meter.

In imposing the requirements for the egress system, the code requires that illumination be supplied at all times when the building is occupied. However, in applying this requirement, the code intends that illumination be provided for those portions of the egress system that serve the parts of the building that are, in fact, occupied. Parts of the exiting system that would not be serving the occupants of the building need not, at that time, be illuminated.

It should be noted that the wording in the UBC prior to the 1997 edition did not require exit illumination "within individual dwelling units, guest rooms and sleeping rooms." This wording would accept the lights being turned off in rooms such as patient sleeping rooms in hospitals, jail cells or dormitory-type rooms, such as army barracks. While the wording in the 1997 UBC does not specifically address these types of sleeping rooms, it would not seem reasonable to prohibit the lights from being turned off in a location where people are trying to sleep. The code change that modified this wording did not discuss any intended change in the application of these provisions.

1003.2.9.2 Power supply. Normally, the power for illumination of the egress path is provided by the premises' wiring system. However, where the potential life-safety hazard is sufficiently great, it is considered inadequate to simply provide the illumination of the exit system by means of the premises' wiring system. In these cases it is necessary that emergency power—a completely separate source of power—automatically provide illumination of the exits. Separate sources of power are required in Group I, Divisions 1.1 and 1.2 Occupancies and in all other occupancies where the exit system serves an occupant load of 100 or more.

Unless the occupancy or occupant load is specifically mentioned in this section, the emergency power supply is not required. However, Section 403 contains special provisions for buildings subject to the high-rise requirements, and various items, such as alarms or ventilation, may require an emergency system based on requirements in other sections.

When emergency power systems are required, they will generally be supplied by approved storage batteries or another type of approved onsite power-generating system. It is the intent that this power source be automatically available even in the event of the total failure of the public utility system. Therefore, a separate, independent source is generally required. Figure 403-2 in this handbook illustrates one method of complying with the UBC. By referring to the requirements of the Electrical Code, the 1997 UBC will give the building official the option of accepting "separate service" as listed in Article 700 of the *National Electrical Code*®. The acceptance of a separate service should be done cautiously to ensure that it will be available during an emergency. This cautious review is extremely important where the emergency power is being provided from an off-site location.

1003.3.1 Doors. This section applies to doors or doorways that occur at any location in the means of egress system. Although the code will use the term "exit door" throughout this section, these provisions will apply not only to doors that provide access to the four items considered an "exit" in Section 1005 but also include any door or doorway that an occupant must use within the exit-access, the exit or the exit-discharge portion of the egress system. Prior to the 1997 edition of the UBC, the scoping of the door requirements were found in this general section. When Chapter 10 was revised in the 1997 UBC, the scoping provisions were relocated so that each section contained the scoping and the code users knew exactly when the provisions would apply. Some of the requirements for doors is applicable only to specific occupancies and therefore certain provisions were relocated to the specific occupancy sections in Section 1007.

The last sentence of the second paragraph to Section 1003.3.1.1 should also be noted since it will require that at least one exterior door that meets the size requirements of Section 1003.1.3 be provided from every building used for human occupancy. Although the requirements in Section 1003.1.3 will generally apply only when the door serves an occupant load of 10 or more, this specific requirement for the exterior door will apply

Application Example 1003-5

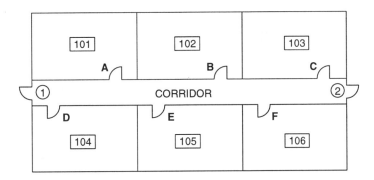

GIVEN: Residential building with units 101 through 106 each having an occupant load of 2.

DETERMINE: Required sizes of doors.

SOLUTION:

1. Doors A through F each serves an occupant load of 2 (which is less than 10). Also, since they are interior doors, they need not satisfy the minimum 3-foot by 6-foot 8-inch (914 mm by 2032 mm) size requirement specified in Section 1003.1.3.

2. Doors 1 and 2 serve a total occupant load of 12. Thus, they are each required to satisfy the minimum 3-foot by 6-foot 8-inch (914 mm by 2032 mm) size specified in Section 1003.1.3. It should be noted that the desired result in this case is not a matter of exit width but of minimum door size. Thus, the total occupant load of 12 should not be divided equally between Doors 1 and 2.

It is interesting to note that if the total occupant load served by Doors 1 and 2 is less than 10, one of the doors must satisfy the minimum size requirement in Section 1003.1.3; the other is not regulated. In fact, one 3-foot by 6-foot 8-inch (914 mm by 2032 mm) door would satisfy the minimum requirement.

regardless of the occupant load. Compliance with these two statements yields some interesting results. See Application Example 1003-5.

Additional doors. The second paragraph of Section 1003.3.1.1 establishes criteria for all egress doors including those that are not required. Such additional egress doors must comply with all provisions of this chapter for exit doors. When these doors are installed for egress purposes, whether required or not, the building occupant would not know if they are part of the egress system or not. Since the building occupant would then expect the door to provide a safe path from the space, it is imperative that such doors and doorways conform to code requirements. It is important to remember the scoping found within each subsection and remember when it applies. An example would be the floor level at doors. Regardless of what the occupant load is and whether the door was provided for "egress purposes," the code will ensure that the occupants would not open a door and find a three-story drop on the other side.

Door identification. The primary gist of the third paragraph of Section 1003.3.1.1 is that exit doors be installed so that they are readily recognized as exit doors and not confused with the surrounding construction. It is important that they be easily distinguishable as doors provided for egress purposes. The corollary of this requirement would also say that exit doors should not be concealed. In other words, they should not be covered with drapes or decorations, nor should they be provided with mirrors or any other material or be arranged in a way that could confuse the building occupant seeking an exit.

1003.3.1.2 Special doors. Based on the provisions in Section 1003.3.1.5, the code generally requires that doors in exiting systems be of the pivoted or side-hinged swinging type. In this section, whenever the door serves an occupant load of 10 or more,

revolving doors, sliding doors and overhead doors are specifically prohibited from being used in the means of egress.

Revolving doors are conditionally acceptable. An exception is made for the installation and use of revolving doors. Revolving doors are finding increasing use in buildings. Where once they were used primarily in cold climates, they are now being installed in all regions primarily as an energy conservation measure. However, it is not permissible to use revolving doors to supply any of the required exit capacity. When used, the door must be an approved revolving door and comply with the specific requirements listed. Although the code requires an "approved" door, the UBC does not provide nor reference any standard since there is no recognized national standard governing revolving doors. Some of the other model codes do contain more specific provisions that were included in the BCMC report on egress systems, which may provide the building official with additional guidance.

At the present time, when revolving doors are installed they must be of a type where the leaves will collapse under opposing pressures. Such doors are required to have a minimum overall width of 6 feet 6 inches (1981 mm). At least one conforming exit door shall be located in close proximity to the revolving door. In such an arrangement, the adjacent swinging door will be used to satisfy exit capacity requirements.

Power-operated doors. Special exceptions are made, however, for certain types of power-operated doors whether they are of the swinging or sliding type. These doors are permitted to be used when they are in compliance with UBC Standard 10-1. Reference is made to that standard for complete details on the use of sliding doors in a means of egress. Essentially, that standard requires that such doors have a capability of swinging, and that they be designed and installed to break away from any position in the opening and swing to the full open position when an

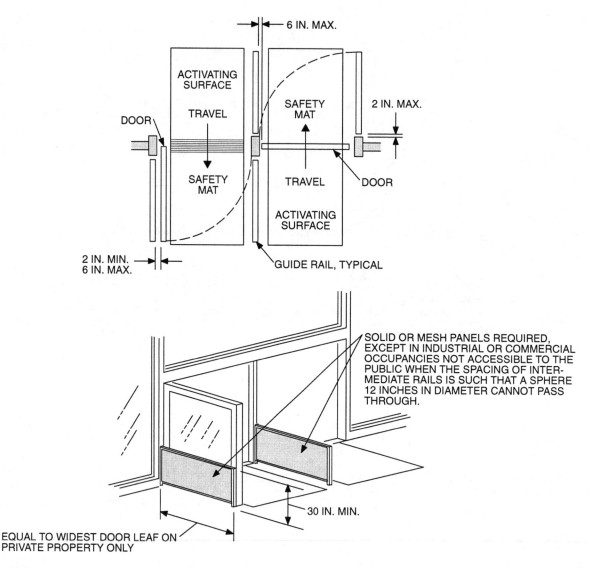

For **SI:** 1 inch = 25.4 mm.

POWER-OPERATED DOORS

FIGURE 1003-6

opening force not exceeding 40 pounds (178 N) is applied at the normal push plate location.

Figure 1003-6 shows that when power-operated swinging doors are used and installed so that they could come in contact with pedestrian traffic, it is necessary to install a guide rail on the swing side of the door that projects out from the door jamb a distance equal to the width of the widest door leaf. These guide rails are required to be a minimum of 30 inches (762 mm) in height and be capable of resisting a horizontal force at the top of the rail of not less than 50 pounds per lineal foot (730 N/m).

The purpose of these guide rails is to provide protection so that the doors, when opened automatically, will not come in contact with pedestrians. In the event the construction of the building or other physical elements provide the same function as the specified guardrails, the separate guardrails need not be provided. At the same time, such guardrails are not necessary in in-

dustrial or commercial occupancies where the general public does not have access to the building spaces.

In that special instance when power-operated swinging doors swing toward approaching traffic, it is necessary that the activating devices begin to function at a point at least 8 feet 11 inches (2718 mm) beyond the door in the open position. Also, the guide rails shall extend 6 feet 5 inches (1956 mm) beyond the door in the open position. The purpose of these, of course, is to permit the door to swing to the open position before the approaching pedestrian traffic reaches the door. Thus, it will be in the open position or at least will not present a potential source of injury to the approaching pedestrian. See Figure 1003-7.

In a provision added in the 1991 edition, and amended in the 1994 edition, horizontal sliding doors complying with UBC Standard 7-8 may be used in elevator lobbies, in smoke barriers for other than Group A or H Occupancies, and when serving an occupant load of less than 50 in any occupancy other than Group

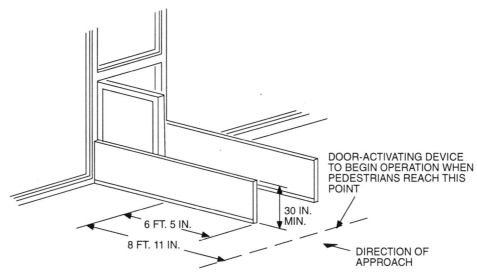

For **SI:** 1 inch = 25.4 mm, 1 foot = 304.8 mm.

POWER-OPERATED DOORS

FIGURE 1003-7

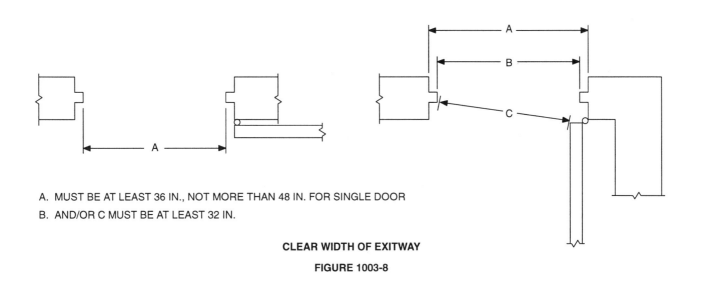

A. MUST BE AT LEAST 36 IN., NOT MORE THAN 48 IN. FOR SINGLE DOOR

B. AND/OR C MUST BE AT LEAST 32 IN.

CLEAR WIDTH OF EXITWAY

FIGURE 1003-8

H. These door systems contain many specific features found in the standard and ensure that they are available as an exit door when needed.

1003.3.1.3 Width and height. As required in Section 1003.3.1.1, every building or structure subject to human occupancy must be provided with at least one exterior exit doorway that complies with the provisions of this section. It specifies that every required exit doorway shall be of such a size as to permit the installation of a door that is at least 3 feet (914 mm) in width and 6 feet 8 inches (2032 mm) in height. This is, of course, one of the standard sizes that door manufacturers produce. However, as the doorway width is the critical dimension, a pair of doors is permitted as long as the required doorway width is provided.

When installed in egress system, doors are required to be arranged so that, when open, the minimum clear width of the exit, in this case the doorway, is at least 32 inches (813 mm), as illustrated in Figure 1003-8. Again, the code requires the net dimension of the clear width provided by the exit component. Thus, when the door is fully opened, it must provide a net unobstructed width of not less than 32 inches (813 mm) and permit the passage of a 32-inch-wide (813 mm) object.

This section applies to every door in the egress system that serves any area having an occupant load of 10 or more. Therefore, in locations in buildings where the doorway is serving a smaller occupant load, it would be permissible to have door openings that are less than 32 inches (813 mm) wide. See Chapter 11 for accessibility requirements. Typically, in residential buildings, door openings to closets, bathrooms and bedrooms where the occupant load is clearly less than 10 may have widths less than 32 inches (813 mm).

The requirement for a minimum 32-inch (813 mm) clear opening on a required exit doorway serving an occupant load of 10 or more provides some interesting results regarding the minimum capacity of any required exit door. Using the formula for capacity presented in Section 1003.2.3 coupled with this requirement for a minimum 32-inch-wide (813 mm) clear opening, it is known that in general, every required exit doorway meeting these specifications will provide an exit capacity for a minimum of 160 persons. This is determined by the fact that the minimum required clear width of such an opening is 32 inches (813 mm). When that dimension is divided by 0.2, the resulting capacity is 160. As a result, every exit doorway meeting the minimum width requirements of the code can serve as an exit for that number of persons.

1003.3.1.4 Door leaf width. Throughout the rest of the code, the intent in specifying dimensions is to provide a minimum width. This particular section is at variance with that general approach, since it limits the maximum width of any single door leaf in a required exit doorway. As shown in Figure 1003-8, no such leaf may exceed 48 inches (1219 mm) in width. The reason for this is that doors often do not receive the maintenance necessary to ensure their continued proper operation. The issue being addressed is that door leaves be reasonably limited in width because wide doors require substantially greater maintenance to ensure reasonable opening effort and this maintenance is too often not provided.

This maximum dimension provides some basic information about door-opening capacities. The maximum width of any door opening, assuming the installation of a pair of 48-inch (1219 mm) door leaves, will approach 96 inches (2438 mm). When that dimension is divided by 0.2, as specified in Section 1003.2.3, the capacity of that exit doorway would be almost 480 persons. By virtue of the limitation on maximum door-leaf width, it is known that no single doorway opening can provide an exit capacity for more than 480 persons. In situations where the required capacity for an individual exit exceeds 480 persons, it will be necessary to provide multiple door openings to accommodate that number.

The limitation on the 48-inch-wide (1219 mm) door leaf does not apply to those doors that do not serve as exit doors, nor does it apply to those doors that serve an occupant load of less than 10.

1003.3.1.5 Swing and opening force. In 1942, 492 people died in the Coconut Grove fire in Boston. One of the significant contributing factors to that loss of life was the fact that the exterior exit doors swung inward. As a consequence, it was not possible to open the doors due to the press of the crowd attempting to exit the building. This incident was the primary reason for changing the existing codes to require that, under certain circumstances, exit doors must swing in the direction of exit travel.

This section requires that every exit door serving an area that has an occupant load of 10 or more persons shall be of the pivoted or side-hinged swinging type. In addition, exit doors serving an area with an occupant load of 50 or more, or those serving any hazardous area as regulated in Section 1007.4.4, shall swing with the flow of egress travel. The door shall swing to a fully open position when subjected to a force not greater than 30 pounds (133.45 N). This force is applied to the latch stile or side of the door. Also, it should be noted that doors on an accessi-

ble route have separate opening force criteria. These criteria are found in Section 4.13.11 of CABO/ANSI A117.1. Most doors are openable with forces less than these maximum limits. However, when in doubt, the actual force required can be easily measured by use of a spring scale.

Limited use of double-acting doors. Double-acting doors are used in a number of instances to facilitate travel in both directions through a door opening. However, the code is concerned that in certain situations double-acting doors should not be used as part of the required exiting system. The UBC intends that every door in the exiting system be installed and maintained available primarily for exiting purposes. The convenience purposes of such doors are subordinate to their need as exits. Therefore, double-acting doors are not to be used any time the occupant load served by the door is 100 or more persons. In addition, double-acting doors are not permitted when the door assembly is required to be a rated fire-protection assembly. One of the necessary features of such a rated assembly is the fact that the doors must be latched and held in the closed position with positive latching. It is difficult to arrange double-acting doors so that they can be effectively latched for this purpose. Additionally, as a part of the fire testing, a through opening between the door and frame is not permitted and therefore a jamb is typically needed to close such a gap. Similar concern applies when the door is part of a smoke- and draft-control assembly. It is particularly difficult to maintain any significant degree of smoke tightness when the door is free-swinging and there are no door stops around the top and sides of the door so that the door can close tightly against them.

Finally, for reasons similar to those relative to the requirements for latching, double-acting doors are not to be used any time the code requires panic hardware on the door or if panic hardware is installed for any reason. Because of the nature of double-acting doors and the fact that they swing in both directions, and because they frequently cause accidents, the code requires that they be provided with a vision panel of not less than 200 square inches (0.129 m^2) so that the door user is able to determine if there is a person at or approaching the door from the other side.

1003.3.1.6 Floor level at doors. This section applies regardless of the occupant load or area served. The purpose is to avoid any surprises to the person passing through the door opening, such as a change in floor level. Therefore, it is necessary that a floor or landing be provided on each side of the doorway. This floor or landing shall not be more than 1 inch (25 mm) lower than the threshold of the doorway. In addition, when the doorway is required to provide access for persons with disabilities, the floor or landing shall not be more than $1/2$ inch (12.7 mm) lower than the threshold. Landings are required to be level, except exterior landings may have a slope of not more than $1/4$ inch per foot (6.4 mm per m) for drainage. See Figures 1003-9 and 1003-10.

Exceptions for individual dwelling units and Group U Occupancies. Exceptions are made for individual dwelling units and Group U Occupancies where it is permissible to open a door at the top step of an interior flight of stairs, provided the door does not swing out over the top step. The same is true for a door or opening at a landing, when the landing is not more than 8 inches (203 mm) lower than the floor level at the doorway. The reason for permitting this type of arrangement in dwelling units

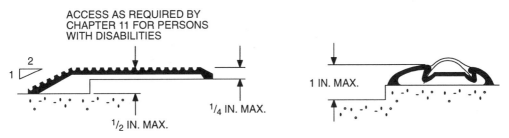

For **SI:** 1 inch = 25.4 mm.

THRESHOLD HEIGHT

FIGURE 1003-9

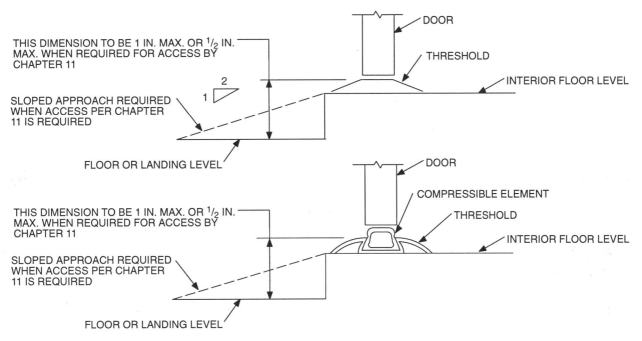

For **SI:** 1 inch = 25.4 mm.

THRESHOLD HEIGHTS

FIGURE 1003-10

is that as a building occupant approaches such a door, in order to open it, he or she must back away from the door. This creates the need for a minimum landing to be traversed before the occupant can proceed to step down onto the stairs or down onto the landing. In this situation with minimal occupant load, the opening may occur at the top of the stair or at the landing, but the door must swing toward the person descending the stair or stepping down onto the landing. See Figures 1003-11 and 1003-12. Also, in such locations it is permissible when screen doors or other doors are installed, especially on the same jamb as the exit door, to swing them over stairs, steps or landings.

The revision in the 1988 UBC, which limited the door to opening on an interior stair and excluded exterior stairways, was an important change that is often overlooked. The primary reason for this change was due to a person needing to stand on a narrow step while attempting to open the door. This often must be

done in nighttime lighting conditions, inclement weather and while holding onto anything the person may be using. These type of conditions create a dangerous situation for the users. Perhaps one of the most common areas where this provision is overlooked is on the sliding glass door, which often leads from a residence out to a patio slab. If the level change between the dwelling and the patio exceeds 8 inches (203 mm), a complying landing must be provided outside the door prior to making any additional changes in elevation. A single step is not permitted.

For building equipment rooms that are not normally occupied, doors need not meet the requirements of Section 1003.3.1.6.

1003.3.1.7 Landings at doors. This section contains the dimensional criteria for landings. It deals primarily with those landings where there is a door installed in conjunction with the landing.

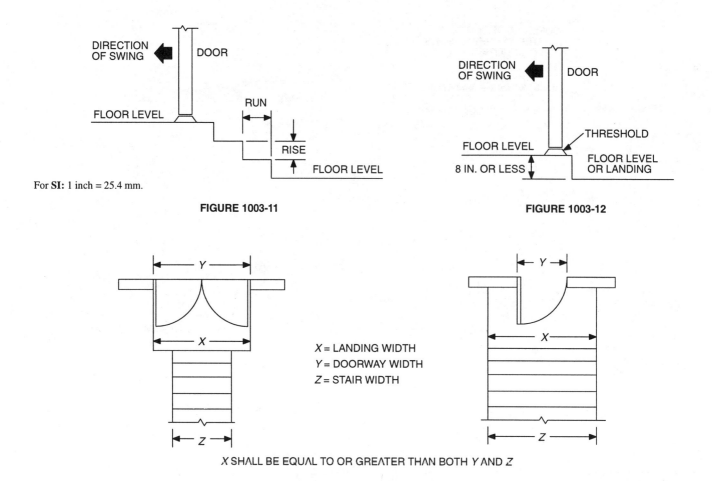

For **SI:** 1 inch = 25.4 mm.

FIGURE 1003-11

FIGURE 1003-12

X = LANDING WIDTH
Y = DOORWAY WIDTH
Z = STAIR WIDTH

X SHALL BE EQUAL TO OR GREATER THAN BOTH *Y* AND *Z*

WIDTH OF LANDINGS AT DOORS

FIGURE 1003-13

Landings that have no adjoining doors are regulated by Sections 1003.3.3.5 and 1003.3.4.4.

Required width of landings. The required width of a landing is determined by the width of the stairway or the width of the doorway it serves. Figure 1003-13 depicts these relationships. The requirement is that the minimum width of the landing be at least equal to the width of the stair or the width of the door, whichever is greater. The code is concerned that doors opening onto landings not obstruct the path of travel on the landing. In this regard, the code establishes two limitations. The first states that when doors open onto landings they shall not project into the required dimension of the landing by more than 7 inches (178 mm) when the door is in the fully opened position. Second, whenever the landing serves an occupant load of 50 or more, doors may not, during the course of their swing, reduce the dimension of the landing to less than one-half its required width. Stated from the positive direction, it requires that doors swinging over landings must leave unobstructed at least one-half of the required width of the landing. While the obstruction of one half of the required width of the landing might seem excessive, it must be remembered that when the door is creating such an obstruction, it is in a position where it is free to swing and the obstruction is not a fixed obstruction. These latter requirements are explained in Figure 1003-14.

Required length of landings. In addition to the width requirements, landings must generally have a length of at least 44 inches (1118 mm) measured in the direction of travel. This restriction applies primarily to landings that serve flights of stairs providing for travel in a straight line. Where one traverses one flight of stairs, crosses the landing and then travels the other flight of stairs, that intermediate landing dimension between flights in the line of travel must be at least 44 inches (1118 mm). Typically, an exception is made for those occupancies with relatively low occupant loads. Therefore, in dwelling units and in Group U Occupancies, the length of the landing need not exceed 36 inches (914 mm). The code requirements are illustrated in Figures 1003-14 and 1003-15.

1003.3.1.8 Type of lock or latch. This section and Section 1003.3.1.5 are particularly focused on the concept of ensuring that everything in the path of travel through the exit system, particularly doors, be under the control of and operable by the person seeking egress. Therefore, as a general statement, this section states that all doors in the egress system are required to be openable from the inside or from the side from which egress is sought, without the need of a key or any special knowledge or effort. If a key or special knowledge or effort is required, in all probability the door could not be readily openable by many building occupants. Such things as combination locks are also

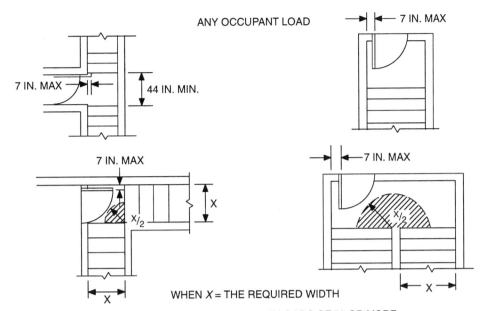

For **SI:** 1 inch = 25.4 mm.

DOORS AT LANDINGS

FIGURE 1003-14

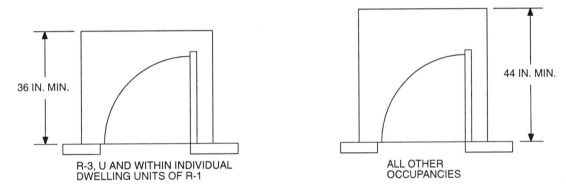

For **SI:** 1 inch = 25.4 mm.

LENGTH OF LANDINGS AT DOORS

FIGURE 1003-15

prohibited on doors in exiting systems. Essentially, the code intends that the hardware installed be of a type familiar to most users—something that is readily recognizable under any condition of visibility, including darkness, and under conditions of fire or any other emergency.

In addition, the hardware must be readily operable. At times one will encounter different types of devices, such as thumb turns, surface bolts or other kinds of hardware. The building official must determine if these special types of operating devices are acceptable. In many instances, it will be necessary to ensure that the building occupant can, in fact, grip the operating device and operate it. Some thumb turns are so small that they are, by their nature, quite difficult to operate.

Another consideration that needs to be remembered in evaluating the acceptability of operating hardware is the fact that this hardware is going to be in place and in use over a substantial period of time. Unfortunately, doors and their operating hardware do not always get the constant maintenance that they should to keep them in operating order. It is imperative, in accordance with Section 3402, that the operation of doors in the egress system be maintained continuously in compliance with this section.

Allowable exceptions to type of lock or latch. The UBC allows two significant exceptions. In allowing these exceptions, it permits certain locking conditions that would appear to conflict with the basic requirement. However, in allowing these exceptions, the code then imposes certain compensating safeguards when the exit doors are to be locked. It is the intent of the code that if the conditions are satisfied, the arrangement then affords essentially an equivalent level of safety as would be provided if the door were, in fact, readily openable at all times without use of a key or any special knowledge or effort.

1. The first exception applies to the main exit in Groups A, Division 3; B, F, M and S Occupancies, and in all churches. It permits certain exterior exit doors to be locked with a key if several conditions are satisfied. The first condition states that the main exit must consist of a single door or a single pair of doors. Thus, if the building is occupied, the main exit will, in all probability, be unlocked. A second condition requires that there be a sign that is readily visible, permanently maintained and located adjacent to the door. This sign is required to read THIS DOOR MUST REMAIN UNLOCKED DURING BUSINESS HOURS. The letters must be at least 1 inch (25 mm) in height and placed on a contrasting background. Both of these requirements are for legibility. The code also requires that, when unlocked, the single door, or both leaves in a pair of doors, must be free to swing.

   Obviously, the sign or the presence of the sign is not going to ensure that the door is unlocked. However, it does advise the occupant that whenever the space is occupied, the law does require that in the interest of reasonable fire safety the door be unlocked. In the event the door is not unlocked, the occupant is advised that his or her life may be at risk. The occupant should seek to alleviate that situation. Note that the use of this exception may be revoked by the building official for due cause.

2. The second exception refers to exit doors from individual dwelling units; Group R, Division 3 congregate residences; and guest rooms in Group R Occupancies. This section essentially prohibits dead bolts in dwelling units if the operation of the dead bolts depends on the use of a key or a special tool. This exception does permit, however, the use of a dead bolt, a security chain or a night latch when the occupant load is 10 or less on the condition that the device be openable from the inside without the use of a key or any special tool and be mounted at a height not exceeding 48 inches (1219 mm) above the finished floor. It follows from the basic requirement of this section, however, that the device must not require any undue effort in order to unlatch the door and gain egress.

Section 1003.3.1.8 also specifically prohibits the use of manually operated edge bolts, surface-mounted flush bolts or surface bolts since these clearly do not conform with the intent of this section. This section was further modified in the 1997 UBC to specifically include "any other type of device that may be used to close or restrain the door other than by operation of the locking device." This new wording did not change any requirements; it is just restating the basic rules. This will address many systems that are being found on doors to provide security such as the magnetic locks at banks and jewelry stores. The general requirements that doors be openable without any special knowledge or effort and that the unlatching must not require more than one operation is the minimum level of safety that the code is looking for.

The last sentence of the second paragraph is often overlooked or is misapplied due to its location after the sentence concerning flush bolts being used on pairs of doors. The general requirement that the unlatching of any leaf require no more than one operation is affected only by the two exceptions listed below it. This limit on the number of operations will apply to any exit door serving any occupant load, whether it is a single door or a

pair of doors. This requirement relates back to the issue of needing special knowledge and the fact that the occupants should not be delayed while attempting to exit a building.

When exit doors are used in pairs, it is anticipated that each leaf in the pair of doors be provided with its own operating hardware. A special arrangement, however, is permitted when the pair of doors is equipped with automatic flush bolts designed so that the act of releasing one of the leaves of the pair releases both leaves. To ensure immediate and reliable operation of the pair of doors, the unlatching of either leaf in the pair must be accomplished by not more than one operation. In the case of Exception 1 discussed above, automatic flush bolts are not permitted to be installed when doors are used in pairs. In other words, each leaf of a pair of doors may be provided with key-locking hardware or a single lock that would restrain both leaves. Of course, both leaves must be unlocked during business hours, no additional operations of a latching device are permitted and the previously mentioned signage is mandatory.

An exception is provided for Group R, Division 3 Occupancies that will permit manually operated edge- or surface-mounted flush bolts and surface bolts, regardless of whether the doors are single leaf or in pairs.

Special application for pairs of exit doors. A second exception recognizes that in certain instances doorway widths are dictated by the need to pass equipment through the openings. As a consequence, doorways, such as those to a boiler room, for example, are frequently substantially larger than would be required for exiting purposes alone. Therefore, where that is the case for a normally unoccupied space, manually operated bolts may be used on the inactive leaf. Thus, the code permits the inactive leaf to be fixed in place without a door closer. As the space is not normally occupied, this exception presents no significant hazard to life safety. The other side of this coin, however, is that any door leaf that is part of the required exit width must comply with all the code requirements that apply to exit doors.

When reviewing the lock and latch provisions, it is important to emphasize that the provisions of the section are applicable to all exit doors, regardless of occupant load or area served.

1003.3.1.9 Panic hardware. This section of the code does not require that panic hardware be installed. Instead, this section establishes what a panic hardware device is and refers to *Uniform Building Code* Standard 10-4, which is the standard that defines panic hardware. When panic hardware is required, it is necessary that the activating member of the device be installed at a height of at least 30 inches (762 mm) but not more than 44 inches (1118 mm) above the floor surface at the door. In addition, the device must be arranged so that a horizontal force not exceeding 15 pounds (66.72 N), when applied in direction of exit travel, will unlatch the door.

Basically, panic hardware is an unlatching device that will operate even during panic situations, so that the weight of the crowd against the door will cause the device to unlatch. It should also be noted that if a door is used in a situation where panic hardware might otherwise be required, it is not necessary to install panic hardware if the door has no means for locking or latching. If the door is free to swing at all times, there is no need to install panic hardware to overcome a lock or latch.

This provision of the code is intended to prevent the type of disaster experienced in the Coconut Grove fire in Boston in

1942. When a panic hardware device is installed on a door leaf, the press of a crowd, which prevented the opening of the door in the Coconut Grove fire, will assure the automatic opening of the door.

Panic hardware on "balanced" doors. Special care must be taken when installing panic hardware on balanced doors. In this instance, push-pad-type panic hardware is to be used and it must be installed on the one-half door width nearest the latch side to avoid locating the pad too close to the pivot point.

Section 1003.3.1.5 requires exit doors to be either side-hinged or pivoted. The typical pivoted door has its top and bottom pivot points located near the edge of the door frame opposite the latch side. Balanced doors are nothing more than a specialized type of pivoted door in which the pivot point is located some distance inboard from the door edge, thus creating a counterbalancing effect. The length of the panic bar is limited for balanced doors because the door cannot be opened if the opening force is applied too close to the pivot point or beyond. Limiting the panic bar length to half the door width ensures that those who use the door will apply opening pressure at a distance sufficiently removed from the pivot point to allow the door to open.

1003.3.1.10 Special egress-control devices. In the 1988 UBC, this section introduced a degree of security to an exit door of a Group B; Group F; Group I, Division 2; Group M; Group R, Division 1 congregate residences serving as a group-care facility and Group S Occupancies. This section allows the use of a door that has an egress-control device with a built-in time delay under specific conditions and when approved by the local building official. These devices were included in the UBC to resolve the problem of exit doors being illegally locked by building operators desperate to stop the theft of merchandise through unsupervised, secondary exits.

The 1994 UBC expanded the applicability for special egress-control devices to additional occupancies. Group I, Division 2 and Group R, Division 1 congregate residences serving as group-care facilities were permitted to be equipped with special egress-control devices. These occupancies were added because it was perceived that they also had security problems that needed to be addressed. The devices are also sometimes needed in nursing homes or group-care facilities where facility operators must restrict patient egress while still maintaining viable exit systems.

It must be emphasized that under the conditions imposed by this section, and within the reliability of the automatic systems required, there will be no delay whatsoever at the exit in an actual fire emergency—the door will be immediately openable.

Special egress-control device conditions. Several conditions should be emphasized at the outset.

1. First, the approval of the building official must be obtained in permit the installation of any special egress-control device.

2. Such devices may be used only in connection with the specifically listed occupancies. In addition, the entire building in which the special egress-control device is installed must be completely protected throughout by both an approved automatic sprinkler system and an approved automatic smoke-detection system. The device must immediately and automatically deactivate on activation of the sprinkler system or detection system and on the loss of electrical power to the egress-control device, to the smoke-detection system or to the exit illumination required by Section 1003.2.9.

There must also be a way of manually deactivating the egress-control device by the operation of a switch located in an approved location. When the operating device is activated, it must initiate an irreversible process that will cause the egress-control device to deactivate whenever a manual force of not more than 15 pounds (66.72 N) is applied for a minimum period of two seconds to the operating hardware. The irreversible process must achieve the deactivation of the device within a time period of not more than 15 seconds from the time the operating hardware is originally activated. To ensure that the time period will not exceed 15 seconds, the code specifies that the egress-control device shall be so constructed that it is not possible to adjust the time period in the field.

Upon activation of the operating hardware, an audible signal shall be initiated at the door so that the person attempting to exit the building will be aware that the irreversible process has been started. At the expiration of the 15-second time period or on automatic deactivation by any of the required systems, the unlatching of the door shall not require more than a single operation.

A sign should be installed on the door within 12 inches (305 mm) of the operating hardware so that the person seeking egress can be informed as to the type and nature of the egress-control device. The sign must read KEEP PUSHING, THIS DOOR WILL OPEN IN ____ SECONDS. ALARM WILL SOUND. In spite of the words "keep pushing," it should be noted that the irreversible process will be commenced when the operating hardware has been depressed for a period not exceeding two seconds; therefore, it is not absolutely necessary to "keep pushing" to unlatch the door. The required sign shall be in letters having a height of at least 1 inch (25 mm) and a thickness of stroke of not less than $1/8$ inch (3.2 mm).

Egress-control device reactivation. The code emphasizes that, regardless of the means of deactivation, relocking of the egress-control device shall only be by manual means at the door. This requirement ensures that to relock the egress-control device, someone must go to the door itself, verify that the emergency no longer exists and only then relock the door by manual means.

1003.3.1.11 Safety glazing identification. This section points out that doors generally are in locations where they would be subject to human impact. Therefore, regardless of the occupant load, if glass doors are used, they are subject to the requirements of Section 2406, which cover safety glazing.

1003.3.2 Gates. This section serves as a reminder that gates within the means of egress system must comply with the requirements related to doors. The exception to Section 1003.3.2.2 overrides the general door requirement that the doors swing and that the length of any leaf cannot exceed 4 feet (1219 mm). This exception is similar to requirement found in the assembly occupancy portion of Section 1007.

1003.3.3 Stairways.

1003.3.3.1 General. This section begins by giving the UBC definition of a stairway. It states that every stairway consisting of two or more risers is required to conform with the provisions of this section. The exception makes it very clear that stairways complying with this section are to be used throughout all occupancies where serving spaces subject to human habitation. As a consequence, only stairs or ladders used solely for access to equipment and those used to climb out of window wells are exempt from the requirements of this section.

Since the provisions for a stairway apply only when there are two or more risers, the code does address single riser "step" conditions to provide a minimum level of safety for those locations. The primary issue regulated for steps is the rise requirements of Section 1003.3.3.3. Without this limitation, the height of a single riser along a means of egress would be unregulated.

1003.3.3.2 Width. The provisions concerning width of stairways are analogous to the provisions relating to corridors discussed in Section 1004. This section provides for minimum stair widths. If the stair is subject to use by a sufficiently large occupant load, the minimum required width of the stair is determined by using the formula stated in Section 1003.2.3. The minimum required clear width of any stair must be at least 44 inches (1118 mm). In the event the stairway serves an occupant load of 49 or less, the required minimum clear width of the stairway is 36 inches (914 mm). Beginning with the 1985 edition, the UBC no longer permits stairs less than 36 inches (914 mm) in width in any occupancy.

Generally, when the code specifies a required width of a component in the egress system, it intends that width to be the clear, net, usable, unobstructed width. As is the case of landings in conjunction with doors, stairways are permitted to have certain limited projections. One permitted projection is for handrails, which may project a maximum distance of 3½ inches (89 mm) from each side of the stair as shown in Figure 1003-16. In addition, stringers, trim and similar decorative features are permitted to project into the required width, but are limited to a maximum projection of 1½ inches (38 mm) on each side of the stairway.

Again, unless a projection into the minimum required width of the stairway is expressly allowed, none is permitted.

1003.3.3.3 Rise and run. This section provides for a maximum riser height of 7 inches (178 mm), a minimum riser of 4 inches (102 mm) and a minimum tread run of 11 inches (279 mm) for each step in a stairway. These limiting dimensions are identified in Figure 1003-17. An exception allows 8 inches (203 mm) and 9 inches (229 mm) for the rise and run, respectively, for private stairways serving an occupant load of less than 10 and for unoccupied roofs. This exception may not be warranted. The 7-inch (178 mm) rise and 11-inch (279 mm) run figures for the steps were new for the 1985 edition and represented a break from tradition. They are based on safety in descending stairs and are the result of much research. Probably at no prior time in the history of codes has the proportioning of stairs had a better foundation in research.[1]

Historically, the pitch angle of stairways has been measured between a plane tangent to the tread nosings and the horizontal. Consequently, the rise and run of steps has been based on comfort in ascending stairs. In fact, one of the reasons given by the proponent of the change to a 7-inch (178 mm) riser height and an 11-inch (279 mm) tread run was ease of climbing for persons with disabilities.

The former figures for riser height and tread run of 7½ inches (191 mm) and 10 inches (254 mm), respectively, had been in the UBC since the first edition in 1927. Until recent years, these dimensions satisfied all the rules commonly in use for stairway geometry. The rules most often applied were:

- The riser height plus tread run shall not be less than 17½ or greater than 18.
- Twice the riser height plus the tread run shall not be less than 24 or greater than 25.

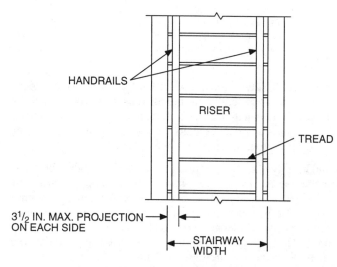

NOTE: Stair stringers may project a maximum of 1½ in. on each side.

For **SI:** 1 inch = 25.4 mm.

PROJECTIONS INTO STAIRWAY WIDTH

FIGURE 1003-16

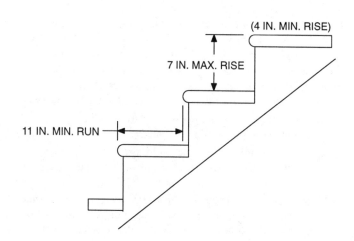

For **SI:** 1 inch = 25.4 mm.

RISE AND RUN

FIGURE 1003-17

- The product of the riser height and the tread run shall not be less than 70 or greater than 75.
- Maximum pitch angle is 37 degrees.

It may be of particular interest to note that the second rule was originated by a French architect in the 17th century.[2] Certainly that formula, as stated, was based on the usability of the stairway and the comfort of the user. However, since that formula was developed, two things have happened. The size of the 95 percentile human being has increased. In other words, as a human race, we have individually become larger. The other change that has occurred since the 17th century is that the length of the inch has changed and has become shorter.

In recent years it became evident that these rules were woefully inadequate as evidenced by the enormous number of accidents—about 800,000 annually— attributed to stairway use. Of these serious accidents, approximately 4,000 were fatal.[1] This unacceptably high rate of accidents and deaths prompted numerous studies to determine the parameters necessary for safe use of stairways.

The results of these research projects revealed that riser heights should be lower than standard practice and should be between $4^1/_2$ inches and $7^1/_4$ inches (114 mm and 184 mm). The same researchers found that the tread run should be greater than standard practice and should be between 11 inches and 14 inches (279 mm and 356 mm), with one study preferring 12 inches (305 mm).

As one descends a stairway, balance is essential for safety. Therefore, the tread run must be of such a dimension as to permit the user to balance comfortably on the ball of the foot. The combination of lower riser height and longer tread run provides the proper geometry to enable the user to accomplish the necessary balance and descend the stairway with reasonable safety. Consistent with the importance of the tread dimension, the method of measurement of the tread is expressly stated. Specifically, tread depth, or run, is that distance measured horizontally between vertical planes passing through the foremost projections of adjacent treads. As such, the tread dimension is the net gain in the run of the stair. Tread dimension is measured in this manner because any tread surface underneath the overhang of a sloping riser or nosing on the tread above is not available to the person descending the stair. Since descending is the more critical direction, proper dimensioning of the tread is of paramount importance. The methods of measuring stair dimensions are illustrated in Figure 1003-17.

Studies of people traveling on stairways have shown that probably the greatest hazard on a stair is the user. Inattention has been identified as the single factor producing the greatest number of missteps, accidents and injuries. Inattention very frequently results from the fact that the user is very familiar with the stair and its surroundings. It often results from a variety of distractions. It is critical to stair safety that the stair user be attentive to the stair. However, stair user attentiveness cannot be codified or dictated. However, stair design and geometry, which usually trigger human error, can be controlled.[1]

A significant safety factor relative to stairways is the uniformity of risers and treads in any flight of stairs. The section of a stairway leading from one landing to the next is defined as a flight of stairs. It is very important that any variation that would interfere with the rhythm of the stair user be avoided. While it is true that adequate attention to the use of the stair can compensate for substantial variations in risers and treads, it is all too frequent that the necessary attention is not given by the stair user.

To obtain the best uniformity possible in a flight of stairs, the maximum variation between the highest and lowest risers and between the widest and the narrowest treads is limited to $3/_8$ inch (9.5 mm). This tolerance is not intended to be used as a design variation, but it does recognize that construction practices make it difficult to get exactly identical riser heights and tread dimensions in constructing a stairway facility in the field. Therefore, the code allows the variation indicated.

The wording regarding uniformity was slightly revised in the 1997 UBC, but it was done more as an editorial issue and should not be viewed as changing the way the provisions are applied. When looking at the prior editions of the code, the rise and run provisions stated that, except as permitted in the sections related to winding, circular and spiral stairways, the minimum 11-inch (279 mm) run and the maximum $3/_8$-inch (9.5 mm) tread variation would be the requirement. Therefore, these alternative types of stairways could have runs that were less than 11 inches (279 mm) at certain locations and could have treads that vary in size and shape. Since the two sentences were repetitive and referred to the alternative stairways listed, it was decided that there was no need to have both sentences. However, when looking at the final outcome, it would appear as if a change has been made. The last sentence of this section now simply states that the treads shall be uniform in both size and shape and that the greatest variation cannot exceed $3/_8$ inch (9.5 mm). This obviously would be a dramatic change to the typical winding stairway which is used, and it would not permit transitioning between a typical straight run stairway and winders. While the stairs would definitely be safer if all treads were exactly identical, the alternative stairs listed in Section 1003.3.3.8 contain no such requirement, and are in fact an exception to the general stairway requirements.

Stairs to and from sloping walks. With respect to variation, it is recognized that stairs frequently descend or rise to areas where the ground or the finished surface is sloping. When this occurs on private property, the code anticipates that the landing of the stairs be leveled so that there will not be any variation in the riser height across the width of the stair at that point. However, from time to time, stairs will land on spaces that are not under the control of the property owner, such as a public sidewalk, for example. Therefore, a certain degree of slope across the width of the stair is permitted, resulting in a variation of the height of the riser from one side of the stair to the other. When this occurs, the height of such riser may be reduced along the slope to less than 4 inches (102 mm), and the maximum permitted slope shall not exceed 3 inches in 3 feet (76 mm in 914 mm) or a slope of 1 unit vertical in 12 units horizontal (8.3% slope). Figure 1003-18 shows this condition.

1003.3.3.4 Headroom. A minimum headroom clearance of 6 feet 8 inches (2032 mm) is required in connection with every stairway. Such required clearance shall be measured vertically from the leading edge of the treads to the lowest projection of any construction, piping, fixture or other object above the stairs. See Figure 1003-19. This specific height requirement overrides the general means of egress requirement found in Section 1003.2.4 and is modified for spiral stairways by Section 1003.3.3.8.3.

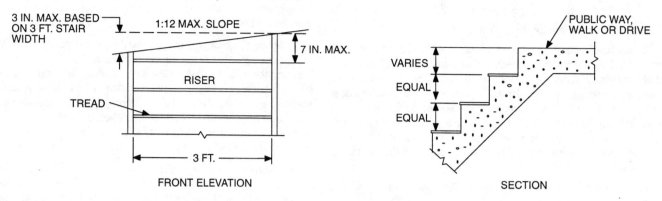

SLOPING PUBLIC WAY, WALK OR DRIVE

3 IN. MAX. BASED ON 3 FT. STAIR WIDTH

1:12 MAX. SLOPE

7 IN. MAX.

RISER

TREAD

3 FT.

FRONT ELEVATION

PUBLIC WAY, WALK OR DRIVE

VARIES

EQUAL

EQUAL

SECTION

For **SI:** 1 inch = 25.4 mm, 1 foot = 304.8 mm.

SLOPING LANDINGS

FIGURE 1003-18

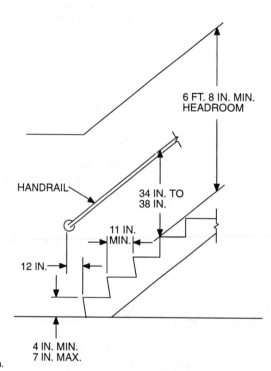

6 FT. 8 IN. MIN. HEADROOM

HANDRAIL

34 IN. TO 38 IN.

11 IN. MIN.

12 IN.

4 IN. MIN. 7 IN. MAX.

For **SI:** 1 inch = 25.4 mm, 1 foot = 304.8 mm.

HANDRAIL AND STAIR DETAIL

FIGURE 1003-19

1003.3.3.5 Landings. Landings are discussed to some extent under Section 1003.3.1.7, which covers landings that are used with adjoining doors. This section covers landings in general as they occur in typical stairs. The basis for determining the required dimensions of landings is simple. Every landing must be at least as wide as the stair it serves. It must also have a dimension measured in the direction of travel of not less than the width of the stairway. However, in those instances where the stair has a straight run between flights, the intervening landing need not be more than 44 inches (1118 mm), measured in the direction of travel. In Group R, Division 3, Group U and within individual units of Group R, Division 1 Occupancies, the 1997 UBC re-

duced this minimum dimension to 36 inches (914 mm). These dimensional criteria for stair landings are illustrated in Figure 1003-20. An exception provides that stairs which serve an unoccupied roof need not comply with the landing requirements specified in this section. However, the stairway must comply with this chapter in all other respects unless it is also exempted from the stairway requirements by the exception in Section 1003.3.3.1.

Shape of landing. It has generally been viewed that the code permits providing a complete curve with a radius equal to the width of the stairway as shown in Figure 1003-21. This view-

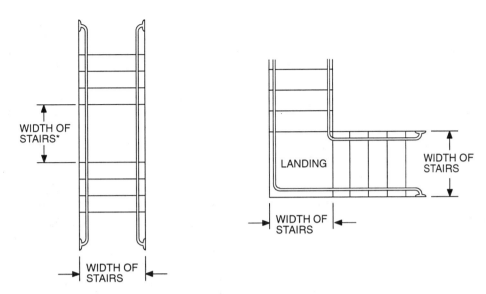

WIDTH OF STAIRS = (1) 36 IN. FOR OCCUPANT LOAD LESS THAN 50
(2) 44 IN. MINIMUM FOR OCCUPANT LOADS OF 50 OR MORE OR AS REQUIRED BY SECTION 1003.3.3.2

*NEED NOT EXCEED 44 IN. IF LANDING OCCURS IN A STRAIGHT RUN OF STAIRS.
36 IN. PERMITTED FOR R-3, U AND INDIVIDUAL UNITS OF R-1 OCCUPANCY.

For **SI:** 1 inch = 25.4 mm.

LANDING DIMENSIONS

FIGURE 1003-20

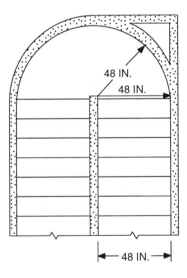

For **SI:** 1 inch = 25.4 mm.

ALTERNATE SHAPE OF LANDING

FIGURE 1003-21

point is based on the fact that at one time the code required that the corners of a landing be splayed. Although this provision was deleted from the code, it was removed based on the belief that the requirement was too restrictive and not because of any problems or concerns. It is important to note that the ascending and descending portions of the stairway runs meet at a level landing.

Distance between landings. Negotiating stairs can sometimes become very difficult, particularly for persons not accustomed to using stairs or for the elderly or disabled. So that this

difficulty does not become excessive, the code limits the maximum vertical rise between landings serving stairs to 12 feet (3658 mm). Aside from the physical exertion necessary, stairs of exceptional length can be intimidating. It is necessary, at vertical intervals not exceeding 12 feet (3658 mm), to provide for places in the stair where the user can rest.

The 12-foot (3658 mm) dimension is not unreasonable. In most instances it will more than accommodate a single-story height so that in most buildings a single flight of stairs could be utilized, if desired, to negotiate travel from one floor to the next adjacent floor. Even though a single flight of stairs is permitted by the code, stairs having an intermediate landing between floors are most commonly used in the majority of buildings.

The wording regarding the need for an intermediate landing was revised slightly during the revision of this chapter for the 1997 edition, although the application was not changed in most cases. Previous editions permitted 12 feet 0 inches (3658 mm) between the landings whereas the current language requires "an intermediate landing" to be provided for each 12 feet 0 inches (3658 mm) of vertical rise. By looking at the entire stairway and looking at the floor or landings at the two extreme ends, an intermediate landing could be placed every 12 feet 0 inches (3658 mm). It would appear, however, that if the stair serves only two adjacent floors that are exactly 12 feet 0 inches (3658 mm) apart, that an intermediate landing is required where previously it was not.

1003.3.3.6 Handrails. Probably the most important safety device that can be provided in connection with stairs is the handrail.[1,3,4] It will never be known how many missteps, accidents, injuries or even fatalities have been prevented by a properly installed, sturdy handrail. Basically, a handrail should be within relatively easy reach of every stair user. In general, all stairways are required to have handrails on each side. However, the code has the following specific conditions allowing the use of only one handrail:

- Stairs are less than 44 inches (1118 mm) in width.
- Stairs serve only an individual dwelling unit or a Group R, Division 3 congregate residence.
- Private stairs are 30 inches (762 mm) or less in height.

Also, stairways having less than four risers and serving only one individual dwelling unit; a Group R, Division 3 congregate residence; or a Group U Occupancy is not required to have any handrails. Chapter 11 should be consulted for all accessibility requirements for stairs; some provisions may be restrictive.

Intermediate handrails. In the event the required width of a stairway must exceed 88 inches (2235 mm), it is necessary to install an intermediate handrail for each 88 inches (2235 mm) of required width. Particular emphasis is placed on the fact that the intermediate handrail requirement is based on the required width of the stairway. In many instances, particularly in the case of monumental stairs, the width of the stairway far exceeds the minimum width required to satisfy exiting requirements. In such instances, it is not necessary to provide intermediate handrails for that portion of the stairway that does not need to meet minimum required egress capacities. However, when intermediate handrails are required, it is important that they be spaced approximately equally across the portion of the stairway they must serve.

With the basic requirements that stairways 44 inches (1118 mm) in width or wider be provided with handrails on each side and that intermediate handrails be provided for each 88 inches (2235 mm) of required width, the resulting configuration places a handrail within relatively easy reach of every stair user.

Handrail height. In the *Uniform Building Code*, the height of handrails has traditionally been established within a range of at least 30 inches (762 mm) and not more than 34 inches (864 mm) vertically above the leading edge of treads of the stairway that the handrails serve. Recent research has shown that handrails will better serve stair users if they are located in a range higher than this traditional location.[1] Higher handrails can be more readily reached by adult stair users, and interestingly enough, handrails at the higher elevation are also more usable by very small persons, including toddlers.

When handrails are required, they should be located at least 34 inches (864 mm) and not more than 38 inches (965 mm) vertically, measured from the nosing of the stair treads to the top of the rail. See Figure 1003-18 for an illustration of UBC requirements for stairs, including handrail height. Handrails must be continuous for the full length of the flight of stairs, and at least one handrail must extend not less than 12 inches (305 mm) beyond the top and bottom risers. See Figure 1003-22. The ends of handrails are to be returned to the wall or shall terminate in newel posts or other similar safety terminals. The emphasis on handrail continuity is to ensure that the handrail extends the full length of the flight of the stairs, thereby affording the stair user support throughout the entire flight. The purpose of the extension of the handrail at the top and bottom of the stairs is to provide minimal additional facility to assist the disabled stair user. This extension is not required for private stairs. The reason for requiring that the ends of handrails be returned to the wall or end in safety terminals is to avoid the possibility of loose clothing or other articles being caught on the projecting end of the handrail. The 1997 UBC included a second sentence to this section that

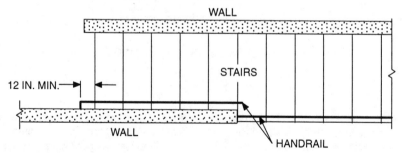

THE HANDRAIL DETAIL SHOWN HERE DOES NOT COMPLY WITH THE "CONTINUOUS" TERMINOLOGY IN THE CODE.

For **SI:** 1 inch = 25.4 mm.

HANDRAIL CONTINUITY

FIGURE 1003-22

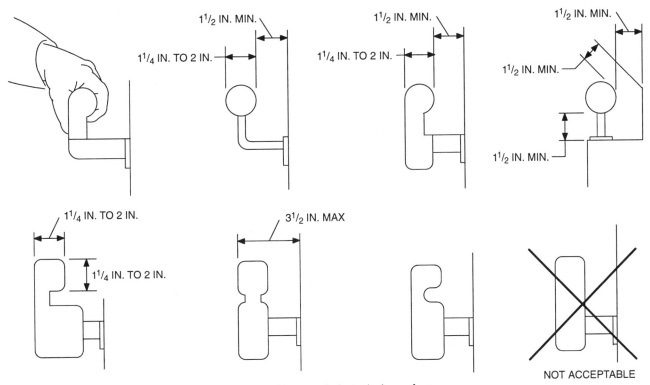

1¹/₂ IN. MIN.

1¹/₄ IN. TO 2 IN.

1¹/₂ IN. MIN.

1¹/₄ IN. TO 2 IN.

1¹/₂ IN. MIN.

1¹/₂ IN. MIN.

1¹/₂ IN. MIN.

1¹/₄ IN. TO 2 IN.

1¹/₄ IN. TO 2 IN.

3¹/₂ IN. MAX

NOT ACCEPTABLE

NOTE: Other shapes may be acceptable if they provide an equivalent gripping surface. See third paragraph of Section 1003.3.3.6.

For **SI:** 1 inch = 25.4 mm.

ACCEPTABLE SHAPES AND INSTALLATIONS—HANDRAIL

FIGURE 1003-23

permitted the handrail to terminate at a starting newel or volute, which is located on the first tread. These types of terminations have been found in residences for years without a record of accidents or lawsuits for an unsafe condition. Having this provision codified will permit this historic practice.

Handgrip size. To be truly effective, handrails must be graspable.[4] Therefore, the handgrip portion of the handrail must not be less than 1¹/₄ inches (32 mm) or more than 2 inches (51 mm) in cross-sectional dimension, or the configuration of the handrail must be such that it provides an equivalent, grippable shape. Many persons (such as small children) are incapable of exerting sufficient finger pressure on a plain surface, such as that provided by a rectangular handrail, or on a handrail of larger cross-sectional dimension. To get adequate support or to adequately grasp the handrail, it is necessary to provide those persons with the shape that the code specifies. With such a shape it is possible for those persons to actually wrap their fingers around that portion of the handrail and, thereby, obtain better support. Also, in view of this desire to make the handrail graspable and considering the requirement that the handrail be continuous, it is necessary to provide a clear space of at least 1¹/₂ inches (38 mm) between the handrail and any abutting construction to avoid injury to fingers. This requirement for the handrail to be continuous has generally been viewed as not only requiring a single uninterrupted rail but has also been used to regulate the method of support so that the handrail is graspable at any point along its length.

Acceptable handrail shapes and installations are shown in Figure 1003-23.

1003.3.3.7 Guardrails. Reference is made to Section 509, which contains the specifications for the installation of guardrails. In many instances stairways are constructed in conjunction with landings, balconies, porches and other building components. When those components are more than 30 inches (762 mm) above the adjacent ground level or surface below, they must be protected by guardrails meeting the requirements of Section 509. However, for the open sides of stairs, compliance with the requirements for handrail heights in Section 1003.3.3.6 is considered sufficient by the code for protection. One item often missed when looking at these two sections is that Section 509 requires that a glazed side of a stairway be protected by a guardrail.

1003.3.3.8 Alternative stairways. The three types of stairs contained in this section (circular, winding and spiral) represent somewhat of an exception to what is normally considered as being a code-complying stair. Where the typical stair is required to have treads of a consistent and uniform size and shape, these three stairs may have different dimensional characteristics from adjacent treads and typically vary from one end of the tread to the other. The fact that these stairs are somewhat of an exception is supported by the language regarding the rise and run requirements found in Section 1003.3.3.3. The only one of these stairs that may be used as a part of the means of egress in all occupancies and locations is the circular stairway.

1003.3.3.8.1 Circular stairways. Circular stairs are the first of three special types of stairways that the code allows as an alternate to the typical straight stair. Figure 1003-24 depicts all three alternative stairs. This one is essentially circular in configuration. The basic requirement is that the inside or, at least, the radius be at least twice the actual width of the stair. This rule ensures a certain degree of curvature deemed acceptable in circular stairs. The only other criterion specified for circular stairs is that

treads have a minimum width of run of not less than 10 inches (254 mm) at the narrow end. In designing the circular stair and relating the inside radius to the width of the stair, it is important in this case that the actual width of the stair, not just the minimum required width, be used. Due to the stair's geometry, this is a fairly comfortable stairway to use.

1003.3.3.8.2 Winding stairways. Winding stairs constitute a second type of special stair provided for limited use. The term "winding stairways" may be a misnomer, as it is not always the stairway that winds. Instead, it is a stairway configuration in

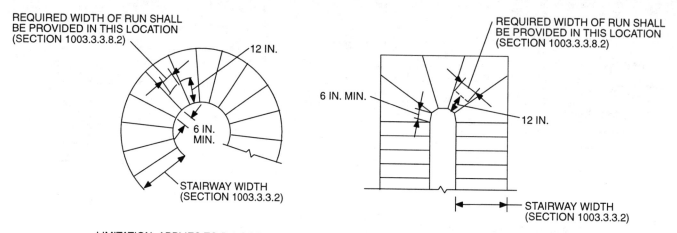

LIMITATION: APPLIES TO R-3 OCCUPANCY AND PRIVATE STAIRWAYS IN R-1 OCCUPANCY.

PLAN VIEW
WINDING STAIRWAY

PLAN VIEW
ALTERNATE USE OF WINDERS

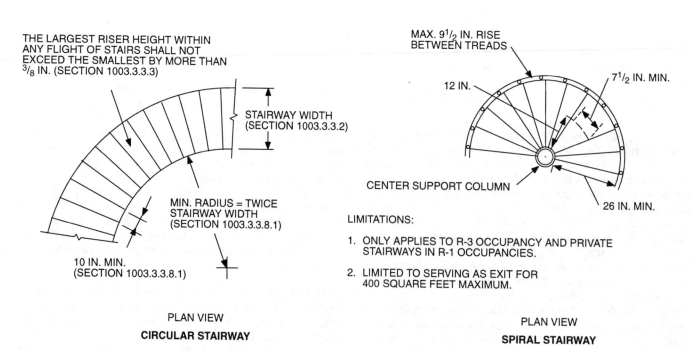

NOTE: Handrails not shown for clarity.

For **SI:** 1 inch = 25.4 mm, 1 square foot = 0.0929 m².

PLAN VIEW
CIRCULAR STAIRWAY

PLAN VIEW
SPIRAL STAIRWAY

WINDING STAIRS

FIGURE 1003-24

which special treads known as winders are used. Winders consist of tapered treads that are narrow on one end and widen out, pie-shaped, toward the opposite side of the stairs. Winders are used primarily for changing the direction of the stair. Winding stairways also include circular stairways whose radii are shorter than required by Section 1003.3.3.8.1. Since they do constitute a change in the rhythm for the stair user, winders are inherently hazardous. While the code does permit them, it allows them only in private stairways, essentially within dwelling units. Even in those instances, they should be used very carefully, and it is particularly important that winders comply with the specified dimensional criteria. In no case should the width of any run be less than 6 inches (152 mm) at the narrow side of the tread. At a point 1 foot (305 mm) from the narrow end of the tread, the tread must have the appropriate required width. In most instances within dwelling units, this minimum required width would be 9 inches (229 mm). Normally, there are a series of winders where they are used in a flight of stairs. Although not required, it would be best from the usability standpoint if each winder was like every other winder with respect to the above dimensional criteria and the rate of taper across the stair.

1003.3.3.8.3 Spiral stairways. Spiral stairs are the third type of special stair that the code permits. Again, however, these are only permitted in private stairs in individual dwelling units. When they are permitted in such occupancies, however, they may be used as the only required path of egress from an area as large as 400 square feet (37.16 m²) but no larger.

A spiral stairway is one where the treads radiate from a central pole. Such stair must provide a clear width of at least 26 inches (660 mm). Each tread must have a minimum dimension of 7¹/₂ inches (191 mm) at a point 12 inches (305 mm) from its narrow end. The stair must have at least 6 feet 6 inches (1981 mm) of headroom measured vertically from the leading edge of the tread. The rise between treads can be as much as, but not more than 9¹/₂ inches (241 mm).

It is important to remember that the locations where a spiral or winding stairway are permitted are very limited. The only time that these two types of stairways may be installed in other than within the individual dwelling units is if it is used only to attend equipment or to climb out of a window well and therefore covered by the exception in Section 1003.3.3.1.

1003.3.3.9 Interior stairway construction. The materials used in the construction of stairways are basically determined in accordance with the requirements of Chapter 6. Materials used for stairways must be in compliance with the appropriate requirements for the type of building in which they are located.

Although Section 1005.3.3.6 prohibits the use of enclosed usable space under stairs inside an exit enclosure, such space is permitted to be used where such enclosed space occurs under a stairway not within an exit enclosure as required by Section 1005.3.3.1. However, when the space is used, it is necessary that the walls, soffits and ceilings of the enclosed space be protected on the enclosed side with materials that would be used for one-hour fire-resistive construction.

Fire department access. Buildings four or more stories in height and that have stairways exiting directly to the exterior are required to provide a means of emergency entry for fire department access. Stair enclosure access is essential for both fire-

fighting and rescue operations. Exterior enclosure doors are often not equipped with locksets or handles, thus requiring exhaustive and time-consuming forced entry. Many multistory buildings do not have interior enclosure access on the ground floor, and this requires firefighters to gain access to the enclosure by using elevators to the second floor, a difficult and dangerous procedure.

If exterior locksets are provided, Section 902.4 of the 1997 *Uniform Fire Code* permits the fire chief to require a key box for entry keys where necessary.

1003.3.3.10 Protection of exterior wall openings. Whenever a stairway is installed as a component in an exiting system, it is important to protect the stair user from potential exposure to any fire that might occur in the building. Therefore, in other than Group R, Division 3 Occupancies and open parking garages, when stairways serve buildings over two stories in height or serve a level where exterior wall openings occur in two or more floors below, all openings in the exterior wall below or within 10 feet (3048 mm) of the stairway must be protected by a self-closing fire assembly having a three-fourths-hour fire-protection rating. This requirement applies to both interior and exterior stairways. The regulations for the interior stairways are found in this section, while the exterior stairs are addressed in Section 1006.3.3.1. The second exception in these two sections is slightly different and provides an additional exception that is dependent on the stair's location. Figure 1003-25 identifies those openings that must be protected for an exterior stairway and Figure 1003-26 covers the protection for interior stairs. This protection for an stairway is important if the stairway is going to be usable as a means of egress component in a fire emergency.

As stated above, the second exception regarding the interior and exterior stairways is different. These exceptions are based on the stairs location, additional protection or an alternate route. If the openings below and adjacent to an interior stairway are protected, then the stair openings may be left unprotected. The main issue is to protect the egress path. Whether the protection is at the stairway or at the location of the hazard is ultimately immaterial. When using exterior stairs, if the arrangement is such that there are two separated, remote exterior stairways serving the same exterior exit balcony, protection of the openings adjacent to the exterior stairs is not required. In this arrangement, the building occupant would have the option of proceeding to the other stairway should one of them become exposed to a building fire. Again, this arrangement and its components are in exterior locations where the heat and other products of combustion have the opportunity to dissipate to the atmosphere. Therefore, the potential exposure to the stair user is not as severe as it would be in an interior location.

1003.3.3.11 Stairway to roof. To provide for easy access to roof surfaces and to facilitate firefighting in buildings four or more stories in height, at least one stairway is required to extend to the roof. This stairway to the roof must comply with all code requirements, including those for minimum headroom. The stairway to the roof is not a requirement, however, on steeper roofs where the slope exceeds 4 units vertical in 12 units horizontal (33% slope). Even though a stairway to the roof is not required for the steeper roofs, the roof hatch required by Section 1003.3.3.12 would still be needed.

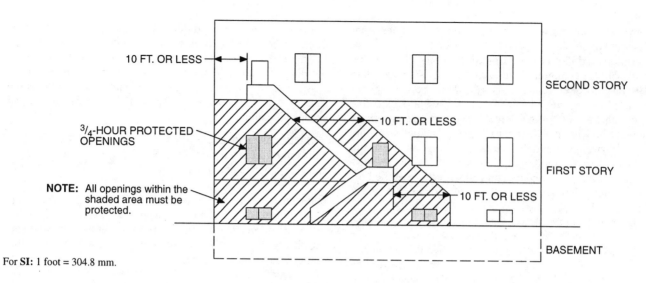

EXTERIOR STAIRWAY PROTECTION

FIGURE 1003-25

10 FT. OR LESS

3/4-HOUR PROTECTED OPENINGS

NOTE: All openings within the shaded area must be protected.

SECOND STORY

10 FT. OR LESS

FIRST STORY

10 FT. OR LESS

BASEMENT

For SI: 1 foot = 304.8 mm.

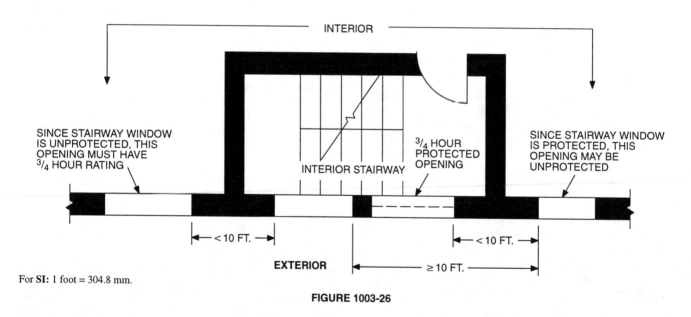

INTERIOR

SINCE STAIRWAY WINDOW IS UNPROTECTED, THIS OPENING MUST HAVE 3/4 HOUR RATING

3/4 HOUR PROTECTED OPENING

INTERIOR STAIRWAY

SINCE STAIRWAY WINDOW IS PROTECTED, THIS OPENING MAY BE UNPROTECTED

< 10 FT.

< 10 FT.

EXTERIOR

≥ 10 FT.

For SI: 1 foot = 304.8 mm.

FIGURE 1003-26

1003.3.3.12 Roof hatches. In buildings of four or more stories in height, all required interior stairways that extend to the top floor of the building shall have, at the highest point of the stair enclosure, a hatch opening to the exterior. The hatch must have a minimum dimension of 2 feet (610 mm) and a cross-sectional area of not less than 16 square feet (1.5 m²). The basic purpose of the hatch is to provide a means of ventilating the stair shaft in the event of a fire. Therefore, a fixed ladder is not required to gain access to the roof. In the event the stair is located in a pressurized enclosure, or if the stair continues to the roof and has an opening onto the roof, the openable hatch need not be provided.

1003.3.3.13 Stairway identification. This section is maintained under the code change procedures of the International Fire Code Institute. This section specifies a system whereby any persons, particularly firefighters, inside a stairway in a building four or more stories in height will be provided with information

telling them where they are in the building and where the stairway leads to both above and below that point. This required sign can be critically important for firefighting purposes and is frequently useful to other building occupants.

As set forth in UBC Standard 10-2, this sign shall be at least 12 inches square (304.8 mm square). The identification or location of the stairway shall be placed at the top of the sign in 1-inch (25 mm) letters. Beneath the stairway identification or location, the stairway's upper terminus must be identified. This information must state whether the stair provides access to the roof. Also required is identification of the floor level of the building in which the sign is located. The floor level number is to be located in the center of the sign in numerals having a height of 5 inches (127 mm) and a stroke thickness of 3/4 inch (19.1 mm). For basement levels, the floor number is to be preceded by the letter "B," and for mezzanines, the letter "M" must be used. Following the floor level identification number, there must then be stated the upper and lower terminus of the stairway, again in letters 1 inch (25 mm) high. These signs shall be of a type approved by the building official and shall be maintained in an approved manner. A sample sign complying with these requirements is shown in Figure 1003-27.

1003.3.4 Ramps.

1003.3.4.1 General. With the exception of ramped aisles in assembly rooms, whenever a ramp is used as a component anywhere in a means of egress, it is necessary that the ramp comply with the provisions of this section. Note that where ramps are used as part of the egress system, every ramp must meet these standards regardless of the occupant load served. The same is true for stairways.

Ramped aisles in assembly rooms shall conform to the provisions of Section 1004.3.2. Also, all ramps located within an accessible route of travel shall be made to conform to the requirements found in Chapter 11.

1003.3.4.2 Width. Because requirements for the widths of ramps are identical to those requirements for widths of stairways, see the discussion of Section 1003.3.3.2. The only item of difference is that the factors from Table 10-B, which are used for stairways, are larger than that for ramps.

1003.3.4.3 Slope. Whenever any ramp is used in an exit system and is required to conform to the requirements of Chapter 11, the slope of such ramp shall not be steeper than 1 unit vertical in 12 units horizontal (8.3% slope). Other ramps in exit systems that are not required to be accessible to the disabled may be steeper, but may not be steeper than a slope of 1 unit vertical in 8 units horizontal (12.5% slope).

1003.3.4.4 Landings. While ramps required to be accessible to the disabled may be as steep as 1 unit vertical in 12 units horizontal (8.3% slope), any ramp having a slope steeper than 1 unit vertical in 20 units horizontal (5% slope) must have landings at the top and at the bottom. Prior to the 1997 edition, the UBC did not require the landings at the terminations until the ramp had a slope steeper than 1 unit vertical in 15 units horizontal (6.7% slope). The lower slope made the provisions consistent with those found in the Americans with Disabilities Act Accessibility Guidelines. The ramps are also required to have at least one intermediate landing for each 5 feet (1524 mm) of vertical rise. With adoption of the 1992 version of CABO/ANSI A117.1 into Chapter 11, requirements for ramps that must be usable by persons with disabilities are now more restrictive as they apply to the distance between landings. When Chapter 11 is applicable, only 2$\frac{1}{2}$ feet (762 mm), rather than 5 feet (1524 mm), of vertical rise is permitted between landings. Intermediate landings and top landings are required to have a dimension measured in the direction of ramp run of not less than 5 feet (1524 mm). Landings at the bottom of ramps must extend at least 6 feet (1829 mm) in the direction of the ramp run. These larger-than-normal dimensions are required to reasonably ensure that disabled persons in wheelchairs will have sufficient space to maneuver both on the top and intermediate landings as well as in the area at the bottom approaching the ramp. See Figure 1003-28.

In all cases where doors enter onto or swing over ramps, the doors may not, during the course of their swing, reduce the minimum dimension of the landing to less than 42 inches (1067 mm).

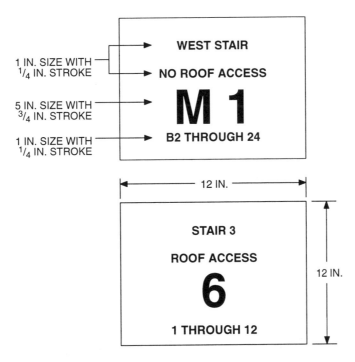

For **SI:** 1 inch = 25.4 mm.

APPROVED SIGN AT EVERY LANDING OF BUILDINGS
FOUR STORIES OR MORE IN HEIGHT

STAIRWAY IDENTIFICATION

FIGURE 1003-27

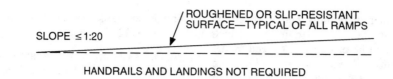

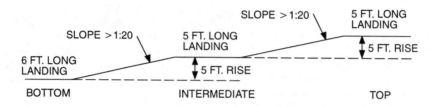

HANDRAILS AND LANDINGS REQUIRED

FIGURE 1003-28

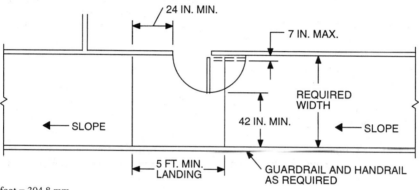

For **SI:** 1 inch = 25.4 mm, 1 foot = 304.8 mm.

INTERMEDIATE RAMP LANDINGS

FIGURE 1003-29

In all cases there must be at least 42 inches (1067 mm) of width available on the ramp even while the door is swinging. When fully opened, no door may reduce the required width of the ramp by more than 7 inches (178 mm). This 7-inch (178 mm) dimension was new in the 1997 UBC. Prior editions had limited the obstruction from the door to $3^1/_2$ inches (89 mm), but in order to be consistent with the requirements for landings at doors and the width of a corridor, this provision was modified.

A provision concerning the dimensional criteria for ramps that must conform to accessibility requirements by Chapter 11 was added in the 1985 edition. When a door swings over the landing of such a ramp, it is necessary that the landing extend 2 feet (610 mm) beyond the latched edge of the door, measured with the door in the closed position. In addition, this ramp must have a length in the direction of travel of not less than 5 feet (1524 mm). As stated previously, these dimensional criteria are intended to provide reasonably adequate space on the landing for both the disabled user and the swing of the door. See Figure 1003-29.

1003.3.4.5 Handrails. Whenever any ramp used in a required exit system has a slope steeper than 1 unit vertical in 20 units horizontal (5% slope), the ramp shall be provided with handrails

in accordance with the requirement for handrails for stairways contained in Section 1003.3.3.6. In the case of ramps, however, intermediate handrails are not required; neither are handrails required on the side of ramped aisles serving fixed seating. Where ramps must be provided by Chapter 11, handrails are required, not based on ramp slope, but on rise or run. As stated in Section 4.8.5 of CABO/ANSI A117.1-1992, ramp handrails are required when the rise is greater than 6 inches (152 mm) or the run is greater than 6 feet (1829 mm). As discussed above, the slope at which handrails are required was modified from the previous slope of 1 unit vertical in 15 units horizontal (6.7% slope) to the current 1unit vertical in 20 units horizontal (5% slope) in the 1997 UBC.

1003.3.4.6 Guardrails. Ramps that extend more than 30 inches (762 mm) above grade or the floor below and are open on one side or both sides must be provided with guardrails on the open side or sides. These requirements are based on Section 509.

1003.3.4.7 Construction. For code requirements concerning the construction of ramps, reference is made to the construction requirements for stairways.

1003.3.4.8 Surface. Because a ramp has a sloping surface, the potential for accidents resulting from slips and falls is greatly increased. It is critically important that the surface of the ramp be made slip resistant to help prevent such accidents. It is imperative that very careful attention be given to the selection of materials for ramp surfaces and the methods of finishing such surfaces. Certainly, materials such as terrazzo should be avoided on ramps unless it can be assured that they have been made slip resistant by some process.

There are a number of products on the market available for treating ramp surfaces that are not sufficiently slip resistant. In many instances, the use of these materials has not proven to be completely satisfactory. One method is to install Carborundum strips across the width of the ramp at appropriate intervals. Other available products can be installed on the ramp surface with an adhesive. It is essential that slip-resistant treatments and materials be of a reasonably permanent nature so they can perform the function for which they were installed, while at the same time not become a potential tripping hazard. Therefore, the slip resistance should be proven by tests and be an integral part of the ramp surface.

SECTION 1004 — THE EXIT ACCESS

1004.1 General. The exit access is identified as the initial component of the means of egress system, the portion between any occupied point in a building and a door of the exit. Leading to an exterior exit door or the door of an exit passageway, exit enclosure or horizontal exit, the exit access makes up a vast majority of any building's floor area.

1004.2 Exit-access Design Requirements.

1004.2.1 General. The term "exit-access doorway" is defined for use within Section 1004.2. It describes the point of entry from one portion of a building from another along the path of exit travel. When access to an exit is not direct, an exit-access doorway will occur. There is no requirement for a door in an exit-access doorway, unless identified as an exit-access door.

1004.2.2 Travel through intervening rooms. Basically, the code intends that access to exits be direct from the room or area under consideration. This section, however, makes some modifications where, under certain circumstances, exit paths may be arranged through adjoining rooms or spaces rather than directly into corridors or into other exit elements, such as exit enclosures or exit passageways.

Quite frequently, the means of egress system will be arranged so that egress travel will lead through or into a reception room or lobby. The code is very explicit in Exception 1 that in such instances these foyers, lobbies or reception rooms should not be considered as intervening spaces; they are simply an extension of the previous room or area.

Exception 2 indicates that any room requiring access to only one exit may have that access through an adjoining space. At that point, direct access to an exit or a corridor is required. Therefore, for those rooms where access to at least two or more exits are required, Exception 4 permits only one exit to be arranged to pass through adjoining space. The others must be directly into a corridor or other acceptable element of the means of egress system.

Earlier editions of the code permitted exits to go through only a single adjoining room or space. Currently, Exception 3 permits an exit path to lead through a succession of adjoining spaces up to the point where the accumulated occupant load from those intervening spaces totals nine persons, as represented in Figure 1004-1. At the point where the tenth occupant is accumulated, that occupant may exit through only one more room before entering a corridor, entering an exit enclosure or exit passageway, passing through a horizontal exit, or exiting through an exterior exit door. The path of travel through the intervening spaces should be direct, obvious and unobstructed. While it is now permissible, under the above circumstances, to travel through more than one intervening space, this section notes that it is still necessary to comply with the maximum overall travel distance limits.

Exception 5 applies to one- or two-story Group F, Group S and Group H, Division 5 Occupancies. It is actually an exception to Exception 4, stating that offices and similar administrative areas may have access to two required exits through a single intervening room. For both means of access to enter the same room or area, the building must also be sprinklered throughout and provided with smoke and heat ventilation. The size of the interior room is also limited to 25 percent of the floor area of the major use. Without the use of this exception, the office area may

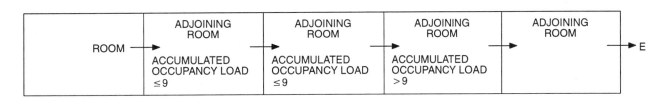

NOTES:
1. No limit on number or type of adjoining rooms in dwelling.
2. Egress shall not pass through:
   a. Kitchens
   b. Rest rooms
   c. Store rooms
   d. Closets or similar spaces

E REPRESENTS:
CORRIDOR
EXIT ENCLOSURE
EXTERIOR EXIT DOOR
HORIZONTAL EXIT
EXIT PASSAGEWAY

TRAVEL THROUGH INTERVENING ROOMS

FIGURE 1004-1

need to be located where it had direct access to the exterior or some other type of exit, or a corridor could be extended through the major use area to the office.

New in the 1997 edition is the introduction of the concept of a "hallway," which the code treats in the same manner as an adjoining or intervening room. The intervening room requirements and exceptions will regulate the use of a hallway. In some cases, depending on the layout of the space, this may create a component that is in many aspects similar to a "non-rated corridor" under the 1994 *Uniform Building Code*. The basis for this comparison is found in the corridor provisions of Section 1004.3.4.3 and the hallway provisions of Section 1004.3.3.

An interior court will be considered as an intervening room unless it provides direct access to an exit and meets the specified width requirements. This is an important distinction since some courts are regulated as intervening rooms in the exit access, while those complying with the exception are considered as a part of the exit access without being viewed as an intervening room. Additionally, courts that are not surrounded on all sides are a part of the exit discharge and regulated by Section 1006 when serving as a portion of the means of egress. Since some interior exit courts are considered as intervening rooms, they permit the occupants to exit into something other than an exit passageway or public way as was previously required. The code previously regulated all courts that had exits going into the court as an "exit court." The interior courts that comply with the exception are basically viewed similar to the way a corridor is considered, the travel distance through the court is still regulated as a portion of the exit access, but the space is not considered as an additional adjoining room.

This section is also concerned with the arrangement of the exit path in that it puts restrictions on certain spaces that are considered to present an undue probability of obstruction to free egress travel. Therefore, the code prohibits the exit path from passing through kitchens, storerooms, restrooms, closets and spaces used for similar purposes where the probability of things obstructing the path of travel is substantially greater. As is so frequently the case throughout the code, exceptions are made for rooms within dwelling units. Neither the restriction against passing through multiple intervening spaces nor the restriction against passing through kitchens, storerooms and similar spaces is applicable in dwelling units.

Also introduced in the 1997 UBC, egress from any occupancy other than a Group H is not permitted to pass through any room containing a Group H Occupancy. This was the first time there had been any restriction on travel through adjacent rooms based solely on occupancy groups. Individuals who are not already within a hazardous area should not be permitted to pass through a hazardous area along their path of travel.

1004.2.3 Access to exits.

1004.2.3.1 General. The *Uniform Building Code* establishes two basic criteria for providing adequate egress for occupants of a building. First, exits must be available from each building level. Second, access to such exits shall be provided from all occupied areas within each level. In all cases, the maximum number of exits required must be maintained until arrival at grade or the public way.

1004.2.3.2 From individual floors. The basis for requiring two means of egress for occupants of the first story is a function of both the use involved and the occupant load. Table 10-A, Column 2, establishes the minimum occupant load level at which at least two means of egress are required from a first story housing the respective uses listed.

For other than the first story, the second basis for requiring two means of egress is related to the location of the occupants of the building with respect to story height and ground level. It states that occupants on stories above the first story and in basements shall have access to not less than two separate means of egress. The code recognizes that basement locations can present particularly difficult fire situations. Basement fires can be fought only by approaching them from above, the most hazardous direction for approaching a fire. Similarly, rescue efforts from basement locations are also complicated by the below-grade location.

The code, then, recognizes that there are certain instances where, even on upper floors of buildings or in basements, the life-safety risk is so minimal that it is reasonable to permit a single means of egress. These exceptions to the requirements for a two-egress minimum are addressed as follows:

1. Second stories having an occupant load less than 10 only require access to one exit.

2. From the basement or the second story, two or more dwelling units may have access to one common exit when such exit serves a total occupant load of 10 or less.

3. Within an individual dwelling unit or Group R, Division 3 congregate residence, access to only one exit or exit-access doorway is required from the second floor or basement when the occupant load is less than 10. The word "floor" is used intentionally so that the exception applies to the second floor level within the dwelling unit whether the second floor happens to be the second floor of a two-story condition or, for example, the tenth floor of a dwelling unit whose first level happens to be located on the ninth story of a building. The code user should be aware that in Exception 2 above, access to only one exit is permitted when the total occupant load is 10 or less while this exception allows access to a single exit when the occupant load is less than 10 based on Table 10-A.

4. When the third floor within an individual dwelling unit or a Group R, Division 3 congregate residence is less than 500 square feet (46.45 m^2), only one means of egress is required from that floor. Again, as in Exception 3, the term "floor" is used here to reflect the level within the dwelling rather than the "story" within the building.

5. An occupied roof of less than 500 square feet (46.45 m^2) on a Group R, Division 3 Occupancy is also permitted to have access to only one exit when located no higher than immediately above the second story.

6. Floors and basements used exclusively for the service of the building may have access to only one exit. The code then carefully points out that the term "service of the building" is to be interpreted as applying to such spaces as equipment rooms, furnace rooms, electrical vaults and similar spaces that are not normally subject to occupancy. Spaces such as storage rooms, laundry rooms, maintenance offices and similar spaces are not to be considered

as providing service to the building, since these spaces are subject to frequent occupancy.

1004.2.3.3 From individual spaces. In this section, the code deals with the number of exits or exit-access doorways that are going to be required to accommodate the occupant load to be served. In what seems to be a self-evident requirement, the first sentence of this section states that every occupied portion of a building must be provided with access to at least one exit or exit-access doorway.

This requirement was first adopted with the 1961 edition of the UBC. Prior to that time, it was assumed that if buildings were occupied, the people obviously had a method of entering the building. Therefore, that same means of entrance was available to serve as a minimum means of egress. Basically, this concept served well for a number of years. However, under that concept it was difficult, in a number of instances which permitted a single-exit situation, to obtain compliance for the various components of the egress system, such as stairs, doors, ramps and other elements. The inclusion of this requirement makes it very clear that a single exit or exit-access doorway is always required. As a consequence, all of its various components are also required to comply with the appropriate provisions of the code relative to those individual components.

Access to at least two exits or exit-access doorways must be provided when the individual or cumulative occupant load served by that portion of the exit access reaches a level specified in Table 10-A. In other words, egress from individual spaces is regulated solely by occupant load.

There are two exceptions that will permit access to only a single exit from a space, room or area:

1. Lobby areas serving elevators may be provided with access to only one exit. This provision was included in the 1991 edition since lobbies are considered as accessory areas to the use that they serve and generally have low occupant loads when in use.

2. Storage, laundry and maintenance uses that do not exceed 300 square feet (27.87 m^2) in floor area may be served by a single exit or exit-access doorway in recognition of the fact that a minimal amount of space is allocated to these uses.

1004.2.3.4 Additional access to exits. Requirements for access to three or four means of egress are based strictly on occupant load. Any area of a building that has an occupant load in excess of 500, up to and including 1,000, shall be provided with access to not less than three exits or exit-access doorways. Any area having an occupant load in excess of 1,000 must be provided with access to not less than four means of egress. Under no circumstances does the *Uniform Building Code* require more than four means of egress from any building or portion thereof based on the number of persons present. It must be noted, however, that additional exits will frequently be required to satisfy the travel distance limits specified in Section 1004.2.5.

1004.2.4 Separation of exits or exit-access doorways. The basic reason for requiring multiple means of egress is that in a fire or other emergency, it is very possible that one of the egress components will be obstructed by the fire and, therefore, not be usable for egress purposes. It is imperative that in that same egress system, all the other required exits or exit-access door-

ways remain available and usable. To ensure that the required egress is sufficiently remote, the code imposes rather strict requirements relative to the location or arrangement of the different required exits or exit-access doorways with respect to each other. The purpose here is to do all that is reasonably possible to ensure that if one means of egress should become obstructed, the others will remain available and will be usable by the building occupants. As a corollary, this approach assumes that because the remaining means of egress are still available, there will be sufficient time for the building occupants to use them to evacuate the building or the building space.

Required separation of two exits. This "remoteness" rule in the *Uniform Building Code* is sometimes referred to as the "one-half diagonal" rule. It has been a part of the *Uniform Building Code* since the 1973 edition and, in recent years, has also found its way into the other model codes. The one-half diagonal rule states that if two exits or exit-access doorways are required, they shall be arranged and placed a distance apart equal to not less than one half of the maximum overall diagonal of the space, room, story or building served. Such minimum distance between the two means of egress, measured in a straight line, shall not be less than one half of that maximum overall diagonal dimension. See Figure 1004-2 for examples of the application of this rule. In compliance with Section 1004.2.3.1, this minimum separation creating multiple means of egress must be maintained until the occupants reach grade or the public way. The 1997 UBC first permitted multiple exits to be combined together once the user has reached grade. Previously, the code required that the exits be continuous and separate until reaching the public way. The provision now permits multiple paths of egress, such as stairs from an exit balcony, to go to a yard or exit court that would have only one way out of it. The modification of the level of protection (separation) is based on the fact that the occupants are out of and off the building and therefore face a reduced level of hazard. The width of the yard or court needs to be sized to accommodate the aggregate load from all the egress paths. The provisions of this section should be viewed in conjunction with the requirements of Section 1006.2.

In past practice, different building officials determined the length of that straight line measurement for egress separation in different ways. In some instances, building officials measured that distance from the near edge of one egress door to the near edge of the other. Other building officials applied the rule as measuring the distance between the center lines or far edges of the two required egress doors. The 1997 edition indicates that this distance is to be measured between the centers of exits or exit-access doorways.

The use of the one-half diagonal rule has been beneficial to *Uniform Building Code* users for many years. It precisely quantifies the code's intent when the code requires that separate means of egress be remote. It does not leave the building official with a vague performance-type statement which can, in many instances, result in a situation where egress separation would be dictated more by the design or desired layout of the building rather than by a consideration for adequate and safe separation of the means of egress.

In applying the one-half diagonal rule to a building constructed around a central court with an egress system consisting of an open balcony that extends around the perimeter of the court, it is important to take the measurement of the diagonal

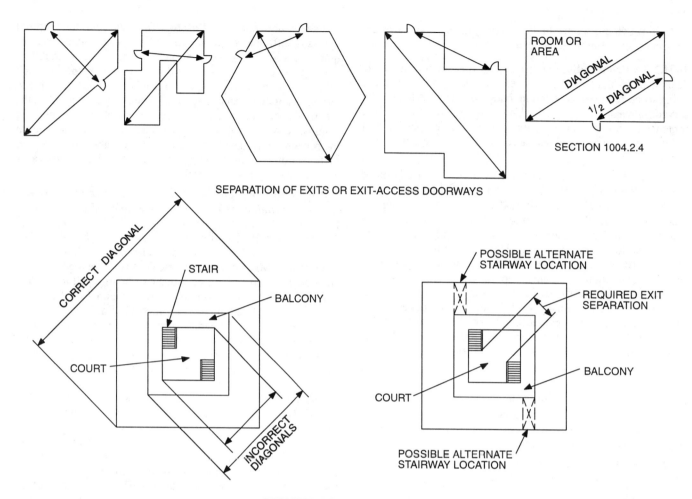

SEPARATION OF EXITS OR EXIT-ACCESS DOORWAYS

SECTION 1004.2.4

REQUIRED EGRESS SEPARATION

FIGURE 1004-2

from which the one-half diagonal dimension is derived at the proper locations. Refer to Figure 1004-2 for examples.

Figure 1004-3 illustrates an exception to the one-half diagonal rule for those buildings, such as core buildings, where the means of egress are sometimes arranged in rather close proximity. The code recognizes the benefits of such a floor arrangement and makes a specific exception in the event there is such a design. If the exits or exit-access doorways are connected by a corridor, the distance determined by one half of the maximum overall diagonal of the space served may be measured along the path of travel inside the corridor between the two exits. It must be stated that the connecting corridor is intended to be of one-hour fire-resistive construction, however the exceptions found in Section 1004.3.4.3 are permitted. When the exception to Section 1004.2.4 is used to ensure that the arrangement does not result in exit enclosures that are too close together, the code specifies that in no event may the straight line distance between the two exit enclosures be less than 30 feet (9144 mm) at any point. This distance should be measured from the closest points between the exit enclosures. This is simply an arbitrary requirement designed to ensure that there is at least minimal separation between the two means of egress.

Additional exits or exit-access doorways. When more than two means of egress are required, the remoteness rule takes on more of a performance character. In such an instance, at least two of the required exits or exit-access doorways shall be arranged to comply with the one-half diagonal rule. The other means of egress must then be arranged at a reasonable distance apart so that if any one of the required exits or exit-access doorways becomes blocked by a fire or any other emergency, the others will be available. Obviously, this performance statement will require some very careful evaluation and judgment on the part of the building official. There may be sufficient basis for applying that same rule when considering each possible pair of egress components in a multiexit situation. The code is not specific in this particular aspect, and proper code administration does require substantial, careful evaluation and judgment on the part of the building official in ensuring that the number of means of egress required are sufficiently remote so that it is not likely that the use of more than one access to an exit will be lost in any fire incident.

1004.2.5 Travel distance. In this section, the code is concerned that the means of egress be accessible in terms of their arrangement so that the distance of travel from any occupied point in the building to an exit is not excessive.

The code, therefore, establishes maximum distances to exits from any occupiable point of the building. This distance is referred to as travel distance. Travel distance is the distance that a

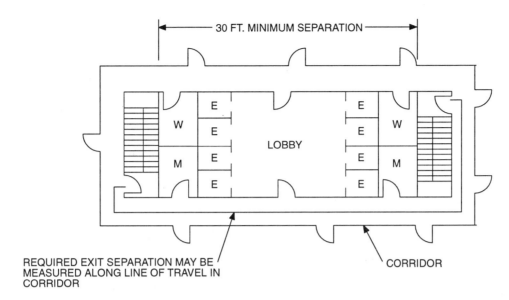

30 FT. MINIMUM SEPARATION

W

E
E

M

E

E

LOBBY

E

E

W

E

E

M

REQUIRED EXIT SEPARATION MAY BE MEASURED ALONG LINE OF TRAVEL IN CORRIDOR

CORRIDOR

For **SI:** 1 foot = 304.8 mm.

CORE ARRANGEMENT OF EXIT ENCLOSURES

FIGURE 1004-3

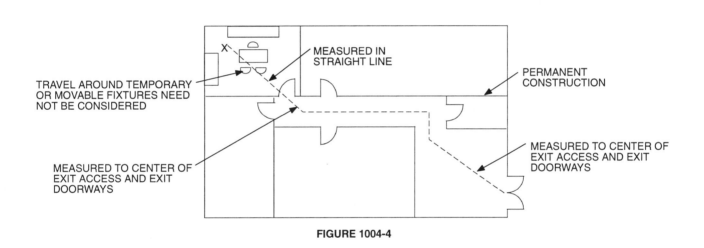

X

MEASURED IN STRAIGHT LINE

PERMANENT CONSTRUCTION

TRAVEL AROUND TEMPORARY OR MOVABLE FIXTURES NEED NOT BE CONSIDERED

MEASURED TO CENTER OF EXIT ACCESS AND EXIT DOORWAYS

MEASURED TO CENTER OF EXIT ACCESS AND EXIT DOORWAYS

FIGURE 1004-4

building occupant must travel from the most remote, occupiable portion of the building to either an exterior exit door, or the door of an exit enclosure, an exit passageway or a horizontal exit.

Each of these four elements in a means of egress system is considered to represent a sufficient level of safety such that the code is no longer concerned about the distance that the building occupant must travel to reach the eventual safe place. On the top floor of the World Trade Center, distance to exits or travel distance is measured on that floor from the most remote occupiable point to the point where the building occupant enters the enclosed exit stair. The fact that the building occupant then has 109 floors of stairway to traverse before exiting the building is not a consideration in dealing with distance to exits. Indirectly, in establishing a maximum distance of travel to a point of reasonable safety, the code is imposing a time factor on the ability of a building occupant to travel from the point of occupancy to a relatively safe place either outside or within the building.

Measurement of travel distance. Travel distance used to be one of the most difficult features of an egress system to determine in either the design or the plan review stage. Travel distance was measured along the path available to the building occupant. See Figure 1004-4. That path is determined by the location of partitions, doors, furniture, equipment and similar objects. Many of these objects are reasonably portable, and, as a consequence, the actual path available was frequently and easily altered. While still requiring travel to be measured around permanent construction and building elements, the 1997 UBC first permitted travel in areas with tables, chairs, furnishings, cabinets and similar temporary or movable fixtures or equipment to be a straight line measurement. The code states that the normal presence of such items is already factored into the permitted travel distance.

1004.2.5.2 Maximum travel distance. Basically, the code states that travel distance to an exit in a nonsprinklered building may not exceed 200 feet (60 960 mm). This was increased by 50 feet (15 240 mm) in the 1997 edition beyond the previous limitation. Then certain modifications are made and travel distance may be increased if additional protective measures are taken or if different protective systems are provided. The first modification states that in a building equipped with an automatic fire sprinkler system throughout the building, travel distance may be increased from the original 200 feet to 250 feet (60 960 mm to 76 200 mm). This was also increased by 50 feet (15 240 mm) from the 1994 and earlier editions. In addition, as depicted in Figure 1004-5, either the 200-foot (60 960 mm) or the 250-foot (76 200 mm) limitation may be increased by an additional 100 feet (30 480 mm) if the increased travel distance is the last portion of the travel distance within a corridor. In other words, either the 200 feet (60 960 mm) in a nonsprinklered building or the 250 feet (76 200 mm) in a sprinklered building may be increased to 300 feet and 350 feet (91 440 mm and 106 680 mm), respectively, if in each instance the last 100 feet (30 480 mm) of travel is within a corridor. In this latter instance, for travel distances between 200 feet and 300 feet (60 960 mm and 91 440 mm) for an nonsprinklered building, the length of the corridor may be reduced. This reduction will be equal to the distance by which the total travel distance is less than 300 feet (91 440 mm). Clearly, however, there is no requirement for corridor protection when the travel distance is 200 feet (60 960 mm).

There are also provisions for two special situations relating to certain occupancies. The first is that in open parking structures, as defined in Section 311.9, travel distance can be as much as 400 feet (121 920 mm) in a building equipped with an automatic sprinkler system, or when not so equipped, the travel distance may be 300 feet (91 440 mm). For the open parking garage, the travel distance for upper floors is measured to the exit stairway whether it is enclosed or not (as permitted in Section 1005.3.3.1). This is because the fire hazard is so low in these structures that the code assumes that once an individual has exited the fire floor, he or she has reached a point of safety equivalent to an enclosed stairway. Greatly increased travel distances are allowed for open parking garages because these structures do not present a life-safety hazard and have an excellent fire- and life-safety record. Tests by the American Iron and Steel Institute and others have supported the finding that open parking garages are low-hazard occupancies.

The other case is in connection with single-story airplane repair hangars, which are essentially very large open areas, and single-story factory and warehouse buildings housing Group F or Group S Occupancies. In these occupancies, travel distances may be as great as 400 feet (121 920 mm). However, to increase travel distance to such a limit, it is necessary that the building be equipped with both a complete automatic fire sprinkler system and with smoke and heat venting as defined in Section 906. If such features are not provided, the maximum allowable travel distance reverts back to the basic distance of 200 feet (60 960 mm). Of course, this can be increased to 300 feet (91 440 mm) if the last 100 feet (30 480 mm) is within a corridor.

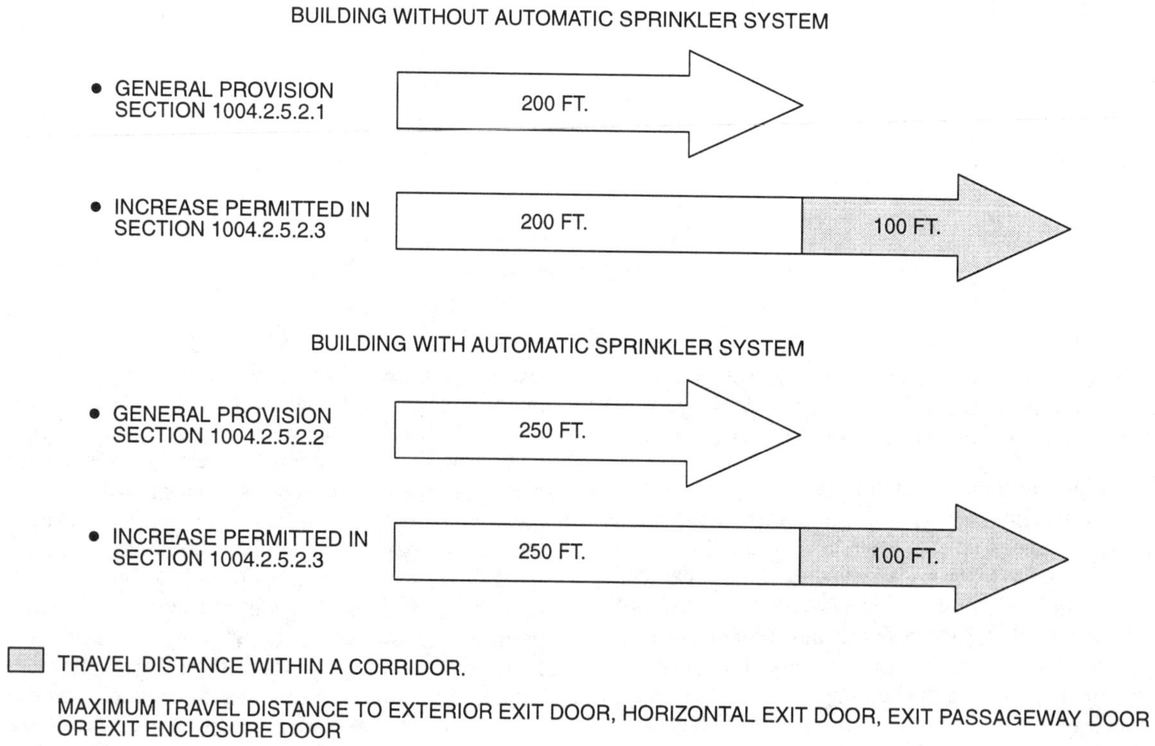

BUILDING WITHOUT AUTOMATIC SPRINKLER SYSTEM

- GENERAL PROVISION
  SECTION 1004.2.5.2.1 — 200 FT.

- INCREASE PERMITTED IN
  SECTION 1004.2.5.2.3 — 200 FT. | 100 FT.

BUILDING WITH AUTOMATIC SPRINKLER SYSTEM

- GENERAL PROVISION
  SECTION 1004.2.5.2.2 — 250 FT.

- INCREASE PERMITTED IN
  SECTION 1004.2.5.2.3 — 250 FT. | 100 FT.

TRAVEL DISTANCE WITHIN A CORRIDOR.

MAXIMUM TRAVEL DISTANCE TO EXTERIOR EXIT DOOR, HORIZONTAL EXIT DOOR, EXIT PASSAGEWAY DOOR OR EXIT ENCLOSURE DOOR

For SI: 1 foot = 304.8 mm.

MAXIMUM TRAVEL DISTANCES

FIGURE 1004-5

To alert code users to the fact that there are other code sections that affect travel distance requirements, Section 1004.2.5.2 lists five locations where special requirements may be found:

1. Section 402.5. Travel distance on an open exit-access balcony within an atrium space, which is limited to 100 feet (30.480 mm).

2. Section 404.4.3. Number of means of egress from mall tenant spaces. This section does not specifically limit travel distance, but rather requires a second means of egress for tenant spaces having a distance of travel to the mall in excess of 75 feet (22 860 mm).

3. Section 404.4.5. Travel distance within mall tenant spaces or covered malls. The section limits travel distance within the mall proper to 200 feet (60 960 mm). The travel distance within individual tenant spaces is also limited to 200 feet (60 960 mm). Note that the tenant space travel distance may no longer be measured to the entrance into the mall, but rather to exterior exit doors, horizontal exits, exit passageways or exit enclosures.

4. Section 1007.3. This section establishes special travel distance limitations for educational occupancies.

5. Section 1007.4. This section establishes special travel distance limitations for hazardous occupancies.

Additional discussion about each of these five special requirements is presented in the appropriate section of this handbook. It should be noted that Section 403 formerly contained a provision allowing increased travel distances within high-rise office and residential buildings. This provision was dropped from the 1994 edition since it was belived that these distances were excessive and that the provisions of Section 1004.2.5 were more appropriate.

1004.2.6 Dead ends. This section establishes the limitations on dead-end hallways and corridors. Basically, whenever more than one exit or exit-access doorway is required, the exit access shall be arranged so that occupants can travel in either direction from any point to a separate exit. However, dead ends in hallways and corridors are permitted up to a maximum length of 20 feet (6096 mm). In the event that the conditions of building occupancy permit access to only a single exit, the dead-end limit does not apply. When the basic requirement is for travel in only a single direction to one exit, travel in the opposite direction is not considered to be in violation of the dead-end requirements.

The limitation on dead ends is directed toward avoiding portions of the hallway or corridor system which could result in entrapment of the building occupant by creating a situation where the building occupant following a proper path of travel through the means of egress system might, under fire conditions, take a wrong turn into a portion of the system from which there is no outlet. In such a situation, it is probable that the building occupant will have to proceed all the way to the end of the dead end before learning that there is no way out and, thereafter, have to retrace steps to proceed to an exit.

1004.3.2 Aisles.

1004.3.2.1 General. This section requires that aisles be provided in all occupied portions of the exit access that contain seats, tables, furnishings, displays, and similar fixtures or equipment. Primarily this would have application to occupied-use areas or rooms where it is necessary to provide a circulation system so that building occupants will have reasonable means for moving around in the occupied spaces as well as safe access to corridors and other components of the egress system. It is customary to think of aisles in such facilities as theaters where an aisle system is installed to serve the fixed seating sections. However, this section applies to other occupancies as well. It is necessary to provide circulation systems through open office areas, retail sales areas, factory areas, dining rooms and other areas in buildings. Also, all aisles located within an accessible route of travel must comply with Chapter 11.

1004.3.2.2 Width in occupancies without fixed seats. The minimum required width of aisles will vary according to the occupancy in which the aisles are located, the nature of the use area that the aisles serve, or even, in some instances, the type of occupant served. A minimum aisle width of 24 inches (610 mm) is required for those aisles that are to be used only by employees. When the number of employees is sufficiently large, aisles are required to be wider than 2 feet (610 mm); in such cases, the required width would be determined in accordance with the formula presented in Section 1003.2.3. Based on a factor of 0.2, a 2-foot-wide (610 mm) aisle would accommodate 120 employees.

In public areas of Groups B and M Occupancies, such as open offices, retail sales areas and similar spaces, and in assembly occupancies without fixed seats, the minimum required clear width of an aisle is 36 inches (914 mm) when furniture, tables, merchandise, seating and other obstructions are located on only one side of the aisle. However, when such items are located on both sides of the aisle, the aisle must be at least 44 inches (1118 mm) in clear width. All aisles are to be unobstructed, except for those permitted projections such as handrails, nonstructural trim and doors.

1004.3.2.3.1 Width. Revised in the 1991 edition and further revised in 1994, aisle widths in assembly areas with fixed seats shall be based on the occupant load served in addition to the minimum widths required by this section based on the arrangement of the seating served. When required to be greater than the minimums specified, the clear width of an aisle, in inches (mm), is based on the occupant load within the portion of the area served, aisle slope, whether or not there is smoke protection, and other factors.

Calculated width of aisles. The method for calculating the required width of aisles for assembly occupancies was revised in the 1994 edition. This revision was made because the width of aisle determined under the 1991 UBC provisions was believed to result in excessively wide aisles, particularly for large occupancy assembly buildings. The method for determining aisle widths is based on the concept that very large assembly areas do not present the same level of risk as smaller uses, and, as a result, factors for calculating aisle width decrease as the total number of seats increases.

The method for calculating widths has two distinct categories. These are buildings with and buildings without smoke-protected assembly seating. Thus, the first thing that must be established is the category in which the aisles must be analyzed. Section 1002 defines smoke-protected assembly seating as "seating served by a means of egress and is not subject to blockage by smoke accumulation within or under a structure." Unfortunately, no additional guidance was provided as to how this could be achieved until the 1997 edition. Section 1008.7 now regulates smoke-protected assembly seating in regard to roof height, smoke control and travel distance.

If it is determined that a building has smoke-protected assembly seating, a second requirement is that an approved life-safety evaluation be conducted. Unlike "smoke-protected assembly seating," the term "life-safety evaluation" is not defined in the code. Thus, the building official needs to establish the criteria for an acceptable evaluation. Such things as pedestrian flow rates, movement characteristics of persons using exit systems, the nature of the means of egress system beyond the aisles, location of potential hazards, staff response capabilities, facility preplanning and training, and other items relating to occupant safety would most likely need to be considered. Should it be determined that a building is not smoke-protected or no life-safety evaluation has been performed, the aisle width will need to be calculated using the more stringent nonsmoke-protected conditions.

Three factors used for calculating aisle widths apply to both smoke-protected and nonsmoke-protected structures. The first two apply to aisles with steps, while the third applies to ramped aisles. These factors are:

- Factor *A* (steps):

A = 1.00 when riser heights are 7 inches (178 mm) or less

A = when riser heights exceed 7 inches (178 mm)

- Factor *B* (steps):

B = 1.00 when a handrail is provided within 30 inches (762 mm) horizontal distance of any point of a step

B = 1.25 when a handrail is not provided within 30 inches (762 mm)

- Factor *C* (ramps):

C = 1.00 when a ramp has a slope of 1:10 or less

C = 1.10 when a ramp used as an ascending path of exit travel has a slope steeper than 1:10

The code provision for Factor *C* states that the 1.10 value applies to ramps when they are used for ascent, with the implication being that steeper ramps used only for exit descent may use a *C* factor equal to 1. Remember that here the code is addressing exiting. The ramp may serve both for ingress and egress to the seating area, but as a means of egress, it well may have unidirectional flow. The increased ramp width for ascending aisles is because pedestrian travel rates up steeper ramps (here defined as those steeper than 1:10) are slower than rates on flatter ramps or on descending ramps. The three factors, *A*, *B* and *C*, are used in conjunction with either Table 10-B, which is for nonsmoke-protected seating, or Table 10-C, which is for smoke-protected seating. Application Example 1004-6 shows how the calculated width of exit provisions would be applied.

It should be noted that although the 1994 edition was revised in the interest of decreasing the aisle width requirements for large occupancy assembly buildings, a reduction actually only occurs in smoke-protected buildings. For the nonsmoke-protected condition, regardless of size, the width of ramped aisles actually increased by 10 percent.

When egress is possible in two directions, the shape of an aisle can no longer be of an "hourglass" configuration. The clear width shall be uniform throughout. A tapered aisle is allowed only for dead-end aisles. Also, when aisles converge to form a single aisle, the width of that single aisle shall not be less than the combined required width of the converging aisles. There is no penalty for providing aisles that are wider than the minimum code requirement.

When seating is arranged in rows, the clear width shall not be less than the following, while still conforming to the calculated-width-of-aisle provisions:

1. Forty-eight inches (1219 mm) for stairs when seating is provided on both sides of an aisle.
2. Thirty-six inches (914 mm) for stairs when seating is provided only on one side of an aisle.
3. Twenty-three inches (584 mm) between a stair handrail and the nearest seat when the rail is within the aisle.
4. Forty-two inches (1067 mm) for level or ramped aisles when seating is provided on both sides of an aisle.
5. Thirty-six inches (914 mm) for level or ramped aisles when seating is provided on only one side of an aisle.
6. Twenty-three inches (584 mm) between a stair handrail and the nearest seat when an aisle serves no more than five rows on only one side.

This section must be used in concert with other provisions of Section 1004.3.2 for aisles to completely define and arrange a seating area. The minimum clear width between rows of seats is 12 inches (305 mm) measured between the rearmost projection of the seat in the forward row and the foremost projection of any portion of the seat in the row behind, when the rows have 14 or less seats. If automatic or self-rising seats are used, such as in movie theaters, the minimum clear width shall be measured with the seat up. See Figure 1004-7.

Such clear width must be increased whenever the number of seats in a row exceeds 14, but in no case shall the number of seats in any row exceed 100. The increased width when seating rows are served by aisles or doors at both ends of a row is the minimum 12 inches plus 0.3 inch (305 mm plus 7.62 mm) for each additional seat over 14; the width need not exceed 22 inches (559 mm). The row length limits may be increased per Table 10-E in smoke-protected assembly seating facilities.

Clear width, in inches = 12 inches + 0.3 inch/seat (× - 14 seats)

For **SI:** Clear width, in mm = 305 mm + 7.62 mm/seat (× - 14 seats)

= the number of seats in a row

By interpreting the formula, we find that the maximum clear width occurs when the number of seats in a row is 48. Section 1004.3.2.4 has other limitations that must be considered in the design. See Figure 1004-8.

For rows of seating served by an aisle or doorway at only one end of a row, the formula for the clear width is the minimum 12 inches plus 0.6 inch (305 mm plus 15 mm) for each seat over seven, but, again, the clear width need not exceed 22 inches (559 mm). This is similar to the previous provision with one major difference: A maximum 30-foot (9144 mm) path of travel is per-

Application Example 1004-6

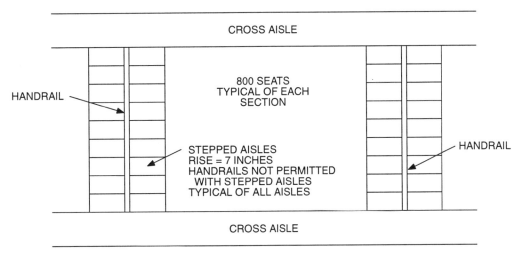

For **SI:** 1 inch = 25.4 mm.

10,000 SEAT ARENA

FIGURE 1004-6

GIVEN: Information in Figure 1004-6.

Case I—Smoke-protected assembly seating for which a life-safety evaluation has been provided.

Case II—Nonsmoke-protected assembly seating.

DETERMINE: Required aisle width for both cases.

SOLUTION:

Case I—Use Table 10-C. For a 10,000 seat arena, the width equation for stairs is 0.130 AB per seat served, with a rise of 7 inches (178 mm), A = 1.00, and with no handrails, B = 1.00. Thus, the width of exit equation resolves to:

$$0.130 \times 1.00 \times 1.00 = 0.130$$

and the required width of aisle becomes:

$$400 \times 0.130 = 52 \text{ inches or } 4.33 \text{ feet (1321 mm)}$$

Since 52 inches (1321 mm) exceeds the minimum required width of 48 inches (1219 mm), it becomes the governing width.

Case II—Use Table 10-B. For nonsmoke-protected assembly seating, the width equation is the same for all conditions. For stairs, this equation is 0.300 AB. Factors A and B are the same as in Case I, so the equation resolves to:

$$0.300 \times 1.00 \times 1.00 = 0.300$$

and the required width of aisle becomes:

$$400 \times 0.300 = 120 \text{ inches or } 10 \text{ feet (3048 mm)}$$

Thus, the aisle required for nonsmoke-protected assembly seating is more than twice as wide as the aisle required for smoke-protected assembly seating.

mitted from the occupant's seat to a point where there is a choice of two directions of travel to an exit. This can be to the adjacent two-way aisle or along a dead-end aisle to a cross-aisle or doorway. For smoke-protected assembly seating, single direction travel distance can be increased from 30 feet to 50 feet (9144 mm to 15 240 mm) and Table 10-E will allow an increase in row length.

1004.3.2.4 Aisle termination. In an arrangement of a seating area, all aisles serving the seating area must end in a cross aisle, foyer or doorway. In large facilities, it is not uncommon to find a number of aisles leading to a number of cross aisles. The required width of a cross aisle is the same as that for converging aisles: the combined required widths of the aisles leading to the cross aisle. Although dead-end aisles are allowed, their length is

limited to 20 feet (6096 mm) except when the seats served by the dead-end aisle are not more than 24 seats from another aisle measured along a row having a minimum clear width of 12 inches plus 0.6 inch (305 mm plus 15 mm) for each additional seat over seven in a row. When seats have no backrests, dead ends in vertical aisles are only limited to 16 rows. For smoke-protected assembly seating, up to 21 rows are permitted in a dead-end vertical aisle. Horizontal dead-end aisles are also allowed in greater lengths in these types of facilities. Cross aisles shall also end in an aisle, foyer, doorway or vomitory.

1004.3.2.5 Aisle steps.

1004.3.2.5.1 Where prohibited. When aisles have a slope of 1 unit vertical in 8 units horizontal (12.5% slope) or less, steps in the aisle are prohibited because in low-slope aisles occupants

(Continued on page 203)

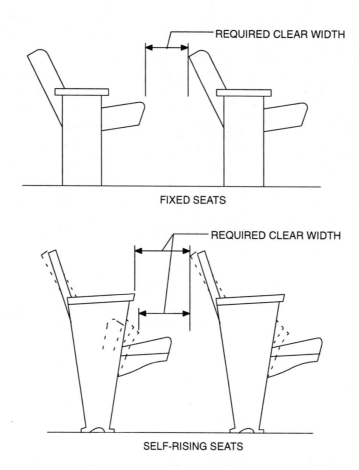

FIXED SEATS

SELF-RISING SEATS

WHEN ALL THE SEATS IN ROW ARE OF THE SELF- OR AUTOMATIC-RISING TYPE, THE REQUIRED 12-INCH CLEARANCE MAY BE MEASURED WITH THE SEATS IN THE UP POSITION.

For **SI:** 1 inch = 25.4 mm.

FIGURE 1004-7

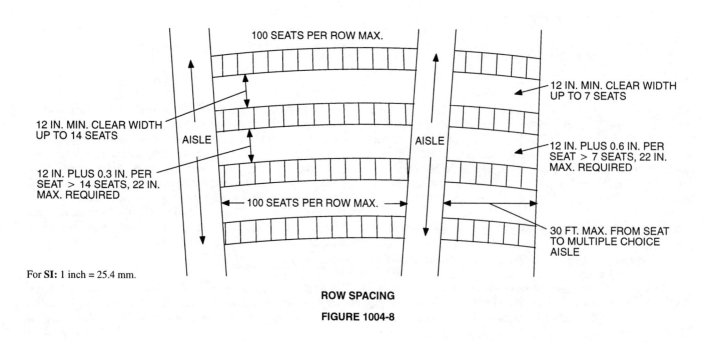

For **SI:** 1 inch = 25.4 mm.

ROW SPACING

FIGURE 1004-8

(Continued from page 201)

have a tendency to not notice steps as readily as they would in the steeper aisles. Continuous surfaces are safer surfaces.

1004.3.2.5.2 Where required. When an aisle has a slope steeper than 1 unit vertical in 8 units horizontal (12.5% slope), a series of risers and treads should be used. These risers and treads shall extend the entire width of the aisle, shall have a rise of no more than 8 inches (203 mm) or less than 4 inches (102 mm), and shall be uniform the entire flight. The tread shall not be less than 11 inches (279 mm) and shall be uniform throughout the flight. Variations in run or height between adjacent treads or risers shall not exceed $^3/_{16}$ inch (4.8 mm).

One provision that helps the user of an aisle notice a step is the provision requiring a contrasting strip or other approved marking on the leading edge of each tread.

In an exception to the riser height provision, riser heights may be increased to 9 inches (229 mm) and may be nonuniform when the slope of the aisle and seating area is the same. This exception can be used only when it is demonstrated that sight-lines would otherwise be impaired. Variations may also exceed $^3/_{16}$ inch (4.8 mm) between risers, provided the exact location of such variation is clearly identified with a marking strip distinctively different from the contrasting marking strip. This marking shall be on the nosing or leading edge of the tread adjacent to the non-uniform riser.

1004.3.2.6 Ramp slope. The maximum slope of a ramped aisle should not be steeper than 1 unit vertical in 8 units horizontal (12.5% slope). An aisle that needs a steeper slope than 1:8 should use steps. If the ramp is within an accessible route of travel, Chapter 11 should be consulted for accessibility requirements.

The surface of the ramp shall be slip-resistant whether the ramp is within an accessible route of travel or not.

1004.3.2.7 Handrails. Handrails must comply with Section 1003.3.3.6 and must have rounded terminations or bends. All aisles having a slope steeper than 1 unit vertical in 15 units horizontal (6.7% slope) and all aisle stairs shall have handrails. The handrails can be placed on either side of or down the center of the aisle served and can project into the required width no more than $3^1/_2$ inches (89 mm).

Handrails may be omitted where the slope of the aisle is not greater than 1 unit vertical in 8 units horizontal (12.5% slope) with fixed seating on both sides, or where a guardrail that conforms to the size and shape requirements of a handrail is located at one side. The first exception has the fixed seating as a substitute for handrails. The second exception intends that a handrail be provided on the side opposite the seating when seating occurs on only one side of the aisle. This side may be open, requiring a guardrail or it may be a wall.

Handrails located within the aisle width shall not be continuous but, shall provide gaps at intervals not exceeding five rows. The width of these gaps should not be less than 22 inches (559 mm) or more than 36 inches (914 mm). This is to provide access to seating on either side of the rail and to facilitate the flow of users on the aisle. Intermediate handrails located 12 inches (305 mm) below the main handrail are required to prevent users from ducking under the handrail and hindering flow. Also, they provide a handrail for toddlers who may be using the aisle.

1004.3.3 Hallways.

1004.3.3.1 General. Requirements for "hallways" have been added due to the elimination of the occupant load-driven fire-resistive construction requirements for corridors. Although not specifically defined, for exit-access design purposes, a hallway will be considered equivalent to passing throught an intervening room as stated in Section 1004.2.2. The important issue for hallways is that, in general, they will not require any type of rated construction or protection. If the exit-access design requirements cannot be satisfied by complying with the intervening room, travel distance or exit separation provisions, then a corridor or other arrangement would be needed.

Definition of a hallway or corridor. For the purpose of this discussion, a corridor is considered similar to a hallway. The term "hallway" is very difficult to define. Over the years, a number of attempts have been made but in each instance it was possible to point out deficiencies in the various proposed definitions. Essentially, the determination as to when a hallway exists is left to the building official, who may seek some guidance from the appropriate dictionary referred to in Section 201.

For the purpose of the code, however, a hallway is essentially a space where the building occupant has very limited choices as to paths or directions of travel. The available path is restricted, and it is usually bordered by other occupied use spaces. As a consequence, it is potentially exposed to fires that might occur in those enclosed spaces unknown to anyone in the egress system. Generally speaking, in a building space of this type, the occupant has only two choices as far as directions of travel through the egress system are concerned. For that reason, it is sometimes necessary for the building official to evaluate the plan layout of an area and determine whether the space presents the potential fire-hazard exposure to building occupants as any regular, well-defined hallway might. If the determination is that the fire-exposure potential is the same, the building space should be made to comply with the requirements for hallways. To assist the building official in this determination, one exception in Section 1004.3.4.3 exempts a corridor from the fire-resistive requirements if the corridor has a width of at least 30 feet (9144 mm). Such a space would also not be considered a hallway, but rather a room.

This section probably gives a little better guidance as to what is not a hallway. It specifically states that partitions, rails, counters, filing cabinets, space dividers, furniture and similar types of equipment that do not exceed a height of 6 feet (1829 mm) above the floor are not to be considered as creating hallways. Essentially, the purpose of the height limitation is that in most instances a building occupant in spaces enclosed by such low-height features is able to detect a fire by smell, sight or sound. Consequently, such low-height dividers are not considered as creating hallways even though they may effectively limit the choice of paths of travel available to the building occupant. Corridors, on the other hand, are required to be fully enclosed by walls, a floor, a ceiling and permitted protected openings.

1004.3.3.2 Width. Relative to the required width of hallways, it is the intent of this provision that, if there are occupied building spaces with a certain occupant load and all of those building occupants have access to the hallway, that hallway serving that occupant load must be available to the building occupants, regardless of the number of egress paths. Again, the assumption in requiring multiple means of egress is that at least one of those means will be lost in a fire emergency. Therefore, all the other required paths of egress travel must remain available to serve as required egress for the total occupant load of the spaces.

Required hallway width. Every hallway determined to be serving an occupant load of 50 or more must be at least 44 inches (1118 mm) in clear width. Hallways serving an occupant load of 49 or less are required to have a minimum width of 36 inches (914 mm). This includes residential dwellings to ensure accessibility to individual rooms within the structure for purposes of moving furniture, appliances and other bulky material. The accessibility requirements of Chapter 11 may have more restrictive provisions and should, therefore, be consulted. Also, special requirements regarding hallway widths in Group E and Group I Occupancies are addressed in Section 1007.

As stated, this section provides for minimum required widths of hallways. At the present time, the code is not completely clear on how the required hallway width is determined when the occupant load is large enough to require hallway widths in excess of these minimums. There have been two interpretations relative to the manner in which the required width of hallways is to be determined. The first utilizes the formula that appears to be required by the provisions of Section 1003.2.3.2 and Table 10-B. This section states that the minimum required width of the hallway, in inches (mm), would be determined by multiplying the total occupant load tributary to that hallway by 0.2.

The same section also provides the formula for determining the minimum required width of any component in the means of egress system. In addition, it says that the minimum required width is to be divided approximately equally among the separate egress components that are available. Under these provisions, given a simple building with occupied spaces on each side of a hallway and exterior exit doors at the extremities of the hallway, the width of the hallway would be determined by taking the entire occupant load of the spaces served and multiplying that occupant load by 0.2. The result would be the minimum required width of the hallway in inches (mm). However, in determining the required width of the exits at the extremities of the hallway, the code is very explicit in that those egress widths are determined by taking the same total occupant load that has access to the hallway and multiplying that number by 0.2 to obtain the total required egress width. The code then specifically provides that the total required egress width be divided between the two separate doorways at the extremities of the hallway. Following the same rule for the determination of both the minimum width of the hallway and the minimum width of the doorways to which the hallways leads will always result in a hallway that is twice as wide as the doorway to which it leads. This is not consistent with good fire-protection and life-safety engineering. Bringing a hallway full of people to an doorway that is only one-half the width of the hallway could result in a potentially hazardous situation.

The other interpretation as to the determination of the required minimum widths of hallways is that the width should be related to the required width of the exit to which the hallway leads. This is the preferred interpretation. The most logical procedure for determining hallway widths is to determine the required width of the exits at the end of the corridor and to size the hallway to provide that same minimum width. See Application Example 1004-9. Therefore, the better application of the provi-

sions contained in the two sections referred to above would be to mutually equate the required width of the hallways and the required width of the exits that the hallway serves. However, the minimum required width of 44 inches (1118 mm) must be maintained for the corridor when serving an occupant load of 50 or more and 36 inches (914 mm) when serving an occupant load of 49 or less.

Based on Section 1003.2.4, all hallways in the means of egress system are required to have a minimum height of not less than 7 feet (2134 mm), measured to the lowest projection from the ceiling. Therefore, there must be at least 7 feet (2134 mm) of clear headroom, measured from the walking surface of the floor to the nearest object overhead. Light fixtures, beams, signs and architectural features must be maintained not less than 7 feet (2134 mm) above the floor.

This provision appears to conflict with the minimum size requirements for egress doors. In the event of a door, the opening must be such as to permit the installation of a door having a height of 6 feet 8 inches (2032 mm). Therefore, the 7-foot (2134 mm) minimum clearance required for hallways is not a requirement at doorways even though the doors might be arranged in a cross-corridor configuration. Building occupants are accustomed to reduced headroom through doorways but should not be surprised by low-hanging projections from the ceilings of hallway and corridors.

Generally, when the code specifies a required width of a component in a means of egress system, it intends that width to be the clear, net, usable, unobstructed width. As is the case of landings in conjunction with doors, hallways are permitted to have certain limited projections. A door opening into a hallway may not, during the course of its swing, reduce the width of the hallway by more than one half of its required width. When fully opened, the door may not project into the required width of the hallway by more than 7 inches (178 mm).

Similarly, handrails may project into hallways but must not exceed a total of 7 inches (178 mm). As in stairs, handrails are normally thought of as occurring on each side of a hallway. In such an arrangement, it is permissible to have each handrail project $3^1/_2$ inches (89 mm).

Again, as discussed in connection with Section 1003.3.1.6, it might be better to think of the permitted obstruction of a door during the course of its swing from the positive side. So stated, each door, when swinging into a hallway, must leave unobstructed at least one half of the required width of the hallway during the course of its swing. At least one half of the required width of the hallway must be available for use by the building occupants.

In applying the requirements for projections into hallways, the code imposes these limitations on doors on a door-by-door basis. It is desirable that doors be arranged so as not to have two doors directly opposing each other on opposite sides of the hallway. Better design would avoid this arrangement. The intent of the code is that at least one half of the required width of the hallway be available for use by the building occupant.

In addition to handrails and doors, certain other limited projections are permitted. Such things as door moldings, casings, chair rails, baseboards and other decorative features are permitted to project into the required width a maximum of $1^1/_2$ inches (38 mm) on each side of the hallway.

Application Example 1004-9
Section 1004.3.4.2

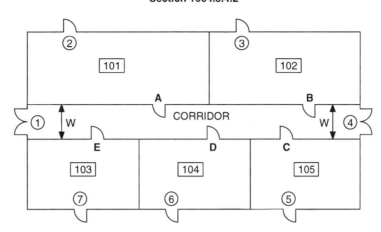

REQUIRED WIDTH OF CORRIDOR

FIGURE 1004-9

GIVEN: See Figure 1003-1. Occupant loads for each room are the same as for Application Example 1003-1. These were 160 for Room 101; 120 for Room 102; and 100 each for Rooms 103, 104 and 105.

DETERMINE: The required minimum width, *W*, of the corridor.

SOLUTION: The occupant load from Room 101 that is required to be considered when calculating the egress width is one half of 160, or 80; one half of 120, or 60 for Room 102; and one-half each of 100, or 50 for Rooms 103 through 105. Thus, the total occupant load required to be considered in the corridor in calculating egress width is:

$$80 + 60 + 50 + 50 + 50 = 290$$

Since, as they may elect to continue exiting to the left or to the right toward Doorway 1 or 4, leave each of Rooms 101 through 105 by way of Doorways A, B, C, D and E, the corridor width then needs to be calculated on the basis of only one half of the total occupant load exiting via the corridor ($1/2 \times 290 = 145$ occupants). The required minimum calculated egress width at the corridor is then 29 inches (737 mm) (145×0.2). However, Section 1004.3.4.2 specifies a minimum width of 44 inches (1118 mm) for a corridor serving an occupant load of 50 or more and 36 inches (914 mm) when the corridor serves an occupant load of 49 or less. The required minimum in this example is 44 inches (1118 mm).

1004.3.3.3 Construction. Unless required by some other provision of the code, hallways are not required to be of fire-resistive construction. They may also have walls of any height. When such walls, partitions, counters and similar space dividers are limited to 6 feet (1829 mm) in height, they are not even considered as forming a hallway.

1004.3.3.4 Openings. There are no limitations on the amount or type of openings permitted in a hallway, unless protection of openings is required by some other provision of the code. Any number of unprotected doors, windows and air openings are permitted.

1004.3.3.5 Elevator lobbies. Unless another provision of the code would require smoke- and draft-control assemblies, elevators that open into hallways need not be provided with elevator lobbies. This is consistent with the allowance for other unprotected openings.

1004.3.4 Corridors.

1004.3.4.1 General. This section sets forth the requirements for corridors serving as a portion of the exit access. It applies any time a corridor is created and such corridor is required or cannot be considered as a hallway. See Application Example 1004-10 for the application of this provision. The *Uniform Building Code* does not contain a definition of the term "corridor." However, Chapter 4 addresses the unique features of covered mall build-

ings. Chapter 11 should also be consulted if the corridor is within an accessible route of travel.

1004.3.4.2 Width. The width of corridors is regulated in the very same manner as for hallways in Section 1004.3.3.2. These projections into the required width permitted for hallways are also permitted for corridors.

1004.3.4.3 Construction. When a hallway serves an occupant load of 10 or more in Group R, Division 1 or in Group I Occupancies or when a corridor is required or created in all other occupancies, the walls and ceilings are required to be of fire-resistive construction. See Cases 1, 2, 3 and 3A of Figure 1004-11. When the hazards reach the specified levels, it is appropriate to afford those persons in the corridor some additional protection from potential fire occurring in the enclosed spaces bordering the corridor. Therefore, a minimum separation for the corridor of one-hour fire resistance is deemed necessary.[5]

Fire-resistive corridor exceptions. A series of exceptions to the corridor requirement lists a number of special circumstances where it is believed that the one-hour fire-resistive separation is not necessary. The first applies to buildings one story in height housing Group F, Division 2 and Group S, Division 2 Occupancies. The basic reason for this is that, as defined in Chapter 3, Group F, Division 2 and Group S, Division 2 Occupancies contain primarily noncombustible materials. The probability of a fire occurring in the spaces adjacent to the corridor is minimal.

Application Example 1004-10
Sections 1004.3.4.3 and 1004.3.4.3.1

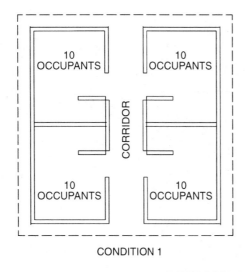

CONDITION 1

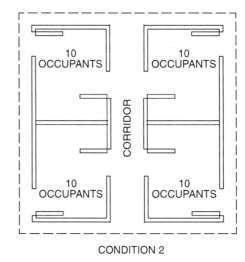

CONDITION 2

RATED CORRIDOR REQUIREMENTS

FIGURE 1004-10

GIVEN: Two office buildings as shown in Figure 1004–10. Note that in Condition 2 each room has an exit directly to the exterior.

DETERMINE: The number of occupants served by the corridor in Condition 1 and in Condition 2.

SOLUTION: The corridor shown in Condition 1 serves as the sole exit for four offices, each having an occupant load of 10 persons; therefore, the corridor serves a total occupant load of 40 persons.

In Condition 2, each office contains an exit directly to the exterior. Since each office has an occupant load of less than 30 persons, each office requires only one exit, which can be provided by these direct exterior exits. Therefore, the corridor does not serve as a required exit and is not regulated by Section 1004.3.4. However, the corridor width must comply with Section 1004.3.4.2 since the corridor is serving as an exit even though it is not a *required* exit.

It should be noted that the corridors in this example could be designed as hallways.

The second exception establishes a condition whereby corridors in excess of 30 feet (9144 mm) in width need not be separated by one-hour fire-resistive construction where all the occupancies served by the corridor have at least one exit totally independent from the corridor. Prior to the inclusion of Section 404 in the code, this exception allowed typical mall construction. Therefore, a mall more than 30 feet (9144 mm) in width, which is simply another form of corridor, was not required to be separated from adjacent tenant spaces by one-hour fire-resistive construction, nor were the openings between the mall and the tenant spaces required to be protected.

It is still acceptable to construct covered mall buildings under this exception, provided the building is in full compliance with all the other applicable provisions of the code. However, for a covered mall building, Section 404 provides a complete and comprehensive treatment of this special type of use.

The third exception recognizes that certain occupancies such as jails, prisons, reformatories and similar places of detention must, by virtue of the nature of their use, have certain features that would not be in conformity with the requirement for one-hour fire-resistive separation of corridors. In Group I, Division 3 Occupancies, which are designed with open-front cells as portions of the corridor walls, the requirement for fire-resistive construction of the corridor and protection of the openings is ex-

empted. In granting the exception, the code takes into account the special requirements of the use.

The fourth exception to this corridor construction requirement, added to the 1985 UBC, applies to office spaces. This exception states that corridor walls and ceilings need not be fire resistive within office spaces having an occupant load of 100 or less when the entire story is equipped with a complete automatic sprinkler system throughout and when a smoke-detection system is installed throughout the corridor system serving such office. Alarms must be audible in all areas served by the corridor. It should be made clear that this exception applies in offices within a building on a story-by-story basis. Under Exception 4, the code does not require that the automatic sprinkler system be installed throughout the entire building. An example is presented in Figure 1004-12.

Exception 5 was added to the 1994 UBC and is similar to Exception 4 in that it permits nonrated corridor construction within office spaces having an occupant load of 100 or less. The difference between the two exceptions is that Exception 5 applies to buildings that are fully sprinklered. Because of the added protection provided by a complete sprinkler system, a smoke-detection system in the corridors is not required.

Exception 6 was added to the 1997 UBC and is similar to Exceptions 4 and 5. In this case, the occupant load serving the non-

(Continued on page 208)
(Continued on page 208)

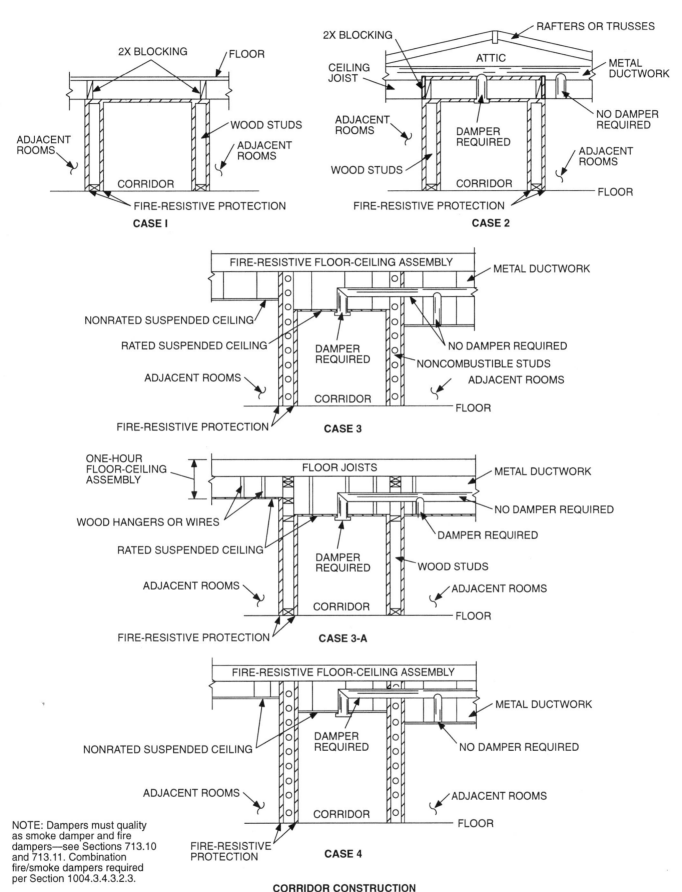

CORRIDOR CONSTRUCTION

FIGURE 1004–11

NOTE: Dampers must quality as smoke damper and fire dampers—see Sections 713.10 and 713.11. Combination fire/smoke dampers required per Section 1004.3.4.3.2.3.

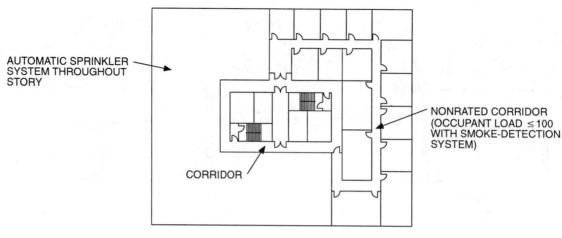

CORRIDOR CONSTRUCTION

EXCEPTION 4 TO SECTION 1004.3.4.3

FIGURE 1004-12

(Continued from page 206)

rated corridor is not limited when the corridor is located within an office space of a Type I, Type II F.R. or Type II One-hour building. An automatic sprinkler system and smoke-detection system is also required.

Generally speaking, when the corridor walls are required to be one-hour fire resistive, the construction must extend from the floor to the floor above so as to completely separate the corridor space from adjacent occupied use areas. The several methods used to comply with Section 1004.3.4.3.1 are shown in Figure 1004-11.

If the entire story has a ceiling that is a membrane of a one-hour fire-resistive floor or roof assembly, the corridor walls may terminate at the ceiling line. See Figure 1004-11, Case 3A. Thus, the corridor walls below the ceiling line are protecting the corridor laterally from adjacent spaces and the ceiling protects the corridor vertically. It is important to note that the construction of the ceiling is not necessarily required to be a complete one-hour fire-resistive floor-ceiling or roof-ceiling assembly. The justification for this position is that a complete one-hour separation is not intended as much as the prevention of smoke migration between the corridor and adjacent occupied spaces is intended for a reasonable period. This could be for preventing smoke from entering the corridor from adjacent rooms as well as preventing smoke from entering the adjacent room should the corridor become contaminated. As implied in Figure 1005-6, Case 1, any floor construction with the blocking as shown is also considered to satisfy the modified one-hour fire-resistive envelope requirement.

Another arrangement that would meet the code requirement is illustrated in Case 3, Figure 1004-11. The corridor walls extend to the floor or roof above and are protected on the side of the occupied use spaces by a fire-resistive membrane extending from floor to floor. In this case, the ceiling over the corridor may be considered part of a fire-resistive floor or roof assembly, and the corridor side of the ceiling protected by appropriate ceiling materials would satisfy the fire-resistance rating for the assembly. Alternatively, the code provides that the corridor ceiling could be of the same construction as permitted for corridor walls

as shown in Case 2, Figure 1004-11. This last provision is essentially an exception. In all probability, typical wall construction might not pass the one-hour test when tested in a horizontal position. However, this arrangement is considered to be adequate protection for the corridor separating it from the spaces above.

By establishing specific requirements for fire-resistive construction for corridor walls and ceilings, the code is essentially attempting to get a minimal separation between the exit corridor and the occupied use spaces. Any arrangement of the one-hour fire-resistive construction that effectively intervenes between these use spaces and the corridor would satisfy this requirement.

Having effectively protected the corridor as described above, the code then permits nonrated ceilings to be suspended below the fire-resistive ceiling provided for corridor protection. In such cases, however, such ceilings must be of noncombustible materials. In that event, it is not necessary to provide any further fire-resistive construction as shown in Case 4 of Figure 1004-11.

Corridor ventilation. Ventilation of corridors is required for certain occupancies and types of construction. Consult the light, ventilation and sanitation provisions of the occupancy and type of construction for each building under consideration. There are many restrictions as to the design of such a system. For these restrictions, the code refers the reader to Section 601.1 of the *Uniform Mechanical Code.*

1004.3.4.3.2 Openings. All openings are required to be protected except under three separate conditions. Corridors excepted from fire-resistive requirements may have unprotected openings. So may openings in corridors on the exterior walls of buildings. In a very unique provision, it states that corridors in multitheater complexes may have unprotected openings under special conditions.

1004.3.4.3.2.1 Doors. Whenever the corridor walls and ceilings are required to be of one-hour fire-resistive construction as discussed above, openings through that construction must also be protected to maintain the integrity of the separation. Therefore, whenever such fire-resistive construction is required, every interior door opening into the corridor from any other building space must be protected by a door assembly having a 20-minute fire-protection rating. Such 20-minute assemblies are referred to in the UBC as smoke- and draft-control assemblies. Their primary purpose is to minimize smoke leakage around the door and through the opening. For this reason, these doors shall not contain louvers and should not have excessive undercuts.

This protection is intended to be a two-way protection. At different times it is as important to protect the occupied use spaces from smoke in the corridor as it is under most other circumstances to protect the corridor from smoke that might be generated by a fire occurring within the use spaces. The 20-minute fire-protection rated assembly must be in compliance with UBC Standard 7-2, Part II. Essentially, this standard provides for the same test of the door as for other fire-door assemblies, except that the fire test for the 20-minute smoke- and draft-control assembly does not include the hose stream test. In addition, Part II requires the door assembly be tested for smoke infiltration.

The door and the frame are required to be appropriately labeled or otherwise identified to establish the rating of the assembly, followed by the letter "S." The name of the manufacturer of the door and the name of the service conducting the inspection of the materials and workmanship during the manufacturing process must be provided. Whether this is achieved by labeling or another type of identification or even by certification, it is important that the building official be satisfied that the assembly complies with the test standard.

For a smoke- and draft-control door to do its job, it is essential that the door be closed and, as with all fire doors, latched. Since these doors penetrating fire-resistive corridor construction are intended primarily to minimize smoke leakage, it is necessary that they be maintained self-closing or, if automatic closing, be arranged so that the closing is accomplished automatically by actuation of a smoke detector. In addition, such smoke- and draft-control doors are to be provided with a gasket around the sides and across the top of the door where the door meets the stop to further inhibit smoke leakage.

An exception permits the installation of a view port through the door for purposes of observation. These view ports must be installed under the limitations of and in accordance with the conditions specified in the exception.

Glazing in fire-rated doors. Glazing in fire-rated doors is allowed and can have unlimited area, provided that the door with the glazing is tested and labeled with the appropriate fire rating for the protection of the opening. The results of the test data for

the acceptance of a fire-rated door are not required as the agencies allowed to label such fire door assemblies are highly regulated and frequently inspected to ensure confidence in their labels.

1004.3.4.3.2.2 Windows. To maintain an effective and protective separation at the corridor wall, it is necessary to protect other penetrations as well. The code permits windows along corridor walls but requires that when they are installed they must have a three-fourths-hour fire rating in accordance with Sections 713.8 and 713.9.

The aggregate area of all openings other than doors is limited. Such cumulative area cannot exceed 25 percent of the surface area of the corridor wall measured on the side of the room that the wall is separating from the corridor. In making this 25-percent calculation, it is permissible to assume the entire area of the wall on the room side even though a portion of that area might be taken up by doors. This gross area is usable in calculating the maximum percentage of area for windows. Where the ceilings are of different heights, the lower ceiling establishes the gross area whether it is in the corridor or in the room. See Figure 1004-13.

1004.3.4.3.2.3 Duct openings. Ducts penetrating fire-resistive-rated corridor walls must also be protected, and the method of protecting such ducts is specified in Sections 713.10 and 713.11.

Skylights in corridors. Skylights may be installed in corridors since the skylights open to the exterior. As with exterior doors and windows, the UBC does not require a rated assembly for the protection of exterior openings. Any provisions regarding limitations in use are based on the material of the skylight itself or on the skylight's proximity to the property line.

Special corridor construction provisions. Refer to Section 1007 for Group E, H, I and R Occupancies for special provisions on corridor construction for these specific occupancies.

1004.3.4.4 Intervening rooms. It is required that corridors not be interrupted by intervening rooms and that they be continuous either to exterior exit doors, exit enclosures, horizontal exits or exit passageways. For example, the corridor indicated as serving the enclosed office spaces in Figure 1004-14 may not empty into an open office space. The absence of doors at the ends of the corridor as indicated in Figure 1004-15 still creates a noncomplying condition. The plan in Figure 1004-16 where the corridor is shown to be 10 feet (3048 mm) wide must still comply with the corridor requirements. However, a point could be reached where the building official could consider it as part of the open office

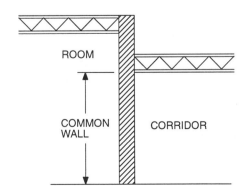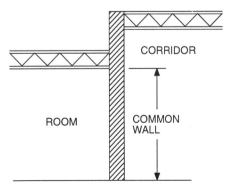

FIGURE 1004-13

209

space. Exercising good judgment is absolutely essential in such situations. This provision carries out the basic concept, which states that once a building occupant progresses to a certain level of safety—in this case the safety afforded by a corridor—that level of safety is not thereafter reduced as the building occupant proceeds through the remainder of the exit system. Therefore, the building occupant having once reached a corridor is not thereafter brought out of the corridor and reintroduced into other occupied use space of the building. The corridor must be continuous. However, here again the code emphasizes that it is possible to permit corridors to be conducted through foyers, lobbies and reception rooms. These are not to be considered as intervening spaces as long as they are constructed in accordance with the requirements for the corridor they serve.

1004.3.4.5 Elevators. This section, added in the 1991 UBC, states that lobbies must be provided for all elevators opening into corridors. These lobbies are to be provided at each floor containing such corridors and shall provide a complete separation as required by Section 1004.3.4.3.1. All the openings into the lobby wall should be protected as required by Section 1004.3.4.3.2.

There are three exceptions to these provisions. The first is that a separation need not be provided in an office building between Group B Occupancies and a street floor lobby, provided that the entire street-level floor is protected by an automatic sprinkler system. The second exception applies when elevator shaft enclosures are not required to meet the requirements of

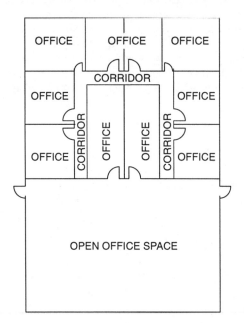

FIGURE 1004-14

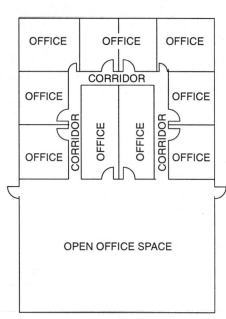

INTEROFFICE CORRIDORS

FIGURE 1004-15

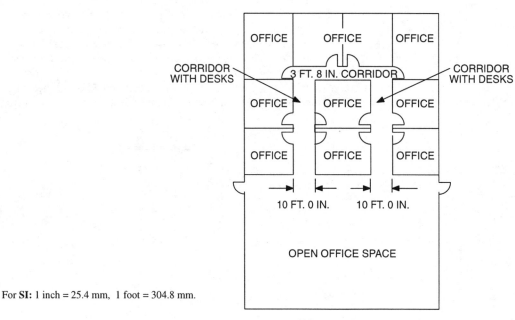

For **SI:** 1 inch = 25.4 mm, 1 foot = 304.8 mm.

FIGURE 1004-16

Section 711. The third exception is when additional doors are provided in accordance with the exception to Section 3007, which allows doors at the point of access to an elevator car, provided that they are readily operable from the car side without a special tool, key or special knowledge.

All elevator lobbies shall comply with Section 3002, which allows only hoistway and elevator car doors at the point of access to the car, unless they meet the requirements of the exception mentioned in the preceding paragraph.

SECTION 1005 — THE EXIT

1005.3.3.1 General. Consistent with the general requirements for the enclosure of vertical openings as set forth in Section 711, all vertical openings for every interior stairway, ramp or escalator must be similarly enclosed within fire-resistive construction. Since vertical openings provide probably the most readily available paths for fire spreading upward from floor to floor through buildings, it is extremely important that such vertical openings be adequately enclosed. This enclosure is required to protect and separate the vertical exitway from potential fire and the products of combustion in other spaces of the building.

Several exceptions from the enclosure requirements, however, are provided:

- In other than Groups H and I Occupancies, an enclosure is not required for a stairway, ramp or escalator that serves only one adjacent floor. Any two such atmospherically interconnected floors shall not communicate with other floors.
- Escalators installed in Group B or M Occupancy need not be enclosed when in compliance with Sections 304.6 and 309.6.
- Stairways in Group R, Division 3 Occupancies and stairways within individual dwelling units in Group R, Division 1 Occupancies need not be enclosed.
- Stairs in open parking garages as defined in Section 311.9 need not be enclosed.

Over the years the provisions of the first exception have been subject to a several interpretations. As a result, the exception was amended for the 1994 edition. Prior editions contained the phrase "and does not connect with corridors or stairways serving other floors." This phrase caused the problems. The limitation now states that when any two floors are open one to the other, neither may be open to yet another floor. This is to prevent the formation of an unprotected vertical shaft through more than two stories. This does not mean that the floors under consideration cannot have access to other floors. They can, but complying enclosures must be provided in order to do so.

Although this section mentions escalators, escalators are not permitted to provide any required exit capacity and are not an acceptable means of egress component.

1005.3.3.2 Construction. The degree of fire resistance required for exit enclosures is dependent on either the type of construction in which the exit is located or the height of the building. Where the construction is Type I or Type II fire resistive, and in all cases in buildings four or more stories in height, the enclosing construction must be two-hour fire resistive. In all other instances, required enclosures of exits may be one-hour fire-resistive construction.

Glazing complying with Sections 713.7, 713.8 and 713.9 may be used for exit enclosures in sprinklered parking garages housing private, pleasure-type vehicles.

1005.3.3.3 Extent of enclosure. One of the basic concepts governing safe means of egress design is that once a building occupant, as that occupant proceeds through the exit system, is brought to a certain level of safety, that level of safety is not reduced for that occupant throughout the rest of the exit system. Therefore, once an enclosure is required for an exit component, it is necessary that the enclosure be continuous and provide continuous protection throughout the remainder of the system until the building occupant reaches at least the exterior of the building. Consistent with this concept, it is required that the enclosures of exits be continuous and that they protect all the portions of the path of travel until arrival at the exit discharge or the public way.

Fire-resistive enclosure continuity. Therefore, as vertical exitways reach successive floors, if there is any travel on that floor or in the corridor on that floor, the enclosure construction must be arranged to also protect that portion of travel. In addition, when the occupant reaches the floor level that provides access to the exterior of the building, any travel on that floor level must be similarly enclosed. The required enclosure for this portion of the exit is the same as that required for the enclosure of the exit stairway that it serves. Again, this protection must be continuous to the exterior of the building. Any openings in such exit passageway providing for that horizontal travel must also be protected with fire-protection assemblies as required for openings in the vertical enclosure that it serves. It must also be stressed that openings into the exit passageway that connect the stairway to the building exterior must not only comply with Section 1005.3.3.5 requirements for fire-protection rating, type of door closure and heat-transmission limitations, but these openings are also limited to those openings necessary for exiting a normally occupied space.

In those few instances where it is permitted to have stairways without enclosing protection as specified in Section 1005.3.3.3, it is not necessary to provide an enclosed, protected corridor or exit passageway to the exterior of the building from those unenclosed stairs.

Continuity exception. An exception to the requirement for the continuity of exit enclosures is permitted in office buildings, Group 1, Division 1.1 hospitals and nursing homes. A maximum of 50 percent of the exits may pass through a street-floor lobby, provided this part of the exit system affords the width required to serve the occupant load. Also, the lobby must provide unobstructed travel through to the exterior of the building. Utilization of this exception is permitted when the entire floor of the building. Utilization of this exception is permitted when the entire floor of the building that contains the lobby is protected with an automatic sprinkler system.

This is an example where the code appears to depart from the basic premise of the concept of continuity of protection by allowing the enclosing construction to not extend to the exterior of the building. However, when it does so it imposes the condition that the entire floor level be completely protected with an automatic sprinkler system. In this limited situation, the installation of the sprinkler system compensates for the lack of the enclosure and provides a level of safety equivalent to that which would be afforded to the building occupant if the enclosure had been made continuous to the outside. Where the street-floor lobby is an extension of an exit passageway that requires protection in accordance with Sections 1005.3.3.3 and 1005.3.3.5, such protection is required for the lobby.

1005.3.3.4 Barrier. The barrier required by this section prevents persons from accidentally continuing into the basement. Directional exit signs as specified in Section 1003.2.8 are also required.

1005.3.3.5 Openings and penetrations. Since the vertical exitways in buildings are so fundamental to the safety of building occupants and their ability to safely exit a building in a fire emergency, the code is careful to protect the integrity of the enclosure of the vertical exitway in every way possible. In addition to the fire-resistive construction required of the enclosure, the openings that are permitted to penetrate the fire-resistive enclosure of the vertical exitway are narrowly limited. This section establishes very clearly that only those openings necessary to provide exit facilities for the occupants of the building spaces and openings in the exterior walls are permitted.

Since the exterior walls of an enclosed vertical stairway are not protecting the stairway from other building spaces, openings through the exterior wall and to the atmosphere are permitted. In fact, in buildings that are so located on the property that there would be no requirement for the fire-resistive construction of the exterior wall or for the protection of the openings in such wall, the exterior wall of a stair enclosure could be eliminated entirely. However, such openings must comply with the appropriate requirements of the code relating to the location of those openings with respect to property lines or to other potential exterior fire exposures.

This provision also makes it clear that it is the intent of the code to prohibit openings from nonoccupant spaces directly into the exit enclosure. Therefore, it is not permitted to provide openings from such spaces as storerooms, equipment rooms, machinery rooms, electrical rooms and similar rooms directly into the vertical exit enclosure.

Other penetrations into the exit enclosure are prohibited unless necessary to service or protect the exit enclosure. All such penetrations shall be made in a manner that will maintain the structural and fire-resistive integrity of the enclosure and shall be detailed on the plans in compliance with the second paragraph of Section 106.3.3.

When openings for exit doorways are provided in exit enclosures, it is necessary that they be protected with a fire-rated assembly. Where the enclosing construction must be two-hour fire resistive, the assembly protecting the opening must have a one and one-half-hour fire-protection rating. Where the enclosing construction need only be one-hour fire resistive, the assembly protecting the opening must have a one-hour fire-protection rating. To properly protect the penetration of the stair enclosure, such doors must be maintained either as self-closing doors or as automatic-closing doors by activation of a smoke detector. Requirements for the installation of such automatic-closing doors are specified in Section 713.2.

In addition to the normal requirement for fire doors, the *Uniform Building Code* is concerned that fire doors installed in openings in vertical exit enclosures be capable of limiting the temperature transmission through the door. It specifies that the temperature rise above ambient temperature be limited to a maximum of 450°F (232°C) at the end of 30 minutes of the normal fire test.

The purpose of the enclosed vertical exitway and the protection of openings into that enclosure is to protect the building occupants while they are exiting the building. It is intended that in a properly enclosed and protected vertical exitway, building occupants from the floors above the fire floor will be able to pass through the fire floor inside the enclosure and eventually pass down and out of the building. The end-point limitation on temperature transmission through the fire door, then, is literally to protect the person inside the enclosure from excessive heat radiation from the fire door as he or she passes through the fire floor. This limitation on temperature transmission for such doors is unique to the UBC and will better protect persons inside the enclosed exitway.

1005.3.3.6 Use of space under stairway or ramp. To protect as well as possible the integrity of this most important element of the exit system, any enclosed space under a stair or a ramp inside an exit enclosure must not be used for any purpose. It is the express intent of the code that such spaces be maintained free of any combustibles or any other contents that could conceivably interfere with the use of the exit for exit purposes. In those instances where such space inside the exit enclosure is not enclosed but open, the code also prohibits the use of that space for any purpose. One of the conditions frequently found in buildings is that building operators or tenants find such spaces convenient for use as storage spaces or paint lockers. Such use could easily adversely impact the use of the enclosed exit stair as an exit.

It is possible, however, that the space could be used given proper construction and arrangement of the exit enclosure. The use of such space is prohibited only if it occurs inside the exit enclosure. If the protective construction of the exit enclosure can be arranged so that it intervenes between the space under the stair and the stairway or ramp itself, that space is no longer in the exit enclosure and is usable. In such an arrangement, however, there may be no opening between that space and the stair enclosure. Access to the space must be provided by means other than the exit enclosure. This arrangement can frequently be achieved by providing the necessary fire resistance in the construction of the stairs. Such an arrangement and the use of space under the stair for an elevator machine room is shown in Figure 1005-1.

1005.3.3.7 Pressurized enclosure. Under certain conditions of building occupancy, protection of the vertical exitways over and above that required in the more usual situations is warranted. Therefore, under certain conditions it is necessary that the vertical exit be pressurized. A pressurized enclosure is a special arrangement of the vertical exitway to minimize, if not prevent, the infiltration of smoke and other products of combustion into the actual stairway. Therefore, a pressurized enclosure is one where the building occupant does not enter the stair enclosure directly from the occupied space of the building. Rather, an arrangement is made whereby occupants enter the stairway through a vestibule that is mechanically ventilated and then trav-

(Continued on page 214)

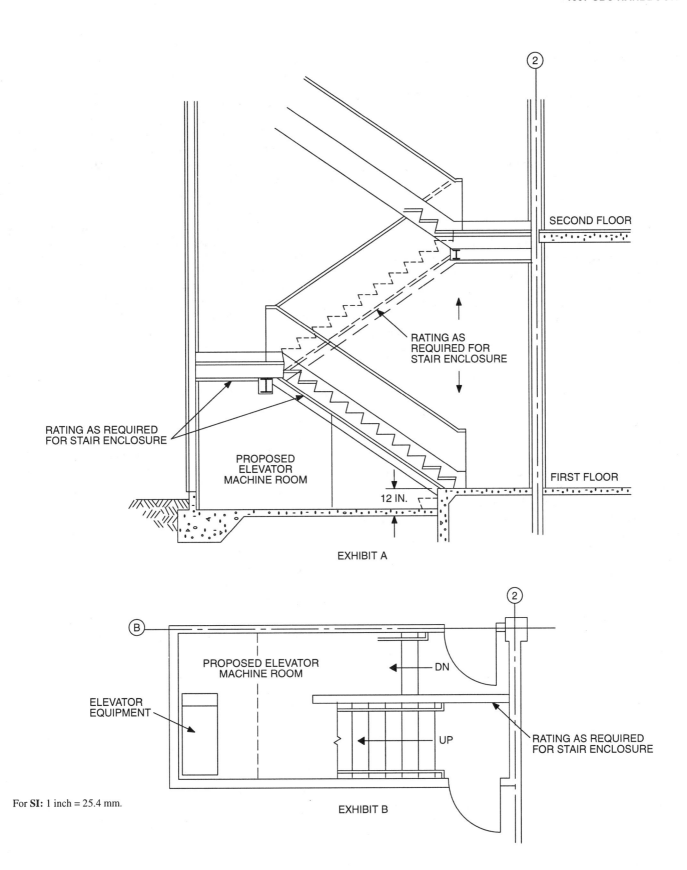

RATING AS
REQUIRED FOR
STAIR ENCLOSURE

SECOND FLOOR

RATING AS REQUIRED
FOR STAIR ENCLOSURE

PROPOSED
ELEVATOR
MACHINE ROOM

FIRST FLOOR

12 IN.

EXHIBIT A

PROPOSED ELEVATOR
MACHINE ROOM

DN

ELEVATOR
EQUIPMENT

UP

RATING AS REQUIRED
FOR STAIR ENCLOSURE

For **SI:** 1 inch = 25.4 mm.

EXHIBIT B

USE OF SPACE UNDER STAIRS AND RAMPS

FIGURE 1005-1

(Continued from page 212)

el from the vestibule through a separate door opening into the actual enclosed stairway.

When required. It is required that all exits in buildings be pressurized enclosures whenever the building has a floor used for human occupancy that is located more than 75 feet (22 860 mm) above the lowest level of fire department vehicle access. This condition is recognized as the definition of a high-rise building found in Section 403. However, required exits in all buildings meeting the high-rise definition must be pressurized enclosures, whereas Section 403 applies only to Group R, Division 1 Occupancies and Group B offices.

In a pressurized stair, the system is arranged so that, through mechanical pressurization to a positive level, the stair enclosure is maintained essentially free of contamination by the products of combustion. The specifications require that the stairway enclosure be provided with a controlled relief vent at its upper portion and that it be supplied with sufficient air to discharge at least 2,500 cubic feet per minute (1180 L/s) through the relief opening at the designed pressure difference. The mechanical equipment supplying the air must be activated by operation of an approved fire alarm system or, when there is no such system, by initiation of a smoke detector located outside the stair enclosure within 5 feet (1524 mm) of the vestibule entry.

Pressurization for the enclosure shall be accomplished in the manner set forth in Section 905.

A bit of history. Prior to the 1994 edition, the UBC contained a section that set forth provisions for "smokeproof" enclosures. These smokeproof enclosures were required at the same height as the pressurized enclosures specified in the 1994 edition. There were, however, two options for providing a smokeproof stairway enclosure: by natural ventilation and by mechanical ventilation. The mechanical option was quite similar to the pressurized enclosure now required by the UBC, while the natural ventilation option is no longer available for new construction. Many older buildings, however, still have this type of smokeproof enclosure. The prior provisions for providing a smokeproof enclosure by mechanical means contained a fairly detailed, prescriptive outline of what was needed to achieve the "smokeproof" enclosure. Almost all these prescriptive requirements have vanished from the pressurized enclosure provisions of Section 1005.3.3.7 and the smoke-control provisions of Section 905 to which they are related. Those needing more information about the older types of smokeproof enclosure should refer to an earlier version of this handbook.

1005.3.3.7.1 Vestibules. Pressurized enclosures are required to be provided with a pressurized entrance vestibule. The vestibule is intended to accomplish three things. First, it eases the demand placed on the pressurization system for the stairway enclosure by providing a buffer between a fire floor and the enclosure. This is accomplished by establishing pressure differences between the vestibule and a fire floor and between the vestibule and the enclosure. The vestibule must have a positive pressure relative to the fire floor and negative pressure relative to the enclosure.

Second, the vestibule provides an area of refuge where persons with disabilities can remain temporarily while awaiting instructions or assistance during an emergency. In fact, the code specifically requires that the vestibule have sufficient area to accommodate one wheelchair space, with Section 1104.2.3

requiring that each space must not be less than 30 inches by 48 inches (762 mm by 1219 mm). These set-aside spaces shall not obstruct the required exit width nor shall they be located where they will interfere with fire department hose connections and valves. To enhance safety and allow fire command personnel to identify locations where building occupants may have sought refuge, each vestibule must be provided with an approved occupant sensing device that will register the presence of an occupant at the fire-control room. More information about areas of refuge is presented in the discussion of Chapter 11.

Third, the vestibule is intended to provide a staging area for firefighters to launch an attack on the fire without compromising the integrity of the stairway enclosure to which it is attached. Vestibules are required by Section 904.5.3 to contain the standpipe outlet connections. It must also contain two-way communication capability, which is connected directly to the fire-control room, and it must be provided with emergency illumination at a level of 30 footcandles (323 lx) at the floor.

Extent of enclosure. From the wording in Section 1005.3.3.7.1, one might conclude that the required vestibule is outside of the stairway enclosure. This, however, is not what is intended. Figure 1005-2 shows the configuration intended by the code. To fulfill its purpose of providing a smoke-free exitway and serving as an area of refuge, the vestibule must be within the confines of the two-hour enclosure walls.

The complex matter of smoke management and smoke control requires particularly competent design. Just as a high-rise building's structural safety depends on well-detailed, properly designed structural systems, the building's fire and life safety depends on well-detailed, properly designed fire- and smoke-control systems. More information is available in *Smoke Control in Fire Safety Design*.[6]

1005.3.4 Exit passageways.

1005.3.4.1 General. Exit passageways serving as an exit in a means of egress system shall comply with the requirements of Section 1005.3.4.

Travel distance in exit passageways. Once a building occupant is inside an exit passageway, there is no subsequent limitation on travel distance. However, the exit passageway must be continuous to a public way. As an exit component, must also be separated from other occupied-use spaces of the building to provide a protected path of travel for the building occupants seeking exit. Exit passageways are required to be enclosed with walls, floors and ceilings of fire-resistive construction, and the degree of fire resistance required is as specified for the type of construction in which the passageway is located. In no event, however, may the enclosing and separating construction of an exit passageway be less than one-hour fire resistive. Unless a more restrictive requirement applies by virtue of the application of some other provision of the code, openings into exit passageways must be protected by assemblies having a fire-resistive rating of not less than one hour. As is the case with enclosures of exit stairs, there may be no openings into exit passageways other than those serving normally occupied spaces, which are required for exiting from those spaces.

Uses of exit passageways. Exit passageways are commonly used in several different exiting situations. It is required in Section 1005.3.3.3 that interior stairways be enclosed and that the enclosure extend completely to the exterior of the building, in-

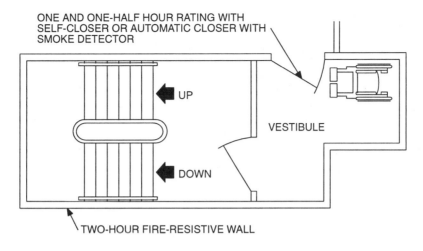

ONE AND ONE-HALF HOUR RATING WITH
SELF-CLOSER OR AUTOMATIC CLOSER WITH
SMOKE DETECTOR

UP

DOWN

VESTIBULE

TWO-HOUR FIRE-RESISTIVE WALL

PRESSURIZED ENCLOSURE

FIGURE 1005-2

cluding, if necessary, an exit passageway on the floor of the building leading to the exterior. When used in this configuration, the exit passageway assumes the same fire-protection requirements as for the stairway it serves.

A growing use of exit passageways is in connection with covered mall buildings. Since most tenant spaces in covered malls require more than one exit, and since Section 404.4.5 limits travel distance within individual tenant spaces of 200 feet (60 960 mm), it is common practice to construct an exit passageway to serve as the secondary exit from the rear of a series of tenant spaces. The exit passageway leads to exterior openings in the building at a limited number of locations so that it is not necessary to have an exterior exit door from each individual tenant space.

Another example of the use of exit passageways in covered mall buildings results from the fact that travel distance in the mall is also limited to a maximum of 200 feet (60 960 mm). It will occasionally be necessary between major exits from the mall to introduce an exit passageway or provide an additional exit to satisfy the requirements limiting travel distance. By the use of such exit passageways, it is possible to locate the main entrance/exit points to the mall building at substantially greater intervals.

A historic use of exit passageways is in buildings that have very large floor areas. In such buildings it is sometimes not possible to get the building occupants to the exits within the limitations of the permitted travel distance. Therefore, an exit passageway is used to literally bring the exit to the interior of the spaces and to the building occupant so that it is possible for any building occupant to reach and enter into the exit passageway within the permitted travel distance. This type of exit passageway is frequently accomplished by constructing, in effect, a special type of fire-resistive corridor. It can also be accomplished by constructing either an overhead, fire-resistive, enclosed passageway or a tunnel. By these latter means it is possible to avoid manufacturing processes and other functions at floor level within the building.

Again, it should be noted that once in an exit passageway, the building occupant is considered to be in a relatively safe location and travel distances within the exit passageway are not limited, just as travel distances within enclosed exit stairs in very tall buildings are not limited.

Detailed requirements. In most cases the primary differences between an exit passageway and an exit corridor lie in the respective requirements for opening protection and the fact that the passageway requires a complete enclosure, including ceiling and floor of at least one-hour fire-resistive construction.

1005.3.5 Horizontal exits. The horizontal exit may well be the least understood and most under-utilized component in an exit system. It can be a very effective method for providing adequate required exiting capacity while at the same time realizing some very substantial construction cost and space savings.

A horizontal exit consists essentially of separating a floor into parts by dividing it with construction having a two-hour fire-resistive rating. Such construction completely divides the floor of the building. The construction of this wall divides the floor into fire compartments. The concept of the horizontal exit is to permit each of these fire compartments to serve as an area of refuge for occupants in one or more of the fire compartments in the event of a fire emergency. Building occupants in the compartment of fire origin may then pass through the two-hour fire-resistive horizontal exit into the compartment of refuge. They thereby gain sufficient protection and sufficient time for either the extinguishment of the fire and the elimination of the fire threat or the orderly use of the remaining exits from the compartment serving as the area of refuge.

Probably the horizontal exit is used most frequently in hospitals and in detention and correctional facilities where total evacuation from the building may present numerous physical and other problems. If in a health-care facility it is necessary to move patients from their rooms in a fire emergency, it is desirable to avoid the need for moving them vertically by stairs. Therefore, if an arrangement can be provided whereby patients would only be subject to horizontal movement, the safety of the building occupant can be far more easily achieved. While horizontal exits are most frequently used in the referenced types of occupancies, they can often be used quite effectively in any occupancy. In fact, in those instances where occupancy separations of two-hour fire resistance or greater are provided, and in all situations where conforming area separation walls are installed, the resulting arrangement is tailor-made for use as a horizontal exit.

Section 1005.3.5.1 defines a horizontal exit as a wall that completely divides a floor of a building into two or more separate exit-access areas to afford safety from fire and smoke in the exit-accesss area of incident origin. The requirement that the two-hour wall be constructed as required for a two-hour occupancy separation is very significant. This analogy is made to ensure the protection of openings and penetrations in the wall.

When properly constructed and installed, a horizontal exit may serve as a required exit. It may, in fact, be substituted on a one-for-one basis for other types of exits. However, in no instance may horizontal exits be used as the only exit from a portion of a building or to provide more than one half the total required number of exits from any building space.

An arrangement of the use of a horizontal exit may be illustrated by the following example: An office building containing three floors having an occupant load of 600 persons per floor has a two-hour fire-resistive area separation wall extending completely through the building and dividing it into two approxi-

mately equal sections, each containing stairways. By utilizing the two-hour fire-resistive wall as a horizontal exit and providing passage of the appropriate width from each compartment to the other through the two-hour wall, it is possible to eliminate one of the enclosed stairways from each of the compartments. By use of the horizontal exit, a building that would otherwise be required to have four enclosed exit stairs would now need only two, since each compartment is, in addition to the stairway, provided with a horizontal exit. Figure 1005-3 depicts possible arrangements for horizontal exits.

1005.3.5.3 Openings and penetrations. In all instances when protection of openings in two-hour fire-resistive walls is required, such opening protection must consist of an assembly having a fire-protection rating of at least one and one-half hours. Openings through a horizontal exit are required to be protected, and thus must have a minimum fire-resistive rating of one and one-half hours. When installed through a horizontal exit wall, these openings must be self-closing, as is typical for one and one-half-hour assemblies, or they must be automatic closing, smoke detector-actuated assemblies identical to those required by Item 3 of Section 713.6.1 for fire doors installed across a corridor. In fact, when a horizontal exit is installed across a corridor or when a corridor terminates at a horizontal exit, the smoke detector-actuated automatic-closing assemblies must be used.

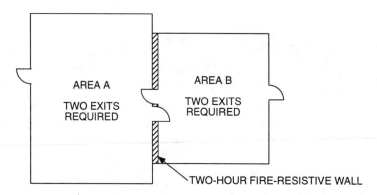

HORIZONTAL EXIT SHALL NOT SERVE AS THE ONLY EXIT FROM AN AREA.

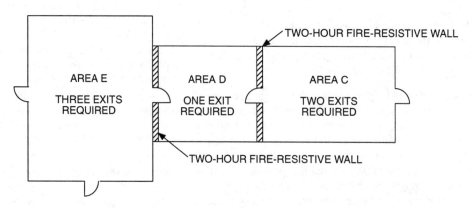

WHEN TWO OR MORE EXITS ARE REQUIRED, NOT MORE THAN ONE-HALF THE TOTAL NUMBER OF EXITS AND ONE HALF OF THE EXIT WIDTH MAY BE HORIZONTAL EXITS.

HORIZONTAL EXITS

FIGURE 1005-3

As is the case with any exit door, doors in horizontal exits must swing in the direction of exit travel when serving an occupant load of 50 or more as provided in Section 1003.3.1.5. When the horizontal exit is to be used for exiting in both directions, it will be necessary to provide separate exit doors for the separate directions to satisfy this requirement.

1005.3.5.4 Refuge area. The area of refuge in a horizontal exit configuration must be sized to provide sufficient space for the total occupant load of both the fire compartment and the compartment of refuge for a limited period of time. It is necessary for building occupants to remain in the area of refuge only long enough to permit the extinguishment of the fire and the elimination of the fire threat or to allow the combined occupant load of the two compartments to utilize the remaining exit facilities from the compartment of refuge. If, for example, it would take the entire occupant load of the floor five minutes to evacuate that floor under another exiting configuration, it would then take the occupant load of that floor 10 minutes to evacuate the compartment of refuge utilizing the remaining exit.

To reasonably accommodate the combined occupant loads in the compartment of refuge, the code requires that there be provided at least 3 square feet (0.27 m^2) of net clear floor area for each ambulatory occupant. In Group I, Division 1.1 Occupancies, it is required that there be provided at least 15 square feet (1.4 m^2) of clear floor area for each ambulatory person and at least 30 square feet (2.8 m^2) for each such nonambulatory occupant. As in hospitals, such nonambulatory occupants will frequently be brought into the compartment of refuge either in a hospital bed or on a gurney.

It is also important to provide such required area for occupants in spaces that will, in fact, be available to the occupants of the building as they enter the compartment of refuge. Such space can be provided in corridors, hallways and other public spaces, as long as it is sufficient to accommodate the total occupant load at the appropriate rate of area per person. While these area figures will permit a rather dense occupancy in the area of refuge, it must be remembered that the occupancy of that space is only temporary and that the occupants of the area of refuge will continue to evacuate the area of refuge by use of the remaining exits. In a fire emergency, such space per person is considered adequate for a short period of time.

In the design of a horizontal exit system, it must be emphasized that it is not necessary to accumulate the total occupant load of the two compartments and then provide exit capacity for that total occupant load from each of the compartments. Were that the case, the horizontal exit would really provide no benefit. Also, in designing a horizontal exit arrangement, one simply treats the separated compartments as if they were, in fact, separate buildings. Each compartment is provided with an exit system that is in compliance with all of the various criteria for a total exit system from a building. The only difference is that in this configuration one of the exits from the separated compartments is a horizontal exit into the compartment of refuge. To support this statement, it is noted that the definition in Section 1004.2.5.1 for travel distance identifies the horizontal exit as one of the end points for measuring travel distance. Once a building occupant gets to and passes through a horizontal exit, the code considers that occupant to be in an area of safety at least equivalent to the level of safety afforded by an enclosed exit stairway.

SECTION 1006 — THE EXIT DISCHARGE

1006.1 General. This section regulates the exit discharge portion of the egress system. This is the last portion of the three-part means of egress system and is the portion between the point where an occupant leaves an exit and continues until they reach a public way. For conceptual ease, all exterior travel is considered as a part of the exit discharge. This will include exterior exit stairways, exterior exit balconies, exit courts and yards. In lieu of extending the exit discharge to the public way, an exception permits the use of a safe dispersal area. For buildings that are a great distance from the public way, or that have problems with the access to it, the exception permits the building official to accept a level of safety equivalent to reaching the public way. The building official shall size and locate the safe dispersal areas based on a variety of factors, including occupant load served, mobility of occupants, construction type, height and fire protection features of the building, and degree of hazard of the occupancy. In no case shall the dispersal area be located within 50 feet (15 240 mm) of the building.

To reduce potential obstruction within the path of egress travel, the exit discharge at grade is required to be permanently maintained. There must be no alterations that would reduce the egress capacity or obstruct the exitway.

1006.2.1 Location. The general location provisions for the exit discharge are located in this section. The first sentence that requires the exit discharge to be at grade or have direct access to grade to important since it will provide the tie to Sections 1006.2.2 and 1006.2.3 for the situations where the exit discharge is at other than grade level. The prohibition against reentering the building is to ensure that the user does not go back into any portion of the building once they have reached the exit discharge. This prohibition can be viewed as excluding the reentry into exit enclosures, exit passageways or any portion that would be considered as a part of the exit access.

Due to exposure potential from adjacent property, exit discharge components other than exit courts and yards are prohibited in areas where building openings are prohibited or required to be protected by Table 5-A.

1006.2.2 Access to grade. The provisions of this section apply when exits occur at other than grade level. They primarily deal with the use of exterior exit balconies and the need for at least two paths of exit travel from the upper floors of a building. In a manner similar to hallways and corridors, the path of travel must be arranged so that there are no dead ends exceeding 20 feet (6096 mm) in length. Exception 1 allows an occupant load of less than 10 to have only one path of travel from the point which an exit discharges. Exception 2 permits a single path of exit travel where exterior exit stairways are accessed directly from an exit. The exceptions do not alter the number of exits that are required from a level by Section 1004.2.3.2.

1006.2.3 Travel distance. Travel distance to the public way or a safe dispersal areas is not limited once an occupant reaches grade level. However, since some exit discharge may occur at other than grade level, a travel distance limitation is mandated. In buildings not equipped with an automatic sprinkler system throughout, this maximum distance is 200 feet (60 960 mm). In a fully sprinklered building, the limitation is 250 feet (76 200 mm). This travel distance begins at a point where the occupant leaves an exit and continues until reaching grade level. These travel distances are in addition to the distances that an occupant travels within the exit access in order to reach the exit.

The fact that additional travel distance is given for exterior paths at other than the grade level was first introduced in the 1997 edition of the UBC. Previously, this distance would have been included as a part of the general travel distance requirements. The distance of travel on unenclosed stairways or ramps with the exit discharge is to be included in the travel distance limitation.

1006.3 Exit Discharge Components.

1006.3.1 General. The general concept of the exit discharge portion of the means of egress is that the components be sufficiently open to the exterior to prevent the accumulation of smoke and toxic gases.

1006.3.2 Exterior exit balconies.

1006.3.2.1 General. An exterior exit balcony is one the components of the exit discharge. It is defined as a balcony, landing or porch projecting from a wall of a building and used for egress purposes.

1006.3.2.2 Width. The minimum required width of exterior exit balconies is consistent with that established for hallways and corridors. Such width shall not be less than 36 inches (914 mm) when serving an occupant load of less than 50, otherwise, the minimum is 44 inches (1118 mm). In no case shall the width ever be less than that specified in Section 1003.2.3. Projections and obstructions into an exterior exit balcony are also limited in the same manner as hallways and corridors.

1006.3.2.3 Construction. When an exterior exit balcony projects from the wall of a Type I or Type II building, it must be of noncombustible construction. When projecting from a Type III, IV or V building, the projection may be of either noncombustible or combustible construction. Regardless of the type of construction, fire-resistive construction is not required unless the balcony serves an occupant load of 10 or more in a Group R, Division 1 or Group I Occupancy. Under these conditions, walls of an exterior exit balcony shall be of not less than one-hour construction and ceilings must not be less than that required for a one-hour floor or roof system.

Since there is potential exposure to a fire condition for occupants utilizing an exterior exit balcony during evacuation of a building, a minimum level of fire protection is mandated. However, there is no requirement for the protection of openings in such walls. In addition, exterior sides of these balconies need not be of fire-resistive construction and when the building is of combustible construction, the balcony roof assemblies may be of heavy-timber construction having no concealed spaces.

1006.3.2.4 Openness. One of the features of an exterior exit balcony is its openness to the atmosphere, limiting the amount of smoke and toxic gas accumulation. To qualify as part of the exit discharge, the balcony must be at least 50 percent open on the long side. It is also necessary that the open areas above the guardrail be distributed to allow for adequate natural ventilation.

1006.3.3 Exterior exit stairways.

1006.3.3.1 General. An exterior exit stairway serves as an exit discharge component in the means of egress system. To be classified as an exterior stair, it must be open on at least two adjacent sides. The open sides must than adjoin open areas such as yard, exit courts or public ways. By limiting the number of sides enclosed by the building, an exterior stair will be sufficiently open to the exterior to prevent the accumulation of smoke and toxic gases. Any stairway that does not comply with this criteria is considered an interior stairway.

1006.3.3.2 Construction. Exterior stairways are required to be constructed of materials consistent with the type of construction of the building. Unlike interior stairways, there can be no enclosed usable space under exterior exit stairways. In fact, the open space under such stairways is not allowed to be used for any purpose.

1006.3.3.3 Protection of exterior wall openings. Whenever an exterior exit stairway is installed as a component in a means of egress system, it is important to protect the stair user from potential exposure to any fire that might occur in the building. Therefore, in other than Group R, Division 3 Occupancies and open parking garages, or unless two separated exterior stairways are served by a common exterior exit balcony, when exterior stairways serve buildings over two stories in height or serve a level where exterior wall openings occur in two or more floors below, all openings in the exterior wall below or within 10 feet (3048 mm) of the exterior stairway must be protected by a self-closing fire assembly having a three-fourths-hour fire-protection rating. Figure 1003-25 identifies those openings that must be protected. This protection for a exterior stairway is important if the stairway is going to be usable as an exit component in a fire emergency.

1006.3.4 Exterior exit ramps.

1006.3.4.1 General. When an exterior exit ramp serves as a component of the exit discharge, it shall be addressed in the same manner as an exterior exit stairway.

1006.3.5 Exit courts.

1006.3.5.1 General. An exit court is defined as any yard or court located on the property with the building it serves, which is also used as access to a public way for one or more required exits. As such, the code requires that every exit court discharge into a public way. In the case of exit courts abutting a public way, this is accomplished very easily. Occasionally, however, the building official may approve the use of a safe dispersal areas as the end point of the means of egress system. In such situations, the exit court need only lead to the discharge area. See Figure 1006-1.

1006.3.5.2 Width. The minimum required width of an exit court is determined in the same manner as is the minimum required width of a hallway or corridor. An exit court must provide at least 44 inches (1118 mm) of clear width in all occupancies except Group R, Division 3 and Group U Occupancies, where the width may be reduced to 36 inches (914 mm). When exit courts are subject to use by a sufficiently large occupant load, the required width may be wider than 44 inches (1118 mm). Such greater width would be determined in accordance with the appli-

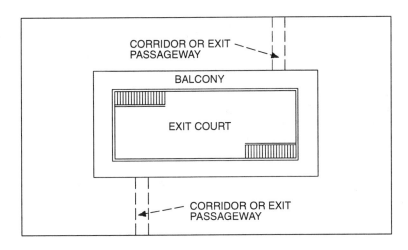

TYPICAL EXIT COURT

FIGURE 1006-1

cable provisions of Section 1003.2.3 based on the occupant load served. Whatever the required width of the exit court, there must be at least 7 feet (2134 mm) of unobstructed headroom.

In no event may the minimum required width be less than that required by the above paragraph. However, should the actual width of an exit court be greater than the minimum required and it becomes necessary to reduce the width of the court as the building occupants proceed toward the public way, such reduction in width cannot be an abrupt change. The changes must be effected by making an angle of not more than 30 degrees with the axis of the exit court so that the reduction in width is a gradual one.

1006.3.5.3 Construction and openings. Since an exit court is a component in a means of egress system, building occupants utilizing that component must be afforded sufficient protection to reasonably ensure that they will reach the safety of the public way. Therefore, any time an exit court serves an occupant load of 10 or more and is less than 10 feet (3048 mm) in width, the walls of the exit court must be of one-hour fire-resistive construction for a height of 10 feet (3048 mm) above the floor of the court. By this means a fire-resistive separation is maintained between the persons in the court and occupied use spaces of the building. Should any openings through the portion of the exit court wall be required to be fire resistive, those openings must be protected by assemblies having a fire-protection rating of not less than three-fourths hour.

SECTION 1007 — MEANS OF EGRESS REQUIREMENTS BASED ON OCCUPANCY

1007.2 Group A Occupancies.

1007.2.1 Main exit. This section provides special exiting requirements for Group A Occupancies. The first specification is that every Division 1, 2 and 2.1 Occupancy must be provided with a main exit. The minimum required width of this main exit is determined by either of two criteria. The rule that would produce the larger required width for the main exit is the one that would govern the required minimum size.

In these occupancies, every main exit must have sufficient width to accommodate one half of the total occupant load. In addition, its width shall not be less than the total required widths of all aisles, exit passageways and stairways that lead to the main exit. Finally, the main exit must be connected by appropriate exit components to ensure that the occupants have continuous and unobstructed access to a public way.

Basically, the requirement that the main exit be adequate to accommodate 50 percent of the total occupant load takes into account a characteristic of human nature. The majority of the occupants are, in all probability, not completely familiar with the facility and its exit system. As a consequence, in the event of an emergency it is typical that people will attempt to reach the exit through which they entered. This natural tendency could put an unduly large load on the main exit if it were not sized according to this requirement.

1007.2.2 Side exits. In addition to requiring that the main exit accommodate 50 percent of the total occupant load, it is also necessary that every auditorium in Group A, Divisions 1, 2 and 2.1 Occupancies be provided with exits on each side. These side exits are required to be of sufficient capacity to accommodate two thirds of the total occupant load, with the exits on each side accommodating at least one third. These side exits must be separate exits and are required to open directly to a public way or into an exit or exit discharge leading to a public way. Where side exits are provided, there must be a cross aisle leading directly to that exit so that from a cross aisle it is not necessary to utilize any other aisle in the auditorium to gain access to the side exit. Egress to and through the side exits is essentially direct by virtue of these cross aisles.

1007.2.3 Balcony exits. Consistent with the basic requirement for number of exits contained in Section 1004.2.3.2, every balcony that has an occupant load of more than 10 must be provided with a minimum of two remote, separate exits. In some Group A Occupancies, more than one balcony is provided. These requirements for balcony exits apply to any and all balconies in the building. In all cases the exits required from balconies must open directly into an exterior stair, an approved stairway or a ramp. As is the case of the side exits from the main auditorium, balcony exits shall also be accessible by means of a cross aisle. In addition, the basic number and distribution of exits shall be as required by Sections 1004.2.3.2 and 1004.2.4 and other applicable provisions of Chapter 10.

1007.2.5 Panic hardware. The Group A Occupancy is one of those occupancy groups that requires the installation of panic hardware. Therefore, any exit door in this occupancy that is serving an occupant load of 50 or more and is provided with a latching or locking device must also be provided with panic hardware in accordance with the provisions in Section 1003.3.1.9. If the door is not lockable and is free to swing for exiting purposes, it is not necessary to install the panic hardware, since there is no lock or latch to overcome.

Key locks on main exit doors. Special exception is made for churches and for other Group A, Division 3 Occupancies, whereby it is permitted to key lock the main exit door under certain specified conditions. However, this can be done only when the main exit consists of a single door or a single pair of doors. The basic objective of this provision is to ensure that the main exit is a single opening. If, in that situation, the building is occupied, in all probability the occupants entered through the main exit. Therefore, the main exit is unlocked and available for emergency egress. In the event the occupant load of the building is such that the main exit must consist of more than one opening to provide sufficient capacity to accommodate the occupant load, this exception may not be used.

When the key-locking device is permitted, a readily visible sign reading THIS DOOR MUST REMAIN UNLOCKED DURING BUSINESS HOURS must be located immediately adjacent to the doorway. Lettering of the sign shall be at least 1 inch (25 mm) high and be on a contrasting background.

When unlocked, all leaves of the main exit doorway must be free to swing without operation of any latching device. When a pair of doors is installed in the opening, the doors must be arranged so that both leaves will unlock simultaneously by a single unlocking action. The use of any flush bolt, edge bolt, surface bolt or any other device to restrain any door leaf is expressly prohibited.

The building official is specifically granted authority to withdraw permission to use this exception for locking of the main exit door should the arrangement not be maintained in keeping with the terms of the exception.

Facilities such as stadiums may be enclosed by fencing or similar enclosures. The requirement for panic hardware does not apply to gates through such enclosures, provided the gates are under constant and immediate supervision while the stadium is occupied. However, there must be a safe dispersal area of a size sufficient to accommodate the occupant load of the stadium based on 3 square feet (0.28 m²) per person and located between the stadium and the fence or other enclosure. Such dispersal area must not be less than 50 feet (15 240 mm) from the stadium that it serves.

1007.3 Group E Occupancies.

1007.3.1 Definitions. This section contains special requirements that apply to Group E Occupancies. These special requirements are to be used in conjunction with the general exiting provisions of Chapter 10. If any provision within these special requirements differs from a similar provision elsewhere in Chapter 10, the special provisions of this section govern.

Because of the nature of some of the special provisions relating to Group E Occupancies, it is necessary to provide special definitions of certain terms used.

Definition of room. For the purposes of this section, a space is to be considered to be a room if it is bounded by any obstruction to exit travel on more than 80 percent of its perimeter. In some school configurations, areas are identified by means of furniture, part-height partitions, filing cabinets, bookcases and other types of furnishings. When these are used to define a space or area and occur on at least 80 percent of the perimeter, that space or area is identified as a room. For the purpose of determining the unobstructed perimeter, any opening that has a clear width of less than 3 feet (914 mm) and a height of less than 6 feet 8 inches (2032 mm) is not to be considered part of the unobstructed perimeter.

As used in this section, an interior room is one that does not have direct access to an exit corridor and whose only exit is through an adjoining or intervening room.

Definition of separate means of egress system. This section will also discuss providing separate means of egress systems. A separate means of egress system is defined as a path of exit travel that is separated from other required exits by construction that adequately separates the atmospheres of the two space to effectively preclude contamination of the atmospheres in both separated sections by the same fire. In other words, separate means of egress systems provide smoke compartmentation by dividing the spaces with a smoke barrier to separate the two atmospheres.

1007.3.2 Separate means of egress systems required. Whenever any room as defined above has an occupant load of more than 300, at least one of its exits must be into a separate means of egress system. For that number of occupants, it is desirable that the two required exits lead through separate atmospheres. In addition, where the occupant load is large enough to require more than two exits, not more than two of the exits provided may be through the same atmosphere or separate means of egress system.

1007.3.3 Travel distance. All rooms in Group E Occupancies shall be arranged so that no point within the room is more than 75 feet (22 860 mm) from a corridor or an exit. In one- or two-story buildings that are equipped throughout with a complete smoke-detection system, this distance-to-exits limitation may be increased to 90 feet (27 432 mm). In all buildings housing Group E Occupancies that are provided with a complete automatic sprinkler system, this distance to exits may be as much as 110 feet (33 528 mm).

In all portions of unsprinklered buildings, travel distances are limited to 150 feet (45 720 mm) measured along the path of travel. In Group E Occupancies, however, increased travel distances are permitted. First, for buildings not more than two stories in height where complete smoke-detection systems are installed, the travel distance may be increased to 175 feet (53 340 mm). Second, where a complete automatic sprinkler system is installed, the travel distance may be as much as 225 feet (68 580 mm). These distances may be increased an additional 100 feet (30 480 mm) when the last portion of travel occurs within a corridor. It should be pointed out that increase in travel distance is permitted based on the fact that the portion of the travel is within a one-hour fire-resistive corridor. In this instance, the permitted increases are cumulative. See Figure 1007-1.

1007.3.4 Travel through intervening rooms. When exits are provided through adjoining or intervening rooms, the basic requirements of Chapter 10 are applicable also to Group E Occupancies. As in all cases, the length of travel that occurs within an intervening room must be calculated as part of the overall travel distance. It is reemphasized here that when travel does involve passing through an intervening room, the path through that intervening room must be direct, obvious and unobstructed. If, however, the intervening room consists of a kitchen, storeroom, restroom, closet, laboratory using hazardous materials, industrial shop or similar-type spaces, it is not permitted that such an intervening room be utilized to provide a path of exit travel for any

interior room or space. Foyers, lobbies or reception areas, when constructed as required for exit corridors, are not to be interpreted as constituting intervening rooms.

Smoke-detection system requirements. Whenever any interior room has an occupant load of more than 10, a smoke-detection system must be installed throughout the area of common atmosphere through which the exit serving that interior room must pass. This smoke-detection system must be complete and must extend to the atmospheric separation, or smoke barrier, which creates the separate exit system. Such detectors must be arranged to sound an alarm that is audible in the interior room. They must also be interconnected with the school's fire alarm system. Rooms used exclusively for mechanical or for public utility service and rooms formed by enclosures that extend less

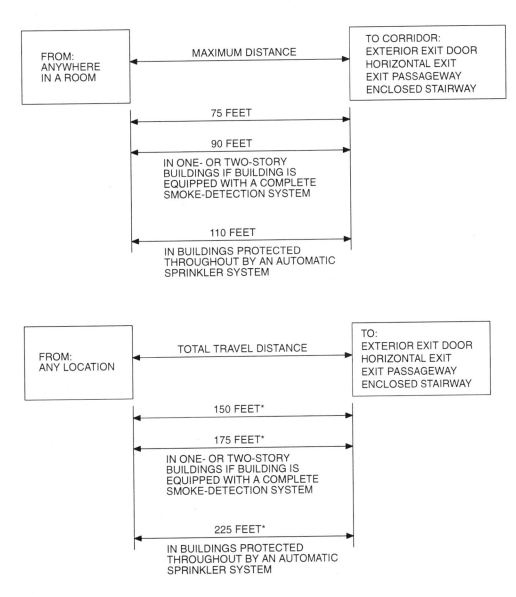

*May be increased up to an additional 100 feet when the last portion of travel occurs within a corridor.

GROUP E OCCUPANCY TRAVEL DISTANCE

FIGURE 1007-1

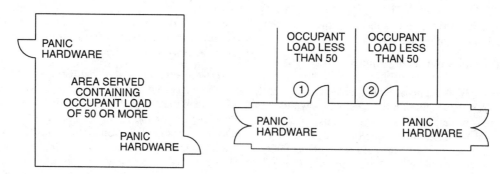

Doors require panic hardware where indicated unless they are not provided with lock or latch. Note that doors serving a corridor must have panic hardware, regardless of occupant load. Doors marked 1 and 2 do not require panic hardware since each serves an occupant load of less than 50.

**PANIC HARDWARE REQUIREMENT
GROUP E OCCUPANCIES**

FIGURE 1007-2

than two thirds of the floor-to-ceiling height and do not exceed 8 feet (2438 mm) are exempted from the smoke-detection system requirement.

1007.3.5 Hallways, corridors and exterior exit balconies. General corridors and hallways provisions of Section 1004.3.3 and 1004.3.4 will apply.

The code previously required all corridors (and hallways) in Group E Occupancies to be rated. The rating was required regardless of the occupant load.

Any change in elevation of less than 2 feet (610 mm) in a hallway, corridor or exterior exit balcony shall be by means of a ramp. Change cannot be achieved by steps.

Corridor width requirements. Several different corridor width requirements are applicable in Group E Occupancies. Basically, the minimum required width of corridors serving Group E Occupancies may never be less than 44 inches (1118 mm) in clear width. When the occupant load served by the hallway, corridor or exterior exit balcony is more than 100, the required clear width must then be at least 6 feet (1829 mm). When the occupant load served by the corridor is sufficiently large, the minimum required width is determined by using the formula contained in Section 1003.2.3 and adding an additional 2 feet (610 mm).

The minimum requirement of 6 feet (1829 mm) when the corridor serves more than 100 persons and the additional 2 feet (610 mm) required to be added to the normal corridor width calculations recognize that in Group E Occupancies it is customary to locate lockers along the sidewalls of the corridor. These additional increments in corridor width then permit such activities to occur without unduly interfering with the flow of occupants through the corridor system.

1007.3.7 Exit serving auditoriums in Group E, Division 1 Occupancies. School buildings often have an auditorium or similar assembly use. When this occurs, the auditorium as well as the classrooms and other spaces in the building are normally served by the same exit system. If the building is to be used in such a fashion that it is probable that both the assembly and the other spaces of the building will be fully occupied simultaneous-

ly, the exiting system must obviously be sufficient to accommodate the combined occupant load of all the spaces. This section states, however, that in the event the different building spaces will not be used simultaneously, the exiting system need provide only that capacity sufficient for whichever condition of use would require the greatest width through the exit system. This determination is made by the building official.

1007.3.9 Basement rooms. Required exit stairways from basements are prohibited from entering corridor spaces on the first floor. Such exit stairways must open directly to the outside of the building. The code clearly intends that there be no communicating opening from basement areas into the exiting system on the ground floor.

1007.3.10 Panic hardware. These special provisions for Group E Occupancies contain slightly different requirements for providing panic hardware. In all instances, doors serving as exits from corridors must be provided with panic hardware to overcome any locking or latching device installed on the door. This applies to exit doors from hallways or corridors, regardless of the occupant load served. In addition, other exit doors throughout a Group E Occupancy must be similarly provided with panic hardware whenever such doors serve an occupant load of 50 or more. See Figure 1007-2.

1007.3.11 Fences and gates. Typically, the premises on which Group E Occupancies are located are fenced or otherwise similarly enclosed. Unless properly designed, such enclosures could conceivably interfere with exiting from the building and from the premises, thereby preventing the building occupants from actually reaching the public way.

This practice of fencing school grounds and locking gates in such fences is permissible if within the fenced-in area there is provided an adequate dispersal area in a safe place to accommodate the occupant load of the building. To properly serve this function, the dispersal area must be at least 50 feet (15 240 mm) from the building it serves and must be of such size as to afford at least 3 square feet (0.28 m^2) of space per occupant. In no case may any portion of the means of egress system leading to such dispersal areas be provided with gates unless such gates are made to comply with all applicable exit requirements.

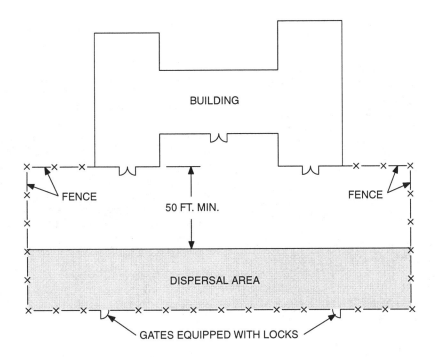

Fences and gates equipped with locks are permitted if a safe dispersal area at least 50 feet from the building is provided. The dispersal area must be a sufficient size to provide an area of not less than 3 square feet per person.

For **SI:** 1 foot = 304.8 mm, 1 square foot = 0.0929 m^2.

FENCES AND GATES
GROUP E OCCUPANCIES

FIGURE 1007-3

When such dispersal areas are provided, they, in turn, must be provided with exits. These required exits must be in conformity with the provisions of Section 1008 for exits from such dispersal areas. See Figure 1007-3.

1007.4 Group H Occupancies. As required by Section 1004.2.3, every Group H Occupancy must have at least one exit. At least two separate exits must be provided for every portion of a Group H Occupancy that has a floor area of 200 square feet (18.6 m^2) or more. Group H, Division 4 Occupancies having a floor area of less than 1,000 square feet (92.9 m^2) are permitted to have one exit.

The potential life-safety hazard in a Group H Occupancy is such that when it is necessary to evacuate this type of use, exit from such spaces must be almost immediate. For that reason, several of the requirements relating to exiting from Group H Occupancies are substantially more restrictive than from other occupancies. The first example is a requirement for the second exit from relatively small spaces. To further ensure reasonably safe exit from such hazardous spaces, egress paths in Group H, Divisions 1, 2 and 3 Occupancies are also more severely limited. No portion of any room within these occupancies may be more than 75 feet (22 860 mm) from an exit. The 100-foot (30 480 mm) corridor increase in Section 1004.2.5 is available. Furthermore, to facilitate rapid escape from these occupancies, exit doors from these occupancies shall not be provided with a latch or lock unless it is panic hardware.

Special exit door requirements. In addition, requirements relating to the protection of hazardous spaces are also more severe. Exit doors leading from such spaces must swing in the direction of exit travel, regardless of the occupant load served. Such doors must have a minimum fire-protection rating of three-fourths hour and may not have more than 100 square inches (0.0645 m^2) of wired glass in steel frames. The doors must also be maintained self-closing or must be automatic closing by one of the arrangements specified in the definition of automatic-closing fire assemblies in Section 713.2.

Provisions have been added to the code relating to Group H, Division 6 and Division 7 Occupancies. In such occupancies the travel distance to an exit is limited to 100 feet (30 480 mm) unless the provisions permitting the 100-foot (30 480 mm) corridor increase is used. Fabrication area is defined in Section 207. See also discussion in Section 307.11 addressing the Group H, Division 6 Occupancy.

1007.5 Group I Occupancies.

1007.5.1 Minimum size of means of egress. Since in Group I Occupancies it is frequently necessary to move occupants in wheelchairs, on gurneys or in beds, it is necessary to ensure that exit doors are of sufficient width to permit the ready passage of such equipment. Therefore, means of egress components subject to such use must have a clear width of not less than 44 inches (1118 mm). Other aisles may have a clear width of not less than

32 inches (813 mm). Absolutely no projections are permitted into the required clear width.

1007.5.4 Corridors. Throughout Group I Occupancies all exit corridors must provide a minimum clear width of at least 44 inches (1118 mm) or as determined by Section 1003.2.3, whichever is greater. Within such occupancies, however, certain corridors are subject to use by nonambulatory persons. Again, such persons are moved in wheelchairs, on gurneys, or in the standard hospital bed. To safely accommodate this kind of use, corridors that serve nonambulatory persons must have a minimum clear width of 8 feet (2438 mm). An exception is made, however, for corridors serving surgical areas of Group I, Division 1.2 Occupancies, allowing a reduced width of 6 feet (1829 mm), provided the corridors meet certain requirements. While individual doorway clear-width dimensions are 44 inches (1118 mm), corridors must have the additional width because it is regularly necessary to accommodate two-way traffic in such corridors. In addition, because of the nature of the use of the corridors, there shall be no change in elevation whatsoever along the corridor, unless such change in elevation is achieved by ramps complying with the provisions of Section 1003.3.4.

Exceptions to corridor protection requirements. Corridors are required to comply with the construction and opening protection requirements of Section 1004.3.4. However, in hospitals and nursing homes, classified as Group I, Division 1.1 Occupancies, a number of necessary exceptions were added to facilitate the primary functioning of these types of health-care facilities. These exceptions recognize the special needs of these occupancies to provide the most efficient and effective health-care services.

Therefore, the first exception makes provisions for the location of nurses' stations and similar spaces necessary for doctors' and nurses' charting and communications in positions that need not be separated from the corridors. Essentially, then, these special-use areas are permitted to be located in the corridor. When this arrangement occurs, however, it is necessary that the construction surrounding the nurses' station be as required for corridors. It is only the corridor separation provisions that are excepted.

Similarly, to provide appropriate waiting spaces for visitors, exceptions are included that allow such waiting spaces to be unseparated from the corridors. One reason for this is to permit the waiting areas and similar spaces to be located to permit direct visual supervision by the health-care facilities staff. In exchange for the elimination of the corridor separation, certain conditions are imposed on the location of such waiting spaces. It is necessary that the space and the corridors into which the space opens be located in the same smoke compartment. Then, in addition to the requirement for the direct visual supervision, such space is required to be protected by an approved electrically supervised automatic smoke-detection system.

Omission of door closers. One of the most controversial issues relative to the arrangement of health-care facilities, such as hospitals and nursing homes, is the matter of the installation of door closers on doors to patient sleeping rooms. The health-care industry has long believed it is more important to the proper delivery of health-care services that the doors to the patient rooms not be self-closing and constantly closed. Therefore, in recognition of this special need, an exception now permits the deletion

of the closers on doors to patient sleeping rooms in hospitals and nursing homes.

Corridor glazing. Consistent with the exception for door closers are additional requirements relative to glazed openings in corridor walls. Exception 4 permits fully tempered or laminated glass in either wood or metal frames, provided the glazed area does not exceed 25 percent of the area of the corridor wall on the room side. Exception 5 goes further by stating that the total area of glass in the corridor wall is not limited when glazing is fixed, $1/4$-inch-thick (6.4 mm) wire reinforced glass set in steel frames and the size of the individual glazed panel is not in excess of 1,296 square inches (0.836 m^2). These two latter provisions also make possible special arrangements where it is desirable to view certain hospital spaces from the corridor without having the visitor enter such space. The primary example of this is the neonatal nursery.

1007.5.6 Basement exits. For rooms located in basements in Group I Occupancies the appropriate number of exits must be provided as required in Section 1004.2.3. In addition, at least one of those exits, accessible to every room, must lead directly to the exterior of the building at grade level.

1007.5.7 Ramps. To ensure that buildings housing Group I, Divisions 1.1 and 1.2 Occupancies are adequately accessible to nonambulatory patients housed therein, every such building must be provided with a ramp leading from the first story to the exterior at grade level. Such ramps are required by the provisions of Chapter 11 for use by persons with disabilities. Therefore, the slope of such ramps may not be steeper than 1 unit vertical in 12 units horizontal (8.3% slope), as specified in Section 1003.3.4.3.

1007.5.8 Hardware. As in Groups A and E Occupancies, all exit doors serving an area having an occupant load of 50 or more shall be provided with panic hardware to overcome any latching or locking device. While not requiring panic hardware as such, all patient room doors must be provided with hardware so that the doors are readily openable from both the corridor and the room sides without the use of keys.

Locking devices in hospitals and nursing homes. An exception added in the 1988 edition of the UBC allows certain locking devices on patient room doors in hospitals and nursing homes classified as Group I, Division 1.1 Occupancies when approved by the building official. These specially approved locking devices must be arranged so that they are readily openable from the patient room side and are readily operable by the facility staff from the opposite side. This special arrangement permits keys to be required for the patient room doors. However, when keys are necessary, they must be in the possession of staff and readily available at a prominent location adjacent to the rooms having lockable doors. Also see Section 1003.3.1.10 for special egress-control devices that may be used in Group I, Division 2 Occupancies.

Locking devices in detention and correctional facilities. These provisions for hardware primarily concern Group I Occupancies such as hospitals, sanitariums and similar spaces. Group I Occupancies also include detention and correctional facilities, such as prisons, penitentiaries, correctional facilities, reformatories and similar Group I, Division 3 Occupancies. By their nature, it is necessary that the occupants in these facilities be restrained. A revised exception to the 1991 UBC allows approved locks or safety devices in Group I, Division 3 Occupancies when it is necessary to forcibly restrain the personal liberties of inmates or patients.

1007.6 Group R Occupancies.

1007.6.2 Floor-level exit signs. When people who are sleeping or are not familiar with the exit system are suddenly awakened by an emergency condition, they may not be able to determine which way they should go to an exit due to a heavy accumulation of smoke. Therefore, when exit signs are required by Section 1003.2.8.2, additional floor-level exit signs, internally or externally illuminated or of the self-luminous type, shall be provided in all interior exit corridors serving the guest rooms of hotels and motels in a Group R, Division 1 Occupancy. This requirement may be considered restrictive in apartments where the occupants are more familiar with exit paths.

The bottom of these floor-level signs must be placed not less than 6 inches (152 mm) or more than 8 inches (203 mm) above the floor; for placement at exit doors, floor-level signs must be located within 4 inches (102 mm) of the door frame.

SECTION 1008 — REVIEWING STANDS, GRANDSTANDS, BLEACHERS, AND FOLDING AND TELESCOPING SEATING

Through the years Section 1008 has proven to be somewhat confusing to code users. This is probably because the code attempts to cover several types of grandstand construction in a single section when the subject most likely should have been addressed in at least three sections. For example, folding and telescoping seating was first introduced in the 1979 UBC as a separate section. Although folding and telescoping seating shares features with other types of bleachers and grandstands, it is still unique. Thus, it first appeared in its own section, which tended to emphasize the fact that this type of seating was unique.

Although not stated in the code, Section 1008 addresses at least three distinct types of grandstands:

- Permanent structures most often used for watching sporting events. These may be either open-air structures such as Yankee Stadium or the Rose Bowl, or they may be enclosed, domed structures such as the Astrodome or the Tacoma Dome. This type of grandstand generally is constructed of reinforced concrete, masonry or structural steel, but is sometimes of wood-frame construction. These grandstands are permanent in nature and would never be used as temporary seating.

- Temporary open-frame skeletal-type grandstands may be erected either outdoors or within a building and are most often erected for viewing parades, golf or tennis tournaments, automobile races, and other transient events. Such stands are most often constructed with a steel structural frame with wooden seats and decks. Figure 1008-1 depicts this type of stand. These stands are also used at schools for events, such as high school football, and at little league ball fields. Some of these latter installations are often left up year around and thus no longer qualify as temporary seating facilities. This distinction is very important when it comes to establishing

aisle widths and handrail requirements. See Sections 1008.5.4.3, 1008.5.5 and 1008.5.6.

- Folding and telescoping seating, which is installed almost exclusively in gymnasiums and is used to provide a limited amount of seating for viewing sporting events.

Grandstand provisions first appeared in the 1964 edition of the UBC, with revisions appearing in the 1973 edition. The 1973 version contained most of the original 1964 provisions and is similar to provisions found in the 1988 edition. Under these prior provisions, required aisle widths remained consistent until the 1997 edition. The 1997 version first eliminated unique requirements for open-air grandstands and bleachers, as they are now regulated under the general requirements of Section 1008.5.

Temporary grandstands installed within a building are really not much different than the same type of grandstand installed outdoors. They are often installed in large roofed multi-use buildings, where grandstand configuration must be changed to suit different activities, such as ice shows, rodeos and basketball games. Permanent grandstands, however, bear more of a relationship to theater seating than to what one commonly thinks of as sporting event or grandstand-type seating. To make the subject a bit more confusing, some arenas have a lower level where seating can be arranged in different configurations, while an upper level has fixed seating.

If a code user is not already familiar with the various shapes and forms that have been used over the years for event viewing, the provisions of Section 1008 can become very confusing. The many changes that occurred in the 1991 edition tended to make the distinction between "grandstand"-type seating and "theater"-type seating even more obscure. Although the discussion that follows attempts to show how the individual provisions of Section 1008 should be applied, their application to a particular grandstand configuration must rest with the building official.

1008.1 Scope. This section deals with reviewing stands, grandstands, bleachers, and folding and telescoping seating.

1008.2 Definitions. Certain special terms apply to the facilities regulated by this section. For code purposes, it is necessary that they be specifically defined.

Bleachers and grandstands are both tiered or stepped seating facilities. They are only differentiated in that bleachers provide seating without backrests.

Folding and telescoping seats are structures that provide tiered seating that can be reduced in size and moved without dismantling.

Footboards are that part of the seating facility, other than an aisle or a cross aisle, on which the occupant walks to reach a seat. Essentially, footboards are the walking surface provided between seating rows.

A safe dispersal area is an area large enough to accommodate the total capacity of the seating facility and the building which it serves at the rate of not less than 3 square feet (0.28 m²) per person and at a location at least 50 feet (15 240 mm) from the stand or the building. It provides a safe area for temporary use by the occupants prior to further egress from the dispersal area.

Permanent stands and temporary seating facilities are differentiated by the duration of use. If the seats are in place for more

(Continued on page 227)

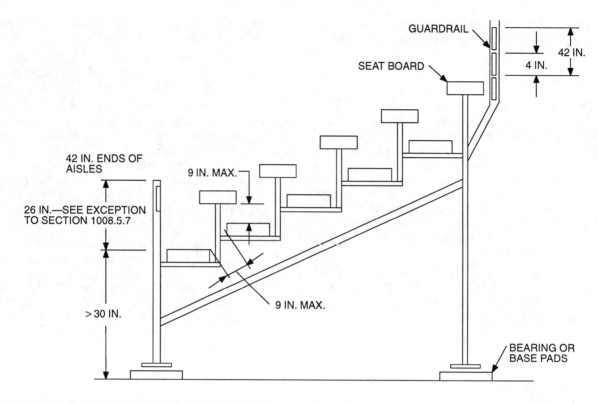

42 IN.
4 IN.
GUARDRAIL
SEAT BOARD

42 IN. ENDS OF AISLES

9 IN. MAX.

26 IN.—SEE EXCEPTION TO SECTION 1008.5.7

9 IN. MAX.

> 30 IN.

BEARING OR BASE PADS

AISLES MAY BE OMITTED WHEN ALL OF THE FOLLOWING CONDITIONS EXIST:
1. SEATS ARE WITHOUT BACKRESTS.
2. THE RISE FROM ROW TO ROW DOES NOT EXCEED 16 INCHES PER ROW.
3. THE ROW SEATING DOES NOT EXCEED 28 INCHES UNLESS THE SEATBOARDS AND FOOTBOARDS ARE AT THE SAME ELEVATION.
4. THE NUMBER OF ROWS DOES NOT EXCEED 16 IN HEIGHT.
5. THE FIRST SEAT BOARD IS NOT MORE THAN 12 INCHES ABOVE GRADE.
6. SEATBOARDS ARE CONTINUOUS FLAT SURFACES.
7. SEATBOARDS PROVIDE A WALKING SURFACE WITH A MINIMUM WIDTH OF 11 INCHES.

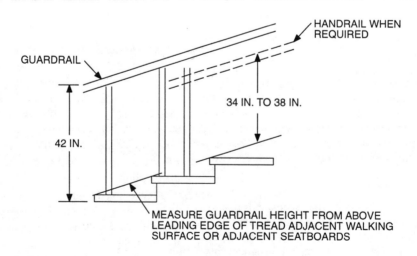

HANDRAIL WHEN REQUIRED

GUARDRAIL

34 IN. TO 38 IN.

42 IN.

MEASURE GUARDRAIL HEIGHT FROM ABOVE LEADING EDGE OF TREAD ADJACENT WALKING SURFACE OR ADJACENT SEATBOARDS

For **SI:** 1 inch = 25.4 mm, 1 foot = 304.8 mm.

SIDE AISLE

GRANDSTANDS AND BLEACHERS

FIGURE 1008-1

(Continued from page 225)

than 90 days, they are classified as permanent. If not, they are classified as temporary.

Finally, reviewing stands are elevated platforms accommodating not more than 50 persons. Normally, if they are provided with seating, the seats are loose chairs. If the reviewing stand provides accommodations for more than 50 persons, it is subject to the requirements for grandstands. See Figures 1008-1 and 1008-2.

1008.3 Height of reviewing stands, grandstands, bleachers, and folding and telescoping seating. Reference is made to the provisions of Section 303.2 where, in Section 303.2.2.3, grandstands, bleachers or reviewing stands are regulated in height according to their type of construction and the materials used. When of Type III One-hour, Type IV or Type V One-hour construction, they shall not exceed a height of 40 feet (12 192 mm) to the highest level of seatboards; when of Type III-N or Type V-N, they shall not exceed a height of more than 20 feet

(6096 mm). When the structural frame is constructed of combustible materials and the stand is located indoors, the height is limited to a maximum of 12 feet (3658 mm).

1008.5 General Requirements.

1008.5.1 Row spacing. As in other types of seating, it is required that there be a clear space between rows of not less than 12 inches (305 mm), measured horizontally between the back or backrest of each seat and the foremost projection of the seat immediately behind it. In addition, there is a specification for the minimum back-to-back spaces between rows of seats. Such minimum back-to-back spacing shall be 22 inches (559 mm) for seats without backrests, 30 inches (762 mm) for seats with backrests and 33 inches (838 mm) for chair seating.

1008.5.2 Rise between rows. The maximum permitted rise between rows of seats is limited to 16 inches (406 mm) unless the seat spacing back-to-back is 40 inches (1016 mm) or more. In that case, the maximum rise between rows of seats may exceed

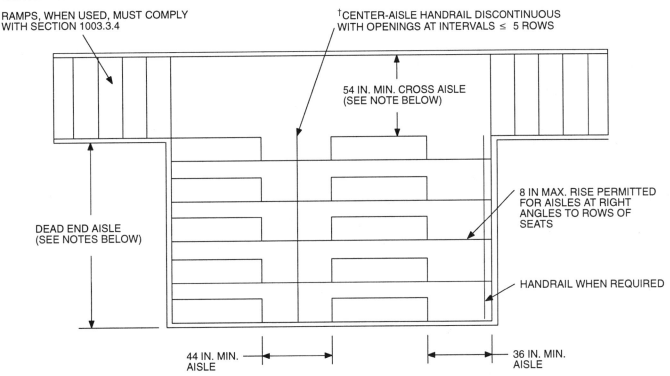

GRANDSTANDS, BLEACHERS AND TELESCOPING SEATING
(SECTION 1008.5)

FIGURE 1008-2

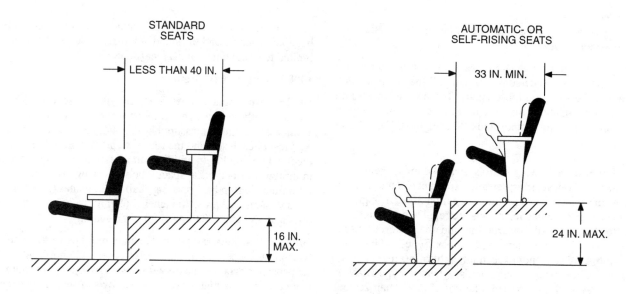

STANDARD
SEATS

LESS THAN 40 IN.

16 IN.
MAX.

AUTOMATIC- OR
SELF-RISING SEATS

33 IN. MIN.

24 IN. MAX.

For **SI:** 1 inch = 25.4 mm.

GRANDSTAND SEATING

FIGURE 1008-3

the 16-inch (406 mm) limitation. When automatic or self-rising seats are used, the rise may be increased to 24 inches (610 mm), provided the back-to-back spacing between rows is at least 33 inches (838 mm). The basic requirement for rise between rows and the exception for self-rising seats are illustrated in Figure 1008-3.

1008.5.3 Seating capacity determination. As with other types of continuous seating surface, the occupant load of such facilities is based on the assumption that there be at least one person for each 18 inches (457 mm) of seating surface.

1008.5.4 Aisles. Generally speaking, it is necessary to provide aisles through all seating sections subject to the requirements of Section 1004.3.2. However, under certain circumstances, aisles need not be provided, and access to and egress from the seats may be over the seating facilities themselves. Where such is the case, aisles may be omitted on the conditions that: (1) the seats are without backrests, (2) the rise from row to row does not exceed 6 inches (152 mm) per row, (3) the row spacing does not exceed 28 inches (711 mm) unless the seat boards and footboards are at the same elevation, (4) the number of rows in the facility does not exceed 16, (5) the first or lowest seating board is not more than 12 inches (305 mm) above grade or floor below or cross aisle, (6) the seat boards are continuous flat surfaces, and (7) the seat boards provide a walking surface at least 11 inches (279 mm) in width. To eliminate aisles from the seating facility, all seven conditions must apply.

Aisles serving seats on both sides of the aisle are required to have a minimum width of 44 inches (1118 mm). When seats occur on only one side of the aisle, the aisle must be a minimum of 36 inches (914 mm) wide.

For temporary seating facilities, aisle widths need only comply with the minimum width specified in Section 1008.5.4.3. Compliance with Section 1004.3.2.3 is not required. This is also true for cross aisles. Their width need only comply with Section 1008.5.5. Aisle widths for permanent grandstands, on the other

hand, must be evaluated under Section 1004.3.2.3; when these widths are greater than the minimums of Section 1008, the minimum widths calculated from Section 1004.3.2.3 will govern.

1008.5.5 Cross aisles and vomitories. When required or provided, cross aisles and vomitories must have a minimum clear width of 54 inches (1372 mm) and shall also extend continuously to an exit or exterior perimeter ramp. For permanent stands, this minimum shall be compared to that required by Section 1004.3.2.3 and the greater shall then be used.

1008.5.6 Stairways and ramps. When provided, stairways and ramps must comply with the requirements of Section 1003.3.3.3 for rise and run and Section 1003.3.4.3 for slope, respectively. However, in bleachers and grandstands, when the aisles are serving the seating sections and are arranged so that they are at right angles to the rows of seats, the maximum permitted rise in such stepped aisles may be as much as 8 inches (203 mm). Consistent with this dimensional limitation, all aisles which terminate more than 8 inches (203 mm) above grade shall be provided with a conforming stairway or ramp extending the aisle to grade level. The width of such a stairway or ramp must be at least equal to the width of the aisle that it serves.

Handrails shall be provided on all stairways and ramps as required by Sections 1003.3.3.6 and 1003.3.4.5, except that only one handrail need be provided along one side or down the center line of stairways that serve as aisles within a seating facility at right angles to the seats. For temporary seating facilities, handrails need not be provided for stepped aisles within the seating area. See Figure 1008-1. Other stairways and ramps, however, must have complying handrails. For example, the stairways at the front of the grandstand shown in Figure 1008-1 would be required to have handrails. A minimum clear width of 48 inches (1219 mm) between the seats shall be provided for aisle stairways having handrails in the center of the aisle. When seating is provided along both sides of an aisle, the handrails shall have openings at intervals not exceeding five rows and a clear width of at least 22 inches (559 mm), but not greater than 36 inches (914 mm). Intermediate rails are required approximately 12 inches (305 mm) below the top handrail when the rail is located in the middle of the aisle stairs.

1008.5.7 Guardrails. All portions of elevated seating facilities that are more than 30 inches (762 mm) above the grade or floor level must be protected on the perimeter by guardrails or the equivalent to protect against falls from the facility. Construction of the guardrails shall be in accordance with Section 509 and shall comply with the design criteria of Table 16-B. All such guardrails must extend a minimum of 42 inches (1067 mm) above the leading edge of the tread adjacent walking surface, adjacent walking surface or adjacent seatboards. Guardrails, however, may be reduced in height to 26 inches (660 mm) when located immediately in front of the front row of seats so as not to interfere with the sight line of occupants in the front row. In addition, these guardrails need not meet the 4-inch (102 mm) maximum spacing limitation; however, a midrail must be provided. The guardrail height reduction, however, applies only to those portions immediately in front of the seating, and does not apply if the guardrail is located at the end of an aisle or is needed to protect the open side of a cross aisle at the bottom of the seating facilities. See Figure 1008-1.

In some grandstands and in many bleachers there will be an open vertical space between the footboards and the seats above. Whenever the footboards are located more than 30 inches (762 mm) above the grade or ground level, such vertical open space must be limited to a maximum height of 9 inches (229 mm). This requirement also protects objects or even occupants from sliding into or perhaps even falling through such vertical open space. See Figure 1008-2.

1008.5.8 Toeboards. Wherever guardrails are required, there shall also be installed a toeboard along the edge of the walking surface. This shall not apply, however, to the ends of footboards.

Such a toeboard shall consist of a 4-inch-high (102 mm) vertical barrier that must be installed along the edge of the walking platform. The purpose of the toeboard is twofold. One purpose is to prevent persons from slipping on the walking surface and projecting into or through the guardrail, and the other is to provide some protection against objects accidentally sliding off of or falling from walking surfaces of the seating facility. See Figure 1008-4.

1008.5.9 Footboards. In bleachers and grandstands, all rows of seats above the third row, or where the seating surface is more than 2 feet (610 mm) above grade, must be provided with footboards to provide access between the rows of seats to the individual seat location. In some instances, bleachers and grandstands can be arranged so that the same surface serves both for the seating and for the footrest. In such cases, it is not necessary that separate footrests be provided. However, the platform used for both seating and footrest must be at least 24 inches (610 mm) in width to accommodate both purposes. See Figure 1008-5. By virtue of the provisions of Section 1008.5.4, footboards must be provided whenever aisles are required, and such footboards must have a minimum width of based on the row to row spacing When projected horizontally, there shall be no horizontal gaps exceeding $1/4$ inch (6.4 mm) between footboards and seat boards. See Figure 1008-1. When at aisles, gaps at footboards shall also be limited to $1/4$ inch (6.4 mm).

1008.6 Grandstands, Bleachers, and Folding and Telescoping Seating within Buildings. For the most part, any such structure installed within a building must comply with the requirements of Section 1008 and Chapter 10 unless there is an expressly stated exception. Two exceptions apply to seating without backrests. In such seating facilities there may be as many as nine seats between any seat and an aisle or a maximum of 20 seats per row. In such facilities, dead ends in vertical aisles may be permitted to serve as many as 16 rows.

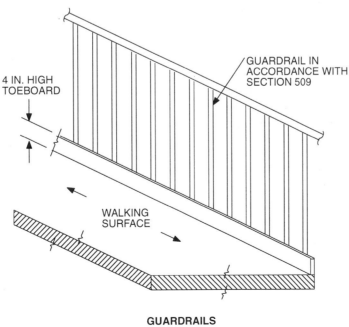

For **SI:** 1 inch = 25.4 mm.

GUARDRAILS

FIGURE 1008-4

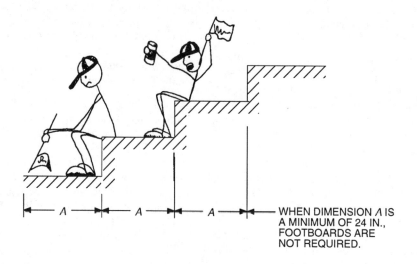

WHEN DIMENSION $\wedge$ IS A MINIMUM OF 24 IN., FOOTBOARDS ARE NOT REQUIRED.

For **SI:** 1 inch = 25.4 mm.

PLATFORM SEATING

FIGURE 1008-5

1008.7 Smoke-protected Assembly Seating.

1008.7.1 General. For seating in an assembly area to be considered as smoke-protected, it must comply with provisions for roof height, smoke control and travel distance. When such requirements are met, the clear width of aisles may be reduced in accordance with Section 1004.3.2.3.1. Additional benefits are also addressed elsewhere in Chapter 10.

1008.7.2 Roof height. Whenever smoke-protected assembly seating is covered by a roof, a minimum clearance of 15 feet (4572 mm) is required between the highest aisle or aisle accessway and the lowest portion of the roof. By providing an adequate roof height above the occupiable portion of the building or structure, a smoke containment area is created. Smoke control or removal would then limit smoke migration into the egress environment.

1008.7.3 Smoke control. To maintain a means of egress system essentially smoke-free, a smoke control system complying with Section 905 must be provided. As stated in Section 905.1, a smoke-control system should be designed to provide a tenable environment for the evacuation or relocation of occupants. When it can be satisfactorily demonstrated to the building official, a design incorporating a natural venting system is permitted. Such a system must accomplish equivalent results to an automatic smoke-control system.

1008.7.4 Travel distance. In smoke-protected assembly seating, a maximum travel distance of 200 feet (60 960 mm) is permitted from each seat to the nearest entrance to an egress concourse. Up to another 200 feet (60 960 mm) of travel is permitted from the egress concourse entrance to an approved egress stair, ramp or walk at the building exterior. When the assembly seating is located in an outdoor facility, and all portions of the means of egress are open to the outside, the maximum travel distance is 400 feet (121 920 mm). This distance is measured from each seat to an approved egress stair or walk at the exterior of the building. When the seating facilities are of Type I or Type II noncombustible construction, the travel distance may be unlimited.

REFERENCES

[1]Pauls, Jake L. (1984). What can we do to improve stair safety? *Building Standards,* 53(3):9-12, 42-43, and 53(4):13-16, 42.

[2]Fitch, James Marston, John Templar and Paul Corcoran (1974). The dimensions of stairs. *Scientific American,* October.

[3]National Bureau of Standards (1935). *Design and Construction of Building Exits,* Miscellaneous Publication, M151. United States Government Printing Office, Washington, D.C.

[4]Sheedy, Paul (1985). Stair railings. *Building Standards,* 54(2):4-9.

[5]Koyamatsu, T. J. (1983). Corridor protection—Combustible and noncombustible construction. *Building Standards,* 52(5):8-10, 50.

[6]Butcher, E. G., and A. C. Parnell (1979). *Smoke Control in Fire Safety Design,* E. and F.N. Spon., London.

Chapter 11

ACCESSIBILITY

This chapter first appeared in the 1991 UBC and resulted in a dramatically increased number of requirements for the accessibility and usability of buildings. Prior to the 1991 code, the UBC contained a limited number of provisions in Chapters 5 and 33 that related to access for persons with disabilities. The provisions in the 1991 code were a major step in a process that began in 1971 when the International Conference of Building Officials approved a number of code changes to the *Uniform Building Code* that were intended to make buildings more accessible to and usable by persons with disabilities.

While ICBO was developing these accessibility provisions for the UBC, BOCA and SBCCI were developing similar regulations for their own building codes. These independent developments resulted in confusion in the regulatory, design and construction community. As a result, the Board of Directors of CABO requested that BCMC review the accessibility regulations and suggest revisions to all of the model codes that would result in national uniformity.

In October 1987, BCMC began developing regulations that set forth when, where and to what degree access must be provided for persons with disabilities. This task was completed when the BCMC report of June 8, 1992, was used as the basis for a code change adopted by ICBO's membership in September 1992 in Dallas, Texas. The BCMC effort resulted in the provisions in the *1993 Accumulative Supplement to the UBC* and the 1994 UBC. These provisions were also adopted in the 1993 BOCA NBC and the 1994 SBC.

SECTION 1101 — SCOPE

1101.3 Design. This section adopts CABO/ANSI A117.1-1992 as an adopted design standard to be used to ensure that buildings and facilities are accessible to and usable by persons with disabilities. With this section providing the accessible design and construction standards for buildings, the remaining sections of the chapter provide the "scoping" provisions that set forth when, where and to what degree access must be provided.

The importance of this section and the requirements it imposes should not be overlooked. As stated, buildings shall be designed and constructed to the minimum provisions of this chapter and CABO/ANSI A117.1 to be considered accessible. Therefore, prior to applying the code provisions for accessibility, it is important for the code user to review a number of elements found in Section 4 of CABO/ANSI A117.1. Though these items are not completely addressed in the UBC, they are an important part in making a building accessible. Such elements include, but are not limited to, space allowance and reach ranges, accessible route, protruding objects, and ramps.

Space requirements can vary greatly depending on the nature of the disability, the physical functions of the individual, and the skill or ability of the individual in using an assistive device.

However, it is generally accepted that spaces designed to accommodate persons using wheelchairs will be functional for most people.

The 1997 edition of the UBC will include an exception to this section to allow Type B dwelling units to comply with Section 1106, Type B Dwelling Units. A discussion of this revision will follow in Section 1102.

SECTION 1102 — DEFINITIONS

It is important to note that the definitions of this section are specifically for this code and may have different meanings from definitions in other accessibility provisions or regulations, such as the Americans with Disabilities Act. Additional definitions that apply to these provisions can be found in Section 3.4 of CABO/ANSI A117.1.

The term "accessible" takes on a very broad meaning by requiring compliance with Chapter 11. Space requirements must be addressed for all portions of a building to be considered accessible or to provide an accessible route within a building. Space requirements apply to adequate maneuvering space, clearance width for doors and corridors, and height clearances.

Location of controls, switches and other forms of hardware becomes a function of forward and parallel reach ranges if they are to be considered accessible. To assist persons with limited dexterity, controls and other forms of hardware need to be operable without tight gripping, grasping or twisting of the wrist.

People with visual impairments are provided with accessible routes, by the inclusion of provisions for clear and unobstructed routes that are free of protrusions created by benches, overhanging stairways, poles, posts and low-hanging signs. Many hazards can be eliminated by using different textural surfaces in the accessible route to alert sight-impaired persons. Visually impaired or partially sighted persons can be assisted with proper signage of the correct size, surface and contrasts. Signage is also provided for the hearing impaired. Directional signage should always be clear, concise and appropriately placed.

An accessible route is defined in both the UBC and CABO/ANSI A117.1 and is discussed in Section 4.3 of that document. Accessible routes have a number of components, such as walking surfaces with a slope not steeper than 1:20 maximum, marked crossings at vehicular ways, clear floor spaces at accessible elements, access aisles, ramps, curb ramps and elevators. Each component must comply with specific applicable standards and requirements.

Several key elements to review when addressing accessible routes are the requirements related to protruding objects and to ramps. An accessible route may contain a number of protruding objects which can affect its use. These objects are ordinary building elements, such as telephones, water fountains, signs, directories and automatic teller machines. Protruding objects and other such obstructions are regulated by Section 4.4 of CABO/ANSI A117.1.

Ramps with proper slopes may serve as acceptable means of egress and as part of an accessible route. A sloped surface that is steeper than 1:20 is considered to be a ramp and is required to comply with both the requirements of UBC Section 1003.3.4 and of Section 4.8 in CABO/ANSI A117.1. To be considered acceptable, ramps shall have a slope not steeper than 1:12, with a maximum rise for any ramp not to exceed 30 inches (762 mm) and a minimum width of at least 36 inches (914 mm).

The 1997 edition also includes several revisions to Chapter 11 and the following new definitions:

DWELLING UNIT — TYPE A is a dwelling unit that is designed and constructed for accessibility in accordance with CABO/ANSI A117.1.

DWELLING UNIT — TYPE B is a dwelling unit that is designed and constructed for accessibility in accordance with Section 1106.

GROUND FLOOR DWELLING UNIT is a dwelling unit with a primary entrance and habitable space at grade.

MULTISTORY DWELLING UNIT is a dwelling unit with habitable or bathroom space located on more than one story.

The revisions in Section 1101, Scope; Section 1102, Definitions; Section 1103.1.9.3, Building Accessibility for Multi-Unit Dwellings; Section 1103.2, Building Accessibility Design and Construction Standards; Section 1105, Facility Accessibility; and Section 1106, Type B Dwelling Units are a BCMC package of code changes incorporating the provisions that bring the residential accessibility provisions in line with HUD's Fair Housing Guidelines. These provisions were initially based on the revised BCMC Accessibility report dated October 5, 1993, which addressed bathroom and kitchen accessibility. This proposal was amended to reflect the work done by the ANSI residential accessibility task force. The main change in this revision is the addition of the adaptable units, or Type B units. This revision allows designers and developers the option of providing a properly sized unit without having to provide, at the time of construction, all the accessibility features that can be added easily at a later date when needed.

SECTION 1103 — BUILDING ACCESSIBILITY

The first exception in Section 1103.1.1 was written to list the specific areas where access is not required. However, since it is impossible to envision every conceivable location that should be exempt from the access requirements, Exception 2 is provided for the building official's use. Exception 2 allows the building official to use discretion in exempting portions of buildings from accessibility features based on a determination that work in an area would not reasonably be performed by a person with a disability. Building officials, however, should exercise extreme care in using this exception. The disabled community can provide well-documented cases where employment has been denied due to the lack of facilities which could be made accessible. One example would be a small grocery store with a raised platform for the cashier position. If the building official decides that a person in a wheelchair cannot possibly manage or work in the store, the ramp from floor level to the cashier's level may be

omitted. In some cases, due to the size and nature of the store, accessible restrooms might not be provided with the features necessary for employee accessibility. Where this occurs, it is much easier for the store to deny employment to persons with disabilities. If it can be shown that a readily achievable alteration could accommodate a disabled employee, employment cannot be denied because of a lack of accessibility.

Unlike Exception 2, which places subjective decision-making responsibilities on the building official, Exception 3 recognizes that some activities directly associated with construction projects will not be safe for persons with certain physical disabilities. Therefore structures, sites and equipment used or associated with construction are not required to be accessible. The limited scope of this exception is important since the accessibility provisions generally do apply to temporary buildings. It is also necessary to note that where pedestrian protection is required by Chapter 33 and Table 33-A of the UBC, such walkways are required to be accessible.

1103.1.2 Group A Occupancies. Group A Occupancies consist of assembly uses as defined in Section 303.1.1. Facilities regulated under these provisions include such uses as restaurants, theaters, auditoriums and stadiums. The following elements are typically common to most assembly occupancies and are regulated by Chapter 11:

- Wheelchair spaces
- Assistive listening devices
- Accessible routes
- Accessible entrances
- Signs
- Stairways
- Elevators
- Platform lifts
- Egress and areas of refuge
- Bathing and toilet facilities
- Drinking fountains and water coolers
- Telephones
- Seating, tables, service counters
- Alarms
- Doors

Obviously, all of these elements are not found in every building, and the code does not specifically require them in *all* Group A Occupancies. However, whenever these elements are provided in Group A Occupancies, they must be designed, installed, constructed and maintained in an accessible condition.

The exception in Section 1103.1.2 eliminates the requirement for an elevator or ramp system to a mezzanine under strict conditions. Again, caution should be exercised when determining the "same services" mentioned in this exception. It is generally accepted that same services not only address actual food and drink service, but also address decor, views and ambiance, etc. It is equally important that a specific accessible space or area *not* be set aside and restricted for use only by people with disabilities.

1103.1.3 and 1103.1.8 Group B and Group M Occupancies. The phrase "shall be accessible as provided in this chapter" addresses most of the same items that are required for other facilities, including accessible routes, accessible entrances, signs, doors, stairways, elevators, platform lifts, egress, areas of refuge, bathing and toilet facilities, drinking fountains, seating, tables, work surfaces, service counters and automatic teller machines.

The requirements for assistive listening systems or devices are located in Section 1105.4.8.2.

It is important to note the difference between the terms "when provided" and "required" as used in Chapter 11. For example, not all occupancies are required to have public restrooms; however, "when public restrooms are provided," they are required to be accessible.

The same criteria applies to a number of other items such as drinking fountains, fixed seating, etc., that may not be required in certain occupancy groups or divisions, but once in place, they must then be accessible. However, all occupancies are required to have certain accessible elements in new construction. These include, but are not limited to, accessible routes, entrances and doors.

1103.1.4 Group E Occupancies. Again, the phrase "shall be accessible as provided in this chapter" addresses the same items, as previously mentioned. When these items are provided, they are required to be accessible. This includes assistive listening devices.

1103.1.5, 1103.1.6 and 1103.1.10 Groups F, H and S Occupancies. Groups F, H and S Occupancies should be treated in the same manner as other commercial uses. The absence of provisions for assistive listening systems presumes the absence of assembly spaces in these occupancies.

1103.1.7 Group I Occupancies. All Group I Occupancies, including nursing homes, hospitals, nurseries, sanitariums, jails, prisons and reformatories, are equally regulated for public-use, common-use and employee-use areas. Treatment and examination rooms are also regulated equally. All must be accessible.

These are a number of varying requirements within the Division 1.1 requirements for Group I Occupancies. Hospitals that specialize in the treatment of conditions affecting mobility are required to have *all* patient rooms, including the toilet rooms and bathrooms, accessible.

Hospitals that do not specialize in treating conditions that affect mobility are required to have at least 10 percent of their patient rooms accessible for their patient population, including the associated toilet rooms and bathrooms. It is assumed that, in most cases, not more than 10 percent of the hospital's patients would need accessible rooms.

In nursing homes and long-term care facilities, at least 50 percent of the patient rooms, and their associated bathrooms are required to be accessible. This increase in the percentage of accessible rooms recognizes that patients or residents of these facilities may be ambulatory on admission, but may become nonambulatory or have further mobility limitations during their stay.

1103.1.9 Group R Occupancies. Rooms or spaces available to the general public and spaces available for use of residents that serve Group R, Division 1 Occupancy accessible dwelling units shall be accessible. Where recreational facilities are provided

serving accessible dwelling units, at least 25 percent, but not less than one of each type in each group of such facilities, shall be accessible. All recreational facilities of each type on a site shall be considered to determine the total number of each type that are required to be accessible. This requirement recognizes that not all recreational facilities need to be accessible nor would such a requirement be feasible. However, at least one of every four recreational facilities shall be available to someone with a disability. Further, each *type* of recreational facility, such as a basketball court, a handball court, a weight room, an exercise area, a game room or a TV room in each *group* of such facilities (e.g., one recreation building housing all of these types of recreational facilities), must be fully accessible. Each type of recreational facility on a site, such as a racquetball court in an apartment complex, is considered to determine the total number required to be accessible. Thus, if there were 12 racquetball courts on the site, at least three of the courts would need to be accessible. If they were evenly distributed in two separate buildings, one building would need to contain at least one accessible court, and another would need at least two accessible courts to meet the overall 25 percent rule. If the courts were located in four separate buildings, each building would require at least one accessible facility, even if the total exceeded the overall 25 percent requirement.

1103.1.9.2 Hotels, lodging houses and congregate residences. This section requires that a certain number of rooms and specific facilities in these uses be accessible. As an example, a new hotel with 650 rooms shall be constructed with at least eight accessible guest rooms, based on the following calculation:

first 30 guest rooms	= 1 accessible room
(650 rooms - 30 rooms) ÷ 100 =	
6.2 additional rooms	= 7 accessible rooms
Minimum total required	= 8 accessible rooms

At least four of those rooms (50 percent × 8 = 4) are required by this section to have a roll-in shower. In addition to the accessible units, guest rooms for the hearing impaired are required. Using the same example of a new hotel with 650 guest rooms, Table 11-B indicates that at least 2 percent, or 13 rooms, would be required to have visible and audible alarm-indicating appliances, that are activated by both the in-room smoke detector and the building's fire protection system.

The 1997 edition of the UBC will require access for congregate residences, which include fraternity or sorority houses, halfway houses, convents, monasteries, etc., under the same conditions as required for hotels and lodging houses.

1103.1.9.3 Multi-unit dwellings. This section, previously titled Apartment Houses in the 1994 edition, includes accessibility requirements for Group R, Division 1 Occupancy apartment houses containing four or more dwelling units and Group R, Division 3 Occupancies where there are four or more dwelling units in a single structure. For such occupancies, all units shall be Type B dwelling units in accordance with the requirements of Section 1106. The accessibility requirements for a Type B dwelling unit are generally less restrictive than that for a Type A dwelling unit which is based on CABO/ANSI A117.1 requirements.

In Group R, Division 1 apartment occupancies containing more than 20 dwelling units, at least 2 percent, but not less than one of the dwelling units shall be a Type A dwelling unit. The total number of units on a site shall be considered in determining the required number of accessible dwelling units.

Five exceptions to these requirements are included in this section. The first four exceptions relate to buildings without elevator service and are self-explanatory as worded in the code. The fifth exception relates to buildings that are required to have raised floors at the primary entrances as measured from the elevations of the vehicular and pedestrian arrival points in order to accommodate the base flood elevation. Where no such arrival points are within 50 feet of the primary entrance, the closest arrival point shall be used.

1103.1.11 Group U Occupancies. Item 1 contains a provision that could possibly be overlooked. The garage or carport may not, on its own merit, be required to be accessible, but once an accessible parking space is placed in the structure, then the structure must be accessible. Making the structure accessible could then be the basis for considering an accessible route from the major use structure to the garage.

Item 2 is an interesting provision concerning buildings that had previously not been required to be accessible. Agricultural buildings must provide some nominal accessible features for employees and the general public. Therefore, fruit and vegetable stands may now be required to have some accessible features.

1103.2.1 General. When accessibility is required by this chapter, it shall be designed and constructed in accordance with this chapter and CABO/ANSI A117.1 requirements. The 1997 edition of the UBC now includes an exception for Type B dwelling units provided they comply with the requirements of Section 1106.

1103.2.2 Accessible route. An accessible route is a continuous, unobstructed path of travel connecting all accessible elements and spaces of a building or facility. It includes corridors, floors, ramps, elevators, lifts and clear floor space at fixtures. Code users should review the accessible route provisions in Section 4.3 of CABO/ANSI A117.1. When UBC Appendix Chapter 11 is adopted, exterior portions of an accessible route must be evaluated and may include parking access aisles, curb ramps, crosswalks at vehicular ways, walks, and ramps and lifts.

The exception to the first paragraph has been revised in the 1997 edition to exclude Group M Occupancies with five or more tenants rather than use of the terms multitenant Group M retail and wholesale occupancies as stated in the previous edition. Also, the occupant load limitation of 50 has been eliminated thereby setting 3,000 square feet ($278.7m^2$) as the area limitation for this exception. Deleting the occupant load criteria will allow different uses above or below accessible levels which may have different occupant load factors. Modification of this exception to allow Group M retail and wholesale occupancies to also use the square footage exception eliminates certain enforcement confusion.

The exception to the first paragraph of this section applies to buildings where elevators may not be required. A building of less than three stories in height or a building that has less than 3,000 square feet ($278.7 m^2$) above and below an accessible level may be exempt from some of the accessibility requirements, unless the building contains offices of health-care providers, transportation facilities and airports, or a shopping com-

plex with five or more tenants. The three-story exemption is based on the provisions of Section 3003.4.1.

This exception eliminates an elevator or other means of vertical access; however, it does not reduce or eliminate the obligation of compliance with other provisions for accessibility. While the floor either above or below the accessible grade-level floor would not be required to meet the applicable accessibility standards, any facilities provided on these floors would also be required to be provided on the accessible floor. For example, if toilet or bathing facilities are located on the floor either above or below the accessible floor, then these same facilities are required on the accessible floor and shall be constructed as accessible facilities. However, if the elevator is not required, but one is provided, then it too must meet accessibility standards.

In other words, the intent of the second paragraph of the section is to provide equal means of access. An interior stairway and an exterior ramp fails the equality test.

The exception to the third paragraph is a unique provision that is limited to one use. As Figure 1103-1 indicates, the accessible route for Group R, Division 1 apartments may be a vehicular route based on this exception. For example, this exception could apply to an apartment complex where common- or public-use areas, such as laundry rooms, storage facilities and recreation rooms, are located in various buildings on a steeply sloped site.

1103.2.3 Accessible entrances. In general, at least one entrance, but not less than 50 percent of all entrances to a building or individual tenant space, must be accessible.

In Figure 1103-2, two entrances (Doors A and B) are considered to be entrances to the entire building. As such they should be accessible. Doors C and D are *tenant* entrances and should not necessarily be considered as building entrances; they may be exempt from these provisions since there are accessible entrances provided into each tenant space. In addition, doors used exclusively for loading and service would also be excluded when determining the total number of entrances to a building or tenant space under the exception to the first paragraph. A required entrance which also accesses a tenant space can be used for both purposes without increasing the number of accessible entrances. One easy requirement to remember is that if there is only one entrance into a building or tenant, that entrance must be accessible. In addition to the exception for entrances used exclusively for loading and service, a second exception was added to the 1997 edition for entrances to spaces not required to be accessible as provided for in Section 1103.

The second paragraph of this section was added to ensure that certain entrances comply with the accessible route provisions. These entrances are the connection between accessible buildings and accessible site elements.

An important aspect of accessibility and accessible entrances is obviously the door assembly and its related components, including the threshold, hardware, closers and opening force. Important requirements that affect doors and their accessibility are in Section 1004 of the UBC and Section 4.13 of CABO/ANSI A117.1.

Landings on both sides of doorways are also important accessibility features. When access for persons with disabilities is required, a floor or landing shall not be more than $1/2$ inch (12.7 mm) lower than the threshold of the doorway according to Section 1003.3.1.6 of the UBC. This reduction from 1 inch (25 mm)

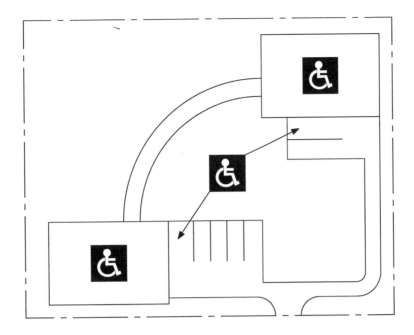

FIGURE 1103-1

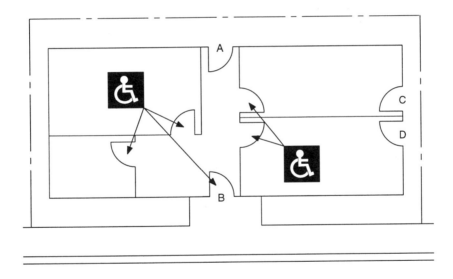

FIGURE 1103-2

is intended to reduce any complex maneuvering required to move across the threshold while operating the door.

Door hardware—including handles, pulls, latches, locks or any other operating device on accessible doors—is required to be of a shape that is easy to grasp with one hand and does not require a tight pinching, tight grasping or twisting of the wrist to operate. Many individuals have great difficulty operating door hardware that does not include push-type, U-shaped handles or lever-operated mechanisms.

Door surface hardware, in the form of kickplates, can effectively reduce the maintenance needed for an accessible door. To be effective, the kickplate should be as wide as the door and extend to a height of 12 inches (305 mm) from the bottom edge.

The kickplate reduces the abuse the door receives from wheelchair footrests or walkers which must be pushed against the door.

Door closers with delayed action capability are also important and allow a person more time to maneuver through a door. These closers are required to be adjusted so that from an open position of 90 degrees, the time required to move the door to an open position of 12 degrees will be a minimum of five seconds. Door closers are required to have minimum closing forces in order to close and latch the door; however, for other than fire doors, maximum force levels are set to limit the force levels for pushing or pulling open doors. Opening forces and the methods used to measure them are specified in Section 4.13.11 and Appendix A of CABO/ANSI A117.1.

Minimum maneuvering clearances at doors, other than those that are for automatic or power-assisted doors, are based on a combination of forward and side reach limitations, the direction of approach, and the minimum clear width required for wheelchairs. They also permit enough space that a slight angle of approach can be gained, which then provides additional leverage or opening force by the user. Without these required clearances, there is a possibility of interference between the edge of the door and the footrest on a wheelchair. This could render the door inaccessible to someone using a wheelchair.

Before these accessibility provisions were added, the accessibility provisions for doors in the UBC addressed the width and height, number, placement or location, swing and fire-resistive ratings, and closing devices. With the new provisions, minimum maneuvering clearances at doors become an extremely important part of the design, review, construction, inspection and maintenance of buildings in providing accessibility.

In addition to the traditional provisions for doors, CABO/ANSI A117.1 contains many detailed provisions and illustrations that are found in Section 4.13.6 and Appendix B.

Care should be exercised when considering the maneuvering space necessary to make doors accessible. An inadvertent reversal of the latch side to hinge side may render a door inaccessible to an individual in a wheelchair.

Paragraph 3 has been added to the 1997 edition of the code requiring the primary entrance to either Type A or B dwelling units to be located on an accessible route from public or common areas. The primary entrance to the dwelling unit should not be to a bedroom.

1103.2.4.2 Other signs. The purpose of this section is to provide signage at certain inaccessible facilities and elements enabling individuals to locate the nearest accessible facilities and elements. Section 4.28 of CABO/ANSI A117.1 contains the detailed provisions for signage. In addition, directional signage shall be provided at all separate-sex toilet or bathing facilities indicating the location of the nearest unisex room.

SECTION 1104 — EGRESS AND AREAS OF REFUGE

With increased access to buildings based on this chapter's provisions, it became apparent that safe egress for people with disabilities was needed. Therefore, the code requires that accessible spaces be provided with accessible means of egress or with areas of refuge where occupants may remain temporarily.

An example to illustrate this provision is an auditorium with multilevel tiers of seating. While the amount of egress from the tier is provided for in Chapter 10, only two accessible means of egress would be required from any accessible space. Therefore, a tier could be required to provide three or more means of egress, but only two accessible means of egress need be provided.

1104.1.2 Stairways. Increasing the width of stairs to 48 inches (1219 mm) between the handrails allows for the minimum amount of space needed to assist persons with disabilities in the event of building evacuation. The provisions for an area of refuge or horizontal exit address the increased time needed for egress. The provided exceptions apply to:

1. A single dwelling unit or guest room,

2. A building where it is anticipated that an automatic sprinkler system would suppress or control a fire,

3. An exit stairway that begins beyond a horizontal exit or

4. In an open parking garage where there is a reduction in combustibles due to the type of construction and an increase in smoke removal through open ventilation.

1104.1.3 Elevators. Unlike Chapter 10, which specifically prohibits considering an elevator as an approved means of egress, this section requires an elevator for egress under certain conditions. In buildings over four stories in height, ramps and stairs cannot adequately serve as egress for individuals in wheelchairs. Therefore, at least one elevator must be used. Increased protection for the occupants using the elevators is provided by either automatic sprinklers or access from an area of refuge or a horizontal exit. Standby power is also required in order to maintain service during emergencies.

1104.1.4 Platform lifts. A platform lift is specifically excluded as an acceptable element of means of egress. This prohibition applies to all occupancy groups and uses, except as part of an interior egress route within dwelling units. In other than dwelling units, the maintenance of the lift as well as the complexity and delay in utilizing a platform lift are considered substantial obstacles in providing an acceptable means of egress for persons in wheelchairs. Section 1105.3 specifically sets forth accessibility requirements for the use of platform lifts.

1104.2 Areas of Refuge. By definition, an area of refuge is an area "where persons unable to use stairs can remain temporarily in safety to await instructions or assistance during emergency evacuation." Unfortunately, the term "temporary" is not defined, so a number of provisions are applied to an area of refuge to increase the level of protection for anyone using it. These provisions include pressurization in some cases to prevent smoke intrusion, a size large enough to accommodate wheelchairs without reducing exit width, smoke barriers of one-hour construction with smoke- and draft-control assemblies, dampers for any duct which penetrates the smoke barrier, two-way communication systems, and instructions on the use of the area under emergency conditions. The two-way communication system is intended to allow a user of the area of refuge to identify his or her location and needs to a central control point. Obviously, it is important that someone be available to answer the call for help when a two-way communication system is provided. An additional public phone can be used to notify the emergency services when the central control point is not constantly attended. The system is not required in buildings of four stories or less.

Each area of refuge shall be identified by a sign stating that it is an area of refuge and with the international symbol of accessibility.

1104.2.3 Size. Each area of refuge shall be sized to accommodate one wheelchair space not less than 30 inches by 48 inches (762 mm by 1219 mm) for each 200 occupants, or portion thereof, based on the occupant load of the refuge area and areas served by the refuge area. Since wheelchair spaces are not permitted to reduce the required exit width nor interfere with access to or use of fire department hose connections and valves, the designer needs to consider access to fire-protection equipment and exit width when placing wheelchair spaces in the area of refuge.

SECTION 1105 — FACILITY ACCESSIBILITY

This section provides scoping provisions to ensure that certain elements or areas within buildings where specific services are provided or activities are performed are made accessible. Certain components in CABO/ANSI A117.1 or other accessibility regulations have not been included in this section. Items such as telephones, swimming pools, and shelving and display for mercantile occupancies were eliminated since these were not considered to be regulated by the building code. Requirements for Type B dwelling units are included in Section 1106.

1105.2.1 Bathing facilities. With the exception of a facility intended for a single occupant and not for common or public use, at least one of all other fixtures or elements in a bathing facility must be accessible. The exception for "executive" bathrooms here and in Section 1105.2.2 was added in the 1994 UBC and represented a fairly significant change in the code, but in application it simply creates greater uniformity since many jurisdictions had previously enforced the code this way. The term "accessible" applies to the doors, clear floor space, operable parts and dispensers, medicine cabinets and mirrors, among other things.

Bathing facility requirements for recreational facilities have been added to the 1997 UBC requiring that an accessible unisex bathing room be provided where separate-sex bathing facilities are provided. Where each separate-sex bathing facility has only one shower fixture, unisex bathing facilities will not be required.

To be considered accessible, a number of items related to the bathtub and its location need to be considered. For example, clear floor space in front of the bathtub is necessary to allow transfer of a person from a wheelchair to the tub. For a bathtub without a seat at the head of the tub, a clear space of 30 inches by 60 inches (762 mm by 1525 mm) for a parallel approach or 48 inches by 60 inches (1219 mm by 1525 mm) for a forward approach shall be provided. If a seat is provided at the head of the tub, the clear space shall be 30 inches by 93 inches (762 mm by 2360 mm) minimum. These requirements are in Appendix B of CABO/ANSI A117.1.

Another important element in making bathing facilities accessible is the proper installation of grab bars. Many persons with disabilities rely on grab bars and handrails to assist them in maintaining their balance or transferring onto a fixture. People brace their arms between the grab bar or handrail and the wall to give them more leverage and stability. The required clearance of $1^1/_2$ inches (38 mm) between the grab bar or handrail and the support is a safety feature to prevent arms from slipping through the openings and causing injuries. It also provides for the usability of the grippable area of a grab bar. Grab bar and handrail provisions do allow alternate shapes as long as the grip is similar to one provided by a cross section with a range of $1^1/_4$ inches (32 mm) to $1^1/_2$ inches (38 mm). Many other bathing facility features are addressed in the CABO/ANSI standard for accessibility, and the reader is directed to this standard for further requirements and illustrations.

1105.2.2 Toilet facilities. Fixtures in dwelling units that are adaptable and in accessible dwelling units must comply with CABO/ANSI A117.1. Noticeable differences in the requirements for dwelling units as compared to all other occupancies include the allowance for adaptable units, for doors to swing into the clear floor space and for a minimum 15-inch (381 mm) height of the water closet instead of 17 inches (430 mm).

In other than dwelling units, the main components of toilet facilities are the water closet, the toilet stall, and the urinal; and the main accessibility issues are the clear space, door swing, transfer capability, height of fixture, grab bars and controls. The CABO/ANSI A117.1 contains the details and many illustrations which depict these requirements.

Accessible unisex toilet requirements for Groups A and M Occupancies have been added to the 1997 UBC where six or more male and female water closets are required. These occupancies generally have high occupant loads with a minimum stay of approximately one hour for the occupants.

1105.2.4. Unisex bathing and toilet rooms. Specific provisions have been added to the 1997 UBC on accessibility requirements for unisex bathing and toilet rooms. Such bathing and toilet rooms are required to comply with this section and CABO/ANSI A117.1-1992. These requirements are a simpler and more concise interpretation of the BCMC recommendations for unisex toilet/bathing facilities and are generally consistent with the intent of BCMC. The primary issue relative to unisex toilet/bathing facilities is that some people with disabilities use the assistance of persons of the opposite sex and, therefore, require a toilet or bathing facility that accommodates both persons.

1105.2.4.2 Location. Unisex toilet and bathing rooms shall be located on an accessible route. Unisex toilet rooms shall be located not more than one story above or below separate-sex toilet facilities. The accessible route from any separate-sex toilet room to a unisex toilet room shall not exceed 500 feet (152 400 mm). The one-story/500-foot limitation is currently in the model plumbing or building code. This requirement may effectively increase the total travel to two stories/1,000 feet (304 800 mm) for someone requiring the use of the unisex facility because the distance is measured from the separate-sex facility. The increase is viewed as justified based on the premise that persons needing such facilities will be assisted, which will reduce travel time in a wheelchair, as well as the requirement that such facilities be provided on an accessible route via elevators.

Additionally, in passenger transportation facilities and airports, the accessible route from separate-sex toilet facilities to a unisex toilet room shall not pass through security checkpoints. The restriction regarding crossing through security checkpoints in airports and similar facilities is intended to eliminate any potential delays which may cause missed flights/connections.

1105.3 Elevators, Stairways and Platform Lifts. A number of elements have specific accessibility requirements and must be considered carefully during both the design and construction of elevators. These elements include automatic operation, call buttons, hall signals, tactile signage on hoistway entrances, door protective and reopening devices, door and signal timing for hall calls, door delay for car calls, inside dimensions for elevator cars, floor surfaces, illumination levels, car controls, car position indicators and emergency communication. Provisions for each of these elements are intended to provide the accessibility of the elevator. For example, features such as automatic operation and automatic self-leveling with a tolerance of $^1/_2$ inch (12.7 mm) make the entry into the elevator car by someone in a wheelchair possible in a way similar to the threshold requirements for accessible doors.

Code users should review and compare the dimensions in CABO/ANSI A117.1 with those specified in UBC Sections 3003.4.7 and 3003.5. The importance of providing an elevator that can accommodate an ambulance stretcher cannot be emphasized too strongly.

The limited acceptance of platform lifts was added in the 1994 UBC. Before that edition, platform lifts were prohibited from being used as a part of the accessible route within a building. Although these lifts can be found in many locations, their installation had generally been limited to providing access in existing construction. The reluctance to accept these lifts in new construction was based on perceptions that the internal changes in elevation could be designed to accommodate ramps, elevators, etc., and was also based on questions regarding reliability and maintenance of these lifts.

To use the platform lifts in lieu of an elevator, they must comply with Section 4.11 of CABO/ANSI A117.1 and be approved by the building official. They also must be installed in one of the four listed locations and, perhaps most importantly, be capable of independent operation. The requirement for independent operation would prohibit not only providing someone to assist the lift user but also the common practice of requiring the user to obtain a key or other such device in order to use the lift. It should be noted that the acceptance of these lifts is limited to providing access and that their use as a portion of the means of egress is restricted by Section 1104.1.4.

1105.4.1 Drinking fountains. This section ensures that at least one half of the drinking fountains provided are made accessible. This is another of the many provisions where it is important to focus on the word "provided" and note that the provision does not require drinking fountains.

1105.4.2 Fixed or built-in seating or tables. For spaces at accessible fixed tables or counters, at least one table in the facility shall be provided for wheelchairs. When more than one is required by this section, then they shall be evenly distributed around the facility so as not to isolate an accessible area from the rest of the establishment.

1105.4.3 Storage. At least one accessible storage facility, when provided, shall be accessible according to CABO/ANSI A117.1.

1105.4.4 Customer service facilities. This section provides nominal accessibility provisions that are intended to allow persons with disabilities to use these facilities without much assistance. Other features commonly found in these uses would have to comply with other provisions in this chapter.

1105.4.5 Controls, operating mechanisms and hardware. To be able to operate controls, operating mechanisms and hardware, a clear floor space and reach ranges for either forward or parallel approaches must be provided.

1105.4.6. Alarms. Audible and visible alarms are intended to alert sight-impaired and hearing-impaired persons in case of emergencies. The general application of alarm systems addresses areas not designed for sleeping, such as offices. Additional methods are needed for awakening sleeping persons with hearing impairments. Audible signals need to have both an intensity and frequency that will attract attention and alert persons who may have a partial hearing loss.

Visual signaling emergency lights shall be integrated into the building or facility alarm system. It is important to note that these provisions apply whenever an alarm system is provided.

1105.4.7 Rail transit platforms. Detectable warnings should be standardized to assist in the universal recognition and reaction of persons using these platforms. Detectable and tactile warning devices also serve guide dogs and should contrast visually with the adjoining surfaces in a light-on-dark or dark-on-light application.

1105.4.8 Assembly areas.

1105.4.8.1 Wheelchair spaces. In stadiums, theaters, auditoriums and similar occupancies, at least one wheelchair location shall accommodate a minimum of two wheelchairs. The requirements for the wheelchair locations can be found in Section 4.32 of CABO/ANSI A117.1. The wheelchair locations are required to be adjacent to an aisle and immediately adjacent to a fixed or removable seat on one side.

The dispersion of wheelchair spaces within an assembly area is regulated by the third paragraph and Table 11-A. As an example, it is determined through the following calculation that a new area with a seating capacity of 18,000 would require at least 94 wheelchair spaces:

$$6 \text{ spaces} + [(18,000 \text{ seats} - 500 \text{ seats}) \div 200 \text{ spaces/seat}]$$
$$= 93.5 \text{ spaces}$$

Minimum number of total wheelchair
spaces required = 94 spaces

The provision intends that these 94 wheelchair spaces not be restricted to one location and, further, based on the availability of accessible routes, that these spaces be dispersed throughout a multilevel facility. Wheelchair spaces should be an integral feature of any seating plan to provide individuals with physical disabilities with a choice of admission prices and a line of sight comparable to that provided to the general public.

1105.4.8.2 Assistive listening systems. Assistive listening systems are required to be installed where audible communications are an integral part of the use of the space. Such spaces having fixed seating and an occupant load of 50 or more shall have permanently installed systems. This also applies to those spaces of any occupant load with fixed seating and having an audio-amplification system in place. Areas or spaces with an occupant load of less than 50 that do not have permanently installed audio-amplification systems may either permanently install an assistive listening system or have the electrical outlets or other supplementary wiring necessary to support a portable system.

These systems are intended to augment a standard public address or other audio system by providing signals that are free of background noise to individuals who use special receivers or their own hearing aids. Further provisions found in CABO/ANSI A117.1 require that when a production includes a live oral presentation, the assistive listening systems should be placed within 50 feet (15 240 mm) of the presentation. This will enable persons with impaired hearing to speech-read the facial expressions of performers. In motion picture theaters, fixed seats served by a listening system shall be placed at any location in the theater that has a complete view of the screen. AM and FM radio frequency systems, infrared systems, induction loops, hard-wired earphones and other equivalent devices are all permitted.

Signage such as the international symbol of access for hearing loss shall be installed to notify patrons of the availability of the listening systems. The signage is required to comply with the provisions of Section 4.28 of CABO/ANSI A117.1.

SECTION 1106 — TYPE B DWELLING UNITS

This section includes the compliance standards for Type B dwelling units, which are new in the 1997 UBC. For a discussion on this section, refer to the discussion on the new definitions to Section 1102 in this handbook.

Chapter 12

INTERIOR ENVIRONMENT

Light and ventilation requirements for all occupancies were consolidated into Chapter 12 in the 1994 UBC.

SECTION 1202 — LIGHT AND VENTILATION IN GROUPS A, B, E, F, H, I, M AND S OCCUPANCIES (NONRESIDENTIAL OCCUPANCIES)

1202.1 Light. For certain defined nonresidential occupancies, portions customarily occupied by human beings are required to be provided with either artificial light or with natural light supplied via exterior glazed openings. Natural light requirements for nonresidential occupancies are identical to those in Section 1203.2 for Group R Occupancies. These light requirements apply to Groups A, B, E, F, H, I, M and S Occupancies. There are no code-specified light requirements, natural or artificial, for Group U Occupancies.

1202.2 Ventilation.

1202.2.1 General. The provisions of Section 1202.2.1 establish general ventilation requirements for occupancies other than residential, with the exception of Group U Occupancies, for which there are no requirements. The first paragraph addresses areas other than toilet rooms, which are covered in the second paragraph. While Section 1202.2.1 covers general requirements, subsequent sections address ventilation for specific occupancies and use areas, such as motor vehicle storage garages.

The general requirement is that all enclosed portions of buildings customarily occupied by human beings are required to be provided with ventilation either through openable exterior openings or by means of a mechanically operated system. Table 12-1 lists light and ventilation requirements for both nonresidential and residential occupancies.

Note that both Sections 1202.1 for light and 1202.2 for ventilation state that the requirements apply to "all enclosed portions of [buildings] customarily occupied by human beings." Thus, the code does not require that those areas not normally occupied, such as storage rooms or equipment rooms, meet Section 1202 requirements. This is not to imply that there are no requirements for light and ventilation in areas not normally occupied, since other codes, such as the Mechanical Code, do contain requirements for lighting, ventilation, combustion air and the like.

TABLE 12-1
GENERAL LIGHT AND VENTILATION REQUIREMENTS[1]

	NONRESIDENTIAL OCCUPANCIES: GROUPS A, B, E, F, H, I, M AND S	RESIDENTIAL OCCUPANCIES: GROUP R	COMMENTS
Light Natural[2]	$1/10$ of floor area No minimum area requirement	$1/10$ of floor area 10 square foot minimum	No light requirements for Group U Occupancies
Artificial[3]	Permitted	Permitted for kitchen only	
Ventilation Natural[4]	$1/20$ of floor area No minimum area requirement	$1/20$ of floor area 5 square foot minimum	No ventilation requirements for Group U Occupancies
Mechanical	15 cubic feet per minute outside air per occupant[5] No minimum number of air changes	15 cubic feet per minute outside air per occupant[6] two air changes per hour	
Toilet Room Ventilation Natural[4]	3 square feet fully operable or vertical duct not less than 100 square inches for the first water closet plus 50 square inches for each additional water closet	$1/20$ of floor area $1^1/2$ square foot minimum	Residential requirement applies to bathrooms, water closet compartments, laundry rooms and similar uses
Mechanical[7]	Four air changes per hour	Five air changes per hour[8]	

For **SI:** 1 foot = 304.8 mm, 1 square foot = 0.0929 m², 1 cubic foot per minute = 0.47L/s.

[1]Light and ventilation:
Group R Occupancies—Requirements apply to guest rooms and habitable rooms.
All other occupancies—Requirements apply to all enclosed portions customarily occupied by human beings. See Sections 1202.2.2 through 1202.2.7 for special requirements.
[2]Natural light to be provided by means of exterior glazed openings that open onto a court or yard complying with Section 1203.4.
[3]See Section 1003.2.9 for exit illumination requirements.
[4]Natural ventilation to be provided by means of openable exterior openings that shall open onto a court or yard complying with Section 1203.4.
[5]Mechanically operated systems shall provide ventilation in all portions of the building during time building is occupied.
[6]Mechanically operated systems shall provide ventilation in guest rooms, dormitories, habitable rooms and in public corridors during time building is occupied.
[7]System shall be connected directly to the outside, and the point of discharge shall be at least 3 feet from any opening that allows air entry into occupied portions of the building.
[8]Bathrooms that contain only a water closet or lavatory, or combination thereof, and similar rooms may be vented with an approved mechanical recirculating fan or similar device designed to remove odors from the air.

1202.2.3 Group H Occupancies. Due to the hazardous nature of dusts, mists, fumes, vapors and gases that may be emitted by hazardous materials, Group H Occupancies are generally required to have special mechanical ventilation systems. The special requirements for these systems are established in Chapter 5 of the Mechanical Code and Section 8003.1.8 of the Fire Code. It should be noted that there are some cases, such as storage of flammable solids (see UFC Section 8003.1.8), which do not require special mechanical ventilation. It should also be noted that the Fire Code contains additional provisions requiring exhaust from areas containing toxic and highly toxic gases to be processed through a treatment system prior to discharging to the atmosphere.

Ventilation systems required for control of hazardous dusts, mists, etc., are required to operate continuously. The code requires an emergency shutoff control to be installed outside of ventilated areas as an emergency means of disengaging the ventilation system to prevent escape of hazardous materials to atmosphere if deemed necessary. Though the code intends to require ventilation to be in operation at all times, requests for alternate methods of compliance are common for buildings located in severe climates. Jurisdictions will sometimes accept ventilation systems that will operate on detection of small quantities of vapors, gases, etc., in the protected area as an alternate method. Systems of such an alternate design must be reliably designed and operated in a manner which prevents hazardous concentrations of vapors, gases, etc., from accumulating. Since there are no provisions in the code that specifically allow such a design, detection-activated ventilation systems must be approved by jurisdictions on a case-by-case basis.

1202.2.4 Group H, Division 4 Occupancies. Group H, Division 4 Occupancies do not have the concentrated movement of vehicles normally found in Group S, Division 3 Occupancies; therefore, the requirements in Section 1202.2.4 do not specify the same volume of exhaust ventilation as is required for Group S, Division 3 Occupancies. Section 1202.2.4 requires exhaust ventilation at a rate of 1 cubic foot per minute per square foot (0.044 L/s/m^2) of floor space, and as indicated in the next section of this handbook, this is the amount recommended by ASHRAE Standard 62, "Ventilation for Acceptable Indoor Air Quality."

This section also requires engine repair stalls to be equipped with exhaust connections and requires connecting offices and waiting rooms to be equipped with conditioned air under positive pressure to minimize migration of vehicle exhaust into these spaces.

The exception allows buildings with substantial openings, such as canopy-style or similar buildings, to omit power-ventilating equipment.

1202.2.7 Group S parking garages. In the specific case of parking garages, the code has ventilation requirements which are based in part on ASHRAE standards, which recommend ventilation of from 1 to 1^1/$_2$ cubic feet per minute per square foot (0.044 L/s/m^2 to 0.71 L/s/m^2) of floor space, depending on the number of vehicles in motion at any given time.

The requirement for 1^1/$_2$ cubic feet per minute per square foot (0.71 L/s/m^2) of floor area can be modified based on criteria established by the American Conference of Industrial Hygienists

(ACIH), including a threshold limit value established by ACIH for carbon monoxide of 50 parts per million, with peaks of 200 parts per million for short duration. The threshold limit value is the concentration which an individual can tolerate based on a continuous exposure during an eight-hour working day. Occasional occupants may safely be exposed to higher concentrations for short periods of time.

Garages where vehicles are frequently in operation and motion require large-capacity ventilation systems. Tests conducted on 1970-year model automobiles indicated that the average carbon monoxide emission rate of vehicles operating under low-speed garage conditions is approximately 0.7 cubic foot per minute (0.33 L/s). The maintenance of a concentration of carbon monoxide at 50 parts per million requires that the ventilation system exhaust 14,000 cubic feet per minute (6608 L/s) for each automobile in operation. The number of cars in operation at any given time is a variable determined by the use of the garage, method of collecting parking fees, and the size and shape of the garage. Most garages will have an average instantaneous movement rate of from 2 to 4 percent of capacity with peak levels of from 5 to 20 percent for apartments and shopping centers. The peak levels for office buildings are from 10 to 40 percent. Peak loads for theater and sports arena area parking garages can run as high as 90 percent. The exhaust quantities specified in the code are adequate for instantaneous movement rates of 3.2 percent and short-term peaks of 13 percent. However, in an exception to this provision, added in the 1991 UBC, mechanical ventilation of a Group S, Division 3 parking garage is not necessary when openings that comply with the provisions for Group S, Division 4 open parking garages are provided. In this case, the ventilation will be provided by natural means.

SECTION 1203 — LIGHT AND VENTILATION IN GROUP R OCCUPANCIES

The light and ventilation requirements in this section of the UBC and, in fact, in other model codes as well, are carryovers from the beginning of this century when conditions in tenement houses were pitiful at best and downright unhealthy in most cases. As a result, New York City, for example, developed its "Tenement House Law" in 1901, which later became known as the "Multiple Dwelling Law." This law was specifically intended to ameliorate the unsanitary and unhealthful conditions existing in the tenement houses of that period. Thus, requirements for light and ventilation, room size, ceiling height, etc., were created. As other agencies, such as ICBO's predecessor, the Pacific Coast Building Officials Conference, developed building regulations, these requirements carried over from the New York Tenement House Law and found their way into other codes. These requirements have been modified somewhat over the years and expanded, but the intent today is the same as the original intent, which is to provide healthful, livable conditions in residential buildings.

1203.2 Light. The *Uniform Building Code* requires that habitable rooms (which are rooms used for living, sleeping and food preparation, as defined in Section 209) have natural light provided by exterior wall openings. The area of the exterior wall openings is computed based on the nominal size of the opening and not the net glazed area for windows and fully glazed doors. Where doors are only partially glazed, the net glazed area would be used to compute the amount of opening provided for light. Although artificial light may be used as a substitute for natural light anywhere within a nonresidential occupancy, the only permitted substitution for habitable rooms in a residential occupancy is the kitchen. This substitution is permitted because it is often difficult to design dwelling units in multiunit buildings that are able to provide sufficient light to all areas of the kitchen.

1203.3 Ventilation. All habitable rooms are required by the code to have ventilation, and where exterior wall openings are used to provide ventilation, the requirement is for one-half the amount used for natural light. The code also requires that bathrooms, laundry rooms, water closet compartments and similar spaces be ventilated.

Although public corridors do not require natural light, they do require exit lighting as required in Chapter 10, and furthermore, the code requires that public corridors be provided with ventilation. The code permits mechanical ventilation. For bathrooms, water closet compartments, laundry rooms, etc., the mechanical ventilation system is required to be connected directly to the outside. Bathrooms that contain only a water closet or water closet and lavatory may utilize an approved mechanical recirculating fan that is designed to remove odors from the air. The code considers that bathtubs and showers generate sufficient moisture so that an openable window or mechanical ventilation system connected directly to the outside is required. An exception has been added to the 1997 UBC for laundry rooms in Group R, Division 3 Occupancies. Currently, automatic washers in any wash cycle do not emit humidity into the space; they are sealed units. Also, dryers are already venting all humidity to exterior of structures, thus no need for additional mechanical exhausting. Combustion air is already admitted to this structure so this venting does/will not create a negative pressure.

Where openable windows are used, the code requires that they face onto a street, public alley, yard or court located on the same lot as the building. However, required exterior openings may be skylights or may open onto a porch as allowed by the exceptions to Section 1203.1.

Section 1203.1 established what are, in reality, some exceptions for the natural light and natural ventilation requirements in Sections 1203.2 and 1203.3. The first paragraph establishes the degree of "openness" required between two adjoining rooms in order for the two to be considered as one for the purpose of light and ventilation. The second paragraph contains two key exceptions: (1) exterior openings may open into a roofed porch meet-

ing three stated conditions, and (2) skylights may be used to provide natural light and, if openable, to provide ventilation.

The consolidated light and ventilation requirements are now found in Chapter 12. Some provisions that you might assume would apply to both residential and nonresidential uses actually do not apply. Specifically, this is true for the provisions of Section 1203.1 discussed earlier. Even though the yard and court requirements of Section 1203.4 appear in Section 1203, Light and Ventilation in Group R Occupancies, they apply to nonresidential occupancies because both Sections 1202.1 and 1202.2 specifically reference Section 1203.4. Also, the provisions of Section 1203.1 specifically reference Section 1203.4. However, the provisions of Section 1203.1 are not likewise cross-referenced and, at least in standard code usage, would not apply. This apparent inconsistency has undoubtedly occurred because residential and nonresidential light and ventilation requirements were, until the 1994 edition, in separate occupancy chapters that were usually modified only within themselves in order to address specific needs. Now with a consolidated chapter, differences in application have become more apparent.

1203.4 Yards or Courts. The *Uniform Building Code* contains provisions for yards and courts where they are used to provide light and ventilation for exterior openings in the building. Most modern-day zoning ordinances also have requirements for yards and courts, and quite often these are more than adequate to provide the light and ventilation required by the code.

To be considered as providing adequate light and ventilation, each yard or court must have a minimum width of 3 feet (914 mm) with eaves limited as discussed in Section 503. In addition, these yards and courts must be increased in width, depending on the height of the building. The intent for the tall building is to have an increased court width so that light coming into the court will be able to reach the lower stories of the building, and this is only possible where the width of the court is in proper relationship to the height of the court. The requirements in the code are an obvious compromise between optimum light at the bottom of a court and the need to build as much building area on the property as possible for economic purposes.

Inner courts that are enclosed by the walls of the buildings, sometimes referred to as lightwells, obviously need some means to remove accumulated trash at the bottom and also a means to provide circulation of air for ventilation purposes. In keeping with this intent, the code requires that an air intake be provided at the bottom of courts for buildings more than two stories in height and requires that all courts be provided with access for cleaning.

Chapter 13

ENERGY CONSERVATION

SECTION 1301 — SOLAR ENERGY COLLECTORS

This section provides requirements for solar energy collectors on roofs of buildings that are consistent with the model document for code officials on solar heating and cooling of buildings. Prepared by CABO for the Department of Energy, this document intends that collectors that function as building components—that is, collectors that are constructed integrally with the roof—shall comply with the provisions of the code regulating roofs and roof coverings. Where collectors are an add-on type of item, such as being above or on an existing roof, they are not permitted to reduce the fire-resistance or fire-retardancy classification of the roof-covering materials, with certain exceptions for one- and two-family dwellings, noncombustible collectors and collectors that comply with Section 2603.14.

Chapter 14

EXTERIOR WALL COVERINGS

This chapter establishes the basic requirement for exterior wall coverings, namely that they shall provide weather protection for the building at its exterior. The other important item necessary for complete weather protection, the roof system, is addressed in the next chapter. Chapter 14 presents general weather protection criteria and specific requirements for veneer and vinyl siding. Specific requirements for such things as wood siding and portland cement plaster are addressed in chapters that specifically address the type of material under consideration. For example, Section 2310 provides requirements for wood-based exterior wall covering materials, while Chapter 25 addresses gypsum board and plaster.

SECTION 1402 — WEATHER PROTECTION

This section provides specifications for the protection of the interior of the building from weather; therefore, there are requirements for:

- Protection of the interior wall covering from moisture that penetrates the exterior wall covering.
- Flashing and counterflashing of openings in exterior walls.
- Flashing and counterflashing of parapets and copings at the edge of the roof.
- Weatherproofing of balconies, landings and other similar-type surfaces that are exposed to the weather.
- Dampproofing of basement walls.

As most exterior wall coverings are permeable by moisture, the code requires that there be a moisture barrier or weather-resistive barrier placed under the exterior wall covering and over the studs whose purpose is to prevent moisture infiltration to the interior wall surfaces. Further, the code establishes those materials outlined in UBC Standard 14-1 as providing the required weather-resistive characteristics. In the case of other materials, they shall be equal to those specified in the standard. Asphalt-saturated rag felt is also considered to be a conforming-type weather-resistive barrier.

This section also provides six cases where the weather-protective barrier may be omitted—for example, where there is no human occupancy, where the exterior covering is either water repellent or of approved weatherproof materials, and other similar cases.

The code also requires that all intersections of vertical and horizontal surfaces be flashed and counterflashed to prevent water intrusion at these locations. Roof and wall intersections and parapets are especially troublesome, as are exterior wall openings exposed to the weather and, particularly, those exposed to wind-driven rain.[1]

Even though the code in this area may not cover the subject as thoroughly as some wish, it intends that the exterior envelope of

the building be weatherproofed so as to protect the interior from the weather. Furthermore, for buildings of human occupancy, the interior must be sanitary and livable. Therefore, whether prescribed in the code or not, any place on the envelope of the building which provides a route for admission of water or moisture into the building is required to be properly protected.

The requirements of Section 1402.3 are intended to protect wood members used in the framing of balconies and landings from dry rot. Where the balcony or landing is sealed underneath, water and moisture are not allowed to dissipate, and dry rot is the eventual result. These areas should have a minimum slope of $^1/_4$ unit vertical in 12 units horizontal (2% slope) to help ensure adequate drainage.

Section 1402.5 is new to the 1997 UBC and requires window wells to extend below the window sill height for obvious drainage purposes.

SECTION 1403 — VENEER

Although the definition for "veneer" in Section 1403.2 includes plastic veneer along with brick, concrete, stone, tile and metal, Section 1403 is primarily concerned with masonry, stone, terra cotta or ceramic tile installations. Plastic veneer is addressed in Section 2604. It is interesting to note that, in the 1927 edition of the UBC, regulations for the installation of veneer considered only those cases where veneer was installed over a masonry backing wall. Since that time, veneer has evolved from being an ornamental facing on masonry walls to an ornamental facing on all types of walls, including wood and metal stud walls.

1403.1 Scope. The code requires that all veneer comply with this chapter, except for wainscots not exceeding 4 feet (1219 mm) above the adjacent walking surface. Wainscots are low enough that if they were to not comply with the code, their failure would not endanger life and would not create a significant property loss.

Exterior veneer attached to wood-frame construction is limited to a height of 30 feet (9144 mm) above the foundation. This limitation is based on the amount of shrinkage that can take place in wood-frame construction of that height. Therefore, either the adhesive bond or the anchorage between the veneer and the wood framing will become seriously strained unless an analysis approved by the building official shows that the differential movements can be tolerated by the attachment of the veneer to the wood framing.

1403.2 Definitions. The code intends by the definition of veneer that it be a *nonstructural* facing of masonry, concrete, metal, plastic or similar approved material. It is intended to provide ornamentation, protection or insulation. On this basis, face brick that are laid with common brick so as to provide a composite structural assembly are not considered veneer, as they act structurally along with the common brick. To be considered veneer, the material must not act structurally with the backing insofar as consideration of structural strength of the assembly is concerned. However, in many cases the veneer does act structurally with the backing and problems can result.

Veneer can be either adhered or anchored and either exterior or interior, depending on its method of attachment to the backing and whether or not it is applied to a weather-exposed surface.

1403.3 Materials. Even though veneer is used nonstructurally, the code requires that materials used for veneer comply with the appropriate chapters of the code relating to the materials used. Further, the code requires that anchors, supports and ties be noncombustible and corrosion resistant. The requirement for corrosion resistance cannot be stressed too highly, as these materials, when used on the exterior of a building, must support the veneer properly for the life of the building. As they are constantly subjected to alternate cycles of wetting and drying, they must be of corrosion-resistant materials as defined in this section.

1403.4 Design.

1403.4.1 General. In addition to the requirements of this section, the code requires that the design of veneer and its attachments comply with the requirements of Chapter 16 (structural forces). This essentially requires that veneer be designed to resist all gravity loads prescribed by the code as well as lateral loads. However, in some cases, such as for anchored veneer in Section 1403.4.3, the lateral load design for anchored veneer effectively utilizes a seismic coefficient of 2.0.

In keeping with the nonstructural concept of veneer, it may not support any load other than its own weight and the vertical dead load of any veneer above. Furthermore, the backing surface to which it is attached is required by the code to be designed to support the additional vertical and lateral loads that are imposed by the veneer.

One aspect of veneer design that is troublesome is the problem of differential movements between the veneer and its backing, as well as differential movements of the supports. These differential movements are created by temperature changes, shrinkage, creep and deflection due to loading. Even though the code considers veneer to be nonstructural, adhered veneer is bonded to its backing so that it must act with the backing, and stresses created by temperature changes, shrinkage, creep and deflection will be transmitted to the veneer. Types of veneer other than adhered veneer also will receive transmission of these stresses from the backing because in many cases the veneer is tightly bonded to the backing by cement plaster or cement grout.

The transmission of stress from the backing surface to the veneer in many cases creates spalling, cracking and buckling of the veneer.[2] Therefore, for the cases where the veneer has a tight bond to its backing, control joints should be installed in the veneer at proper intervals to prevent too large a stress buildup in the veneer.

1403.4.2 Adhered veneer. Where adhered veneer and its application is designed rather than following the prescriptive requirements of Section 1403.5, the code requires that the adhesive materials withstand a shearing stress of 50 psi (345 kPa). This requirement excludes ceramic tile for the reason that prescrip-

tive code provisions for ceramic tile in Table 14-A have been shown by experience to provide adequate adhesion.

1403.4.3 Anchored veneer. Where the prescriptive requirements of Section 1403.6 are not followed, the code requires that the attachment of anchored veneer be designed to resist a horizontal force equal to twice the weight of the veneer. Although a design for twice its weight seems excessive for veneer, it is not difficult to obtain adequate strength in the anchorage to accomplish this design requirement. Past experience with improperly anchored veneer has been disastrous. In fact, for a good many years the insurance companies writing earthquake insurance have excluded exterior masonry veneer from coverage on wood-frame buildings unless the premium was substantially increased to include the veneer. This policy was based on very poor performance of masonry veneer in past earthquakes.

1403.5 Adhered Veneer. As with all exterior wall coverings, the code requires that exterior veneer and its backing provide a weatherproof covering for the exterior wall.

The code does not restrict the length and height of veneered areas for adhered veneer, except as may be required to control expansion and contraction as limited under Section 1403.1.1. As previously discussed in this handbook, one method to control distress due to differential movements is to limit the areas with control joints.

The provisions of this section are prescriptive, and where a design is not provided in accordance with Section 1403.4, these provisions have been shown by experience to be adequate. Figure 1403-1 shows a typical installation of adhered veneer over wood-stud construction.

1403.6 Anchored Veneer. The *Uniform Building Code* requires that anchored veneer be supported on noncombustible supports, except that Section 2307 does permit anchored veneer to be supported on a treated-wood foundation. However, as discussed earlier, Section 1403.1.2 limits the height above the foundation for veneer attached to wood-frame construction to 30 feet (9144 mm).

Where anchored veneer is applied to a surface more than 30 feet (9144 mm) above the foundation, the UBC requires that, in Seismic Zones 2, 3 and 4, the veneer be supported by noncombustible corrosion-resistant structural framing. Furthermore, the structural framing is limited to a 12-foot (3658 mm) spacing vertically, above the 30-foot (9144 mm) height. Moreover, the deflection of the horizontal structural framing which supports the veneer is limited to $1/600$ of the span under the loading created by the veneer.

The deflection limitation and the limitation on vertical spacing of horizontal structural supports are intended by the code to limit the differential interaction of the veneer with its backing so as to prevent cracking, spalling and buckling of the veneer surfaces.

The provisions of Section 1403.6.4 relating to application are intended to apply only where a design is not provided in accordance with Section 1403.4. These provisions also have been developed through experience over the years and have been found to provide reasonable performance. Figures 1403-2 through 1403-5 illustrate the various application requirements specified in this section. See the *Uniform Building Code* for a complete description of the application for the various assemblies.

(Continued on page 253)

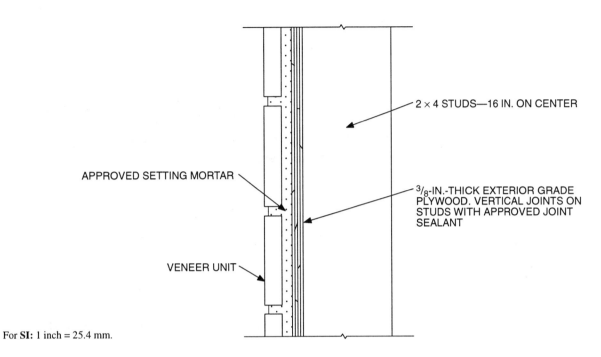

2 × 4 STUDS—16 IN. ON CENTER

APPROVED SETTING MORTAR

$^3/_8$-IN.-THICK EXTERIOR GRADE PLYWOOD. VERTICAL JOINTS ON STUDS WITH APPROVED JOINT SEALANT

VENEER UNIT

For **SI:** 1 inch = 25.4 mm.

APPLICATION OF ADHERED VENEER

FIGURE 1403-1

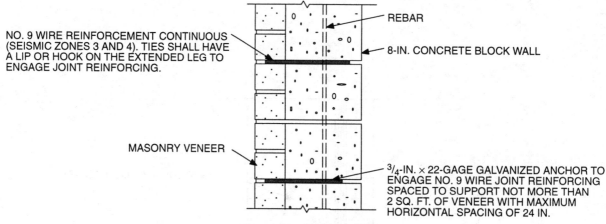

NO. 9 WIRE REINFORCEMENT CONTINUOUS
(SEISMIC ZONES 3 AND 4). TIES SHALL HAVE
A LIP OR HOOK ON THE EXTENDED LEG TO
ENGAGE JOINT REINFORCING.

REBAR

8-IN. CONCRETE BLOCK WALL

MASONRY VENEER

$^3/_4$-IN. × 22-GAGE GALVANIZED ANCHOR TO
ENGAGE NO. 9 WIRE JOINT REINFORCING
SPACED TO SUPPORT NOT MORE THAN
2 SQ. FT. OF VENEER WITH MAXIMUM
HORIZONTAL SPACING OF 24 IN.

A. TO CONCRETE BLOCK WALL

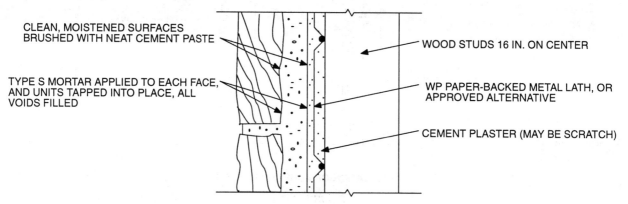

CLEAN, MOISTENED SURFACES
BRUSHED WITH NEAT CEMENT PASTE

TYPE S MORTAR APPLIED TO EACH FACE,
AND UNITS TAPPED INTO PLACE, ALL
VOIDS FILLED

WOOD STUDS 16 IN. ON CENTER

WP PAPER-BACKED METAL LATH, OR
APPROVED ALTERNATIVE

CEMENT PLASTER (MAY BE SCRATCH)

B. TO WOOD STUDS AND PAPER-BACKED METAL LATH

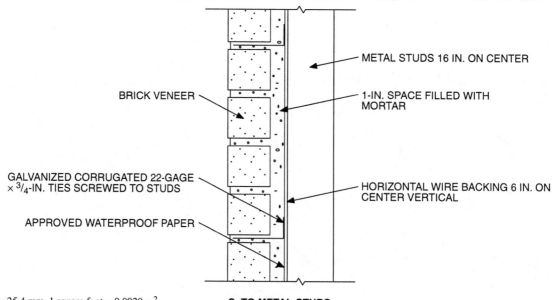

BRICK VENEER

METAL STUDS 16 IN. ON CENTER

1-IN. SPACE FILLED WITH
MORTAR

GALVANIZED CORRUGATED 22-GAGE
× $^3/_4$-IN. TIES SCREWED TO STUDS

HORIZONTAL WIRE BACKING 6 IN. ON
CENTER VERTICAL

APPROVED WATERPROOF PAPER

For **SI:** 1 inch = 25.4 mm, 1 square foot = 0.0929 m^2.

C. TO METAL STUDS

**APPLICATION OF ANCHORED VENEER MASONRY AND STONE UNITS
(5-INCH MAXIMUM THICKNESS)**

FIGURE 1403-2

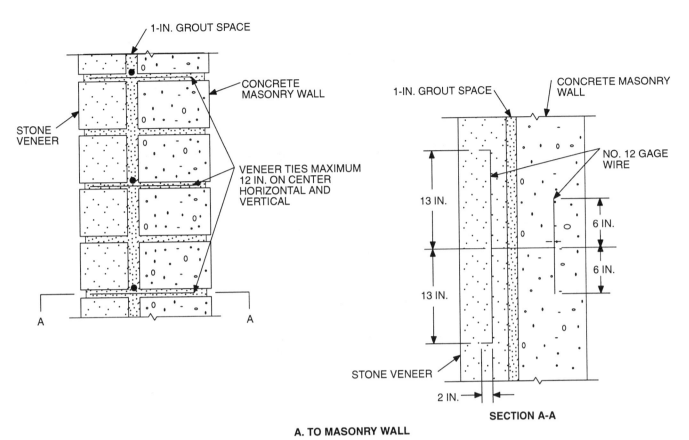

1-IN. GROUT SPACE

CONCRETE MASONRY WALL

STONE VENEER

VENEER TIES MAXIMUM 12 IN. ON CENTER HORIZONTAL AND VERTICAL

A

A

A. TO MASONRY WALL

1-IN. GROUT SPACE

CONCRETE MASONRY WALL

NO. 12 GAGE WIRE

13 IN.

6 IN.

13 IN.

6 IN.

STONE VENEER

2 IN.

SECTION A-A

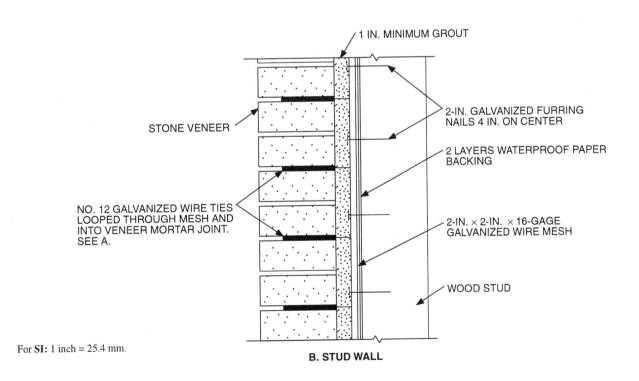

1 IN. MINIMUM GROUT

STONE VENEER

NO. 12 GALVANIZED WIRE TIES LOOPED THROUGH MESH AND INTO VENEER MORTAR JOINT. SEE A.

2-IN. GALVANIZED FURRING NAILS 4 IN. ON CENTER

2 LAYERS WATERPROOF PAPER BACKING

2-IN. × 2-IN. ×16-GAGE GALVANIZED WIRE MESH

WOOD STUD

For **SI:** 1 inch = 25.4 mm.

B. STUD WALL

APPLICATION OF ANCHORED VENEER STONE UNITS UP TO 10 INCHES MAXIMUM THICKNESS

FIGURE 1403-3

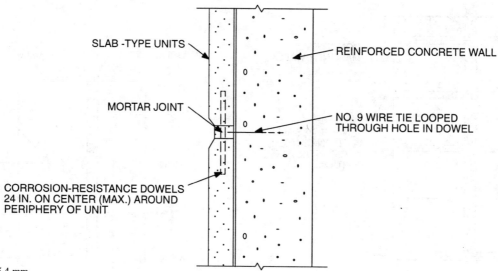

SLAB -TYPE UNITS

REINFORCED CONCRETE WALL

MORTAR JOINT

NO. 9 WIRE TIE LOOPED THROUGH HOLE IN DOWEL

CORROSION-RESISTANCE DOWELS 24 IN. ON CENTER (MAX.) AROUND PERIPHERY OF UNIT

For **SI:** 1 inch = 25.4 mm.

APPLICATION OF SLAB-TYPE UNITS
(2-INCH MAXIMUM THICKNESS)

FIGURE 1403-4

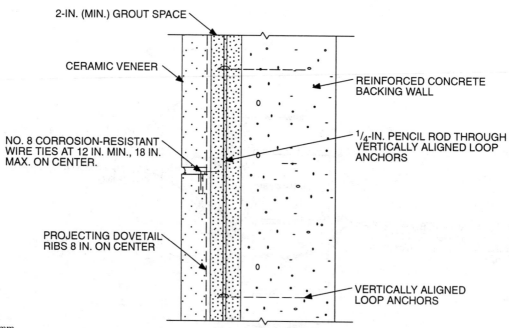

2-IN. (MIN.) GROUT SPACE

CERAMIC VENEER

REINFORCED CONCRETE BACKING WALL

NO. 8 CORROSION-RESISTANT WIRE TIES AT 12 IN. MIN., 18 IN. MAX. ON CENTER.

$1/4$-IN. PENCIL ROD THROUGH VERTICALLY ALIGNED LOOP ANCHORS

PROJECTING DOVETAIL RIBS 8 IN. ON CENTER

VERTICALLY ALIGNED LOOP ANCHORS

For **SI:** 1 inch = 25.4 mm.

APPLICATION OF TERRA COTTA OR CERAMIC UNITS

FIGURE 1403-5

(Continued from page 248)

SECTION 1404 — VINYL SIDING

This new section in the 1994 UBC establishes material standards and sets forth installation requirements for vinyl siding.

Uniform Building Code Standard 14-2 establishes requirements and testing methods for extruded single-wall siding manufactured from rigid PVC compound. To help the building official determine if a particular siding material is code-complying, Section 14.205 of the standard requires each carton to be labeled "conforms to UBC Standard 14-2."

Siding regulated by Section 1404 may be installed on exterior walls of buildings of Type V construction where wind speed according to Figure 16-1 does not exceed 80 miles per hour (129 km/h) and the building height is limited to 40 feet (12 192 mm) in Exposure C. More severe wind or height conditions would require submittal of data showing compliance with Chapter 16. However, most areas in the continental United States fall within the specified wind speed and exposure limit, and most Type V buildings are under 40 feet (12 192 mm) in height. Although not specifically stated, the code intends that the construction type be nonrated unless test data are provided to show that an exterior wall utilizing vinyl siding has undergone fire testing to qualify as at least a one-hour fire-resistive assembly. It is anticipated that vinyl siding will be used on wood-frame construction, even though any type of construction could be classified as Type V construction.

1404.2 Application. Vinyl siding must be installed over a wood-based sheathing material listed in Section 2310 and must satisfy the weather-resistive barrier requirements of Section 1402.1. The section's second paragraph sets forth specific requirements regarding the nailing of siding. Along with these specific requirements, the section's first paragraph states that "siding and accessories shall be installed in accordance with approved manufacturer's instructions."

REFERENCES

[1]Goldberg, Alfred (1985). *Design Guide to the 1985 Uniform Building Code.* GRDA Publications, Mill Valley, California, pages 6-10 to 6-12.

[2]Plewes, W. G. (1978). "Measured Stress in a Ceramic Veneer on Concrete Columns." Proceedings of the North American Masonry Conference, August, pages 116-1 to 116-12. Edited by James L. Noland and James E. Amrheim. Boulder, Colorado.

Chapter 15

ROOFS AND ROOF STRUCTURES

The provisions in Chapter 15 for roof construction and covering are intended to provide a weather-protective barrier at the roof and, in most circumstances, to provide a fire-retardant barrier to prevent flaming combustible materials, such as flying brands from nearby fires, from penetrating the roof construction. The chapter is essentially prescriptive in nature and is based on decades of experience with the various traditional roofing materials. These prescriptive rules are very important to ensuring satisfactory performance of the roof covering even though the reason for a particular requirement may be lost. The provisions are based on an attempt to prevent observed past unsatisfactory performances of the various roofing materials and components.

Those measures that have been shown by experience to prevent past unsatisfactory performance generally are included in the manufacturer's instructions for application of the various roofing materials. In many cases, the manufacturer's instructions are incorporated in this code by reference. The code intends, then, that they be followed as if they were part of the code.

The 1997 edition of the UBC includes various code revisions intended to emphasize that fire-retardant roofs are tested and listed as an assembly of roofing materials and not generally a roof covering itself. It also makes the appendix chapter more compatible with the code and simplifies its organization.

The overriding safety need for roofs is the resistance to external fire factors. The enforcement of this chapter is driven by Table 15-A and the UBC Standard 15-2, fire-retardant requirements. Fire-retardant roofs are tested and listed only as assemblies. A roof covering by itself cannot be a listed fire-retardant roof. Therefore, the regulations should clearly separate assemblies and coverings to enforce construction of listed roof assemblies to the level that we enforce listed wall and floor-ceiling assemblies.

SECTION 1502 — DEFINITIONS

As with other industries supplying specialty building products, the roof-covering industry has a language of its own, and in order to properly understand and apply the provisions of the UBC, the unique terms employed in the UBC must be understood. Several publications contain excellent glossaries of the terms used by the roofing industry.[1,2]

. The 1997 edition of the UBC includes several revisions to the definitions in the previous editions. The revision to the definition of "equiviscous temperature (EVT)" is applicable to asphalt and other mopping bitumens (e.g., coal tar pitch) already referenced in Table 15-G. This revision is consistent with that understood by industry and stated in ASTM D 1079-95, "Standard Terminology Relating to Roofing, Waterproofing, and Bituminous Materials." The revised definition of "wood shakes, treated," permits the use of preservatively treated red pine tapersawn shakes.

SECTIONS 1503 AND 1504 — ROOF-COVERING REQUIREMENTS AND ROOF-COVERING CLASSIFICATION

The *Uniform Building Code* generally requires Class A and Class B roof coverings for most buildings. These are roof coverings that provide protection for the roof against severe and moderate fire exposures, respectively. These exposures are external and are generally created by fires in adjoining structures, wild fires (brush fires and forest fires, for example), and fire from the subject building that extends up the exterior and onto the top surface of the roof. Wild fires and some structure fires create flying and flaming brands that can ignite nonrated roof coverings. With regard to clay tile roofing, which is defined in Section 1504.2 as a noncombustible roof covering, it is of interest to note that the Spanish missionaries shipped clay roofing tile to North America to protect their mission buildings from fire caused by flaming arrows shot onto the roofs by hostile Native Americans.[3]

The roof-covering classifications required by the code, which are related to occupancy and type of construction, are delineated in Table 15-A.

Section 1504 defines fire-retardant roofing, noncombustible roof covering and nonrated roofing:

- A fire-retardant roof is a roofing assembly complying with UBC Standard 15-2 and listed as a Class A, Class B or Class C roof.

  For a roof-covering material to qualify as a Class A, Class B or Class C roof-covering assembly, it must have successfully passed the appropriate test specified in UBC Standard 15-2. The difference among the three classifications is in the severity of the testing. One portion of the testing procedure is the burning brand, described in Section 15.202.4 of UBC Standard 15-2. From Standard 15-2, it can be seen that there is a fair dropoff in brands, with a Class B brand being 25 percent the size of a Class A brand, and a Class C brand being less than 1 percent the size of a Class A brand.

- Noncombustible roof coverings are the roof covering materials listed in Section 1504.2.

- Nonrated roof coverings as described in Section 1504.3.

  Roof coverings that are considered nonrated roof coverings are approved for use by the UBC in those cases where a nonrated roof covering is permitted by Table 15-A. These roof coverings have been shown by experience to provide the necessary resistance to weather as intended by the code when the qualities of the materials comply with the appropriate UBC standard.

It is the intent of the UBC that all buildings have a Class A or Class B roof covering (sometimes referred to as fire-retardant roof coverings in this code), with few exceptions:

- The code permits nonrated roof coverings (those not qualifying as fire retardant) to be used on Group R, Division 3, or Group U Occupancies housed in Type III, IV or V buildings. This exception to the general rule is based on the fact that the combustibility of the building construction permitted by the UBC to house these occupancies is comparable to the combustibility of a nonrated roof covering.

- The code permits Group R, Division 1 Occupancies not greater than two stories in height housed in Type III, IV or V buildings, and with a projected roof area* of not more than 3,000 square feet (278.7 m²), to utilize nonrated roof coverings, provided there is a minimum of 10 feet (3048 mm) from the edge of the roof to the property line on all sides, except for street front property lines. The rationale for this exception is somewhat similar to that described in the previous item. Also, the area of the roof is limited as well as the number of stories so as to limit the application to small buildings. The required clearance of 10 feet (3048 mm) from a property line is intended to reduce the probability of fire spread from one roof to another.

The 3,000-square-foot (278.7 m²) limit on the projected area of the roof is an absolute limit and may not be increased by the use of area separation walls. One way of rationalizing the 3,000-square-foot (278.7 m²) limitation as being absolute is to assume that an area separation wall provides the equivalent of a property line between two buildings. As a result, the requirement that the edge of the roof be at least 10 feet (3048 mm) from the property line would not be met in this case.

SECTION 1505 — ATTICS: ACCESS, DRAFT STOPS AND VENTILATION

1505.1 Access. Because enclosed attics provide an avenue for the undetected spread of fire in a concealed space, the code requires that access openings be provided into the attic so that firefighting forces may gain entry to fight the fire. To be of any value, the access opening must be of sufficient size to admit a firefighter with fire-suppression gear and must also have enough headroom so that entry into the attic may be secured. Access is required to attics of buildings with combustible ceiling or roof construction. Access would not be required for buildings of noncombustible construction except as mentioned below.

A public hallway is the best location for attic access openings, so that fire department personnel will not have to open private offices, apartments or hotel rooms in order to enter the attic. Prior to the 1991 edition, the code required this location in buildings of three or more stories. The current provision still requires attic access to be located in a corridor or hallway, but it also allows the access to be located in any readily accessible location. By the term "readily accessible," the UBC intends that the attic access opening be available for use without the need to move furniture and other items, although the use of a ladder may be required. Again, a preferred location would be in the hallway of

an apartment or a hotel suite, but the access opening may also be located in a closet when it is not necessary to move items in order to gain access. Attic access may be provided through a wall as well as through a ceiling. In split-level buildings with multiple attics, an attic access opening must be provided to each attic space.

The *Uniform Building Code* requires that the access opening not be less than 22 inches by 30 inches (559 mm by 762 mm). However, if the attic contains mechanical equipment, the opening will need to be enlarged to at least 30 inches by 30 inches (762 mm by 762 mm) to comply with access requirements of the Mechanical Code. Also, the access requirements of the Mechanical Code would be applicable whether or not the ceiling or roof framing is combustible.

1505.2 Draft Stops. The code requires that combustible attics be provided with draft stops as outlined in Section 708 to prevent the rapid spread of fire.

1505.3 Ventilation. During cold weather, condensation is deposited on cold surfaces when, for example, warm, moist air rising from the interior of a building and through the attic comes in contact with the roof deck. This alternate wetting and drying due to condensation creates dry rot in the wood, and preventive measures are required. Therefore, the code indicates that "where determined necessary" the building official may require that the attic be ventilated. Ventilation of the attic prevents moisture condensation on the cold surfaces and, therefore, will prevent dry rot on the bottom surface of shingles or wood roof decks. Where atmospheric or climatic conditions or construction details are such that moisture will not likely condense on the underside of the roof, the building official has the authority to not require the attic ventilation. Figure 1505-1 provides three examples of attic ventilation. In areas where the moisture condensation is a particular problem or where the normal requirement for attic ventilation cannot be provided, ventilation of the attic by mechanical exhaust fans may be required. Exhaust fans are particularly beneficial in all cases due to the extra movement of the air provided.

Something often overlooked when sizing attic vents is that the code requires that the area provided be the net free area. The net free area can be as much as 50 percent less than the gross area. For example, one manufacturer's 24-inch (610 mm) square gable vent [gross area = 576 square inches (371 6112 mm²)] is listed in their catalog as having a net free area of 308 square inches (198 709 mm²), which is about 53 percent of the gross area. The manufacturer's literature needs to be consulted in order to obtain free area information.

Where eave or cornice vents are installed, insulation shall not block the free flow of air. A minimum of 1 inch (25 mm) of air space is required between the insulation and roof sheathing.

Ventilation openings are required by the code to be screened in order to prevent entry of vermin. This requirement is specific with no alternate, as health sanitarians have indicated that a 1/4-inch (6.4 mm) mesh is required to address both the problem of smaller openings being blocked by debris and spider webs and of larger openings permitting access to small rodents. Therefore, there is no option to the 1/4-inch (6.4 mm) size.

(Continued on page 258)

*Projected roof area means the area of the roof projected on a horizontal plane. Also, it is the horizontal or plan area encompassed within the perimeter of the roof.

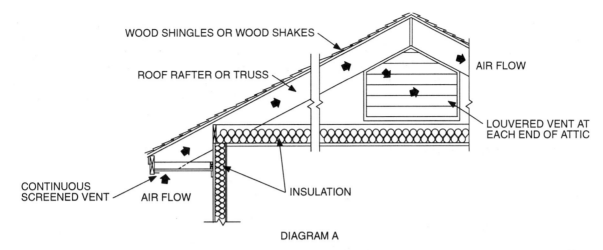

WOOD SHINGLES OR WOOD SHAKES

ROOF RAFTER OR TRUSS

AIR FLOW

LOUVERED VENT AT EACH END OF ATTIC

CONTINUOUS SCREENED VENT

AIR FLOW

INSULATION

DIAGRAM A

VENTILATION FOR GABLE ROOF WITH ATTIC

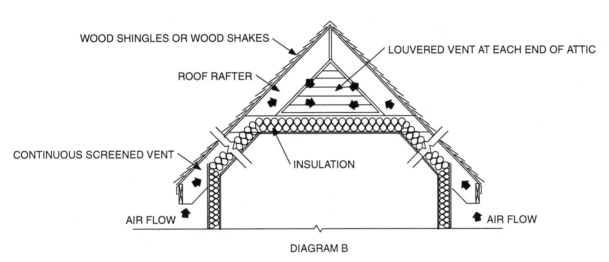

WOOD SHINGLES OR WOOD SHAKES

LOUVERED VENT AT EACH END OF ATTIC

ROOF RAFTER

CONTINUOUS SCREENED VENT

INSULATION

AIR FLOW

AIR FLOW

DIAGRAM B

VENTILATION FOR CATHEDRAL CEILING WITH PARTIAL ATTIC

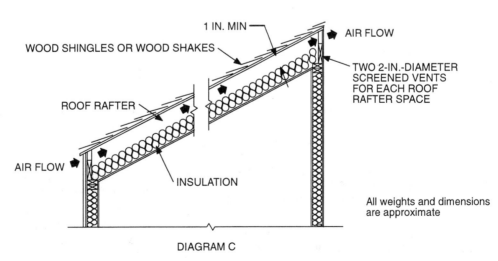

1 IN. MIN

AIR FLOW

WOOD SHINGLES OR WOOD SHAKES

TWO 2-IN.-DIAMETER SCREENED VENTS FOR EACH ROOF RAFTER SPACE

ROOF RAFTER

AIR FLOW

INSULATION

All weights and dimensions are approximate

For **SI:** 1 inch = 25.4 mm.

DIAGRAM C

VENTILATION FOR SHED ROOF

FIGURE 1505-1

(Continued from page 256)

Two exceptions provide for reduced ventilation under certain conditions. These exceptions have been permitted under the Department of Housing and Urban Development minimum property standards and the CABO *One and Two Family Dwelling Code* for many years without negative experience and, thus, represent acceptable alternatives.

SECTION 1506 — ROOF DRAINAGE

Positive roof drainage is required for essentially two reasons:

1. To prevent ponding of water and the consequent rapid deterioration of the roof-covering material, including potential for early failure of the roof covering.

2. To prevent ponding and the resulting failure of the roof structure or, alternatively, the demand for increased strength of the roof structure to support ponding.

Although the UBC offers the alternative of structurally designing a roof to support any accumulation of water on roofs, water ponding is highly detrimental to the roof covering and, as a result, the roof must be designed with a positive drainage slope of $^1/_4$ unit vertical to 12 units horizontal (2% slope). This drainage slope generally will provide positive drainage and will not permit water ponding.

Where the roof does not drain over the edge, the UBC requires roof drains to be provided at each low point of the roof. Clearly, the design of the roof drains should be such as to convey the water from the largest practical rainstorm tributary to the roof drain. Many areas, such as the Southwest, have infrequent rainfall, and it is quite probable that roof drains will become blocked due to an accumulation of leaves and other debris. For this reason the UBC requires that overflow drains be provided for each roof drain. The inlet flow line of the overflow drain must be located no more than 2 inches (51 mm) above the low point of the roof.

Where the roof drain is located adjacent to a parapet wall, the code provides that overflow scuppers in the adjacent parapet may be used, provided they have an area three times that required for the roof drain and the inlet flow line is located no more than 2 inches (51 mm) above the low point of the roof.

An alternate to the separate overflow scupper and roof drain is to provide in one scupper a combined overflow and drain. Figure 1506-1 shows a schematic detail of this type of drain. The opening is four times the required drain size—one time for the drain itself and three times for the required overflow with a minimum height of 4 inches (102 mm). This detail has the advantage of creating fewer holes in the roof that are potential avenues of leaks. It is also of sufficient size to prevent the accumulation of trash and debris. For this type of detail, flashing must be carefully detailed and executed in the field to ensure that the flashing extends up the parapet above the highest probable waterline at the low point of the roof.

To secure the intent of the code, the UBC requires that overflow drains be connected to drain lines that are independent from the roof drains. If the two drains are connected to a common drain line, it becomes easily apparent that a blockage of the common drain line would affect both the roof drain and the overflow and would defeat the purpose of the overflow.

Except for Group R, Division 3 and Group U Occupancies, the code prohibits roof drainage water from a building to flow over public property. The intent is not necessarily preventing drainage water from flowing over "public property" in general, but rather preventing drainage water from flowing over a sidewalk or pedestrian walkway that is between the building and the public street or thoroughfare.

There are at least two problems that arise when roof drainage water is allowed to flow over a public sidewalk:

1. Under proper conditions of light and temperature, algae will form where the water flows across the sidewalk and create a hazardous, slippery walking surface.

2. During heavy rainstorms, the velocity and force of the water emitting from the drain can create hazardous walking conditions for pedestrians.

Therefore, the usual procedure is to carry the roof drain lines inside the building through the wall of the building and under the sidewalk through a curb opening into the gutter.

SECTION 1507 — ROOF-COVERING MATERIALS AND APPLICATION

1507.2 Identification. Certainly, roofing materials must comply with quality standards embodied in the UBC standards for Chapter 15. Furthermore, identification of the roofing materials is mandatory in order to verify that they comply with the quality standards.

In addition to bearing the manufacturer's label or identifying mark on the material, prepared roofing and built-up roofing materials are required by the code to carry a label of an approved agency having a service for inspection of material and finished products during manufacture. This, in essence, refers to the inspection services provided by organizations such as Underwriters Laboratories Inc.® (UL®) and Factory Mutual (FM). Other organizations also provide this type of service, and they can be determined by referring to the evaluation reports issued by ICBO ES.

Because UL and FM generally do not provide inspection and labeling services for shingles (except when specifically treated for fire retardancy), the code requires that shingles be identified by an approved inspection bureau or agency showing the grade of the material. The use of the word "approved" by the code intends to convey the meaning established for the definition of "approved" in Chapter 2. These agencies are quite often trade-related agencies and their listing can be found in the evaluation reports of ICBO ES.

Asphalt is required by the code to carry information indicating the flash point of the material and the name of the manufacturer. Fires in roofing kettles at the jobsite occur often enough to make it imperative that the flash point be identified.

Ferrous roofing materials and fasteners in general are required by the code to be corrosion resistant. Clearly, the roof will be subjected to moisture and, therefore, corrosion-resistant materials and fasteners are required.

1507.3 through 1507.14 Application. *Uniform Building Code* Tables 15-B-1 through 15-F contain the basic requirements of the UBC for the installation of the various roof-covering materials. In addition, the following paragraphs cover additional specific application requirements.

Built-up roofs. Figures 1507-1 through 1507-3 show three typical examples of the application of built-up roofing to both nailable and nonnailable decks. It should be noted for built-up roofs as well as for others that the code requires the application to be made to clean and dry decks. A clean and dry deck is essential to obtain proper adhesion of the roofing membrane to the deck. Also, if the deck is not dry, the entrapped moisture will eventually work its way to the surface of the roofing membrane under pressure and cause blistering.

In addition to the spot mopping shown in Figure 1507-3, another method is to use strip mopping or, as sometimes used in the industry, the term "channel mopping." The National Roofing Contractor's Association prefers application by a mechanical spot-mopper.[1]

After the base ply has been attached to the deck, the successive plies are then embedded in 20 pounds (9.07 kg) of hot asphalt per roofing square, which is applied continuously so that at no place will adjacent plies of felt touch. Thus, the asphalt must not only be applied continuously, but must also be of a fluid consistency. As the plies of felt are laid, they are broomed (the embedment of the roofing felt in the asphalt by the use of a broom to smooth out the ply and obtain proper adhesion to the asphalt below the ply).

A flood coat of 50 pounds (22.68 kg) of hot asphalt or 60 pounds (27.22 kg) of hot coal tar per roofing square is applied to the top surface of the felts, and either 300 or 400 pounds (136.1 or 181.4 kg) of roofing aggregate is spread into the flood coat. Alternatively, a mineral-surfaced cap sheet may be used in lieu of the roofing aggregate, particularly on the steeper roof slopes (≥ 2:12).

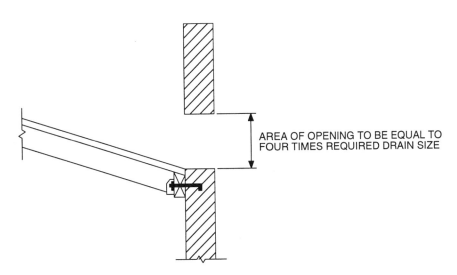

CONDITION WITHOUT LEADER AND DOWNSPOUT

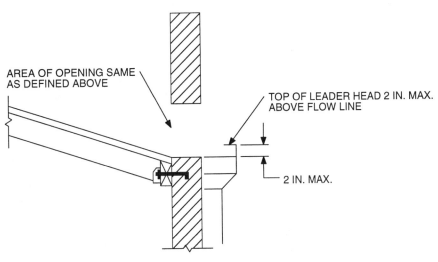

For **SI:** 1 inch = 25.4 mm.

CONDITION WITH LEADER AND DOWNSPOUT

FIGURE 1506-1

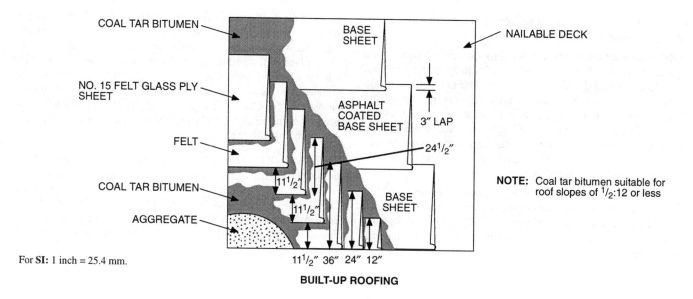

For SI: 1 inch = 25.4 mm.

BUILT-UP ROOFING

NAILABLE DECK APPLICATION

FIGURE 1507-1

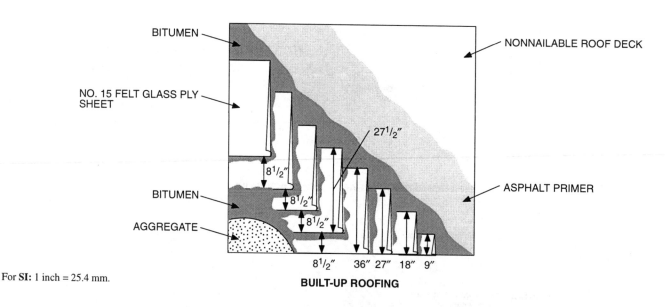

For SI: 1 inch = 25.4 mm.

BUILT-UP ROOFING

APPLICATION TO NONNAILABLE DECK BY SOLID MOPPING

FIGURE 1507-2

The temperature limitations specified in the code for asphalt application are intended to maintain the asphalt within the proper viscosity range for application. This will result in a uniform coat of asphalt between the plies of the roofing membrane, which will meet the code requirement of providing not less than 20 pounds (9.07 kg) of asphalt per roofing square. The proper application temperature for asphalt is referred to as the equiviscous temperature (EVT). The actual application temperature should be maintained at plus or minus 25°F (14°C) from the EVT.

The maximum heating temperatures given in the code are based on the premise that the asphalt should not be heated for more than four hours above the finished blowing temperature created in the asphalt blowstill. Asphalt is processed by taking the heavy asphaltic residue remaining after distillation and heating this residue to about 500°F (260°C) in a blowstill. Air (or sometimes pure oxygen) is then blown through the asphalt from the bottom of the blowstill to a fume draw-off system.

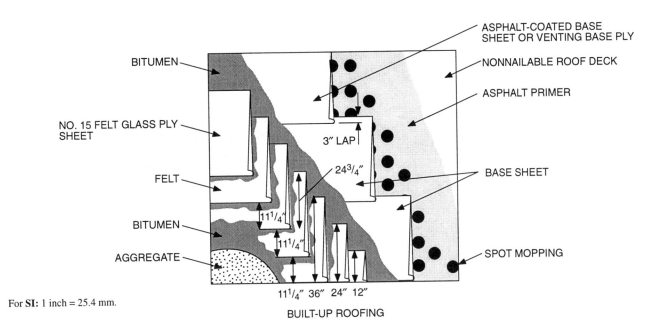

BITUMEN

NO. 15 FELT GLASS PLY SHEET

FELT

BITUMEN

AGGREGATE

ASPHALT-COATED BASE SHEET OR VENTING BASE PLY

NONNAILABLE ROOF DECK

ASPHALT PRIMER

3″ LAP

24³/₄″

11¹/₄″

11¹/₄″

BASE SHEET

SPOT MOPPING

11¹/₄″ 36″ 24″ 12″

BUILT-UP ROOFING

For **SI:** 1 inch = 25.4 mm.

APPLICATION TO NONNAILABLE DECK BY SPOT MOPPING

FIGURE 1507-3

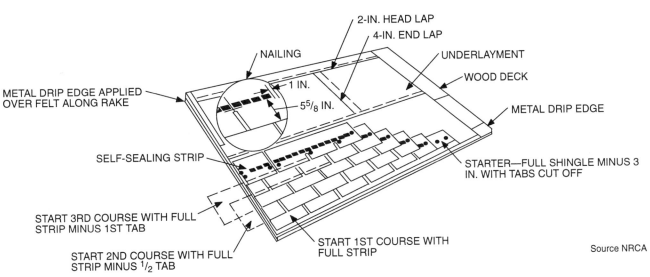

2-IN. HEAD LAP

4-IN. END LAP

NAILING

UNDERLAYMENT

WOOD DECK

METAL DRIP EDGE APPLIED OVER FELT ALONG RAKE

1 IN.

5⁵/₈ IN.

METAL DRIP EDGE

SELF-SEALING STRIP

STARTER—FULL SHINGLE MINUS 3 IN. WITH TABS CUT OFF

START 3RD COURSE WITH FULL STRIP MINUS 1ST TAB

START 1ST COURSE WITH FULL STRIP

START 2ND COURSE WITH FULL STRIP MINUS ¹/₂ TAB

Source NRCA

THREE-TAB, SQUARE BUTT STRIPS—CUTOUTS ARE CENTERED OVER THE TABS IN THE COURSE BELOW

For **SI:** 1 inch = 25.4 mm.

ASPHALT ROOFING SHINGLES APPLICATION HIGH SLOPE (4:12 MINIMUM)

FIGURE 1507-4

Low-melt Type I asphalts have a maximum limit of 475°F (246°C), and the higher-melt types are limited to 525°F (274°C). For obvious reasons, the maximum temperature must be limited to the flash point of the material. Realistically, the maximum temperature should be maintained at least 25 to 30°F (14 to 17°C) below the flash point.

The maximum limit of 425°F (218°C) for coal-tar pitch is based on the fact that when heated to extreme temperatures for long periods of time, the softening point of coal-tar pitch will rise. This raising of the softening point may result in application temperatures that are too low and that will cause heavy moppings. Heavy moppings can result in roofing problems such as slippage.

Asphalt shingles. Figure 1507-4 shows a typical installation of asphalt shingles as required by the UBC. However, the UBC

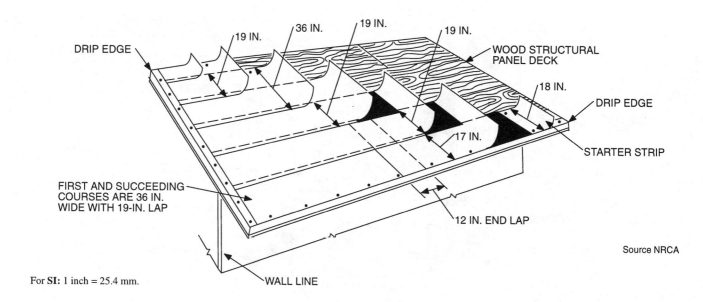

LOW SLOPE (LESS THAN 4:12) UNDERLAYMENT APPLICATION

FIGURE 1507-5

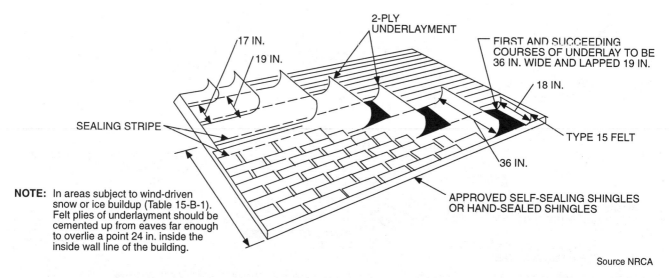

APPLICATION OF ASPHALT SHINGLE SLOPES BETWEEN 2:12 AND 4:12

FIGURE 1507-6

permits application on a roof that has a slope of less than 4:12 in accordance with Table 15-B-1.

Where the roof slope is less than 4:12, water drainage from the roof is slowed down and has a tendency to back up under the roofing and cause leaks. Also, the effect of ice dams at the eaves is more pronounced on "low-slope" roofs and, as a result, special precautions are necessary to ensure satisfactory performance of the roofing materials. Thus, the code requires that the underlayment be laid with two layers of shingled Type 15 felt, which provides two thicknesses of the underlay at any point. The code also specifies double coverage of the shingles. The usual methods of laying asphalt shingles provide double coverage, although the language in the table would seem to imply that this is not the case. Figure 1507-5 shows the method of the underlayment application, and Figure 1507-6 shows the method for shingle application for "low-slope" roofs.

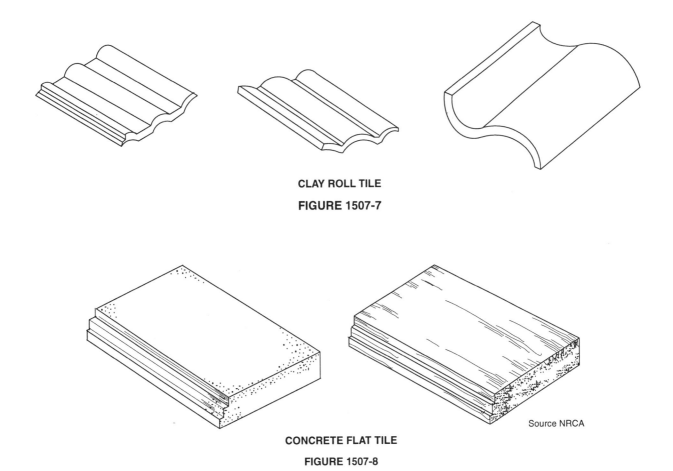

CLAY ROLL TILE

FIGURE 1507-7

Source NRCA

CONCRETE FLAT TILE

FIGURE 1507-8

The code requires that underlayment of one layer of Type 15 felt be provided under asphalt shingle roof coverings with a slope at least equal to 4:12. Where the roof slope is less than 4:12, underlayment is required for the same reasons described above for low-slope roofs.

Clay or concrete tile. Tile is among the oldest of roofing materials, and clay tile was used by the builders of ancient Greece and Egypt.[3] Clay and concrete tile come in two generic configurations—roll tile and flat tile. Figures 1507-7 and 1507-8 give examples of some of the configurations for roofing tile. Either roll tile or flat tile may be interlocking, and Figure 1507-8 shows an example of interlocking tiles. It will be noted that the ribs along the long edge of each tile are designed such that each adjacent tile has ribs which overlap and interlock with the adjoining tile. *Uniform Building Code* Tables 15-D-1 and 15-D-2 contain application requirements for these tiles.

Figure 1507-9 is an example of the application of roll tile and also provides details for ridge covering and the closure at a gable rake. Interlocking clay or concrete tile roofs may be installed over either a solid deck or spaced wood sheathing.

Wood shingles. Wood shingles may be applied on either solid or spaced sheathing, on roofs with a minimum slope of 3:12 when the exposure to the weather is reduced in accordance with Table 15-C, and without underlayment. Figures 1507-10 and 1507-11 show typical applications of wood shingles.

Wood shakes. Wood shakes are applied on roofs with a minimum slope of 4:12 on either spaced or solid sheathing and with-

out an underlayment. However, 18-inch-wide (457 mm) strips of Type 30 felt interlayment are required to be shingled between the courses of wood shakes.

As with other special requirements for shingle and tile roofs laid on a low slope or laid in areas where wind-driven snow is a factor, the extra precautions are required to prevent the backup of water on the roof and under the shingles with the resulting leaks into the building. Figure 1507-12 illustrates an example of wood-shake application on a roof with a slope of 3:12. The difference between this detail and application on a roof with a slope of 4:12 or greater is the roof underlayment in accordance with Footnote 1 to Table 15-B-2. It should also be noted that the application of wood shakes on a slope of 3:12 is not automatically permitted by the code and requires that the approval of the building official be obtained. When granting an approval, the building official should consider such items as the severity and frequency of storms and the likelihood of high-velocity wind-driven rains.

Both wood shingles and wood shakes are required by the code to have certain maximum exposures to the weather, and in the case of shingles this exposure is dependent on the roof slope. These exposures for roofs with slopes of 4:12 or greater provide a minimum of three thicknesses of shingle with an overlap of $1^1/_2$ inches (38 mm) [1-inch overlap (25 mm) for 16-inch-long (406 mm) shingles] and have been shown through experience to be the maximum exposure which will provide a leak-free roof.

Other roof coverings. Other roof coverings, such as corrugated asbestos-cement roofing, asbestos-cement shingles,

(Continued on page 266)

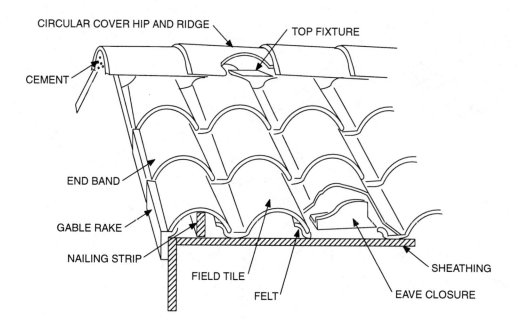

CIRCULAR COVER HIP AND RIDGE

TOP FIXTURE

CEMENT

END BAND

GABLE RAKE

NAILING STRIP

FIELD TILE

FELT

SHEATHING

EAVE CLOSURE

APPLICATION OF ROLL TILE

FIGURE 1507-9

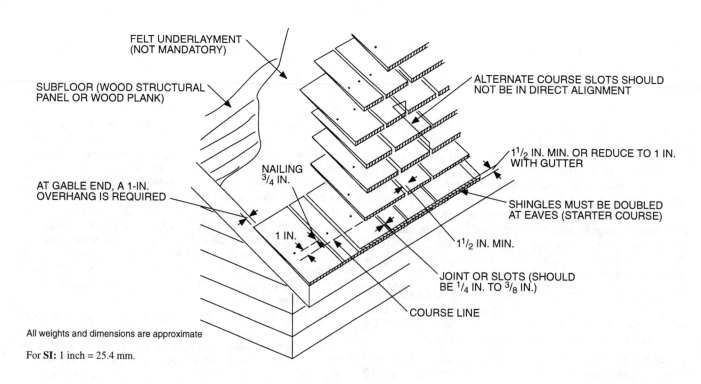

FELT UNDERLAYMENT
(NOT MANDATORY)

SUBFLOOR (WOOD STRUCTURAL
PANEL OR WOOD PLANK)

AT GABLE END, A 1-IN.
OVERHANG IS REQUIRED

NAILING
$3/4$ IN.

1 IN.

ALTERNATE COURSE SLOTS SHOULD
NOT BE IN DIRECT ALIGNMENT

$1^{1}/_{2}$ IN. MIN. OR REDUCE TO 1 IN.
WITH GUTTER

SHINGLES MUST BE DOUBLED
AT EAVES (STARTER COURSE)

$1^{1}/_{2}$ IN. MIN.

JOINT OR SLOTS (SHOULD
BE $1/_{4}$ IN. TO $3/_{8}$ IN.)

COURSE LINE

All weights and dimensions are approximate

For **SI:** 1 inch = 25.4 mm.

WOOD SHINGLE APPLICATION

FIGURE 1507-10

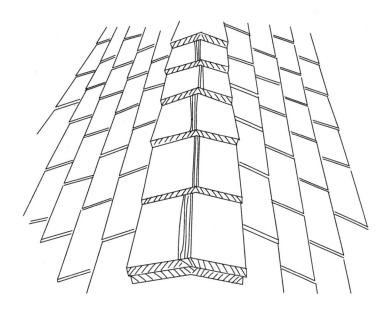

APPLICATION OF WOOD SHINGLES AT RIDGES

FIGURE 1507-11

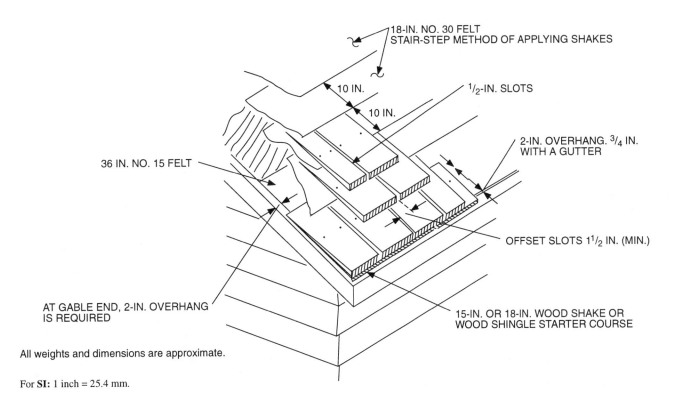

18-IN. NO. 30 FELT
STAIR-STEP METHOD OF APPLYING SHAKES

10 IN.

10 IN.

¹/₂-IN. SLOTS

2-IN. OVERHANG. ³/₄ IN.
WITH A GUTTER

36 IN. NO. 15 FELT

OFFSET SLOTS 1¹/₂ IN. (MIN.)

AT GABLE END, 2-IN. OVERHANG
IS REQUIRED

15-IN. OR 18-IN. WOOD SHAKE OR
WOOD SHINGLE STARTER COURSE

All weights and dimensions are approximate.

For **SI:** 1 inch = 25.4 mm.

WOOD SHAKE APPLICATION

FIGURE 1507-12

(Continued from page 263)

flat-sheet metal roofing, sheet roofing (roll roofing) and slate shingles, are required by the code to be applied "in an approved manner." Thus, the manufacturer's recommendations should be followed with any restrictions required by the UBC, such as requiring solidly sheathed roof decks for the installation of flat-sheet metal roofing. Several publications provide detailed recommendations for the application of roll roofing.[1,4]

Installations in severe climate areas. When shingle, shake or tile roofs are installed in areas subject to wind-driven snow or roof ice buildup, the code imposes special underlayment requirements to help protect against water leakage into the interior of the building. In these areas, the freezing and thawing along the cold-exposed edge of the eave creates ice dams, which in turn prevent the water from running down and off the roof. Without proper eave flashing, the water will back up and leak into the interior of the building. For tile roofs, the same special underlayment requirements mandated for snow and ice areas are also imposed within special wind regions as shown in Figure 16-1 of the code.

Underlayment requirements are found in Tables 15-B-1, 15-B-2, 15-D-1 and 15-D-2. These tables set forth requirements in four categories: temperate climate for high- or low-sloped roofs and severe climate for high- or low-sloped roofs. Although the requirements for severe climate installations are quite similar, they do vary somewhat depending on the material and roof slope. In addition, other conditions may be imposed. For example, wood shake roofs are required to be installed over solid sheathing in severe weather areas. The appropriate application table must be consulted for each type of installation.

In addition to the underlayment requirements set forth in the application tables, Section 1508 requires that in severe climates metal valley flashing underlayments must be solid-cemented to the roof underlayment for all shingle types when the slope is less than 7 units vertical in 12 units horizontal (58.3% slope).

Slope of roof. The *Uniform Building Code* places limits on roof slope insofar as roofing applications are concerned in the following cases and for the following reasons:

- The maximum slopes of built-up roof coverings are limited based on the cold-flow characteristics of the roofing asphalt, and also on whether a mineral aggregate is placed as the top surfacing of the roofing membrane. Types I and II roofing asphalt and coal tar pitch have cold-flow characteristics, and, on slopes greater than $1/2$ unit vertical in 12 units horizontal (4% slope), will flow downslope to the lower areas so that the higher points of the slope will have less waterproofing than the code desires. Page 137 of the *Manual of Built-Up Roof Systems* contains a detailed discussion of this principle of cold flow.[2]

To prevent downslope slippage, Table 15-E in the code requires that the various felts be blind nailed through tin caps into the deck or wood nailers or wood insulation stops when:

1. The roof slopes greater than 1 unit vertical in 12 units horizontal (8.3% slope) for gravel-surfaced roofs.

2. The roof slopes greater than 2 units vertical in 12 units horizontal (16.7% slope) for smooth cap-sheet roofs.

Blind nailing (back nailing) is a nailing procedure used to prevent slipping by nailing the layers of felt so that the nails are covered by successive layers of overlapping felt. Tin caps are used to prevent the tearing of the plies.

- In the case of mineral aggregate surfacing, Footnote 1 to Table 15-F in the code limits the maximum slope to 3:12, which is intended to prevent the aggregate and the flood coat in which it is embedded from sliding down slope during application as well as during hot weather.[2]

Furthermore, the code requires that built-up roofing on slopes exceeding 3 units vertical in 12 units horizontal (25% slope) be installed with the plies laid parallel to the slope of the roof and that surfacing other than gravel be utilized. Clearly, gravel will not remain in place on a roof of such a slope. Roofing felts are applied parallel to the slope of the deck because the felts are stronger in the longitudinal direction and are less likely to split.

- Shingle and tile roofs are required by the code to have minimum slopes because of roof drainage. If the shingles and tiles are installed on roofs with a slope less than that required by the code, water drains more slowly and tends to back up, infiltrate under the roofing and create leaks. Also, low-slope applications increase the susceptibility of the roof to damage by wind, and, in colder climates, wind-blown snow may infiltrate under the roofing material and cause leaks. Therefore, *Uniform Building Code* Table 15-B-1 provides special requirements such as underlays and, in the case of asphalt shingles, either self-sealing shingles or hand-sealing shingles to prevent wind uplift.

SECTION 1508 — VALLEY FLASHING

Improper installation of flashing is the greatest cause of failures of roof-covering systems.[2] Whenever one plane of a roof intersects another plane, flashing is required where the planes intersect. Thus, flashing is required at valleys and intersections of the roof with vertical surfaces, such as walls, parapets, sides of chimneys, etc. Furthermore, flashing is required around all edges of the roof, such as at eaves and rakes, to prevent the entry of water underneath the roofing. The code requires that flashing materials, when of metal, be noncorrosive. Whenever copper and ferrous metals are used together for flashing, they should not be placed in direct contact because of the likelihood of galvanic action. The dissimilar metals should either be separated from each other or electrically isolated so that galvanic action will not occur.

1508.1 Valleys. Although all areas of flashing are important, the UBC emphasizes details for valley flashing in this section.

Valleys generally exist at the intersection of two sloping roof surfaces at a change in plan. For example, an L-shaped building will have a valley at the reentrant corner of the L extending upward to the ridge line. As water runs off the roof from both sloping surfaces into the valley, the valley is particularly susceptible to leaks unless the flashing is properly installed. A typical detail of sheet metal valley flashing with a splash diverter is shown in Figure 1508-1. In this case, the splash diverter aids in preventing runoff water down one side of the valley from running up the other side under the shingles.

(Continued on page 268)

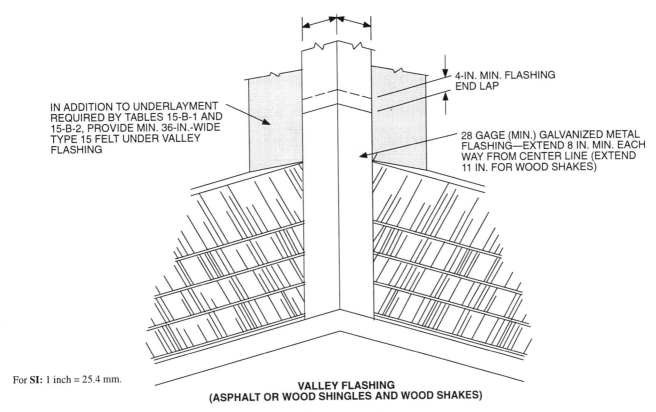

IN ADDITION TO UNDERLAYMENT
REQUIRED BY TABLES 15-B-1 AND
15-B-2, PROVIDE MIN. 36-IN.-WIDE
TYPE 15 FELT UNDER VALLEY
FLASHING

4-IN. MIN. FLASHING
END LAP

28 GAGE (MIN.) GALVANIZED METAL
FLASHING—EXTEND 8 IN. MIN. EACH
WAY FROM CENTER LINE (EXTEND
11 IN. FOR WOOD SHAKES)

For **SI:** 1 inch = 25.4 mm.

**VALLEY FLASHING
(ASPHALT OR WOOD SHINGLES AND WOOD SHAKES)**

FIGURE 1508-1

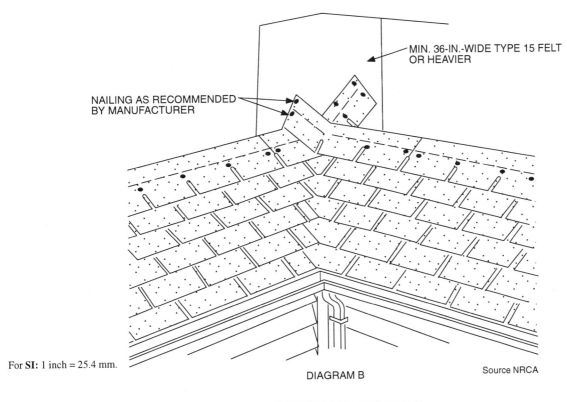

MIN. 36-IN.-WIDE TYPE 15 FELT
OR HEAVIER

NAILING AS RECOMMENDED
BY MANUFACTURER

For **SI:** 1 inch = 25.4 mm.

DIAGRAM B

Source NRCA

**ALTERNATE VALLEY FLASHING
(ASPHALT SHINGLES)**

FIGURE 1508-2

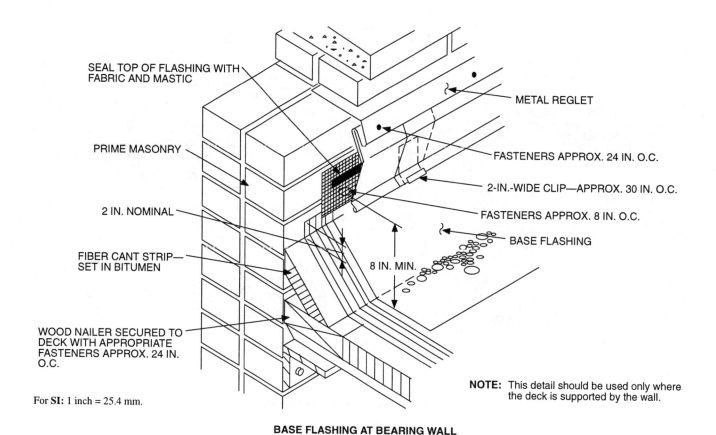

SEAL TOP OF FLASHING WITH
FABRIC AND MASTIC

METAL REGLET

PRIME MASONRY

FASTENERS APPROX. 24 IN. O.C.

2-IN.-WIDE CLIP—APPROX. 30 IN. O.C.

2 IN. NOMINAL

FASTENERS APPROX. 8 IN. O.C.

BASE FLASHING

FIBER CANT STRIP—
SET IN BITUMEN

8 IN. MIN.

WOOD NAILER SECURED TO
DECK WITH APPROPRIATE
FASTENERS APPROX. 24 IN.
O.C.

NOTE: This detail should be used only where
the deck is supported by the wall.

For **SI:** 1 inch = 25.4 mm.

BASE FLASHING AT BEARING WALL

FIGURE 1509-1

(Continued from page 266)

1508.2 Asphalt Shingles. Figures 1508-1 and 1508-2 provide examples of valley flashing as required by the UBC. Figure 1508-1 applies to asphalt or wood shingles or shakes, and Figure 1508-2 is specifically detailed for asphalt shingles.

1508.3 Metal Shingles. Valley flashing for metal roofs is identical to that shown in Figure 1508-1.

1508.4 Asbestos-cement Shingles, Slate Shingles, and Clay and Concrete Tile. Roof valley flashing for these materials as required by the code is very similar in nature to that shown in Figure 1508-1, except for dimensional differences.

1508.5 Wood Shingles and Wood Shakes. Roof valley flashing for wood shingles is illustrated in Figure 1508-1. The 8-inch (203 mm) dimension for asphalt and wood shingles is required by the code to be 11 inches (279 mm) for wood shakes.

SECTION 1509 — OTHER FLASHING

In addition to the roof valley flashing, this section also requires flashing where the roof intersects vertical surfaces such as chimneys, dormers, plumbing stacks, plumbing vents and other appurtenances which penetrate the roof. In addition to flashing, the code requires that counterflashing be provided. Counterflashing is sometimes referred to as cap flashing and is the flashing embedded in the vertical surface that caps over the flashing materials that extend up from the roof surface. Figures 1509-1 through 1509-4 depict some cases of roof flashing at vertical surfaces.

SECTION 1510 — ROOF INSULATION

During these days of energy consciousness, the use of roof insulation will become more and more prevalent, as it has distinct benefits not only in energy conservation but also in building occupant comfort. Insulation also provides a smooth uniform substrate for application of the roofing materials. In fact, the code requires that the insulation be of a rigid type suitable for application of roof-covering materials. For foam plastic insulation used under roof coverings, see the discussion in this handbook under Section 2602.

When used with a required fire-retardant roof covering, insulation is required by the code to be of a type approved for the type of deck and roofing assembly applied. Where the roofing assembly is a tested assembly, the insulation to be used will be that type of insulation used during the test. Where one of the nonrated assemblies referred to in Section 1504.3 is used, the insulation should be no more combustible than the usual plywood-sheathed roof deck. There are several insulation materials listed by UL for use with metal roof deck construction, and these insulation materials should be approved for use under fire-retardant roofing materials over both noncombustible and combustible decks.

The intent of the code for the use of a vapor retarder installed between the deck and insulation for built-up roofing is to prevent the migration of moisture from the interior of the building upward into the insulation and roofing materials, thereby causing degradation. One problem with the use of a vapor retarder is that if the summer temperatures are high with high relative

(Continued on page 270)

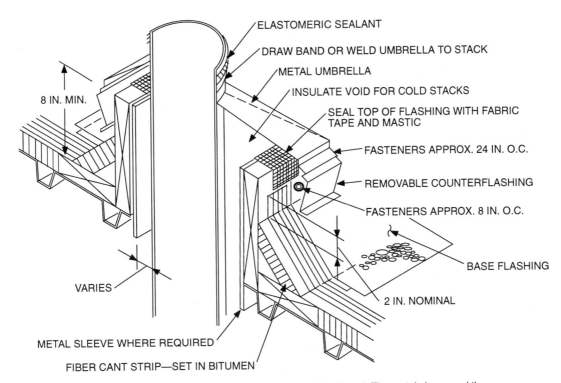

8 IN. MIN.

ELASTOMERIC SEALANT

DRAW BAND OR WELD UMBRELLA TO STACK

METAL UMBRELLA

INSULATE VOID FOR COLD STACKS

SEAL TOP OF FLASHING WITH FABRIC TAPE AND MASTIC

FASTENERS APPROX. 24 IN. O.C.

REMOVABLE COUNTERFLASHING

FASTENERS APPROX. 8 IN. O.C.

BASE FLASHING

2 IN. NOMINAL

VARIES

METAL SLEEVE WHERE REQUIRED

FIBER CANT STRIP—SET IN BITUMEN

NOTE: This detail allows the opening to be completed before the stack is placed. The metal sleeve and the clearance necessary will depend on the temperature of the material handled by the stack.

For **SI:** 1 inch = 25.4 mm.

STACK FLASHING

FIGURE 1509-2

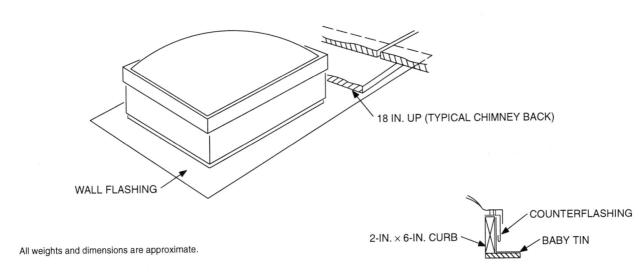

18 IN. UP (TYPICAL CHIMNEY BACK)

WALL FLASHING

COUNTERFLASHING

2-IN. × 6-IN. CURB

BABY TIN

All weights and dimensions are approximate.

For **SI:** 1 inch = 25.4 mm.

FLASHING AT SKYLIGHT (WOOD ROOF)

FIGURE 1509-3

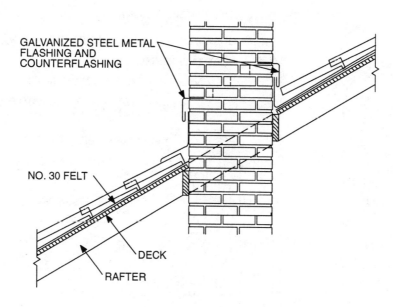

GALVANIZED STEEL METAL
FLASHING AND
COUNTERFLASHING

NO. 30 FELT

DECK

RAFTER

CHIMNEY FLASHING DETAIL

FIGURE 1509-4

(Continued from page 268)

humidity, the vapor retarder will act to prevent downward flow of vapor and, as a result, moisture may gather in the insulation and cause degradation. Fortunately, unless conditions are severe, the roofing membrane itself will act as a vapor retarder to prevent downward migration of moisture into the insulation.

SECTION 1511 — PENTHOUSES AND ROOF STRUCTURES

Penthouses and roof structures are regulated by the UBC as if they were appurtenances to the building rather than occupiable portions.

In fact, if a penthouse is used for any purpose other than shelter of mechanical equipment or shelter of vertical shaft openings, the code requires that it be considered an additional story of the building.

As intended by the UBC, roof structures are equipment shelters, equipment screens, platforms that support mechanical equipment, water tank enclosures and other similar structures generally used to screen, support or shelter equipment on the roof of the building. This section does not regulate towers and spires, which are treated separately in Section 1512.

The *Uniform Building Code* regulates penthouses, roof structures, towers and spires to prevent hazardous conditions due to structural inadequacy and to ensure proper use as equipment shelters.

1511.1 Height. The code does not regulate the height of penthouses and roof structures on Type I buildings, as Table 5-B permits an unlimited height for Type I buildings. However, for other buildings where Table 5-B establishes a height limit, the code limits the height of penthouses and roof structures to 28 feet (8534 mm) above the height of a story. As Section 1511.2 limits the aggregate area of all penthouses and roof structures to

one-third the area of the roof, the additional 28 feet (8534 mm) in height permitted for penthouses and roof structures does not pose any significant fire- and life-safety hazard, due to other restrictions that the chapter places on construction. Prior to the 1994 edition, the 28-foot (8534 mm) height was permitted only for penthouses and other roof structures that enclosed tanks or elevators. Others were limited to a height of 12 feet (3658 mm). This 12-foot (3658 mm) limitation proved to be inadequate for the clearances needed for modern mechanical equipment, so the 28-foot height (8534 mm) is now allowed for all conditions.

1511.3 Prohibited Uses. As the code has reduced requirements for construction of penthouses and roof structures, it is logical, then, that their use should be limited as specified in this section. Thus, if other uses are made of penthouses or other roof structures, it also seems logical that they should be constructed as would be required for an additional story of the building. It is the intent of the code that a penthouse or roof structure not be used to create an additional story above that permitted by Section 506.

1511.4 Construction. The intent of the code is that penthouses or roof structures be constructed with the same materials and the same fire resistance as required for the main portion of the building. However, due to the nature of their use, the code does permit exceptions where the exterior walls of penthouses and roof structures are at least 5 feet (1524 mm) [or in some cases 20 feet (6096 mm)] from the property line.

In the case of unroofed mechanical equipment screens, fences and similar enclosures provided in Exception 4, the code permits combustible construction, provided the height of the structure is no more than 4 feet (1219 mm) above the adjacent roof surface. As this exception applies only to one-story buildings, the fire hazard is not significantly increased, as firefighting forces will have reasonable access to the roof from the exterior of the building.

SECTION 1512 — TOWERS AND SPIRES

The *Uniform Building Code* intends that towers and spires be considered separately from penthouses and roof structures. The towers contemplated in this section are towers such as radio and television antenna towers, church spires, and other towers and spires of similar nature that do not support or enclose any mechanical equipment and that are not occupied. Towers supporting tanks and mechanical equipment would be limited by Section 1511. As the provisions of Section 1512 are nearly identical to those in the 1927 edition of the UBC, the rationale for the provisions is lost in antiquity. However, as with penthouses and roof structures, the code intends to obtain construction and fire resistance consistent with that of the building to which they are attached. Furthermore, high towers are required to be constructed of noncombustible materials, regardless of building construction [depending on use of the tower, either more than 75 feet (22 860 mm) above grade or 25 feet (7620 mm) above the roof].

Although this section requires a wind load design only for towers and spires, Chapter 16 of the code requires that any penthouse, roof structure, tower or spire be designed for lateral forces in accordance with that chapter. It is interesting to note that as these provisions in Chapter 15 are essentially a holdover from the 1920s, the provisions and requirements may not seem to be consistent with the other design provisions of Chapter 16. It must be remembered, however, that in the 1920s wind load design was not as sophisticated as it is today, and earthquake-resistant design was almost unheard of outside of California. In particular, heavy, massive buildings of reinforced concrete or masonry were considered to be wind resistant as a result of their weight, and usually no detailed structural calculations were made for wind resistance. Because quite often there was no specific wind load design for the building, the code required a specific design of towers and spires to resist wind and required tower framing to extend through the building and directly to the ground.

REFERENCES

[1]National Roofing Contractor's Association (1985). *The NRCA Roofing and Waterproofing Manual.* Chicago, Illinois.

[2]Griffin, C.W. (1982). *Manual of Built-Up Roof Systems,* Second Edition. McGraw-Hill Book Company, Inc., New York City.

[3]*Masonry Design West,* September-October 1986. Pinedale, California.

[4]Asphalt Roofing Manufacturers Association [1966 (revised 1974)]. *Manufacture, Selection and Application of Asphalt Roofing and Siding Products.* New York City.

Chapter 16

STRUCTURAL DESIGN REQUIREMENTS

Chapter 16 has been retitled in the 1997 edition of the UBC to more correctly reflect the chapter scope. The major changes to this chapter in the 1997 code were submitted in two parts by the Structural Engineers Association of California (SEAOC).

The first part is a strength design package of code changes designed to incorporate the strength design or load and resistance factor design (LRFD) concept, terminology, loads and load factors into Chapter 16 and each of the material design chapters in the UBC. These changes are made in parallel with allowable stress design (ASD) rather than replacing it. The basic conversion from working stress to strength design is consistent with the direction of all material code requirements in the U.S. and with the National Earthquake Hazards Reductions Program (NEHRP) seismic provisions, which serve as a source document for building codes other than the UBC.

The second part of the code changes include major revisions to the seismic provisions of Chapter 16, which are discussed under Division IV—Earthquake Design.

Chapter 16 has also been reformatted in order to make the provisions more logically organized and therefore easier to use, and to bring the provisions closer in line with the ASCE 7 standard. Separate sections have been developed for dead load and live load, previously mixed into the floor and roof design sections. All miscellaneous design loads specified in Chapter 16 have been collected into a single section, Section 1611, Other Minimum Loads, making them much easier to locate. One set of factored load combinations, applicable to all materials (except concrete for the time being), is included for Chapter 16. This is an important step toward standardizing strength design (LRFD).

Reformatting of the materials chapters is also made in order to clearly differentiate between general requirements which apply regardless of design method, strength (LRFD) requirements, and ASD requirements. Additional reformatting is also made to move toward adoption of national standards.

Division I—GENERAL DESIGN REQUIREMENTS

SECTION 1601 — SCOPE

Chapter 16 contains general building code requirements for the structural engineering design of all buildings and structures regulated by the code. These design requirements cover both design for gravity loads (live loads and dead loads) plus lateral loads due to wind, earthquake and lateral soil pressure.

The chapter essentially establishes the loads for which buildings and structures should be designed, and the methods for determining these loads. The method of design to resist these loads is in general left up to the designer, except Division IV also prescribes design methods. However, in this latter case, Section 104.2.8 of the code would permit an alternate method of design, provided the building official finds that the alternate design meets the criteria established in Section 104.2.8 and in Division IV insofar as strength and ductility are concerned. Additionally,

Section 1629.10 permits alternate design concepts as long as equivalent ductility and energy absorption are provided.

SECTION 1602 — DEFINITIONS

In the definition of live load, the code intends that the definition refers only to those loads superimposed on the structure by the use or occupancy of the building. Therefore, roof loads such as snow loads are not use and occupancy related and, therefore, are not classified as live loads.

On the other hand, crane loads comprise a combination of dead and live loads. All loads involving the crane machinery, such as the trolleys, cables, hooks, etc., are dead loads, but the lifted load or so-called hook load is related to the use and occupancy and, therefore, is a live load. Furthermore, as will be seen in Table 16-B, crane loads also involve impact loads.

Load duration, although defined, is not discussed in Chapter 16 (but is discussed in Chapter 23) and can either be a continuous application of a load or the load may be intermittently applied. In this latter case, the load duration will be the sum of the lengths of the periods of application of this same load.

Additional definitions important for the use of strength design (LRFD) and allowable stress design (ASD) have been included in the 1997 UBC. These definitions are dervied from the ASCE 7 standard, but have been modified as needed for use in Chapter 16.

SECTION 1603 — NOTATIONS

The 1997 UBC includes notations in Division I for consistency with ASCE 7 and the 1994 NEHRP *Recommended Provisions for Seismic Regulations for New Buildings*. Additional notations and symbols are included in Division III—Wind Design, Division IV—Earthquake Design and Division V—Soil Profile Types.

The notations E, E_h, E_m and E_v in this chapter have been selected for clarity. To remain consistent with allowable stress and current design requirements, the earthquake load for strength design has been modified to include a nominal margin for vertical earthquake forces. The definition of the proposed earthquake loads is consistent with ASCE 7 and 1994 NEHRP provisions. The factor Ω replaces $^3/_8 R_w$ from previous codes.

SECTION 1605 — DESIGN

1605.1 General. The intent of Chapter 16 is that all buildings be structurally designed and constructed to safely withstand the loads specified in the UBC, except for certain wood-frame buildings. The exception to this section permits the specification and prescriptive-type criteria in the conventional framing provisions in Chapter 23 to be considered as adequate to resist all of the loads specified in the code. However, the exception begins with the words "Unless otherwise required by the building official," so that if the building official finds that there are some unusual circumstances involved, such as excessive irregularity in the floor plans or elevations, the building official may require that a structural design be provided. However, the intent of the code is—and this will be discussed in more detail in Section 2320—to permit wood-frame buildings designed and constructed completely in accordance with Section 2320 to be considered as complying with Section 1605.1. For these buildings, the code intends that these provisions be allowed only when specific conditions exist such as those described under Section 2320.1.

Nevertheless, state law may prescribe more restrictive provisions than Section 2320.1 and may require that any building over two stories in height, for example, be designed by a licensed engineer or architect. Where this is the case, state law will prevail.

1605.2 Rationality. While the code in general does not intend to specify the design method used by the engineer, it does intend that the design method be rational and in accordance with well-established principles of mechanics. Departures from this latter requirement can still be made based on the provisions of Section 104.2.8 when approved by the building official. For example, the structural adequacy of a building may not admit to a rational analysis; a program of full-scale testing may be the only reasonable way to determine its structural behavior. If the testing program shows that a certain building can safely resist the loads required by the code, the building official may approve the construction of the building.

This section was expanded in the 1982 edition to include criteria regarding load paths and certain other general criteria for design to resist lateral forces. Originally, the criteria for the design to resist lateral forces were in Division III, addressing the subject of earthquake loads. However, the provisions now listed in this section are equally applicable to wind, and, therefore, they have been gathered together in this one section and made applicable to lateral forces of both wind and earthquake.

There is, however, one section (Section 1605.2.3, Anchorage), which originally was in Division III and addressed the subject of wind loads. This provision is equally applicable to both wind and earthquake and was moved to this section. Many of these sections are discussed in the publication SEAOC entitled *Recommended Lateral Force Requirements and Commentary* (Blue Book). This document should be consulted for a more thorough discussion.

Section 1605.2.3 addresses the anchorage of the various components of a building to resist the uplift and sliding forces which result from the application of the code-prescribed lateral forces. This section intends that all members be tied together or anchored to resist the uplift and sliding forces. This section differentiates between the uplift and sliding forces to be resisted in general and the lateral support required by Section 1611.4 for concrete and masonry walls.

SECTION 1606 — DEAD LOADS

For the 1997 edition, the 1994 UBC sections on floor design, roof design, reduction of live loads, special loads, etc., have been reorganized into more logical groupings of dead loads, live loads, snow loads, wind loads, earthquake loads and other minimum loads. This conversion was necessary in order to use

LRFD and ASD load combinations (for example, the 1994 UBC lets you substitute snow loads for roof live load, while in ASCE 7 these are treated with two separate loads in load combinations). In addition, it was desirable to have the reformatting follow the general organization of ASCE 7.

New Section 1611 gathers all other minimum load requirements from Chapter 16 into one place. This will be of great assistance to designers who previously had to search through the code provisions for scattered load requirements. Several editorial changes are included in this section.

1606.2 Partition Loads. In those uses where the partitions are subject to change in locations such as office buildings and flexible-plan school buildings, the code requires that the floor system be designed to support a uniformly distributed dead load of 20 pounds per square foot (0.96 kN/m^2). It should be noted that the uniformly distributed load of 20 pounds per square foot (0.96 kN/m^2) is considered by the code to be a dead load. Thus, it should be included with other dead loads in factored load combinations.

Access floor systems (as defined in Chapter 2) may be designed (at the option of the designer) for a less uniformly distributed partition dead load of 10 pounds per square foot (0.48 kN/m^2). This latter permissible reduction is due to the fact that access floor systems are most often installed in open areas where it is not desirable to erect and move partitions about, as would be the case for a general office floor.

SECTION 1607 — LIVE LOADS

1607.2 Critical Distribution of Live Loads. As continuous framing will receive bending moments created by loads on adjacent spans or even on spans that are beyond adjacent spans, the code intends that where loads are uniformly distributed, they be arranged so as to create maximum bending moments in any given span. This may require a design to consider so-called "skip" loading or alternate span loading, as shown in Figure 1607-1. In the case of continuous beams or girders, full live loads on adjacent spans with no live load on spans beyond may also be required in the design to determine the maximum negative bending moments at the supports. However, this section intends that all conditions of loading be considered in addition to uniformly distributed loads. Where concentrated loads can have variable locations, this condition should also be considered.

1607.3 Floor Live Loads. The *Uniform Building Code* in this section charges the designer to use the unit live loads set forth in Table 16-A and specifies that these loads shall be considered minimum live loads. The second paragraph intends that for industrial or commercial occupancies, when the actual live load can be determined at the time of the design, it be considered when it would create larger loads than those specified in Table 16-A. Furthermore, the code requires that special design provisions be made where machine or apparatus loads are involved which would cause a greater load than Table 16-A would specify for that use.

In other words, floors shall be designed for the maximum live loads to which they are likely to be subjected during the life of the building based on its intended use, but in no case shall the design loads be less than those set forth in Table 16-A.

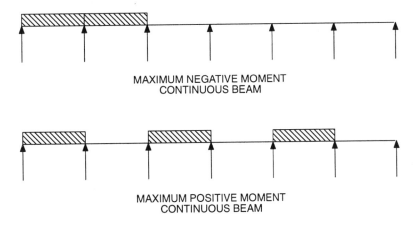

MAXIMUM NEGATIVE MOMENT
CONTINUOUS BEAM

MAXIMUM POSITIVE MOMENT
CONTINUOUS BEAM

DISTRIBUTION OF LIVE LOADS

FIGURE 1607-1

1607.3.3 Concentrated loads. Many uses are susceptible to the movement of equipment, files, machinery, etc. Therefore, the code requires that floors for those uses, which are listed in Table 16-A, be designed for the concentrated load indicated placed on a space $2^1/_2$ feet (762 mm) square whenever this load, on an otherwise unloaded floor, produces stresses greater than those caused by the uniform loads required by the code. As this concentrated load can take many forms in the real world, and as the design structural engineer usually does not know in advance what form the load will take and how it will be applied, the best compromise to cover most situations is to consider the concentrated load to be applied through a rigid base $2^1/_2$ feet (762 mm) square.

The code also requires garages and other areas where motor vehicles are stored to be designed for concentrated loads or, alternatively, the uniform loads as specified in Table 16-A. In the case of a general storage garage where all types of vehicles are parked, the code requires that a pair of loads be considered, with each load representing 40 percent of the gross weight of the maximum-size vehicle which will be accommodated. In the case of garages for storage of private pleasure-type vehicles, the code prescribes a single 2,000-pound (8.9 kN) load over a 20-square-inch (12 903 mm²) area.

It is interesting to note that for general-purpose storage garages the codes does not prescribe the area of application of the load: that is, whether it be a point load or that it cover some specified area. Therefore, the structural designer would most likely follow *Minimum Design Loads for Buildings and Other Structures,* which recommends an area of 20 square inches (12 903 mm²) for application of the load the same as for private garages.

For all of the concentrated loads just discussed in this section, the intent of the code is that the concentrated load be placed on the floor in such a position as to create maximum stresses in the structural members on an otherwise unloaded floor as far as live load is concerned. Therefore, the loading condition, either uniform or concentrated, which provides the maximum stresses in the structural members would be used for the design of the floor system.

1607.3.5 Live loads posted. In this section, the code charges the owner of a commercial or an industrial building with posting

signs in conspicuous locations. These signs must specify the actual live load for which the floor system has been designed. Also, the code charges the occupant of the building with the responsibility of maintaining the actual loads at a level below those posted. The intent, of course, is to prevent the overloading of floors, and the code assumes that by posting the live loads for which the floor system was designed, the occupant of the building will be more likely to maintain the actual loads below the posted live loads. It should emphasized that this requirement for posting live load signs applies to commercial buildings as well as industrial buildings. Therefore, offices, retail sales areas, etc., should also have live load signs posted conspicuously about the premises where there is a likelihood of overloading.

1607.4 Roof Live Loads.

1607.4.2 Distribution of loads. Where roof structural members are detailed to provide continuity, this section permits the consideration of alternate span loading to just two cases. Understandably, full dead load on all spans will be considered in either case. The two cases are:

* Full live load on adjacent spans.

* Full live load on alternate spans.

Full live load on adjacent spans creates maximum negative moments at the supports, while loading alternate spans with full live load creates higher positive bending moments. The exception provides for those cases where the design roof live load is 20 pounds per square foot (0.96 kN/m²) or more, or where the design is for snow loads and the requirements of Section 1614 are met.

The rationale behind the exception is twofold:

1. The 20-pound-per-square-foot (0.96 kN/m²) or greater roof live load is considered to be a severe enough loading condition on the roof so that alternate or adjacent span placement of live loads is not necessary. As roof live loads consist mainly of the loads created by maintenance workers, including their equipment and materials, the code considers that any unbalance created by roof live loads is more than compensated for by a design for 20 pounds per square foot (0.96 kN/m²) or more over the entire roof area.

2. When the roof is designed to resist snow loads, the provisions of Section 1614 are considered by the code to provide ample strength in the roof structural members to accommodate the occasional unfavorable distribution of any roof live loads.

In a provision added in the 1994 edition of the *Uniform Building Code*, alternate span live loads need not be considered in the design of light-gate steel roof purlins or decking that serve as both the structural support and roof covering of the building. Four loading conditions have been provided; the one that creates the most critical loading situation is added to the full dead load. This was felt to more accurately reflect the live loads that this type of roofing will actually experience.

1607.4.3 Unbalanced loading. This section considers unbalanced loading as a distinct separate situation from alternate span and adjacent span loading for continuous structural systems. In this section the *Uniform Building Code* intends unbalanced loading to apply to trusses and arches. The placement of live load on one-half the span for trusses and arches can create a reversal of stress in some of the members due to a change in the shear pattern. Therefore, half-span loading should be considered, as depicted in Figure 1607-2. In half-span loading, the loading of the central half of the span for arches and domes should also be considered.

1607.4.4 Special roof loadings. The code requires that the design of roof members of greenhouses account for a minimum concentrated load of 100 pounds (444.8 N). The intent of the code is that this load be so placed on any structural member as to create maximum bending moments and shears. Also, the load is added to the uniformly distributed load required by the code. The rationale behind the requirement for the 100-pound (444.8 N) concentrated load is that greenhouse roofs are normally designed for only a 10-pound-per-square-foot (0.48 kN/m²) live load, which does not provide adequate safety against concentrated loads due to workers and their materials on the roof.

1607.5 Reduction of Live Loads.

The *Uniform Building Code* permits reductions in live loads for both roofs and floors based on, among other things, the tributary area supported by the member under consideration. In addition, the live load reduction for roofs is also a function of the slope of the roof, as it becomes less probable that the loads on a roof member will be at maximum levels as the roof slope increases.

In the case of roofs, Table 16-C provides two methods for computing the live load reduction:

- **Method 1.** The code requires specified live loads that become smaller as a series of stepped functions based on the tributary area supported by the loaded member and the slope of the roof.

- **Method 2.** This method is similar to the provisions for live load reductions for floors and provides a continuous reducing function based on tributary area supported by the member under consideration and the slope of the roof.

The rationale for reductions of live load as permitted by the code is that it is highly improbable, for large tributary loaded areas, that the member under consideration will be loaded over that entire area with the full live load delineated in Tables 16-A and 16-C. Figure 1607-3 illustrates the tributary areas for various structural elements.

The code establishes a minimum tributary area of 150 square feet (13.94 m²) as the threshold for live load reductions computed from Formula (7-1), which is plotted in Figure 1607-4. The *Uniform Building Code* does not permit a reduction in live load for assembly areas on the theory that they must be considered to be fully occupied under normal conditions of occupancy, and a reduction, therefore, would not be appropriate. Live loads in excess of 100 pounds per square foot (4.79 kN/m²) are not permitted reductions, except that for storage live loads exceeding 100 pounds per square foot (4.79 kN/m²), the design live loads on columns may be reduced 20 percent. The maximum live load reduction permitted is 40 percent for members receiving loads from one level only and 60 percent for other members (such as columns or transfer girders).

Formula (7-2) was derived so that if a structural member supporting a tributary area of sufficient size to qualify for the maximum reduction allowed by the formula were subjected to the full design load over the entire area, the overstress would not exceed 30 percent.[1]

It will be noted from Formula (7-2) that the maximum reduction is proportional to the ratio of dead load to live load. Therefore, for heavy framing systems with a high dead load, the reduction is permitted to be greater than it would be for lighter framing systems. Thus, it follows that the concept of relating the maximum live load reduction in the formula to the ratio of dead load to live load is in harmony with a standard principle of structural engineering which holds that for a given magnitude of overload on a structural system, that system with the heavier dead load

(Continued on page 278)

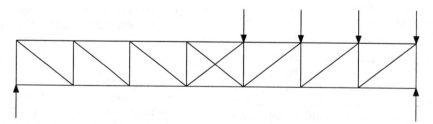

LOAD ON MIDDLE PANEL DIAGONALS CHANGES FROM 0 STRESS FOR BALANCED LOADING TO TENSION OR COMPRESSION FOR UNBALANCED LOADING

UNBALANCED LOAD ON TRUSS

FIGURE 1607-2

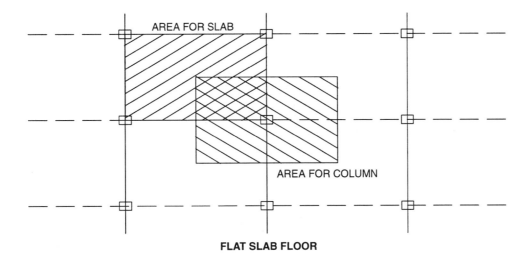

FLAT SLAB FLOOR

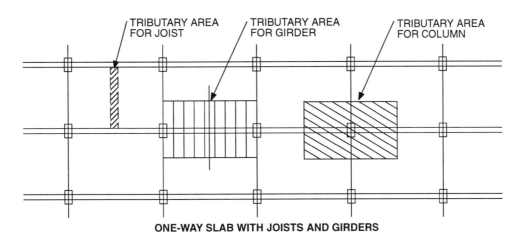

ONE-WAY SLAB WITH JOISTS AND GIRDERS

TRIBUTARY AREAS

FIGURE 1607-3

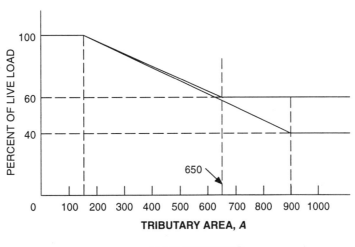

FLOOR MEMBERS

FIGURE 1607-4

COLUMNS

BEAMS AND GIRDERS

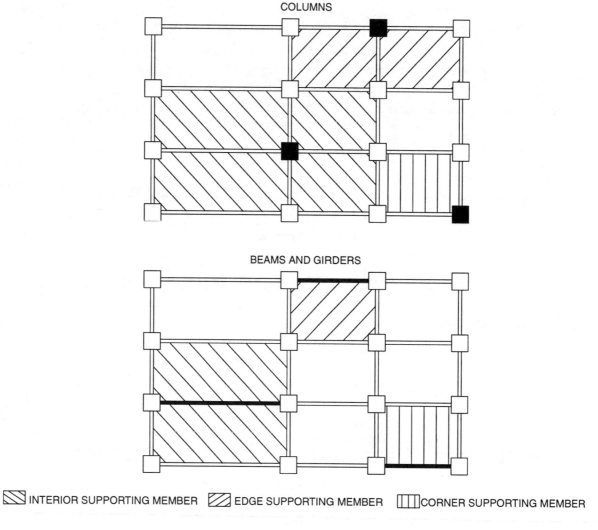

INTERIOR SUPPORTING MEMBER   EDGE SUPPORTING MEMBER   CORNER SUPPORTING MEMBER

INFLUENCE AREAS

FIGURE 1607-5

(Continued from page 276)

will be overstressed proportionally less than one with a lighter dead load. For example, if a floor system weighing 30 pounds per square foot (1.44 kN/m^2) and designed for a live load of 40 pounds per square foot (1.92 kN/m^2) were subjected to a 20-pound-per-square-foot (0.96 kN/m^2) overload, the amount the structural system would be overstressed is about 30 percent, assuming the system was designed to support just the design live load of 40 pounds per square foot (1.92 kN/m^2). If this floor had a dead load of 60 pounds per square foot (2.88 kN/m^2), the overstress would be only 20 percent, again assuming that the system were designed to support just the 40-pound-per-square-foot (1.92 kN/m^2) live load.

In the case of storage live loads exceeding 100 pounds per square foot (4.79 kN/m^2), it is not uncommon in these types of uses for several adjacent floor panels to be fully loaded. However, actual live load surveys have shown that it is highly improbable that the average live load per story will exceed 80 per-

cent of the posted live load.[2] On this basis, the code permits a reduction of 20 percent for the design of columns.

In the case of garages used for storage of passenger cars, the UBC limits the permitted reduction to 40 percent of the live load.

1607.6 Alternate Floor Live Load Reduction. This section has been provided as an alternate to the allowable reduction from Section 1607.5. This floor live load reduction is consistent with the ASCE 7 floor live load reduction provisions. It is based on the influence area that has been shown to provide structural reliability for the various structural effects.

Influence areas are depicted in Figure 1607-5 and are greater than the tributary areas of the members identified. For example, the influence area for an interior column is four times the tributary area. It should be noted, however, that the maximum reduction allowed for these members that support loads from one level is 50 percent of the unreduced live load and 40 percent for other members. For a more thorough discussion, one should consult the commentary in ASCE 7.

SECTION 1611 — OTHER MINIMUM LOADS

1611.4 Anchorage of Concrete on Masonry Walls. Concrete on masonry exterior walls of buildings are subject to horizontal forces of either winds or earthquakes, and these may be in combination with other lateral forces such as soil pressure. In order to resist these horizontal forces, the walls must be supported laterally, and the code requires that the walls be anchored to the floors, roofs and other structural elements that provide required lateral support for the wall.

Walls of concrete or masonry will be subjected to earthquake forces, and exterior walls will also be subjected to wind forces. Damage in the past due to high-velocity winds or earthquakes has shown a weakness in walls that are not anchored properly to their supports. In fact, many failures resulted during the 1971 San Fernando earthquake and the 1994 Northridge earthquake because of inadequate anchorage. Therefore, the code requires that the anchorage of masonry and concrete walls to elements providing lateral support be designed to resist either the horizontal loads specified in Chapter 16 or 280 pounds per lineal foot (2.92 kN/m) of wall, whichever creates the higher loading. For design of elements of the wall anchorage system in Seismic Zone 4, refer to Section 1633.2.8.1 for special loading requirements (420 pounds per lineal foot). Furthermore, where the spacing between anchors exceeds 4 feet (1219 mm), the code requires that the wall be designed to resist the loading between anchors in bending. Understandably, any anchors required for masonry walls of hollow units or cavity walls must be embedded in a reinforced grouted structural element of the wall. The cross-references are intended to call attention to earthquake design requirements related to anchorage of walls to floor and roof diaphragms.

1611.5 Interior Wall Loads. In this section, the code provides minimum criteria for the design of interior partitions so they will be able to resist normal loads of occupancy without deflecting excessively. Also, it is intended that they will be anchored at the ceiling and floor line. Furthermore, in the case of fire-resistive walls, the design criteria provide resistance against the pressures that build up during a fire, and as a result the walls have enough strength and stiffness to provide the required fire endurance. In accordance with Section 1605.1, wood-frame partitions constructed in accordance with the conventional provisions of Section 2320 are deemed to meet this requirement. Brittle finishes include plaster. Flexible finishes would be those that can distort $L/120$ without cracking, such as gypsum board and wood paneling.

The intent of the exception is to require anchorage only of flexible folding or of portable partitions. Anchorage is required to be designed to resist the loads specified in the UBC.

1611.6 Retaining Walls. The retaining wall design prescribed in the UBC is to follow accepted engineering practice. Moreover, the code also specifies a design that appears to be based on either or both of the Coulomb and Rankine theories of earth pressure. The design active earth pressure on a retaining wall

may be considered equivalent to that produced by a fluid weighing 30 pounds per cubic foot (4.71 kN/m³). This design equivalent fluid pressure of 30 pounds per cubic foot (4.71 kN/m³) is really only appropriate for cantilever walls that can be expected to deflect laterally at the top due to earth pressure. Other retaining wall systems should be designed in accordance with the recommendations of soil report. The safety factor against sliding of 1.5 and overturning of 1.5 is a typical safety factor prescribed for this type of cantilevered structure.

1611.7 Water Accumulation. The provisions of Section 1506 addressing the subject of roof drainage are intended to prevent the accumulation of water above the overflow drain inlet level where roofs are designed to slope to roof drains. Section 1506 also requires that either roof drains be provided or that the roof be designed so that it drains over the edge of the roof. Furthermore, Section 1611.7 requires, in addition to the slope for proper drainage, that the structural members be analyzed for deflection so that proper camber will be introduced to cause the roofs to drain.

The alternative to adequate drainage intended by the code is that the roof structure be designed to support the accumulated or ponded water and, furthermore, be designed to account for the progressive deflections created by the ponded water. This phenomenon of progressive deflections is very critical in lightweight roof structures where the ratio of the weight of ponded water to the dead weight of the roof structure is relatively high. Division III of Chapter 23 and Division III of Chapter 22 of the UBC should be consulted when designing roofs with glued-laminated wood or steel structural members, respectively.

Minimum Design Loads for Buildings and Other Structures contains an expanded commentary for ponding due to snow loads and rainfall loads. In addition, the American Institute of Timber Construction's *Timber Construction Manual* contains additional information and methodology for the design of wood roofs to resist ponding loads.[3]

1611.8 Hydrostatic Uplift. The intent of the UBC is to require that hydrostatic uplift pressure be considered in the design of foundation slabs and other horizontal members subject to water pressure.

1611.10 Heliport and Helistop Landing Areas. In this section, the UBC intends that the design of touchdown areas be regulated only when the touchdown area is on a building. In those cases, the criteria in the UBC are essentially the same as those promulgated earlier by the City of Los Angeles and are intended to provide a minimum loading criterion of one of the following:

- The weight of the helicopter.
- A uniform live load of 100 pounds per square foot (4.9 kN/m²), which may be reduced in accordance with Section 1607.5.
- The landing impact effect of the helicopter. Where the craft is equipped with hydraulic shock absorbers, the effect will be less than if equipped with rigid or skid-type landing gear.

SECTION 1612 — COMBINATION OF LOADS

This new section in the 1997 UBC revises the load factors and load combinations stated in Section 1603.6 of the 1994 code.

Also, Section 1603.5 of the 1994 code on stress increases has been deleted in the 1997 code since the new Section 1612 will include all required design load combinations and appropriate stress increases where stated.

New Section 1612 provides LRFD and ASD load combinations. It is important to move toward one set of load combinations applicable to all materials in lieu of different combinations in each material chapter. The proposed load combinations are largely based on ASCE 7, but are somewhat modified to address specific concerns. The term "f_1" has been introduced to solve an editorial problem in ASCE 7. The term "f_2" has been added to deal with the larger probability of simultaneous occurrence of snow and seismic under some conditions.

Two sets of allowable stress design load combinations are proposed in Section 1612.3. The basic load combinations in Section 1612.3.1 are substantially based on ASCE 7 provisions. Instead of providing for a one-third increase in allowable stresses for combinations including wind and earthquake, a factor of 0.75 is applied to the combined transient loads in Formula (12-11). This factor is based on the low probability of simultaneous occurrence of all the transient loads at design load level. This treatment of combinations of loads can be more rationally justified than an increase of the allowable stresses. See the ASCE 7 standard and commentary for further discussion.

The alternate load combinations in Section 1612.3.2 maintain the current allowable stress increases, while not permitting reduction of combined transient loads. These combinations are intended to allow the designer to continue using current methods. Hopefully these combinations can be eliminated after a transition period.

SECTION 1613 — DEFLECTION

The *Uniform Building Code* limits the deflections of structural members in this section for two reasons:

- To limit cracking of plaster ceilings.
- To provide for serviceability and usability of the floor systems

The latter reason for controlling deflections is necessary in order to ensure the proper fit of partitions and equipment on floors of commercial structures. Also, for structural members with high strength-to-weight ratios, the deflection limits are necessary to prevent springiness and annoying vibrations of the floor system.

The code intends that when the span tables in Chapter 23 are used for joist and rafter spans, the deflection criteria on which the tables are based shall be used. Where the dead load exceeds 50 percent of the live load, Table 16-D shall govern.

The allowable deflection in Table 16-D of $L/240$ for those members loaded with live load plus K times the dead load is designed to provide a limit for those structural systems that exhibit long-term creep, such as wood and reinforced concrete. In the case of wood structural elements, the dead load for seasoned lumber would need to be greater than the live load in order for the $L/240$ criterion to be the more restrictive. In the case of reinforced concrete structural members, the dead load would need to be slightly less than the live load to make the $L/240$ criterion

more restrictive than $L/360$ (83 percent of the live load where the K factor equals 0.6).

Division II—SNOW LOADS

The 1997 edition of the UBC relocates the snow load design provisions into Division II, beginning with Section 1614.

SECTION 1614 — SNOW LOADS

In this section, the code requires that a design to resist snow load should be made whenever such loading will result in larger members or connections. The language "where such loading will result in larger members or connections" is used because even where a roof is designed for a snow load on the roof of 20 pounds per square foot (0.96 kN/m^2) [which at first glance seems equivalent to a nominal 20-pound-per-square-foot (0.96 kN/m^2) live load], the design to resist the snow load would result in larger members or connections. This is because the code does not permit reductions in snow load as it does for live load based on tributary area. Furthermore, this section requires that unbalanced snow loads be considered. Consequently, in what might appear nominally to be equal loadings [that is, a 20-pound-per-square-foot (0.96 kN/m^2) roof live load versus a 20-pound-per-square-foot (0.96 kN/m^2) roof snow load], the snow load design actually would result in larger members and connections.

As snow on the roof of a building rarely accumulates evenly, the code intends that the designer investigate conditions of imbalance by requiring that roof designs consider unbalanced snow loading. One case would be the loading of one slope of a gable roof with snow while the other slope is unloaded. If this creates a more unfavorable condition in the design of the roof structure members, then it is the loading that should be considered. This type of loading covers the case where the snow may be removed from one side of the roof due to sliding or melting.

As most roof failures due to snow loads are created by significant accumulations of snow at valleys, parapets, roof structures and offsets in roofs, as shown by Figure 1614-1, the code requires that these potential accumulations be considered in the design. However, the code specifies no criteria for the determination of how these potential accumulations are to be handled. Division I of Appendix Chapter 16 does contain a methodology for considering unbalanced snow loads as well as drifts on multilevel roofs. Therefore, even through Appendix Chapter 16 may not have been adopted, a rational approach would be to follow the procedures outlined for unbalanced roof snow loads and drifts on multilevel roofs.

Section 1614 further charges the building official with establishing the magnitude of the roof snow loads. To make this determination, the building official may use Division I of Appendix Chapter 16 as a guide or, alternatively, enlist the aid of a local structural engineer's association.

The *Uniform Building Code* permits a reduction in roof snow loads for roofs with slopes exceeding 20 degrees. This is due to the fact that on slopes even as low as 10 degrees, snow will slide, and as a result a reduction in the roof snow load is appropriate for sloping roofs. It is the intent of the code that snow is able to slide from the roof to utilize this reduction factor. If snow is impeded from sliding, such as on roofs with multiple gables or roofs with a high parapet, a reduction factor may not be used. In fact, for

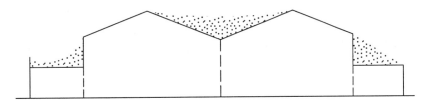

POTENTIAL SNOW ACCUMULATION, GABLE ROOF WITH SIDE SHEDS

FIGURE 1614-1

multiple-gable roofs, the code intends that the roof be designed for accumulation of snow in the valleys between adjacent gables.

Division III—WIND DESIGN

SECTION 1615 — GENERAL

The provisions in Division III were originally distilled from the wind load provision in American National Standards Institute (ANSI) A58.1—1972 with some provisions from ANSI A58.1—1982 included (basically the wind speed map and some revised coefficients). Since that time, the standard has been transferred to the American Society of Civil Engineers (ASCE) who under an ANSI approved maintenance procedure, published a slight revision and redesignation in 1988 (ASCE Standard 7—1988). Indeed, the q_s and C_e factors were changed in the 1991 UBC to create a pressure profile equivalent to ASCE 7—1988. When the code referred to "approved national standards"being allowed as an alternative to the UBC method, it was referring to this ASCE document as well as other documents related to specific industries or structures such as towers, tanks, flagpoles and so forth. The 1997 UBC refers overtly to these documents in Section 1604. The reader may refer to the original documents for historical commentary. However, a more comprehensive commentary is available from the Structural Engineers Association of Washington.[4]

UBC wind pressures are calculated in a manner similar to ASCE 7 except that only four coefficients are used. In other words, the UBC is a simplification of the ASCE 7 methodology that tends to be closer to pure research data and requires a more exacting analysis. For the UBC to apply to design of many buildings and structures, certain assumptions were made about what the structure will be like. These assumptions limit the UBC's applicability to a height of 400 feet (121 920 mm) when using Method 1 as discussed later. They are also limited to structures that are subject to dynamic loads (those with a large height to width ratio of 5 or more or high period of vibration). Chapter 6 of ASCE 7—1995, as alluded to above, is now the main national standard that one may use to design for wind resistance of these exempted buildings or structures. ASCE 7 and other national standards may be used for structures subject to vortex shedding, such as from structures with cylindrical shapes or subject to icing.

The reader should realize, however, that Chapter 6 of the new ASCE 7—1995 is now somewhat different from the UBC method. The major difference is that the basis of the wind speed map has been changed to a 3-second gust wind speed instead of the UBC's Basic (Fastest Mile) Wind Speed (see the definitions be-

low). The new basic wind speed map is considerably different than that in the 1997 UBC, although the equations in ASCE 7 were adjusted to produce wind pressures that are equivalent to those calculated from an equivalent fastest mile wind speed. Nevertheless, since the fastest mile wind speed data has not been kept by the Weather Bureau since the early 1980's and large wind storms have caused a change in the data, there may still be localities that have a net effective increase in wind speed and wind pressures. The second biggest change is a requirement to design for wind speed-up effects at or near the crest of isolated hills, ridges or escarpments. Depending on slopes, height and other conditions, the pressures may double at the top of these topological features.

Prior knowledge of wind direction is not required, and winds are assumed to come from any horizontal direction. The provisions in ASCE 7 that depend on wind direction are not included in the UBC. The design of open-frame towers is complicated, and they should be designed in accordance with procedures such as ASCE 7. However, a simplified procedure that is intended to be on the conservative side has been included so that open-framed towers of limited height may be designed by this code.

SECTION 1616 — DEFINITIONS

BASIC WIND SPEED. The minimum basic wind speeds to be used for design are shown in the UBC in Figure 16-1, which was taken from ANSI A58.1-1982 and represented the latest research available at the time these provisions were promulgated. The map is based on a 50-year mean recurrence interval, which has traditionally been accepted as providing a reasonable risk. For important structures such as essential facilities outlined in Table 16-K, however, the code specifies an importance factor of 1.15, which is reasonably consistent with a 100-year recurrence interval. The basic wind speed map also reflects special wind regions, such as those in southern California for Santa Ana winds, which may include the channeling effect due to canyons or gorges. Therefore, the building official has the option of requiring higher wind speeds where the records so indicate. Tornadoes have not been considered in the development of the wind speed contours shown on the map.

EXPOSURE. Built-up or rough terrain can cause a substantial reduction in wind speed because of turbulence. ASCE 7 establishes four conditions of exposure, three of which, Exposures B, C and D, are included in this part. However, the definitions have been changed to eliminate dependence on wind direction. Exposure A should not be used without detailed analysis. For this reason, it has been excluded from these provisions, and designers wishing to use this exposure must follow procedures such as those in ANSI A58.1. Exposure B will be applicable in most urban areas, but structures in flat and open country should be designed for Exposure C. Exposure D applies to areas adjacent to bodies of water where the basic wind speed is 80 miles per hour or greater and the surrounding terrain is flat and unobstructed.

PARTIALLY ENCLOSED STRUCTURE OR STORY. For the purposes of applying the factors in Table 16-H, a definition for partially enclosed structures is given. Windows and doors must be designed and detailed to resist the loads specified for elements and components in order to *not* be considered openings. A definition of openings is also provided for clarity.

Special glazing such as tempered or laminated glass is not required unless necessary to comply with the code requirements for strength. Impact resistance from missiles is not required.

SECTION 1620 — DESIGN WIND PRESSURES

Equation (20-1) represents a more simplified design procedure than the corresponding equations in ASCE 7. The *Uniform Building Code* uses a three-coefficient equation with the coefficients selected from three tables; ASCE 7 uses more complex equations and requires the computation of most coefficients. The development of the coefficients in the code will be described more fully under the descriptions of the tables.

The designer should be cautioned that since total wind forces may be lower in some cases than in previous UBC designs, wind drift limitations, when applicable, should be proportionately reduced to maintain the same building stiffness.

SECTION 1621 — PRIMARY FRAMES AND SYSTEMS

1621.1 General. Prior to the 1982 edition, the traditional method in the *Uniform Building Code* for determining wind forces on buildings was to apply horizontal pressures on the vertical projected area and apply vertical uplift forces on the horizontal projected area. This procedure works well for most regular square or rectangular structures, but gives incorrect joint moments when applied to gabled frames. Therefore, two methods of design are included to provide for the special problem of the gabled rigid frame. ASCE 7 requires that the leeward wall suction be constant and equal to that at the roof level. This provision is included in Method 1, but in order to include it in Method 2, it was necessary to limit applicability of Method 2 to buildings 200 feet (60 960 mm) or less in height.

Overturning stability can be computed by either method. In accordance with ASCE 7, horizontal and vertical forces must be assumed to act simultaneously. The traditional factor of two-thirds applied to the dead load resistive moment has been retained and included in this section. However, it should be noted that the overturning stability applies to the primary load-resisting elements of the structure in addition to the overall structure.

For the overall structure with a height-to-width ratio of 0.5 or less in the wind direction considered, and with a maximum height of 60 feet (18 288 mm), the code permits a one-third reduction in the combination of effects of uplift and overturning. This was justified by the results of wind tunnel tests.

SECTION 1622 — ELEMENTS AND COMPONENTS OF STRUCTURES

Wind pressures are higher on small areas than on large areas due to the gust effects, which are more pronounced on the small areas. Whereas ASCE 7 provides a separate table of velocity pressures to apply to parts and portions of structures, the UBC modifies the C_q values. The C_q values in this code for elements and components are the sum of external pressures, internal pressures and the increase for small tributary areas. The increase is based on a tributary area of 10 square feet (0.93 m^2). To reduce the local pressure effect for larger areas, Footnote 2 of Table 16-H has been added.

Much higher negative pressure increases occur near discontinuities such as eaves, corners, ridges or rakes. The majority of wind damage observed after severe windstorms has been the result of these high localized pressures. The most significant increase in design requirements, as compared to the 1979 and earlier editions of the UBC, has been in this area. Suctions on small areas close to the discontinuities may be even higher than indicated by the C_q values in the table.

The high negative pressures near discontinuities are generally combined with areas of much lower pressure. Hence, a dual method of analysis is given for elements and components. For example, a wall girt 20 feet (6096 mm) long in an enclosed structure would be designed for an outward C_q of 1.2 along its entire length or an outward C_q of 1.5 along the 10 feet (3048 mm) of its length nearest the corner, with no pressure on the remaining 10 feet (3048 mm). One difference between ANSI A58.1-1982 and the 1972 edition was that negative pressures are to be calculated using velocities at the mean roof height. This provision is still included in the UBC.

SECTION 1624 — MISCELLANEOUS STRUCTURES

This paragraph is similar to earlier editions of the UBC in that it allows lower wind forces on miscellaneous structures. The reduction is comparable to reducing the wind recurrence interval below 50 years.

TABLE 16-F — WIND STAGNATION PRESSURE (q_s) AT STANDARD HEIGHT OF 33 FEET (10 058 mm)

The theoretical pressure (stagnation pressure) developed by the wind's impinging on a vertical surface at sea level and standard atmospheric pressure is determined from the well-known formula, $q_s = 0.00256V^2$. The velocity V in miles (km) per hour used in this expression is based on the "fastest mile"; that is, the velocity is averaged over the time it takes a mile of air to pass a given point. Local fluctuations in this velocity cause the gusting effects, which will be discussed later. A height of 33 feet (10 058 mm) has been adopted as the standard height for measuring wind velocity. The stagnation pressure q_s is measured in pounds per square foot (kN/m^2).

TABLE 16-G — COMBINED HEIGHT, EXPOSURE AND GUST FACTOR COEFFICIENT (C_e)

This table provides coefficients that allow for the effects of height, gust factor and exposure conditions. The coefficients C_e were derived using the procedures outlined in ANSI

A58.1-1972. The pressures resulting from the procedures in ASCE 7 are essentially the same.

The values for C_e were computed by combining height and gust factors from ANSI A58.1 and rounding to the nearest hundredth. The values conform to the procedures in ANSI A58.1 in that the values of C_e were computed for the midrange of each height bracket. For example, the value of the 30- to 40-foot-high (9144 to 12 192 mm) range is calculated for 35 feet (10 668 mm). The exception is the range 0 to 15 feet (0 to 4572 mm), which is calculated for the height of 15 feet (4572 mm).

TABLE 16-H — PRESSURE COEFFICIENTS (C_q)

The coefficients C_q were calculated by combining the appropriate coefficients in ANSI A58.1-1982. The rationale for developing these coefficients follows.

Primary Frames and Systems

Two methods are presented. The projected area method is easier to apply but may not be correct for some rigid-frame systems. It does apply to overturning stability on all structures. The coefficients have been developed as follows:

Vertical Projected Area (Horizontal Forces)

Windward wall	0.8 inward	ANSI Figure 2
Leeward wall	0.5 outward	ANSI Figure 2
Combined	1.3	

The 1.4 factor for buildings taller than 40 feet (12 192 mm) is an increase to account for ANSI A58.1-1982's constant leeward wall suction that was discussed under Section 1622.

Horizontal Projected Area (Uplift Forces)—Enclosed and Unenclosed Structures

External suction	0.7 upward	ANSI Figure 2

Horizontal Projected Area (Uplift Forces)—Partially Enclosed Structures

External suction	0.7 upward	ANSI Figure 2
Internal pressure	0.5 upward	
Combined	1.2 upward	

(A combination of the maximum values of external pressures and internal pressure from ANSI Table 9 is excessively conservative when applied to primary frames and systems. Internal pressures have been omitted for enclosed and unenclosed structures and taken as 0.5 rather than the value given in ANSI Table 9 for open structures.)

The "normal force" method should be applied to rigid frames where the moments in joints or members can be affected by the point of load application. These coefficients were developed as follows:

Windward wall	0.8 inward	ANSI Figure 2
Leeward wall	0.5 outward	ANSI Figure 2
Wind perpendicular to ridge		
Leeward roof or flat roof	0.7 outward	ANSI Figure 2
Windward roof		
Slope < 2:12	0.7 outward	
Slope 2:12 to < 9:12	0.9 outward or 0.3 inward	
Slope 9:12 to 12:12	0.4 inward	
Slope >12:12	0.7 inward	

(These roof coefficients for windward slopes are a simplification of ANSI Figure 2.)

Wind parallel to ridge and flat roofs		
Enclosed structures	0.7 outward	ANSI Figure 2
Partially enclosed structures	1.2 outward	(See comments on Method 2 and Table 16-H, Footnote 1.)

(Partially enclosed structures or stories are defined as those having more than 15 percent of any windward projected area open and in which the area of opening on all other projected areas is less than half of that on the windward projection.)

Elements and Components

Elements and components have increased pressures due to local effects. An additional factor of 0.1 is added to approximate the difference between ANSI Table 5 for buildings and ANSI Table 6 for parts and portions. It is intended to apply to areas up to 10 square feet (0.93 m^2). For larger tributary areas, the load reduction in Footnote 2 applies.

Coefficients were derived as follows:

Wall Elements:

All structures
External pressure	0.8 inward	ANSI Figures 3 and 4
Internal pressure	0.3 inward	ANSI Figures 3 and 4
Parts and portions	0.1 inward	
Combined	1.2 inward	

Enclosed and unenclosed structures
External pressure (side walls)	0.8 outward	ANSI Figures 3 and 4
Internal pressure	0.3 outward	ANSI Figures 3 and 4
Parts and portions	0.1 outward	
Combined	1.2 outward	

Partially enclosed structures
External pressure	0.7 outward	ANSI Figures 3 and 4
Internal pressure	0.8 outward	ANSI Figures 3 and 4
Parts and portions	0.1 outward	
Combined	1.6 outward	

Roof Elements:

Enclosed and unenclosed structures

Slope < 7:12
External pressure	0.8 outward	ANSI Figures 3 and 4
Internal pressure	0.4 outward	ANSI Figures 3 and 4
Parts and portions	0.1 outward	
Combined	1.3 outward	

Slope 7:12 to 12:12 Outward or inward pressure	1.3	Same as above

For slopes >12:12, use wall element values.

Local Pressures

Higher pressures exist near discontinuities. These pressures apply over a distance of 10 feet (3048 mm) or 0.1 times the least width, whichever is smaller, from the discontinuity. There is some controversy regarding the values and the area over which they should apply. American National Standards Institute recommendations have been modified in some cases.

Wall Corners:

1.5 outward or 1.2 inward   ANSI-82, Figures 3 and 4

Canopies or Overhangs at Eaves, Rakes or Ridges:

Varies from 3.1 to 2.1 for slopes   ANSI Figures 3 and 4 less than 2:12

Roof Eaves, Rakes or Ridges without Overhangs:

Varies from 2.6 to 1.6 for slopes   ANSI Figures 3 and 4 less than 12:12

TABLE 16-K — OCCUPANCY CATEGORY

Wind importance factor. The importance factor for the specified occupancy categories which must be operational after a wind storm is based on a recurrence interval greater than that considered for other structures. Rather than provide wind maps for various recurrence intervals, the use of the importance factor accomplishes the required result in a simpler fashion.

Division IV—EARTHQUAKE DESIGN

This division on earthquake design provisions has undergone major revisions in the 1997 edition of the UBC. A majority of these revisions had been under development since 1993 by SEAOC and its ad-hoc subcommittees on strength and strong ground motion and include the following:

1. Incorporation of load combinations consistent with ASCE 7 and 1994 NEHRP recommended provisions for seismic regulations for new buildings. (Section 1612)

2. Introduction of a new Reliability/Redundancy Factor, ρ, to recognize design redundancy. (Sections 1628 and 1630)

3. A simplified seismic lateral-force procedure for select applications not requiring a rigorous design procedure. (Sections 1629.8.2 and 1630.2.3)

4. Changes in the primary seismic base shear equations for consistency with 1994 NEHRP equation with some modifications. (Section 1630.2.1)

5. Changes in the soil profile type for consistency with 1994 NEHRP. A new Division V is added to Chapter 16 to pro-

vide a procedure for determining soil profile types and categorization of sites.

6. Introduction of overstrength factors Ω_o and R. R is a numerical coefficient representative of the inherent overstrength and global ductility capacity of lateral-force-resisting systems and "Ω_o" is a seismic amplification factor required to account for structural overstrength. (Tables 16-N and 16-P)

7. Adjustments in the drift requirements for consistency with strength design requirements. (Sections 1630.9 and 1630.10)

8. Dynamic analysis procedures have been adjusted to be consistent with the strength design parameters, and a new section has been added on requirements for elastic and nonlinear time-history analysis. (Section 1631)

9. Revisions in the nonstructural components design provisions for consistency with 1994 NEHRP provisions. (Sections 1632, 1633 and Table 16-O)

10. Modifications to provisions for nonbuilding structures to reflect conversion to strength design. (Section 1634 and Table 16-P)

11. Introduction of a near-source effect design provision to account for the increase in ground motions for sites closer to known earthquake faults in Seismic Zone 4. (Section 1629.4.2)

12. Revisions in the seismic design requirements for shear walls. (Sections 1630.4.3 and 1921.6.6)

13. Revisions in the seismic design of elements supporting discontinuous structural systems. (Section 1630.8.2)

14. Revisions to the collector elements design requirements. (Section 1633.2.6)

Except for a few exceptions, the earthquake regulations in the UBC are similar to the *Recommended Lateral Force Requirements and Commentary*,[5] which includes a comprehensive and detailed commentary.

The following cross-reference table will correlate the 1997 UBC earthquake design provisions by code section with the appropriate code and commentary included in Appendix C of the 1996 SEAOC *Recommended Lateral Force Requirements and Commentary.*

CROSS-REFERENCE TABLE FOR EARTHQUAKE DESIGN PROVISIONS
1997 UBC AND 1996 SEAOC APPENDIX C

UBC CODE SECTION	SECTION TITLE	SEAOC/APPENDIX C SECTION
Division I—General Design Requirements		
1602	Definitions	—
1603	Notations	1603.0
1612	Combinations of Loads	1612.0
1612.2	Load Combinations Using Strength Design or LRFD	1612.2
1612.3	Load Combinations Using Allowable Stress Design	1612.3
1612.4	Special Seismic Load Combinations	1612.4
Division IV—Earthquake Design		
1626	General	1641
1627	Definitions	1642
1628	Symbols and Notations	1643
1629	Criteria Selection	1644
1629.1	Basis for Design	1644.1
1629.2	Occupancy Categories	1644.2
1629.3	Site Geology and Soil Characteristics	1644.3
1629.4	Site Seismic Hazard Characteristics	1644.4
1629.5	Configuration Requirements	1644.5
1629.6	Structural Systems	1644.6
1629.7	Height Limits	1644.7
1629.8	Selection of Lateral-force Procedure	1644.8
1629.9	System Limitations	1644.9
1629.10	Alternative Procedures	1644.10
1630	Minimum Design Lateral Forces and Related Efforts	1645
1630.1	Earthquake Loads and Modeling Requirements	1645.1
1630.2	Static Force Procedure	1645.2
1630.3	Determination of Seismic Factors	1645.3
1630.4	Combination of Structural Systems	1645.4
1630.5	Vertical Distribution of Force	1645.5
1630.6	Horizontal Distribution of Shear	1645.6
1630.7	Horizontal Torsional Moments	1645.7
1630.8	Overturning	1645.8
1630.9	Drift	1645.9
1630.10	Story Drift Limitation	1645.10
1630.11	Vertical Component	1645.11
1631	Dynamic Analysis Procedures	1646
1631.1	General	1646.1
1631.2	Ground Motion	1646.2
1631.3	Mathematical Model	1646.3
1631.4	Description of Analysis Procedure	1646.4
1631.5	Response Spectrum Analysis	1646.5
1631.6	Time-history Analysis	1646.6
1632	Lateral Force on Elements of Structures, Nonstructural Components and Equipment Supported by Structures	1647
1632.1	General	1647.1
1632.2	Design for Total Lateral Force	1647.2
1632.3	Specifying Lateral Forces	1647.3
1632.4	Relative Motion of Equipment Attachments	1647.4
1632.5	Alternative Design	1647.5
1633	Detailed Systems Design Requirements	1648
1633.1	General	1648.1
1633.2	Structural Framing Systems	1648.2
1634	Nonbuilding Structures	1649
1634.1	General	1649.1
1634.2	Lateral Force	1649.2

(continued)

CROSS-REFERENCE TABLE FOR EARTHQUAKE DESIGN PROVISIONS
1997 UBC AND 1996 SEAOC APPENDIX C—(continued)

UBC CODE SECTION	SECTION TITLE	SEAOC/APPENDIX C SECTION
1634.3	Rigid Structures	1649.3
1634.4	Tanks with Supported Bottoms	1649.4
1634.5	Other Nonbuilding Structures	1649.5
1635	Earthquake-recording Instrumentations	1650
Division V—Soil Profile Types		
1636	Site Categorization Procedure	1662
1636.1	Scope	1662.1
1636.2	Definitions	1662.2
Tables 16-A through Tables 16-U	All design table numbers match	Tables 16-A through Tables 16-U
Figure 16-2	Seismic Zone Map	Figure 104-1
Figure 16-3	Design Response Spectra	Figure 16-4

SECTION 1629 — CRITERIA SELECTION

Section 1629.8.1, in selection of a seismic lateral-force design procedure, states that any structure may be, and certain structures as defined in Section 1629.8.4 shall be, designed using the dynamic lateral-force procedures stated in Section 1631. Sections 1629.8.2 and 1629.8.3, however, define the conditions that a building or structure must meet in order to use a static lateral-force design procedure rather than the more-rigorous dynamic analysis.

1629.8.2 Simplified static. This seismic lateral-force design procedure is new in the 1997 UBC and applies to Occupancy Category 4 or 5 (see Table 16-K) buildings of any occupancy not more than three stories in height, excluding basements, that use light-frame construction and other buildings not more than two stories in height, excluding basements. As shown by Figure 1629-1. The actual design procedure is specified in Section 1630.2.3 and makes use of conservative base shear formulas that

envelop the general building code requirements. The proponents of this code change believed that the user of these requirements for these very limited structures should have a procedure that can be quickly and conservatively used without full application of the static force procedure stated in Section 1630.2. It is intended that the simplified static procedure will result in a safe design with significantly less effort in the calculation of the required lateral forces for these building types.

SECTION 1630 — MINIMUM DESIGN LATERAL FORCES AND RELATED EFFECTS

In Section 1630.1, a new factor, ρ, defined as a redundancy/reliability factor, is introduced in the 1997 code. The use of the ρ factor in the earthquake design loads (Equation 30-1) is intended to encourage the use of redundant lateral-force-resisting systems in buildings and structures by penalizing nonredundant ones through higher lateral-force requirements. The ρ factor was

APPLICABILITY:

- [✓] OCCUPANCY CATEGORY 4 OR 5
- [✓] ALL TWO-STORY STRUCTURES
- [✓] ALL THREE-STORY STRUCTURES OF LIGHT-FRAME CONSTRUCTION

$$V = \frac{3.0C_a}{R} W$$

$$F_x = \frac{3.0C_a}{R} w_i$$

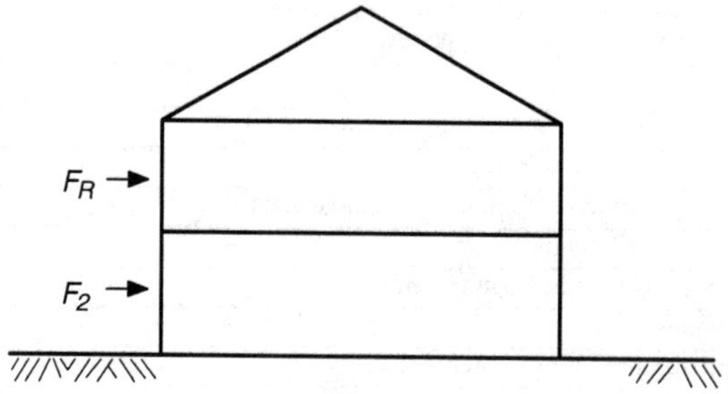

SIMPLIFIED DESIGN BASE SHEAR

FIGURE 1629-1

based on results of a SAC joint venture study of welded steel moment-resisting frames and observations from the 1994 Northridge earthquake and others. The ρ factor, which is defined by Equation (30-3), ranges from 1.0 to 1.5 with factors greater than 1.0 applying to what is determined to be the less-redundant configured lateral-force-resisting systems.

Also new in the 1997 code is a Ω_o factor, which is defined as a seismic-force amplification factor that is required to account for structural overstrength. Values of Ω_o are shown in Table 16-N for various basic structural systems. This factor has application for use of Equation (30-2) for E_m, the estimated maximum earthquake force that can be developed in the structure as

set forth in Section 1630.1.1. Utilization of the overstrength factor is needed to establish design loads for specific elements of the structure that are required to remain elastic during the design basis ground motion; for example, a discontinuous shear wall that bears on columns. For further background on the determination and use of Ω_o factors, it is suggested that the commentary on Section 1645.3 of the 1996 edition of the *Recommended Lateral Force Requirements and Commentary, Appendix C* (SEAOC Blue Book) be reviewed.

1630.2 Static Force Procedure. The primary base shear formulas in Section 1630.2.1, as shown in Figure 1630-1, have been

$$V = \frac{C_v I}{RT} W \qquad \text{(LONG PERIOD STRUCTURES)}$$

$$V = \frac{2.5 C_a I}{R} W \qquad \text{(SHORT PERIOD STRUCTURES)}$$

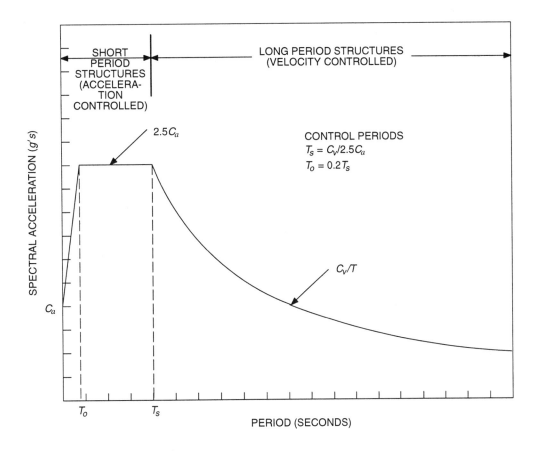

NOTES:

1. Constant velocity portion is a function of $\frac{I}{T}$ not $\frac{I}{T^{2/3}}$.

2. Plateau in the constant acceleration portion varies with soil profile.

STATIC FORCE PROCEDURE—BASE SHEAR EQUATIONS

FIGURE 1630-1

replaced by formulas that are consistent with the 1994 NEHRP formulas, with a few modifications. A single R factor, defined as the numerical coefficient representative of the inherent over-strength and global ductility capacity of the lateral-force-resisting system, is included in the new design base shear formula. Also new are C_a and C_v factors that are site-dependent ground motion coefficients that define the ground-motion response within the acceleration and velocity-controlled ranges of the design-response spectrum. The C_a and C_v factors vary with soil profile type and seismic zone factor as shown in Tables 16-Q and 16-R.

The 1997 UBC also specifies the minimum base shear required for design of buildings and structures in Seismic Zone 4 to be is based on N_a and N_v factors, which are near-source factors used in the determination of C_a and C_v in Seismic Zone 4. These factors relate to both the proximity of the building or structure to known faults and earthquake magnitudes and slip rates as set forth in Tables 16-S, 16-T and 16-U. The incorporation of N_a and N_v factors in the minimum design base shear in Seismic Zone 4 is intended to recognize the amplified ground motions that occur at close distances to faults.

Division V—SOIL PROFILE TYPES

SECTION 1636 — SITE CATEGORIZATION PROCEDURE

This new division in the 1997 UBC describes the procedure for determining Soil Profile Types S_A through S_F in accordance with Table 16-J.

REFERENCES

[1]The National Bureau of Standards (1952). *Live Loads on Floors and Buildings,* Building Materials and Structures Publication No. 133. Washington, D.C., page 26. (To obtain a copy, order Publication No. COM 7311055 from the National Technical Information Service, Springfield, Virginia 22161.)

[2]American Society of Civil Engineers (1996). *Minimum Design Loads for Buildings and Other Structures,* ASCE 7-95. New York City.

[3]The American Institute of Timber Construction (1985). *Timber Construction Manual.* John Wiley and Sons, Incorporated, New York City.

[4]Wind Subcommittee, SEAW (1995). *Wind Commentary to the Uniform Building Code.* Seattle, Washington. (To obtain a copy, order from SEAW, P.O. Box 4250, Seattle, WA 98104.)

[5]Seismology Committee, SEAOC (1996). *Recommended Lateral Force Requirements and Commentary.* Sacramento, California.

Chapter 17

STRUCTURAL TESTS AND INSPECTIONS

SECTION 1701 — SPECIAL INSPECTIONS

1701.1 General. The *Uniform Building Code* is unique among the model building codes in its requirement for continuous or periodic inspection provided by special inspectors for certain types of work. Most building departments do not have the staff of inspectors to provide detailed inspections on large and complicated projects. This is also true for other projects where the nature of the construction is such that extra care in quality control must be exercised in order to assure compliance with the code. Also, it is questionable whether this type of inspection service should be provided at public expense. For these reasons, special inspection for certain types of work as listed in this section is mandated by the code. The code specifies that the special inspector be employed by the owner (or the engineer or architect acting as the owner's agent), thus avoiding the possibility of conflict of interest were the special inspector to be employed by the contractor. It should be noted that if the building official finds that the proposed project or element of construction is of a minor nature then special inspection may be waived.

1701.2 Special Inspector. The code intends that the special inspector be a specially qualified person who can demonstrate competency to the satisfaction of the building official. This usually requires an examination of the special inspector's knowledge of the type of work to be inspected. The test should determine that the special inspector not only knows the trade but also the code requirements for the work. In this regard, ICBO maintains a program of testing and certification for special inspectors.

A fairly common practice of permitting the architect or engineer—through periodic observational visits to the project—to act as a special inspector is not within the intent of the code, except as required in Section 1702. This is true unless the individual is specifically qualified to inspect the work involved and spends the requisite amount of time on the job to provide either the continuous or periodic inspections required by the code.

1701.3 Duties and Responsibilities of the Special Inspector. It is the duty of the special inspector to not only observe the work assigned for conformance with the code but also to furnish inspection reports to the building official, engineer or any other designated person. If discrepancies are found in the work, the special inspector should call them to the immediate attention of the contractor for correction. If the discrepancies are not corrected, the special inspector should notify the design engineer and the building official. When the inspector has completed the inspection, the code requires that a final report be submitted to the building official and engineer stating that, to the best of the special inspector's knowledge, the inspected work complies with the approved plans and specifications and the code.

1701.7 Approved Fabricators. The *Uniform Building Code* also states that special inspections required by the code will not be required where the work is done on the premises of an approved fabricator. The requirements of the code are such that if the fabricator meets the qualifications described in the code and is approved by the building official, the fabricator's quality control procedures are expected to be such that a special inspector is not required for work accomplished in the fabricator's shop. See discussion in Sections 1704.1 through 1704.6 of this handbook.

SECTION 1702 — STRUCTURAL OBSERVATION

Due to the critical nature of construction in Seismic Zones 3 and 4, this section requires that the engineer or architect of record be employed by the owner to provide observational visits to the site to obtain compliance with the structural drawings. This requirement is triggered by the following conditions:

1. The structure is defined in Table 16-K as Occupancy Category 1, 2 or 3, or

2. The structure is required to comply with Section 403, or

3. The 1997 edition of the UBC will require structural observation for structures in Seismic Zone 4 where the near-source factor, N_a from Table 16-5, used in the structural design exceeds 1.0. The need for structural observation for designed structures located close to faults capable of producing large-magnitude earthquakes has been clearly demonstrated by the damage experienced in previous earthquakes. An exception has been added for single one- and two-story commercial buildings and one- and-two story dwellings and accessory garages, or

4. When so designated by the architect or engineer of record, or

5. When such observation is specifically required by the building official.

SECTION 1703 — NONDESTRUCTIVE TESTING

This section includes the testing requirements for structural steel welding and is applicable to welded, fully restrained connections between primary members of ordinary moment frames and special moment-resisting frames for structures in Seismic Zones 3 and 4. Testing must be done by nondestructive methods for compliance with approved standards and job specifications. The testing must be a part of the special inspection requirements of Section 1701.5 and shall be established by the person responsible for structural design and as shown on the plans and specifications.

The 1997 edition of the UBC expanded this section to include the welded, fully restrained connections between primary members of ordinary moment frames in addition to the special moment-resisting frames as a result of the 1994 Northridge earthquake. The discovery of fractured connections at the welded column-to-beam connections occurred in both ordinary moment frames and special steel moment-resisting frames. This additional testing requirement is necessary to supplement existing welding inspection and testing requirements to minimize similar behavior in future earthquakes.

SECTION 1704 — PREFABRICATED CONSTRUCTION

When a structure or components of a structure are prefabricated off site, the building official has no opportunity to make the inspections which would normally be made for site-built construction. Therefore, this section contains requirements that, if followed, give reasonable assurance that the construction of the prefabricated components or buildings will comply with the provisions of the code.

1704.1 General. In the context of the UBC, a prefabricated assembly is a "structural" unit. Where the components are nonstructural, this section does not apply.

1704.4 Connections. The intent of this section is that the connecting devices which are used to connect prefabricated assemblies should be capable of developing the strength of the members connected. However, it excepts those designs that are specified in Chapter 16 for members of a structural frame. There are cases where the code has specific requirements for the design of connections in braced frames and for the connections of cross bracing for elevated water tanks.

1704.6 Certificate and Inspection. There are three different sets of conditions under which prefabricated assemblies are approved for installation in a building:

1. Where the assembly is fabricated under continuous inspection by a special inspector in accordance with and when required by Section 1701.

2. Where the assembly is readily accessible for inspection at the site.

3. Where an approved agency as defined in Chapter 2 provides a certificate of approval which certifies that the prefabricated assembly has been inspected by agency personnel and meets all the requirements of the code.

The code still requires the jurisdiction to inspect the placement of the prefabricated assembly in the building to determine compliance with the code.

Chapter 18

FOUNDATIONS AND RETAINING WALLS

SECTION 1801 — SCOPE

This chapter contains provisions and requirements for the design of foundations for buildings and other structures, requirements for excavations and fills, and requirements for retaining wall structures. The provisions in Chapter 18 for excavations and fills are intended to apply to the specific site where a building or a structure will be located. Chapter 33 in the appendix contains requirements for more extensive excavations, grading and earthwork and includes requirements for fills and embankments.

The provisions in Chapter 18 are based on general principles of soil mechanics, and any standard textbook on this subject should be consulted for those desiring the basic rationale for these principles.[1]

Although Section 1612 of the UBC requires buildings, structures, and all portions thereof to be designed by either strength design, load and resistance factor design, or allowable stress design, Section 1802 requires the allowable bearing pressures, allowable stresses and design formulas provided in Chapter 18 to be based on allowable stress design.

SECTION 1803 — SOIL CLASSIFICATION—EXPANSIVE SOIL

1803.1 General. In this section, the code provides the definitions and classifications of the soils to be used in this chapter. These are to be in accordance with UBC Standard 18-1, which is based on ASTM Standard E 2487, that provides for the classification of soils under the Unified Soil Classification System.

1803.2 Expansive Soil. In the context of the UBC, expansive soils are those soils that shrink or swell in accordance with changes in the soil moisture content. Other related problems of soil, such as frost heave, are not considered in this section.

The *Uniform Building Code* specifies the standard to be used for the determination of the expansion index, which is a measure of the expansiveness of the soil. The code further requires that the expansive soil be classified in accordance with Table 18-I-B based on the expansion index determined in accordance with UBC Standard 18-2. If the soil expansive index varies with depth, the variation is to be included in the engineering analysis of the expansive soil effect on the structure.

Although the specific provisions in the UBC for expansive soils were first adopted into the 1970 edition of the UBC, problems with expansive soils have plagued the construction industry for several decades. However, it was not until the early 1950s that the problems of expansive soils became of such a magnitude that these problems and research measures were discussed in technical journals.[2]

Even though "expansive soils are present or prevalent in a majority of the 50 states of the United States as well as in numerous countries around the world,"[2] the provisions of the UBC were developed in the 1960s by concerned building officials and soils engineering professionals in southern California.[3]

This section also requires that where the expansion index determined in accordance with UBC Standard 18-2 is greater than 20, structure foundations shall require special design considerations. These special design considerations usually take the form of designing the foundation system to resist a specified amount of swell in the foundation soils.

SECTION 1804 — FOUNDATION INVESTIGATION

In this section, the UBC requires that the soil at each building site be classified (in accordance with Table 18-I-A and UBC Standard 18-1) "when required by the building official." It is the intent of the code that the soils be classified whenever alterations are made to a building that will change the bearing pressures on the soil for existing buildings or where additions are made or new buildings erected which require new foundations. Under these circumstances, the soils at the site require classification, as the new foundations could not otherwise be designed.

Except for those structures of stud-bearing wall construction which are eligible to use the provisions of Table 18-I-C for foundation design, the code gives the building official authority to require a soils investigation prepared by an engineer or architect licensed by the state to practice as such. In most states of the United States, the soil investigation would be made by a geotechnical engineer. The building official also has authority to require such an investigation for sites on which stud-bearing wall buildings are to be erected where there is any question about the adequacy and classification of the soils.

On the other hand, the code does not make it mandatory to determine the soils' classification by a soil investigation. For those structures, usually of limited size and weight, which can utilize the allowable foundation pressures delineated in Table 18-I-A, there may not be any need for a foundation investigation. Only where there is question as to the proper soil classification would a foundation investigation be required for these lightweight structures.

The potential for seismically induced soil liquefaction and soil instability must also be investigated in Seismic Zones 3 and 4, with few exceptions. Liquefaction is treated in the same manner as a number of other geotechnical issues. The potential for such an occurrence should be analyzed by a professional to assist in the determination of an adequate foundation system.

Where a foundation investigation has been made, the building official is given authority by the code to require that the geotechnical engineer making the investigation submit a written report of the investigation. Although the language in the first paragraph of Section 1804.3 seems to imply that a report might not be required, it is inconceivable that a report of the investigation would not be required.

In order that the report of the foundation investigation provides necessary information to ensure compliance with the code and to ensure a safe foundation system, the code requires that the report include at least the five items enumerated in Section 1804.3.

In addition to giving the building official the authority to require special foundation investigations and foundation design provisions to safeguard buildings against the effects of expansive soils or soil liquefaction, the code also requires that the foundation design of any building include the effect of adjacent loads where footings are placed at different elevations. Furthermore, since 1976 the code has required that provisions must be made to control surface water around buildings. Although the requirements in the appendix in Chapter 33 require the control of surface water in the areas in which grading operations are to take place, the earlier editions of the UBC had no such similar requirements for building sites where no grading operations were to take place.

SECTION 1805 — ALLOWABLE FOUNDATION AND LATERAL PRESSURES

In accordance with the UBC, allowable foundation bearing and lateral pressures are determined in two ways:

1. The values to be used are based on a foundation investigation conducted in accordance with Section 1804.

2. The values may be obtained from Table 18-I-A on rock or nonexpansive soil for lightweight buildings as delineated in this section.

As indicated earlier, the soil classifications are based on the Unified Soils Classification System from ASTM Standard E 2487. In addition to allowable bearing pressures, Table 18-I-A includes allowable lateral bearing and values for frictional and sliding resistance. The allowable foundation bearing pressure and the values for frictional and sliding resistance were developed considering the limited-size structures for which the table will be used and the fact that these are lightweight structures in general. If a professional foundation investigation is made and higher values are indicated by the soils analysis, these higher values are permitted to be used when approved by the building official.

The values for bearing pressures on rock are conservatively based since the rock condition is not known without a soil investigation. Values for the other categories consider a failure against shear using a safety factor of 3 and a settlement of less than $1/2$ inch (12.7 mm) based on the assumption of loose dry granular soil or a moderately soft, underconsolidated clay. The values for lateral bearing pressures will be discussed under Section 1806.8.

SECTION 1806 — FOOTINGS

1806.1 General. The general requirements for footings in the UBC are that they:

- Be constructed of solid masonry or concrete or treated wood in conformance with Chapter 18, Division II of the UBC.

- Extend below the depth of frost penetration.

- Extend at least 6 inches (152 mm) above the adjacent finished grade when supporting wood.

- Have a minimum depth as shown in Table 18-I-C unless a foundation investigation recommends a different depth.

Good construction practice holds that buildings should not be founded on or within frozen ground. This is mandatory in order to prevent damage to the exterior walls and other walls bearing on the frozen soil. The volume changes (frost heave) which take place during freezing and thawing are such as to produce excessive stresses in the foundations in buildings and, as a result, create extensive damage to the walls which are supported thereon. Thus, the code requires that foundations be extended below the depth of frost penetration. The depth of frost penetration and thus the minimum depth of foundations varies throughout the United States, and Figure 1806-1 gives some guidance for the depth of frost penetration. However, local jurisdictions should establish the depth of frost penetration for their jurisdiction based on field experience.

In addition to the requirement for footings extending below the depth of frost penetration, footings should also be at such depth as to be below the zone of seasonal moisture variations in the upper soil layers. Thus, the depth requirement in areas of heavy seasonal rains will be greater than those areas with more arid climates. However, for areas of moderate rainfall and where frost penetration is not a consideration, the depths indicated in Table 18-I-C are required.

Buildings and foundation systems in areas subject to scour and water pressure due to wind and wave action should be designed in accordance with approved national standards such the *Shore Protection Manual.*

1806.3 Bearing Walls. Clearly, the foundation system supporting bearing walls is required to be of a size to support all loads. In the case of stud-bearing walls where an engineering design is not provided, the code requires that the foundations for these types of structures comply with the criteria established in Table 18-I-C, unless expansive soils of a severity to cause differential movement are known to exist. The purpose of Table 18-I-C is to provide footing size and depth criteria which can be used in conjunction with conventionally framed wood-stud bearing walls. This table is based on anticipated loads on foundations due to wall, floor and roof systems. Thus, the first column of the table labeled "Number of Floors Supported by the Foundation" is intended to reflect the number of floor levels which are supported by the foundation under consideration. It is not intended that Table 18-I-C be tied to the definition of "story" contained in Section 220.

In Figure 1806-2, a two-story building is shown by Example 1. Although the structure is a two-story building for the purpose of area and height limitations, it is considered to have only one supported floor when applying the provisions of Table 18-I-C. In this example, the foundation supports only the upper floor level since the lower floor is a slab-on-grade and, thus, is not supported by the foundation. Example 2 illustrates a two-story condition where the foundation supports a roof and two floors. The appropriate foundation size for Example 2 is based on the number of supported floors being two.

The two exceptions to the requirements for bearing-wall footings are as follows:

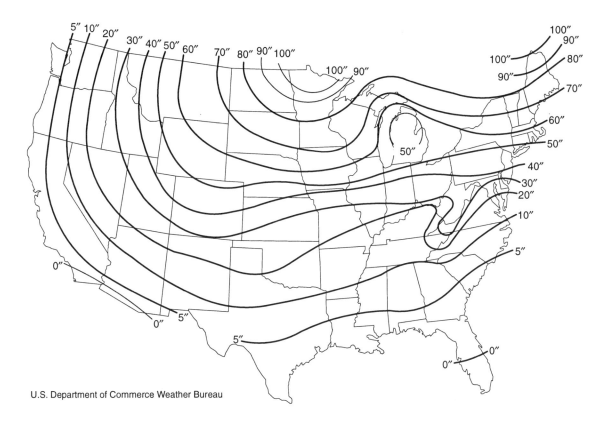

U.S. Department of Commerce Weather Bureau

FROST PENETRATION DEPTHS

FIGURE 1806-1

1. Small [not over 400 square feet (37.2 m²) in floor area] wood- or metal-frame buildings not used for human occupancy may rest on a mud sill supported directly on the ground.

2. Any building may be supported by wood poles embedded in the earth in accordance with Section 1806.8. Wood poles are required to be preservatively treated, and steel poles shall be protected against corrosion where the soil constituents are such as to be corrosive.

1806.4 Stepped Foundations. The code requires that foundations for buildings be essentially level. This means that the bottom bearing surface, as well as the top of the foundation wall which supports the walls must be level. However, a slope of 1 unit vertical in 10 units horizontal (10% slope) is permitted, but when the slope is steeper, the foundation is required to be stepped.* Figure 1806-3 schematically shows a stepped foundation. Although the code places no restriction on a stepped foundation except that the top and bottom surfaces be level, the figure shows a recommended overlap of the top of the foundation wall beyond the step in the foundation to be larger than the vertical step in the foundation wall at that point. This recommendation is based on possible crack propagation at an angle of 45 degrees. In order to keep this effect to a minimum, it is also recommended that the height of each step in the foundation not exceed 1 or 2 feet (305 or 610 mm). Other measures to protect

against cracking, such as special reinforcing details, would of course take care of the problem. However, a footing which has no engineering design and which is on competent soil materials most likely will not be reinforced.

1806.5 Footings on or Adjacent to Slopes.

1806.5.1 Scope. The provisions of this section apply only to buildings placed on or adjacent to slopes steeper than 1 unit vertical in 3 units horizontal (33.3% slope).

1806.5.2 Building clearance from ascending slopes. The criterion for the location of buildings adjacent to the toe of an ascending slope is depicted in UBC Figure 18-I-1. Figure 1806-4 of this handbook depicts the criteria expressed in this item for the determination of the location of the toe of the slope where the slope exceeds 1 unit vertical in 1 unit horizontal (1% slope).

As indicated in this item, the setback required by the code is intended to provide protection to the structure from shallow failures (sometimes referred to as sloughing) and protection from erosion and slope drainage. Furthermore, the space provided by the setback provides access around the building and helps to create a light and open-air environment.

1806.5.3 Footing setback from descending slope surface. In this item, the code restricts the placement of footings adjacent to or on descending slopes so that both vertical and lateral support are provided. The criteria for this condition are as shown in UBC

---

*However, the top of the footing may be sloped, provided a structural design is submitted with details for proper anchorage of the sill plate and wall studs.

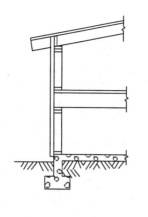

EXAMPLE 1

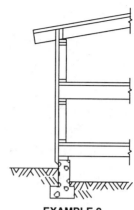

EXAMPLE 2

FOUNDATIONS FOR STUD BEARING WALLS—MINIMUM REQUIREMENTS[1,2,3,4]

| NUMBER OF FLOORS SUPPORTED BY THE FOUNDATION[5] | THICKNESS OF FOUNDATION WALL (inches) × 25.4 for mm | | WIDTH OF FOOTING (inches) | THICKNESS OF FOOTING (inches) | DEPTH BELOW UNDISTURBED GROUND SURFACE (inches) |
	CONCRETE	UNIT MASONRY	× 25.4 for mm		
1	6	6	12	6	12
2	8	8	15	7	18
3	10	10	18	8	24

[1]Where unusual conditions or frost conditions are found, footings and foundations shall be as required in Section 1806.1.
[2]The ground under the floor may be excavated to the elevation of the top of the footing.
[3]Interior stud bearing walls may be supported by isolated footings. The footing width and length shall be twice the width shown in this table and the footings shall be spaced not more than 6 feet (1829 mm) on center.
[4]In Seismic Zone 4, continous footings shall be provided with a minimum of one No. 4 bar top and bottom.
[5]Foundations may support a roof in addition to the stipulated number of floors. Foundations supporting roofs only shall be as required for supporting one floor.

FOUNDATIONS FOR STUD BEARING WALLS

FIGURE 1806-2

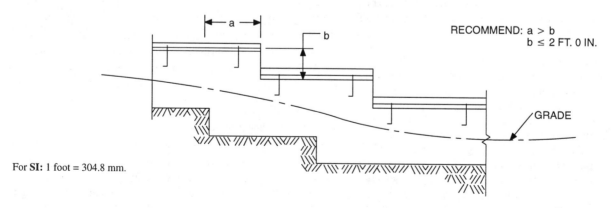

For **SI:** 1 foot = 304.8 mm.

STEPPED FOUNDATIONS

FIGURE 1806-3

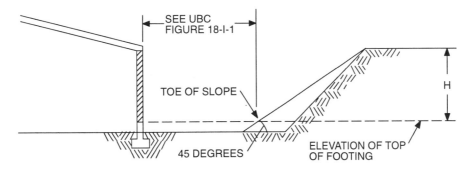

BUILDINGS ADJACENT TO ASCENDING SLOPE EXCEEDING 1 TO 1

FIGURE 1806-4

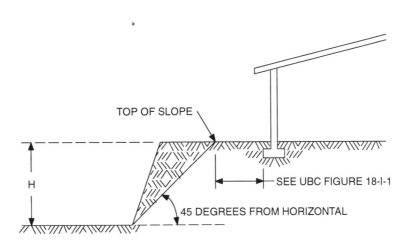

BUILDINGS ADJACENT TO DESCENDING SLOPE EXCEEDING 1 TO 1

FIGURE 1806-5

Figure 18-I-1. It is possible to locate buildings closer to the slope than the indicated setback in UBC Figure 18-I-1, and in fact it is possible to locate the footing of the structure on the slope itself. In these two latter cases, it will be necessary to provide an adequate depth of embedment of the footing so that the face of the footing at the bearing plane is set back from the edge of the slope at least the distance required by the code.

Figure 1806-5 depicts the condition where the descending slope is steeper than 1 unit vertical in 1 unit horizontal (1% slope) and shows the proper location of the top of the slope as required by the UBC. The setback at the top of descending slopes will primarily provide lateral support for the foundations. The area so allocated also provides space for lot drainage away from the slope without creating too steep a drainage profile, which could create erosion problems. Furthermore, this space also provides for access around the building.

1806.5.4 Pools. Figure 1806-6 portrays the code criteria for the design of swimming pool walls which are near the top of a descending slope. The requirement that the pool wall be self-sufficient to retain the water without support from the soil is designed to protect against failure of the pool wall should localized minor sliding and sloughing take place so that the soil support would

be lost. The pool setback should be established as one-half the building footing setback required by UBC Figure 18-I-1.

1806.5.5 Foundation elevation. Figure 1806-7 depicts the requirements of the code in this item for the elevation for exterior foundations with respect to the street, gutter or point of inlet of a drainage device. The elevation of the street or gutter shown is that point at which drainage from the site reaches the street or gutter.

This requirement is designed to protect the building from water encroachment in case of heavy or unprecedented rains and may be modified on the approval of the building official if the building official finds that positive drainage slopes are provided to drain water away from the building and that the drainage pattern is not subject to temporary flooding due to landscaping or other impediments to drainage.

1806.5.6 Alternate setback and clearance. This item provides that the building official may approve alternate setbacks and clearances from slopes provided the building official is assured that the intent of this section has been obtained. To this end, the UBC gives the building official authority to require a foundation investigation by a qualified geotechnical engineer to show that

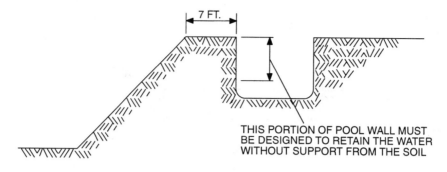

For **SI:** 1 foot = 304.8 mm.

SWIMMING POOL ADJACENT TO DESCENDING SLOPE

FIGURE 1806-6

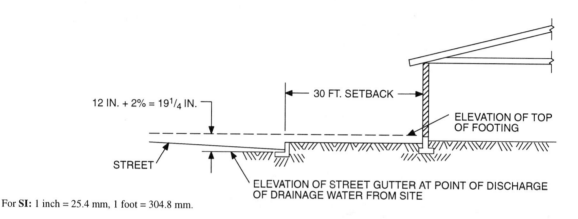

For **SI:** 1 inch = 25.4 mm, 1 foot = 304.8 mm.

FOOTING ELEVATION ON GRADED SITES

FIGURE 1806-7

the intent of the code is met. This item also specifies the parameters that must be considered by the geotechnical engineer in the investigation.

1806.2 Footing Design. In this section, the code requires that footings be structurally designed in accordance with the structural provisions of this code and also be designed to minimize differential settlement when necessary and the effects of expansive soils when present. There is also a reference to Division III of Chapter 18 in the UBC for the design of slab-on-grade footings in order to resist the effects of expansive soils.

Expansive soils, according to estimates, account for annual residential building losses of about $2 billion. This damage has been caused by severe cracking of slab-on-grade footings due to the soil movement of expansive soils. This movement may either cause an expansive soil heave, due to excessive moisture, or, alternatively, cause loss of support for the footing due to loss of moisture.

1806.6 Foundation Plates or Sills. This section prescribes the size and spacing of foundation bolts and is intended to apply to those buildings where no engineering design is provided when such buildings comply with the conventional framing provisions of Section 2320. The 1997 edition of UBC will require $5/8$-inch-diameter (16 mm) steel bolts embedded at least 7 inches

(178 mm) into concrete or masonry for sill plate connections to the foundation in Seismic Zone 4. The $1/2$-inch-diameter (12.7 mm) bolt size will continue to be the standard requirement in other seismic zones. The code's minimum sill bolt size [$1/2$ inch (12.7 mm)] and spacing had remained unchanged for the past 51 years, during which time substantial increases in minimum seismic lateral loads for design of buildings have occurred. The wood required for the sill plates is either preservatively treated wood or foundation-grade redwood. Section 2306.4 provides exceptions to the requirement for treated wood or foundation-grade redwood for areas where moderate or slight hazard to termite damage prevails.

Section 1806.6.1, new in the 1997 edition, sets forth additional requirements in Seismic Zones 3 and 4 for sill bolts in three-story raised wood floor buildings and for plate washer sizes for each bolt. Buildings in these seismic zones having three stories above a cripple wall should have the sill plate connection designed since the cripple wall bracing and stud size and spacing in such buildings are generally required to be designed. The new requirement for square plate washers (2 inches by 2 inches by $3/16$ inch minimum) (51 mm by 51 mm by 4.8 mm) are prescriptively required to compensate for the very common construction practice of oversize bolt holes in the plates and to reduce the resulting tendency for longitudinal splitting of the plate from seismic loading where the bolt does not bear tightly against the hole in the sill.

Section 1806.7, also new in the 1997 edition, will require horizontal (longitudinal) reinforcement at the top and bottom of all continuous footings, as stated, for buildings or structures located in Seismic Zones 3 and 4.

1806.8 Designs Employing Lateral Bearing. The design criteria for the use of poles embedded in the ground or in concrete footings in the ground and unconstrained at the ground surface were developed for the Outdoor Advertising Association of America, Inc. The research was conducted at Purdue University from 1938 to 1940, and continued in 1947 at the University of Notre Dame. The results of this research were used by an association for the design of outdoor advertising structures which had previously utilized trussed A-frame supporting systems. Charts and a nomograph were developed, which the association used for the design of poles as cantilever uprights for support of its outdoor advertising structures. These data were subsequently submitted through the ICBO code change process and were incorporated into the 1964 edition of the UBC.

The criteria relate to lateral bearing and apply to a vertical pole considered as a column embedded in either earth or in a concrete footing in the earth and used to resist lateral loads. In order for the pole to meet the conditions of research which resulted in the code formula, the code requires that the backfill in the annular space around a column not embedded in a concrete footing be either of 2,000-pound (13.78 MPa) concrete or of clean sand thoroughly compacted by tamping in layers not more than 8 inches (203 mm) in depth.

The original design criteria established for the Outdoor Advertising Association of America, Inc., resulted in a $^1/_2$-inch (12.7 mm) lateral pole deformation at the surface of the ground. These criteria were also based on field tests conducted in a range of sandy and gravelly soils and of silts and clays.

The *Uniform Building Code* employs allowable lateral bearing stresses in UBC Table 18-I-A, which are considerably lower than those developed for the Outdoor Advertising Association of America; consequently, Footnote 3 to the table permits a doubling of the lateral bearing values for isolated poles and poles supporting structures which can tolerate the $^1/_2$-inch (12.7 mm) movement at the ground surface.

The limitations imposed by Section 1806.8.4 are intended for both structural stability and serviceability. The limitation of the frictional resistance on silts and clays is consistent with Footnote 6 to UBC Table 18-I-A, which also limits the sliding resistance to one-half the dead load.

The limitations on the types of construction which utilize the lateral support of poles are based on the brittle nature of the materials. In order to prevent excessive distortions which would cause the cracking of these brittle materials, the code limits the use of the poles unless some type of rigid cross bracing is provided to limit the deflections to those that can be tolerated by the materials.

SECTION 1807 — PILES—GENERAL REQUIREMENTS

1807.1 General. In this section it is the intent of the UBC that the building official may, if deemed necessary, require a foundation investigation as the basis for the design and construction of pile foundations. Furthermore, the code specifies the minimum elements that must be included in the investigation.

Practically, the building official will require a foundation investigation. If the site conditions are such that pile foundations are required, a foundation investigation will usually be necessary to determine as much information about the subsurface conditions as possible. In fact, most pile foundation systems cannot be installed with any reasonable assurance of satisfactory performance unless they are based on a foundation investigation. However, there may be a few cases where personal knowledge of the site based on history and other field observations may be such that the building official would not require a foundation investigation. Even so, these circumstances should be few and far between.

1807.2 Interconnection. Prior to the 1988 edition, this provision was in Section 2312 addressing earthquake design. Interconnection of piles and caissons is necessary to prevent differential movement of the components of the foundation during an earthquake. It is well known that a building must be thoroughly tied together if it is to successfully resist earthquake ground motion.

1807.3 Determination of Allowable Loads. The *Uniform Building Code* specifies that the determination of allowable loads shall be based on three methods:

1. An approved formula.
2. Load tests.
3. Foundation investigation.

In most cases, the allowable loads will be determined by a combination of Items 2 and 3. However, there may be circumstances where the soil conditions, such as granular soils, and the types of piles selected are such that the use of an approved dynamic pile-driving formula can be an aid to a qualified practitioner in establishing reasonable but safe allowable loads for the foundation system. Nevertheless, in report B of "Pile-driving Formulas—Progress Report,"[4] "The use of a complicated formula is not recommended since such formulas have no greater claim to accuracy than the more simple ones."[4]

The dynamic pile-driving formula included in the 1970 and earlier editions of the UBC was dropped from the code because of its unreliability for cohesive soils. The deletion was also prompted by the likelihood that the formula would be misapplied by individuals untrained in the use of such formulas. It is interesting to note that the earliest editions of the UBC utilized the so-called Engineering News formula,

$$R = \frac{12WH}{S + c}$$

which is the most simple of the dynamic pile-driving formulas. Later, in 1937, the Pacific Coast formula was adopted in the UBC until its deletion prior to the 1973 edition of the code. This was one of the more complex dynamic pile-driving formulas and was based on a dynamic pile-driving formula developed by Terzaghi. However, as stated previously, in the hands of a qualified practitioner, a dynamic pile-driving formula does have some utility even though the UBC no longer provides such a formula.

1807.4 Static Load Tests. The three methods of determining the allowable axial load on a single pile specified in this section have been in use for several decades in one form or another. The methods outlined in the UBC have been simplified greatly from those in other codes such as, for example, the Foundation Code of the City of New York, adopted in 1948. It must be emphasized that the static load test provides only the allowable load on the one pile tested at that specific location on the site. However, load tests can be valuable when supervised by a geotechnical engineer as part of the foundation investigation.

1807.5 Column Action. Understandably, the code requires that piles standing unbraced in air, water or material not capable of providing lateral support shall be designed in accordance with the column formulas of the code. Obviously, water and air do not provide lateral support. On the other hand, most soils do provide lateral support, although exceptionally loose and unconsolidated fills might conceivably be inadequate to provide lateral support.

1807.6 Group Action. It is a recognized principle of foundation engineering that friction piles placed in groups in most soils do not have a capacity equal to the number of piles times the allowable load on one pile by itself. Therefore, the UBC requires that where soil conditions are such that the group action of piles is not equal to the sum of the individual capacities, a reduction be taken and that it be based on any rational method or formula approved by the building official. The building official's decision will usually be based on an analysis of the foundation investigation prepared by a soils engineer.

1807.7 Piles in Subsiding Areas. Where piles are driven through subsiding soils and derive their support from underlying firmer materials, the subsiding soils add additional load to the piles through so-called negative friction. This negative friction is actually a downward friction force on the piles, which increases the axial load on the piles. The code permits an increase in the allowable stress on the piles if an analysis of the foundation investigation indicates that the increase is justified.

1807.8 Jetting. The code does not permit jetting of piles except as specifically approved by the building official. This is usually only after reviewing a geotechnical engineering report of the soil conditions and with the recommendation of a geotechnical engineer. Water jetting disturbs the soil and can be particularly detrimental to existing pile foundations. When used, the water jet should be removed prior to reaching the desired pile tip elevation and the pile should then be driven to the required resistance.

1807.9 Protection of Pile Materials. This section is one of the more important provisions of the code relative to pile foundations. The durability of the pile materials must be such as to assure the required service life of the superstructure. The pile materials specifically referred to in the code when properly installed and treated will provide the required durability. The man-

ner in which certain soil constituents, water and deleterious materials and organisms affect the various pile materials are:

- **Wood piles.** The primary deleterious action on wood piles is that of fungi, which cause what is commonly known as "wood rot." Fungi require food, air and moisture in order to exist. Therefore, if wood piles are continually submerged in water, air is not available and the piles are not subject to attack by fungi. However, the old expression "here today and gone tomorrow" is applicable to the level of the water table. In many parts of the country, the existing water table has been drawn down to such a degree that any wood piles formerly completely submerged are now exposed to attack by fungi. Depending on complete submergence of wood piles is dangerous. The wise course of action is to use piles that have been preservatively treated.

  In marine environments, wood piles may be attacked by marine borers, and here again preservative treatment is indicated to protect the piles.

- **Concrete piles either cast in place against the earth or precast.** Reinforced concrete is a highly durable pile material, and the primary deleterious substances that attack concrete are acids and sulphates. In the case of acids, it is best to use an alternative pile material if the acid attack is potentially destructive, as coating piles may be ineffective due to soil abrasion during driving. In the case of high alkaline soils with sulphate salts, Type V portland cement may be used. Where the exposures are only moderate, a Type II portland cement will usually be adequate. If the piles are in a marine environment, Type V or Type II portland cement is also indicated to provide the necessary sulphate resistance.

- **Steel piles.** Under most circumstances, for steel piles embedded in undisturbed natural soil there is little likelihood of rusting, and protection is unnecessary. However, if the soil is pervious and groundwater moves freely through the soil, some rusting to a moderate extent may occur. Also, acidic fill soils may be corrosive. It usually is not necessary to protect steel piles, except possibly in marine environments, in acidic fills or in the fluctuating water table zone of pervious soils. Even under these latter conditions, experience shows that serious corrosion occurs very seldom to unprotected steel piles.[5]

1807.10 Allowable Loads. This section appears to be essentially an exception to the provisions of Section 1807.2, but in reality is an alternate provision for establishing presumptive skin friction values for uncased cast-in-place concrete piles. If a value exceeding the presumptive value of 500-pound-per-square-foot (24 kPa) skin friction is desired, such increase is required to be based on a foundation investigation.

Under certain circumstances, such as when the pile extends through cohesive soils, such as clays, to a bearing stratum of compact sand and gravels, both skin friction and end bearing act together to support the pile. However, the nature of the load sharing between the two and whether in fact both exist simultaneously can be determined only by an analysis of a foundation investigation. Thus, the code requires that in order to assume that both skin friction and end bearing act simultaneously, the assumption must be justified by means of a foundation investigation.

1807.11 Use of Higher Allowable Pile Stresses. The allowable stresses in Section 1808 are quite conservative based on the assumption that uncertainties in driving and other unknown factors will contribute to less-than-desirable foundation attributes. Uncertainties include piles not driven straight due to the tips being deflected by unaccounted-for boulders, etc. In the case of cast-in-place concrete piles that are cast against the earth, intrusion of soil into the concrete of the pile can create the uncertainties which call for conservatism. However, it may be determined on the basis of a foundation investigation that these problems do not exist for the particular type of pile foundation being utilized and, as a result, an increase in allowable stresses may be justified.

SECTION 1808 — SPECIFIC PILE REQUIREMENTS

1808.1 Round Wood Piles. The durability of wood piles was discussed in Section 1807 along with the need for preservative treatment. The *Uniform Building Code* notes that wood piles conform to ASTM Standard D 25-87, which is, in effect, a grading standard for wood piles.

As explained in the second paragraph of Section 1808.1.2, the values in Chapter 23, Division III, Part I, for compression parallel to the grain and extreme fiber in bending are based on load sharing, which occurs when piles are grouped in clusters at each pile cap. Where a pile is used singly, the code requires a further safety factor of 1.25 for compression parallel to the grain and 1.3 for extreme fiber in bending. These safety factors are based on the concept that where a pile is used singly it is more probable that it will be loaded to its maximum capacity than if it were used in a group of piles.

1808.2 Uncased Cast-in-place Concrete Piles. This section refers to concrete piles cast in place against the earth in drilled or bored holes. The limitations placed on these piles and the conservative allowable stresses are due to the reasons discussed in Section 1807, where possible uncertainties may be encountered. These may be water infiltration into the bore hole which could weaken the concrete, or granular soil constituents may slough off and restrict the cross section. Although the code requires that care be exercised in the placement of the concrete in this type of pile, these uncertainties still exist.

1808.3 Metal-cased Concrete Piles. These piles consist of a metal shell which is driven to the proper elevation and then filled with concrete. They do not have the problems associated with concrete piles cast against the earth; therefore, the code permits a higher allowable stress in the concrete where the shells meet the criteria itemized in Section 1808.3.3. The criteria itemized are intended to provide a shell that will maintain its proper size and shape and will not admit water and soil constituents into the pile.

Unless the sequence of pile driving is accomplished with great care, it is possible to damage recently placed concrete in existing piles. Therefore, it is common practice to delay concreting of piles and leave a number of empty shells between recently filled concrete piles and newly driven shells. Thus, the code has a requirement that no shell can be driven within four and one-half average shell diameters of a shell which has been filled with concrete less than 24 hours. This provision is intended to protect against damaging the freshly cast concrete in the shell casings.

1808.4 Precast Concrete Piles. This section refers to non-prestressed concrete piles. Because of the stresses created in handling as well as the dynamic stresses caused by driving, these piles are very heavily reinforced and conservatively designed. As a result, they are highly resistant to damage created by pile-driving operations.

1808.5 Precast Prestressed Concrete Piles (Pretensioned). Comments made with regard to precast concrete piles in Section 1808.4 also are applicable here.

1808.6 Structural Steel Piles. Structural steel piles are most commonly H piles and steel pipe piles. As with other pile materials specified in this chapter, the allowable stresses and design criteria for steel piles are also very conservative, and again, this is due to the possibility of uncertainties involved in the foundation materials beneath the structure.

The minimum dimensions specified in this section for H piles are intended to provide a compact section with relatively heavy projecting elements (flange projections), which have a high resistance to twisting. As these piles may be very long, the effects of uncertainties such as pile curvature and accidental eccentricity are minimized by the code-prescribed dimensional limitations. All of the HP sections rolled in the United States meet these dimensional limitations.

The steel pipe, by virtue of its closed section and code-prescribed size limitations, provides a compact section with high twisting resistance.

1808.7 Concrete-filled Steel Pipe Piles. These piles are differentiated from metal-cased concrete piles by the fact that the steel pipe is the primary load-carrying element. Due to the composite action, the pile stresses are determined in accordance with Chapter 19.

SECTION 1809 — FOUNDATION CONSTRUCTION— SEISMIC ZONES 3 AND 4

This section is a result of the complete rewrite of the UBC earthquake provisions by SEAOC and reference to their commentary is recommended.[6]

In Section 1809.2 of the 1997 edition of the UBC, the one-third stress increase mentioned in previous editions is deleted in order to be consistent with changes made in Chapter 16. When substantiated by a geotechnical investigation report, increases in allowable bearing pressure should be allowed. Such increases have more to do with increased deformation limits and decreased factor of safety than with increases in soil strength. Therefore, the reference to the Chapter 16 stress increases is eliminated so that increases can be made as specifically justified. The geotechnical engineer should be aware of which Section 1612.3 load combinations are to be used for design.

It should, however, be noted that Footnote 2 in Table 18-1-A allows a one-third increase in the allowable foundation pressure shown when considering load combinations that include wind or earthquake loads as permitted by Section 1612.3.2. Because these vertical bearing pressure permitted by Table 18-1-A are conservative, the one-third increase was believed to be justified.

REFERENCES

[1]Terzaghi, Karl, and Ralph B. Peck (1967). *Soil Mechanics in Engineering Practice,* Second Edition. John Wiley and Sons, Inc., New York City.

[2]National Research Council (1986). Commentary on Ground Failure Hazards, *"Ground Failure,"* No. 3. National Academy Press, Washington, D.C., Spring.

[3]Department of the Army. Corps of Engineers (1984). *Shore Protection Manual,* Volumes I and II.

[4]Committee on the Bearing Value of Pile Foundations (1941). Pile-driving Formulas—Progress Report. *Proceedings,* ASCE, May.

[5]Romanoff, Melvin, and W. J. Schwerdtfeger (1972). "NBS Papers on Underground Corrosion of Steel Piling," NBS Monograph 127. United States Government Printing Office, pages 21-38.

[6]Seismology Committee, SEAOC (1990). *Recommended Lateral Force Requirements and Commentary.* San Francisco, California.

Chapter 19

CONCRETE

The contents of this chapter are patterned after, and in general conformity with, the provisions of Building Code Requirements for Reinforced Concrete (ACI 318-95) and Commentary—American Concrete Institute (ACI 318 R). Italics have been used in this chapter to indicate where the *Uniform Building Code* differs substantively from the ACI standard.

To make reference to the ACI commentary easier for users of the code, the section designations of this chapter have been made similar to those found in ACI 318-95. The first two digits of a section number indicate this chapter number ("19") and the balance matches the ACI chapter and section designation wherever possible. Thus, UBC Section 1904 indicates the section is in UBC Chapter 19 and similar provisions are found in Chapter 4 of ACI 318-95.

Those individuals desiring an analysis of the code provisions that are not printed in italics are referred to the *Commentary of the ACI Building Code, ACI 318*-95. Commentary on the provisions of Chapter 19 unique to the *Uniform Building Code* is provided in this chapter of the handbook and the *Analysis of Revisions to the 1997 Uniform Codes.*

Chapter 19 in the 1997 edition of the UBC has been reformated and revised to be consistent with all materials chapters in the UBC. Eight divisions are established as follows:

DIVISION	BEGINNING SECTION	TITLE
I	1900	General
II	1901	(From American Concrete Institute)
III	1923	Design Standard for Anchorage to Concrete
IV	1924	Design and Construction Standard for Shotcrete
V	1925	Design Standard for Reinforced Gypsum Concrete
VI	1926	Alternate Design Method
VII	1927	Unified Design Provisions
VIII	1928	Alternative Load-factor Combination and Strength Reduction Factors

SECTION 1900 — GENERAL

This section is located in Division 1 of Chapter 19 and sets forth the general requirements for the design of cast-in-place or precast concrete, plain, reinforced or prestressed.

All concrete structures shall be designed and constructed in accordance with the requirements of Division II and the additional requirements contained in Section 1900.4 of this division, as follows:

1900.4 Additional Design and Construction Requirements

Anchorage. Anchorage of bolts and headed stud anchors to concrete shall be in accordance with Division III.

Shotcrete. In addition to the requirements of Division II, design and construction of shotcrete structures shall meet the requirements of Division IV.

Reinforced gypsum concrete. Reinforced gypsum concrete shall be in accordance with Division V.

Minimum slab thickness. The minimum thickness of concrete floor slabs supported directly on the ground shall not be less than 3 $1/2$ inches (89 mm).

Unified design provisions for reinforced and prestressed concrete flexural and compression members. It shall be permitted to use the alternate flexural and axial load design provisions in accordance with Division VII, Section 1927.

Alternative load-factor combination and strength-reduction factors. It shall be permitted to use the alternative load-factor and strength-reduction factors in accordance with Division VIII, Section 1928.

The design methods for design of concrete structures shall be in accordance with strength design (load and resistance factor design) in conformance with the requirements of Division II or allowable stress design in conformance with the requirements of Division VI, Section 1926.

SECTION 1907 — DETAILS OF REINFORCEMENT

1907.5.4. This section does not permit welding of crossing bars in Seismic Zones 3 and 4. Moreover, Exception 2, which permits welding of crossing rebar in Seismic Zones 0, 1 and 2, requires that data be submitted to the building official to show that there is no detrimental effect on the action of the structural member as a result of the welding of crossing rebar.

Welding, including tack welding, of crossing bars for assembly creates a metallurgical notch effect at each point which is welded, and this can seriously weaken the bar. This operation can be performed safely only when under competent control, such as with welders certified to weld rebar, and under continuous inspection by a qualified special inspector. For these reasons, this section does not permit welding of crossing rebar in Seismic Zones 3 and 4 on steel required by the design; the UBC requires justification for such welding in Seismic Zones 0, 1 and 2.

SECTION 1912 — DEVELOPMENT AND SPLICES OF REINFORCEMENT

1912.14.3.6. This section clarifies that welded splices and mechanical connections are required to provide the same prescribed clearances and coverage as those for reinforcement. Some confusion had occurred since previous editions of the code had not addressed the clearances and coverages required for welded splices and mechanical connections.

1912.15.4.3. The provisions that previously required the staggering of mechanical connections have been relaxed. These connections need not be staggered provided the proper coverage and clearances are maintained and strain and stress comply with the listed criteria. The previous provisions were believed to be too restrictive for mechanical connections.

SECTION 1914 — WALLS

1914.3.8. This section permits interchanging the minimum requirements for horizontal and vertical steel in precast panels which are not restrained along vertical edges to inhibit temperature expansion or contraction. In many cases, construction practices utilize precast concrete wall panels with a relatively short horizontal dimension, and quite often they are not tied at their vertical edges. Therefore, a minimum ratio of horizontal steel reinforcement area to gross concrete area of 0.0012 is acceptable when the panels are not restrained against temperature expansion or contraction. The deformed bars should not be larger than No. 5 with a yield strength not less than 60,000 psi (413.4 MPa).

1914.8 Alternate Design Slender Walls. These provisions are commonly used for "tilt-up" wall design and are based on the recommendations of a Structural Engineers Association of Southern California ad-hoc committee. These recommendations are found in what is called the "yellow" book, which contains a description and discussion or commentary of the recommendations.

SECTION 1915 — FOOTINGS

1915.8.3.2. This provision as revised in the 1997 code allows the connection tensile strength of precast wall element bases to be based on the calculated forces subject to the minimum tie and design requirements of Section 1916.5.1.3, Items 2 and 3. The 1997 edition of the UBC also allows, in the exception to this provision, the connecting of tilt-up wall elements to an adjacent floor slab as an alternative to connecting them to the foundation.

SECTION 1917 — COMPOSITE CONCRETE FLEXURAL MEMBERS

1917.5.1.1 and 1917.5.1.2. These sections have been provided to give criteria for the full transfer of horizontal shear forces. Section 1917.5.1.1 lists four conditions that must be met. The first is that sufficiently clean and roughened surfaces of the interconnected elements is provided to assure a good bond. The second condition is that ties are adequate for horizontal shear.

SECTION 1918 — PRESTRESSED CONCRETE

1918.9 Minimum Bonded Reinforcement. Section 1918.9.2.2 includes additional provisions for bonded rebar in unbonded posttensioned prestressed concrete construction, which provide for additional safety against unprecedented loading. When subject to large overloads, these members do not inherently provide excess capacity for energy dissipation.

1918.9.2.3. This section contains provisions that clearly specify the intent of the code in that the maximum spacing limitations do not apply to the spacing of bonded reinforcement in prestressed members with unbonded tendons. The purpose of the bonded rebar in prestressed members with unbonded tendons is to provide crack control when the tensile stresses at service load exceed the modulus of rupture of the concrete. Also, bonded rebar ensure proper flexural performance at ultimate member strength. Thus, there is no reason to require a maximum spacing of the bonded rebar in prestressed members with unbonded tendons as long as the proper amount is supplied and distributed uniformly over the precompressed tension zone.

SECTION 1921 — REINFORCED CONCRETE STRUCTURES RESISTING FORCES INDUCED BY EARTHQUAKE MOTIONS

This section is based heavily on Chapter 21 of the *ACI Building Code,* although it has been amended extensively by the structural engineers associations of the West Coast states to include provisions deemed important in areas of high seismic risk, such as the West Coast. As amended for the *Uniform Building Code,* Chapter 21 of the *ACI Building Code* is an update to the current state of the art for the design and detail of reinforced concrete structures in Seismic Zones 3 and 4 for earthquake resistance. Also included are special requirements for frames in Seismic Zone 2, but no provisions for structures in Seismic Zones 0 and 1 are included. It is believed that the basic provisions of Chapter 19 are adequate for reinforced concrete structures in Seismic Zones 0 and 1.

The *Uniform Building Code* revisions to Chapter 21 relate to items provided in prior editions of the UBC, which were deemed to be important enough to retain in the UBC. Such items include the revised load factors in Section 1612.2.1; welding of reinforcing steel in accordance with UBC Standard 19-1; revisions of the requirements for special transverse reinforcement in columns above and below discontinuities and stiffness changes; anchorage of shear wall reinforcement in edges of structural shear walls; provisions for columns where the nominal strength, ϕP_n, of the column is less than the sum of the shears, V_e, for all the beams framing into the column above the level under consideration; provisions for shear wall boundary zone design and detailing requirements; and inspection requirements for reinforced concrete moment frames.

The language in Chapter 21 referring to structural walls has been changed to "shear walls" in the UBC as it was believed that the term "shear walls" more properly conveys the meaning and intent of the provisions. Requirements were added to those of Chapter 21 addressing the subject of coupling beams, which are horizontal members interconnecting shear walls. Earthquake damage has shown coupling beams to be very vulnerable and subject to excessive damage. As a result, the provisions in the UBC are an attempt to develop adequate shear resistance in the coupling beams to prevent these common failures. Relatively recent research on short beams with a clear span-to-depth ratio of less than 4 has shown that full-length diagonal bars are needed to provide the required ductility under load reversals in the inelastic range.

The design criteria in the wall pier provisions in Section 1921.6.13 are intended to apply when wall piers resist a significant portion of the in-plane wall force. Required special transverse reinforcement should extend into walls or spandrels above and below the wall pier.

Further commentary on these items can be obtained from the *Recommended Lateral Force Requirements and Commentary* published by SEAOC.[1] Chapter 4 explains in detail the provisions described above and provides additional insight on the provisions of Chapter 21, which are included in Section 1921.

SECTIONS 1922 THROUGH 1926 — STRUCTURAL PLAIN CONCRETE, ANCHORAGE TO CONCRETE, SHOTCRETE, REINFORCED GYPSUM CONCRETE AND ALTERNATE DESIGN METHOD

These sections have been unique to the *Uniform Building Code* for a many years and cover special subjects deemed important by the members of ICBO. These provisions cover such subjects as shotcrete (pneumatically placed concrete), plain concrete, and of anchor bolts embedded in concrete.

The plain concrete provisions found in Section 1922 have been extensively revised to be in general conformance with Chapter 22 of ACI 318-95. Section 1923, Anchorage to Concrete, was revised in the 1994 edition to accommodate the areas of the shear and tension interaction diagram where the strength values calculated using the interaction equation are greater than the direct shear or tension strength values. This now requires

that all the concrete strength equations be considered. This is a result of considerable work by the Structural Engineers Association of California. Section 1924 includes deign and construction standards for shotcrete and Section 1925 covers reinforced gypsum concrete. Section 1926 covers the alternate design method (formerly known as working stress design), and all provisions for the alternate design method are gathered together in this one section for easy reference.

SECTIONS 1927 AND 1928 — UNIFIED DESIGN PROVISIONS FOR REINFORCED AND PRESTRESSED CONCRETE FLEXURAL AND COMPRESSION MEMBERS, AND ALTERNATIVE LOAD-FACTOR COMBINATION AND STRENGTH REDUCTION FACTORS

These last sections in Chapter 19 are new in the 1997 UBC and provide for alternative flexural and axial load design provisions and alternative load-factor and strength-reduction factors, which are based on Appendices B and C of ACI 318-95.

REFERENCE

[1]Seismology Committee, SEAOC (1996). *Recommended Lateral Force Requirements and Commentary.* San Francisco, California.

Chapter 20

LIGHTWEIGHT METALS

Chapter 20 of the UBC is patterned after and in general conformity with the provisions of *Specifications for Aluminum Structures* of the Aluminum Association, dated December 1986. Those desiring an analysis should refer to the commentary contained in the above specifications. Also, a separate publication entitled "Commentary and Specifications for Aluminum Structures" is available. Both publications are available from the Aluminum Association, Inc., 900 19th Street, N.W., Washington, D.C. 20006.

Chapter 21

MASONRY

Chapter 21 presents general requirements first and then provides specific requirements depending on the type of masonry and design method. This chapter was reformatted in its entirety in the 1994 UBC. The 1997 edition made additional revisions primarily to coordinate with the changes to Chapter 16, i.e., strength design load combinations, ΔM notations, etc. The following list outlines the organization of Chapter 21 as it appears in Volume 2 of the 1997 UBC:

For an analysis of these provisions, the reader is referred to the comprehensive commentary to Chapter 21 of the UBC prepared by The Masonry Society. The Masonry Society is located at 2619 Spruce Street, Suite B, Boulder, Colorado, 80302-3808.

Chapter 22

STEEL

Chapter 22 has been reformatted in the 1997 UBC and is intended to give the user a clear indication of what provisions and design standards are applicable. The 1997 code also made additional revisions to coordinate with the changes to Chapter 16, i.e., design load combinations, Δ_M and Ω_o notations, etc.

Chapter 22 of the UBC is patterned after, and in general conformity with, the provisions of the *Specification for Structural Steel Buildings—Allowable Stress Design and Plastic Design for Structural Steel Buildings* and *Load and Resistance Factor Design for Structural Steel Buildings* published by the American Institute of Steel Construction. Those individuals desiring an analysis of these provisions are referred to the commentary included with the specifications. These specifications are available from the American Institute of Steel Construction, Inc., 1 East Wacker Drive, Suite 3100, Chicago, Illinois, 60601. Seismic design provisions of Chapter 22, which are unique to the *Uniform Building Code,* are based on the Structural Engineers Association of California's (SEAOC) recommended lateral force requirements and input from other professional engineering organizations.

Those persons interested in the background and rationale behind Divisions IV and V are urged to review the commentary to the *Recommended Lateral Force Requirements and Commentary* (Blue Book) prepared by the Seismology Committee of SEAOC. This publication is available through ICBO.

The following list outlines the organization of Chapter 22 as it appears in Volume 2 of the 1997 UBC.

Chapter 23

WOOD

Chapter 23 has been reformatted in the 1997 UBC due to adoption of the ANSI/NFoPA NDS-91, National Design Specification for Wood Construction by reference. The National Design Specification for Wood Construction, ANSI/NFoPA NDS-91, revised 1991 edition, and supplement to NDS-91 are published by American Forest and Paper Association (NFoPA).

Various 1994 UBC code sections and tables with equivalent sections and tables in NDS-91 have been deleted in the 1997 UBC. Adoption of the NDS-91 by reference includes certain amendments as stated in this chapter. The format change is consistent with other material design chapters in the 1997 edition. Additional changes to this chapter include revisions resulting from the effects from the 1994 Northridge earthquake, which primarily apply to Seismic Zones 3 and 4.

The following is a summary index for Chapter 23:

Chapter 23	Wood
Division I	General Design Requirements (Sections 2301-2305)
Division II	General Requirements (Sections 2306-2315)
Division III	Design Specifications for Allowable Stress Design of Wood Buildings (Sections 2316-2319)
Division IV	Conventional Light-frame Construction (Section 2320)
Division V	Design Standard for Metal Plate Connected Wood Truss (Section 2321)
Division VI	Design Standard for Structural Glued Built-up Members—Plywood Components (Sections 2322-2327)
Division VII	Design Standard for Span Tables for Joists and Rafters (Sections 2328-2333)
Division VIII	Design Standard for Plank-and-beam Framing (Sections 2334-2336)

The following publications contain commentary relating to the design and construction of wood structures:

National Design Specification—Wood Construction[1]
American Forest and Paper Association

Wood Handbook No. 72[2]
United States Department of Agriculture

Western Wood Use Book[3]
Western Wood Products Association

Timber Construction Manual[4]
American Institute of Timber Construction

For this reason, this handbook will refer to one or more of these resources where the information in the publication provides adequate commentary to the provisions of the UBC. As the structural provisions of Chapter 23 of the UBC are based heavily on the *National Design Specification—Wood Construction*, that publication will be cited whenever there is a commentary or discussion available to explain the parallel provisions in the UBC.

Division I—GENERAL DESIGN REQUIREMENTS

SECTION 2302 — DEFINITIONS

2302.1 Definitions. The terms defined in this section have a specific meaning for Chapter 23 and thus are defined herein. Other terms have their ordinary dictionary meanings. Symbols included in this section in the 1994 edition are now shown in appropriate code sections.

SECTION 2303 — STANDARDS OF QUALITY

The standards listed as "UBC Standard" are a part of the code. The other standards are recognized standards. One significant addition is Item 5.4, which cities ASCE-16, Load and Resistance Factor Design Standard for Engineered Wood Construction as a recognized design standard.

SECTION 2304 — MINIMUM QUALITY

2304.1 Quality and Identification. As lumber and, particularly, wood structural panels are highly variable in strengths and other mechanical properties, the code requires that these materials (defined in the first paragraph of this section) conform to the applicable standards or grading rules specified in the code. Furthermore, the code requires that they be identified by a grade mark or a Certificate of Inspection issued by an approved agency. The grade mark is also required to be placed on the material by an approved agency.

Obviously, the proper use of a wood structural member cannot be determined unless it has been identified as to grade and species, nor can the span tables in Chapter 23 be applied without this same information.

From time to time, bogus or counterfeit grade stamps appear on lumber in the field, and it is highly important that designers and enforcement personnel be familiar with the approved grade stamps. Some of these marks are shown in Figure 2304-1.

2304.2 Minimum Capacity or Grade. The quality of materials used in the construction of buildings and structures is one of the more important factors affecting the serviceability, structural capacity and durability of the structure. This fact is as true for wood members as it is for other construction materials. Therefore, the code requires that lumber used structurally be at least of the minimum grades set forth in the table in this chapter.

Approved end-jointed lumber is, as far as the UBC is concerned, the equivalent of regular sawn lumber, and therefore the code permits its use wherever regular sawn lumber is specified.

1. Panel Grade
2. Span Rating
3. Thickness
4. Exposure Durability Classification
5. Mill Number
6. Species Group Number
7. Product Standard PS 1-83
8. Product Standard PS 1 Grade Conformance Where Applicable
9. Tongue and Groove
10. National Evaluation Service Report Number
11. FHA Use of Material Bulletin Number

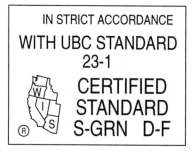

THE AWPB QUALITY MARK

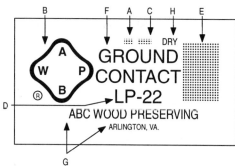

A. Year of treatment
B. American Wood Preservers Bureau Trademark
C. The preservative use for treatment
D. The applicable American Wood Preservers Bureau quality standard
E. Trademark of the agency supervising the treating plant
F. Proper exposure conditions
G. Treating company and plant location
H. Dry or KDAT if applicable

SOME TYPICAL LUMBER GRADE STAMPS

FIGURE 2304-1

The use of the term "approved" is intended to convey the need for quality control over the production of these glued products, and also to establish the qualification tests for the type of end joint utilized. The standards for proof testing of end-jointed lumber are outlined in guideline standards referenced in Part IV of Chapter 35. An example of end-jointed lumber is shown in Figure 2304-2, which illustrates a finger-jointed end joint.

2304.3 Timber Connectors and Fasteners. The code intends that Table 23-II-B-1 provide minimum requirements for the number and size of nails connecting wood members. This table is essentially designed to accommodate nondesigned construction, but still provides minimum requirements even for designed construction. Details such as end and edge distances and nail penetration are required to be in accordance with the applicable provisions of Division III, Part III. Where required, corrosion-resistant fasteners shall be either zinc-coated, aluminum alloy wire or stainless steel.

Connections between wood members that depend on joist hangers or framing anchors, or other mechanical fastenings that are not otherwise covered by this code, may be used, subject to the approval of the building official. The ICBO Evaluation Ser-

vice, Inc., has issued several evaluation reports covering these types of fastenings and should be consulted.

Table 23-II-B-2 is new in the 1997 UBC, which gives roof nailing schedules for wood structural panels. The table specifies the nailing based on the roof fastening zone and the regional wind speed. For mean roof heights over 35 feet (10 668 mm), the roof diaphragm nailing must be designed.

Also, the word "roof" has been deleted from Item 26 of Table 23-II-B-1 because roof nailing for wood structural panels is shown in new Table 23-II-B-2.

2304.5 Dried Fire-retardant-treated Wood. After treatment, it is mandatory that fire-retardant-treated wood be dried to the maximum moisture content outlined in the code. This is necessary for several reasons:

- **Strength reduction.** The fire-retardant-treatment process itself results in some reduction in the strength of wood. As high moisture content also causes a reduction in strength, it is important that the moisture content be limited as indicated in the code so that there will not be a compounding of strength-reducing factors.

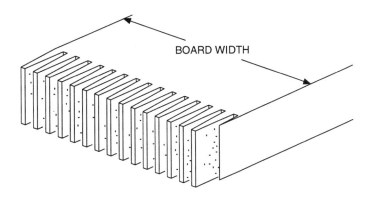

FINGER-JOINTED END JOINT

FIGURE 2304-2

- **Corrosiveness.** Fire-retardant-treatment chemicals themselves are quite corrosive to metal fasteners. Where the moisture content of the treated wood is too high, the corrosivity of the treated wood is even higher and contributes to greater corrosion of metal fasteners.

- **Dimensional changes.** See the discussions in Sections 604.3 and 2308.

2304.6 Size of Structural Members. Although the sizes of lumber referred to in this code are nominal sizes (see definition in Section 2302), design computations for determining the required sizes shall be based on the actual net dimensions of the material after dressing and not based on the nominal sizes. For example, the sectional properties of a nominal 2-inch by 4-inch (51 mm by 102 mm) piece are required to be determined on the basis of actual net size, which is $1^{1}/_{2}$ inches by $3^{1}/_{2}$ inches (38 mm by 89 mm). See the discussion in the *National Design Specification—Wood Construction.*

2304.7 Shrinkage. For the reasons discussed under Sections 604.3.3 and 2308 regarding cross-grain shrinkage of lumber, the code requires in this section that where lumber is fabricated in a green condition, regardless of the number of stories, the possible detrimental effects of cross-grain shrinkage should be given consideration in the design.

2304.8 Rejection. Even though the lumber furnished for a job may comply with the grading rules for the grade specified, a piece of lumber intended for use as a structural member may have such a combination of permissible defects that the structural strength is substantially below that typical for the grade. When this situation occurs, this section gives the building official the authority to deny permission for the use of the member.

SECTION 2305 — DESIGN AND CONSTRUCTION REQUIREMENTS

This new section provides an index to the design requirements for wood structures that are covered in Chapter 23. This format is similar to other material design chapters in the 1997 edition of the UBC.

Section 2304 of the 1994 UBC has been integrated into the various design divisions in the 1997 edition. The 1994 hand-

book provided a discussion on this section, which included adjustment of stresses for duration of load, size of members, slenderness of member, form factor, modulus of elasticity, temperature, and fire-retardant treatment that was based, in part, on the *Western Wood Use Book.* With the new format for the 1997 edition and the adoption of the *National Design Specification for Wood Construction* (ANSI/NoFPA NDS-1991) as amended in Division III, it is suggested that the user refer to the commentary for this NDS publication.

Division II—GENERAL REQUIREMENTS

SECTION 2306 — DECAY AND TERMITE PROTECTION

2306.1 and 3302 Preparation of Building Site. In order to prevent decay and to eliminate an avenue of entrance for termites and other insects, the code requires that the area of the site to be occupied by the building to be free of all stumps, roots, and any loose or casual lumber.

2306.2 Wood Support Embedded in Ground. The provisions of this section intend, as the title indicates, to protect against decay and termite infestation. The *Wood Handbook No. 72* contains an extensive discussion on the protection of wood from decay and termite infestation, which is illustrated in Figures 2306-1 through 2306-7. The provisions in this section are based on this reference. Some comments about the specific provisions of the UBC are in order:

- In the case of wood embedded in the ground or in direct contact with the earth, the UBC does not permit the use of wood of natural resistance to decay. The hazard associated with ground contact is too high for these decay-resistant woods. Therefore, the code permits only the use of preservatively treated wood.

- When the code requires that under-floor areas be accessible, a minimum 18-inch by 24-inch (457 mm by 610 mm) access opening is specified. Where the access opening opens to the exterior of the building, the code requires it to be screened or covered to prevent the entrance of insects and animals. Also, it is the intent of the code that all portions of the under-floor area be accessible and free of obstructions created by pipes, ducts, etc. In addition to providing accessibility for inspection, the clearances required by the code between the earth and joists or girders, as shown in Figure 2306-1, facilitate cross-ventilation of the under-floor space.

- The 1982 edition of the code departed from the traditional method of specifying under-floor ventilation, and the code now relates under-floor ventilation to the area of under-floor space. In those areas where groundwater conditions are not considered excessive, the code permits operable louvers to cover the required ventilation openings and permits a reduction in the required ventilation openings where a vapor retarder is used to reduce the evaporation of ground moisture into the crawl space.

- Where wood structural members support moisture-permeable floors or roofs, such as concrete slabs, experience has proven the need for durable wood in those cases where the permeable slabs are exposed to weather. An alternative is to provide an impervious moisture barrier between the permeable floor or roof and the wood structural member. The intent of the code would also be secured if the surface of the permeable floor or roof were treated so that it would not be permeable.

- Where waterborne preservatives are used for treatment, the code requires that the wood members be dried to a 19 percent moisture content, which is the typical moisture content required for use in structures.

Section 2306.12 gives the building official authority to require durable wood for structural members exposed to the weather in those geographical areas where experience has demonstrated a specific need. In many cases, balconies, porches and similar projections are exposed to severe weather conditions along ocean fronts and lake fronts and do not have protective overhangs above them. Under these circumstances, water can accumulate in joints and on the surface, thus creating alternate cycles of wetting and drying which are conducive to decay. Where these conditions prevail, the building official has the authority to require preservatively treated wood or wood of natural resistance to decay.

SECTION 2307 — WOOD COMBINED WITH MASONRY OR CONCRETE

Wood structural members are subject to long-term creep, which increases the deflection, particularly where a high dead load is present. Thus, the code does not permit wood members to permanently support the dead load of masonry or concrete, since the deflection created by the long-term creep has the potential to cause severe cracking in the masonry or concrete.

The exceptions cover specific cases, such as supporting a structure on wood piles, which have been used successfully for over 100 years. Although Exception 1 permits masonry or concrete nonstructural floor or roof surfacing of not more than 4 inches (102 mm) in thickness to be supported by wood members, this exception is generally utilized for thinner materials up to about 1 1/2 inches (38 mm) in thickness. Thicker concrete or masonry floor surfacing can be accommodated, however, by rigid control of deflections. Exception 3 provides controls for the support of masonry veneer on a treated-wood foundation and for the support of interior wall veneer on wood floors with exceptionally tight controls on the design for deflection.

SECTION 2308 — WALL FRAMING

This section provides performance criteria for designs where wood stud walls support more than two floors and a roof. In such cases, an analysis of the effects of wood cross-grain shrinkage on the structure as well as on its plumbing and mechanical systems is required.

As explained in this handbook, the amount of cross-grain shrinkage of the wood depends on the moisture content at the time the building is erected, as well as on the amount of drying that occurs after construction has been completed. For taller buildings, this effect can be substantial; in fact, the effects of

(Continued on page 317)

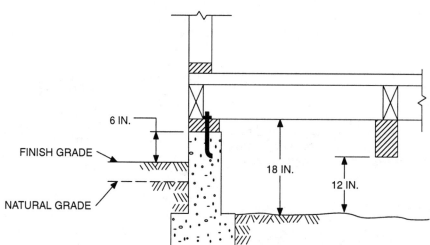

For **SI:** 1 inch = 25.4 mm.

UNDER-FLOOR CLEARANCE

FIGURE 2306-1

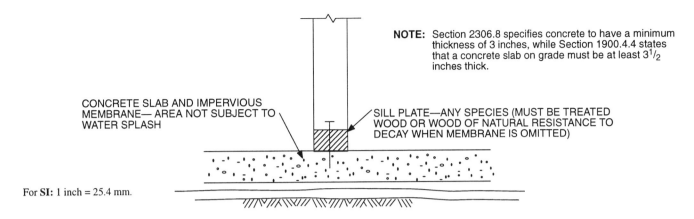

NOTE: Section 2306.8 specifies concrete to have a minimum thickness of 3 inches, while Section 1900.4.4 states that a concrete slab on grade must be at least 3¹/₂ inches thick.

CONCRETE SLAB AND IMPERVIOUS MEMBRANE— AREA NOT SUBJECT TO WATER SPLASH

SILL PLATE—ANY SPECIES (MUST BE TREATED WOOD OR WOOD OF NATURAL RESISTANCE TO DECAY WHEN MEMBRANE IS OMITTED)

For **SI:** 1 inch = 25.4 mm.

PROTECTION AGAINST DECAY PLATES, SILLS AND SLEEPERS

FIGURE 2306-2

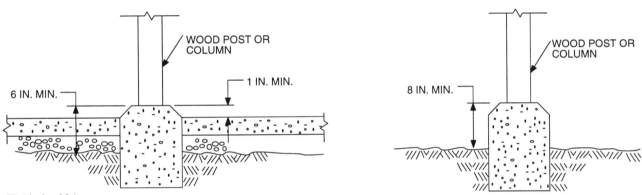

WOOD POST OR COLUMN

6 IN. MIN.

1 IN. MIN.

WOOD POST OR COLUMN

8 IN. MIN.

For **SI:** 1 inch = 25.4 mm.

PROTECTION AGAINST DECAY COLUMNS AND POSTS

FIGURE 2306-3

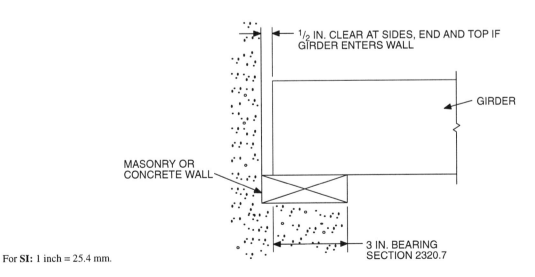

¹/₂ IN. CLEAR AT SIDES, END AND TOP IF GIRDER ENTERS WALL

GIRDER

MASONRY OR CONCRETE WALL

3 IN. BEARING SECTION 2320.7

For **SI:** 1 inch = 25.4 mm.

PROTECTION AGAINST DECAY GIRDERS

FIGURE 2306-4

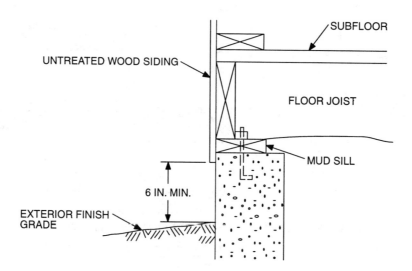

For **SI:** 1 inch = 25.4 mm.

WOOD SEPARATION FROM EARTH

FIGURE 2306-5

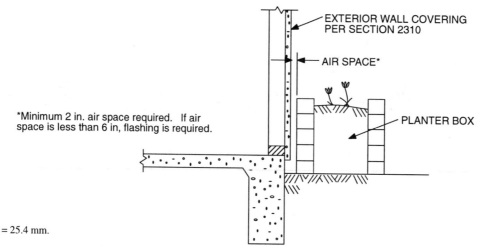

*Minimum 2 in. air space required. If air
space is less than 6 in, flashing is required.

For **SI:** 1 inch = 25.4 mm.

PROTECTION AGAINST DECAY PLANTER BOXES

FIGURE 2306-6

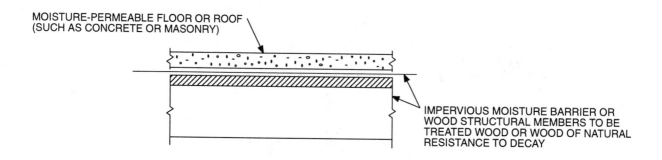

PROTECTION AGAINST DECAY STRUCTURES EXPOSED TO THE WEATHER

FIGURE 2306-7

(Continued from page 314)
cross-grain shrinkage have created the illusion of plumbing stacks rising up through the roofs of buildings. Other detrimental effects where the shrinkage is not compensated for include changes of the roof gradient so that roof drainage patterns may be changed. Furthermore, the effects of cross-grain shrinkage can change the gradient of the drainage system in a building to such an extent that its operation is adversely affected.

SECTION 2310 — EXTERIOR WALL COVERINGS

The intent of the UBC is that exterior wall coverings:

- Protect the interior of the building from the weather. This may require the installation of a weather-resistive barrier beneath the exterior wall covering as discussed in Section 1402.1.

  Where wood structural panel products are used for exterior siding, such as plywood, particleboard or hardboard, the code requires that the joints occur over framing members and be protected with continuous wood battens, approved caulking, flashing, vertical or horizontal shiplaps or any other method approved by the building official which will waterproof the joints. Alternatively, these panels may be applied over lumber and wood structural panel sheathing. In this latter case, the double layers provide for an overlapping of joints and, therefore, prevent direct penetration of water.

- Be of sufficient strength to span between the studs or other structural members. The strengths or thicknesses of most of the exterior wall-covering materials listed in this section are based on a stud spacing of 16 inches (406 mm) on center. However, there are a few cases where the thickness is based on a 24-inch (610 mm) spacing.

- Have sufficient durability to withstand, for the life of the building, the weathering effects of the elements to which they are exposed. Thus, where wood structural panels are used, the code requires that they be of exterior types. Other materials must be of a weather-resistant type of material, such as cedar shingles, or the material must be finished with a weather-resistive finish, such as exterior paint.

SECTION 2312 — SHEATHING

2312.1 Structural Floor Sheathing. The *Uniform Building Code* requires that structural floor sheathing serves two primary purposes:

1. Provides support of the superimposed loads placed on it by the use and occupancy of the building.

2. Provides lateral support for the top of the floor joists.

In keeping with the first purpose, the UBC prescribes in this section performance criteria for the strength and stiffness of the structural floor sheathing. Also, criteria are prescribed for the flooring system, including the finish floor, underlayment and subfloor, where used. The code also states that the span tables in Chapter 23 relating to floor sheathing materials meet the requirements of the performance criteria outlined in this section.

2312.2 Structural Roof Sheathing. The three primary criteria established by the UBC for structural roof sheathing are that:

1. The sheathing must have adequate strength to support the roof live loads or other loads to which it may be subjected.

2. The sheathing shall provide an adequate base for the proper performance of the roof-covering materials.

3. The sheathing shall provide lateral support for the top of the rafters and truss compression chords when nailed directly to these members.

As with structural floor sheathing, the code provides performance criteria for the strength and stiffness of the sheathing. Similarly, it is intended that the span tables for roof-sheathing products in Chapter 23 be deemed to meet the performance strength requirements of this section.

SECTION 2313 — MECHANICALLY LAMINATED FLOORS AND DECKS

A laminated lumber floor or deck designed in accordance with this section provides the equivalent of a solid-wood deck and may be designed as if it were a solid-wood deck of the same thickness. However, the code requires a conservative design for bending strength in that continuous spans are designed using the moment coefficients for a single span.

Because this type of floor or deck is labor intensive, it is not often used. When it is used, it is used primarily for heavy-timber construction. However, strength is generally not a controlling criterion with this type of deck; therefore, lower grades of lumber can usually be incorporated into the design.

One feature of the code related to construction of these decks that creates homogeneity is the requirement for nailing of adjacent laminations. As the laminations are thoroughly side nailed and the nails are required to penetrate two laminations and half of the third, the floor or deck does act essentially as a homogeneous material.

SECTION 2314 — POST-BEAM CONNECTIONS

Post and beam connections which meet the intent of the code are shown in Figures 2314-1 and 2314-2. However, the lower right diagram in Figure 2314-2 shows a connection to the footing with toenails between the post and the treated-wood plate which may not provide resistance to uplift or lateral displacement.

SECTION 2315 — WOOD SHEAR WALLS AND DIAPHRAGMS

This section contains provisions for the design and construction of lumber and wood structural panel diaphragms for the resistance to lateral forces in either horizontal diaphragms or vertical shear walls. The word "diaphragm" for vertical assemblies is used interchangeably with "shear wall." The design of fiberboard-sheathed diaphragms is covered in Section 2315.6.

The use of diaphragms sheathed with either lumber or wood sructural panels such as plywood, particleboard and fiberboard has evolved principally since the Long Beach earthquake of March 10, 1933. Wood diaphragms are particularly efficient structural systems for resisting lateral forces as they utilize com-

(Continued on page 319)

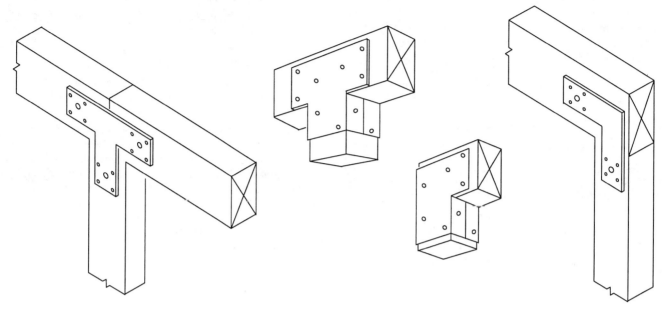

POST-TO-GIRDER CONNECTIONS

FIGURE 2314-1

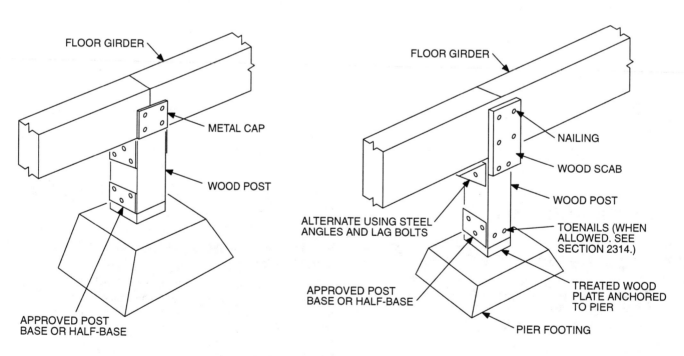

POST-GIRDER CONNECTION

FIGURE 2314-2

(Continued from page 317)

ponents that are already being used to carry gravity loads. Therefore, the modification of the components into lateral- force-resisting systems can be carried out relatively inexpensively, and as a result, these systems enjoy wide usage, particularly for one- and two-story buildings.

A thorough discussion of the design and construction of wood diaphragms is contained in the *Western Wood Use Book*. This reference discussion covers in detail the provisions for diaphragms as contained in this section of the UBC and, furthermore, provides the rationale and design theories for the use of wood diaphragms.

It should be noted that the 1997 edition allows the use of particleboard for structural diaphragm purposes only when used as a vertical diaphragm (shear wall), subject to the conditions, allowable shear, and diaphragm dimension ratios as specified in Tables 23-II-I-2 and 23-II-G. The use of fiberboard for structural diaphragm purposes is similarly limited to shear walls as specified in this section subject to the conditions and allowable shear as specified in Table 23-II-J.

As wood diaphragms are relatively flexible, the deflections created by lateral forces can be significant; therefore, the code places restrictions on the use of wood diaphragms in rotation. Rotation of a horizontal diaphragm is created by asymmetrical placing of the vertical resisting elements, asymmetrical loading or both. The translational forces plus rotation may create excessive deflections. Also, rotation may not be possible for a wood diaphragm on a building with a long, narrow shape where the narrow end is open and without lateral resistance. In this case, structural collapse under lateral loading is probable.

For these reasons, the code limits the geometrical properties of the shape in plans of wood-frame buildings where rotation of wood diaphragms is to be utilized and prohibits rotation completely in buildings of masonry or concrete construction.

Included in the 1997 UBC is Figure 23-II-1, which basically illustrates shear wall aspect ratio definitions so that Table 23-II-G aspect ratio limitations can be consistently applied. These are the definitions most commonly used in current practice and are appropriate for inclusion in the UBC.

Table 23-II-G has also been revised in the 1997 edition to reduce the maximum height-to-width ratios for vertical diaphragms or shear walls in Seismic Zone 4. Previous allowed narrower shear walls experienced excessive deflection problems as a result of the 1994 Northridge earthquake.

Tables 23-II-I-1 and 23-II-I-2, which define the allowable shear for structural panel and particleboard shear walls were also revised in the 1997 edition.

In Seismic Zones 3 and 4, where allowable shear values exceed 350 pounds per foot (5.11 N/mm), foundation sill plates and all framing members receiving edge nailing from abutting panels shall be not less than a single 3-inch (76 mm) nominal member, and foundation sill plates shall not be less than a single 3-inch (76 mm) nominal member.

In shear walls where total wall design shear does not exceed 600 pounds per foot (8.76 N/mm), a single 2-inch (51 mm) nominal sill plate may be used, provided anchor bolts are designed for a load capacity of 50 percent or less of the allowable capacity and bolts have a minimum of 2-inch by 2-inch by $^3/_{16}$-inch-thick

(51 mm by 51 mm by 5 mm) plate washers. Plywood joint and sill plate nailing shall be staggered in all cases.

Shear walls with high shear demand sustained major damage or complete failure during the Northridge earthquake due to inadequate nail edge distance into 2-inch (51 mm) nominal framing members.

2315.2 Wood Members Resisting Horizontal Forces Contributed by Masonry and Concrete. The general prohibition of using wood members to resist horizontal forces contributed by masonry or concrete in buildings is based on deflection and deformation compatibility. The deflection of wood members and systems when subjected to loads from masonry or concrete can be excessive and, as a result, can cause distress in the concrete or masonry members.

However, the second exception permits wood structural panel-sheathed shear walls in masonry or concrete buildings up to two stories in height under specified conditions. These conditions are intended to increase the stiffness of the wood framing and thus control deflections.

Division III—DESIGN SPECIFICATION FOR ALLOWABLE STRESS DESIGN OF WOOD BUILDINGS

Part I of the new division, Allowable Stress Design of Wood, adopts the ANSI/NFoPA NDS-91 National Design Specification for Wood Construction and the supplement to the 1991 NDS by reference with certain amendments as stated in Division III. This division, beginning with Section 2316, includes the design requirements previously covered in Sections 2306 through 2310 of the 1994 edition for horizontal member design, column design, flexural and axial loading, compression at angle to grain, and tension design. Also included are provisions for the design of structural glue-laminated timber and structural connections. For a discussion on the above design elements, the user should refer to the appropriate commentary in the NDS-91 publication.

Part II of Division III, Plywood Structural Panels, sets forth the allowable unit stresses for construction and industrial softwood plywood in accordance with Table 23-III-A.

Part III of Division III, Fastenings, beginning with Section 2318, replaces Section 2318 of the 1994 edition for timber connectors and fasteners.

Part IV of Division III, Allowable Stress Design for Wind and Earthquake Loads, beginning with Section 2319, replaces the wood shear wall and diaphragm design requirements that were previously shown in Sections 2314 and 2315 of the 1994 UBC.

SECTION 2318 — TIMBER CONNECTORS AND FASTENERS

The 1-inch (25 mm) diameter size limit placed on large-diameter bolt connections was added in the 1994 *Uniform Building Code* based on lumber testing that showed a reduction in bolt strength at low moisture contents. Allowable lateral design values for bolts in shear in seasoned lumber of Douglas fir-larch and Southern Pine and shown in Table 23-III-B-1 and 23-III-B-2.

The basic criteria for the design construction and allowable loads on timber fastenings are provided in Chapter 23, Division III, Part I. This standard is based essentially on the provisions of the *National Design Specification—Wood Construction NDS-1991.* In addition to the NDS-91 Commentary, the *Western Wood Use Book* contains similar material but with explanatory materials.

As stated in Section 2304.3, fasteners for pressure-preservative-treated and fire-retardant-treated wood are required to be of hot-dipped zinc-coated galvanized, stainless steel, silicon bronze or copper.

In the case of light metal plate connectors for wood trusses, Section 2321 of Chapter 23, Division V, is based on the 1995 design specifications of the Truss Plate Institute. Section 2304.4.4 also contains requirements for the quality control inspections of each truss manufacturer's plant. These requirements are somewhat more rigorous than usual for quality control inspections.

In Seismic Zones 3 and 4, toenails shall not be used to transfer lateral forces in excess of 150 pounds per foot from diaphragm to shear walls, drag struts (collectors) or other, or from shear walls to other elements. The use of toenails as a shear transfer mechanism should be limited to those instances when the level of force is nominal. Although a properly installed toenail can withstand the loads allowed by code, toenails are often not installed properly (for example, with an improper angle resulting in minimal edge distances and reduced penetrations) yielding a detail of questionable integrity when subjected to cyclic loading. An exception to this requirement exists for structures built in accordance with Section 2320.

Division IV—CONVENTIONAL LIGHT-FRAME CONSTRUCTION

SECTION 2320 — CONVENTIONAL LIGHT-FRAME CONSTRUCTION DESIGN PROVISIONS

2320.1 through 2320.5 General. Section 2320 is designed to provide prescriptive construction details and methods for light wood-frame construction, as depicted in Figures 2314-1, 2314-2, and 2320-1 through 2320-25. Light wood-frame construction is, in the parlance of the UBC, that construction which utilizes 2-inch (51 mm) nominal-width [sometimes 3-inch (76 mm)] wood studs at 16 or 24 inches (406 or 610 mm) on center to comprise the walls. Wood joists are used to frame the floors and roofs and are usually of 2-inch (51 mm) nominal lumber at 16 or 24 inches (406 or 610 mm) on center.

To resist lateral loads, wall bracing is specified based on past experience. The intent of these provisions is that they are prescriptive and do not ordinarily require a structural design to comply with the code. Where the construction conforms with the provisions of Section 2320.1, no structural design is indicated. However, in the case of unusual shape, size or weight, or if the construction involves split levels or when the building is not provided with braced wall lines, as noted in Sections 2320.4.4 and 2320.5.4, the code requires a structural design. Buildings shall be considered to be of unusual shape when the building official determines that the structure has framing irregularities, offsets, split levels or any configuration that creates discontinuities in the seismic load path and may include any of the conditions described in Sections 2320.5.4.1 through 2320.5.4.6. The designer has the option under any circumstances to design the building using other provisions of the code.

In this latter case, strict and specific compliance with the provisions of Section 2320 is not required.

The provisions of Section 2320 are based on experience gained over the last 60 years or more. In general, these types of provisions are reasonably quick to adopt modifications where experience shows they are inadequate. An example of such modification is the change in bracing requirements, which resulted from experience gained in the 1971 San Fernando, 1987 Whittier, and the 1994 Northridge, California earthquakes. However, where it appears these types of provisions are over-conservative, change is not so rapid unless research has shown any portion of the provisions to be overconservative. Nevertheless, over the years many constructors of light wood-frame construction have developed methods and systems for this type of construction that have resulted in cost savings. As a result, light wood-frame construction has become very cost-effective.

To address the issue of spacing of braced wall lines, the code has specific prescriptive provisions depending upon the structure's exposure to high winds and seismicity. For example, a two-story nonresidential structure located in Seismic Zone 3 and exposed to wind speeds greater than 80 mph will require a braced wall line every 25 feet (7620 mm) on center in both the longitudinal and transverse directions. Illustrations of the provisions of Sections 2320.4 and 2320.5 are depicted in Figure 2320-18.

The intent of the code as far as Section 2320 is concerned bears repeating. The *Uniform Building Code* intends that a building constructed of light wood-frame construction and in compliance with the provisions of Section 2320 be deemed to be in compliance with the engineering provisions of the code. An exception to this intent, of course, is the unusual-sized building or building of unusual shape or split-level located in Seismic Zones 3 and 4. However, the mere fact that the building is located in one of these seismic zones is not a valid reason to require an engineering design. Buildings that are of unusual shape, size or split-level construction as outlined in Sections 2320.4.4 and 2320.5.4 will require an engineering design when such construction is located in a seismic zone. (Also see the discussion of the exception to Section 1605.1.) Moreover, if the building is designed in accordance with other provisions of the code, the UBC does not intend that the building comply with the provisions of Section 2320, which may have been modified by the design.

2320.7 Girders. Although the provisions of Section 2320 are prescriptive in nature, the design of girders to support floor loads contains so many variables that tables of girder spans are not considered practical for the UBC. However, the code does provide prescriptive girder sizes, span and spacing for girders in single-story construction supporting loads from a single floor. Beyond this narrow prescriptive limit, the code requires that girders be designed to support the actual loads specified by the code. Figures 2314-1 and 2314-2 show details to comply with the requirements specified in this section.

2320.8 Floor Joists. In this section, the code specifies that spans for floor joists shall be in accordance with Tables 23-IV-J-1 and 23-IV-J-2. To properly use these tables, floor joist spans must be checked for deflection as well as for strength. Therefore, when using these tables, the modulus of elasticity and the allowable stress in bending for repetitive members must be obtained from Tables 23-IV-V-1 and 23-IV-V-2.

For example, if the permissible span is desired for 2 by 6 joists spaced 16 inches (406 mm) on center and the joists are specified to be No. 1 grade Douglas fir, the first step is to enter Table 23-IV-V-1 under the species heading "Douglas Fir—Larch." The next step is to enter the column under the size classification. Within the row size designated "2 × 6" and reading across from the No. 1 grade, the normal allowable stress in bending is found to be 1,495 pounds per square inch (psi) (10.3 N/mm^2). Reading further across under the column headed "Modulus of Elasticity," the figure of 1,700,000 psi (11 713 N/mm^2) will be found.

With these data one can turn to Table 23-IV-J-1 with the size and spacing of 2 by 6 joists at 16 inches (406 mm) on center. Under the column headed with a 1.7, which represents the modulus of elasticity of 1,700,000 psi (11 713 N/mm^2), a span of 9 feet 11 inches (2108 mm) is indicated. At the end of the table, one finds that the minimum allowable bending required is 1,306 psi (9.0 N/mm^2). As this fiber stress is below the permitted fiber stress of 1,495 psi (10.3 N/mm^2), the deflection is the governing factor in this case and the maximum allowable span is 9 feet 11 inches (3023 mm).

Framing details for floor joists are depicted in Figures 2320-1 through 2320-9.

(Continued on page 329)

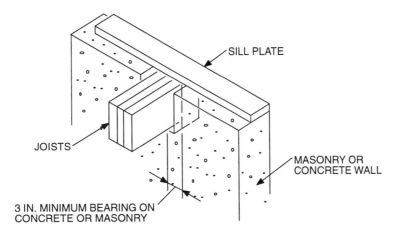

JOISTS BEARING ON CONCRETE OR MASONRY

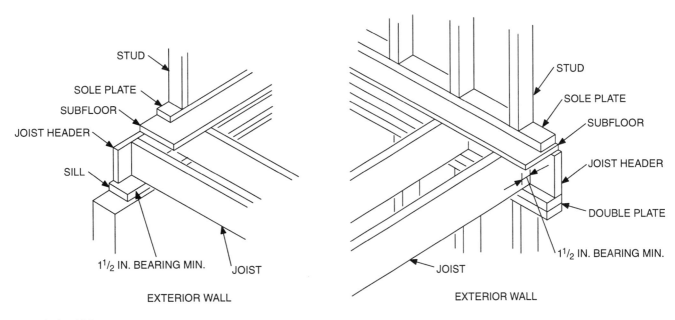

For **SI:** 1 inch = 25.4 mm.

JOISTS BEARING ON WOOD

FIGURE 2320-1

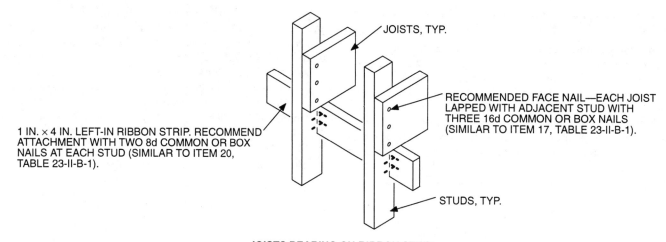

JOISTS, TYP.

RECOMMENDED FACE NAIL—EACH JOIST LAPPED WITH ADJACENT STUD WITH THREE 16d COMMON OR BOX NAILS (SIMILAR TO ITEM 17, TABLE 23-II-B-1).

1 IN. × 4 IN. LEFT-IN RIBBON STRIP. RECOMMEND ATTACHMENT WITH TWO 8d COMMON OR BOX NAILS AT EACH STUD (SIMILAR TO ITEM 20, TABLE 23-II-B-1).

STUDS, TYP.

JOISTS BEARING ON RIBBON STRIP

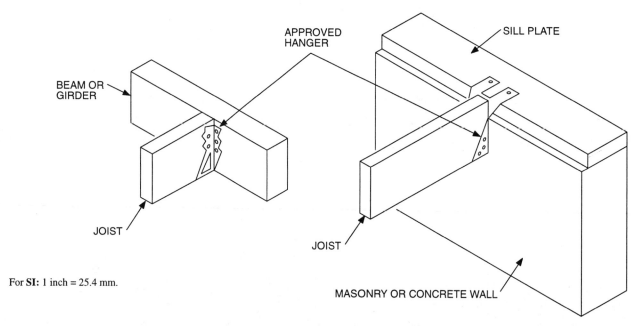

APPROVED HANGER

SILL PLATE

BEAM OR GIRDER

JOIST

For **SI:** 1 inch = 25.4 mm.

JOIST

MASONRY OR CONCRETE WALL

JOISTS SUPPORTED BY APPROVED ANCHORS

FIGURE 2320-2

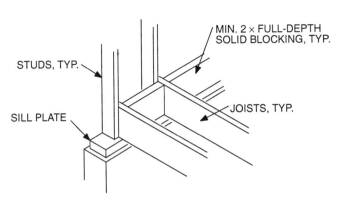

JOISTS ATTACHED TO ADJACENT STUDS

JOISTS ATTACHED TO BAND OR RIM JOIST

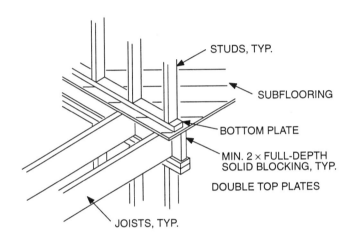

**JOISTS LAPPED OVER PARTITION WITH BLOCKING
BETWEEN JOISTS**

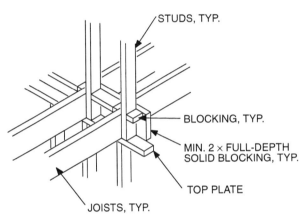

**JOISTS LAPPED OVER PARTITION AND NAILED TO
ADJOINING STUD**

FIGURE 2320-3

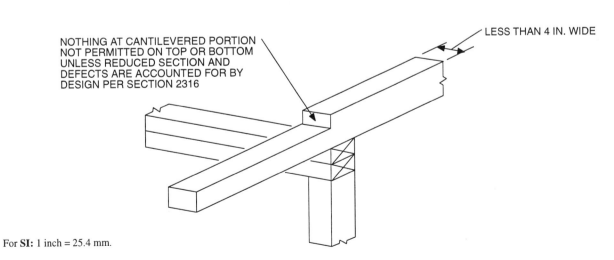

For **SI:** 1 inch = 25.4 mm.

NOTCHING OF CANTILEVER

FIGURE 2320-4

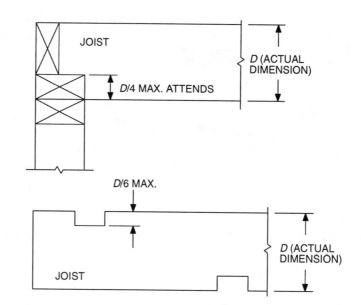

CUTTING AND NOTCHING LIMITATIONS

NOTE: Notching not permitted in middle of ¹/₃ of span

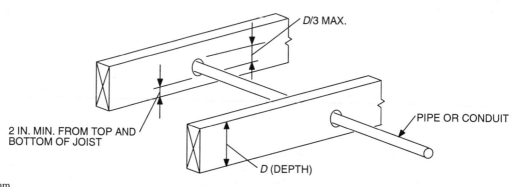

For **SI:** 1 inch = 25.4 mm.

BORED HOLES IN JOISTS

NOTCHING AND BORING LIMITATIONS—FLOOR JOISTS

FIGURE 2320-5

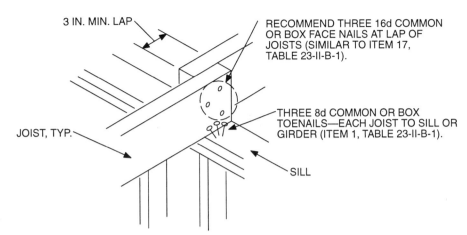

3 IN. MIN. LAP

RECOMMEND THREE 16d COMMON OR BOX FACE NAILS AT LAP OF JOISTS (SIMILAR TO ITEM 17, TABLE 23-II-B-1).

THREE 8d COMMON OR BOX TOENAILS—EACH JOIST TO SILL OR GIRDER (ITEM 1, TABLE 23-II-B-1).

JOIST, TYP.

SILL

For **SI:** 1 inch = 25.4 mm.

JOIST LAPPING OVER BEAM, GIRDER OR PARTITION

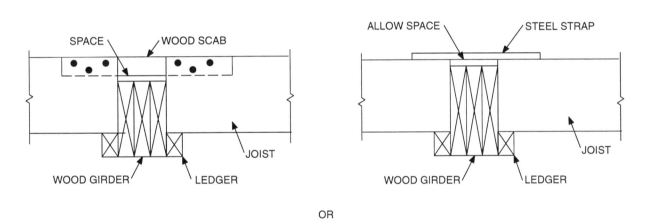

SPACE WOOD SCAB

JOIST

WOOD GIRDER LEDGER

ALLOW SPACE STEEL STRAP

JOIST

WOOD GIRDER LEDGER

OR

RECOMMEND THREE 8d COMMON OR BOX NAILS EACH END WITH METAL STRAP, OR THREE 16d COMMON OR BOX NAILS EACH END WITH WOOD STRAP (6 NAILS TOTAL EACH STRAP).

RECOMMEND WOOD OR METAL TIE STRAP

SILL (OR BEAM OR GIRDER)

JOIST, TYP.

CENTER LINE OF SPLICE AT CENTER LINE OF SUPPORTING MEMBER

For **SI:** 1 inch = 25.4 mm.

FLOOR JOISTS TIED OVER WOOD BEAM, GIRDER OR PARTITION

FIGURE 2320-6

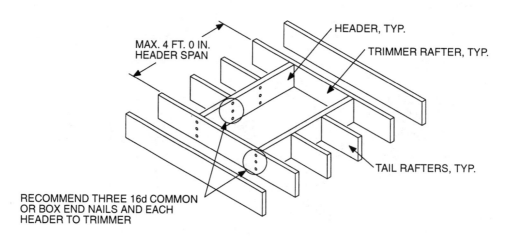

MAX. 4 FT. 0 IN.
HEADER SPAN

HEADER, TYP.

TRIMMER RAFTER, TYP.

TAIL RAFTERS, TYP.

RECOMMEND THREE 16d COMMON
OR BOX END NAILS AND EACH
HEADER TO TRIMMER

For **SI:** 1 foot = 304.8 mm.

FRAMING AROUND OPENINGS—HEADER SPAN ≤ 4 FEET

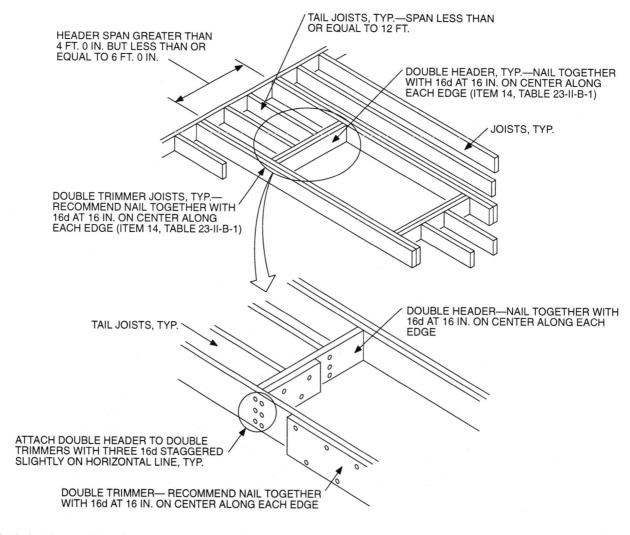

HEADER SPAN GREATER THAN
4 FT. 0 IN. BUT LESS THAN OR
EQUAL TO 6 FT. 0 IN.

TAIL JOISTS, TYP.—SPAN LESS THAN
OR EQUAL TO 12 FT.

DOUBLE HEADER, TYP.—NAIL TOGETHER
WITH 16d AT 16 IN. ON CENTER ALONG
EACH EDGE (ITEM 14, TABLE 23-II-B-1)

JOISTS, TYP.

DOUBLE TRIMMER JOISTS, TYP.—
RECOMMEND NAIL TOGETHER WITH
16d AT 16 IN. ON CENTER ALONG
EACH EDGE (ITEM 14, TABLE 23-II-B-1)

TAIL JOISTS, TYP.

DOUBLE HEADER—NAIL TOGETHER WITH
16d AT 16 IN. ON CENTER ALONG EACH
EDGE

ATTACH DOUBLE HEADER TO DOUBLE
TRIMMERS WITH THREE 16d STAGGERED
SLIGHTLY ON HORIZONTAL LINE, TYP.

DOUBLE TRIMMER— RECOMMEND NAIL TOGETHER
WITH 16d AT 16 IN. ON CENTER ALONG EACH EDGE

For **SI:** 1 inch = 25.4 mm, 1 foot = 304.8 mm.

FRAMING AROUND OPENINGS—HEADER SPAN > 4 FEET

FIGURE 2320-7

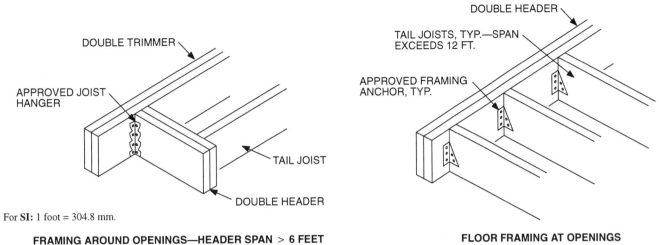

For **SI:** 1 foot = 304.8 mm.

FRAMING AROUND OPENINGS—HEADER SPAN > 6 FEET

FLOOR FRAMING AT OPENINGS

FIGURE 2320-7—(Continued)

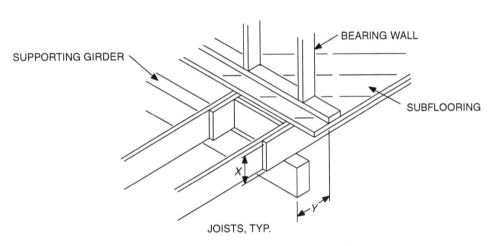

DISTANCE *Y* MUST NOT EXCEED DIMENSION *X*

SUPPORT OF BEARING PARTITION—PERPENDICULAR TO JOISTS

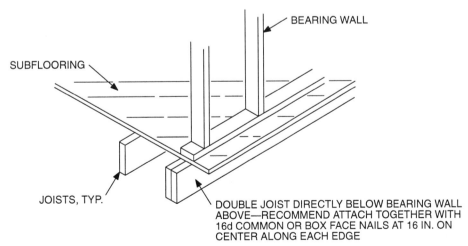

For **SI:** 1 inch = 25.4 mm.

SUPPORT OF BEARING PARTITION—PARALLEL TO JOISTS

FIGURE 2320-8

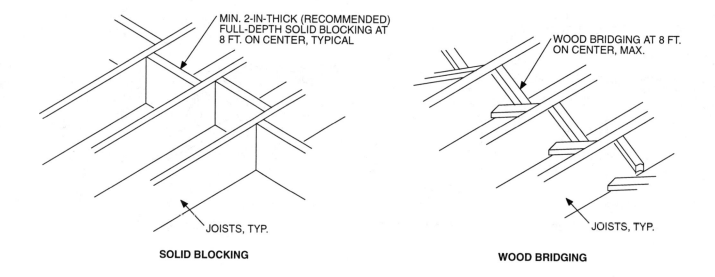

MIN. 2-IN-THICK (RECOMMENDED) FULL-DEPTH SOLID BLOCKING AT 8 FT. ON CENTER, TYPICAL

WOOD BRIDGING AT 8 FT. ON CENTER, MAX.

JOISTS, TYP.

JOISTS, TYP.

SOLID BLOCKING

WOOD BRIDGING

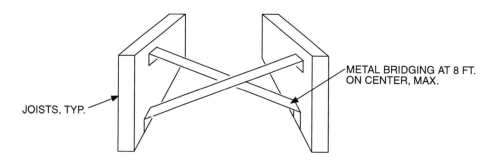

JOISTS, TYP.

METAL BRIDGING AT 8 FT. ON CENTER, MAX.

METAL BRIDGING MUST BE APPROVED BY BUILDING OFFICIAL

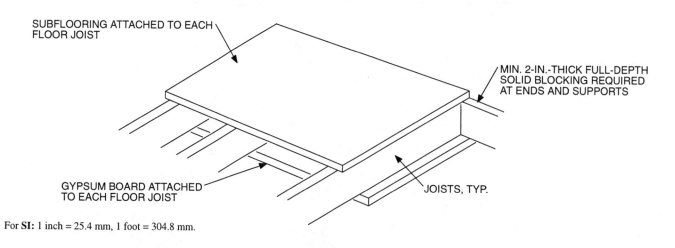

SUBFLOORING ATTACHED TO EACH FLOOR JOIST

MIN. 2-IN.-THICK FULL-DEPTH SOLID BLOCKING REQUIRED AT ENDS AND SUPPORTS

GYPSUM BOARD ATTACHED TO EACH FLOOR JOIST

JOISTS, TYP.

For **SI:** 1 inch = 25.4 mm, 1 foot = 304.8 mm.

ALTERNATE TO SOLID BLOCKING OR BRIDGING

FIGURE 2320-9

(Continued from page 321)

2320.9 Subflooring. Flooring systems may consist of a subfloor on which may be placed an underlayment or a combination subfloor/underlayment system, upon which a finished floor-surfacing material may be applied. The finished floor-surfacing material may either be wood-strip flooring, tongue-and-groove flooring, various types of resilient floor coverings such as vinyl asbestos tile, or carpet. For the noncombined subfloor/underlayment system, underlayment is required to provide a smooth, even surface to which the finished flooring will be attached. However, in some cases, the underlayment is required to add strength to the subflooring such as that shown in system choice 3, Figure 2320-11. On occasion, depending on the strength of materials used, any one of the three components described above may be absent, or any two or all of them may be combined into one layer.

Lumber subflooring, for example, may be omitted when the joist spacing does not exceed 16 inches (406 mm) and 1-inch (25 mm) nominal tongue-and-groove wood-strip flooring is applied perpendicular to the joists. In this case, the 1-inch (25 mm) nominal tongue-and-groove wood-strip flooring is considered to be adequate in strength to support the loads required by the code.

Subflooring is classified by the UBC as follows.

2320.9.1 Lumber subfloor. Details for lumber sheathing used as subflooring are shown in Figure 2320-10. Allowable spans for lumber subflooring are set forth in UBC Tables 23-II-D-1 and 23-II-D-2. The span tables are based on the thickness of the floor sheathing, the orientation of the sheathing with respect to the joists (either perpendicular or diagonal) and the board grade of the lumber being used.

2320.9.2 Wood structural panels. Wood structural panels may be manufactured for use as either structural subflooring or combination subfloor-underlayment. The allowable spans for structural subflooring and combination subfloor-underlayment are based on the wood structural panels' face grain (strength axis) parallel to its supporting members or its being continuous over two or more spans and with the face grain placed perpendicular to the supports. These qualifications are very critical in determining the permissible spans. Most wood structural panels are considerably stronger when their face grain is perpendicular to the supports and continuous over two or more spans. Panels with multiple spans have greater capacity than when they are simply supported between two joists.

To create a stiffer floor and to prevent squeaking of the floor system after the building has been in use, the subfloor may be glued to the joists. This gluing prevents the relative movement between the panel and the joist that takes place when people walk on the floor and, thus, provides additional stiffness. Where the panel is glued to the floor, the code permits the spacing of fasteners to be a maximum of 12 inches (305 mm) on center at all supports, which is somewhat larger than the spacings required in Table 23-II-B-1. Figure 2320-11 depicts the five choices of systems indicated in Footnote 1 to Table 23-II-F-1 for wood structural panel combination subfloor-underlayment.

2320.9.3 Plank flooring. Plank flooring may either be designed in accordance with the general engineering provisions of the code or Table 23-IV-A may be used for 2-inch (51 mm) tongue-and-groove planking where all joints occur over supports. Random planking layup is permitted by the code as long as it con-

forms to the specifications in this item and as depicted in Figure 2320-12.

2320.9.4 and 2320.10 Particleboard and particleboard underlayment. Particleboard can be used as underlayment, structural subflooring or as combined subfloor-underlayment. Where used as underlayment, the code permits Type PBU particleboard. Where particleboard is used as a structural subfloor or as combined subfloor-underlayment, the code specifies Type 2-M-W or 2-M-3 particleboard, which is most often made with phenol-formaldehyde resin binders which not only have high wet strength but are also highly resistant to moisture and heat. The code specifies Type 2-M-W or 2-M-3 particleboard for structural subflooring and combination subfloor-underlayment, as they are subject to wetting from rainfall until the building has been completely enclosed and weatherproofed. Therefore, the high durability and strength under high moisture conditions provided by Type 2-M-W or 2-M-3 particleboard are necessary.

The 1997 edition has deleted UBC Standard 23-4, Wood particleboard. Particleboard is now listed as a recognized standard through American National Standard for Particleboard, ANSI A208.1-93. Appropriate code revisions are based on this standard.

2320.11 Wall Framing.

2320.11.1 Size, height and spacing. The size, height and spacing of studs in bearing walls is depicted in Figure 2320-13 in accordance with the requirements of Table 23-IV-B. As stated in Footnote 1 to UBC Table 23-IV-B, the listed stud heights in the table may be increased when an engineering analysis shows the increase in height is justified. To qualify as lateral support, the points of support must be placed perpendicular to the plane of the wall.

2320.11.2 Framing details. Framing details as related to the top plate requirements of the code for bearing partitions are depicted in Figures 2320-14 through 2320-16.

Interior nonbearing partitions are permitted to be capped with a single plate with a splice detail and tie details at corners and wall intersections, as described in the code.

All stud walls are required by the code to have a bottom or sill plate with not less than a nominal 2 inches (51 mm) in thickness and with a width not less than that of the wall studs. This is necessary to provide a nailing surface for the bottom edge of the wall sheathing. The latter requirement is also to keep the compression-perpendicular-to-grain stress on the sill plate from reaching excessive values and causing too large a deformation. This is particularly important because of the characteristic of wood framing to shrink across the grain as it dries. If the compression-perpendicular-to-the-grain deformation of the sill plate is too great and it is combined with cross-grain shrinkage, problems arise such as those described in this handbook under Section 2308.

2320.11.3 Bracing. The bracing requirements for light-frame construction are depicted in Figure 2320-17. As described in the code, exterior walls and main cross partitions are required to be braced to resist wind and seismic forces. Main cross partitions are defined as those partitions (usually bearing partitions) that cross the building either transversely or longitudinally and that have sufficient length of wall without openings to provide the bracing required under this item. In fact, if in the judgment of the

(Continued on page 333)

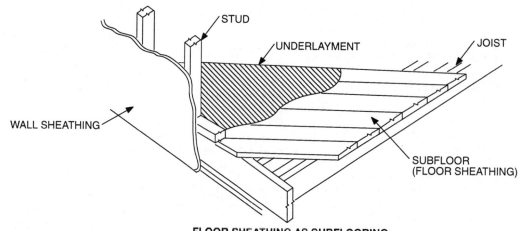

FLOOR SHEATHING AS SUBFLOORING

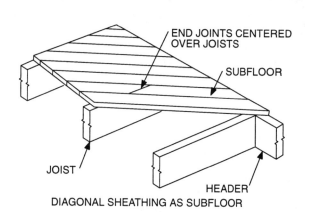

DIAGONAL SHEATHING AS SUBFLOOR

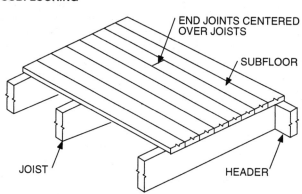

STRAIGHT SHEATHING AS SUBFLOOR

SUBFLOOR (FLOOR SHEATHING) ORIENTATION

LUMBER SUBFLOORING

FIGURE 2320-10

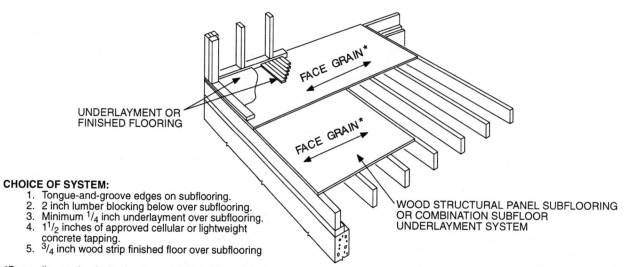

CHOICE OF SYSTEM:
1. Tongue-and-groove edges on subflooring.
2. 2 inch lumber blocking below over subflooring.
3. Minimum $^1/_4$ inch underlayment over subflooring.
4. $1^1/_2$ inches of approved cellular or lightweight concrete tapping.
5. $^3/_4$ inch wood strip finished floor over subflooring

*Depending on the design loads, panel thickness and the panel span rating, the face grain (strength axis) of the wood structural panel may be oriented parallel or perpendicular to the supporting members below.

For **SI:** 1 inch = 25.4 mm.

PLYWOOD SUBFLOORING

FIGURE 2320-11

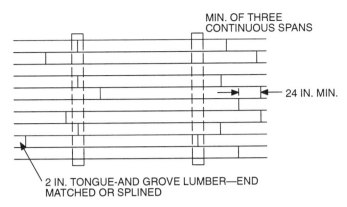

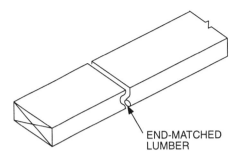

MIN. OF THREE
CONTINUOUS SPANS

24 IN. MIN.

2 IN. TONGUE-AND-GROVE LUMBER—END
MATCHED OR SPLINED

END-MATCHED
LUMBER

For **SI:** 1 inch = 25.4 mm.

PLANK FLOORING

FIGURE 2320-12

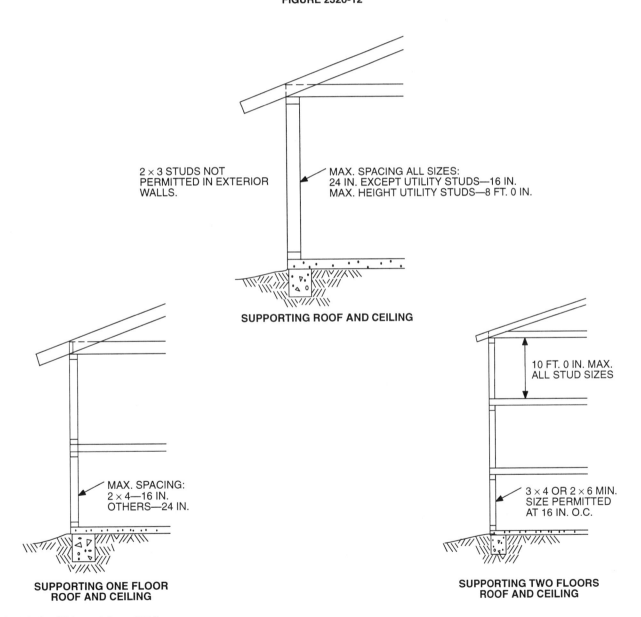

2 × 3 STUDS NOT
PERMITTED IN EXTERIOR
WALLS.

MAX. SPACING ALL SIZES:
24 IN. EXCEPT UTILITY STUDS—16 IN.
MAX. HEIGHT UTILITY STUDS—8 FT. 0 IN.

SUPPORTING ROOF AND CEILING

MAX. SPACING:
2 × 4—16 IN.
OTHERS—24 IN.

**SUPPORTING ONE FLOOR
ROOF AND CEILING**

10 FT. 0 IN. MAX.
ALL STUD SIZES

3 × 4 OR 2 × 6 MIN.
SIZE PERMITTED
AT 16 IN. O.C.

**SUPPORTING TWO FLOORS
ROOF AND CEILING**

For **SI:** 1 inch = 25.4 mm, 1 foot = 304.8 mm.

BEARING WALLS AND STUDS SPACING

FIGURE 2320-13

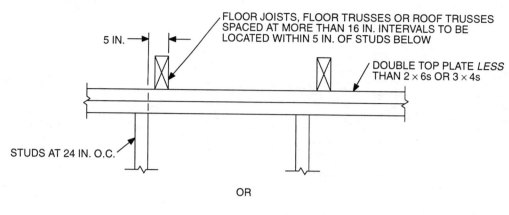

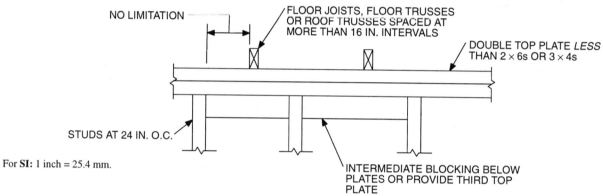

For **SI:** 1 inch = 25.4 mm.

TOP PLATE LIMITATIONS—BEARING PARTITIONS

FIGURE 2320-14

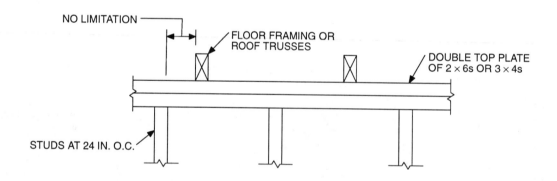

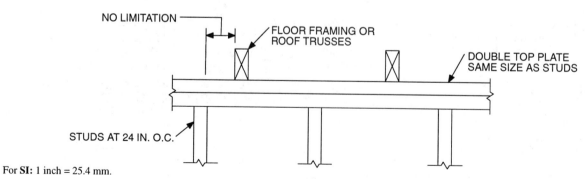

For **SI:** 1 inch = 25.4 mm.

TOP PLATE LIMITATIONS—BEARING PARTITIONS

FIGURE 2320-15

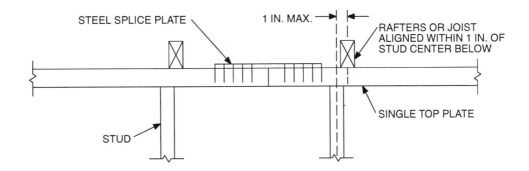

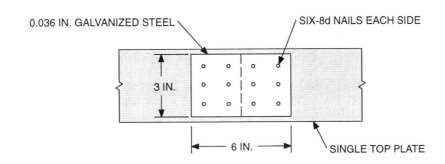

RAFTERS, JOISTS AND TRUSSES ARE CENTERED OVER THE STUDS WITH A TOLERANCE OF NOT MORE THAN 1 INCH.

For **SI:** 1 inch = 25.4 mm.

SINGLE TOP PLATE SPLICE—BEARING PARTITIONS

FIGURE 2320-16

(Continued from page 329)

building official the spacing of main cross partitions with bracing is too great, the building official may require, as discussed in Section 1605.1, an engineering design to show that the building can withstand the loads prescribed by this code.

An item worth noting that was revised in the 1994 *Uniform Building Code* is the placement of braced wall panels. In previous versions of the code, placement of braced wall panels near ends of braced wall lines were to occur "as near thereto as possible." This provision became difficult to enforce and nonuniformity in code enforcement and construction became more prevalent. To increase uniformity, the code was revised to require wall bracing to start at no more than 8 feet (2438 mm) from each end of a braced wall line. Also, the code required bracing elements within a braced wall line to occur in line with one another. However, an offset in the bracing of one panel to another of 4 feet (1219 mm) is permitted.

The 1997 edition further revised the bracing requirements to prohibit Method 1 (let-in braces) to be used in Seismic Zones 2B, 3 and 4 as a required braced wall panel as a result of its performance during the 1994 Northridge earthquake.

2320.11.4 Alternate braced wall panels. In previous code editions, the braced wall panel provisions for conventional construction have required a minimum 4-foot (1219 mm) panel length. However, construction practices for braced wall panels adjacent to garage door openings employed lengths considerably less than 4 feet (1219 mm). Therefore, the 1994 code was revised to permit braced wall panels to be a minimum 2 feet

8 inches (813 mm) in length if certain construction methods, as outlined in this section, are used. The provisions found in this section of the code denote braced wall panel requirements for sheathing material, thickness, size, fasteners and steel tie-down device requirements. Figure 2320-19 depicts these provisions.

2320.11.5 Cripple walls. Cripple walls (sometimes referred to as foundation stud walls or knee walls) are stud walls usually less than 8 feet (2438 mm) in height that rest on the foundation plate and support the first immediate floor above.

The code requires a minimum height of 14 inches (356 mm) for cripple wall studs, and this minimum is based on the length necessary to properly fasten the studs to the foundation wall plate and the double-wall plate above. Where the 14-inch (356 mm) minimum is not possible, the code then requires that the cripple wall be framed with solid blocking. Under this circumstance, the cripple wall studs, even though shorter than 14 inches (356 mm) in length, should be installed with wall plates as required by Section 2320.11.2 and with the solid blocking tightly fit between each stud. This solid blocking performs three purposes: it provides a level uniform bearing surface for the support of the floor above, it transmits lateral forces from the floor to the foundation and it reduces the "racking" effects of the studs during seismic or high-wind activity. Wood structural panel sheathing may also be used to brace these walls provided adequate nailing is supplied along the foundation sill and top plates.

Where cripple studs exceed 14 inches (356 mm) in height, the code places two requirements on them:

- Foundation stud walls having a stud height exceeding 14 inches (356 mm) shall be braced in accordance with Table 23-IV-C-2. This new table in the 1997 UBC will, in all cases, require a wood structural panel for cripple walls exceeding 14 inches (356 mm) in height. This table was needed to differentiate between bracing required at the cripple wall level where normally only exterior walls are provided compared to the bracing prescribed in Table 23-IV-C-1 for main story levels where interior partitions share the lateral load demands.

- Where foundation stud walls exceed 4 feet (1219 mm) in height, they shall be framed with studs having the size required for an additional story. Thus, for a building that would be considered to be two stories in height with a crawl space beneath the first story but having foundation stud walls with the studs greater in height than 4 feet (1219 mm), the code would require that the studs be framed with either 3 by 4 or 2 by 6 members, as would be required for the first story of a three-story building.

2320.11.6 Headers. As with floor girders, headers and lintels support such varying loads that a table of spans for headers and lintels is not considered practical for the UBC. Therefore, the code requires that they be designed to support the actual loads specified by the code. Each end of a lintel or header is required by the code to have a minimum length of bearing of $1^1/_2$ inches (38 mm) for the full width of the lintel. Figure 2320-20 portrays typical framing around an exterior wall opening, including the lintel and the trimmer or jamb stud on either side of the opening.

2320.11.7 Pipes in walls. Figures 2320-21 and 2320-22 depict the requirements of this item relative to placement of plumbing pipes in walls.

2320.11.8 Bridging. Where stud partitions do not have adequate sheathing to brace the studs laterally in their weak or smaller dimension, and the studs have a height-to-least-thickness ratio exceeding 50, the studs are required to have bridging (in this case, solid blocking) with a minimum nominal thickness of 2 inches (51 mm) and a width the same as the studs. This blocking should be installed at such heights as to reduce the height-to-least-thickness ratio below 50. For 2 by 4 studs this will require placement of the blocking over 6 feet 3 inches (1905 mm) maximum over the height of the wall.

2320.11.9 Cutting and notching. Drawings 1 and 2 of Figure 2320-23 depict code requirements for cutting and notching of studs.

2320.11.10 Bored holes. Drawings 3 and 4 of Figure 2320-23 depict the code requirements for bored holes in studs.

2320.12 Roof and Ceiling Framing.

2320.12.1 General. The code intends that the framing details for roofs in this section apply only to roofs having a minimum slope of 3 units vertical in 12 units horizontal (25% slope). For roofs flatter than a slope of 3 units vertical in 12 units horizontal (25% slope), the side thrust becomes so large as to exceed the capabili-

ties of conventional framing. Although the code specifies that the members supporting rafters and ceiling joists of roofs with a slope less than 3 units vertical in 12 units horizontal (25% slope) be designed as beams, struts back to interior bearing partitions may be used to provide support for the ridge board, hip and valley rafters. Figure 2320-24 shows rafter framing details which comply with the code. It can be seen from the diagram that the horizontal thrust at the wall plate line must be resisted by either ceiling joists nailed to the rafters or by rafter ties where the joists are not parallel to the rafters.

Figure 2320-25 shows the framing and rafter tie requirements of the code. Where the rafters are not parallel to the ceiling joists and rafter ties are provided, the rafter ties must be as close to the plate line as possible, as indicated by the note on the lower drawing.

Figure 2320-26 depicts the code requirements for the use of purlins and struts to reduce the span of rafters. Where the roof slope is less than 3 units vertical in 12 units horizontal (25% slope), the code requires that members supporting rafters such as ridge boards, for example, be designed as beams. However, as previously discussed, struts can be installed from a partition up to the ridge board to reduce the span.

2320.12.8 Blocking. As with all other horizontal beams, the code requires that roof rafters and ceiling joists be supported laterally to prevent rotation and lateral displacement in accordance with Section 2316 and Section 4.4.1.2 of 1991 ANSI/NFoPA. Thus, 2 by 4 rafters or joists would not require any lateral support, but 2 by 6 ceiling joists would require their ends to be held in position by full-depth solid blocking, bridging, nailing or bolting to other framing members, approved hangers or other acceptable means.

Although the code requires solid blocking at points of bearing for roof trusses to support them laterally, other methods are acceptable if they provide the same amount of restraint to rotation and displacement as would be provided by solid blocking. This requirement is in the code primarily to prevent displacement or rotation of roof trusses during construction. After the roof diaphragm is in place and the ceiling membrane is in place (when attached directly to the truss lower chords), the roof trusses are effectively stayed against rotation or lateral displacement. However, blocking may be required to provide shear transfer from the diaphragm to the wall bracing.

2320.12.9 Roof sheathing. For lumber roof sheathing, the code requirement is the same as for lumber subfloors, and the bottom two drawings of Figure 2320-10 should be consulted for details.

The code requires that wood structural panels used for roof sheathing be bonded by intermediate or exterior glue and that any wood structural panel roof sheathing exposed on the underside be bonded with exterior glue. These requirements are based on the fact that moisture quite often gets beneath the roof covering. This causes delamination of plies bonded with interior glue. Therefore, wood structural panels should be bonded by intermediate or exterior glues in order to prevent delamination.

2320.12.10 Roof planking. The code requirement for roof planking is very similar to that for plank flooring except that no lumber surface layer is required on top of the planking.

TABLE 23-IV-C-1—BRACED WALL PANELS[1]

| SEISMIC ZONE | CONDITION | CONSTRUCTION METHOD[2,3] | | | | | | | | BRACED PANEL LOCATION AND LENGTH[4] |
		1	2	3	4	5	6	7	8	
0, 1 and 2A	One story, top of two or three story	X	X	X	X	X	X	X	X	Each end and not more than 25 feet (7620 mm) on center
	First story of two story or second story of three story	X	X	X	X	X	X	X	X	
	First story of three story		X	X	X	X[5]	X	X	X	
2B, 3 and 4	One story, top of two or three story		X	X	X	X	X	X[6]	X	Each end and not more than 25 feet (7620 mm) on center
	First story of two story or second of three story		X	X	X	X[5]	X	X[6]	X	Each end and not more than 25 feet (7620 mm) on center but not less than 25% of building length[6]
	First story of three story		X	X	X	X[5]	X	X[6]	X	Each end and not more than 25 feet (7620 mm) on center but not less than 40% of building length[6]

[1]This table specifies minimum requirements for braced panels which form interior or exterior braced wall lines.
[2]See Section 2320.11.3 for full description.
[3]See Section 2320.11.4 for alternate braced panel requirement.
[4]Building length is the dimension parallel to the braced wall length.
[5]Gypsum wallboard applied to supports at 16 inches (406 mm) on center.
[6]Not permitted for bracing cripple walls in Seismic Zone 4. See Section 2320.11.5
[7]The required lengths shall be doubled for gypsum board applied to only one face of a braced wall panel.

TABLE 23-IV-C-2—CRIPPLE WALL BRACING

| SEISMIC ZONE | CONDITION | AMOUNT OF CRIPPLE WALL BRACING[1,2] |
		× 25.4 for mm
4	One story above cripple wall	$3/8''$ wood structural panel with 8d at $6''/12''$ nailing on 60 percent of wall length minimum
	Two story above cripple wall	$3/8''$ wood structural panel with 8d at $4''/12''$ nailing on 50 percent of wall length minimum or $3/8''$ wood structural panel with 8d at $6''/12''$ nailing on 75 percent of wall length minimum
3	One story above cripple wall	$3/8''$ wood structural panel with 8d at $6''/12''$ nailing on 40 percent of wall length minimum
0, 1 and 2	One story above cripple wall	$3/8''$ wood structural panel with 8d at $6''/12''$ nailing on 30 percent of wall length minimum
0, 1, 2 and 3	Two story above cripple wall	$3/8''$ wood structural panel with 8d at $4''/12''$ nailing on 40 percent of wall length minimum or $3/8''$ wood structural panel with 8d at $6''/12''$ nailing on 60 percent of wall length minimum

[1]Braced panel length shall be at least two times the height of the cripple wall, but not less than 48 inches (1219 mm).
[2]All panels along a wall shall be nearly equal in length and shall be nearly equally spaced along the length of the wall.

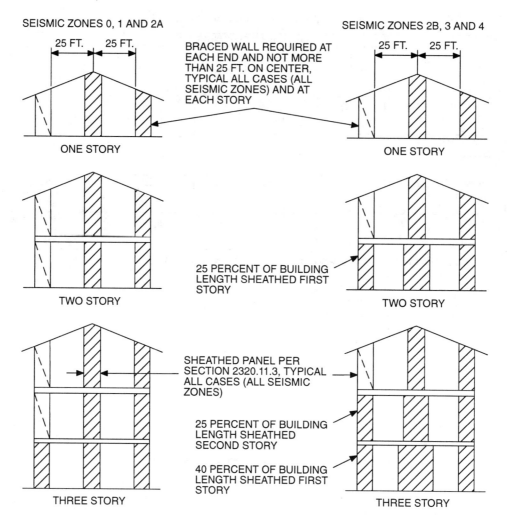

SEISMIC ZONES 0, 1 AND 2A

25 FT.   25 FT.

ONE STORY

TWO STORY

THREE STORY

BRACED WALL REQUIRED AT EACH END AND NOT MORE THAN 25 FT. ON CENTER, TYPICAL ALL CASES (ALL SEISMIC ZONES) AND AT EACH STORY

SEISMIC ZONES 2B, 3 AND 4

25 FT.   25 FT.

ONE STORY

25 PERCENT OF BUILDING LENGTH SHEATHED FIRST STORY

TWO STORY

SHEATHED PANEL PER SECTION 2320.11.3, TYPICAL ALL CASES (ALL SEISMIC ZONES)

25 PERCENT OF BUILDING LENGTH SHEATHED SECOND STORY

40 PERCENT OF BUILDING LENGTH SHEATHED FIRST STORY

THREE STORY

NOTE: Measurements are to center line of panels, 25 feet on center.

For **SI:** 1 foot = 304.8 mm.

WALL BRACING

FIGURE 2320-17

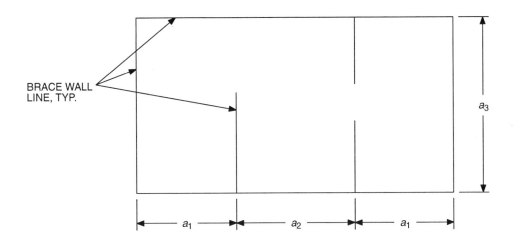

BRACE WALL LINE, TYP.

SEISMIC ZONES 0, 1, 2 AND 3
BASIC WIND SPEED $\leq$ 80 MPH

$a_1 = a_2 = a_3 = 34$ FEET MAXIMUM
BASIC WIND SPEED > 80 MPH

$a_1 = a_2 = a_3 = 25$ FEET MAXIMUM
EXCEPTION: ONE- AND TWO-STORY GROUP R, DIVISION 3 BUILDINGS

$a_1 = a_2 = 34$ FEET MAXIMUM, PROVIDED MAXIMUM SINGLE ROOM SIZE IS 900 SQUARE FEET PER DWELLING UNIT

a_1 = DISTANCE BETWEEN EXTERIOR AND INTERIOR BRACED WALL LINES

a_2 = DISTANCE BETWEEN INTERIOR BRACED WALL LINES

a_3 = DISTANCE BETWEEN EXTERIOR BRACED WALL LINES WITH NO INTERIOR BRACED WALL LINE BETWEEN EXTERIOR WALLS

SEISMIC ZONE 4

$a_1 = a_2 = a_3 = 25$ FEET MAXIMUM
EXCEPTION: ONE- AND TWO-STORY GROUP R, DIVISION 3 BUILDINGS

$a_1 = a_2 = 34$ FEET, PROVIDED MAXIMUM SINGLE ROOM SIZE IS 900 SQUARE FEET PER DWELLING UNIT

For **SI:** 1 foot = 304.8 mm, 1 square foot = 0.0929 m^2.

ADDITIONAL BRACED WALL LINE REQUIREMENTS FOR CONVENTIONAL CONSTRUCTION

FIGURE 2320-18

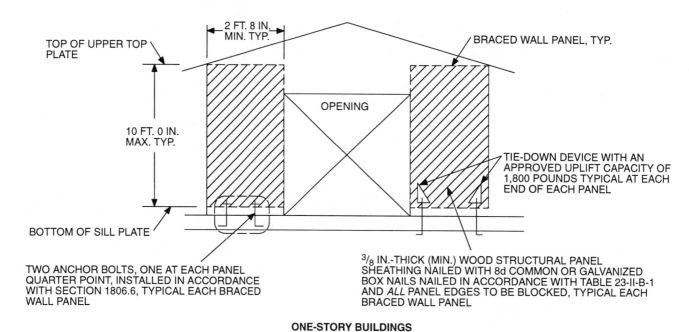

TOP OF UPPER TOP PLATE

2 FT. 8 IN. MIN. TYP.

BRACED WALL PANEL, TYP.

10 FT. 0 IN. MAX. TYP.

OPENING

TIE-DOWN DEVICE WITH AN APPROVED UPLIFT CAPACITY OF 1,800 POUNDS TYPICAL AT EACH END OF EACH PANEL

BOTTOM OF SILL PLATE

TWO ANCHOR BOLTS, ONE AT EACH PANEL QUARTER POINT, INSTALLED IN ACCORDANCE WITH SECTION 1806.6, TYPICAL EACH BRACED WALL PANEL

$3/8$ IN.-THICK (MIN.) WOOD STRUCTURAL PANEL SHEATHING NAILED WITH 8d COMMON OR GALVANIZED BOX NAILS NAILED IN ACCORDANCE WITH TABLE 23-II-B-1 AND *ALL* PANEL EDGES TO BE BLOCKED, TYPICAL EACH BRACED WALL PANEL

ONE-STORY BUILDINGS

For **SI:** 1 inch = 25.4 mm, 1 foot = 304.8 mm, 1 pound = 4.45 N.

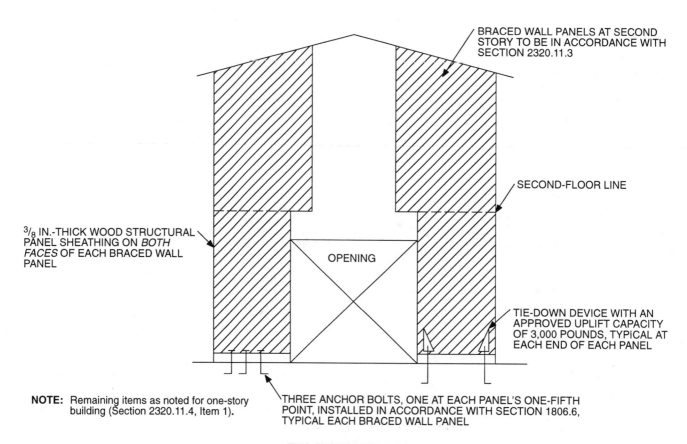

BRACED WALL PANELS AT SECOND STORY TO BE IN ACCORDANCE WITH SECTION 2320.11.3

$3/8$ IN.-THICK WOOD STRUCTURAL PANEL SHEATHING ON *BOTH FACES* OF EACH BRACED WALL PANEL

SECOND-FLOOR LINE

OPENING

TIE-DOWN DEVICE WITH AN APPROVED UPLIFT CAPACITY OF 3,000 POUNDS, TYPICAL AT EACH END OF EACH PANEL

NOTE: Remaining items as noted for one-story building (Section 2320.11.4, Item 1).

THREE ANCHOR BOLTS, ONE AT EACH PANEL'S ONE-FIFTH POINT, INSTALLED IN ACCORDANCE WITH SECTION 1806.6, TYPICAL EACH BRACED WALL PANEL

TWO-STORY BUILDINGS

For **SI:** 1 inch = 25.4 mm, 1 foot = 304.8 mm, 1 pound = 4.45 N.

ALTERNATE BRACED WALL PANELS

FIGURE 2320-19

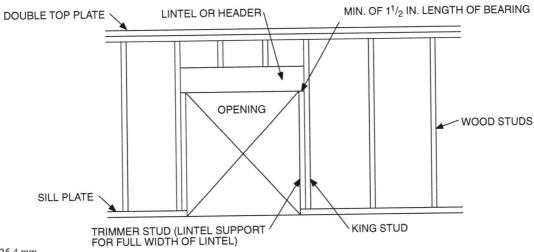

For **SI:** 1 inch = 25.4 mm.

LINTEL OVER WALL OPENING

FIGURE 2320-20

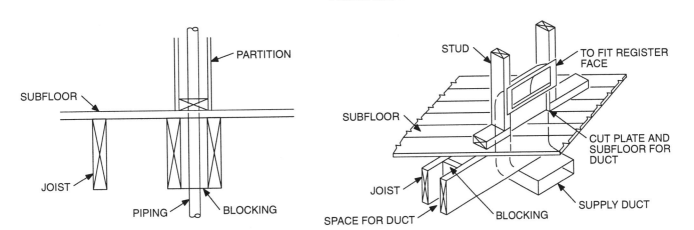

FLOOR FRAMING TO ACCOMMODATE PIPING AND DUCTWORK

FIGURE 2320-21

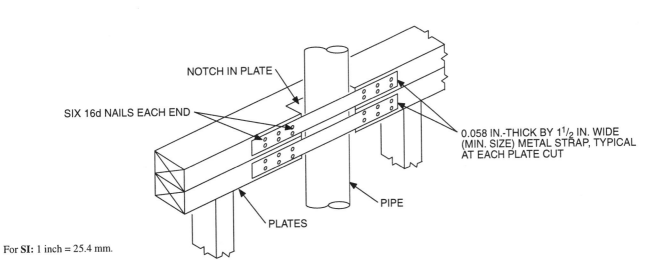

For **SI:** 1 inch = 25.4 mm.

PLATE FRAMING TO ACCOMMODATE PIPING

FIGURE 2320-22

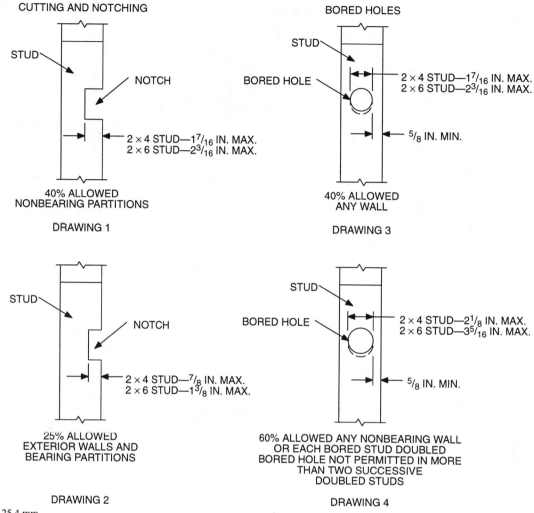

CUTTING AND NOTCHING

STUD

NOTCH

2 × 4 STUD—1⁷/₁₆ IN. MAX.
2 × 6 STUD—2³/₁₆ IN. MAX.

40% ALLOWED
NONBEARING PARTITIONS

DRAWING 1

BORED HOLES

STUD

BORED HOLE

2 × 4 STUD—1⁷/₁₆ IN. MAX.
2 × 6 STUD—2³/₁₆ IN. MAX.

⁵/₈ IN. MIN.

40% ALLOWED
ANY WALL

DRAWING 3

STUD

NOTCH

2 × 4 STUD—⁷/₈ IN. MAX.
2 × 6 STUD—1³/₈ IN. MAX.

25% ALLOWED
EXTERIOR WALLS AND
BEARING PARTITIONS

DRAWING 2

STUD

BORED HOLE

2 × 4 STUD—2¹/₈ IN. MAX.
2 × 6 STUD—3⁵/₁₆ IN. MAX.

⁵/₈ IN. MIN.

60% ALLOWED ANY NONBEARING WALL
OR EACH BORED STUD DOUBLED
BORED HOLE NOT PERMITTED IN MORE
THAN TWO SUCCESSIVE
DOUBLED STUDS

DRAWING 4

For **SI:** 1 inch = 25.4 mm.

**MAXIMUM ALLOWED NOTCHING AND DRILLING FOR NORMAL
CONSTRUCTION WITH 2 BY 4 STUD**

FIGURE 2320-23

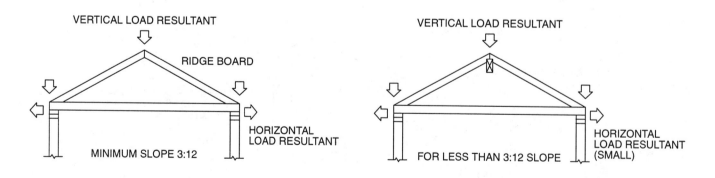

VERTICAL LOAD RESULTANT

RIDGE BOARD

HORIZONTAL
LOAD RESULTANT

MINIMUM SLOPE 3:12

VERTICAL LOAD RESULTANT

HORIZONTAL
LOAD RESULTANT
(SMALL)

FOR LESS THAN 3:12 SLOPE

NOTE: For open beam or sloped ceilings, the ridge beam must be a designed member in order that horizontal forces are reduced.

ROOF FRAMING

FIGURE 2320-24

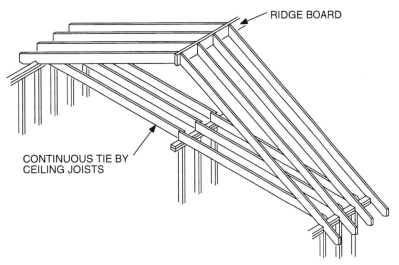

ROOF FRAMING WITH CEILING JOISTS PARALLEL TO RAFTERS

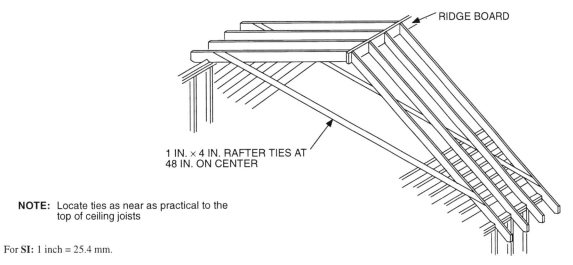

NOTE: Locate ties as near as practical to the top of ceiling joists

For **SI:** 1 inch = 25.4 mm.

ROOF FRAMING WITH CEILING JOISTS NOT PARALLEL TO RAFTERS

RAFTER TIES

FIGURE 2320-25

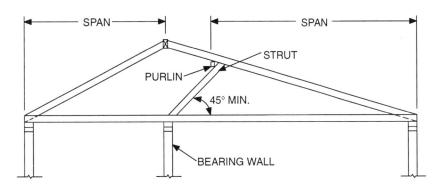

NOTE: Rafters must frame opposite each other at the ridge (Section 2320.12.3).

PURLINS

FIGURE 2320-26

REFERENCES

[1]American Forest & Paper Association (1991). *National Design Specification for Wood Construction.* Washington, D.C.

[2]United States Department of Agriculture (1974). *Wood Handbook No. 72.* United States Government Printing Office.

[3]Western Wood Products Association (1983). *Western Wood Use Book.* Portland, Oregon.

[4]American Institute of Timber Construction (1985). *Timber Construction Manual.* John Wiley and Sons, Incorporated, New York City.

Chapter 24

GLASS AND GLAZING

Chapter 24 regulates glass and glazing for essentially two reasons:

1. To protect against breakage due to building distortion under lateral loads or due to wind loads applied more or less perpendicularly to the surface of the glass.

2. To protect against accidental impact by individuals adjacent to the glazing.

SECTION 2401 — SCOPE

2401.1 General. This chapter applies to exterior glass and glazing in all occupancies except Groups R and U Occupancies less than four stories in height and in low-wind areas. Because these latter two occupancies do not have a record of any problems with exterior glass and glazing (except for human impact), they are subject only to the provisions of Section 2406 addressing safety glazing. The code intends that all exterior or interior glazing subject to human impact in all occupancies in all buildings comply with Section 2406.

SECTION 2402 — IDENTIFICATION

Since glass is not manufactured at the building site and is usually incorporated into assemblies which are not manufactured at the building site, the code requires that the glass and glazing be identified as to type and thickness so that the building inspector may determine compliance with this chapter as far as permitted areas of glass are concerned.

SECTION 2403 — AREA LIMITATIONS

Exterior glass and glazing are subject to the same loads as the exterior cladding of a building; therefore, the code requires that glass and glazing be designed for the same wind loads specified in Part II of Chapter 16 for cladding. This design will also include the increased pressures on local areas at discontinuities. Based on the specified wind loads in pounds per square foot (kg/m^2), the area of the individual glass lights is required by the code to be determined from the areas set forth in UBC Graph 24-1 as adjusted by Table 24-A. Table 24-A provides adjustment factors for glazing materials other than plate, float or sheet glass.

The building inspector is then able to determine whether the glass or glazing in a building is in conformance with the code by knowing the type of glass and thickness from the identification and by utilizing Graph 24-1 and Table 24-A. The areas shown in Graph 24-1 are based on square glass lights and are considered to be adequate for rectangular shapes up to a length-to-width ratio of 5 to 1. The graph also assumes that the glass will be installed in a more or less vertical position and will have firm supports on all four edges.

SECTION 2404 — GLAZING SUPPORT AND FRAMING

Glass firmly supported on all four edges is considerably stronger than a glass light with one or more free edges. As a result, where the glass does not have firm support on four edges, the code requires that a design for the glass be submitted to the building official for approval. In this latter case, the design would be based on the number and location of free edges.

Section 2404.2 was added to the 1994 edition to limit deflection of the framing members for each glass pane.

SECTION 2405 — LOUVERED WINDOWS AND JALOUSIES

The requirements for louvered windows are based on there being no edge support on the longitudinal edges. Moreover, for safety purposes the code requires that the exposed glass edges be smooth. For the same reason, wired glass, when used in jalousies or louvered windows, shall have no exposed wire projecting from the longitudinal edges.

SECTION 2406 — SAFETY GLAZING

2406.2 Identification. The code requires identification for safety glazing for similar reasons as for ordinary annealed glass not subject to human impact. However, in the case of safety glazing the requirement carries more detail since improperly installed annealed glass in areas of human impact can create such a serious hazard. Therefore, it is doubly important that the glazing material be identified so that everyone can be assured that the proper glazing material is in place. Not only does proper marking assist in the inspection process, it also helps identify a location where safety glazing must be installed should future replacement be required. The code specifically requires the use of permanent labels and identification marks for glazing installed in hazardous locations.

2406.3 Human Impact Loads. The code requires that glazing in hazardous locations subject to human impact comply with Part I of UBC Standard 24-2. Part I of the standard is essentially the test standard developed by the Consumer Product Safety Commission (CPSC) when it determined that the former standards (such as Part II of UBC Standard 24-2) were inadequate to properly protect the public from injury due to accidental impact with glazing. The code excepts polished wired glass in smoke- and draft-control and fire assemblies from compliance with Part I if it complies with Part II of the standard. The problem is that wired glass cannot pass the test requirements of Part I, but its use is necessary in fire assemblies. Also, the code considers it adequate for glazing of fixed panels, such as in Items 6 and 7 of Section 2406.4. The other eight locations listed in Section 2406.4 are considered to be too hazardous to permit wired glass. Except for wired glass, other glazing materials used in fire assemblies installed in hazardous locations must comply with Part I of the standard.

2406.4 Hazardous Locations. This section lists ten specific hazardous locations where safety glazing is required. Some of these locations are shown in Figures 2406-1 through 2406-8. In addition to the hazardous locations shown in the eight drawings, safety glazing is also required for a number of other conditions, including fixed and sliding panels of sliding door assemblies, storm doors, bathtub and shower enclosures, pool and spa enclosures, and glass railings.

Figure 2406-1 illustrates several locations where safety glazing may or may not be required. To facilitate discussion, each panel has been numbered. Panel 1 is not required to have safety glazing because a protective bar has been installed in compliance with Exception 2, the requirements of which are illustrated in Figure 2406-2. Panels 2 and 3 will be discussed along with Panels 8 and 9. Panels 4 and 7 require safety glazing because they are door side lights. Exception 2 does not apply to panels adjacent to a door, so even though Panel 7 has been provided with a protective bar, safety glazing is still required. Figures 2406-3 and 2406-4 illustrate when safety glazing is required for panels adjacent to a door. This requirement applies for both fixed and operative panels. Where there is an intervening wall or a permanent barrier as shown in Figure 2406-5, safety glazing would not be required.

Panels 8 and 9, as well as Panels 2 and 3, fall under Item 7 of Section 2406.4. Under this item, all four stated conditions must occur before safety glazing is required. These conditions are:

1. The area of an individual pane must be greater than 9 square feet (0.84 m^2);

2. The bottom edge must be less than 18 inches (457 mm) above the floor;

3. The top edge must be more than 36 inches (914 mm) above the floor; and

4. One or more walking surfaces must be within 36 inches (914 mm) measured horizontally from the glazed panel.

Panels 2 and 3 do not require safety glazing because their bottom edges are not less than 18 inches (457 mm) from the floor. If Panels 8 and 9 have a walking surface within 36 inches (914 mm) of the interior, safety glazing would be required. Otherwise, it would not. [Remember that from the exterior side as shown in Figure 2406-1, the bottom of the panel appears to be greater than 18 inches (457 mm) above the exterior walking surface, so the exterior condition would have no bearing on the determination.] Panels 5 and 6 are glass doors, which require safety glazing. All ingress and egress doors (except jalousies), unframed swinging doors, and glazing in storm doors require safety glazing. There are several exceptions. If openings in a door will not pass a 3-inch-diameter (76 mm) sphere, the door is exempt, as are assemblies of leaded, faceted or carved glass used for decorative purposes. The latter exception not only applies to

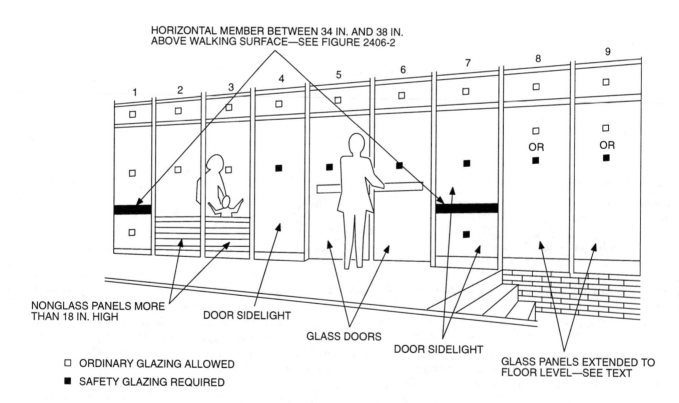

HORIZONTAL MEMBER BETWEEN 34 IN. AND 38 IN.
ABOVE WALKING SURFACE—SEE FIGURE 2406-2

NONGLASS PANELS MORE THAN 18 IN. HIGH

DOOR SIDELIGHT

GLASS DOORS

DOOR SIDELIGHT

GLASS PANELS EXTENDED TO FLOOR LEVEL—SEE TEXT

□ ORDINARY GLAZING ALLOWED

■ SAFETY GLAZING REQUIRED

For **SI:** 1 inch = 25.4 mm.

HAZARDOUS LOCATIONS

FIGURE 2406-1

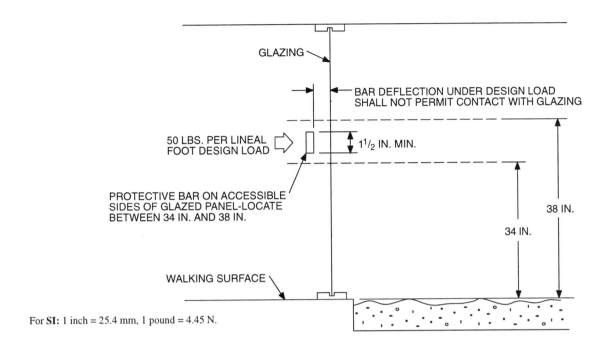

GLAZING

BAR DEFLECTION UNDER DESIGN LOAD
SHALL NOT PERMIT CONTACT WITH GLAZING

50 LBS. PER LINEAL
FOOT DESIGN LOAD

1$^1/_2$ IN. MIN.

PROTECTIVE BAR ON ACCESSIBLE
SIDES OF GLAZED PANEL-LOCATE
BETWEEN 34 IN. AND 38 IN.

38 IN.

34 IN.

WALKING SURFACE

For **SI:** 1 inch = 25.4 mm, 1 pound = 4.45 N.

FIGURE 2406-2

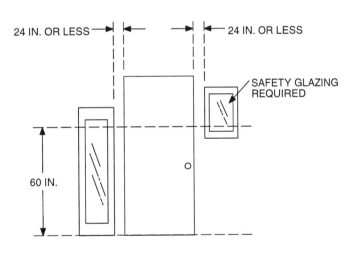

24 IN. OR LESS

24 IN. OR LESS

SAFETY GLAZING
REQUIRED

60 IN.

For **SI:** 1 inch = 25.4 mm.

GLASS IN SIDELIGHTS—ELEVATION

FIGURE 2406-3

doors, but also to side lights and other glazed panels covered by Item 7.

Figure 2406-6 illustrates the condition where a window occurs within a shower. If this window is less than 60 inches (1524 mm) above a standing surface and drain inlet, then safety glazing would be required. This same requirement applies not only to showers but also to windows installed adjacent to hot tubs, whirlpools, saunas, steam rooms and bathtubs. Because of the presence of moisture, all of these locations represent slip hazards and need safety glazing to prevent injury in case of a fall.

Glass in railings, baluster panels and in-fill panels, regardless of height above a walking surface, require safety glazing. This requirement was added as Item 8 to the 1988 UBC. See Section 2406.6.

Items 9 and 10 were added to the 1994 UBC. Figure 2406-7 illustrates the requirements of Item 9, which was revised on the 1997 UBC. The provision applies to walls and fences used as a barrier for either indoor or outdoor swimming pools and spas. Before safety glazing is required, the glazed panels must be within 5 feet (1524 mm) of the pool or spa water's edge and have its bottom edge less than 60 inches (1524 mm) above the deck-

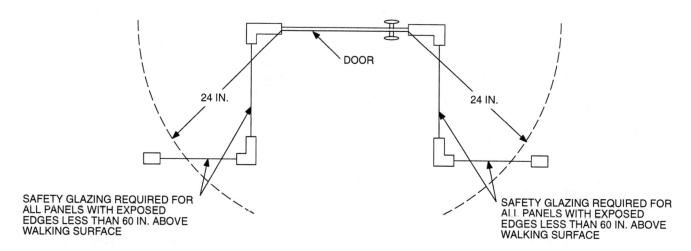

For **SI:** 1 inch = 25.4 mm.

GLASS IN SIDELIGHTS—PLAN

FIGURE 2406-4

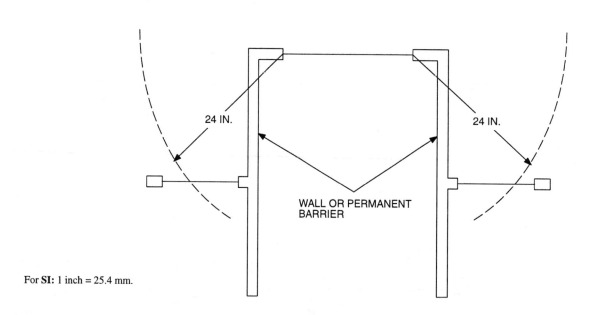

For **SI:** 1 inch = 25.4 mm.

FIGURE 2406-5

ing. Item 10 requires the installation of safety glazing for walls enclosing stairway landings or walls within 5 feet (1524 mm) of the top or bottom of stairways when the bottom edge of the glazing is less than 60 inches (1524 mm) above the walking surface. Figure 2406-8 illustrates the applications of Item 10.

2406.5 Wardrobe Doors. Section 2406.5 contains requirements for glazing in wardrobe doors. These requirements apply only where there is no backing for the mirrors. In this case the impact test standard is based on Part II of UBC Standard 24-2, except that the impact testing is modified to require more im-

pacts from the impacting object, thus providing a more difficult test to pass than the one provided by Part II.

2406.6 Glass Railings. The increasing use of glass, usually tempered, to act as balustrade panels, prompted the inclusion of these provisions in the 1988 edition of the UBC. *Webster's Third New International Dictionary of the English Language, Unabridged,* copyright 1986, defines balustrade as "a row of balusters topped by a rail or a low parapet or barrier." Balusters are technically vase shaped, but in recent years have become merely vertical posts used structurally to support a rail. These provisions will help provide uniform regulation by identifying the

(Continued on page 349)

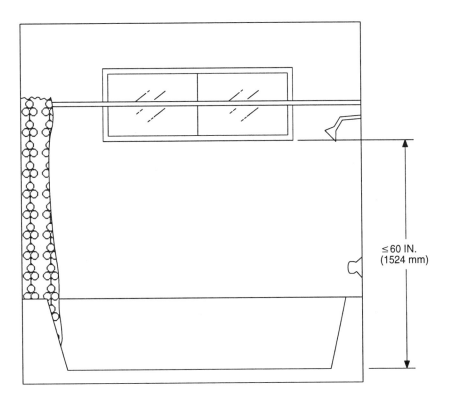

FIGURE 2406-6

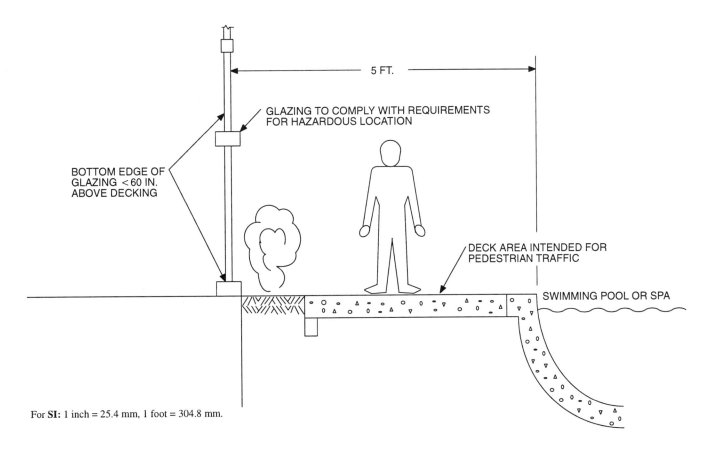

For **SI:** 1 inch = 25.4 mm, 1 foot = 304.8 mm.

FIGURE 2406-7

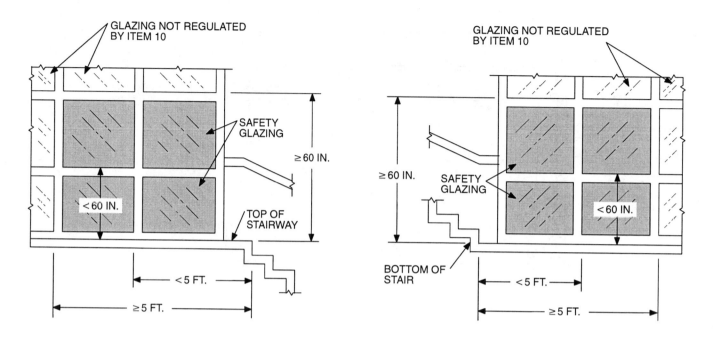

GLAZING NOT REGULATED BY ITEM 10

SAFETY GLAZING

≥ 60 IN.

< 60 IN.

TOP OF STAIRWAY

< 5 FT.

≥ 5 FT.

GLAZING NOT REGULATED BY ITEM 10

≥ 60 IN.

SAFETY GLAZING

< 60 IN.

BOTTOM OF STAIR

< 5 FT.

≥ 5 FT.

ELEVATION

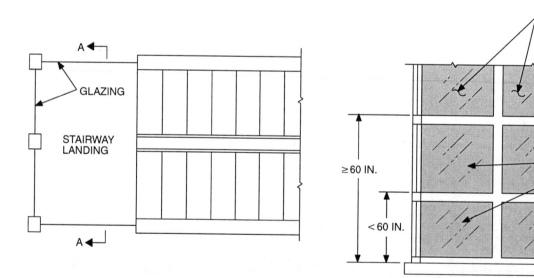

A

GLAZING

STAIRWAY LANDING

A

For **SI:** 1 inch = 25.4 mm, 1 foot = 304.8 mm.

GLAZING NOT CONSIDERED TO BE IN HAZARDOUS LOCATION

≥ 60 IN.

SAFETY GLAZING

< 60 IN.

STAIRWAY LANDING

SECTION A-A

PLAN

FIGURE 2406-8

(Continued from page 346)

specific types of safety glazing that may be used structurally (as balustrade panels). Fully tempered or laminated heat-strengthened glass are the only types considered by the code to be structurally adequate for this use so critical to life safety. Design criteria are also included by reference to Chapter 16. However, the building official will have to approve the basic strengths used in the design, as they are not provided in the code.

SECTION 2407 — HINGED SHOWER DOORS

This section is related to an individual becoming trapped in a small shower compartment rather than to glass and glazing hazards and would seem to logically belong in Chapter 29.

SECTION 2408 — RACQUETBALL AND SQUASH COURTS

These provisions, new to the 1988 edition, prescribe the test criteria for safety glazing materials used in squash and racquetball courts.

SECTION 2409 — SLOPED GLAZING AND SKYLIGHTS

Sloped glazing and skylights consist of glazing installed in roofs or walls that are on a slope of 15 degrees or more from the vertical. The provisions of the UBC are intended to protect these glazed openings from flying firebrands and to provide adequate strength to carry the loads normally attributed to roofs. The provisions are also intended to protect the occupants of a building from the possibility of falling glazing materials.

2409.2 Allowable Glazing Materials. Glazing materials and protective measures for sloped glazing and skylights are outlined in this section. The materials and their characteristics and limitations are as follows:

- **Laminated glass.** Laminated glass is usually furnished with an interlayer of polyvinylbutyrate, which has a minimum thickness of 0.030 inch (0.76 mm) for frames greater than 16 square feet (1.5 m^2) or those higher than 12 feet (3658 mm) above a walking surface. All others the minimum thickness is 0.015 inch (0.38 mm). Such glass is highly resistant to impact and, as a result, requires no further protection below.

- **Tempered glass.** Tempered glass is glass that has been specially heat treated or chemically treated to provide high strength. When broken, the entire piece of glass immediately breaks into numerous small granular pieces. Because of its high strength and manner of breakage, tempered glass had been considered in the past to be a desirable glazing material for skylights without any protective screens. However, as a result of studies by the industry which show that tempered glass is subject to spontaneous breakage such that large chunks of glass may fall under this condition, the UBC now requires screen protection below tempered glass.

- **Annealed glass.** Annealed glass is subject to breakage created by impact, has very low strength and is unsatisfactory as a glazing material in skylights and sloped glazing.

Annealed glass has a further unsatisfactory characteristic for use as a skylight as it breaks up under impact into large sharp shards which, when they fall, are hazardous to occupants of a building. Annealed glass is permitted a very limited use in sloped glazing and skylights as discussed under Section 2409.3.

- **Heat-strengthened glass.** Heat-strengthened glass is glass that has been reheated to just below its melting point and then cooled. This process forms a compression on the outer surface and increases the strength of the glass. However, heat-strengthened glass has the unsatisfactory characteristic of breaking into shards, as does annealed glass. Thus, heat-strengthened glass requires screen protection below the skylight to protect the occupants from falling shards.

- **Wired glass.** Wired glass is resistant to impact and, when used as single-layer glazing, requires no additional protection below.

- **Approved rigid plastics.** See discussion in this handbook under Section 2603.7.

2409.3 Screening. The use of protective screens was discussed somewhat in Section 2409.2. Multiple-layer glazing systems are now used quite often for skylights and sloped glazing due to energy conservation requirements. Where this is the case and where the layer of glazing facing the interior is laminated glass, the code permits the omission of the protective screen below the skylight. However, when heat-strengthened, fully tempered and wired glass is used as the layer facing the interior, screen protection is required below the skylight.

The exception permitting fully tempered glass in near vertical wall sections is based on the low height plus the very low probability of breakage.

Annealed glass may be used only (and is permitted without screening) under the following three circumstances:

1. Where the accessible area below is permanently protected from falling glass.

2. In greenhouses under the limitations outlined in Exception 3.

Where the size of the panel and height above the walking surface or accessible area is limited, Exception 4 allows unscreened glazing based on the incidence of injury due to breakage being extremely low. The use of the exception is limited to installations within an individual dwelling unit.

2409.4 Framing. This is an omnibus section containing requirements related to:

- Combustibility of materials, and
- Leakage protection of the skylight juncture with the roof.

This section logically requires that skylight frames be constructed of noncombustible materials when erected on buildings for which the code requires noncombustible roof construction. Where combustible roof construction is permitted by the code, combustible skylight frames are also permitted.

The provision requiring a curb at least 4 inches (102 mm) above the plane of the roof for mounting skylights is intended to provide a means for flashing between the skylight and the roofing to prevent leaks around the margin of the skylight. The 4-inch (102 mm) curb then provides a vertical surface up which the flashing can be extended and to which counterflashing may be attached to cover the flashing.

2409.5 Design Loads. In keeping with the intent of the code, this section of the UBC requires that skylights be designed to carry tributary roof loads as required in Section 1605. As Graph 24-1 and Table 24-A refer to glazing in a more or less vertical plane subjected to short-time wind loads, the factor of 2.67 has

been applied to provide necessary safety for glazing in a horizontal plane subjected to gravity loads.

2409.6 Floors and Sidewalks. The provisions of this section are intended to provide adequate strength for skylights or light-transmitting panels in sidewalks or floors. Thus, the design would be as required by the code for sidewalks or floors in Chapter 16, except where the light-transmitting panel is protected by a guardrail. In this latter case, the code requires that the strength be based on roof loads as specified in Section 1605.

Chapter 25

GYPSUM BOARD AND PLASTER

This chapter regulates the covering materials for walls and ceilings:

- To provide weather protection for the exterior of the building.
- To secure the material to the wall and ceiling framing so that it will remain in place during the expected life of the building.
- To resist lateral forces on wood stud vertical diaphragms in accordance with Section 2513.

Where these materials are used or required for fire-resistive construction, the code requires that they also comply with the provisions in Chapter 7.

SECTION 2501 — SCOPE

This chapter of the UBC covers the installation requirements for wall- and ceiling-covering materials, including their method of fastening and, in the case of plaster, the permitted materials for lath, plaster and aggregate.

Although plaster has many uses, including ornamental and decorative work, its use in the UBC is regulated purely as a wall- and ceiling-covering material.

The *Uniform Building Code* regulates the installation of wall- and ceiling-covering materials as well as the quality standards for the materials themselves. The primary wall- and ceiling-covering materials in use today are gypsum wallboard, lath and plaster, and wood paneling. As wood paneling is covered in Chapter 23, it follows then that Chapter 25 regulates gypsum wallboard, lath and plaster. However, in this section the code permits the installation of other wall- and ceiling-covering materials, provided the materials have been approved. On this basis, the ICBO ES reports can be consulted for other materials.

Gypsum wallboard is a relatively new material for covering walls and ceilings. On the other hand, plaster is among the oldest of building materials in current use. The use of gypsum plaster dates back to about 4000 B.C. when the Egyptians applied it to the interior and exterior of the pyramids.[1]

SECTION 2503 — VERTICAL ASSEMBLIES

2503.1 General. Vertical assemblies (walls and partitions) are required by this section to be designed in accordance with the engineering chapters of the codes for proper performance of the wall covering. If the wall or partition construction and assembly are not designed to resist the loads prescribed in the code, the wall-covering materials will undoubtedly fail or at least perform inadequately. The provisions of Section 1610 and the deflection limitations are particularly important in this regard.

2503.2 Wood Framing. The minimum dimensions required by this section for wood supports for lath or gypsum board are intended to prevent fastener failures and surface distortion due to warping of the wood supports.

2503.3 Studless Partitions. Figure 2503-1 shows a solid plaster studless partition. As its name implies, it is a partition constructed solidly of plaster and lath without framing studs. Thus, the lath and plaster form the structural elements of the partition to resist lateral loads. These partitions are used as nonbearing partitions, but they must meet the deflection and load-carrying requirements specified in Section 1610.

SECTION 2504 — HORIZONTAL ASSEMBLIES

The code requirements for the design and framing of horizontal assemblies (ceilings) are intended to achieve the same results as described for vertical assemblies.

As visualized by the UBC, suspended ceilings generally consist of ceiling framing in which a metal grid of either metal channels or T-bars is suspended by steel wire ties from the structure above. Light fixtures and acoustical, fire-resistive or other types of panels are inserted between the metal framing members. *Uniform Building Code* Table 25-A provides framing requirements for suspended ceilings. However, it should be noted that where a suspended ceiling is designed in accordance with the prescriptive requirements of UBC Standard 25-2, the provisions of Table 25-A do not apply.

Although a suspended ceiling system may be structurally designed to utilize any type of framing and framing members that meet the intent of the code as far as strength and load-carrying capability are concerned, most suspended ceiling systems constructed today are constructed in accordance with the provisions of UBC Table 25-A or UBC Standard 25-2.

Lightweight suspended ceilings. *Uniform Building Code* Standard 25-2 prescribes construction that may be used for lightweight suspended ceilings. The standard is referenced by Footnote 1 to Table 25-A. At this point it is worth noting that Part III of the standard addresses lateral-force bracing requirements for these lightweight ceilings. Although the use of Standard 25-2 is optional—that is, a structural design showing compliance with Chapter 16 could be provided—there are two sections in Part III that are intended to be mandatory for all lightweight suspended ceiling construction: Sections 25.213 and 25.214. (The intent that these are mandatory provisions is borne out by Footnote 11 to Table 16-N.) These two sections provide specific installation requirements for light fixtures and mechanical service equipment. Of particular importance in Seismic Zones 3 and 4 is the requirement that light fixtures and mechanical services be independently supported from the structure above.

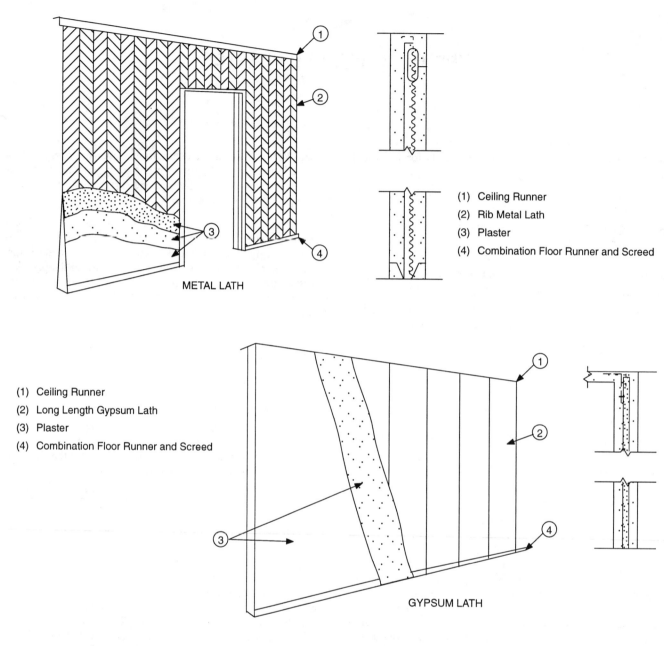

(1) Ceiling Runner
(2) Rib Metal Lath
(3) Plaster
(4) Combination Floor Runner and Screed

METAL LATH

(1) Ceiling Runner
(2) Long Length Gypsum Lath
(3) Plaster
(4) Combination Floor Runner and Screed

GYPSUM LATH

SOLID PLASTER STUDLESS PARTITION
FIGURE 2503-1

SECTION 2505 — INTERIOR LATH

2505.1 General. Because gypsum plaster, gypsum board and gypsum lath are subject to deterioration from moisture, the code restricts their use to interior locations and weather-protected surfaces and requires that interior gypsum lath not be installed until the installation has been weather protected. The protection with an approved moisture barrier required by the code for interior wood framing, which is covered with portland cement plaster, tile or similar material and which is subject to water splash, is to prevent alternate wetting and drying which can cause fungus attack (dry rot).

2505.2 Application of Gypsum Lath. Since gypsum lath functions as the plaster base, it must be properly installed to avoid cracking and premature failure of the plaster. Gypsum lath has a special paper on the side to be plastered, which is mechanically engaged by the long crystals formed when gypsum plaster sets; as a result, a very tight adhesive and mechanical bond is created between the base coat of plaster and the gypsum lath.

Because of this tight bond, discontinuities in the lath can create cracking of the plaster. Therefore, the code requires that the ends of the gypsum lath boards be staggered so they do not all occur on the same stud or ceiling joist. Where the joints are continuous, the code requires that they be reinforced with strip lath. The strip lath is usually a strip of expanded metal lath that is fastened to the gypsum lath along the discontinuity to reinforce the plaster.

Proper installation requires the edges of the gypsum lath to be in moderate contact. However, where the joint gaps exceed $3/8$ inch (9.7 mm), they should be covered with metal strip lath or cornerite. Cornerite is similar to metal strip lath except it is formed into a right angle to reinforce interior corners where two plaster surfaces join.

2505.3 Application of Metal Plaster Bases. Metal lath has another function in addition to acting as a plaster base. It also acts as a plaster reinforcement.

As metal lath provides a relatively flexible base for the plaster, lath continuity is even more important to prevent cracking. Structural discontinuities occur with metal lath at the edges and ends of the sheets. The problem of discontinuities can be overcome by proper overlapping of the sheets at edges and supports and by securely fastening the ends of sheets together where end laps do not occur over supports. A typical metal stud interior lath and plaster partition is depicted in Figure 2505-1.

SECTION 2506 — EXTERIOR LATH

2506.3 Backing. Proper application of exterior plaster requires that the base coat be thoroughly pushed through the lath to provide a proper mechanical bond. For this reason, it is necessary (and required by the code) that the lath or the backing for the lath provide sufficient rigidity to permit the proper application of plaster. A common method of providing the backing for exterior plaster over open wood-stud framing is to horizontally fasten 18-gage wire backing (string wire) to the studs at 6 inches (152 mm) on center.[2] It is important that the wire be stretched tightly across the studs to provide the proper rigidity for the backing.

Because metal lath or paperbacked wire fabric lath has reinforcing ribs to provide the necessary rigidity, the code requires no further backing for these materials.

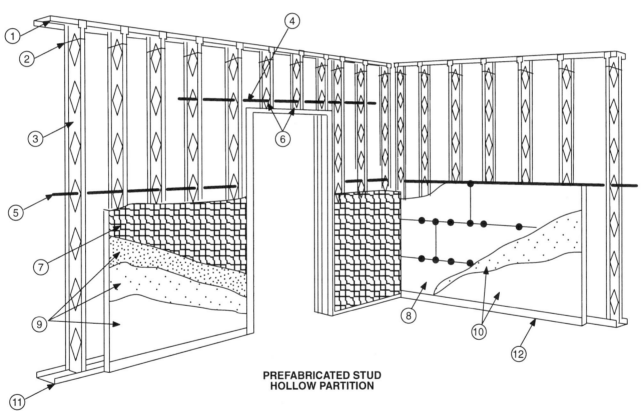

**PREFABRICATED STUD
HOLLOW PARTITION**

(1) Ceiling Runner Track	(8) Gypsum Lath (clipped on)
(2) Stud Shoe (wire tied)	(9) Three Coats of Plaster (Scratch, Brown, Finish)
(3) Prefabricated Stud	(10) Two Coats of Plaster (Brown, Finish)
(4) Door Opening Stiffener	(11) Floor Runner Track
(5) Partition Stiffener	(12) Flush Metal Base
(6) Jack Studs	
(7) Metal or Wire Fabric Lath (wire tied)	

LATH AND PLASTER APPLICATION TO INTERIOR METAL STUD PARTITION

FIGURE 2505-1

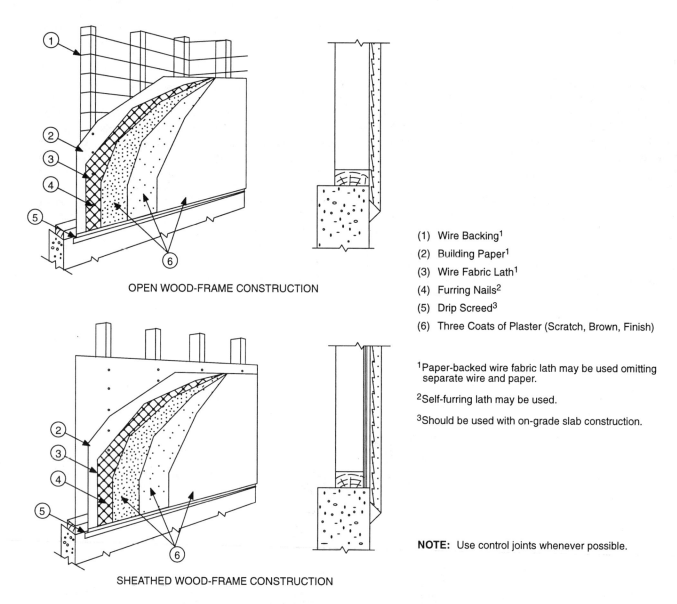

OPEN WOOD-FRAME CONSTRUCTION

SHEATHED WOOD-FRAME CONSTRUCTION

(1) Wire Backing[1]

(2) Building Paper[1]

(3) Wire Fabric Lath[1]

(4) Furring Nails[2]

(5) Drip Screed[3]

(6) Three Coats of Plaster (Scratch, Brown, Finish)

[1]Paper-backed wire fabric lath may be used omitting separate wire and paper.

[2]Self-furring lath may be used.

[3]Should be used with on-grade slab construction.

NOTE: Use control joints whenever possible.

LATH AND PLASTER APPLICATION TO EXTERIOR WOOD STUD WALLS

FIGURE 2506-1

2506.4 Weather-resistive Barriers. The code requires a weather-resistive barrier to be installed behind exterior plaster for the reasons discussed for the provisions of Section 1402. Furthermore, the code requires that when the barrier is applied over wood-base sheathing such as plywood, for example, the barrier shall be two layers of Grade D paper. This requirement is based on the observed problems where one layer of a typical Type 15 felt is applied over wood sheathing. The wood sheathing eventually exhibits dry rot because moisture penetrates to the sheathing. Cracking is created in the plaster due to movement of the sheathing caused by alternate expansion and contraction. Field experience has shown that where two layers of building paper are used, penetration of moisture to the sheathing is considerably decreased, as is the cracking of the plaster due to movement of the sheathing caused by wet and dry cycles. The Grade D paper is specified because it has the proper water vapor

permeability to prevent entrapment of moisture between the paper and the sheathing.

2506.5 Application of Metal Plaster Bases. Metal lath plaster bases require a mechanical bond to the plaster and actual embedment in the plaster in order to reinforce it. Thus, the code requires that the lath be furred out from the vertical supports or backing a minimum of $1/4$ inch (6.4 mm). An exterior lath and plaster wall of wood-stud construction is illustrated in Figure 2506-1.

Water can penetrate exterior plaster walls for a variety of reasons. Once it penetrates the plaster, the water will run down the exterior face of the weather-resistive barrier until it reaches the sill plate or mudsill. At this point the water will seek exit from the wall, and if the exterior plaster is not applied to allow the water to escape, it will exit through the inside of the wall and

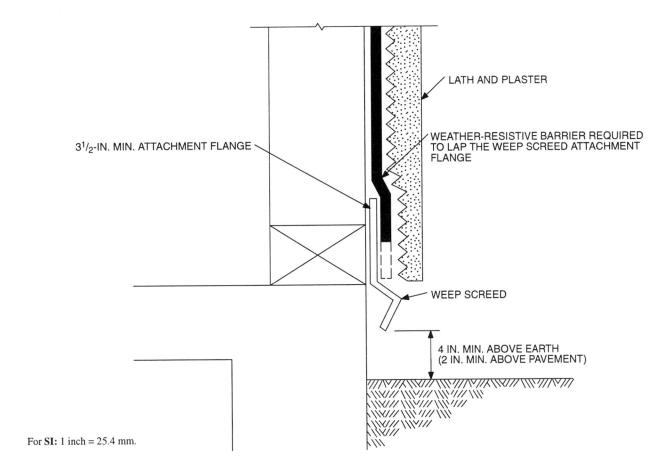

3¹/₂-IN. MIN. ATTACHMENT FLANGE

LATH AND PLASTER

WEATHER-RESISTIVE BARRIER REQUIRED TO LAP THE WEEP SCREED ATTACHMENT FLANGE

WEEP SCREED

4 IN. MIN. ABOVE EARTH (2 IN. MIN. ABOVE PAVEMENT)

For **SI:** 1 inch = 25.4 mm.

FIGURE 2506-2

leak into the building. Thus, the code requires a weep screed which, when constructed as shown in Figure 2506-2, will permit the escape of the water to the exterior of the building.

Added in the 1994 edition is a provision requiring that the weather-resistive barrier lap the weep screed's vertical flange. This revision was made to correlate weep screed requirements with the weather-resistive barrier requirements in Section 1402.1. Although Section 2506.5 does not specify the amount of overlap, at least 2 inches (51 mm) should be provided in keeping with the weather-resistive barrier lap requirements of Section 1402.1.

SECTION 2507 — INTERIOR PLASTER

2507.1 General. Multicoat plastering has been the standard in the western world for at least 100 years.[2] It is generally the consensus of the industry that, particularly where plaster application is by hand, multicoat work is necessary for control of plaster thickness and density. Most of the materials used for plaster densify under hand application due to the pressure applied to the trowels, and it is believed that this change in density is more controllable and will be of a more uniform nature where the plaster is applied in thin, successive layers. For these reasons, the UBC requires three-coat plastering over metal or wire lath and two-coat work applied over other plaster bases approved for use

by the code. Reducing the requirement for plaster bases other than metal or wire lath is based on the rigidity of the plaster base itself. More-rigid plaster bases are not as susceptible to variations in thickness and flatness of the surface. In fact, it may be considered that the first coat applied in three-coat work on a flexible base, such as wire lath, is used to stiffen that base to provide the rigidity necessary to attain uniform thickness and surface flatness.

Fiber insulation board does not have the qualities necessary for a good performing plaster base. It absorbs excessive moisture from the plaster mix, creating problems of workmanship, and it does not have the stability and rigidity required for a proper functioning plaster base. Also, in the colder and damper climates, the fiberboard insulation retains the moisture absorbed from the plaster for a relatively longer period of time than other bases, causing premature failure of the plaster. For these reasons, the code prohibits its use as a plaster base.

Portland cement plaster is highly susceptible to drying shrinkage during curing. Therefore, the scratch and brown coats in dry climates will generally require moist curing where water spray is applied to the base coat for a period of at least 24 hours for interior work. Certainly, if the job conditions are such that moisture will be retained in the plaster for the required time period, moist curing is not required.

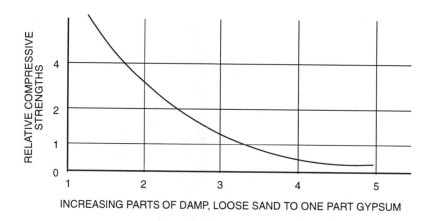

**RELATIVE COMPRESSIVE STRENGTHS FOR GYPSUM BASECOAT
PLASTERS WITH SAND AGGREGATE**

FIGURE 2507-1

Because portland cement plaster does not bond properly to gypsum plaster bases, the code prohibits its use over gypsum plaster bases. However, the code permits exterior plaster to be applied on horizontal surfaces, soffits, etc., over gypsum lath and gypsum board when used as a backing for metal lath.

Plaster grounds are utilized to establish the thickness of plaster and usually are wood or metal strips attached to the plaster base. The intent is that plaster grounds are used as a guide for the straightedge in determining the thickness. In many cases, door and window frames are used as plaster grounds.

2507.2 Base Coat Proportions. The proportions required by the code for plaster mixes are based on a long history of the use of plaster and are those that have been found to generally give satisfactory results under most conditions. As the amount of aggregate is increased in proportion to the amount of cementitious material, additional water is usually required to maintain workability; as a result, the strength of the plaster mix is relatively reduced.

Figure 2507-1 illustrates the relationship between proportions of damp, loose sand aggregate to gypsum plaster in a plaster mix using the amount of water necessary to provide a workable mix. These relative values are only approximate for average conditions, but do represent the trend in strength as compared to the amount of aggregate in the mix.

The art of proportioning plaster mixes does not have the scientific basis as the proportioning of concrete mixes, for example, and is primarily based on the history of satisfactory uses of the various mix proportions. There are many factors that affect the proportions utilized in plaster mixes, but these primarily affect the amount of water necessary more than the proportions of aggregate to cementitious binder. For example, the type of plaster base and the weather (including temperature and wind) have a pronounced effect on the amount of water necessary for a workable mix.

2507.3 Base Coat Application. In plaster work, a base coat is any coat beneath the finish coat. This is true whether the plaster is of two-coat or three-coat application. In three-coat work, the first coat is usually referred to in the trade as the "scratch" coat.

It is usually applied over flexible bases, such as metal or wire fabric lath, and is intended to stiffen the base and provide a mechanical bond to the base. Also, as its name implies, the first coat is scratched with a scarifying tool which provides horizontal ridges or scratches that are intended to provide mechanical keys for the application of the second coat (or brown coat). The brown coat usually constitutes the major bulk of the plaster and, consequently, materially affects the membrane strength. As a result, proportioning and workability are critical, and the mix should have high plasticity for proper application. The term "brown coat" is utilized by the trade to differentiate the relative color of the second coat to the finish coat, which is usually much lighter in color and is sometimes white, depending on the constituents.

2507.4 Finish Coat Application. The base coats in plaster work provide the strength for the plaster membrane but generally do not provide a proper surface texture for a finished surface. Therefore, a thin, almost veneer, coat of plaster is applied to the base coats as a finish coat. The finish coat may be applied in such a manner as to provide an ornamental or decorative finish, or it may be applied as a smooth surface to act as a flat base over which paint and wallpaper may be applied.

2507.5 Interior Masonry or Concrete. Nonlath plaster bases, such as masonry or concrete, provide special problems for plaster as follows:

1. **Concrete.** Because concrete generally has a denser and tighter finish than masonry, a proper plaster bond to concrete requires special preparations. As concrete does not have the suction properties that are present with masonry, the bond between the plaster and concrete surface must be completely mechanical. The surface must be rough, clean and damp. Also, it must be free of any efflorescence. If the surface of the concrete is not adequately rough in order to provide the proper mechanical bond, it may be prepared as follows:

   • If preparation of the surface is to begin before the concrete has completely set, the necessary roughness may be obtained by scarifying the surface with some type of scoring tool or with stiff heavy-duty wire brushes.

- If preparation of the concrete surface is necessary after the concrete has hardened, the surface may be brush hammered or scarified by chisels or other types of scarifying tools.

- Another common method, which is that specified in the code, is to apply a rich mixture of portland cement, sand and water as a dash coat. This application, in which the material is "dashed" on the surface with a coarse brush, may be used only where portland cement plaster is to be applied to the concrete surface.

- Where gypsum plaster is to be applied to a concrete surface, proprietary chemical bonding agents and bond plasters are used as a surface preparation for concrete surfaces. Their use must be approved by the building official.

Where ceiling surfaces of concrete are to be plastered, the code requires that the total thickness of base coat plaster be as set forth in UBC Table 25-D. It will be noted from the table that for ceiling applications on concrete surfaces, the requirement is for a thinner coat than that required for other applications. This is due primarily to the difficulty of acquiring an adequate bond between the plaster and the concrete surface. As the application is horizontal, the weight of the plaster base coat must be kept to a minimum. If it becomes necessary to require a greater thickness due to the unevenness of the concrete surface, the code requires that metal lath or wire-fabric lath be attached to the concrete ceiling to act as the necessary anchorage and reinforcement to support the additional weight.

2. **Masonry.** A masonry plaster base must be prepared in a similar manner to a concrete plaster base when considering cleanliness, dampness and freedom from dust and efflorescence. Furthermore, masonry must present a reasonably flat surface without large indentations or protrusions which will affect the evenness and uniform thickness of the plaster. For this reason, mortar joints should be struck flush.

Masonry plaster bases have varying degrees of suction but generally provide a good adhesive as well as mechanical bond. Most masonry plaster bases have enough suction so that special bonding agents will not be required to provide the proper bond between the plaster and plaster base. However, where harder and denser masonry materials which have very low suction characteristics are used, preparation of the surface as required for concrete surfaces may be necessary, such as mechanical scoring or the use of special bonding agents. Partition tile is manufactured for use in partitions to be plastered and is scored during manufacture to create a mechanical bond.

Conversely, where the masonry surface has too high a suction, particularly for portland cement plasters, the suction can be reduced by dampening the surface of the masonry just prior to plastering. Where dampening is necessary, the surface should be damp, but there should be no free water on the surface, which would indicate a saturated condition.

SECTION 2508 — EXTERIOR PLASTER

2508.1 General. Portland cement plaster is the only material approved by the code for exterior plaster. Gypsum plaster deteriorates under conditions of weather and moisture, which are prevalent on the exterior surfaces of buildings. Exterior portland cement plaster is required by the code to be applied in not less than three coats when applied over metal or wire-fabric lath for the same reasons as discussed for interior plaster. When the portland cement plaster is applied over other approved plaster bases, the code requires only two-coat work. The code permits plaster work that is completely concealed to be of only two coats, provided the total thickness is that required by UBC Table 25-F, since the finish coat of plaster is to provide a surface for exterior finishes (such as paint) and to provide a visibly aesthetic appearance. Thus, where the plaster surface is to be completely concealed, it is not necessary to provide a finish coat.

The code requires that the exterior plaster be installed to completely cover, but not extend below, the lath and paper on wood or metal stud exterior wall construction supported by an on-grade concrete floor slab. This requirement, combined with the requirement in Section 2506.5 for a weep screed, is intended to prevent the entrapment of free moisture and the subsequent channeling of the moisture to the interior of the building. This requirement is depicted in Figure 2508-1.

Admixtures such as plasticizers should not be added to portland cement unless approved by the building official. Some admixtures can have deleterious effects which more than offset the desired improvement in plasticity. It is preferable that plasticizers be added during the manufacture of the cement in order to ensure product uniformity and proper proportions. When plastic cement is used, the code does not permit any further additions of plasticizers as it is assumed that the amount added during the manufacturing process is adequate and is the maximum permitted. Hydrated lime and lime putty are time-tested plasticizers used with portland cement plaster, and their use is permitted by the code in the amounts set forth in UBC Table 25-F.

2508.4 Environmental Conditions. Portland cement plaster is affected by freezing in the same manner as portland cement mortar or portland cement concrete. The application to frozen bases or those covered with frost will not only weaken the bond of the plaster to its base, but will also freeze the layer of plaster adjacent to the frozen base. When portland cement plaster is applied during freezing weather or applied to a frozen base, or if it is mixed with frozen ingredients, it loses a high proportion of its strength and, therefore, does not meet the intent of the code.

2508.5 Curing and Interval. The code requires the moist-curing and time intervals between coats for the same reasons as discussed for interior plaster in Section 2507.

2508.6 Alternate Method of Application. While the majority of experts on the application of plaster generally agree that the first two coats of portland cement plaster should be cured as required by Section 2508.5, there is an increasingly large number who feel that the brown coat could be applied without requiring moist curing of the scratch coat but at least allowing the scratch coat to harden to a condition of sufficient rigidity to accept the second coat. This alternate method of application is also considered by its proponents to be stronger than when the scratch coat has been cured as required by the code. This is due to a manufacturer's claim that a superior bond is produced between the two

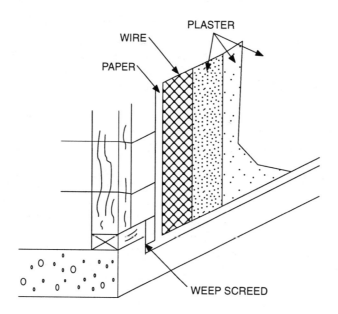

**TERMINATION OF EXTERIOR PLASTER AT ON-GRADE
CONCRETE FLOOR FOR STUD WALLS**

FIGURE 2508-1

coats of plaster when the second coat is applied to a set but un-cured base coat.

To develop a quicker set, the code permits the addition of calcium aluminate cement up to 15 percent of the weight of the portland cement. These high-alumina cements are characterized by a faster set time than portland cement. Because the high-alumina cements do not possess the same high strength and qualities as portland cement in plaster mixes, the code limits their proportion of the total mix.

SECTION 2509 — EXPOSED AGGREGATE PLASTER

Exposed aggregate plaster is a plaster finish used mostly on exterior cement plaster walls, although its use is not restricted to these applications. The intent of using exposed aggregate plaster is to provide an architecturally pleasing surface and texture to the exterior of a building. Two of the more common exposed aggregate finishes are pebble finish and marblecrete. In the former case, the pebbles are usually thrown or dashed against the bedding coat, and then a trowel or other suitable tool is used to press the pebble aggregate into the bedding coat. In the case of marblecrete, marble chips are applied to the bedding coat, and, again, they may be lightly tamped into place with a trowel or other suitable tool.

The code requires that the materials used for the aggregate be nonreactive and moderately hard (3 or harder on the Mohs hardness scale of minerals). The mineral which is used as the identifier for the hardness of 3 is calcite, which in its common form is represented by limestone and marble, to name two examples. By requiring at least this hardness, the code intends to approximate ordinary sand aggregate plaster in durability. For the same reason, the code establishes a minimum compressive strength for the exterior bedding coat of 1,000 pounds per square inch (6894.8 kPa).

Type S lime is a special hydrated lime for masonry purposes, and its use is required in the exterior bedding coat to increase the high early plasticity and water retention. For the increased plasticity, the code requires the relatively richer gypsum plaster for the interior bedding coat.

SECTION 2510 — PNEUMATICALLY PLACED PLASTER (GUNITE)

Pneumatically placed portland cement plaster, also referred to as Gunite in this section, is generically placed with pneumatically placed mortar and pneumatically placed concrete as shotcrete. The plaster differs from pneumatically placed concrete in the proportions of its constituents. The term "Gunite" is a registered trademark and refers to a proprietary system of shotcrete and materials for the handling and deposition of shotcrete.

As pneumatically placed plaster is applied, a certain amount of the material bounces away from the surface to which it is being applied. This material is referred to as rebound. The amount varies depending on several variables, such as air-pressure and placement conditions. This variation ranges from about 30 percent for vertical surfaces to about 20 percent for horizontal or sloping surfaces.[3]

The rebound material must not be used again as plaster because of its low cement content and variable quality, depending on the conditions of application.[3] However, the code permits its use after recovery as a portion of the sand aggregate in the plaster mix, but it must not exceed 25 percent of the total sand in any batch.

When properly proportioned and applied, pneumatically placed plaster is very dense and achieves a high compressive strength. It is particularly useful where the plaster will be used for structural purposes, such as on shear walls of wood and metal stud construction, to resist lateral loads.

SECTION 2511 — GYPSUM WALLBOARD

2511.1 General. For reasons discussed earlier in this chapter, the code does not permit gypsum wallboard to be installed on weather-exposed surfaces or on interior surfaces until weather protection has been provided. See definition in Section 224 for weather-exposed surfaces.

2511.2 Supports. The maximum support spacings permitted by the code are intended to provide a relatively rigid wallboard surface without excessive deflection. See also the discussion in this handbook under Section 1610.

2511.3 Single-ply Application. The application of gypsum wallboard is specified in this chapter for nonfire-resistive construction or construction where diaphragm (shear wall) action is not required. Chapter 7 and fire test reports will establish the means of fastening and supporting the ends and edges of gypsum wallboard for fire-resistive assemblies. In the case of stud walls required for diaphragm action, UBC Table 25-I establishes the sizes and spacing of fasteners as well as the conditions of end and edge support.

The code requires the fit of gypsum wallboard sheets to be such that the edges and ends are in moderate contact. However, wider gaps are permitted in concealed spaces where fire-resistive construction or diaphragm (shear wall) action is not required. This requirement is based primarily on appearance. Therefore, where the wallboard application is concealed, it is not objectionable to have wider gaps than those resulting from moderate contact. However, where the wallboard surface is exposed as it normally is, moderate contact is required so that there will be no objectionable cracking when the joint between sheets is finished.

Uniform Building Code Table 25-G contains the requirements for size and spacing of fasteners. The omission of fasteners specified in this section is qualified in the UBC by the expression "except on shear-resisting elements or fire-resistive assemblies." This qualifying exception is intended to indicate that where a fire test report or UBC Table 25-1 indicates that fasteners are required on supports or edges, the fastening may not be omitted.

The intent of the requirement that the fastener head not fracture the face of the paper is to provide a tight fastening but not damage the plaster board to the extent its nail-holding power may be affected. Proper construction procedure for the nailing of gypsum wallboard panels is to use a drywall hammer which has a crowned head and to use wallboard nails which have concave heads. Figure 2511-1 illustrates the case where a drywall hammer is used and the drywall nail is not overdriven. The intent is to create a dimple in the plaster board with no projection of the nail head above the plaster board.

2511.4 Two-ply Application. Two-ply application of gypsum wallboard is generally intended to increase the fire resistance of the assembly, increase the shear-resisting strength of the assembly or increase the sound transmission class for the assembly. Chapter 7 specifies the fastener size and spacings required for fire-resistive construction, and UBC Table 25-H provides fastener sizes and spacing for nonfire-resistive construction and nonshear wall construction. Table 25-I provides the fastener sizes and spacings for shear wall construction.

2511.5 Joint Treatment. Although in this section the UBC requires joint treatment for single-layer fire-rated assemblies, the code also specifies exceptions where the wallboard is to receive a decorative finish or any other similar application which is considered to be equivalent to the joint treatment. In addition, an ex-

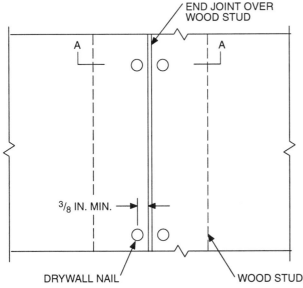

ELEVATION OF WALL

For **SI:** 1 inch = 25.4 mm.

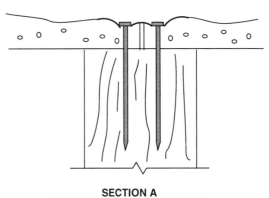

**SECTION A
SHOWING CORRECT DIMPLING**

GYPSUM WALLBOARD NAILING

FIGURE 2511-1

ception indicates that the joint treatment is not required for assemblies tested without joint treatment. Also, joint treatment is not required where joints occur over wood-framing members. In general, joint treatment does not materially increase the fire rating, and many partitions have passed the fire test without joint treatment. As indicated earlier in this section for single-ply application, joint treatment is primarily used for aesthetic reasons and to prepare a satisfactory base for the application of surface finishes such as paint or wallpaper. However, where fire tests indicate that joint treatment was used in the test, the code requires that joint treatment be applied. Moreover, where the fire test report or the assemblies listed in UBC Tables 7-B and 7-C do not state whether or not joint treatment is required, then Section 2511.5 requires that joint treatment be applied.

SECTION 2512 — USE OF GYPSUM IN SHOWERS AND WATER CLOSETS

This section was added to the 1988 UBC and revised in the 1994 edition. The code intends that water-resistant gypsum board be used as a base for tile or wall panels for tubs, showers or water closet compartment walls. It is used in these locations due to its moisture-resistant qualities. However, in locations subject to continuous moisture, such as in saunas, steam rooms or gang showers, even water-resistant gypsum board exhibits unsatisfactory performance. Except for tubs, showers and water closet compartment walls, regular gypsum board may be used as a backing for tile or wall panels. Prior to the 1994 edition, water-resistant gypsum board was prohibited for use in ceiling installations due to problems with sagging. The material may now be installed on ceilings, provided framing spacing does not exceed 12 inches (305 mm).

SECTION 2513 — SHEAR-RESISTING CONSTRUCTION WITH WOOD FRAME

2513.1 General. The prohibition against using cumulative shear values where different materials are applied to the same wall is based on the fact that different materials will have different strengths and deflection characteristics. Therefore, where plywood is used on one side and gypsum wallboard on the other side of a wall, the load on the shear panel will cause failure of the weaker material (gypsum wallboard) first so that the stronger material (plywood) must resist the entire load without significant assistance from the gypsum wallboard.

Where identical materials are used on both sides of the shear wall, the code provides for the addition of the shear values even when the fastener requirements provide different shear values. The use of the word "additive" also covers the case where the materials have the same shear values. Because the behavior of identical materials under load is the same, load sharing is permitted by the code. This is also true where the gypsum wallboard panels have different thicknesses.

It is important that gypsum wallboard shear walls be identified on the plans to differentiate them from nonshear wall construction. The fastener size and spacing, conditions of edge and end support of panels, size of end posts, and shear connection at base should be detailed or set out in a schedule.

It is always important to read table footnotes, but in the case of Table 25-I, it is extremely important that Footnote 1 be read, particularly when considering designs in Seismic Zones 3 and 4. In these two zones, the design value for gypsum-based products must be reduced by 50 percent.

2513.2 Masonry and Concrete Construction. The code prohibits the use of the materials specified to be used in vertical diaphragms, which resist lateral forces imposed by masonry or concrete construction, because the deflections created may be excessive for the masonry or concrete. The determination of the deflection for these materials in vertical diaphragms is subject to uncertainty, unlike the determination for plywood shear walls.

2513.4 Height-to-Length Ratio. The maximum allowable height-to-length ratios indicated in this section are based on comparison of test results of these assemblies with other tested assemblies having similar shear values and rigidities as shown in UBC Table 23-I-I.

2513.5 Application. Test results of shear walls constructed of the materials listed in this section have shown that the staggering of end joints increases the stiffness of the shear wall and, as a result, reduces the deflection. For this reason, the UBC requires staggered end joints.

The requirement that blocking required by UBC Table 25-I have the same cross-sectional dimensions as the studs is necessary for two reasons:

1. To provide an adequate bearing surface to fasten two adjacent sheets which butt over the blocking.
2. To provide the same depth as the stud to prevent the stud from twisting.

The code requires that gypsum lath be applied perpendicular to the studs. Perpendicular application increases the bracing strength of the material, as each board ties several framing members together rather than just two. Gypsum lath, gypsum sheathing and gypsum wallboard are stronger in their longitudinal direction, and the perpendicular application places the stronger dimension of the board across the framing members.

REFERENCES

[1]Diehl, John R. (1965). *Manual of Lathing and Plastering.* Gypsum Association Edition, Publishers Associations, New York, page 42.

[2]California Lathing and Plastering Contractors Association (1977). *Plaster Metal Framing Systems/Lath Manual.* Building News, Inc., page 75.

[3]Waddell, Joseph J. (1989). *Concrete Manual.* International Conference of Building Officials, Whittier, California, page 299.

Chapter 26

PLASTIC

This chapter covers several topics all related to the use and installation of various types of plastic materials. Included are foam plastic insulation, light-transmitting plastics and plastic veneer. One plastic material not addressed in Chapter 26 is vinyl siding, which is covered in Chapter 14.

SECTION 2602 — FOAM PLASTIC INSULATION

2602.1 General. During the early 1970s the Federal Trade Commission (FTC) investigated the claims made by some manufacturers in the plastics industry of "slow-burning" or "nonburning" as related to foam plastic insulation materials. With assistance from the former National Bureau of Standards (NBS), now called the National Institute of Standards and Technology (NIST), the FTC concluded that these claims were in fact erroneous due to improper testing. Because of the earlier criticisms aimed at the claims, the code changes that were finally adopted into the *Uniform Building Code* were of necessity somewhat conservative.

The provisions were developed by the Society of the Plastics Industry, Inc. (SPI), after numerous meetings, hearings and seminars relating to the hazard characteristics of the materials.

During this time, SPI funded an extensive program of research that reviewed the then-current test procedures, with a goal of establishing new test procedures where necessary to properly reflect the hazard of the material as it would actually be used, in place, in buildings.

The code provisions developed as a result of the extensive research were centered on two basic concepts:

1. A limitation of the flame spread and smoke developed to 75 and 450, respectively.

2. Separation of the foam plastic insulation from the interior of the building by an approved thermal barrier. The adequacy of the thermal barrier is related to its index, which is determined by testing in accordance with UBC Standard 26-2. The code requirement currently is for an index of 15, which is related to the time during which the thermal barrier is expected to remain in place under fire conditions.

2602.2 Labeling and Identification. In addition to the flame-spread and smoke-developed criteria, the code also requires that the containers of foam plastic and foam plastic ingredients be labeled by an approved agency to show that the material complies with the code. There are many foam plastic products on the market that do not comply with the code and that were not intended for use in construction. The labeling requirement is intended to prevent the misapplication of products not designed for this use.

2602.4 Thermal Barrier. The test standard in UBC Standard 26-2 utilizes a small-scale furnace with the time/temperature re-

lationship maintained within the furnace the same as required in the standard fire-endurance test specified in UBC Standard 7-1. The thermal barrier is applied over $^1/_2$-inch-thick (12.7 mm) calcium silicate board to provide reproducibility of results. The calcium silicate board eliminates variables which would result if the thermal barrier is applied over various types of foams or foams having varying densities.

This section of the code also requires a demonstration by approved testing that the thermal barrier will remain in place for the required 15-minute time period. The testing to determine if the barrier will remain in place requires that the barrier be applied over foam plastic of the type for which recognition is requested. Based on testing, it has been found that regular $^1/_2$-inch-thick (12.7 mm) gypsum wallboard fastened in accordance with the UBC will qualify as remaining in place for 15 minutes.[1]

Siding backer board. Where it is desired to insulate exterior walls under exterior siding, the code permits foam plastic to be used as a backer board for the siding containing a potential heat of not more than 2,000 Btu per square foot (22.7 MJ/m^2). The determination of the potential heat is based on a relatively new test standard (UBC Standard 26-1) that was developed by NBS (now NIST). The thermal barrier is not required under these circumstances as long as the siding backer board is separated from the interior of the building by not less than 2 inches (51 mm) of mineral fiber insulation or the equivalent.

The code also permits the siding backer board without a thermal barrier when the siding is applied as residing over existing wall construction. This is reasonable considering the separation provided by the existing construction and the limitations on the potential heat imposed by the code.

Masonry or concrete construction. See Figure 2602-1. When foam plastics are encapsulated within concrete or masonry walls, or floor or roof systems, the code does not require a thermal barrier as long as the foam plastic is covered by a minimum of 1-inch (25 mm) thickness of the masonry or concrete.

Attics and crawl spaces. See Figure 2602-2. This item describes specific methods used to protect foam plastics located within attics and crawl spaces (in lieu of a thermal barrier having an index of 15) where entry is provided only for services of utilities. The phrase "where entry is provided only for services of utilities" is intended to restrict these reduced requirements for a thermal barrier to those unused areas where there are no heat-producing appliances. Thus, the reduced provisions are intended to provide a barrier whose only purpose is to prevent the direct impingement of flame on the foam plastic.

Cold storage construction. Cold storage uses provide a unique use for foam plastic insulation in that thicknesses are generally required to be greater than 4 inches (102 mm) for proper thermal insulation, although 4 inches (102 mm) is about the maximum that can be tested. The code, in all other cases, places limits on the thickness of the foam plastic insulation to

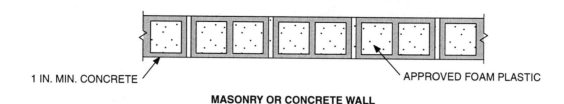

1 IN. MIN. CONCRETE —   APPROVED FOAM PLASTIC

MASONRY OR CONCRETE WALL

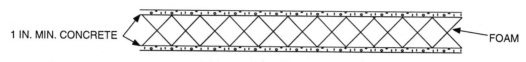

1 IN. MIN. CONCRETE —   FOAM

For **SI:** 1 inch = 25.4 mm.

ROOF OR FLOOR SANDWICH PANEL

ENCAPSULATED FOAM PLASTIC

FIGURE 2602-1

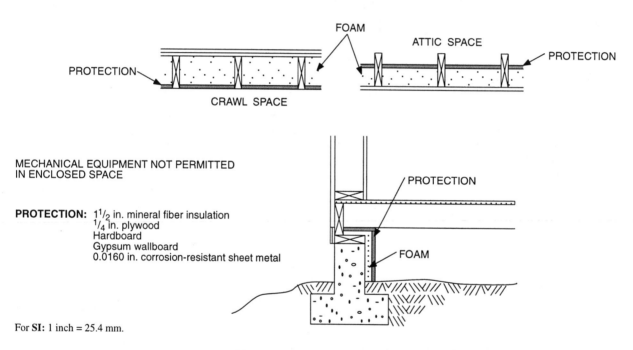

PROTECTION: $1^{1}/_{2}$ in. mineral fiber insulation
                 $1/_{4}$ in. plywood
                 Hardboard
                 Gypsum wallboard
                 0.0160 in. corrosion-resistant sheet metal

For **SI:** 1 inch = 25.4 mm.

FOAM PLASTIC, ATTIC AND CRAWL SPACES

FIGURE 2602-2

that which was tested. However, due to the nature of the use in cold storage facilities, the ignition hazards are not great. Therefore, the code permits foam plastic insulation in greater thicknesses even though tested in a thickness of 4 inches (102 mm). The intent is that the foam plastic will be provided with a protective thermal barrier having an index of 15. In the case of interior rooms within a building, the foam plastic is required to be protected on both sides with a thermal barrier having an index of 15.

Provisions are included to permit freestanding coolers and freezers without a thermal barrier, provided the foam plastic has a flame-spread rating of 25 or less; has minimum allowable flash and self-ignition temperatures of 600°F and 800°F (316°C and 427°C), respectively; and the foam is protected by 0.032-inch-thick (0.8 mm) aluminum or 0.0160-inch-thick (0.4 mm) steel. The cooler or freezer and the portion of the building where the cooler or freezer is located must be sprinklered in this case. Again, the code presumes that with a low-hazard use, such as a cold storage and freezer box, the metal covering will prevent the actual impingement of any flames on the foam plastic, and the sprinkler system will provide the cooling necessary to maintain proper low temperatures to prevent ignition of the foam plastic.

Where freestanding coolers and freezers have an aggregate floor area of less than 400 square feet (37.2 m[2]), the code contains an exception which, in effect, provides for no thermal barrier and no sprinkler protection as long as the foam plastics comply with the general provisions of Section 2602.3.

Exterior garage doors. In Group U, Division 1 Occupancies, a thermal barrier is not required in exterior garage doors since such do not pose a great risk to the occupants. Other doors containing foam plastic are covered in Section 2602.5.5.

2602.5 Special Provisions. Sections 2602.3 and 2602.4 cover the general use of foam plastic insulation, and this section covers specific cases and applications. These are as follows:

Noncombustible exterior walls. For one-story buildings, metal-clad sandwich panels with foam plastic cores with thicknesses up to 4 inches (102 mm) are permitted to be installed without a thermal barrier, provided the metal cladding complies with the provisions outlined in the code and, furthermore, the building is protected with automatic fire sprinklers. In this case, the code assumes that the protection and cooling effect provided by automatic sprinklers is a reasonable alternative to the thermal barrier.

In addition, the requirements for foam plastic insulation allow the material in buildings that are of fire-resistive or noncombustible construction. Section 2602.5.2.2 applies to exterior walls of such buildings of any height. It requires that the wall be tested in accordance with UBC Standard 26-4 or 26-9. These tests provide a method of evaluating the wall's resistance to fire spread from story to story. Section 2602.5.2.2 also requires that test data be provided to show that if a fire-resistive rating is required, the rating of the wall containing the foam maintains the required rating. Moreover, the foam plastic insulation:

1. Must be separated from the interior of the building with a thermal barrier having an index rating of 15.

2. Must not have a potential heat content of more than 6,000 Btu per square foot (68.2 MJ/m^2) of wall area, and neither the exterior coating nor the foam plastic can have a flame-spread rating of more than 25, nor can the smoke-development rating exceed 450.

Roofing. This item covers three different cases (see Figure 2602-3 for the first two cases) involving roof-covering assemblies:

1. The use of foam plastic insulation as part of a Class A, B or C roofing assembly in which the foam plastic and the roof covering are tested as an integral unit. The test standard used is the Standard Test for Determination of Fire Retardancy of Roof Coverings, UBC Standard 15-2. In this case, the code requires that the plastic foam have a minimum flame-spread rating of 75 and that it be separated from the interior of the building by a thermal barrier having an index of 15. Clearly there is no need for limitations on smoke development, as the tars and asphalt used in roofing assemblies would have a smoke-developed rating greatly exceeding 450.

2. This case again involves the use of Class A, B or C roof assemblies in which the foam plastic insulation is also considered to be an integral part of the assembly. Here, a nationally recognized test standard for insulated roof decks should be utilized, although the Class A, B or C roofing assembly must also, by itself, meet the criteria of UBC Standard 15-2. Factory Mutual's Fire Test Standard for Insulated Roof Deck Construction could serve as an appropriate test since it is listed as a recognized standard. This test standard for insulated roof deck construction should be adequately conservative so that assemblies passing either of the two test methods in the standard are considered to meet the intent of the code without any limit on flame spread or smoke development. Furthermore, no thermal barrier is required.

3. The last case involves nonrated roofing assemblies or roofing coverings as described in Section 1504.4. As there are generally no test standards for these prescriptive assemblies, the code provides that they may be applied over foam plastic when the foam is separated from the interior of the building by $^1/_2$-inch-thick (12.7 mm) wood structur-

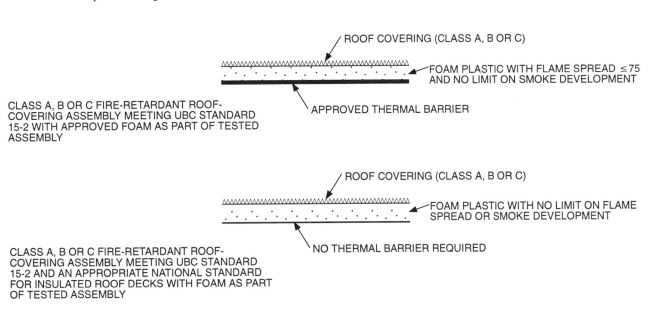

CLASS A, B OR C FIRE-RETARDANT ROOF-COVERING ASSEMBLY MEETING UBC STANDARD 15-2 WITH APPROVED FOAM AS PART OF TESTED ASSEMBLY

ROOF COVERING (CLASS A, B OR C)

FOAM PLASTIC WITH FLAME SPREAD ≤75 AND NO LIMIT ON SMOKE DEVELOPMENT

APPROVED THERMAL BARRIER

ROOF COVERING (CLASS A, B OR C)

FOAM PLASTIC WITH NO LIMIT ON FLAME SPREAD OR SMOKE DEVELOPMENT

NO THERMAL BARRIER REQUIRED

CLASS A, B OR C FIRE-RETARDANT ROOF-COVERING ASSEMBLY MEETING UBC STANDARD 15-2 AND AN APPROPRIATE NATIONAL STANDARD FOR INSULATED ROOF DECKS WITH FOAM AS PART OF TESTED ASSEMBLY

FOAM PLASTIC USED WITH ROOF COVERINGS

FIGURE 2602-3

al panel sheathing bonded with exterior glue. The edges of the wood structural panel sheathing must be supported by blocking or be tongue-and-groove construction or of any other approved type of edge support. In this case, the thermal barrier is waived as well as the smoke-developed rating.

Based on the rationale that the $^1/_2$-inch-thick (12.7 mm) wood structural panel provides an adequate separation for ordinary roof-covering assemblies, it is also acceptable for a tested assembly. Thus, it is the intent of the UBC that any roof-covering assembly installed over foam plastic may be installed with only a $^1/_2$-inch (12.7 mm) wood structural panel separation between the assembly and the interior of the building. Where the $^1/_2$-inch (12.7 mm) wood structural panel separation is utilized, it is important to recognize that the joints must be protected even though the roofing specimen used during the fire-retardancy test might have been installed over wood structural panels with abutted joints without any supplemental protection.

Doors. Pivoted or side-hinged doors not required to have a fire-resistive rating are permitted to be installed without the thermal barrier, provided the door facings are of sheet metal of the thicknesses prescribed in this section. The rationale behind the waiver of the thermal barrier is that the foam plastic is completely encapsulated within the sheet metal facings, and the quantity of foam plastic in doors so protected is quite small.

2602.5.5 Garage doors. Garage doors used in other than Group U Occupancies that contain foam plastic are allowed based on the development of UBC Standard 26-8. Previous to the standard, these doors were not allowed without a thermal barrier or by complying with Section 2602.5.4. This was a cumbersome requirement for the manufacturers and one that was proved not necessary given the new test methodology. These criteria were used successfully by the ICBO Evaluation Services prior to their incorporation into the UBC. This section is intended to regulate the commercial applications of overhead, sectional and tilt-up types of doors.

2602.6 Specific Approval. In this section the code provides for those cases where foam plastic products and their protective coverings do not comply with the specification requirements of Section 2602. These specific approvals are based on testing which is related to the actual end use of the products. The code refers to UBC standards as test standards for determining specific approvals, and, in addition, there are others which utilize some variation of the room test and are designed for testing exterior wall applications. Of the UBC standards, UBC Standard 26-3 is a relatively new standard that was adopted after several years of development and establishes criteria for the so-called room test or corner test.

SECTION 2603 — LIGHT-TRANSMITTING PLASTICS

2603.1 General.

2603.1.1 Scope. It is the intent of this section to regulate the use of light-transmitting plastics—those plastics used in the building envelope or with interior lighting to transmit light to the interior of the building. Light-transmitting plastics are regulated because they are combustible materials. The unregulated use of

combustible materials in the roof structure and for the exterior walls can possibly defeat the intent of the provisions of the code relating to types of construction. Thus, Section 2603 regulates these materials so that they do not materially affect the other requirements of the code regarding types of construction.

2603.1.2 Approval for use. Any use of light-transmitting plastic materials must be approved by the building official and be based on technical data submitted to substantiate their use. As a basis of this approval, the building official will refer to Chapter 2 for the definition of "plastic materials, approved." The definition includes criteria for the approval of plastic materials and also classifies plastic materials as either CC1 or CC2, classifications which are defined in UBC Standard 26-7, Method of Test for Determining Classification of Approved Light-transmitting Plastic. The ICBO ES reports also contain data referencing certain assemblies of light-transmitting plastics, such as skylights.

2603.1.4 Combination of glazing and exterior wall panels. Light-transmitting plastics can be used in exterior walls as glazing for windows and as light-transmitting panels. It is the intent of the code that where both plastic-glazed windows and exterior wall panels are used, the applicable area, height, percentage and separation requirements are those in the code for light-transmitting exterior wall panels.

2603.1.5 Combination of roof panels and skylights. Light transmission through the roof can be obtained either by skylights glazed with light-transmitting plastics or by roof panels utilizing light-transmitting plastics. Where they are combined, the code specifies that they shall be subject to the area, percentage and separation requirements which apply to roof panel installations. In this case and with exterior walls, the requirements for the panels are more restrictive than for either plastic-glazed openings or skylights.

2603.4 Glazing of Unprotected Openings. Since plastic glazing materials are combustible, their use is limited to openings not required to be fire protected. In the case of building construction other than Type V-N, their use is restricted. The glazing of openings not required to be fire protected in Type V-N construction is essentially unlimited as to the area, height, percentage and separation requirements applicable to the individual glazed openings.

For plastic-glazed openings in buildings other than Type V-N, restrictions are placed on the area, height, percentage and separation requirements for the individual glazed openings because plastic glazing materials are combustible. In Type V One-hour construction, unprotected combustible materials must be limited in accordance with their areal extent and separation. Because of the combustibility of plastic glazing, the code requires flame barriers at each floor level for multistory buildings to prevent the transmission of flame from one story to another by way of the combustible openings.

As with other provisions of the code limiting the height of combustible materials above grade, this section also limits the height of plastic materials above grade to 65 feet (19 812 mm).

2603.5 Light-transmitting Exterior Wall Panels. Exterior wall panels are regulated for the same reason as plastic glazing in openings. However, because exterior wall panels are sheet materials, they generally constitute larger unbroken areas than plastic glazing for openings do; as a result, their burn rate characteristics are more critical than those for plastic glazing in openings.

2603.6 Roof Panels. Plastic roof panels are regulated on the basis of whether or not the roof of the building is required to have a fire-resistive rating. Thus, the combustibility of the roof assembly is not a factor because the code considers noncombustible roof construction and combustible roof construction to be affected in about the same way as far as the amount and extent of plastic roof panels are concerned.

Because plastic roof panels constitute unprotected openings in the roof, the code requires that they be separated from each other by 4 feet (1219 mm) horizontally. Furthermore, their location on the roof is regulated in the same fashion as wall openings with respect to proximity to a property line or public way.

Because Class CC1 plastics have a slower burn rate than Class CC2 plastics, the code limits Class CC2 plastics to smaller areas than allowed for Class CC1 materials. As with exterior wall panels, the actual numbers relating to area, height and separation requirements must be somewhat arbitrary, but are reasonable code limits determined by a consensus of knowledgeable experts.

2603.7 Skylights.

2603.7.1 General. In this section the requirements for skylights are more detailed than those for roof panels in Section 2603.6 because there is no limit on the type of construction or fire-protection requirements for the roof assembly. Furthermore, skylights have unique requirements, such as those for flashing and resistance to burning brands. Also, as plastic-glazed skylights provide an unprotected combustible assembly in the roof, limitations must be placed on the area, percentage and separation of each unit. Also, each unit's location on the roof relative to property lines is regulated in a similar fashion as plastic roof panels are regulated.

The problems of plastic-glazed skylights are related to flashing at the intersection with the roof and to their ability to resist the effects of flying, burning brands. Therefore, the code, with one exception, requires that they be mounted on a curb at least 4 inches (102 mm) above the plane of the roof so that proper flashing may be accomplished. The exception involves self-flashing skylights on roofs of dwellings which have a minimum slope of 3 units vertical in 12 units horizontal (25% slope). This slope should provide adequate roof drainage to accommodate self-flashing skylights. The slope requirements for flat or corrugated plastic- glazed skylights and the rise requirement for dome-shaped skylights are based on the skylights' ability to shed flying brands. However, when the glazing material in the skylights can pass the Class B burning brand test specified in UBC Standard 15-2, there is no limitation on slope, either of flat or corrugated glazed skylights, or on rise in the case of dome-shaped skylights.

The requirement for the protection of the edges of plastic-glazed skylights or domes is to prevent the rapid spread of fire along the roof, as the edges of the plastic glazing material ignites more readily than the interior portions. The edges of some types of plastic ignite no more readily than the interior, and where tests show that the edges offer equivalent fire protection to the protection specified by the code, their use in skylights is warranted. Also, where Class C roof coverings are permitted by the code, there is no need for the protection of the edges.

As with roof panels, the various limitations on area, percentage and separation of skylights are somewhat arbitrary and, as with roof panels, are based on a consensus among knowledgeable experts on what is reasonable.

2603.7.2 Plastics over stair shafts. The intent of this section is to permit the use of approved plastics as vents for stairways and shafts, provided they can be vented by the use of a firefighter's ax or similar tool. However, the limitations in Section 2603.7.1 regarding materials, area, percentage and separation of skylights are maintained.

2603.8 Light-diffusing Systems. Light-diffusing systems regulated in this chapter are of two types:

1. Light-diffusing systems that are generally suspended below the light fixtures in a building and, in some cases, may cover the complete areal extent of a room.

2. Light diffusers that are attached directly to individual light fixtures.

The light-diffusing systems (sometimes referred to as luminous ceilings) are regulated by the UBC either as interior finish (to comply with the requirements in Chapter 8) or as "drop-out" systems which fall from their mountings under action of heat before ignition. On this latter basis, the code in this section provides the four criteria that must be met to qualify as a drop-out-type ceiling. The intent of these four requirements is twofold:

1. To ensure that the diffusing systems remain in place except during fire conditions, at which time the temperature criteria are such that they will fall out of their mountings before ignition.

2. The light-diffusing systems are limited in size in order to prevent a premature fallout due to excessive length or weight. The limitation on the percentage of area covered by light-diffusing systems in exits is to prevent blocking the exit if the panels were to fall.

Obviously, if plastic light-diffusing systems were to interfere with the effective spray pattern of sprinkler systems, the code should not permit their use. This potential problem is more troublesome with those systems which do not have fallout characteristics. If tests show that the design of the diffusing system is such that the effectiveness of sprinkler operation is not reduced, the code permits their installation. Drop-out panels should be designed to fall out of their supports at a temperature reasonably below the activation temperature for the sprinklers so that they will not have a detrimental effect on the flow and spray characteristics of the sprinklers.

2603.12 Greenhouses. Even though they are combustible materials, approved plastics are permitted by the code to be used in greenhouses in lieu of plain glass due to the very low occupant load and fuel load.

2603.13 Canopies. The criteria in this section for approved plastic panels installed in canopies over motor vehicle pumps are intended to isolate the combustible materials from other buildings so that if the materials become ignited, they will not present an exposure problem to other buildings.

2603.14 Solar Collectors. This section regulates plastic covers on solar collectors under the specified limitations. The provisions are intended to create a reasonable limitation on the buildings which may utilize the plastic covers on solar panels. As with skylights and roof panels, the limitations on the plastics are intended to limit the total amount of combustible material on the roofs of buildings. These limitations are reasonably consistent with the requirements of Sections 2603.6 and 2603.7.1, Item 5. The exception deletes the requirements for approved plastics where the plastic covers have a thickness of 0.010 inch (0.3 mm) or less, as the amount of combustibles is relatively low for these thinner materials.

Although not stated in this chapter, it is the intent of the code that, where solar collectors utilizing plastic covers are placed on buildings having skylights or roof panels of approved plastics, the limitations on area and percentage of cover applicable to roof panels must be applied to the total area of roof panels or skylights and solar collector covers.

SECTION 2604 — PLASTIC VENEER

Since it is a combustible material, plastic veneer used in the interior of a building is required by the code to comply with the interior finish requirements of Chapter 8.

Where plastic veneer is used on the exterior of a building, the code requires that the veneer be of approved plastic materials as defined in Chapter 2. This places severe restrictions on the combustibility and smoke development of the plastic materials. Be-cause plastic materials are combustible, the code limits their attachment on any exterior wall to a height no greater than 50 feet (15 240 mm) above grade. Furthermore, the UBC limits the area of plastic veneer to 300 square feet (27.9 m^2) in any one section and requires each section to be separated vertically by a minimum of 4 feet (1219 mm). The 4-foot (1219 mm) separation helps control rapid vertical spread of fire. The code anticipates that local firefighting forces can effectively fight a fire that involves plastic veneer up to a height of about 50 feet (15 240 mm). Also, if the plastic veneer involves too large of an area, it is conceivable that a fire could overtax local firefighting forces. The exception applies to Type V-N buildings where the walls are not required to have a fire-resistive rating. In this case, the plastic materials do not present a greatly different hazard than the unprotected wood construction.

REFERENCE

[1]Nosse, John N. (1979). Enforcement of foam plastic regulations. *Building Safety*, 48(2): 14-16, 18, 20. (This March-April issue of *Building Safety* was a special combined issue jointly published by ICBO, BOCA and SBCCI. This issue superseded the March and/or April issues of the magazines usually published by the three model code agencies.)

Chapters 27, 28 and 29

SPECIALTY CODES

Electrical, Mechanical and Plumbing

Three chapters were added to the 1994 UBC: one for each of the primary specialty codes used to regulate building service equipment. Chapter 27 is for electrical systems and merely contains a reference to the Electrical Code. Chapter 28 is for mechanical systems and contains both a reference to the Mechanical Code and specific requirements for refrigeration system machinery rooms. The last of the specialty code chapters, Chapter 29, is for plumbing systems. Chapter 29 references the Plumbing Code and contains provisions for the number of required fixtures and water closet compartment geometry. A discussion of the provisions in Chapters 28 and 29 follows.

addresses exit requirements for refrigeration machinery rooms and requires the doors to be tightfitting and self-closing.

Section 2802 states that "nothing contained herein shall be used to limit the height or area of the building or the machinery room." The intent here is to isolate refrigeration machinery rooms, but not to apply Group H, Division 7 area or height limitations to the machinery room or to the building in which they are housed nor to apply the mixed occupancy provisions of Section 504.3. There is no specific area limitation placed on machinery rooms, but since the *Uniform Mechanical Code* has strict limits on access to and use of machinery rooms, no one is going to make one any larger than necessary.

Chapter 28

MECHANICAL SYSTEMS

Chapter 29

PLUMBING SYSTEMS

SECTION 2802 — REFRIGERATION SYSTEM MACHINERY ROOM

This section was added so that those who use the UBC would be aware of the requirements of the Mechanical and Fire codes as they affect machinery room installations. A refrigeration machinery room is defined in the *Uniform Mechanical Code* as a space designed to safely house compressors and pressure vessels. Chapter 11 of the UMC covers refrigerants, and Section 1106.1 establishes when a refrigeration machinery room is required.

Refrigeration machinery rooms are considered to be health hazard occupancies and are classified as Group H, Division 7 because many of the new refrigerants replacing CFCs pose a greater health risk, which the code needs to address. As such they must be separated from other occupancies and be located on the property as required for Group H, Division 7 Occupancy.

An exception is granted for the horizontal portion of the occupancy separation, although it is not expressed in the section as an exception. Section 302.2 requires that structural members supporting a horizontal occupancy separation be protected by equivalent fire-resistive construction. The exception permitted for refrigeration machinery rooms is that the supporting structural members need only comply with type-of-construction requirements, not with occupancy separation requirements.

For example, the separation required between a Group H, Division 7 and a Group B Occupancy is one hour. If the building housing the Group B Occupancy is Type V-N construction, the structural supporting elements need not have one-hour protection because the occupancy separation is intended to restrict the potential spread of toxic refrigerants, not fire spread. This intent justifies the reduction in fire-resistive rating. One interesting thing about the occupancy separation is that neither Section 2802 nor Section 302 address how the doors for the separation must fit or seal. For this, one must go to Section 1020.2, which

SECTION 2902 — NUMBER OF FIXTURES

Section 2902 establishes the number of plumbing fixtures which must be provided for various occupancies. However, these requirements are minimal and, except for a Group E Occupancy, set forth no user/fixture ratio that a designer may use as a guide for providing adequate toilet facilities. Appendix Chapter 29, however, was added in the 1994 UBC and provides such information. This appendix chapter is also referred to in the discussion of Section 2903.

The number of accessible unisex toilet and bathing rooms added in the 1997 UBC is also to be included in the determination of the number of fixtures in a building. These elements are not intended to be in addition to the count generated from Table A-29-A.

2902.2 Group A Occupancies. This section does not establish the number of fixtures required, but it does require one lavatory for every two water closets for each sex. Although the section does not specifically state that you must provide separate facilities for each sex, the requirement for the number of lavatories strongly implies that you must do so.

2902.3 Groups B, F, H, M and S Occupancies. This section requires that toilet facilities be provided for employees, not the general public, and that when more than four persons are employed, there shall be a facility for each sex. The second paragraph of the section addresses toilet facilities in food establishments, requiring, among other things, that hand-washing facilities be provided in the water closet room or nearby. Interestingly, there is no requirement to provide hand-washing facilities in the general provision. Determining the number of employees in a given establishment, particularly smaller ones, is not easy, since the code provides no guidance. It would not be appropriate to use Table 10-A since the table considers total anticipated occupancy, which would include customers as well as employees. A visit to a similar establishment may be required.

One aspect of this section that is often overlooked is that all buildings on a given site are not required to have toilet facilities. Section 2902.3 allows toilet facilities to be located in an adjacent building on the same property. The section does require this location to be convenient, but it does not specifically define the term. The dictionary defines convenient as being near at hand, so whether or not an adjacent location is convenient becomes a judgment call.

2902.4 Group E Occupancies. This is the one part of Section 2902 that includes a ratio for the number of fixtures. A certain number of water closets, urinals and lavatories are required for boys and girls, and this number depends on whether the facility is an elementary or secondary school. With the ever-changing organization in education, it may not be as clear today when secondary schooling begins as it was over 30 years ago when the provisions first appeared in the code.

2902.5 Group I Occupancies. These occupancies must have toilet facilities as required by the preceding section for employees and must, beginning with the 1994 edition, have additional facilities for occupants other than employees when the employee facilities are not generally accessible. This provision was added because often patients and visitors do not have access to employee facilities.

2902.6 Group R Occupancies. In keeping with the intent of the code to provide healthful, livable living conditions in residential buildings, Section 2902.6 requires certain minimum sanitary facilities for residential buildings. Hotels must have at least one water closet for each sex when public water closet compartments are furnished. Dwelling units require a minimum of a kitchen equipped with a kitchen sink and a bathroom provided with a water closet, lavatory, and either a bathtub or shower. Lodging houses and congregate residences require at least one bathroom provided with a water closet, lavatory, and either a bathtub or shower. The sinks, bathtubs, showers and lavatories are also required to be equipped with hot and cold running water necessary for their normal use. The use of the word "normal"

intends that bar sinks, for example, need not be provided with hot water since hot water is not necessary for their normal use.

SECTION 2903 — ALTERNATE NUMBER OF FIXTURES

For those who want or need user/fixtures ratios, they have been provided in UBC Appendix Chapter 29. Like all appendix chapters, this one is not legally binding unless specifically adopted, but even when not adopted, it does provide designers with guidance. The appendix chapter contains Table A-29-A, which contains fixture requirements for Groups A, B, E, F, I, M, R and S Occupancies. In addition, educational facilities beyond the secondary level—that is, colleges, universities, adult education centers, and the like—which are not Group E Occupancy, have a unique listing. Note that the Group E Occupancy requirements of Table A-29-A differ from those of Section 2902.4 and will result in slightly more fixtures. Drinking and dining establishments classified as Group B Occupancies are evaluated along with Group A Occupancies.

The table is applied assuming a 50-50 male-female split of the calculated occupancy, and the occupancy is determined not by the use of Table 10-A, but rather as indicated within each section of Table A-29-A. For example, for Group B Occupancies, other than drinking or dining facilities, an occupancy factor of 200 square feet (18.58 m^2) per occupant is used, while for a Group S Occupancy, the factor is 5,000 square feet (464.5 m^2) per occupant.

Because some communities have requirements dictated by health regulatory agencies, particularly for food and beverage uses, the provisions of the local jurisdiction should be consulted.

SECTION 2904 — ACCESS TO WATER CLOSET STOOL

The title of this section may be a bit misleading. It does not address accessibility as covered by Chapter 11. Rather, the section covers the minimum clearances required in front and on the sides of water closet stools.

Chapter 30

ELEVATORS, DUMBWAITERS, ESCALATORS AND MOVING WALKS

Chapter 30 of the UBC was extensively revised for the 1985 edition of the code to provide more-current requirements and to provide detailed requirements for installation and operation in Appendix Chapter 30. For the detailed provisions, Appendix Chapter 30 adopts ASME/ANSI A17.1-1987 with 1988 and 1989 supplements, *Safety Code for Elevators and Escalators,* published by the American Society of Mechanical Engineers.

SECTION 3001 — SCOPE

Chapter 30 applies to all automatic passenger elevators, regardless of the use of the building, number of stories in the building, number of floors served or the vertical distance traveled by the elevator car. There are a few exceptions in the Elevator Code and in UBC Sections 3003.4 and 3003.7. One exception in the Elevator Code is that the requirement for a commandeering switch in automatic elevators does not apply to elevators within dwelling units.

SECTION 3002 — ELEVATOR AND ELEVATOR LOBBY ENCLOSURES

The first paragraph is essentially a cross-reference to Section 711 of the code, which contains the specific requirements for the enclosures of shafts in buildings.

The code requires that lobbies have at least one means of egress that can always be used. This covers situations such as where a floor of an office or a residential building with only one tenant has only one door leading from the elevator door. If the door was locked, a person could possibly become trapped in the lobby as depicted in Figure 3002-1. The tenant door can be locked if the lobby has access to the stairway as shown in Figure 3002-2. A similar provision appears in Section 1003.1.

When an elevator hoistway shaft is not required to have a fire-resistive rating, the code allows the shaft to be constructed with glass. Examples of where this might occur are elevators located on the exterior wall of a building where nonrated construction is permitted by Table 5-A or an elevator located within an atrium. When used, glass must be laminated glass that will pass the test requirements of Part I of UBC Standard 24-2. Laminated glass is required to protect the public from shattered falling glass, which can occur if a part falls from the elevator during operation or during maintenance and repairs.

SECTION 3003 — SPECIAL PROVISIONS

3003.1 Number of Cars in Hoistway. These provisions were extracted from the Elevator Code since they are more appropriate as Building Code requirements. The basis for limiting the number of cars in a single hoistway is to provide a reasonable level of assurance that a multilevel building served by several elevators would not have all of its elevator cars located in the same hoistway. This could result in a single emergency disabling all elevators within the building. For example, if all elevator cars were allowed to be located in the same hoistway, smoke which entered the enclosure during a fire would render all elevator cars unusable. The code provisions will increase the chance that some elevators within a major building would remain operational during a fire or other emergency.

3003.2 Smoke-detection Recall. These provisions describe the performance expected from elevator lobby smoke detectors. The intent of the requirement for a smoke detector is to prevent the elevator doors from opening on any floor where the smoke detector has activated. This requirement correlates with ANSI Standard A17.1.

3003.3 Standby Power. Standby power requirements in this section are an extension of the requirements of Section 403 for

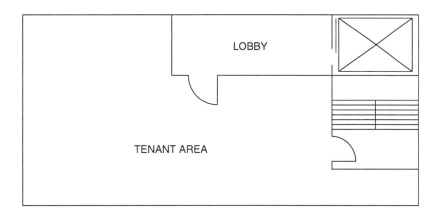

FIGURE 3002-1

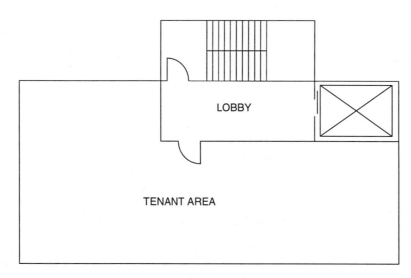

FIGURE 3002-2

high-rise buildings. The requirement that standby power be manually transferable to all elevators in each bank is necessary to improve their reliability during emergency conditions. For example, the elevator to which standby power is connected may be in a hoistway that is unusable due to smoke contamination. In this case, the transferability requirement provides for transferring the emergency power from the elevator in the affected hoistway to an elevator in a hoistway in the same bank which is usable. Also, this requirement provides for transferring the emergency power to the elevator car, which has been designed in accordance with Section 3003.4 to accommodate a wheelchair.

The first exception provides that a single elevator may be the only elevator required to have standby power. In an emergency this permits firefighters to gain access to the top stories of a high-rise building without having to change elevators at one or more intermediate floors.

The second exception provides that standby power need not operate all elevators simultaneously in each bank or group of banks having a common lobby.

The note defining a bank of elevators has been reprinted here, as the definition is pertinent to only this section. A bank of elevators may have more than one hoistway.

3003.4 Size of Cab and Control Locations. Where elevators are provided in buildings three or more stories in height or when they are used to provide access in accordance with Chapter 11, this section of the code requires that at least one elevator serving all floors accommodate a wheelchair. This is appropriate not only to provide access for individuals in wheelchairs but also to provide for movement of wheelchair-bound individuals during fire and emergencies. The provisions relating to the elevator that can accommodate a wheelchair are intended to be consistent with the requirements for access by the physically handicapped, ANSI Standard A117.1.

Section 3003.4 provides detailed requirements for elevator geometry, door-response times, control locations and other items necessary for making elevators safe, accessible and usable. Where compliance with Chapter 11 is required, the provisions of CABO/ANSI 117.1-1992 and Section 3003.4 must be

satisfied. For the most part, these provisions are the same, but there are a few differences. Among these are:

- **3003.4.7 Car inside.** American National Standards Institute 117.1 does not specifically define the inside dimensions of elevator cars, but does provide a reference drawing which matches the dimensions of the UBC [Caution: The Americans with Disabilities Act recommends a car that is 80 inches (2032 mm) wide when car doors are centered]. Figure 3003-1 shows both side-opening and center-opening door configurations. The side-opening door, Figure 3003-1, shows the dimensions listed in Section 3003.4.7.

- **3003.4.8 and 3003.4.10 Car controls and telephone or intercommunicating system.** American National Standards Institute 117.1 limits the highest button and telephone heights to 48 inches (1219 mm) when the approach to the control panel or telephone is from the front.

- **3003.4.11 Floor covering.** American National Standards Institute 117.1 limits carpet pile height to $^1/_2$ inch (12.7 mm).

3003.5 Stretcher Requirements. The ability to transport an individual on a stretcher in an elevator in a multistory building is a basic life-safety consideration. Immediate identification of elevators that accommodate stretchers is necessary so that emergency services personnel can quickly respond to emergency conditions.

3003.7 Restricted or Limited-use Elevators. These provisions are intended to allow the building official to waive the requirements of Section 3003 for elevators which are used in a nonpublic, restricted or limited-use application.

This waiver applies only to the provisions of Section 3003. Therefore, the other requirements in this chapter as well as in Appendix Chapter 30, when adopted, are applicable.

SECTION 3004 — HOISTWAY VENTING

Hoistway ventilation is intended to remove any smoke which may have entered the hoistway which would, of course, render the cars within the hoistway useless. In addition, unvented smoke can eventually spill out of the hoistway into the upper

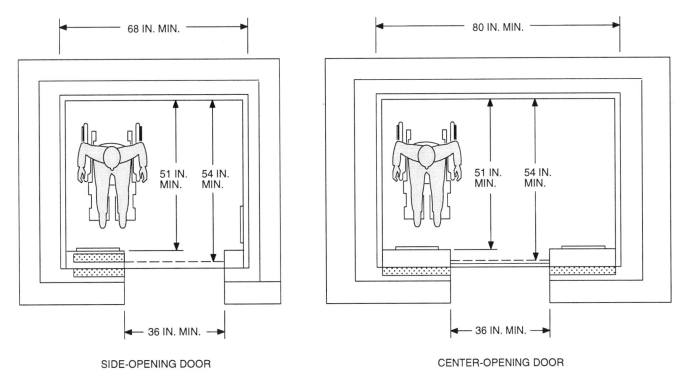

SIDE-OPENING DOOR   CENTER-OPENING DOOR

For **SI:** 1 inch = 25.4 mm.

MINIMUM DIMENSIONS OF ELEVATOR CARS

FIGURE 3003-1

floors of a building. Inadequate top ventilation of the elevator shafts at the MGM Grand Hotel was one cause cited for smoke spreading into upper-story corridors.[1] Normally these vents should be open 100 percent of the time so that they would be immediately available in case of need.

An exception previously found in the 1991 edition, which had permitted automatic venting when normally closed vents were necessary for energy conservation or hoistway pressurization, was removed from this section by the membership. The code states that vents shall be capable of manual operation only. The reason for removing the prior exception is somewhat obscure. Its removal was part of a change to Section 403.7, Item 3, for elevators in high-rise buildings.[2] Although a reason was given for amending Section 403.7, none was given for removing the exception.

For elevators in high rises subject to Section 403, Item 3 of Section 403.7 prohibits elevator hoistways from being vented through the elevator machine room. Although this limitation appears in Section 403 and thus appears to apply only to high-rise buildings, designers would be wise to apply it to any building with an elevator machine room located above the hoistway. In fact, prior to the 1994 UBC, this prohibition against venting hoistways appeared in Section 3004. Deletion from Section

3004 may have been the unintended result of the code change process. As will be discussed in the next section, smoke is a very undesirable commodity when one considers elevator controls.

SECTION 3005 — ELEVATOR MACHINE ROOM

Modern elevator control equipment is solid-state and is extremely sensitive to temperature. For this reason provisions have been developed to keep smoke and heat out of the machine room by requiring that the room be provided with an independent ventilation or air-conditioning system. Proper control of machine room temperatures is considered so vital that machine room ventilation or air-conditioning systems must be connected to standby power when provided for elevators.

SECTION 3006 — CHANGE IN USE

Under the Elevator Code, a change in use, say from a warehouse with only freight elevators to a multiresidential occupancy, would require elevator modifications to assure continued safe use of the equipment. Section 3006 is included with other elevator-related requirements so users of the Building Code will be aware of the change in use provisions of the Elevator Code.

SECTION 3007 — ADDITIONAL DOORS

The prohibition against installing additional doors at the point of access to an elevator car is to minimize the possibility of a person becoming trapped between doors or the possibility of the elevator car being rendered unusable due to blocked access at a particular floor where such an additional door has been closed and locked. The exception permits additional doors under the safeguards described.

REFERENCES

[1]Bush, Vincent R. (1981). Preliminary report—MGM Grand Hotel Fire, Las Vegas, Nevada. *Building Standards,* 50(1):6-9.

[2]International Conference of Building Officials (1991). *Code Change Agenda,* Item 62. *Building Standards*, Part III, July-August, page 32.

Chapter 31

SPECIAL CONSTRUCTION

Chapter 31 of the UBC covers requirements for chimneys, fireplaces and barbecues. Also included is a short paragraph that covers temporary buildings or structures.

SECTION 3102 — CHIMNEYS, FIREPLACES AND BARBECUES

The application of the provisions is general and applies to any chimney, fireplace or barbecue in any type of occupancy, although the primary use is in residential occupancies. Historically, fireplaces and chimneys have been among the worst offenders as far as starting fires is concerned. Some of the earliest building code provisions in our American colonies were concerned with the prevention of fires by prohibiting wood chimneys.[1] As a chimney, fireplace or barbecue is intended to contain a fire within a building which may be constructed of combustible materials, the potential for disaster is obvious, and therefore, so is the necessity for code provisions to regulate these structures.

This section refers to another hazard involved with chimneys, fireplaces and barbecues—the hazard presented by the products of combustion. Generally, the fireplace or barbecue contains the combustion process, while the chimney or flue and necessary connectors transport the products of combustion from the interior to the exterior. Even though the combustion process may be safely contained within a conforming fireplace, the combustion products may accumulate inside the building and reach lethal proportions unless they are properly conveyed from the building. Also, other heating appliances may be connected to a chimney, although their use and installation is regulated by the Mechanical Code.

In addition to the fire-safe design and construction, the proper operation of fuel-burning appliances, fireplaces and barbecues connected to chimneys requires an adequate supply of combustion air and proper conveyance of combustion products from the combustion chamber to the outside air. Again, although these requirements are completely general, the biggest problems usually occur in residential occupancies because it is necessary that the occupants perform certain operations in order to have a safely operating system. For example, the proper operation of a fireplace and chimney requires combustion air, and in a residential occupancy such as a dwelling, it is necessary that the occupants provide this combustion air in some fashion. The usual procedure is to open a window. This becomes even more important in today's tight construction due to energy conservation requirements. The amount of air which infiltrates a dwelling is considerably less than in former years; therefore, it becomes extremely important to provide for combustion air by opening a window or by some other means. Otherwise, oxygen depletion plus accumulation of the products of incomplete combustion (carbon monoxide, for example) are capable of creating a life-threatening interior environment.

3102.3 Chimneys, General.

3102.3.1 Chimney support. Chimneys are subject to considerable stresses due to thermal shock and, as a result, should not support any structural load other than their own weight, unless specifically designed as a supporting member for the additional load. Also, due to its heavy mass, a chimney will tend to settle more than the building structure; as a consequence, the chimney and any part of the building which it supports will settle at a greater rate and to a greater degree than the rest of the building, resulting in damage. If a chimney is subject to structural loads for which it is not designed, the additional stresses created could quite possibly lead to cracks in the chimney. Thus, the chimney would become a hazard due to flames from the firebox penetrating the cracks and igniting combustible construction. Moreover, hazardous conditions are created inside the building due to a buildup of the products of combustion which leak through the cracks.

3102.3.2 Construction. In this section the UBC states a performance criterion regarding the design of the chimney to produce a draft which will ensure its safe operation. The compliance with this latter provision requires that the volume of flue gases and the height and diameter of the chimney be calculated. However, at least for residential chimneys, these calculations are not necessary, and Table 31-B of the code provides data which have been shown over the years to provide the necessary performance.

3102.3.6 Height and termination. The figures in Table 31-B of the UBC for the height termination of chimneys are based on many years of experience with chimneys. At altitudes of 2,000 feet (610 m) or lower, these height terminations have produced satisfactory operation of the chimney. These heights were developed considering the possibility of downward drafts created by eddying, which will neutralize the required upward draft in the chimney as well as the temperature of the flue gases emitting from the top of the chimney.

At altitudes above 2,000 feet (610 m), the height of the chimney should be increased due to the decrease in barometric pressure. As the increased height of the stack creates additional friction, it is sometimes also advisable to increase the diameter of the flue. One common rule of thumb is to increase both the height and diameter of the chimney about 5 percent for each 1,000 feet (305 m) of altitude above the 2,000-foot (610 m) base-line elevation.[2] Mechanical engineers have developed tables to determine the increase in height and/or stack diameter based on the normal barometric pressure and the ratio of sea level pressure to pressure at the site elevation. As these tables are fairly well known, their use may be advisable rather than the use of a rule of thumb, unless local experience has shown otherwise.

3102.3.7 Cleanouts. The code requires that cleanout openings be provided within 6 inches (152 mm) of the base of every masonry chimney as shown in Figure 3102-1. The interior of the

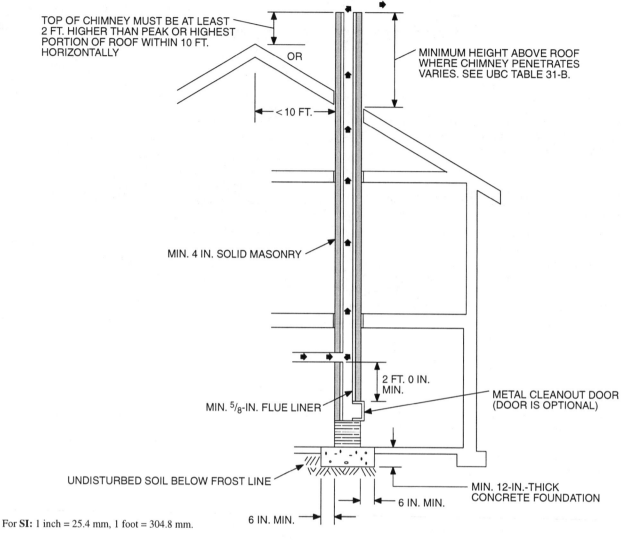

TOP OF CHIMNEY MUST BE AT LEAST 2 FT. HIGHER THAN PEAK OR HIGHEST PORTION OF ROOF WITHIN 10 FT. HORIZONTALLY

OR

MINIMUM HEIGHT ABOVE ROOF WHERE CHIMNEY PENETRATES VARIES. SEE UBC TABLE 31-B.

< 10 FT.

MIN. 4 IN. SOLID MASONRY

2 FT. 0 IN. MIN.

METAL CLEANOUT DOOR (DOOR IS OPTIONAL)

MIN. $^5/_8$-IN. FLUE LINER

UNDISTURBED SOIL BELOW FROST LINE

MIN. 12-IN.-THICK CONCRETE FOUNDATION

6 IN. MIN.

6 IN. MIN.

For **SI:** 1 inch = 25.4 mm, 1 foot = 304.8 mm.

TYPICAL MASONRY CHIMNEY

FIGURE 3102-1

chimney may become coated with carbonaceous deposits as well as with acids, and as a result, the brick in the mortar will be chemically attacked, gradually causing deterioration. The deposits will fall to the bottom of the chimney, and a cleanout will be necessary to remove them. Also, chimney-cleaning operations will result in the accumulation of deposits at the base of the chimney, necessitating a cleanout opening. In the case of a fireplace chimney, the fireplace opening itself provides the cleanout and no further cleanout opening is necessary.

Figures 3102-1 through 3102-5 show the details required by Section 3102 as applied to concrete or masonry chimneys. Although the figures depict residential concrete or masonry chimneys, the details shown for clearance from combustible materials, height of chimney and cleanout opening apply to all types of residential chimneys.

3102.3.8 Spark arrester. These provisions make the requirements for spark arresters on chimneys serving solid-fuel-burning appliances a local decision to be made by the building official. The requirement applies to all solid-fuel-fired

appliances, including fireplaces, and correlates with provisions of the *Uniform Fire Code.*

The Building Code requires the installation of spark arresters on fireplaces and appliances which burn solid or liquid fuel when located in areas where the land is covered with flammable materials or where the roof has less than a Class C roof covering.

3102.4 Masonry Chimneys.

3102.4.3 Reinforcing and seismic anchorage. Chimney behavior during past earthquakes has been very poor. Chimney losses on residential buildings caused by several earthquakes in California over the past 20-plus years have been excessive. In many cases, chimneys were completely detached from the building and thrown to the ground. As a result, the prescriptive requirements of this section regarding anchorage and reinforcing were increased in the 1973 UBC and later editions of the code to correct the observed deficiencies. A minimum $^1/_2$-inch (12.7 mm) grout cover for the vertical reinforcement was added to the 1991 edition. Limits on slope of vertical reinforcement

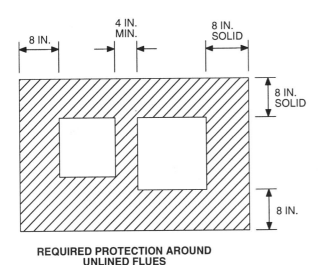

REQUIRED PROTECTION AROUND
UNLINED FLUES

For **SI:** 1 inch = 25.4 mm.

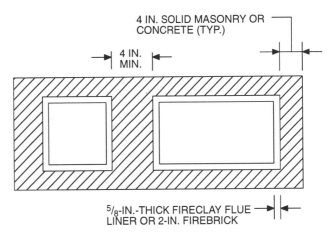

LINED MULTIPLE-FLUE CHIMNEY

LINED AND UNLINED MASONRY CHIMNEYS—RESIDENTIAL
GREATER THICKNESSES ARE REQUIRED FOR UNBURNED CLAY UNITS AND STONE

FIGURE 3102-2

have been added to avoid stress concentrations due to abrupt changes in sections of the chimney. Even where the chimney is completely surrounded by the roof structure, anchorage of the type required for exterior chimneys is recommended, although not required by the UBC This will prevent the chimney from banging or pounding against the roof framing and damaging it. The *Residential Fireplace and Chimney Handbook* contains several examples of chimney reinforcing and anchorage for locations in Seismic Zones 2, 3 and 4.[2]

An acceptance method of anchoring the chimney to the framing is specified in the third paragraph.

3102.4.4 Chimney offset. Limitations on the chimney offset are intended to provide a gradual transition at the offset to prevent critical stress concentrations at the bottom of the offset. Furthermore, the limit of one-third the dimension of the chimney in the direction of the offset and a maximum transition slope limit is intended to maintain structural stability for vertical loads.

3102.4.5 Change in size or shape. Changes in the size or shape of a chimney provide potential areas for leaks or cracks in the chimney. Thus, the code prohibits these changes within the zones specified where the chimney passes through an assembly to prevent fires from starting in a concealed space and spreading undetected.

3102.4.7 Inlets. Limitations on the size of the cleanout cavity have been included to preclude the use of large cavities which could result in an increased fire hazard because of the amount of creosote which could be allowed to accumulate.

3102.5 Factory-built Chimneys and Fireplaces. Factory-built fireplaces are permitted to be used by the UBC where they are approved and installed in accordance with their listing. A factory-built fireplace is a manufactured heating appliance built, as its name indicates, in a factory. The word "approved" in this section carries the connotation provided in the definition of "approved" in Chapter 2. Agencies such as UL provide listing serv-

ices for factory-built fireplaces. The listing not only includes a description of the manufactured unit, but also includes requirements for clearances from combustible materials, hearth details if necessary and other limitations placed on the unit to provide a safe installation. The ICBO Evaluation Service, Inc. (ICBO ES), has also evaluated numerous factory-built heating appliances. Factory-built fireplaces are installed in conjunction with factory-built chimneys so that the complete installation of fireplace and chimney is factory built.

3102.7 Masonry and Concrete Fireplaces and Barbecues.

3102.7.1 General. The provisions of this section are intended to apply to masonry or concrete fireplaces. Figure 3102-3 depicts the typical details and requirements of this section.

3102.7.2 Support. Although the code does not require such a design, it is good practice to proportion the foundation of a masonry fireplace and chimney to have approximately the same bearing pressure as is present under the building structure itself under dead loads. The dead-load bearing pressure for the building structure, particularly if it is a light wood-frame building, is usually quite low, while the bearing pressure on the foundation for a masonry or concrete fireplace and chimney can be several times higher. Where the soil is compressible, differential settlements between the fireplace and chimney and its surrounding structure will be detrimental due to cracking of the finish materials in the vicinity of the fireplace and chimney. Also, firestopping may be displaced so that a draft opening is created.

3102.7.3 Fireplace walls. The Rumford fireplace, designed by Count Rumford in the late 18th century, was common worldwide until about 1850 when coal- and gas-burning fireplaces became popular. There are many historic houses in America that contain originally built Rumford fireplaces. The *Uniform Building Code,* however, favored a particular type of fireplace designed in the 1940s, which is much deeper and lower than the older Rumford design. The firebox depth and throat size requirements were intended to ensure that the fireplace would draw
(Continued on page 377)

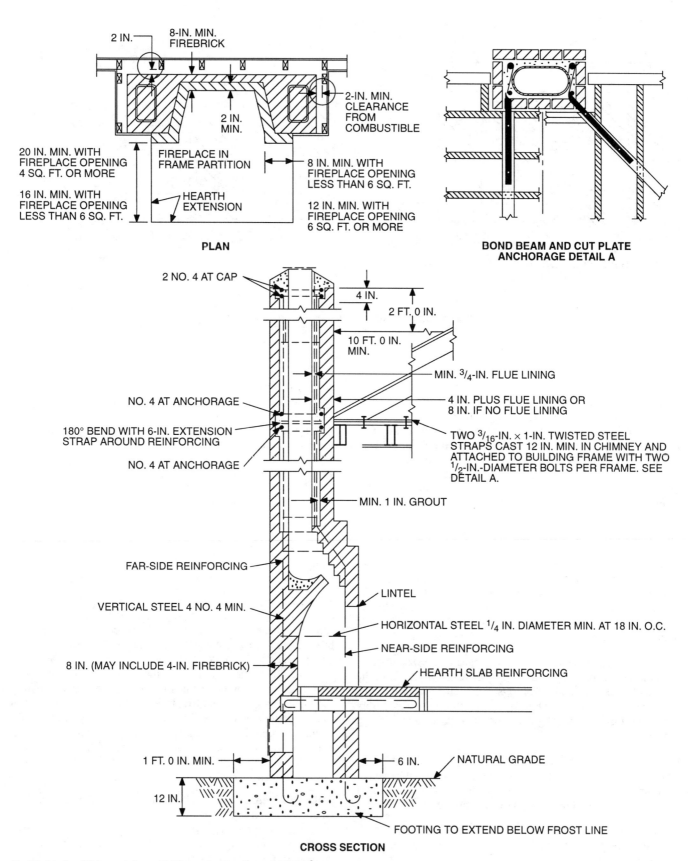

PLAN

**BOND BEAM AND CUT PLATE
ANCHORAGE DETAIL A**

CROSS SECTION

For **SI:** 1 inch = 25.4 mm, 1 foot = 304.8 mm, 1 square foot = 0.0929 m².

FIREPLACE DETAILS

FIGURE 3102-3

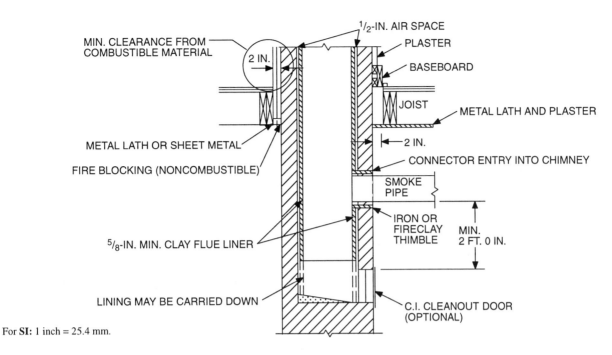

MASONRY OR CONCRETE CHIMNEY DETAILS

FIGURE 3102-4

For SI: 1 inch = 25.4 mm.

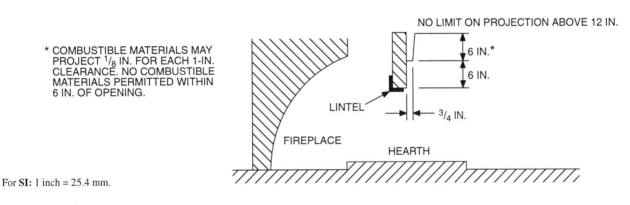

COMBUSTIBLE MATERIALS PROJECTION FROM FIREPLACE

FIGURE 3102-5

For SI: 1 inch = 25.4 mm.

(Continued from page 375)

well, regardless of its efficiency, but these requirements prohibit the construction of a Rumford fireplace.

Rumford fireplaces are tall and shallow to reflect more heat, and they have streamlined throats to eliminate turbulence and carry away the smoke with little loss of heated room air.[3] Section 3102.7.3 now recognizes the Rumford fireplace through an exception added to the 1994 UBC. Figure 3102-6 illustrates the dimensions of a Rumford fireplace.

3102.7.5 Metal heat circulators. As with approved factory-built fireplaces, the word "approved" used in this section has the same meaning. Underwriters Laboratories and other listing agencies list metal heat circulators, and they should be installed in accordance with their listing. Furthermore, ICBO ES has also

issued evaluation reports for a number of these metal heat circulators.

3102.7.8 Clearance to combustible material. Obviously, combustible materials must not be in direct contact with a fireplace or chimney or placed too close to the fireplace opening. Figure 3102-5 illustrates the code requirements relative to the permissible projection from the face of the fireplace for those cases where combustibles are placed closer than 12 inches (305 mm).

3102.7.12 Hearth extensions. Hearth extensions are necessary to keep sparks flying from the fireplace opening from igniting combustible material, such as rugs on the floor. Radiated heat from the fireplace can also ignite combustible flooring materials. The required distance for the hearth extension is related to the size of the fireplace opening, as larger fireplace openings

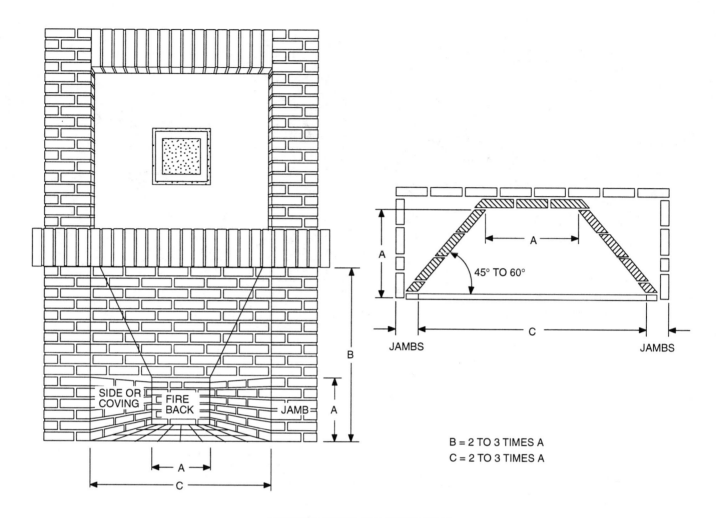

RUMFORD FIREPLACE DIMENSIONS

FIGURE 3102-6

have a potential for radiating heat and throwing larger sparks to further distances.

The code requires that the hearth slab, including its extension, be readily distinguishable from the surrounding or adjacent floor. This is so that it will be obvious to the occupants of the building that rugs and other combustible objects should not be placed on the hearth extension.

3102.7.13 Fire blocking. Although this section refers to the fire blocking requirements in Section 708, it should be noted here that in the case of fire blocking between chimneys and combustible construction, the code requires that the fire-blocking material be noncombustible. Figure 3102-3 includes a detail for this requirement.

Nonconforming fireplaces. Provisions dealing with nonconforming fireplaces, namely those with a shallow depth where decorative gas appliances were most typically installed, have been deleted from the code. The nonconforming fireplace provisions which appeared in the code up through the 1991 edition seem to have evolved from a provision in Section 3706 of the 1927 *Uniform Building Code*. The Building Code section that addressed nonconforming fireplaces did not actually allow the installation of unvented heaters, since the section required com-

pliance with the *Uniform Mechanical Code* which, in Section 327.6, prohibits the installation of unvented fuel-burning room heaters and which, in Section 901.1, allows gas logs to be installed only within a complying fireplace. Since there no longer seemed to be any good reason to preserve provisions for nonconforming fireplaces, the section was removed. For additional historical background, see Code Change Item 372 in Part III of *Building Standards*, November-December, 1992.

SECTION 3103 — TEMPORARY BUILDINGS AND STRUCTURES

Prior to the 1994 edition this section was included with the moved building provisions now found in Section 3405. The section authorizes the erection of temporary buildings and structures such as those erected at construction sites. Temporary reviewing stands and other miscellaneous, temporary structures would also fall under this section. Key provisions for temporary buildings and structures are that they:

- Are erected by special permit.

- Are erected for a limited period of time.

- Are completely removed upon expiration of time limit stated in the special permit.
- Need not comply with the type of construction or fire-resistive requirements of the code.

REFERENCES

[1]O'Bannon, Robert E. (1988). *Building Department Administration.* International Conference of Building Officials, Whittier, California.

[2]Masonry Institute of America (1983). *Residential Fireplace and Chimney Handbook,* Fourth Edition. Los Angeles, California.

[3]Buckley, Jim (1993). What Is a Rumford Fireplace Anyway? *Building Standards*, 62(1): 20-21.

Chapter 32

CONSTRUCTION IN THE PUBLIC RIGHT OF WAY

By using the language "construction in the public right of way," the code is referring to projections of appendages and other projections from the building (except signs*), which are permitted to project beyond the property line of the building site and into the public right-of-way. The intent of the code is that projections from a building into the public right-of-way shall not interfere with the free use of the public right-of-way by vehicular and pedestrian traffic, and shall not interfere with public services, such as fire protection and utilities.

SECTION 3201 — GENERAL

The *Uniform Building Code* requires that any construction which projects into or across the public right-of-way be constructed as required by the code for buildings on private property. Furthermore, the intent is that the provisions of this chapter are not considered as permitting a violation of other laws or ordinances regulating the use and occupancy of public property. Many jurisdictions have ordinances regulating the use and occupancy of public property which go beyond the provisions of this chapter and which may be more restrictive and not permit the projections permitted by this chapter. Where there are no other ordinances that prohibit such construction, it is the intent of this chapter to permit the construction of a connecting structure between buildings either over or under the public way.

These types of permanent uses of the public way are often permitted by the jurisdiction under a special license issued by the public works agency. Where these uses create no obstruction to the normal use of the public way, the jurisdiction, by authorizing connecting structures between buildings on either side of the public way, can derive revenue from the licensing agreement, which can be of assistance in maintaining the public right-of-way.

SECTION 3202 — PROJECTION INTO ALLEYS

Because alleys are relatively narrow as compared to streets, for example, the code does not permit any projection into an alley except for the two exceptions listed:

1. While the exact dimensions of 9 inches (229 mm) specified may be somewhat arbitrary and could just as well be 8 inches or 10 inches (203 mm or 254 mm), the intent is that they be small enough so as not to obstruct vehicular traffic and yet provide some protection for an occupant of a building to look each way before proceeding into the alley.

2. In this exception the code assumes that there will be no utilities or other public facilities below this depth adjacent to the building and, therefore, the exception permits foot-

ings to project 12 inches (305 mm) below the 8-foot (2438 mm) depth.

SECTION 3203 — SPACE BELOW SIDEWALK

In many cases the space below the sidewalk is not used for public purposes, such as utilities, sewers and storm drains (except for catch basins); therefore, where local ordinances do not prohibit the use of the space beneath the sidewalk, the code permits its use by the adjoining property owners. Usually the basement of an adjoining building is extended beneath the sidewalk and is used for any of the uses permitted by the code. This is a revocable permission, as the jurisdiction may find at a later date that there is a public need for the public use of the space beneath the sidewalk.

In any case, the code permits footings which are at least 8 feet (2438 mm) below grade to project beneath the sidewalk not more than 12 inches (305 mm) for the same reasons discussed under alleys.

SECTION 3204 — BALCONIES, SUN-CONTROL DEVICES AND APPENDAGES

The code permits the projection of balconies, unroofed porches and the other items listed in this section above a height of 8 feet (2438 mm) in accordance with Figure 3204-1. The intent of the code is that no projection should be permitted near the sidewalk level and up to 8 feet (2438 mm) in height so that free passage of pedestrians along the sidewalk will not be inhibited. Above the 8-foot (2438 mm) height, projections are permitted as long as they do not interfere with public utilities. It is generally assumed that utility lines for telephone and power will not occupy this zone except for the service entrances to the buildings. There are jurisdictions that have high-voltage power lines running along the sidewalk, and the regulations of the agency that regulates the power companies generally require certain clearances from these lines. Therefore, in addition to the requirements shown in Figure 3204-1, power-line clearances should also be checked, and the requirements of the *National Electrical Code®* should be checked when it is adopted by the jurisdiction.

SECTION 3205 — MARQUEES

A marquee is defined in Section 214 as a permanent roofed structure attached to and supported by the building and projecting over public property. Thus, a marquee is different than an awning based on its permanence. The classic example of a marquee is the theater marquee or the entrance marquee at a hotel.

---

*Permissible projections for signs are found in the *Uniform Sign Code.*

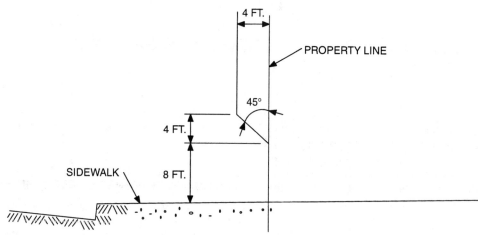

For **SI:** 1 foot = 304.8 mm.

PERMISSIBLE PROJECTION FOR BALCONIES, SUN-CONTROL DEVICES AND APPENDAGES

FIGURE 3204-1

The restrictions placed on the size, projection and clearances for marquees are intended to:

1. Prevent interference with the free movement of pedestrians.

2. Prevent interference with trucks and other tall vehicles using the public street.

3. Prevent interference with the fire department in its fire-fighting operations at a building.

4. Prevent interference with utilities.

Thus, the projection and clearance, length, and thickness of the marquee are regulated to meet the intent of the code. Figure 3205-1 depicts the permissible projection and clearances required for marquees.

SECTION 3206 — AWNINGS

Awnings are regulated for the same reasons just described for marquees. However, the code does not restrict their length along the wall of the building, but in provisions similar to those for marquees, the code does restrict an awning's projection from a building. Figure 3206-1 depicts the permissible projections and clearances for awnings.

SECTION 3207 — DOORS

While the code permits ordinary exit doors from buildings to project not more than 1 foot (305 mm) beyond the property line, power-operated doors and their guide rails are not permitted to project at all. This is due to the nature of the power-operated door and the guide rails. The power-operated door is a mechanical facility, and the guide rails are permanent structures which, if allowed to project, would provide an unreasonable interference to pedestrian traffic along the sidewalk. In fact, it is not uncommon for many jurisdictions by ordinance to permit no door projections of any kind beyond the property line.

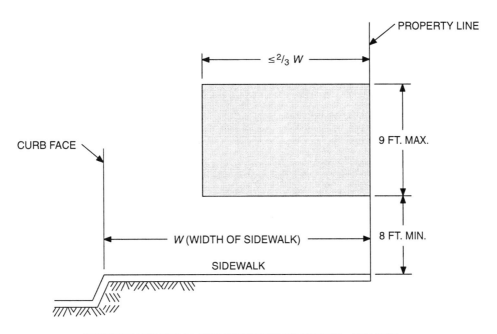

PROPERTY LINE

≤²/₃ W

CURB FACE

9 FT. MAX.

8 FT. MIN.

W (WIDTH OF SIDEWALK)

SIDEWALK

MAXIMUM LENGTH ALONG DIRECTION OF STREET—NO LIMIT

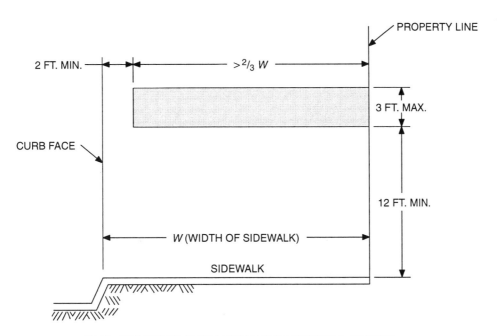

PROPERTY LINE

2 FT. MIN.

>²/₃ W

CURB FACE

3 FT. MAX.

12 FT. MIN.

W (WIDTH OF SIDEWALK)

SIDEWALK

MAXIMUM LENGTH ALONG DIRECTION OF STREET—25 FEET

For **SI:** 1 foot = 304.8 mm.

PERMISSIBLE PROJECTION, HEIGHT AND CLEARANCES FOR MARQUEES

FIGURE 3205-1

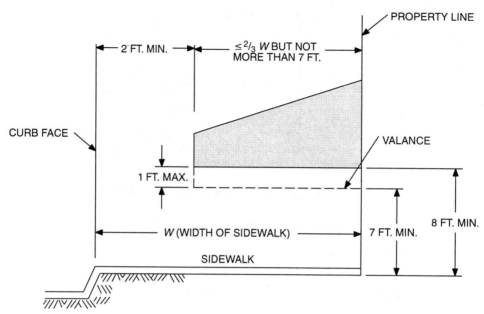

For **SI:** 1 foot = 304.8 mm.

PERMISSIBLE PROJECTIONS AND CLEARANCES FOR AWNINGS

FIGURE 3206-1

Chapter 33

SITE WORK, DEMOLITION AND CONSTRUCTION

This chapter addresses three distinct topics: site excavations and fills, protection of pedestrians during construction or demolition, and preparation of the building site.

Prior to 1994, the excavation and fill provisions of Section 3301 were found in Chapter 29, which contained requirements for the design and construction of foundations and retaining walls. These foundation and retaining wall provisions are found in Division I of Chapter 18. Provisions for excavations and fills have been placed in a separate chapter since they are not directly related to foundation work.

SECTION 3301 — EXCAVATIONS AND FILLS

3301.1 General. The provisions in Section 3301.1 for excavations and fills are intended to apply to the specific site where a building or structure will be located. Section 3301.1 does not address massive grading on a site. For those requirements, one would turn to a local grading ordinance or, if adopted, Appendix Chapter 33, which contains requirements for more extensive excavations, grading and earthwork and includes requirements for fills and embankments. The *Uniform Building Code* limits the slopes for permanent fills or cut slopes for permanent excavations for structures to 2 units horizontal in 1 unit vertical (50% slope). While steeper cut slopes are permitted where substantiating data are submitted, the limitation on filled slopes of 2 units horizontal in 1 unit vertical (50% slope) is an absolute limitation, and filled slopes may not be steeper.

While cut slopes into natural soils may be excavated with a slope steeper than 2 units horizontal in 1 unit vertical (50% slope) depending on the nature of the soil materials and the density, the code reasons that filled slopes must not be steeper than 2 units horizontal in 1 unit vertical (50% slope) to cover unprecedented circumstances such as heavy rains creating supersaturated soils or, in the case of seismic zones, vibration of the soils during an earthquake causing failures of steep filled slopes.

Understandably, the code requires that fill or surcharge loads not be placed adjacent to an existing building or structure unless the existing building or structure is structurally capable of resisting the additional loads caused by the fills or surcharge. See Figure 3301-1. Alternatively, the existing building can be strengthened in order to resist the additional loading.

The code requires that existing footings or foundations which may be affected by an excavation be adequately underpinned or otherwise protected. This concern is with excavations on the same property and under the control of the same individual who has control of the existing buildings. For obvious reasons, it is the intent of the code that excavations in close proximity to an existing footing shall not be made unless proper protective measures are taken for the existing building. These measures may involve underpinning of the existing foundations or shoring and bracing of the excavation so that the existing building foundations will not settle or lose lateral support.

Where the excavation is for a new building foundation and the new footing is at an elevation below, but within reasonably close proximity to, an existing foundation, underpinning is the usual procedure to protect the existing foundation. If the existing footing is for a structure which creates a horizontal thrust, the means of providing lateral support may take the form of a buttressed retaining wall designed to resist the lateral thrust of the existing foundation.

Where buildings are to be supported by fills, the code requires that the fills be placed in accordance with "accepted engineering practice." Thus, fills utilized for the support of buildings must be designed by a geotechnical engineer (soils engineer) utilizing the principles of geotechnical engineering (soils engineering) so

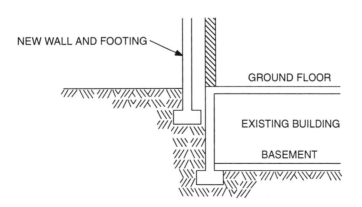

SURCHARGE LOAD ON ADJACENT BUILDING

FIGURE 3301-1

as to provide a proper and adequate foundation for the structure above and one which will limit settlements to tolerable levels.

So that the building official may verify the adequacy of the geotechnical design of the fills, the code requires that a soil investigation report outlining the geotechnical design of the fill materials and a report of satisfactory placement of the fill be submitted for approval.

3301.2 Protection of Adjoining Property. The provisions in this section are based on common law precepts of lateral support. Over the years, common law and, more recently, statute law have established the requirements for lateral support. That is, the owner of a piece of real property shall be entitled to the lateral support of that property by adjacent property. The principle of lateral support covers basically two situations:

1. When the owner of a piece of property desires to cause an excavation to be made on the property to a depth less than a "standard depth" [standard depth is 12 feet (3658 mm) in the UBC], that owner is responsible for protecting the adjacent real property so that it will not cave in or settle due to the removal of lateral support. However, the excavating owner is not responsible for providing lateral support or protection against lateral movement and settlement for any buildings on the adjacent property as long as the excavation does not extend below the standard depth.

   Therefore, if there is a building on the adjacent property, the excavating owner must permit the owner of the adjacent property reasonable access to the property so that the adjacent owner may underpin or take whatever means are necessary to protect his or her building.

2. When an owner wishes to excavate below the standard depth, the owner must not only provide protection to prevent cave-in and settlement of the soil on the adjacent property but must also underpin or otherwise protect the foundations of the buildings on the adjacent property below the 12-foot (3658 mm) depth.

In other words, the excavating owner is responsible for providing lateral support to protect adjacent property from cave-in or settlement regardless of the depth of the excavation. However, the excavating owner is responsible for underpinning the adjacent owner's buildings only where the excavation exceeds the standard depth. These provisions are illustrated in Figures 3301-2 and 3301-3.

SECTION 3302 — PREPARATION OF BUILDING SITE

To prevent decay and to eliminate an avenue of entrance for termites and other insects, the code requires that the area of the site to be occupied by the building be free of all stumps, roots, and any loose or casual lumber. This requirement was formerly included with the wood-frame construction requirements of Chapter 23 of the 1991 UBC.

SECTION 3303 — PROTECTION OF PEDESTRIANS DURING CONSTRUCTION OR DEMOLITION

Both Section 3303 and Chapter 32 regulate the use of public streets and sidewalks. Section 3303 provides those general regu-

lations and criteria for the temporary use of public property which are generally found to apply to most jurisdictions.

As the nature and philosophy of each jurisdiction varies, so do the regulations each promulgates regarding the use of public property and, in particular, the use of streets and sidewalks. Adjacent property owners have rights of access to their property. The public street also provides access for public services such as fire and police protection, street sweeping and maintenance, street lighting, trash pickup, and other services provided by the jurisdiction or its contractors. Utilities serving adjacent property also use the public street for access.

3303.1 General. It is the intent of Section 3303 to regulate temporary use of public property and to secure the safety of pedestrians using the sidewalk or public right-of-way adjacent to building construction operations or demolition.

For obvious reasons, the code requires that any construction materials temporarily stored on the street, any pedestrian walkway or any protection canopy be adequately lighted between sunset and sunrise. This may take the form of warning lanterns on barricades protecting materials storage or on the boundaries of walkways and canopies. Also, incandescent or other illumination may be required on the underside of the protection canopy to provide lighting for the walkway. For simple pedestrian walkways, the public street lighting may be adequate to properly light the walkway.

3303.2 Temporary Use of Streets and Alleys. Most jurisdictions have regulations for the use of public property which are enforced by the public works department or a similar agency. It is the intent of the UBC that wherever other regulations are in effect they shall be followed. Where they conflict with this chapter, the conflict should be resolved by amending this chapter or the regulations of the public works agency.

3303.6 Walkway. A public jurisdiction provides sidewalks and streets for the free passage of vehicular and pedestrian traffic. In the case of pedestrian traffic, the usual procedure is to provide a sidewalk on each side of the street. Therefore, when construction or demolition operations are conducted on property adjacent to the sidewalk, the code requires that a walkway at least 4 feet (1219 mm) wide be maintained in front of the building site for the use of pedestrians. However, in those cases where pedestrian traffic is unusually light, the jurisdiction may authorize the fencing and closing of the sidewalk to pedestrian use.

3303.7 Pedestrian Protection.

3303.7.1 Protection required. Pedestrians must be protected from the potential hazards that exist during construction or demolition operations adjacent to the public way. The type of protection depends on the type of operation being conducted. For example, an excavation directly adjacent to the pedestrian walkway would necessitate a minimum of a guardrail along the side facing the excavation. Also, where the pedestrian walkway extends into the public street, a railing is required on the street side of the walkway to protect the pedestrians from vehicular traffic. *Uniform Building Code* Table 33-A provides the criteria for determining whether or not additional protection is required, depending on the height and proximity of the construction operations to the pedestrian walkway. Depending on these various parameters, the protection required will vary from none to a fence and canopy.

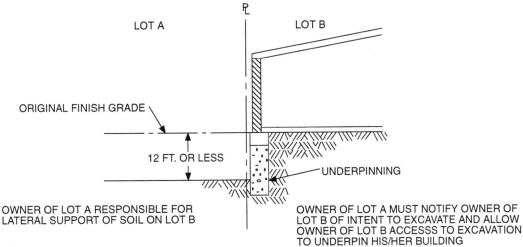

For **SI:** 1 foot = 304.8 mm.

LATERAL SUPPORT—EXCAVATION TO DEPTH OF 12 FEET OR LESS

FIGURE 3301-2

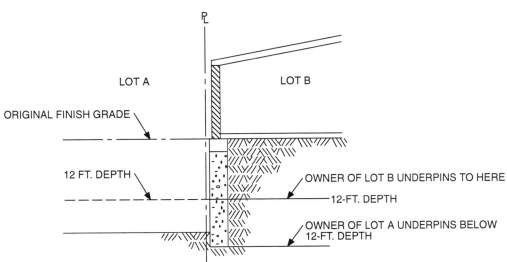

For **SI:** 1 foot = 304.8 mm.

LATERAL SUPPORT—EXCAVATION TO DEPTH EXCEEDING 12 FEET

FIGURE 3301-3

3303.7.2 Railings. The code only requires an open-type guard-rail 3 feet 6 inches (1067 mm) in height when a railing is required; furthermore, when the railing is adjacent to an excavation, the code requires that it be provided with a midrail. However, the jurisdiction may wish to modify these requirements to require a solid fence 5 feet (1524 mm) high in place of the guardrail adjacent to excavations. Today's litigious society almost guarantees that were a child to fall through or climb over the open railing, the jurisdiction would be sued for several million dollars.

3303.7.3 Fences. The intent of the code is that a fence, when required, be solid and sturdy enough to prevent impacts from the construction operations from penetrating the fence and injuring passing pedestrians. Because of this intent the code also requires that the fence extend along the entire length of the building site and that the ends return to the building line so as to provide a complete separation between construction operations and pedestrians.

Although the code requires openings in the fence to be protected by doors which normally are kept closed, the code does not intend to prevent the use of small view ports at eye level so that passing pedestrians may stop and view the construction operations if they wish.

3303.7.4 Canopies. The protective canopy is required for the same reasons as a protection fence—to prevent falling objects from endangering passing pedestrians. Therefore, the code requires that the design be such that the canopy be capable of preventing falling objects from breaking through.

The tight sheathing requirement for the roof is to prevent even small amounts of dust and dirt from falling through onto pedestrians. Pedestrians using walkways adjacent to building sites where construction or demolition operations are taking place have every right to safe passage protected from falling debris and other hazards of the construction operations. Furthermore, they should not be subjected to the indignities of dirt, water and other foreign material sifting through leaks in the canopy.

Since a canopy is intended to protect pedestrians against construction operations, including demolition, the canopy structure should be designed structurally to serve that purpose. Thus, the code provides two means for the design of the canopy:

1. **A structural design** to withstand the actual loads to which it will be subjected, provided the live load is not less than 150 pounds per square foot (7.18 kN/m^2).

2. **A prescriptive design** in accordance with this section of the code where the canopy will not be subjected to live loads greater than 150 pounds per square foot (7.18 kN/m^2).

The exception provides for a permissive design for a live load of 75 pounds per square foot (3.59 kN/m^2) for the protective canopy where the construction operation is the erection of new, small, light-frame buildings.

3303.9 Demolition. As the work of demolishing a building is subject to so many variations and to so many different hazards, the code authorizes the building official to require the submission of plans and a complete schedule of the demolition. For some multilevel buildings and for certain types of demolition operations, it may be necessary to temporarily close the street (this is usually done at night).

Chapter 34

EXISTING STRUCTURES

This chapter covers all aspects of existing buildings, including their occupancy and maintenance as well as additions, alterations or repairs to existing buildings.

Section 3401 establishes that a building in existence when a new code edition is adopted has the right to have its existing use or occupancy continued, provided, however, the use or occupancy was legal at the time the new code edition was adopted and that it is not dangerous to life. Should the owner subsequently want to change the use or occupancy, Section 3405 provides the guidelines for doing so. Other provisions for existing buildings are contained in Appendix Chapter 34, which is primarily intended to present upgrading provisions for use by adopting jurisdictions to improve life safety in existing buildings. Except for glazing and smoke detectors in residential occupancies, no retroactive provisions appear in Chapter 34. In addition to Appendix Chapter 34, a separate document, the *Uniform Code for Building Conservation,* provides a comprehensive code with guidelines that can be adopted by a community to preserve its existing building stock by establishing appropriate threshold levels for safety.

SECTION 3402 — MAINTENANCE

This section has the effect of charging the building official with the responsibility of seeing that all buildings, both existing and new, are maintained properly. This section does not require that the building official develop a schedule for reinspection of existing buildings to determine whether or not they are being properly maintained. However, it does give the building official the authority to make a reinspection of any structure if there is reason to believe that the building has been improperly maintained. As discussed in Section 101.2, vigorous enforcement of this section will have the effect of reducing slums where they exist.

SECTION 3403 — ADDITIONS, ALTERATIONS OR REPAIRS

3403.1 General. The subject of applications to existing buildings has been revised from earlier additions to the code (prior to the 1979 edition). The present provisions are intended to encourage rehabilitation of existing buildings which may have been allowed to deteriorate because they could not comply with the earlier editions of the code. These earlier codes required that the total building, including the existing building, be brought up to the current standards of the code if more than 50 percent of the value of the building was involved in the additions, alterations or reconstruction.

3403.2 When Allowed. The present wording in this section will allow existing buildings to be altered, repaired or modified without complying with all provisions of the code as long as the new

work complies with the code. The code also intends that the new work will not make the existing building unsafe nor should the new work cause any portion of the existing building to be in violation of the code. For example, any new addition or new alterations should not remove or block existing exits.

There are two separate provisions which relate to limiting any altered building to the height, number of stories and area specified for new buildings. At first, these two provisions seem to create a redundancy, but further study reveals that the first addresses the specific case of a change in occupancy and would apply even if no alterations or additions were made to the existing building. The second provision has the effect of not permitting an addition to an existing building if the existing building already is nonconforming due to excessive height, number of stories or area.

Section 3403.2 also intends to permit additions or alterations to existing noncomplying buildings only when such additions or alterations will result in conditions no more hazardous than existing conditions.

The basic requirement of Section 3403.2 is that any structural alteration or repair made to an existing building fully comply with all applicable provisions of the currently adopted code. Prior to the 1994 edition, there were no provisions to address voluntarily increasing the strength or stiffness of an existing building's lateral-force-resisting system. If such work were to be undertaken, then full compliance with the current code would be required. An exception now permits such voluntary strengthening, provided an engineering analysis is submitted to show compliance with stated objectives. This exception permits existing structural elements to be altered and new structural elements to be installed for the purpose of increasing the strength or stiffness of the lateral-force-resisting system. The exception specifies that the design forces need not comply with the current code requirements. No force level is specified. However, the exception states that the capacity of existing structural elements required to resist forces may not be reduced; thus, compliance with forces at least equal to original design force levels seems to be implied.

Before the exception was added to the code, there was a disincentive for improving lateral-force-resisting elements because one had to either provide full compliance or do nothing. Improving the lateral-force-resisting capacity of a building's structural system can be extremely beneficial, even when it is not possible to gain full compliance with current code force levels. This should encourage rather than discourage strengthening. The exception states that work may be undertaken when not required by Section 3401. Since Section 3401 does not specifically address structural work, the intent of the reference is not clear. What is clear from the original proposal is that the exception was intended to apply only when voluntary strengthening of an existing building was proposed. The exception should not be used as a reason for reducing force levels to be taken by existing lateral-force-resisting elements which will be used to brace an addition. Any addition plus existing building elements used to resist lateral forces generated by the addition should comply with current code requirements.

SECTION 3405 — CHANGE IN USE

Because each occupancy group and division thereof contemplates a different level of hazard, the code intends that when a use is changed, and particularly when the change in use increases the level of hazard, the building must be brought to conform to the requirements of the code for the proposed occupancy. Moreover, if the level of hazard has not changed appreciably but the code requirements for the new use are more restrictive in such cases as floor live load or the number and widths of exits, these more-restrictive provisions of the code must be applied to the new use. It is because of this latter situation that in several places the code uses the language "character of occupancies or use" or more often just "character of the occupancy."

The exception to Section 3405 grants the building official broad authority in determining whether or not the new or proposed use is less hazardous than the existing use. Each change of occupancy, therefore, must be analyzed based upon the hazards consequent to the new use. In addition, the fire- and life-safety and structural features of the building must be analyzed to determine if they are as required by the code for the new use. Even though there is no change in occupancy group or division thereof, the character of the occupancy may have changed such that other requirements of the code related to the new use require that the building be altered to comply with these other requirements. For example, consider a Group A, Division 2.1 restaurant where no alcoholic beverages are served. The owner wants to obtain a liquor license so alcoholic beverages can be served, but with no contemplated change in occupant load. Although there is no change in either the occupancy group or division, Section 904.2.3.1 would require that the restaurant be protected with an automatic fire sprinkler system when alcoholic beverages are served if the undivided seating area exceeds 5,000 square feet (465 m^2). Thus, at a minimum, the change in use requires the installation of the sprinkler system.

Therefore, except as provided in the exception to Section 3405, it is the intent of the code that a change of occupancy shall not be made unless the building is made to comply with the requirements of the code that are related to the proposed use. Thus, structural requirements of the code must also be met where they are more restrictive for the new use.

As the exception to Section 3405 grants wide authority to the building official to use judgment in determining which code requirements will be exacted, the building official should develop rules which are to be followed upon a change of occupancy so that even enforcement will result. When the *Uniform Code for Building Conservation* (UCBC) has been adopted, Chapter 5 provides minimum requirements for a change in occupancy. If the UCBC has not been adopted, it does provide provisions in Chapter 5 to guide the building official in the promulgation of rules to enforce Section 3405 of the UBC.

Referring back to the exception in Section 3405 and as previously stated in this commentary, the building official is given broad authority in determining the hazards involved in a change of occupancy. If it is determined that the proposed or new use is less hazardous than the existing use, the building official may approve a change in occupancy without requiring that the building conform to all the requirements of the code for the new use. Given this wide authority, a building official may require that the building comply with only those requirements for the new use which are important to fire and life safety. Under these circumstances, the code permits the building official to choose *not* to require those changes which are deemed unnecessary as far as fire and life safety are concerned, based on the character of the new use.

In those cases where the building official exercises the discretionary authority granted by the exception, the code permits the issuance of a new certificate of occupancy without certifying that the building complies with all the provisions of the code. Thus, the intent of the code is clear that the building official may exercise judgment in determining hazards present in the proposed use and imposing only those requirements of the code which are deemed necessary, commensurate with the hazard involved in the new use.

A practical application. In closing, let us briefly discuss a change of occupancy determination that building officials face all the time—the conversion of a single-family dwelling to an office use. Districts which were formerly residential in nature have seen the expansion of neighboring commercial areas, and now someone wants to save an attractive old Victorian residence and convert it into offices. Does the exception to Section 3405 apply, and if so to what extent? To determine this, the building official must evaluate the fire- and life-safety and structural features of the building to determine if existing conditions satisfy the code and to determine to what extent the new use poses a greater or a lesser hazard than the existing use. For example, the adequacy of the floor system would need to be reviewed since a dwelling requires only a 40-pound-per-square-foot (1.92 kN/m^2) live load while an office use must be designed for a 50-pound-per-square-foot (2.40 kN/m^2) live load and a 2,000-pound (8.96 kN) concentrated load. Floor system structural capacity is thus an important factor to consider. Another item that always arises with such conversions is what to do about exterior wall and opening protection. Many of the dwellings that are converted are historical in nature or, at the very least, are a part of a community's cultural fabric. As a result, there is an understandable desire to maintain their present appearance. In such cases, some jurisdictions permit the use of exterior fire sprinklers to serve as exterior protection. In other jurisdictions, a comparison is made between the fire- and life-safety hazards of the two occupancies. Such things as fire loading, alertness of building occupants, building size and similar considerations may be used by the building official in determining if the converted use poses a greater or lesser hazard than the former one.

Chapter 35

UNIFORM BUILDING CODE STANDARDS

As a companion publication to the UBC, the UBC Standards is unique and provides in one volume most of the major standards referenced in the UBC. Thus, the users of the *Uniform Building Code* are provided with a relatively inexpensive and complete building code, which includes pertinent standards.

Under the adoption of standards policy, there are now six potential methods by which standards may be proposed for adoption. A complete explanation of the criteria associated with each method of adoption may be obtained from Conference headquarters. A brief explanation of Chapter 35 is provided below.

Part I. Chapter 35 is divided into four parts. Part I contains the general provisions which indicate how Part II, Part III and Part IV are to be used. Section 3501 adopts the UBC standards referenced in Part II as a part of the code. As indicated in the sample adoption ordinance at the front of the *Uniform Building Code,* it is suggested that UBC standards be specifically mentioned in the legislation which adopts the *Uniform Building Code* so that there is no doubt as to legislative intent.

The provisions in Section 3503 are a departure from a previous practice of publishing all standards used by the code. Section 3503 recognizes that the designer and builder have a standard of duty to construct buildings that are reasonably safe for persons and property; if they utilize materials that conform with the standards listed in Part IV of Chapter 35, this can be used as prima facie (valid) evidence of meeting the standard of duty.

Section 3504 explains that the standards listed in Part IV are not a part of the code; however, compliance with these standards is prima facie evidence of satisfying the duty to construct buildings that are reasonably safe to persons and property.

Part II. Part II contains a list of the standards that are published in Volume 3 of the *Uniform Building Code*. For the most part, these are the same standards that appeared in the previous edition of the code, some of which have been updated. Three standards of interest are UBC Standards 21-6, 21-7 and 21-8, which are not referenced by the *Uniform Building Code,* but are referenced by the *Uniform Code for Building Conservation.*

Part III. In addition to the UBC standards listed in Part II and the recognized standards listed in Part IV, a few other standards are referenced in various sections of the code. These referenced standards are listed. One referenced standard which is vital for proper application of Chapter 11 is CABO/ANSI A117.1, Accessible and Usable Buildings and Facilities. Another included in this category is ASME/ANSI A17.1 for elevators, which applies when Appendix Chapter 30 is adopted.

Part IV. Part IV contains the recognized standards that are referenced in Sections 3503 and 3504. These standards were published in the previous edition of the code, but for the most part, it was seldom necessary for the building official to use these standards while fulfilling ordinary code enforcement responsibilities. The building official may use the listed recognized standards as appropriate to determine compliance with the minimum levels of quality, performance, durability, strength, safety, fire resistance, effectiveness and suitability. It is anticipated that builders or suppliers of products listed in the recognized standards will provide the code enforcement official with a copy of the referenced standards when they propose to use one of the materials, procedures, tests, etc., which are listed therein.

APPENDIX

The appendix to the UBC contains subjects which the ICBO membership believes should not be a mandatory part of the code but, rather, an optional part, with each jurisdiction adopting all, parts or none of the appendix chapters, depending on its needs for enforcement in any given area. Also, in some cases, provisions are placed in the appendix because they are not thought to be fully developed enough to constitute provisions in the body of the code. Therefore, they are placed in the appendix in order to allow jurisdictions to test the provisions. In this latter case, the provisions may be placed in the body of the code after several years. Provisions of this latter type include the covered mall provisions of Section 404, which were initially contained in an appendix chapter, and those in Chapter 16 for earthquake design. Each appendix chapter contains subject material related to the same numbered chapter in the body of the code. Because of a diversity of topics, many of the appendix chapters contain several divisions.

Appendix Chapter 3

USE OR OCCUPANCY

Division I—DETENTION AND CORRECTIONAL FACILITIES

An appendix section on the construction of detention and correctional facilities was added to the 1991 edition since these Group I, Division 3 Occupancies are unique from other occupancy types of Section 308. Lock-up facilities are designed with security as the primary concern. This appendix chapter allows the designer some flexibility, yet offers sound fire protection for the building and safety for the incarcerated.

Division II—AGRICULTURAL BUILDINGS

The provisions of Division II were developed to address the needs of those jurisdictions (primarily unincorporated county territory) whose primary development is agricultural. In these cases, agricultural property usually consists of large tracts of land on which agricultural buildings are placed, usually with large open spaces and with essentially no congestion. Therefore, the provisions for agricultural buildings classify the structures as Group U, Division 3 Occupancies and include storage, livestock and poultry buildings, milk barns, shade structures, and horticultural structures.

Because of the generally large open spaces that usually surround the buildings and the relatively low occupant load, the limitations imposed on construction, height, area, occupancy separations, location on property and exiting are generally more liberal than the requirements in the body of the code for Group F, Division 2 Occupancies that would generally otherwise apply.

Division III—REQUIREMENTS FOR GROUP R, DIVISION 3 OCCUPANCIES

This division facilitates the provisions of Section 310.1, which references Appendix Chapter 3 as a complete code for construction of detached one- and two-family dwellings. In essence, Appendix Chapter 3, Division III, adopts by reference the 1995 edition of the *One and Two Family Dwelling Code*. This is a code publication of the Council of American Building Officials, an umbrella organization consisting of the International Conference of Building Officials, Building Officials and Code Administrators International, and Southern Building Code Congress International.

This adoption by reference facilitates the adoption of the *One and Two Family Dwelling Code* and gives jurisdictions easy access to alternative requirements that are nationally recognized for the construction of dwellings. The *One and Two Family Dwelling Code* is a comprehensive code that contains requirements for heating and plumbing systems in dwellings as well as requirements for the design and construction of the structure itself. By its adoption, the principles of code uniformity on a national basis are extended.

Division IV—REQUIREMENTS FOR GROUP R, DIVISION 4 OCCUPANCIES

Many jurisdictions believe the need for code provisions that apply to residential group care facilities. These types of facilities can range from child care through care of the infirm and disabled. However, in Division IV of Appendix Chapter 3, the residential group care facility is defined as group care for ambulatory, nonrestrained persons (note that there is no age criteria) who may have a mental or physical impairment. Also, the facility is further qualified by the number of "clients or residents," but this number does not include the facility staff.

The requirements in this division are a combination of the requirements of Chapter 3 in the body of the code for both Group R, Division 1 and Group R, Division 3 occupants, although in some instances the requirements in this division are more restrictive. Even though the occupants are ambulatory, they may be physically impaired and may at one time or another require assistance from the facility staff to properly exit the building. Therefore, these requirements are somewhat more restrictive in the following areas:

- Section 334.1 limits this occupancy to a maximum of two stories in height. Also the basic floor area is limited to 3,000 square feet (278.7 m²), although increases permitted in Sections 504, 505 and 506 are allowed.

- Section 334.2 is similar in concept to Section 310.2.2 in the body of the code as it limits the area above the first story to 3,000 square feet (278.7 m²) unless the building is of at least one-hour fire-resistive construction throughout.

- Section 334.3 provides special occupancy separations between Group R, Division 4 Occupancies and other occupancies. Exception 2 to this section is identical to Exception 3 to Section 302.4 in the body of the code relating to Group R, Division 3 Occupancies.

- Section 335 is virtually identical to the requirements for Group R, Division 3 Occupancies in the body of the code.

- Section 336 has more-restrictive requirements for the number of means of egress and path of exit travel, and this is understandable due to the nature of the occupants. As a result, two means of egress are required from any story or basement, regardless of the occupant load, and the maximum travel distance to exits is limited to 50 percent of that permitted in Chapter 10. Furthermore, emergency exit illumination is required.

- The remainder of this division, Sections 337 through 343, contain requirements which are similar to those in the body of the code.

Appendix Chapter 4
SPECIAL USE AND OCCUPANCY

Division I—BARRIERS FOR SWIMMING POOLS, SPAS AND HOT TUBS

This division, which was added to the 1991 edition, addresses barriers for swimming pools, spas and hot tubs. Drowning is the second leading cause of accidental death in the home for children under five years of age. It has been the number one cause of accidental death in the home for that age group in a number of states, including Arizona, California, Florida and Texas. Over 4,600 drowning and near-drowning incidents are estimated to occur each year in residential swimming pools at an estimated cost of approximately one billion dollars.

The use of effective residential swimming pool barriers is the best way to reduce these losses. A barrier is important to the safety of children since parents cannot be expected to keep children in their line of sight at all times.

Division II—AVIATION CONTROL TOWERS

These provisions, which were new for the 1982 edition of the UBC, are intended to reconcile the differences between the life-safety needs of air-traffic control towers and the life-safety requirements in the body of the code. For example, an air-traffic control tower life-safety requirement demands that controllers in the cab or at the observation level have a 360-degree view. This would not be possible if a stairway enclosure is required into that level. The life and property loss in these towers has been very small even though they have not complied completely with all the code requirements in the past. In developing these provisions, consideration was given to the inherent qualities of the use which makes normal requirements in the body of the code unnecessary. For example, air-traffic control personnel are required to undergo medical examinations to assure they are of sound body and mind. Recognition was also given to the life-safety record of these uses and the specific limitations which are imposed on the allowable size, type of construction, etc. The provisions also require early-warning systems by smoke detectors, and these devices are also required to be a part of an approved fire alarm system having audible alarms in all

occupied areas. Because of the critical nature of the facility, a standby power-generation system is required for towers over 65 feet (19 812 mm) in height.

Appendix Chapter 9
BASEMENT PIPE INLETS

These provisions are intended for those jurisdictions whose fire departments intend to fight basement fires from within the first story with a basement pipe. Basement pipe inlets are not required where the basement is equipped with an automatic fire sprinkler system or where the basement is used for storage of valuable materials or archives and similar items that are adversely affected by water.

Appendix Chapter 11
ACCESSIBILITY

Division I—SITE ACCESSIBILITY

Note: To enforce the requirements of Appendix Chapter 11, the chapter must first be adopted. Section 101.3 of the *Uniform Building Code* states "the provisions in the appendix shall not apply unless specifically adopted."

SECTION 1107 — ACCESSIBLE EXTERIOR ROUTES

The clear intent of these provisions is to provide, in sites with single or multiple buildings or facilities, access to each accessible element from all parking areas and from one accessible element to another on the same site.

An indicator of the critical nature of site development is the requirement for "the most practical direct route." A site with multiple buildings and a number of requirements for accessibility in each or several of those buildings may pose complex site design problems related to direct routes. Early involvement or early attention to the location of multiple accessible elements during site development may tend to eliminate most, if not all, related problems.

SECTION 1108 — PARKING FACILITIES

The number of accessible parking spaces required on a site varies by the total number of spaces provided. For other than specific institutional and residential uses, Table A-11-A is used as the basis for calculating the required number of spaces. Medical care facilities specializing in the treatment of persons with mobility impairments, as well as those facilities providing outpatient medical care, require a larger percentage of accessible spaces than addressed in the table.

In addition, for every eight accessible parking spaces, one accessible van space must be provided. As an example, consider a parking lot with 28 total parking spaces. According to Table A-11-A, one accessible space and one accessible van space shall be provided.

1108.3 Signs. Provisions for signs at accessible parking spaces are found in Section 4.28 of CABO/ANSI A117.1, with the specifications for letter and number heights found in Table 4.28.3. Signs must be placed in a position and at such a height that a vehicle parked in the space will not obscure it. These signs are not required to be installed when the total number of all parking spaces, including the accessible space, does not exceed five.

SECTION 1109 — PASSENGER LOADING ZONES

If a passenger loading zone is provided, it shall have an adjacent access aisle that is a part of the accessible route to the building. The space shall have a vertical clearance of at least 9 feet 6 inches (2895 mm) at the zone and along the vehicle access route on the site.

Division II—ACCESSIBILITY FOR EXISTING BUILDINGS

The provisions of this division were substantially altered in the 1994 UBC. In general the provisions contained in this appendix chapter are less detailed and place a greater reliance on determinations made by the building official. Code users should especially note that the special provisions related to historic preservation and the appeals section were eliminated. The appeals provisions were eliminated since they are addressed by Section 105 of the code.

SECTION 1111 — DEFINITIONS

The definition for alteration should be noted since the provisions which were formerly found in Section 3111 of the 1991 UBC, which applied to additions, were deleted. These provisions were removed as a part of the BCMC recommendations and result in additions being treated in a similar manner as other alterations of existing buildings.

Although the code contains a definition of what is "technically infeasible" in these provisions, the determination of what that is exactly is the building official's responsibility. Unlike new construction, alterations to existing facilities can create a number of unique problems. Each alteration must be evaluated on a case-by-case basis in order to determine the extent of the accessibility modifications.

SECTION 1112 — ALTERATIONS

1112.1.1 Compliance. Asking a number of questions may be helpful in determining compliance with Section 1112.1.1:

1. What is the current level of accessibility?

2. What is the scope of the alteration?

3. How will the alteration affect the current level of accessibility?

4. Does the alteration increase the accessibility or use of the building?

5. If it is technically infeasible, what is the maximum extent the alteration can be made to meet accessibility requirements?

1112.2 Modifications. A number of building elements are addressed in this section due to the importance of their features. To maintain a certain degree of accessibility to these elements, modifications to the standard provisions lessen the degree of

alteration required. However, alterations must occur at these minimum levels, regardless of their perceived technical infeasibility.

SECTION 1113 — CHANGE OF OCCUPANCY

This section was added in the 1994 code so that changes of occupancy would be specifically addressed. This leads to greater uniformity than would be possible if the issue were not specifically treated.

SECTION 1114 — HISTORIC PRESERVATION

The *Uniform Building Code* describes a historic building as one which has been designated by official action as having special historical or architectural significance. Such designation shall be made by the legally constituted authority of the jurisdiction. Again, key elements such as performance and assembly areas, toilets and dressing rooms, and hotel guest rooms must be specifically addressed.

Appendix Chapter 12
INTERIOR ENVIRONMENT

Division I—VENTILATION

Division I of Chapter 12 is an alternative to the ventilation requirements of Chapter 12 in the body of the code. When adopted, the division still allows for the use of natural ventilation. Mechanical ventilation, however, shall be capable of supplying ventilation air in accordance with Table A-12-A rather than as set forth in Sections 1202.2.1 and 1203.3. The division incorporates the latest ventilation rates for mechanical ventilation from ASHRAE 62-1989, Ventilation for Acceptable Indoor Air Quality. This division was added in the 1994 edition.

Division II—SOUND TRANSMISSION CONTROL

Appendix Chapter 12, Division II, is intended to provide regulations governing sound transmission control in residential buildings. It pertains to Group R Occupancy wall and floor-ceiling assemblies separating dwelling units or guest rooms from each other and from public space, such as interior corridors and service areas. These must be provided with airborne sound insulation for the walls and both airborne and impact sound insulation for the floor-ceiling assemblies.

For airborne sound insulation, the separating walls and floor-ceiling assemblies must be provided with insulation equal to that required for a sound transmission class (STC) of 50 (45 when field tested) as defined by recognized standards. The division lists four guideline standards which may be used for determining compliance. These are ASTM E 90 and E 413, Laboratory Determination of Airborne Sound Transmission Class (for STC); ASTM E 492, Impact Sound Insulation (for impact insulation class, or IIC); and ASTM E 336, Airborne Sound Insulation Field Test. Penetrations or openings through the assemblies must be sealed, lined, insulated or otherwise treated to maintain the required ratings. Dwelling unit entrance doors from interior corridors, together with their permanent seals, must have an STC rating of not less than 30, and the permanent seals must be maintained.

Floor-ceiling assemblies between separate units or guest rooms must provide impact sound insulation equal to that required to meet an IIC of 50 (45 when field tested) as defined in ASTM E 492. This standard was developed from HUD Publication FT/TS 24, "Guide to Noise Control in Multifamily Dwellings." Floor covering may be included in the assembly to obtain the required rating but must be maintained as a permanent part of the assembly or must be replaced by another floor covering providing the same sound insulation.

Field- or laboratory-tested wall or floor-ceiling designs having an STC or IIC of 50 or more as determined by recognized standards may be used without additional field testing when, in the opinion of the building official, the tested design has not been compromised by flanking halves. Tests may be required by the building official when evidence of compromised separations is noted.

Field airborne sound transmission test procedures are set forth in ASTM E 314 and E 336. If field testing is done, it must be done under the supervision of a professional acoustician experienced in the field. The acoustician must also forward certified tests to the building official.

The Gypsum Association's *Fire-Resistance Design Manual* contains generic sound transmission control systems which may be accepted by the building official where a laboratory test indicates the requirements of this chapter are met by the system.

Appendix Chapter 13

ENERGY CONSERVATION IN NEW BUILDING CONSTRUCTION

This chapter adopts by reference the *Model Energy Code* promulgated by CABO for those jurisdictions wanting to regulate energy conservation standards.

Appendix Chapter 15

REROOFING

Appendix Chapter 15 was developed to address the problems associated with unregulated reroofing operations. The intent of these provisions is to assure that when an existing building is reroofed, the existing roof is structurally sound and in a proper condition to receive the new roofing. The intent of the code is clearly stated in Section 1515, which requires that no reroofing shall be done until the building official has inspected the existing building and has given written approval for the reroofing. If evidence of ponding is observed, the section directs that corrective measures be taken.

In the case of built-up roofs, the written approval of the building official will generally take one of two possible forms:

1. The building official will require that the existing built-up roof cover be completely removed, and the new roof covering be installed in accordance with Chapter 15 on a proper substrate.
2. The building official may permit the reroofing to be applied over the existing roof under the conditions itemized in Section 1516.1. Under this option, the code requires certain preparatory measures as far as the existing roof covering is concerned so that the reroofing will be applied to a proper substrate.

For shingles and shakes, the building official's approval will generally permit reroofing over the existing roof covering, provided the installation of the new roof covering is in accordance with Section 1517 of this appendix.

Sections 1518, 1519, 1520 and 1521 provide requirements for tile, metal, foam and other roofing materials. Tile roofing may be installed over existing roof coverings subject to the approval of the building official. Substantiation of the ability of the existing roof structure to support the new tile is required.

Appendix Chapter 16

STRUCTURAL FORCES

Division I—SNOW LOAD DESIGN

The snow load design provisions in Appendix Chapter 16 are intended to expand on the provisions for snow loads in Chapter 16 in the body of the code by accounting specifically for unbalanced snow loading and drift effects. These provisions are a distillation of the snow load provisions in ASCE/ANSI A58.1, the design manual of the Metal Building Manufacturers Association (MBMA), and the snow load ordinances of Nevada and Placer Counties, California.[1,2] *Minimum Design Loads for Buildings and Other Structures* (ASCE/ANSI A58.1) and *Low Rise Building Systems Manual* published by MBMA are recommended reading for commentary on the snow load provisions.

Division II—EARTHQUAKE RECORDING INSTRUMENTATION

The provisions for earthquake-recording instrumentation in buildings in Seismic Zones 3 and 4 are intended to provide data from strong-motion earthquakes that, when synthesized, may be used to improve the code requirements for earthquake-resistant design. The intent of the code is that a sufficient number of multilevel buildings (over six stories in height) of various types of construction and configurations will eventually be instrumented so that records obtained from these instruments during strong-motion earthquakes will be representative of most of the buildings to be erected in the future. On this basis the provisions of the code should become more viable as the records are obtained and the results of their analyses incorporated into the code.

To help jurisdictions outside the United States, Appendix Chapter 16 contains a seismic zone tabulation for areas outside the United States. This list was approved for use in the 1976 UBC and has remained unchanged since. Discretion should be used when applying these seismic zones since many changes have occurred since that time.

Division IV—EARTHQUAKE REGULATIONS FOR SEISMIC-ISOLATED STRUCTURES

This division of Chapter 16 was developed by SEAOC's Seismology Committee on a statewide level. The recommended provisions are based on the most current information and practices of the present state-of-the-art in engineering design.

REFERENCES

[1]American Society of Civil Engineers (1987). *Minimum Design Loads for Buildings and Other Structures,* ASCE/ANSI A58.1. New York.

[2]Metal Building Manufacturers Association (1986). *Low Rise Building Systems Manual.* Cleveland, Ohio.

Appendix Chapter 18
WATERPROOFING AND DAMPPROOFING FOUNDATIONS

Appendix Chapter 18 on waterproofing and dampproofing foundations was added to the 1991 UBC to establish uniform criteria for jurisdictions that find such regulations necessary.

Appendix Chapter 19
PROTECTION OF RESIDENTIAL CONCRETE EXPOSED TO FREEZING AND THAWING

Appendix Chapter 19 is provided for those jurisdictions in areas where weathering can damage reinforced concrete. This chapter is specifically designed to address the requirements for Groups R and U occupancies which are three stories or less in height. The essence of these requirements is to increase the strength of the concrete used in various locations in residential buildings depending on the severity of the weathering potential. Figure A-19-1 provides a map of the United States showing those areas where the weathering probability varies from negligible to severe.

The intent of the provisions is to provide criteria for the use of normal-weight aggregate concrete where the site is such as to subject the building to alternating cycles of freezing and thawing. As previously indicated, the chapter requires increased compressive strength of the concrete for the higher weathering potential zones. The chapter also requires air-entrained concrete in the more severe cases since air entrainment provides a tougher concrete that is better able to resist the effects of deicing chemicals and freezing and thawing.

Appendix Chapter 21
PRESCRIPTIVE MASONRY CONSTRUCTION IN HIGH-WIND AREAS

SECTION 2112 — GENERAL

2112.2 Scope. This chapter provides construction material and detailing requirements for masonry structures not more than two stories in height located in areas with basic wind speeds from 80 through 100 miles per hour (mph) (129 through 177 km/h) which are not located in Seismic Zone 3 or 4. The Pacific coastline of Oregon and Washington, a small central area in Nevada, a footprint in the midwest, and the Gulf and Atlantic coastlines are regions in the continental United States where this chapter applies.

Area or occupancy classification of the structure is not restricted by the provisions. Roof and floor framing of wood, steel joists or concrete planks are allowed. Steel joist and concrete plank systems are required to be designed by an engineer or architect in accordance with state statutes.

2112.4 Materials. Material specifications for masonry units, grout and mortar are provided.

2112.6 and 2112.7 Foundations and Drainage. These foundation sizing requirements and drainage provisions also include references to the appropriate tables which are an important segment of the chapter.

2112.8 Wall Construction. Wall construction requirements, such as requirements for thickness and height, are referenced to tables. Also, provisions for walls in Seismic Zone 2 are included. Lintel and wall anchorage provisions are also provided.

2112.10 Lateral Force Resistance. References are provided to illustrate the required lateral-force-resisting system of floor and roof diaphragms and shear walls. The provisions of Section 2112.10.4 regarding interior plywood shear walls should be prudently applied only when complete construction details are provided.

Appendix Chapter 23
CONVENTIONAL LIGHT-FRAME CONSTRUCTION IN HIGH-WIND AREAS

SECTION 2337 — GENERAL

2337.1 Purpose. The focus of this appendix chapter is on reducing, not attempting to eliminate, damages due to high winds. Therefore, empirical procedures were used in its development and "limit" state or member "capacity" design was used in establishing prescribed member sizes.

2337.2 Scope. This section provides boundary conditions for the applicability of this chapter. Referencing conventional light-frame construction is intended to ensure that member sizes are selected to comply with the code requirements and span tables in Chapter 23, specifically those in Section 2320. Uplift requirements are based on a 32-foot-wide structure (9.75 m) with tie straps at the exterior walls only. Other configurations, such as layouts with interior bearing walls, will require special detailing. Limiting the areas to basic wind speeds from 80 through 110 mph (129 through 177 km/h) was considered prudent and realistic. Figure 16-1 in the body of the code illustrates the limited areas of applicability of this chapter: the northwest and southeast coastlines, a footprint in the central plains, and the coastal areas of Alaska.

An exception is provided that permits carports and garages accessory to Group R, Division 3 Occupancies to comply only with the tie-strap requirements for roof-framing members to exterior studs, posts or other supporting members, and with the load path specified for beams, columns and foundations when the opening width is between 12 and 16 feet (3658 and 4877 mm). The 600-square-foot (55.7 m²) area limit was considered reasonable due to the small occupant load and separate building requirement. Also, Section 312.2.1 will not permit garages or carports to exceed one story in height.

2337.4 General. A general reference to conventional light-frame construction provisions is provided to indicate that specific items listed in this appendix chapter are in addition to Section 2320 criteria. The reference to "other methods" is intended to allow portions of structures which vary from these prescriptive requirements to be constructed when approved by the building official if an engineer or architect provides an analysis with appropriate construction details.

The design reference to "approved national standards" for wave action or tidal surge could be met by such publications as the 1984 *Shore Protection Manual,* Volumes I and II, prepared for the Department of the Army, Corps of Engineers, and the *Coastal Construction Manual FEMA-55* published in February 1986 by the Federal Emergency Management Agency (FEMA).

The requirement for all parts of elements to be noncorrosive was placed in the general section to emphasize the provision and ensure it is apparent. This text is also similar to the veneer tie requirements in Section 1403.

2337.5 Complete Load Path and Uplift Ties. The main thrust of this chapter is the detailing requirements shown in Figure A-23-1, which illustrates a complete load path to resist the uplift and horizontal force demand of the wind.

This section contains the charging statement regarding corrosion protection of connections and fasteners and the basic tie strap material and its cross-sectional area.

Section 2337.5.2 specifies that provisions to assure a complete load path for anchoring the exterior walls of the structure apply to cripple walls and walls supported by concrete slabs on grade. The phrase "continuous foundation" refers to concrete slab-on-grade or raised foundation systems, such as interior posts and girders with enclosing continuous exterior footings. The reference to elevated foundations applies when the structural system is supported on wood piles in accordance with Section 2337.10.

Section 2337.5.3 specifies a reduced anchor bolt spacing of 4 feet (1219 mm) on center when the basic wind speed is 90 mph (145 km/h) or greater. This 4-foot (1219 mm) dimension was established as the basic spacing for tie-strap requirements shown in Figure A-23-1.

In Section 2337.5.4, floor-to-foundation tie refers to concrete slab-on-grade, cripple wall, and raised or elevated foundation systems where studs or floor joists are supported on sill plates directly over a concrete foundation or wood girder. Figure A-23-1 and Table A-23-B shows four typical examples.

Section 2337.5.5 specifies that exterior wall stud spacing for 2 by 4 studs should not exceed 16 inches (406 mm) on center when the wind speed is 90 mph (145 km/h) or greater. Table 23-IV-B may be used to select exterior wall studs and their spacing when the basic wind speed is less than 90 mph (145 km/h). The height limitation for bearing or nonbearing assemblies applies if studs are selected from Table 23-IV-B and a specific design is not provided.

In areas of basic wind speeds where the minimum nailing of wall studs to top and bottom or sole plates required in Table 23-II-B-1 is not adequate, it may be prudent to require framing clips or other approved connection methods.

Spacing of required interior shear panels is based on the width of the structure. The basic model for the empirical analysis and "limit" design of the lateral-force-resisting system was based on a plan layout in the shape of two adjoining squares. Judgment should be exercised when the length of the structure greatly exceeds twice its width. As the ratio of length to width increases, the structural system will be stretched beyond its reserve capacity strength (due to deformation limitations) with only exterior foundation walls to transfer lateral forces to the ground.

The wall sheathing requirements in Section 2337.5.6 are based on the concept of limiting the maximum length of openings for exterior walls and required interior shear walls. The phrase "interior main cross-stud partition" was selected to be consistent with Section 2320. Provisions for exterior wall sheathing to extend from the foundation sill plate to roof-level top plates are intended to provide a shear transfer mechanism. The shrinkage effects of floor joists were addressed by allowing panel edges to be backed by 2-inch (51 mm) or wider nominal framing. Essentially, the joint at the floor level between the floor and ceiling surface is the area of concern.

This paragraph lists limiting height-to-length ratios for different sheathing materials, which are identical to requirements currently in the code. Also included are minimum 4-foot-length (1219 mm) and in-plane spacing requirements for required shear panels. These limitations are identical to the prescriptive requirements in Section 2320.

Figure A-23-1 illustrates the required floor-to-floor tie strap and its spacing to which Section 2337.5.7 refers.

Since roof uplift forces are a major contributing factor in damage to roof systems in high-wind areas, the roof-to-wall connection is the keystone of the provisions. The reference to "roof-framing member" in Section 2337.5.8 is intended to apply to prefabricated truss systems when an approved analysis with details is submitted. Whether conventional construction provisions are intended to apply to roof trusses was purposely left to the judgment of the local jurisdiction.

Areas at discontinuities, such as eave overhangs, induce large uplift forces which must be resisted at the exterior wall. Therefore, eave projections are limited to 3 feet (914 mm) unless an analysis and appropriate details to resist the demand are provided.

The uplift demand on larger openings up to 12 feet (3658 mm) in width is addressed by doubling the required tie straps and connecting them to a full-height doubled wall stud. A specific design is required when the opening exceeds 12 feet (3658 mm) in width.

An exception is included to allow garages and carports accessory to Group R, Division 3 Occupancies to have openings large enough to accommodate two full-size automobiles. Detailing requirements are provided for connection of wood post column bases and caps to the concrete footing and roof beam above. The exception is intended to allow the building official to approve available building hardware so that realistic detailing demands are placed on carports or garages serving Group R, Division 3 Occupancies.

Ridge ties shown in Figure A-23-1 are required by Section 2337.5.9 to maintain the integrity of the roof system which will be subject to significant tensile chord forces at the ridge due to uplift effects. Conversely, compression forces may affect the ceiling joist system or bottom chord of any truss members.

2337.6 Masonry Veneer. Required anchor ties for masonry veneer are spaced closer than specified in Section 1403.6.4.2, Item 1, for Seismic Zones 3 and 4, where the anchor tie-spacing requirement for anchored veneer is not more than 2 square feet (0.19 m²) of wall area but not more than 24 inches (610 mm) on center horizontally.

2337.7 Roof Sheathing. Solid roof sheathing to maintain adequate diaphragm action is required. The unsupported edges of plywood or particleboard panels are not intended to require blocking. Blocking noted in the last sentence is intended to occur over exterior walls at the roof diaphragm boundary.

2337.8 Gable-end Walls. Uplift effects of areas at discontinuities induce upward loading which may be limited by reducing the eave overhang. The provision for requiring analysis and details if the eave projection exceeds 2 feet (610 mm) is similar to the eave overhang requirements for a condition not at gable ends.

Performance requirements for out-of-plane bracing of gable-end walls when wall studs are not continuous between the foundation sole plate and the top roof plates are provided. Bracing at intermediate levels or points of support is required.

When gable-end wall studs are discontinuous, they should be connected to out-of-plane bracing at points of support or intermediate floor levels with approved fasteners at each end.

2337.9 Roof Covering. Roof-covering requirements are more difficult to address since testing procedures are so varied and actual installations subjected to high-wind speeds have performed erratically. A performance-oriented approach referencing Chapter 15 and increasing installation requirements is considered prudent at this time.

2337.10 Elevated Foundation. A wood pile system may be permitted to support not more than one story when approved by the building official. This phrasing was necessary since unused under-floor space could be considered a story as defined in Section 220. The provision allows a loft condition when the mezzanine requirements are considered. Elevated systems along

coastlines or inland waterways may require a foundation investigation.

Section 2337.10.2 states that treated wood and corrosion-resistant connections shall be provided at all exposed locations due to location and exposure to atmosphere or the elements.

The wood pile sizes and spacing shown in Section 2337.10.3 are derived from the *Coastal Construction Manual FEMA-55*. Minimum embedment length refers to penetration into firm, suitable natural grade.

In Section 2337.10.4, the span of girders is required to be parallel to potential battering effects due to water surges and floating debris. Framing direction is intended to protect the primary floor members.

In Section 2337.10.5, the minimum size of connection plates and bolting requirements are listed to provide substantial support for and maintain the integrity of the floor girder and pile system.

TABLE A-23-A — WALL SHEATHING AT EXTERIOR WALLS AND INTERIOR MAIN CROSS-STUD PARTITIONS

Wall sheathing requirements referenced in Section 2337.5.6 are tabulated in this table. The heading "LEVEL" in the third column refers to structural levels such as mezzanines and under-floor spaces. The table contains sheathing types required for basic wind speed, exposures, and height of buildings based on story and level divisions.

TABLE A-23-B — ROOF AND FLOOR ANCHORAGE AT EXTERIOR WALLS

Roof and floor anchorages to exterior walls are listed. The phrase "floor to floor" refers to levels and was preferred to "story to story." Floor-to-foundation details require special consideration when the table lists more than four 10d nails as shown for the raised foundation system.

TABLE A-23-C — RIDGE TIE-STRAP NAILING

Ridge tie-strap nailing is specified for four basic wind speeds and three exposures.

FIGURE A-23-1 — COMPLETE LOAD PATH DETAILS

This figure shows a cross section through a typical wood structure and indicates tie-strap spacing and location with references to appropriate tables.

Appendix Chapter 30

ELEVATORS, DUMBWAITERS, ESCALATORS AND MOVING WALKS

Appendix Chapter 30 is intended for those jurisdictions which find it necessary to regulate elevators, dumbwaiters, escalators and moving walks. The provisions are similar to ASME/

ANSI A17.1-1987 (and supplements), *Safety Code for Elevators and Escalators.*

The essential impact of the provisions in Appendix Chapter 30 is to provide administrative regulations so that the jurisdiction may adopt the ANSI *Safety Code for Elevators and Escalators.* Also included are provisions for operation and maintenance and provisions for the abatement of unsafe conditions in elevators.

Appendix Chapter 31
SPECIAL CONSTRUCTION

Division I—FLOOD-RESISTANT CONSTRUCTION

Added to the 1991 *Uniform Building Code,* this division addresses flood-resistant construction and provides jurisdictions with uniform regulations for areas subject to flooding. Hazard Zone A or V must be established when flood-resistant construction is required.

SECTION 3104 — GENERAL

3104.2 Scope. The requirements of this division are essentially in accordance with FEMA and National Flood Insurance Program regulations. The most recent Flood Insurance Rate Map published by FEMA may be considered in establishing the official flood hazard map.

SECTION 3105 — MANUFACTURED STRUCTURES

Under this section, new or replacement manufactured structures are required to be elevated and anchored in accordance with hazard zone requirements.

SECTION 3107 — FLOOD HAZARD ZONES—
A ZONES

3107.2 Elevation. The lowest floor of buildings or structures in a Hazard Zone A should be elevated above or at the base flood elevation unless flood-resistant construction is provided. Some uses are permitted below the base flood elevations when the enclosure requirements of Section 3107.4 are applied.

3107.4 Flood-resistant Construction. When floors usable for human occupancy are provided below the base flood elevation, the following requirements apply:

1. Exterior walls and floors should be impermeable to water.
2. Effects of buoyancy and flood loading should be considered in the structural design.
3. Openings should be provided with approved closures and should be capable of resisting flood forces.
4. Floor and wall penetrations should be sealed, and sewer and storm drain systems must be provided with closure devices.

3107.5 Plan Requirements for Flood-resistant Construction. Buildings or structures with floors below the base flood elevation are required to be designed by an engineer or architect licensed in accordance with state statutes.

SECTION 3108 — COASTAL HIGH HAZARD ZONES—
V ZONES

3108.2 Elevation. In a Hazard Zone V, buildings or structures should be elevated above the base flood elevation.

3108.3 Enclosures below Base Flood Elevation. Only limited obstructions are allowed in areas below the base flood elevation. Structural elements and stored items which may be moved are among the obstructions permitted. Also, breakaway walls or partitions and screening are allowed.

3108.4 Foundations. Requirements for depth of foundation elements considering erosion and effect of scour are provided. Also, loading combinations of wind and wave forces for piles are emphasized.

3108.5 Plan Requirements for Coastal High-hazard Construction. A building or structure in a Hazard Zone V is required to have its foundation and its connections designed by an engineer or architect licensed in accordance with state statutes.

SECTION 3109 — ELEVATION CERTIFICATION

The actual elevation of the lower floor in a Hazard Zone V and the bottom of the lowest horizontal structural member in a coastal high-hazard zone should be certified by a qualified professional.

SECTION 3110 — DESIGN REQUIREMENTS

3110.2 Design Loads. Approved national standards such as the Flood-Proofing Regulations by the United States Army Corps of Engineers may be used as a reference to establish water and impact forces.

3110.3 Load Combinations. Load combinations may be selected by the design engineer and approved by the building official. Load combinations from the publication referenced in Section 3110.2 above may be considered as fulfilling the requirement.

3110.4 Stress Increases. When flood loads are combined with dead or dead and live load combinations using allowable stress design, a one-third increase in stresses is allowed. When strength design using load factors and capacity-reduction coefficients is used, flood loads may be considered as dead loads in dead and live load combinations, and wind loads in other combinations.

3110.5 Overturning. The dead-load-resisting moment shall be 1.5 times the overturning moment due to wind and flood loads acting simultaneously. Friction on piles or caissons should not be used to resist the overturning effect. Sliding resistance to wind and flood forces should also be based on the minimum 1.5 ratio of resistance to actual lateral forces.

Division II—MEMBRANE STRUCTURES

Because regulations for membrane structures are of the type which are not universally adopted, they are placed in the appendix for the convenience of those jurisdictions which regulate membrane structures. The regulations cover all such structures, which include air-supported, air-inflated, cable-supported or frame-supported structures. The intent of the provisions is that, except for the unique features of membrane structures, they otherwise comply with the code as far as occupancy requirements and area are concerned. Membrane structures are limited to one story in height since, at the time the regulations were developed, there was insufficient experience to justify multi-level structures enclosed with a membrane.

In general, membrane structures are considered to be of Type V-N construction except where the membrane is noncombustible, as defined in Section 215. When a noncombustible membrane is used, the membrane structure will be classified as Type II-N construction. An exception permits the use of a noncombustible membrane on a structure which would otherwise comply as Type I or Type II-F.R. where the membrane is used exclusively as a roof and is located more than 25 feet (7620 mm) above any floor, balcony or gallery. This is a similar provision to Sections 602.5 and 603.5. This exception will permit noncombustible membranes to be constructed as roof systems for sports stadiums and similar buildings.

The structural design of membrane structures is subject to the approval of the building official since there were no design standards when the provisions were developed which could be considered to be national consensus standards for the structural design of membrane structures. However, the various trade associations involved, such as the Air-Supported Structures Institute, have developed design standards for their own particular types of membrane structures. The ASCE publication, *Air-Supported Structures,* contains a summary of the design procedures for air-supported structures.[1]

Division III—PATIO COVERS

SECTION 3116 — PATIO COVERS DEFINED

The intent of the UBC is that patio covers are essentially open-type structures used in conjunction with Group R, Division 3 or single dwelling units in Group R, Division 1 Occupancies or with Group U Occupancies. The intent is that they be used for outdoor living purposes or recreation and not for the uses generally ascribed to Group U Occupancies and Group R, Division 3 Occupancies. This section also provides the details and specifications to provide the required amount of openness. A patio structure may also be considered to be an open structure even though the openings are enclosed with insect screening or readily removable plastic panels.

SECTION 3117 — DESIGN LOADS

Design loads are loads normally required for buildings and structures in Chapter 16. In the case of the roof design load, the minimum vertical design load on the roof is 10 pounds per square foot (0.48 kN/m^2), except that snow loads, where applicable, shall be used where they exceed 10 pounds per square foot (0.48 kN/m^2).

Because wind loads are based on a height zone of less than 12 feet (3657 mm), the loads are less than those required by Chapter 16 for the usual type of structure. When the patio cover is to be enclosed with insect screening or the permitted plastic panels, the wind load design shall be applied to the entire structure, assuming that it is fully enclosed. As indicated previously, the insect screening, however, is not considered an enclosure from the standpoint of transmitting light and ventilation from required windows.

REFERENCE

[1]American Society of Civil Engineers (1979). *Air-Supported Structures.* New York, New York.

Appendix Chapter 33
EXCAVATION AND GRADING

Not every jurisdiction is located in an area where the topography of the terrain requires grading operations on private property. In those areas where developers need to grade private property, Appendix Chapter 33 provides appropriate administrative and technical regulations to assure the jurisdiction of reasonable safety against slope failure, landslides and other soil failure hazards.

The provisions in Appendix Chapter 33 were written by a committee of representatives from technical organizations in this field. One committee member, C. Michael Scullin, wrote *Excavation and Grading Code Administration, Inspection and Enforcement,* which contains a detailed commentary with interpretations beginning on page 290.[1] As Mr. Scullin was intimately involved with the development of the provisions, his commentary is recommended reading, and no further commentary will be provided for this chapter except for the discussion of changes that have been made since the 1976 edition of the UBC.

Since Mr. Scullin's commentary on Chapter 33, which was based on the 1976 edition of the UBC, there have been substantial revisions to Appendix Chapter 33, and these are analyzed below.

SECTION 3308 — DEFINITIONS

The definition of "approval" has been revised and now brings the building official into the process. The revisions to the definitions of "soils engineer" and "soils engineering" more properly define the terms. A new definition has been added for "professional inspection" to cover those areas where this term is used.

SECTION 3309 — GRADING PERMIT REQUIREMENTS

3309.3 Grading Designation. Previous Section 3317.2 has been relocated to Section 3309.3 with some editorial changes.

This section clarifies that the type of grading should be identified for the permit since "engineered grading" is more restrictive than "regular grading." Since the building official does not need to be involved in this decision, the phrase "with the approval of the building official" was deleted.

3309.4 Engineered Grading Requirements. This section states the requirements for "engineered grading" at the permit stage. Section 3309.3 requires that the plans be prepared by a civil engineer. Therefore, the phrase "when required by the building official" was replaced with "engineered grading." Thus, the permittee is responsible for the work and to the building official.

Former Sections 3309.3 and 3309.4, which stated requirements for plans and specifications as required according to engineered grading have been combined in Section 3309.4, and the requirements for regular grading are defined separately in Section 3309.8.

Section 3309.4, Item 6, is an editorial change. The requirement has been moved from former Section 3309.5, Soils Engineering Report, and Section 3309.6, Engineering Geology Report, since it is a requirement for the person preparing the plans. Reports frequently contain recommendations that do not apply to grading and should not be included by reference. However, some recommendations are too detailed and lengthy to add to the plans, yet may be unintentionally modified if not added verbatim.

3309.5 Soils Engineering Report. New language has been added to require that the soils engineering report also include corrective measures. These are to include buttress fills, when necessary. Also, recommendations made in the soils engineering report covering the adequacy of sites to be developed by the proposed grading, including the stability of slopes, are required.

3309.7 Liquefaction Study. This provision was added to the 1994 edition with the intent of providing simple guidelines to assist the building official in determining when a liquefaction study should be conducted. The section applies only in Seismic Zones 3 and 4, where liquefaction during a seismic event can result in extensive structural damage.

3309.8 Regular Grading Requirements. Section 3309.8 has been added to cover regular grading and to require the needed minimum information related to the grading for submittal to the building official for approval.

3309.9 Issuance. This section requires the soils engineer to observe and test the engineered grading.

SECTION 3312 — CUTS

3312.1 General. The provisions in this section are similar to those already in the code for fills since it is appropriate to have the same provisions apply to cuts.

3312.2 Slope. Provisions have been added to allow slopes steeper than 1 unit horizontal in 2 units vertical (50% slope) when proper substantiating data are submitted.

SECTION 3313 — FILLS

3313.2 Preparation of Ground. In the earlier editions of the UBC, the last sentence in this section was a definition of "unsuitable soil." This has been deleted since it was redundant and simply stated the obvious. The present last sentence has been revised so that the soils engineer or engineering geologist "accepts" instead of "approves" the fill. Under the revised definition for "approval," the building official makes the approvals, not the soils engineer or the engineering geologist. Because some geographical areas require the placement of rock near the surface because of the availability of materials, the provisions should depend on the engineer preparing the plans to specify what is needed. The deletion permits more or less restrictions as needed for a particular jobsite.

SECTION 3314 — SETBACKS

The requirements for setbacks of buildings on graded building sites have been moved to Chapter 18, as Appendix Chapter 33 relates only to grading operations. The provisions remaining in Section 3314 relate to setbacks of cut-and-fill slopes from site boundaries.

SECTION 3315 — DRAINAGE AND TERRACING

3315.1 General. The language added at the end of this section is to provide a lower limit for graded slopes requiring terracing, which is 1 unit horizontal in 3 units vertical (33.3% slope). It is assumed that slopes flatter than 1 unit horizontal in 3 units vertical (33.3% slope) are not critical as far as drainage and terracing are concerned.

SECTION 3317 — GRADING INSPECTION

3317.6 Building Official. This section is a performance requirement involving inspections by the building official. The frequency of inspections is left up to the judgment of the building official.

SECTION 3318 — COMPLETION OF WORK

3318.1 Final Reports. Item 1 has been revised to indicate that the civil engineer's responsibility is not to approve the work but rather to state to the best of his or her knowledge that the work was done in accordance with the final approved grading plans. Changes have been made to Section 3318.1, Items 2 and 3, so that the consulting soils engineer makes a finding rather than provides an approval. The building official is responsible for providing final approval under the requirements of Section 3318.2.

REFERENCE

[1]Scullin, C. Michael (1983). *Excavation and Grading Code Administration, Inspection and Enforcement.* Prentice-Hall, Inc., Englewood Cliffs, New Jersey.

Appendix Chapter 34

EXISTING STRUCTURES

Division I—LIFE-SAFETY REQUIREMENTS FOR EXISTING BUILDINGS OTHER THAN HIGH-RISE BUILDINGS

SECTION 3406 — GENERAL

The provisions of Section 3406.2 are fraught with problems unless scrupulous attention is given to the rights of the building owners, and due process is granted as discussed in Section 104.2 of this handbook. Also, the blanket time constraints listed in this section can create an impossible enforcement task for the jurisdiction when it is faced with a rush of plans within 18 months of the effective date and then all of the completions occur approximately 18 months thereafter. It would seem more appropriate to follow the provisions of Section 3415 in Division II.

SECTION 3407 — EXITS

The means of egress provisions are intended to obtain reasonably safe exiting from existing buildings that do not comply with the code. For example, the second means of egress from upper floors may be an existing fire escape or an exit ladder device as specified in Section 3407. Although fire escapes and exit ladder devices are not permitted for new construction, their use in existing buildings is warranted since they provide additional safety where only one exit is available.

Stair construction is required to comply with the minimum requirements in UBC Chapter 10 for stairs in dwellings, which is considered to provide reasonable safety for existing buildings.

These provisions also intend to provide corridor protection somewhat similar to that required in Chapter 10, except that the building official is given authority to substitute solid-wood doors not less than $1^3/4$ inches (45 mm) thick for the 20-minute smoke- and draft-control assembly. Also, authority is granted to accept existing wood lath and plaster or $^1/2$-inch (12.7 mm) regular gypsum wallboard. As with all the provisions in this division, these uses of existing materials which will provide some measure of fire safety are intended to meet the objectives of the division without creating undue hardship for the owner of the building.

SECTION 3408 — ENCLOSURE OF VERTICAL SHAFTS

In this section the code intends to provide protection for vertical shafts unless the building is protected by an automatic fire sprinkler system. The code intends that where a building is fully sprinklered, the hazard presented by vertical openings in multistory buildings is not so great as to significantly compromise life safety.

The basic requirement is for a continuous shaft of one-hour fire-resistive construction. However, stairways need not be enclosed in a continuous shaft provided they are cut off at each floor level and exit corridors leading to the stairways are protected with sprinklers.

SECTION 3409 — BASEMENT ACCESS OR SPRINKLER PROTECTION

The intent of this section is identical to that of Section 904.2.2 in the body of the UBC.

SECTION 3410 — STANDPIPES

The provisions in Section 3410 may create a problem where Exception 2 to Section 3408 is utilized for stairways. Without a continuous stair enclosure, it will be difficult for fire department personnel to utilize the standpipe outlets in an efficient manner.

SECTION 3411 — SMOKE DETECTORS

The requirement for smoke detectors has the same rationale as that for Section 310.9 in the code, and in the case of existing buildings, the code permits the detectors to be battery operated.

SECTION 3412 — SEPARATION OF OCCUPANCIES

This requirement has the same rationale as the requirements in Chapter 3 for occupancy separations. However, in the case of one-hour fire-resistive occupancy separations, the building official is given authority to allow the use of existing wood lath and plaster in good condition or $^1/2$-inch (12.7 mm) gypsum wallboard in lieu of the basic protection required for one-hour fire-resistive construction.

Division II—LIFE-SAFETY REQUIREMENTS FOR EXISTING HIGH-RISE BUILDINGS

Even though high-rise buildings in the United States have historically had a good safety record, relatively recent fires in high-rise buildings resulting in substantial life loss and property damage have precipitated the development of proposed minimum requirements to retroactively address existing high-rise buildings. The goal in developing these requirements was to address life-safety concerns first, with property damage considerations being secondary.

There were many other high-rise requirements of Section 403 which also were considered for inclusion in these provisions but after considerable discussion were deemed inappropriate for existing high-rise buildings and were not included. Some of these excluded provisions are as follows:

1. **Compartmentation of nonsprinklered buildings.** Compartmentation as a mandatory requirement to be retroactively applied to existing buildings was considered. However, it was not included on the basis that the more critical buildings as far as life loss is concerned, such as apartment houses and hotels, are already typically inherently compartmented by the partitions that are normally constructed for these types of uses. This is also the case for some office buildings but is not as prevalent as for residential buildings.

2. **Helicopter landing area on roofs.** A helicopter landing area or hovering area may be beneficial, but the mandating of such provisions for existing buildings would in most cases require extensive structural strengthening of the roof structure and other modifications to ensure a reasonably unobstructed hovering or landing area.

Additionally, if a helicopter landing or hovering area is mandated, additional access to the roof of the building must also be mandated for the use of the building occupants and firefighters, with a further increase in the cost of compliance. As a result, this type of provision was not included on the basis of the very low cost-benefit ratio.

3. **Emergency power to all life-safety systems in the building.** Emergency power was also considered as excessive in cost for the benefits to be derived. The requirement for emergency power for exit lighting and signs was deemed sufficient to accomplish the desired life-safety goal for existing buildings.

4. **Stairway pressurization.** Provisions for stairway pressurization were not included on the basis that the costs would be excessive.

5. **Exterior windows for smoke ventilation.** The mandatory requirement for exterior ventilation windows or, alternatively, for major modification of the HVAC system to provide smoke control as required for new structures was felt, again, not to be economically justified in comparison with the benefits to be derived. Moreover, most existing buildings have exterior windows which can be used for ventilation during a fire. Also, the installation of a manual HVAC shutdown is considered to be adequate.

6. **Corridors used as plenums for the HVAC system.** This subject engendered considerable discussion within the code development committee, and a great number of solutions to the problem were suggested, depending on the assumptions made regarding the type of system used. However, the committee was unable to agree on definitive requirements, and it was agreed that dependence would be placed on the manual shutdown of the HVAC system. Where individual room units are utilized for HVAC, it was felt that emergency instructions to the occupants regarding the closing of dampers or stuffing of wet towels into the damper openings would be the best, most cost-effective solution.

7. **Standpipes.** Virtually all existing high-rise buildings are equipped with standpipes and further requirements were deemed unnecessary.

SECTION 3413 — SCOPE

The scope of these provisions for existing high-rise buildings is limited to high-rise office buildings, apartments and hotels. Institutional occupancies are excluded on the basis that such occupancies are usually covered by existing multilayered regulations from federal and state agencies as well as local regulations. The multilayered regulatory system involving hospitals is such that the life safety of the occupants in existing hospitals is at least equivalent to that required by the provisions of this division. The intent of the provisions is to provide requirements to save as many lives as possible through reasonable, minimal life-safety requirements.

SECTION 3414 — GENERAL

These provisions provide for less protection than that required for new buildings, and in the case of exiting systems, the requirements may provide less life safety than prior code requirements. Therefore, it is important to specify that these provisions shall not be construed to allow the elimination of life-safety systems or the reduction in the level of life safety which was required by the code and under which the existing high-rise building was constructed. This is an important life-safety provision.

SECTION 3415 — COMPLIANCE DATA

The criteria and times required for compliance with these regulations are adequately flexible to ensure the enforcement agency is not forced into a corner by impossible compliance dates. The first action required by the code is a notice by the enforcement agency to the owner that the owner's building is potentially subject to these regulations by the enforcement agency. Not only are the compliance data flexible enough to allow the building official to obtain compliance without undue hardship, the provisions also allow the building official to grant extensions of time when hardship has been shown or when practical difficulties require an extension of time.

SECTION 3416 — AUTHORITY OF THE BUILDING OFFICIAL

The intent is that consideration of alternate methods which provide levels of safety equal to or greater than those required by the code should be based on existing structured methods for determining fire- and life-safety alternatives. Examples are evaluation systems, point systems and other methods of systems analysis currently recognized and used by the fire-protection engineering community.

The building official is further authorized to waive specific individual requirements when it can be shown that they are not physically possible or practical and, furthermore, that a practical alternative cannot be provided.

SECTION 3417 — APPEALS BOARD

It is the intent of this section that individuals or owners may seek administrative relief from the requirements imposed by the building official through an appeals board which has been established in accordance with Section 105 of the UBC.

SECTION 3418 — SPECIFIC PROVISIONS AND ALTERNATES

3418.1 Specific Provisions. Table A-34-A is a matrix that contains the basic provisions required for the life-safety protection of existing high-rise buildings. The life-safety requirements are listed in the left-hand column. Across the top are listed the three use classifications as well as the three height zones for each use classification. Therefore, all that is necessary to determine the requirements for a building is to enter the table with the occupancy classification and height zone and then to read vertically downward to determine whether a life-safety provision is required or not. In general, the requirements for Group R, Division 1 Occupancies are more restrictive than for Group B Occupancies.

The occupancy classifications have been divided into three different height zones on the basis of three factors:

1. The lower limit of Height Zone 1 was chosen to agree with the current provisions within the UBC: namely, the maximum external reach capability of fire department suppression and rescue apparatus.

2. The upper limit of Height Zone 1 was predicated on buildings which have occupied floors not in excess of 149 feet (45 415 mm) above the lowest level to which fire department apparatus are capable of effecting total evacuation in a reasonable amount of time.

3. The upper limit of 399 feet (121.6 m) for Height Zone 2 was based on the fire department's ability to pump water.

3418.1.1 Type of construction. Retroactively mandating the installation of an automatic sprinkler system in all existing high-rise buildings was deemed unnecessary and economically unrealistic, except for those buildings which do not have inherent fire resistance in the basic construction. The lack of inherent fire resistance in the basic building presents a sufficient life-safety hazard to warrant the mandatory installation of an automatic sprinkler system. Therefore, Type II-N, III-N or V-N buildings have no inherent resistance against fire and are required to be protected by an automatic sprinkler system. The exception is intended to reduce the cost of the automatic fire sprinkler system where no other regulations require water flow meters or backflow preventers. Backflow preventers in particular can represent a substantial proportion of the total cost of the sprinkler system; where there are no other regulations which require their use, it is the intent of these provisions that they not be required.

Owners of buildings which do not require the mandatory installation of an automatic fire sprinkler system may still wish to provide that protection. When sprinkler protection is voluntarily provided in Type I, II-F.R., II One-hour, III One-hour, IV or V One-hour construction, the provisions provide trade-offs. These will be discussed in the specific life-safety item where a trade-off is permitted. The intent of those who developed these provisions was to encourage automatic fire sprinkler protection wherever possible and to make it mandatory only in those buildings not having inherent fire-resistant qualities. Therefore, it was felt desirable to permit as many trade-offs as possible consistent with life safety in order to make the retrofitting of the building as economical as possible.

3418.1.2 Automatic sprinklers. These partial sprinkler systems are required in all buildings. They are considered an essential part of life safety for existing buildings.

3418.1.3 Fire department communication system. The need for an effective fire department communication system within a high-rise structure cannot be overemphasized. Without the capability of coordinating the fire department personnel, control of the fire, rescue activities and general efficient use of emergency personnel are not possible. The provisions permit the use of portable communication equipment if such equipment provides communication between all critical elements of the building.

3418.1.4 Single-station smoke detectors. Installation of single-station smoke detectors within all dwelling units or guest rooms is deemed appropriate to ensure that sleeping occupants in close proximity to the fire or area exposed to smoke would be given the maximum amount of time to exit the affected area. Such smoke detectors would also result in an earlier detection of the emergency condition and subsequent notification of the fire department.

3418.1.5 Manual fire alarm system. A manual fire alarm system in unsprinklered buildings is considered necessary to expedite the notification of the fire department. This will reduce the fire department emergency response time, and emergency evacuation can be accomplished within a reasonable time following detection of the fire. The installation of the manual fire alarm system is not required in a building that is sprinklered voluntarily. In addition to the control and size limitation of the fire by the sprinkler system, it also provides its own alarm.

3418.1.6 Occupant voice notification system. A perusal of Table A-34-A will show that the installation of an occupant voice notification system is necessary only for apartments and hotels where evacuation of the building may be impractical (namely, in Height Zones 2 and 3). Office buildings in all height zones are not required to have the occupant voice notification system on the theory that the occupants will be alert at the time of a fire and familiar with the location of the exits from their occupied areas.

The purpose of the occupant voice notification system is to permit fire department personnel to systematically notify occupants of the location of areas of refuge and other pertinent information. Additionally, the occupant voice notification system can be used to maintain contact with occupants throughout the public areas of the building and thus minimize the potential for panic.

When a building is equipped with a voluntary automatic sprinkler system (which is not mandated by these provisions), the occupant voice notification system is not required. This trade-off is granted because the automatic sprinkler system will control a fire, thereby restricting its effect on the occupants of adjacent areas or floors and minimizing the concern for the voice notification system's function. In addition, it is reasonable to assume that the fire will occur within an area that in most cases will have compartmentation by partitions and self-closing doors.

Although the occupant voice notification system is waived for buildings containing voluntary sprinklers, these buildings, if equipped with a public address system, are required to have the public address system available for use as an occupant voice notification system.

For purposes of additional economy in the retrofitting of existing high-rise buildings, the occupant voice notification system is permitted to be combined with the fire alarm system; however, constraints have been placed on such a combined system to ensure that the important functions of each system will not be overridden by the other and thus defeat the basic purpose for each installation.

3418.1.7 Vertical shaft enclosures. Openings through two or more floors, except mezzanine floors, which contain a stairway or an elevator shall be provided with vertical shaft enclosure protection as specified in this section. The provisions recognize that openings through floors within existing buildings represent a significant deficiency from the standpoint of fire spread and smoke migration. Thus, this section requires the enclosure of such openings with a minimum of one-hour fire-resistive construction. Where there is an existing enclosure, the code provides for the use of existing materials, provided they are in good condition, and although not stated, they should also be approved by the building official. The choice of the requirement for one-hour fire-resistive enclosures, regardless of the height of buildings, is predicated on providing minimum requirements for reasonable life safety.

Where the floor openings are protected by an existing shaft enclosure, the use of existing materials in good condition is justified. The economic impact of upgrading the construction to present requirements for one-hour fire resistance is not considered technically justified. This approach recognizes that fire test methods establish a way to compare different materials and assemblies and are not indicative of the actual performance of a particular assembly in a real fire situation. For this reason the acceptance of an existing shaft enclosure constructed of typical materials such as wood lath and plaster found in older existing buildings is felt to provide the intended level of protection desired for retroactive requirements. This section also recognizes that existing vertical shaft enclosure construction might contain wired-glass assemblies; therefore, the code requires only that where they are openable, they be fixed closed and the operating devices be rendered inoperable.

In buildings protected by a voluntary automatic sprinkler system, vertical shaft enclosure requirements are modified by Section 3418.2 to provide further economic savings to encourage the installation of the sprinkler system. The intent is that reasonable levels of smoke control will still be maintained by smoke-stop barriers. For vertical shaft enclosures for exit stairways, the requirements for one-hour fire resistance have been eliminated in favor of providing an effective nonrated smoke-control barrier. This reduction appropriately assumes that the automatic sprinkler system will control the fire size such that the need for a fire-resistive rating is minimized.

The enclosure of openings in floors for elevators and escalators in buildings equipped with a voluntary sprinkler system can be eliminated, provided the openings are protected with an approved curtain board and water curtain system. This alternative is equivalent to the protection provided by Section 304.6. The requirement for an enclosure of exit stairways in buildings equipped with a voluntary sprinkler system, even though unrated, is appropriate since exit stairways should be maintained smoke free for the occupants using them.

Openings through floors for other than stairways, elevators or escalators (such as openings for piping, ducts, gas vents, dumbwaiters, and rubbish and linen chutes) are also considered to present a significant problem in terms of smoke and fire spread between floors. Thus, the protection of such openings through two or more floors by the same vertical shaft enclosure protection as required for stairways and elevators is appropriate. It is recognized that this may not always be practical in existing buildings; therefore, the code provides an exception that would permit piping, ducts, gas vents, dumbwaiters, and rubbish and linen chutes of copper or ferrous construction to penetrate the floor, provided the openings are effectively firestopped at each floor line.

3418.1.8 Shaft enclosure opening protection. For the same reasons given for the requirements for shaft enclosure protection, this section requires only either a 20-minute smoke- and draft-control assembly or a $1^3/_4$-inch (45 mm) solid-wood door for installation in existing vertical shaft enclosure construction.

In the case of openings into elevator shafts, the code does not require the same protection as required for other shafts. It is impractical to require elevator doors to provide the same level of smoke and heat protection as dictated for stair enclosures.

In all cases, doors other than elevator doors installed in either new or existing shaft enclosure construction are required to be either self-closing or automatic closing to eliminate the chance of their being left open and thus negating the basic protection provided by a door.

In buildings equipped with a voluntary automatic sprinkler system, opening protectives in vertical shaft enclosures are allowed to be nonrated but at least of $1^3/_4$-inch (45 mm) solid-wood construction on the basis that the sprinkler system will control the fire size and the fire severity will be limited.

3418.1.9 Manual shutoff of heating, ventilating and air-conditioning (HVAC) systems. Manual shutoff control of the HVAC system to reduce migration of smoke throughout a building by way of the air-handling system can be provided at a reasonable cost and can certainly enhance the total life safety provided by these provisions. The necessity for the manual shutoff control is appropriate for both sprinklered and nonsprinklered buildings, although it is recognized that the quantity of smoke generated in a sprinklered building would in most cases be limited.

3418.1.10 Automatic elevator recall system. An approved automatic recall system for the elevators is necessary in an unsprinklered building to eliminate the possibility of elevators being called to the fire floor. In buildings equipped with a voluntary automatic sprinkler system, the chance of elevators being called to a fire floor is minimal; therefore, this appendix section permits the elimination of this requirement for such buildings.

3418.1.11 Unlocked stairway doors. This section, which requires unlocked stairway doors to provide access to the building at every fifth floor level, is based on the fact that it is not feasible in the higher buildings to evacuate the building through the stairways. Thus, occupants need to be able to return into the building at some other floor level, and the code requires that this access be available every fifth level. The code also requires that unlocked doors be identified by a sign stating ACCESS ONTO FLOOR THIS LEVEL. In Height Zone 1 office buildings, the occupants are going to be awake at the time of a fire; therefore, they could reasonably exit the building through the stairs. For hotels and apartment buildings, the occupants may be asleep at the time of a fire, and there could be a delay before they were aware of the emergency and attempted to exit. Therefore, the code requires that these unlocked doors be maintained for all height zones in apartment and hotel buildings.

Since ensuring adequate security is a serious problem, the code does allow the locking of the stairway doors at all floors, provided they are capable of being simultaneously unlocked on all floors from a central location. Furthermore, the code requires that a telephone or other two-way communication system which is connected to an approved emergency service in continuous operation be located at every fifth floor level in stairways in buildings where all the stairway doors are locked.

3418.1.12 Stair shaft ventilation. For stair shaft enclosures which extend to the roofs, these provisions require that the shaft be ventilated by means of a manually openable hatch. Such ventilation will minimize smoke buildup within the shaft and the consequent spread to floors other than the fire floor. The size of the hatch is drawn from the provisions contained in Section 1006.12 in the body of the code.

The exceptions to the use of the hatch for ventilation consider the desirable qualities of smokeproof enclosures and pressurized stairways in remaining clear of smoke.

Buildings equipped with a voluntary automatic fire sprinkler system are permitted by the code to eliminate the stair shaft ventilation since the sprinkler system will control potential fires and, as a result, smoke generation will be held to a minimum.

3418.1.13 Elevator shaft ventilation. These provisions require that elevator shaft enclosures which extend to the roof be vented to the outside with openings. The reason is the same for stair shafts—to prevent a buildup of pressure due to the hot smoke in the shaft and the consequent forcing of hot smoke into other floors of the building. The exception permits an automatic venting device where energy conservation requirements or hoistway pressurization require that the vents normally be closed. Interestingly, this same exception is no longer permitted for new construction.

3418.1.14 Posting of elevators. The posting of the advisory sign required by this section at elevator call stations and within the elevator cab is a minimal cost item and provides occupants with a constant reminder of the appropriate use of exit stairs rather than the elevators in case of a fire emergency.

3418.1.15 Exit stairways. Proper life-safety considerations require that every floor be provided with exits so that any individual has access to a minimum of two exit stairways.

Where an exterior stairway is provided as a second means of egress, Section 1006.11 in the body of the code requires that openings in the exterior walls within 10 feet (3048 mm) of a stairway be protected with fire-protection assemblies. This prevents fire within the building from breaking through the opening and rendering the stairway useless.

3418.1.16 Corridor construction. The basic requirement of this section is for construction similar to the requirements for new buildings in Section 1005 of the UBC. Therefore, corridors serving as an exit for an occupant load of 30 or more are required to have walls and ceilings as required by the code in Section 1005. However, this section does permit the use of existing wood lath and plaster in good condition or $^1/_2$-inch (12.7 mm) gypsum wallboard when approved by the building official. The building official's main concern when approving such materials is that they provide a tight and effective smoke barrier and, particularly in the case of plaster over wood lath, that there is a reasonable thickness of plaster to provide some fire resistance (at least equivalent to the 20-minute smoke- and draft-control assembly permitted for doors in corridors).

In buildings equipped with a voluntary fire sprinkler system, existing corridor construction need not be altered because the sprinkler system will control fires to the extent that existing fire-resistive construction is adequate. However, the statement that the existing corridor construction need not be altered does not convey all of the code's intent. It is still intended that even where the fire sprinkler system is provided on a voluntary basis that the corridor be at least smoketight so that a fire in an adjacent room will not generate smoke which infiltrates the corridor.

3418.1.17 Corridor openings. These provisions require protection of openings in corridors for the same reasons that it is required by Section 1005.8 of the UBC. Although the provisions allow construction not completely in conformance with all of the provisions of Section 1005.8, the essential features of this section for corridor opening protection will provide an effective smoke barrier having some fire resistance. This section does not require any special protection of the openings into corridors for office buildings where the occupants are awake and familiar with the location of exits.

In those buildings equipped with a voluntary automatic sprinkler system, corridor door openings may be protected by assemblies having minimal fire resistance, and protection of duct penetrations is not required. However, the door openings should provide a smoke- and draft-control barrier, and closing and latching hardware must be provided.

3418.1.18 Corridor door closers. Corridor door protection requires that the doors in both sprinklered and nonsprinklered residential buildings be equipped with self-closers or automatic closers actuated by a smoke detector.

3418.1.19 Corridor dead ends. Dead ends for corridors in unsprinklered buildings are limited to 20 feet (6096 mm) when the corridor serves an occupant load of more than 30. The dead-end requirement applies only to apartments and hotels. In hotels, occupants are generally unfamiliar with the means of egress system, and therefore a dead-end limitation is desirable. In apartments, even though the occupants are probably familiar with the exit system, a fire could just as easily occur during the hours when the occupants are asleep and could be disoriented or confused when awakened by a fire. In office buildings, however, the occupants are awake and familiar with the surroundings, and dead-end corridors are not considered to be a sufficient hazard requiring alterations to the exit system.

In buildings equipped with a voluntary automatic sprinkler system, it is assumed that the fire size will be limited by the sprinklers such that dead-end limitations are not justified.

3418.1.20 Interior finish. Retroactive conformance with present code requirements for interior finish in critical means of egress elements, such as corridors, exit stairways and the extensions thereof, are justified on the basis that the exit facilities must be usable at all times by the occupants of the building. Therefore, the flame spread of interior finish in these elements must be restricted to those values required by the code in Chapter 8.

In a similar manner as in Chapter 8, those buildings equipped with a voluntary automatic sprinkler system qualify for a reduction of one classification in the requirements for interior finish in exitways as long as the minimum classification is Class III.

3418.1.21 and 3418.1.22 Exit stairway and corridor illumination. These requirements are essentially the same as those for new buildings, which require that all exits be illuminated with an intensity of not less than 1 footcandle (10.8 lx) at floor level. Exit illumination is an important feature of life safety and can be accomplished relatively inexpensively in existing buildings which do not have adequate exit illumination. The code also requires that the exit illumination be equipped with an independent alternate source of power which could be either a battery pack or an on-site motor generator set. When addressing corridor illumination, the provisions do not apply to office buildings because the occupants are awake and familiar with their surroundings.

3418.1.23 and 3418.1.24 Exit stairway exit signs and exit signs. As for new buildings, and with the same rationale, this section requires exit signs to clearly indicate the location of exit stairways and the direction of egress. As with exit illumination, it is also required that exit signs be illuminated and be equipped with an independent alternate source of power. This may be a battery pack, an on-site motor generator set or an approved self-illuminating type of sign.

3418.1.25 Emergency plan. Due to the anticipated large occupant loads in high-rise buildings and the logistical problems which make access to the fire difficult, it is essential that the building staff have an emergency plan. Such a plan should include first aid capability and systematic notification of occupants. The plan should also require that staff proceed to assigned locations to assist anyone requiring help. This section requires management to submit a plan to the fire department for approval based on criteria and guidelines developed by the fire chief.

3418.1.26 Posting of emergency plan and exit plans. It is essential that occupants of a building be provided with basic emergency information. This is especially true in hotels where the occupants are normally not familiar with the building. This may include, but is not necessarily limited to, exit diagrams, posting of floor numbers on the inside of exit stairs and the posting of other similar information or instructions. Posting locations must be approved by the fire chief.

3418.1.27 Fire drills. The purpose of fire drill requirements is to ensure that the action of the staff and employees during an emergency is orderly. This requirement is deemed reasonable only for hotel occupancies since the staff of an apartment building would be minimal at best. In office buildings, the disruption of normal operations would be excessive, even in single-tenant buildings. Also, occupants of apartment buildings and office buildings are reasonably familiar with their surroundings and should be able to follow the posted emergency plans without too much difficulty. This item also provides that the fire drills be conducted regularly.

3418.2 Sprinkler Alternatives. During the development of these provisions, the committee members were unanimous in recommending that jurisdictions adopting provisions requiring retrofit for existing high-rise buildings should also consider providing tax incentives and other incentives to further encourage the installation of a sprinkler system installation as the principal means of protection for the building.

For these and other reasons, the committee members felt that where a sprinkler system is chosen by the owner, certain allowances by the jurisdiction were thought to be appropriate. Such allowances would include the elimination of sprinkler standby charges and detector check valves. The elimination of the requirement for backflow preventers, such as double check valves, was also considered an important inducement since the hazard due to a possible cross connection between the sprinkler system and the public water supply is minimal.

INDEX

Index is not all inclusive of code items.

B